MW01195046

REVOLUTION AND DICTATORSHIP

Revolution and Dictatorship

THE VIOLENT ORIGINS OF
DURABLE AUTHORITARIANISM

Steven Levitsky

Lucan Way

PRINCETON UNIVERSITY PRESS

PRINCETON & OXFORD

Published by Princeton University Press
41 William Street, Princeton, New Jersey 08540
99 Banbury Road, Oxford OX2 6JX

press.princeton.edu

All Rights Reserved

Library of Congress Control Number: 2022932449

ISBN 9780691169521
ISBN (e-book) 9780691223575

British Library Cataloging-in-Publication Data is available

Editorial: Bridget Flannery-McCoy, Alena Chekanov
Jacket Design: Heather Hansen
Production: Erin Suydam
Publicity: James Schneider (US), Kathryn Stevens (UK)

Jacket Credit: colaimages / Alamy Stock Photo

This book has been composed in Miller

Printed on acid-free paper. ∞

Printed in the United States of America

10 9 8 7 6 5 4 3 2 1

Steve dedicates this book to Liz Mineo and Alejandra Mineo-Levitsky

Lucan dedicates this book to Victor (*dziadzio*) Erlich (1914–2007)

CONTENTS

ACKNOWLEDGMENTS

THIS BOOK IS THE PRODUCT of nearly three decades of collaboration. It emerged out of an argument made in our first book, *Competitive Authoritarianism*, linking the origins of violent regimes to robust authoritarian party-states. In many ways, however, the book would never have been possible without the collaboration of two young scholars who began their careers at the University of Toronto: Adam Casey and Jean Lachapelle. Adam led our effort to code all autocracies since 1900. His encyclopedic knowledge of authoritarian regimes, bulldog intensity, and readiness to challenge our preconceived expectations about specific cases resulted in the "Revolutionary Autocracies Data Set 1900–2015," which is backed up by nearly 500 sources and forms the basis of the book's statistical analysis (the data set is available at https://press.princeton.edu/books/revolution-and-dictatorship and is summarized in appendix III). Jean was primarily responsible for the statistical analysis itself, showing that revolutionary regimes are especially durable (excerpted in appendix I). The book benefited enormously from Jean's careful work and analytical perspicacity. The statistical analysis is presented in greater detail in Jean Lachapelle, Steven Levitsky, Lucan Way, and Adam Casey, "Social Revolution and Authoritarian Durability," *World Politics* 72, no. 4 (2020). We are also thankful to Gabriel Koehler-Derrick and Kai Thaler for their research assistance.

We also could not have written this book without critical institutional support, including a generous grant from the Social Sciences and Humanities Research Council of Canada (Insight Grant No. 435120767, P.I. Lucan Way). The grant allowed us transform the project from a kernel of an idea into a full-blown book. Steve benefited enormously from a faculty leave grant—and countless other forms of support—from the Weatherhead Center for International Affairs at Harvard University. We thank the Harvard Academy for International and Area Studies for generously sponsoring our book conference. Lucan is also thankful for the intrepid enthusiasm and support of his colleagues at the Centre for European, Russian, and Eurasian Studies at the University of Toronto, as well as the outstanding collection at Robarts Library at the University of Toronto.

The book project was enriched by comments from numerous friends and colleagues. James Mahoney, whose own work influenced our book in a variety of ways, provided early encouragement and generous feedback at various points along the way. Dan Slater was a constant source of critical insight from the project's earliest stages. Our long-standing exchange with Dan and his research improved the book in countless ways. The authors also thank Alicia Holland for suggesting the idea of segmented radicalism in Mexico. Eva Bellin, James Mahoney, Tom Pepinsky, Dan Slater, Milan Svolik, and David Waldner generously spent a day digging into our project at a conference, which dramatically improved the book. Mark Beissinger provided constant encouragement and detailed advice on the statistical analysis and made sure that we did not exclude Finland from the analysis. Lynne Viola generously bestowed early encouragement and multiple rounds of feedback on the Soviet chapter. Kevin Luo closely read early versions of the China chapter and helped us to avoid several embarrassing mistakes. Ajmal Burhanzoi, who lived through the Taliban's seizure of power in 1996, provided helpful comments on the Afghanistan case study. Numerous colleagues provided feedback at various stages of the project, including Robert Austin, Nancy Bermeo, Keith Darden, Larry Diamond, Jorge Domínguez, Henry Erlich, Mark Erlich, Tulia Falleti, Diana Fu, Jack Goldstone, Jeff Goodwin, Peter Gourevitch, Frances Hagopian, Randall Hansen, Stephen Hanson, Jingkai He, Alisha Holland, Pavlo Kutuev, Adrienne LeBas, James Loxton, Julie Lynch, Andrei Melville, Anne Meng, Lynette Ong, Mitch Ornstein, Adam Przeworski, Phil Roessler, Mariano Sánchez Talanquer, Ed Schatz, Oxana Shevel, Kai Thaler, Kathleen Thelen, Josh Tucker, Yuhua Wang, Joe Wright, and participants in seminars at Harvard, the University of Toronto, the University of Pennsylvania, Brigham Young University, the University of California, Berkeley, Fudan University in Shanghai, Gothenberg University, the Higher Economic School in Moscow, the Kyiv Polytechnic Institute, the University of Michigan, New York University, the University of Notre Dame, Stanford University, Stockholm University, the University of Sydney, Tulane University, the College of William and Mary, and Yale University.

John Donohue and Amelie Tolvin did a wonderful job proofreading the manuscript and tracking down innumerable missing citations.

We are also indebted to Princeton University Press, particularly Eric Crahan and Bridget Flannery-McCoy. Bridget's engagement with the project and extensive commentary on early chapter drafts dramatically improved the quality of the book.

Finally, some personal notes of gratitude. Ron Suny witnessed Lucan's transformation from spaced-out kid to absent-minded professor and inspired a lifelong interest in Soviet politics. Lucan's wife Zareen and their twin boys, Idris and Kamran, provided encouragement and put up with the mountains of books on Stalin that still litter the house.

Steve thanks his two role models, Liz Mineo and Alejandra Mineo-Levitsky, and dedicates this book to them.

Lucan dedicates this book to his step grandfather, Victor (*dziadzio*) Erlich (1914–2007). Victor was a toddler in Petrograd during the Russian Revolution, suffered the death of his father to Stalinist repression, and barely escaped the Holocaust before migrating to the United States, where he had a long and distinguished career as a professor of Russian literature. Despite his brush with some of the twentieth century's worst tragedies, Victor was preternaturally happy, eminently approachable, and exuded an infectious warmth and humor that persisted until his final breath. He is sorely missed.

CHAPTER ONE

A Theory of Revolutionary Durability

IN JUNE 1941, SOVIET POWER hung by the barest of threads. Over-whelmed by invading Nazi armies, the Soviet Union ceded vast tracts of territory as entire Russian divisions lost contact with their commanders. Across the country, the Red Army disintegrated into bands of fugitives seeking to escape German encirclement. In the central corridors of power, panicked confusion reigned.[1]

One might have expected the Soviet regime to collapse, falling prey to either an uprising by citizens who had suffered years of starvation and repression or a coup by army officers angry at Joseph Stalin's brutal purges and catastrophic meddling in military affairs. Indeed, military disaster during World War I had precipitated the fall of the tsarist regime. More-over, the devastating first weeks of the invasion could be traced directly to Stalin's leadership. He had refused to prepare for an invasion despite numerous intelligence reports that an attack was imminent; in fact, he had ordered the dismantling of existing defense fortifications in the east, leaving the Soviet army largely defenseless in the rear.[2] Several days after the German invasion, Stalin retreated to his dacha, leaving the rest of the leadership in the lurch. A small group of Politburo members ventured out to see him uninvited—a risky move in Stalinist Russia.[3] According to one account, the Soviet leaders found Stalin alone in the dark, slumped in an armchair, seemingly expecting arrest.[4] He later admitted that "any other government which had suffered such losses of territory . . . would have collapsed."[5] Yet Stalin's government survived, and Soviet communism endured for another half century.

The Soviet regime's survival amid extreme adversity highlights a broader phenomenon of great significance. Revolutionary autocracies—those born of violent social revolution—are extraordinarily durable. Soviet communism lasted seventy-four years; Mexico's Institutional Revolutionary Party (PRI) regime ruled for eighty-five years; revolutionary regimes in China, Cuba, and Vietnam remain in power today after more than six decades. Among modern states, only a small handful of Persian Gulf monarchies match this longevity.

Revolutionary autocracies do not merely persist over time. Like the Soviet Union, most of them have survived despite external hostility, poor economic performance, and large-scale policy failure. The Chinese Communist Party held on to power in the face of the catastrophic Great Leap Forward and the "Great Chaos" unleashed by the Cultural Revolution. Vietnam's Communist regime endured the devastation caused by thirty years of war; Cuba's revolutionary regime survived a U.S.-backed invasion, a crippling trade embargo, and the economic catastrophe that followed the Soviet collapse; and the Islamic Republic of Iran endured four decades of intense international hostility, including a bloody eight-year war with Iraq.

Finally, most revolutionary regimes survived the global collapse of communism. During the 1990s, the loss of foreign patrons, economic crisis, and unprecedented international democracy promotion undermined autocracies across the world.[6] Yet many revolutionary regimes—including erstwhile communist regimes in China, Cuba, and Vietnam—remained intact. Indeed, all the communist regimes that survived into the twenty-first century were born of violent revolution.[7] Likewise, in sub-Saharan Africa, the only Soviet client states to survive the end of the Cold War were Angola and Mozambique, both of which emerged out of violent social revolution.

These cases are not anomalies. In a statistical analysis of all authoritarian regimes established since 1900, undertaken with Jean Lachapelle and Adam E. Casey,[8] we find that authoritarian regimes that emerged out of violent social revolution survived, on average, nearly three times as long as their nonrevolutionary counterparts.[9] Revolutionary regimes broke down at an annual rate that was barely a fifth of that of nonrevolutionary regimes.[10] To help visualize these differences, figure 1.1 presents the Kaplan-Meier estimates for the two regime types, along with 95 percent confidence envelopes. It shows that a striking 71 percent of revolutionary regimes survived for thirty years or more, compared to only 19 percent of nonrevolutionary regimes.[11] Importantly, revolutionary origins are

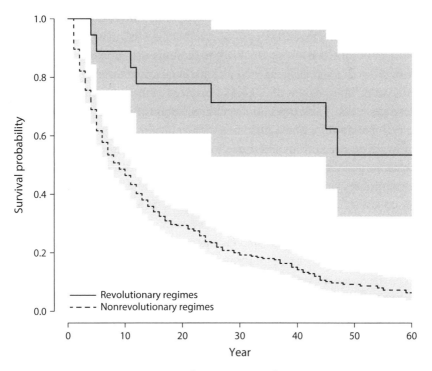

FIGURE 1.1: Kaplan-Meier Survival Curves.

positively associated with regime longevity, even when we control for standard variables such as level of economic development, GDP growth, oil wealth, and type of authoritarian regime (party-based, military, monarchy, or personalist).[12]

The durability of revolutionary regimes is highly consequential. Though rare (we count twenty since 1900), revolutionary autocracies have had an outsized impact on modern world politics. Revolutions expand state power, sometimes dramatically. As Theda Skocpol observed,[13] the destruction of old elites and mobilization of vast human and other societal resources may permit rapid industrial and military advances, enabling states to leapfrog others in the geopolitical pecking order. Thus, the Russian Revolution transformed a predominantly agrarian society into a modern industrial power capable of defeating Germany in World War II and achieving nuclear parity with the United States. The revolution shook the global capitalist system and gave rise to the Cold War rivalry that defined the post-1945 geopolitical order. Likewise, the Chinese Revolution brought the centralization of what had been a weak, fragmented state and fueled the country's emergence as a superpower. Cuba's revolution transformed a peripheral state into one capable of successful military intervention in Africa.

Revolutions also bring war.[14] Dramatic shifts in national power tend to destabilize the regional and even international order, increasing the likelihood of military conflict.[15] Revolutionary governments generate heightened uncertainty and perceptions of threat among both neighboring states and global powers, which increases the likelihood of interstate conflict.[16] Thus, from revolutionary France to Communist Russia and China, to postcolonial Vietnam, to late twentieth-century Iran and Afghanistan, revolutionary governments have often found themselves engulfed in war. Overall, revolutionary governments are nearly twice as likely as nonrevolutionary governments to be involved in war.[17]

Revolutionary regimes also engender new ideological and political models that spread across national borders. The Bolshevik Revolution gave rise to an economic model (state socialism) and a political model (Leninism) that diffused across the globe during the twentieth century. Similarly, the Cuban Revolution gave rise to a new guerrilla strategy that transformed the Latin American Left, polarizing politics across the region for a generation.[18] The Iranian Revolution created a new model of a modern theocracy.

Revolutionary regimes, moreover, have been responsible for some of the most horrific violence and human tragedy in modern history, including the 1932–1933 Ukrainian famine, Stalin's Great Terror, the Great Leap Forward in China, and the Khmer Rouge's genocide in Cambodia.

Finally, revolutionary regimes have posed major foreign policy challenges for Western democracies. Few states were more closely associated with U.S. foreign policy ineffectiveness—if not outright failure—than revolutionary Vietnam, Cuba, Iran, and Afghanistan.

This book seeks to explain the extraordinary durability of modern revolutionary regimes.[19] Drawing on comparative historical analysis, we argue that social revolutions trigger a *reactive sequence* that powerfully shapes long-run regime trajectories.[20] Revolutionary governments' attempts to radically transform the existing social and geopolitical order generate intense domestic and international resistance, often resulting in civil or external war. This counterrevolutionary reaction is critical to long-run regime durability. Counterrevolutionary wars pose an existential threat to newborn regimes, and, in some cases (e.g., Afghanistan, Cambodia), they destroy them. Among revolutionary regimes that survive, however, early periods of violence and military threat produce three key pillars of regime strength: (1) a cohesive ruling elite, (2) a highly developed and loyal coercive apparatus, and (3) the destruction of rival organizations and alternative centers of power in society. These three pillars help to inoculate revolutionary regimes against elite defection, military coups, and mass protest—three principal sources of authoritarian breakdown. Such a trajectory almost always yields durable autocracies.

Defining Revolutionary Regime

A revolution is not a dinner party, or writing an essay, or painting a picture, or doing embroidery; it cannot be so refined, so leisurely and gentle, so temperate, kind, courteous, restrained, and magnanimous.

—MAO ZEDONG[21]

Revolutionary autocracies are political regimes that emerge out of social revolutions. We define a social revolution as the violent overthrow of an existing regime from below, accompanied by mass mobilization and state collapse, which triggers a rapid transformation of the state and the existing social order.[22]

Social revolutions possess four characteristics that jointly distinguish them from other types of regime change. First, they occur from below, in that they are led by mass-based movements that emerge outside the state and regime.[23] These may be armed guerrilla movements (China, Cuba, Eritrea, Vietnam), political parties (Russia), or militant social movements (Iran) that seize power amid mass unrest. In all cases, the revolutionary elite is drawn from outside the preexisting state. Military coups are not social revolutions.

Second, social revolutions involve the violent overthrow of the old regime.[24] This may take the form of a civil war (Mexico, Rwanda), a guerrilla struggle (China, Cuba, Eritrea, Mozambique), or a rapid and violent seizure of power (Russia, Bolivia in 1952, Iran).

Third, social revolutions produce a fundamental transformation of the state.[25] State transformation initially involves the collapse or crippling of the preexisting coercive apparatus.[26] Military chains of command are shattered by mutinies or widespread desertion, preventing the security forces from functioning as coherent organizations. In many cases, preexisting coercive structures simply dissolve (e.g., Mexico, Cuba, Cambodia, Nicaragua, Russia) or, in anticolonial revolutions (e.g., Algeria, Mozambique, Vietnam), are withdrawn. Upon seizing power, revolutionary forces usually dismantle remaining coercive agencies and build new armies, police forces, and bureaucracies—often from scratch.[27]

Fourth, social revolutions involve the initiation of radical socioeconomic or cultural change.[28] Revolutionary governments attempt to impose, by force, measures that attack the core interests of powerful domestic and international actors or large groups in society. Such measures include the systematic seizure and redistribution of property; attempts to eliminate entire social classes (e.g., China, Russia); campaigns to destroy preexisting cultures, religions, or ethnic orders (e.g., Iran, Rwanda); efforts to impose new rules governing social behavior (e.g., Afghanistan, Iran); and foreign policy initiatives aimed at spreading revolution and transforming the regional or international order (e.g., Hungary in 1919, Cuba, Iran, Russia). Because such efforts at radical social transformation trigger substantial resistance, often from powerful places, they are invariably accompanied by a heavy dose of coercion. For this reason, social revolutions are antithetical to the development of liberal democracy.

Our definition of social revolution is demanding.[29] It excludes at least three types of regime change that scholars sometimes describe as revolutionary. First, it excludes cases of mass-based regime change in which states and social structures remain intact, such as the so-called color revolutions in Serbia, Georgia, Ukraine, and Kyrgyzstan; the Arab Spring transitions in Egypt and Tunisia; or Third Wave democratizations in the Philippines (1986) and South Africa (1994).

Second, our definition excludes cases of radical change initiated by actors within the state. So-called revolutions from above,[30] such as those in Turkey under Kemal Ataturk, Egypt under Gamal Nasser, or Ethiopia under Mengistu Haile Mariam, do not meet our definition of revolution because they were led by state officials rather than mass-based regime outsiders. Far from involving the collapse or transformation of the state, revolutions from above are *led* by the state.

Third, we exclude cases that emerge out of violent regime change but do not initiate radical social transformations. These cases—which include China under the Kuomintang (1927–1949), postcolonial Indonesia and contemporary Ethiopia, South Sudan, and Uganda—might be characterized as *political revolutions*, as opposed to *social revolutions*.[31] Regimes that emerge out of political revolutions sometimes share important characteristics with social revolutionary regimes, such as the creation of new armies. As a result, they too are often robust. However, only social revolutions trigger the revolutionary reactive sequence that generates the extraordinary durability observed in countries like Mexico, the Soviet Union, Communist China, and Vietnam. When we use the term "revolutionary regime," then, we refer to regimes born of *social* revolution.

Our definition does not encompass some prominent cases that have been described as revolutionary, such as the postcommunist "refolutions" of 1989–1991.[32] Because the fall of communism in Eastern Europe involved mass uprisings and produced far-reaching socioeconomic transformations, these transitions have been described as revolutionary.[33] They do not meet our criteria, however. With the exception of Romania,[34] postcommunist transitions were peaceful, in that they were driven by either peaceful demonstrations (Eastern Europe) or, in the Soviet case, elections (in 1990) and peaceful protest (after the 1991 putsch).[35] In addition, most postcommunist transitions left important state structures, including preexisting armies, intact.[36]

Our definition also excludes fascist regimes. Although Nazi Germany and Italy under Benito Mussolini have been described as revolutionary,[37] the Nazis and the Italian fascists came to power through institutional means, and with the backing of state officials.[38] States never collapsed.

Our definition of revolution is thus more demanding than those used in much of the contemporary literature. Minimalist definitions, such as those of Mark R. Beissinger, Jack Goldstone, Jeff Goodwin, and others, categorize as revolutions all cases "of irregular, extraconstitutional, and sometimes violent changes of political regime and control of state power brought about by popular movements."[39] By excluding criteria such as state and societal transformation, these definitions broaden the concept of revolution to encompass a wide array of cases, ranging from violent social revolutions in China and Russia to the protest-driven removal of autocrats such as the fall of Ferdinand Marcos in the Philippines, Slobodan Milošević in Serbia, and Zine el-Abidine Ben Ali in Tunisia. Our definition yields a narrower—but more uniform—set of cases.

To identify revolutionary regimes, we compiled a list of all 355 autocracies since 1900 by drawing on data from Barbara Geddes, Joseph Wright, and Erica Frantz's "Autocratic Breakdown and Regimes Transitions" data set (GWF).[40] We then narrowed the set of cases to governments that came to power in an irregular fashion (i.e., not via succession or election) and from outside the state (i.e., *not* via a military coup).[41] Finally, we excluded cases in which new governments did not initiate an effort to radically transform the state and the social order. (Our coding criteria and reason for excluding each nonrevolutionary case may be found in appendixes II and III.)[42]

To ensure that we did not miss any revolutionary governments that collapsed before the end of the first calendar year, thereby failing to meet GWF's inclusion criteria for being a regime,[43] we also examined all 219 autocratic leaders who were in power for at least a day but less than a

Table 1.1 Revolutionary Regimes since 1900

Afghanistan, 1996–2001

Albania, 1944–1991

Algeria, 1962–

Angola, 1975–

Bolivia, 1952–1964

Cambodia, 1975–1979

China, 1949–

Cuba, 1959–

Eritrea, 1993–

Finland, January 28–April 13, 1918

Guinea-Bissau, 1974–1999

Hungary, March 21–July 29, 1919

Iran, 1979–

Mexico, 1915–2000

Mozambique, 1975–

Nicaragua, 1979–1990

Russia, 1917–1991

Rwanda, 1994–

Vietnam, 1954–

Yugoslavia, 1945–1990

---

year.[44] We identified two revolutionary governments that died in their infancy: Finland in 1918 and Hungary in 1919.[45] The fact that we could identify only two such cases increases our confidence that we have not inadvertently failed to identify short-lived revolutionary governments.[46]

Overall, then, we find twenty revolutionary autocracies since 1900; these are listed in table 1.1. In terms of regime longevity, our cases range from those that survived less than a year (Finland, Hungary) to those lasting more than seventy years (China, Mexico, Russia). They include both regimes that emerge out of classic social revolutions, such as those in China, Cuba, Mexico, and Russia, and those founded in radical national liberation struggles, as in Algeria, Angola, Mozambique, and Vietnam. The list also includes some post–Cold War cases that are not always treated as social revolutions, such as Rwanda, where the Rwandan Patriotic Front government took steps to overturn the preexisting ethnic order,[47] and Eritrea, where the Eritrean People's Liberation Front sought to radically overhaul the country's rural social structure.[48]

Seventeen of the twenty regimes listed in table 1.1 are left-leaning. This pattern may be attributed to the fact that radical challenges to the existing social order, a defining characteristic of social revolution, were more likely to be undertaken by leftist (and, more recently, Islamist) forces in the twentieth and early twenty-first centuries. Conservative or right-wing forces usually seek to preserve the existing social order.[49]

Finally, all the regimes encompassed by our definition are authoritarian. This should not be surprising. Because efforts to carry out radical social transformation attack the vital interests or way of life of powerful domestic actors and large societal groups, they require a level of violence and coercion that is incompatible with liberal democracy.[50] Social revolutions may contribute to long-run democratization, for example, by destroying institutions or social classes that inhibit democratic change, as Barrington Moore argued in the case of France.[51] In all revolutionary cases, however, the initial regime was authoritarian.

A Theory of Revolutionary Regime Durability

This book seeks to explain the durability of authoritarian regimes. Durable authoritarian regimes are those in which a single party, coalition, or clique remains continuously in power, usually beyond the lifetime of founding leaders, and often despite adverse conditions.[52] Durable autocracies are less likely to suffer serious contestation, either from within (e.g., coups) or from society (e.g., large-scale protest), even in circumstances—such as economic crisis, major policy failure, or leadership succession—that often give rise to such contestation. Moreover, when regime challenges *do* emerge, durable autocracies are better equipped to thwart them.

The early twenty-first century witnessed a proliferation of research on the sources of authoritarian durability. Some scholars pointed to economic sources of regime stability. One of these is growth. Studies have shown that economic growth helps sustain autocracy by limiting public discontent and providing governments with the resources to both maintain pro-regime coalitions and co-opt potential rivals.[53] Other research highlighted the role of natural resource wealth, particularly oil, in sustaining autocracies.[54] However, few revolutionary regimes have achieved sustained economic growth (at least initially) or possess vast natural resource endowments. In fact, most of them have experienced the kind of severe economic crisis that is widely associated with authoritarian breakdown.

Much of the contemporary literature on authoritarian durability highlights the role of political institutions.[55] Scholars argue that pseudo-democratic institutions such as elections, legislatures, and ruling parties help autocrats gain access to information,[56] co-opt opponents,[57] and provide mechanisms of coordination and cohesion among the ruling elite.[58]

The most prominent institutionalist arguments center on the role of political parties.[59] Ruling parties are said to enhance authoritarian stability by creating incentives for elite cooperation over defection. By providing institutional mechanisms to regulate access to the spoils of public office and by lengthening actors' time horizons through the provision of future opportunities for career advancement, ruling parties encourage long-term loyalty.[60] Those who lose out in short-term power struggles remain loyal in the expectation of gaining access to power in future rounds. Ruling parties thus reduce the incentives for elite defection, which is widely viewed as a major cause of authoritarian breakdown.[61]

Given that most revolutionary regimes are governed by strong ruling parties, revolutionary cases may appear to conform to such theories. Nevertheless, there are limits to the explanatory power of institutionalist approaches. As Benjamin Smith has shown, party-based authoritarian regimes vary widely in their durability.[62] Whereas some party-based regimes survive for decades, even in the face of intense opposition and severe economic crises (e.g., Malaysia, Zimbabwe), others (e.g., Pakistan in 1958, Ghana in 1966) quickly collapse, often at the first sign of duress. Indeed, as we show in this book, the formal existence of a ruling party tells us virtually nothing about its strength.[63]

Furthermore, ruling parties may not exert the independent causal force that is often assigned to them in the literature.[64] Looking back at the origins of many party-based autocracies, we see that ruling parties were often initially weak or nonexistent. Mexico's ruling party was not created until fifteen years after the revolutionary elite took power; Cuba's Communist Party was not established until six years after the revolution, and the party remained inoperative for a decade after its founding. Even the Bolshevik Party, which became the model for Leninist party regimes, was initially weak and riven by internal conflict. In these and other cases, ruling parties strengthened over time, together with processes of state-building and regime consolidation. This sequencing suggests that other, more exogenous, factors may be at work. In other words, strong ruling parties may contribute to durable authoritarianism, but we still need to understand where strong ruling parties come from.

Our statistical analysis offers further evidence that revolutionary origins are associated with more durable party-based authoritarianism.[65] We found that among the party-based authoritarian regimes that emerged since 1900, those with revolutionary origins are considerably more robust than those without such origins. The likelihood that a revolutionary regime will collapse in any given year is less than half that of nonrevolutionary party-based regimes.[66]

Recent scholarly efforts to explain variation in authoritarian durability have taken a historical turn, examining the role of regime origins.[67] This approach may be traced back to Samuel Huntington, who argued more than half a century ago that strong ruling parties were rooted in "struggle and violence."[68] For Huntington, the strength of single-party regimes was grounded in the "duration and intensity of the struggle to acquire power or to consolidate power after taking over the government."[69] Thus, ruling parties that emerged out of violent revolution or prolonged nationalist struggle were most durable, whereas parties that seized and consolidated control of the state "easily, without a major struggle," usually "withered in power."[70] Katharine Chorley,[71] writing a full generation before Huntington, pointed to the critical role of social revolutions in facilitating the construction of strong and loyal coercive agencies. This book expands upon and tests these insights.

There exists a rich tradition of research on social revolutions.[72] Much of this research focuses on the *causes* of revolution. Scholars have long debated the causal role of modernization, class structure, culture, ideology, and leadership.[73] Since publication of Theda Skocpol's pathbreaking book *States and Social Revolutions*,[74] however, there has been a near consensus—to which this book adheres—that state weakness is a necessary condition for revolution.[75] Revolutions occur only where states are disabled by war, decolonization, or the breakdown of a sultanistic regime.[76]

We know less, however, about the *consequences* of revolution, especially for political regimes. Scholars have examined the impact of revolution on culture,[77] redistribution and social equality,[78] and state-building.[79] They have linked revolutions to the development of powerful coercive structures,[80] heightened repression and terror,[81] and war.[82] Nevertheless, there have been fewer efforts to theorize how social revolutions shape political regimes.[83]

THE REVOLUTIONARY REACTIVE SEQUENCE

Building on Huntington,[84] as well as more recent work by scholars such as James Mahoney,[85] Benjamin Smith,[86] and Dan Slater,[87] we argue that developments during a revolutionary regime's foundational period have a profound impact on its long-term trajectory. Revolutionary origins trigger

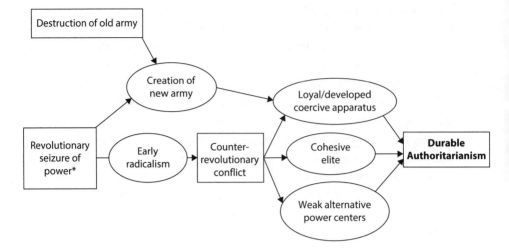

FIGURE 1.2: The Ideal-Typical Revolutionary Reactive Sequence.
* In some cases (e.g., China), the reactive sequence occurs before seizure of power.

what Mahoney calls a "reactive sequence,"[88] or a series of violent conflicts that, if they do not destroy the regime early on, dramatically strengthen state institutions and weaken societal ones, laying a foundation for durable authoritarianism.

In the ideal-typical revolutionary reactive sequence, which is summarized in figure 1.2, early radicalism triggers a violent counterrevolutionary reaction, often supported by foreign powers. This counterrevolutionary reaction is critical to long-run regime durability because it creates an existential threat that reinforces elite cohesion, encourages the development of a powerful and loyal coercive apparatus, and facilitates the destruction of rival organizations and independent centers of societal power. This process of state-building and societal weakening lays a foundation for durable authoritarian rule. In classical cases (e.g., Russia, Cuba, Iran), or what Huntington called the "Western" type of revolution,[89] the reactive sequence begins after the seizure of national power. In some cases (e.g., China, Vietnam, Yugoslavia), however, much of the conflict and transformation occurs *prior* to the seizure of national power (Huntington called this the "Eastern" type of revolution). Notwithstanding this difference in timing, this book shows that the "Western" and "Eastern" revolutionary paths unfold in comparable ways and give rise to similarly durable regimes.

Two alternative revolutionary paths yield less durable regimes. One is a radical path to *early death*, in which revolutionary attacks on powerful domestic and international interests trigger a military conflict that destroys the regime. Hungary (1919), Cambodia under the Khmer Rouge, and Afghanistan under the Taliban (1996–2001) followed this path. The other alternative path is one of *accommodation*, in which revolutionaries initiate far-reaching social change but then temper or abandon most of these measures to avert a counterrevolutionary reaction. This more pragmatic approach often succeeds at limiting violent conflict, but in the absence of such conflict, revolutionary governments are less likely to forge a cohesive elite, build a powerful and loyal coercive apparatus, or destroy independent power centers. Such regimes tend to survive in the short run, but without a durable foundation, they are prone to instability. Opposition challenges—both from within and from society—are more frequent, more potent, and thus more likely to undermine the regime. This was the path followed by regimes in Algeria, Bolivia, and Guinea-Bissau.

THE SEIZURE OF POWER: EARLY RADICALISM AND THE ROLE OF IDEOLOGY

You cannot carry out fundamental change without a certain amount of madness.

—THOMAS SANKARA[90]

In observing the strength of regimes in Mexico and the Soviet Union during the 1950s and 1960s, or in contemporary China and Vietnam, it is easy to forget that most revolutionary autocracies are born weak. Revolutionaries seize power in a context of state collapse, in which preexisting armies, police forces, and bureaucracies have been partially or fully destroyed. Inevitably, then, new revolutionary elites inherit weak states. Rebel armies are often too small, ill equipped, and inexperienced to maintain order across the national territory.[91] In Russia, for example, Bolshevik forces had virtually no presence outside the major cities in October 1917. Likewise, Albanian revolutionaries barely possessed any state structures when Enver Hoxha declared victory in late 1944,[92] and Iranian revolutionaries controlled only a "hastily gathered, disorganized and ill-trained militia" upon seizing power in 1979.[93]

Ruling parties also tend to be weak in the immediate aftermath of revolution. In Cuba, for example, Fidel Castro ruled without a party between 1959 and 1965. Even after being formally established in 1965, the Cuban Communist Party barely functioned.[94] It never even held a congress before 1975, allowing Castro to rule in an "institutional void."[95] Likewise, Mexican revolutionaries lacked a ruling party during their first twelve years in power. Even in Russia, the birthplace of the Leninist party model, the Bolshevik Party was initially plagued by internal conflict and loose discipline.[96]

The absence of a strong party or coercive apparatus leaves revolutionary governments vulnerable to challenges from diverse actors, ranging from ancien régime elites to remnants of the old army to rival political organizations seeking power in the wake of the old regime's collapse. For example, Mexico's revolutionary government confronted remnants of the old Federal Army, landowners, and rival armies led by Francisco (Pancho) Villa and Emiliano Zapata for nearly a decade after the seizure of power. The Bolsheviks faced opposition from the White Armies and other remnants of the tsarist regime, as well as two rival socialist parties: the Mensheviks and the Socialist Revolutionaries (SRs).

Without an effective army or party and surrounded by a multitude of real and potential enemies, new revolutionary governments tend to be vulnerable. As George Pettee keenly observed, victorious revolutionaries take power "not like men on horseback . . . but like fearful children, exploring an empty house, not sure that it is empty."[97]

The aftermath of the seizure of power may be understood as a critical juncture,[98] during which the behavior of the revolutionary elite can have powerful long-term consequences for the regime. Nonrevolutionary governments tend to respond pragmatically to conditions of extreme vulnerability by seeking to broaden their domestic coalitions, build investor confidence, and cultivate international legitimacy in order to attract foreign support. In postcolonial Indonesia, for example, Sukarno sought to forge a broad governing coalition that included nationalist, Marxist, and conservative religious factions.[99] Likewise, when the People's Liberation Movement won power in South Sudan in 2011, it moved to strengthen traditional chiefs and reconcile with competing groups across the country.[100]

Most revolutionary governments do the opposite. Upon seizing power, revolutionary elites launch radical policy initiatives that threaten the vital interests of powerful domestic and foreign actors and disrupt the way of life of much of society.[101] For example, the Bolsheviks abolished private property, halted all bond payments, and repudiated Russia's foreign debts, causing "shock waves" in the international financial system.[102] Similarly, Cuban revolutionaries ignored the advice of their Soviet patrons and attempted to export armed revolution throughout Latin America in the 1960s.[103] This "revolutionary messianism" placed Cuba in the crosshairs of the U.S. government, which posed a direct threat to the regime's survival.[104]

Such radical behavior cannot be understood in strictly power-maximizing terms. Initiatives such as radical land reform, large-scale expropriation of foreign-owned companies, confrontation with neighboring or Western powers, and efforts to wipe out secular culture challenge powerful interests and disrupt the lives of millions of people. For new governments presiding over weak states, such strategies are extraordinarily risky—sometimes fatally so (e.g., Hungary, Afghanistan, Cambodia). Such risk-acceptant behavior is very often driven by ideology.[105] Revolutions "put extreme idealists . . . in positions of power they do not ordinarily have."[106] As Stephen E. Hanson has argued, strong ideological commitments lengthen actors' time horizons. Ideologues operate "secure in the 'knowledge' of long-term success" and thus "rationally forgo the benefits of short-term egoistic behavior in order to advance the cause of the ideological collective."[107] Indeed, there is evidence that revolutionary leaders such as Vladimir Lenin, Béla Kun, Mao Zedong, Pol Pot, Mullah Mohammed Omar, Ho Chi Minh, Ayatollah Ruhollah Khomeini, and Samora Machel were unusually ideological, in that they placed considerable emphasis on utopian or eschatological visions of a new world order.[108]

COUNTERREVOLUTIONARY REACTION

Forrest D. Colburn observed that "just as Newton demonstrated that every action brings about a reaction, so every revolution evokes a counterrevolution."[109] The radical initiatives undertaken by new revolutionary governments almost invariably generate violent reactions, both at home and abroad.[110] Large-scale expropriation of private property, attacks on dominant cultural or religious institutions, and efforts to challenge the existing geopolitical order almost invariably trigger domestic counterrevolutionary movements or external military aggression, or both.[111]

Most revolutions thus spark the emergence of armed counterrevolutionary movements, often backed by foreign powers, which must be defeated if the new regime is to consolidate.[112] The Bolsheviks were thrown into a civil war against White Armies backed by British, French, Japanese, and American forces. The Castro government confronted a U.S.-backed counterrevolutionary campaign that culminated in the 1961 Bay of Pigs invasion. In Mozambique, the Front for the Liberation of Mozambique's (Frelimo) radical agrarian experiments and support for insurgents in Rhodesia led to the emergence of a large Rhodesian- and South African–backed insurgency at home.

Revolutions also provoke *external* wars, often with neighboring states whose governments perceive a threat from the revolutionary government or a window of opportunity in the wake of state collapse.[113] For example, the bloody Iran-Iraq War (1980–1988) was a direct consequence of the

Iranian Revolution, as Saddam Hussein viewed the Khomeini government as a threat.[114] Vietnam's revolutionary government fought a devastating war with the United States, while the Cambodian Revolution led to a war with Vietnam. In the 1990s, Eritrea engaged in military conflict with every country with which it had a land border. Overall, a striking seventeen of our twenty revolutions were followed by a civil or external war.[115]

Postrevolutionary conflicts generate enduring existential threats, often from powerful enemies.[116] Vietnam, for example, was in a state of continuous war—with France and later the United States—for three decades. Cuba's revolutionary regime faced decades of unrelenting U.S. hostility, and its leaders maintained a "siege mentality" as late as the early 2000s.[117]

REVOLUTIONARY LEGACIES: THREE PILLARS OF DURABLE AUTHORITARIANISM

The existential threats posed by counterrevolutionary reactions sometimes prove fatal for regimes. As chapter 7 shows, for example, the Hungarian Soviet Republic collapsed after only five months at the hands of invading Allied-backed Romanian troops. Likewise, revolutionary dictatorships in Cambodia and Afghanistan were destroyed by foreign military responses to their belligerent behavior.

Where regimes survive these counterrevolutionary reactions, however, military conflict generates processes of revolutionary state-building and societal transformation that lay a foundation for durable authoritarianism. The violent conflict triggered by efforts to radically transform the existing social or geopolitical order generates a prolonged perception of extreme threat, which reinforces elite cohesion, contributes to the development of strong and loyal coercive institutions, and facilitates the destruction of alternative centers of societal power. These three legacies serve as crucial pillars of regime durability because they help to inoculate revolutionary regimes against elite defection, military coups, and mass protest—three major sources of authoritarian breakdown.

A Cohesive Ruling Elite

Counterrevolutionary conflict tends to produce a cohesive regime elite, or one in which high-level government or ruling party defection to the opposition is rare, even during crises. Revolutions enhance elite cohesion because they polarize societies, often for decades. Intense polarization sharpens "us–them" distinctions, strengthening within-group ties and fostering perceptions of a "linked fate" among cadres.[118] Revolutionary polarization is often accompanied by an enduring perception of existential threat. Due to continuing counterrevolutionary challenges, most revolutionary regimes face persistent threats to their survival. Such existential threats tend to generate a siege mentality among the revolutionary elite, which creates powerful incentives to close ranks. With the regime's survival perceived to be at stake, elite defection—or even open dissent—is often viewed as treason. As a result, the costs of defection are high.

To be clear, the cohesion generated by revolutionary and counterrevolutionary conflict does not eliminate the factional power struggles that are endemic to all large political organizations. However, postrevolutionary conflict creates powerful obstacles to defection, especially during periods of crisis when the regime's survival is at stake. Thus, revolutionary leaders may compete for power and disagree over policy and strategy, but they almost never attack the regime itself. Due to the heightened cost of defection, elite schisms are less frequent in revolutionary regimes than in other autocracies. In Russia, China, Yugoslavia, Vietnam, Cuba, Albania, Mozambique, Nicaragua—and even the hyper-factionalized Islamic Republic of Iran (see chapter 6)—revolutionary autocracies suffered virtually no defections, often for decades.

The claim that revolutions generate elite cohesion may appear to fly in the face of events in Stalinist Russia, Maoist China, and Cambodia under the Khmer Rouge, where revolutionary governments carried out massive purges of the ruling elite. Indeed, since the time of the Jacobin Terror, revolutions have been said to "devour their own children." However, revolutionary purges are not as common as is sometimes believed—there were no purges, for example, in Cuba, Mozambique, Nicaragua, or Vietnam. Crucially, moreover, purges should not be treated as an indicator of low cohesion. There is broad scholarly agreement that leaders in Russia, China, and Cambodia used purges primarily as means to concentrate power. In other words, Stalin's and Mao's purges were *not* responses to serious threats of defection and opposition.[119] Likewise, years after the Khmer Rouge fell from power, Cambodian foreign minister Ieng Sary acknowledged that widespread claims of elite conspiracies against Pol Pot made during his tenure were simply concocted to justify purges.[120] Where elites are cohesive, dissident officials close ranks (or at least remain silent) even under the worst of circumstances. Thus, the fact that Stalin, Mao, and Pol Pot carried out massive purges *without triggering schisms* suggests a strikingly high degree of cohesion.

A cohesive elite is an important pillar of durable authoritarian rule. Internal schisms often pose a serious threat to authoritarian survival.[121] Those best positioned to remove autocrats are members of the inner circle because they have access to the coercive, administrative, patronage, and media resources needed to challenge the dictator. In autocracies facing economic or other crises, signs of regime vulnerability may induce erstwhile loyalists to abandon ship, which can trigger collapse.[122] For example, Zambia's single-party regime collapsed in 1991 after economic crisis and mounting protest triggered a wave of defections from the ruling United National Independence Party (UNIP). As one defecting UNIP member put it, "Only a stupid fly . . . follows a dead body to the grave."[123]

By contrast, revolutionary elites tend to remain loyal even during severe crises. For example, after Lenin's incapacitation in Russia, perceived threats from Western powers dissuaded Leon Trotsky and other dissident Bolsheviks from challenging Stalin or defecting at a time when such opposition might have succeeded. Instead, Trotsky, a revolutionary war hero who was widely considered Lenin's natural successor (and who personally despised Stalin), pledged loyalty to Stalin's ruling triumvirate even after he was excluded from it.[124] Although they might have used their considerable prestige to oppose Stalin, Trotsky and other dissidents were "paralyzed by fear" at the prospect of creating a rival party.[125] Similarly, Vietnam's Communist Party leadership suffered no defections during the entirety of the war against the United States,[126] and Cuba's Communist Party leadership suffered no defections despite a catastrophic economic crisis in the wake of the Soviet collapse.[127]

A Strong and Loyal Coercive Apparatus

Social revolution and its aftermath tend to produce strong and loyal coercive organizations. While the collapse and reconstruction of the state allows revolutionaries to create new army, police, and intelligence agencies that are fused with, and tightly controlled by, the ruling elite, sustained counterrevolutionary or external military threats almost invariably lead to the development of a large and effective coercive apparatus.

Political-Military Fusion. Because social revolutions are accompanied by the crippling or collapse of prerevolutionary states, revolutionary leaders must build new coercive agencies, often from scratch.[128] Indeed, in nearly all our cases, revolutionary elites built entirely new armies, police forces, and intelligence services.[129]

Revolutionary armies differ from nonrevolutionary ones in several important ways. First, they tend to be tightly fused with ruling parties, creating what Amos Perlmutter and William M. LeoGrande call a "dual elite."[130] Revolutionary army, police, and intelligence forces are led and staffed by cadres from the liberation struggle, and military officials hold top positions in the government and the ruling party. In such cases, it "makes no sense to ask whether the dual elite functions as the agent of the party within the army or the agent of the army within the party. It is both."[131] For example, Cuba's revolutionary regime was marked by a near-total overlap between civilian and military elites.[132] Civilian control over the military was not an issue because civilian leaders "*were* the armed forces."[133] Likewise, in Vietnam, where Communist guerrillas founded the People's Army of Vietnam in the 1940s, effectively fusing party and army leaderships,[134] the military command "was nothing more than a segment of the party leadership."[135] A similar degree of party-army fusion could be observed in China, Mexico, Mozambique, Nicaragua, Yugoslavia, and elsewhere.

Party-army fusion enhances the authority of political leaders, many of whom led the armed struggle. Thus, in Albania, Angola, China, Cuba, Eritrea, Mexico, Mozambique, Nicaragua, Yugoslavia, and elsewhere, party leaders were guerrilla commanders during the revolutionary war. Their military achievements and demonstrated willingness to share battlefield risks earned them "martial prestige."[136]

Building new armies from scratch also allows revolutionary elites to penetrate the armed forces with political commissars and other institutions of partisan oversight and control.[137] Partisan penetration enhances the ruling elite's capacity to monitor militaries and identify potential conspirators. In most cases, such penetration is extraordinarily difficult to achieve. Partisan interference is often fiercely resisted by traditional militaries, whose leaders value their autonomy.[138] For example, Kwame Nkrumah's attempts to introduce political commissars and party cells into the Ghanaian military met strong resistance and contributed to the coup that toppled him in 1966. Such politicization is easier when ruling parties create militaries from scratch.[139] In Albania, China, Cuba, Nicaragua, Rwanda, the Soviet Union, Vietnam, Yugoslavia, and elsewhere, revolutionary leaders successfully established political commissars, party cells, and other institutional mechanisms at all levels of the armed forces to ensure ruling party control.

The fusion of revolutionary party and army structures fosters an unusual degree of military loyalty. In most nonrevolutionary autocracies, militaries retain strong corporate identities and thus view their interests as distinct from those of the government. In postcolonial Burma, for example, military leaders believed that politicians "could not be trusted" with holding the country together.[140] Likewise, the Pakistani army viewed itself as the primary guardian of the national interest and able to run the country more efficiently than civilians.[141] In revolutionary regimes, by contrast, civilian and military elites share an identity.[142] Army commanders view themselves as partners in the revolutionary struggle and thus tend to be staunchly loyal to the revolution and its ideology.[143] Thus, in China, there was little danger of the military betraying the revolution because the military "had *become* the revolution."[144] Likewise, in Nicaragua, Sandinista military officials viewed themselves as "defenders . . . of a revolutionary political project,"[145] and in Iran, the Revolutionary Guard viewed itself as the "principal bastion and perpetuator of revolutionary purity."[146]

Party-army fusion dramatically reduces the likelihood of military coups.[147] Coups were the principal cause of regime collapse—authoritarian and democratic—during the Cold War era.[148] Militaries seized power throughout the developing world in the decades after World War II.[149] According to Naunihal Singh,[150] coups were attempted in 80 percent of sub-Saharan African states, 76 percent of Middle Eastern and North African states, 67 percent of Latin American states, and 50 percent of Asian states during the second half of the twentieth century.[151]

Yet coups are extremely rare in revolutionary regimes. Among our twenty cases, only two regimes—those in Bolivia and Guinea-Bissau— were overthrown by the military.[152] In an analysis conducted with Jean Lachapelle and Adam E. Casey, we found that revolutionary regimes are considerably less likely to suffer coup attempts than nonrevolutionary regimes.[153] Indeed, revolutionary armies have remained loyal even in circumstances that frequently trigger intervention. In China, for example, the military remained loyal to Mao during the Cultural Revolution, even though Mao encouraged violent factional conflict that brought the country to the brink of civil war. In Soviet Russia, Stalin faced no challenge from the army despite purging 90 percent of top military officials in 1937–1938. In Mozambique, the military did not attempt a coup despite a 1992 peace agreement that required Frelimo to disband the military and create a new force that integrated its rival, the Mozambican National Resistance (Renamo).[154] Regimes in Cuba, Iran, and Nicaragua did not suffer coups despite severe economic crises.

In sum, party-army fusion has a powerful coup-proofing effect. Because coups are a leading source of authoritarian breakdown,[155] revolutionary state-building contributes in an important way to regime durability.

A Strong Coercive Apparatus. Social revolutions frequently increase the power and reach of the state.[156] Existential military threats compel revolutionary governments to build a vast security apparatus. Faced

with counterrevolutionary violence and, in many cases, real or threatened foreign invasion, revolutionary governments often must invest
heavily in building up their armies and internal security forces.[157] In
Vietnam, decades of war gave rise to one of the world's largest and most
effective armies.[158] In Cuba, the threat of a U.S-backed invasion led the
Castro government to transform its "ragtag army" of 5,000 soldiers into a
300,000-strong force capable of deterring the United States.[159] In Eritrea,
counterrevolutionary conflict in the 1990s transformed the country from
a weak state into one of the most militarized autocracies in the world—
second only to North Korea.[160]

A developed coercive apparatus—especially one that is tightly wedded
to the ruling elite—enhances a regime's repressive capacity. In addition to
elite schisms and coups, autocrats face potential threats from below.[161] To
combat such challenges, they rely on both low-intensity and high-intensity
repression.[162] High-intensity repression refers to high-visibility acts that
target large numbers of people, well-known individuals, or major institutions. An example is violent repression of mass demonstrations, as in
Mexico City in 1968, Tiananmen Square in China in 1989, or Iran in 2019.
Low-intensity repression refers to less visible, but more systematic, forms
of coercion, such as surveillance, low-profile harassment or detention by
security forces, and intimidation by paramilitary forces.

Revolutionary origins increase the capacity of autocrats to engage in
both low- and high-intensity repression. The vast expansion of the central state apparatus, often in a context of wartime mobilization, enhanced
revolutionary regimes' capacity for surveillance and other forms of low-
intensity repression. The Soviet KGB stationed officials in every significant
enterprise, factory, and government institution and drew on roughly 11
million informers who infiltrated virtually every apartment block in the
country.[163] Vietnam's intelligence agency (Cong an) mobilized as many
as a million agents,[164] which allowed it to penetrate society "down to the
smallest alley."[165] With informants in workplaces and classrooms and
"wardens" overseeing every neighborhood, the Vietnamese state was able
to monitor every active dissident in the country.[166]

Revolutionary governments also possess an unusual capacity for high-
intensity repression. Large-scale and public repression of mass protest
involves considerable risk. Not only is it likely to trigger international
condemnation, but it may erode the domestic legitimacy of the security
forces, which can undermine internal discipline and morale.[167] Due to
fear of prosecution or other forms of public retribution, both security
officials and rank-and-file soldiers may resist orders to repress. For this

reason, governments are often reluctant to order high-intensity coercion, and where such orders are issued, security officials often refuse to carry them out. Indeed, numerous authoritarian regimes have collapsed due to the government's unwillingness—or inability—to repress protest in a consistent and sustained manner. (Twenty-first-century examples include Serbia in 2000, Madagascar in 2002 and 2009, Georgia in 2003, Ukraine in 2004, Kyrgyzstan in 2005 and 2010, and Egypt and Tunisia in 2011.)

By contrast, states that emerge from revolutionary conflict are well equipped to crack down on protest. Years of military struggle give rise to a generation of elites and cadres with experience in violence. Ruling elites that have engaged in violent conflict are more likely to unite behind coercive measures, and, crucially, security officials who belong to those revolutionary elites are more likely to carry out controversial orders to engage in high-intensity repression. Thus, revolutionary ties between government and security forces facilitated the PRI government's brutal repression of student protesters in Mexico City in 1968, the Chinese Communist government's high-intensity crackdown on the Tiananmen Square protesters in 1989, and the Algerian military's crackdown on Islamists in the 1990s. In Iran, the Revolutionary Guard and the Basij—organizations created by revolutionary forces and strengthened by years of counterinsurgency and war—consistently carried out orders to repress during the 2009 Green Revolution protests as well as the 2019 uprisings.

The Destruction of Rival Organizations and Independent Centers of Societal Power

Finally, revolutionary and counterrevolutionary conflict facilitates the destruction of both existing rivals and the social institutions that could serve as the bases for future challenges.[168] Wars allow governments to do things ordinary dictatorships often cannot do. For one, they provide revolutionary elites with both a justification and the means to destroy political rivals. For example, Russia's civil war allowed the Bolsheviks to wipe out other socialist parties, including the Mensheviks and the popular SRs.[169] In Yugoslavia, the revolutionary war allowed the Partisans to destroy the nationalist Chetniks, who had competed for control of the country. By the war's end, almost all potential rivals to the revolutionaries had been destroyed.[170] Likewise, the Vietnamese Communists undertook the violent destruction of rival nationalist and religious organizations during their struggle against the French.[171] By the time the Communist Party gained control of North Vietnam in 1954, all major challengers had been eliminated.[172]

Crucially, moreover, revolutionary and postrevolutionary wars facilitate the weakening or destruction of independent centers of societal power: institutions or social classes whose power, resources, or legitimacy can serve as a basis for opposition. These include local elites, landowning classes, preexisting armies, and traditional monarchic and religious authorities whose "symbolic power" could be used to mobilize opposition to the regime.[173] Thus, Mexico's bloody 1913–1915 civil war weakened landowners and destroyed the old army,[174] while Russia's civil war finished off the last remnants of the tsarist forces and the landowning classes. In Yugoslavia, military conflict during World War II undermined local authority structures, weakening the traditional village chiefs who had long dominated the country,[175] and in China, the revolutionary war and land reform wiped out the dense network of local gentry, foreign and domestic churches, warlords, criminal gangs, secret societies, and clan networks that had limited the reach of the prerevolutionary state.[176]

The destruction of independent power centers weakens the structural bases of future opposition. The mobilization of trade unions, religious institutions, and other civic associations undermined dictatorships in Argentina, Brazil, the Philippines, Poland, South Africa, South Korea, and elsewhere during the Third Wave of democratization. Revolutionary regimes are less likely to face such societal mobilization. In the absence of independent sources of finance, infrastructure, or legitimacy, the organizational bases of opposition effectively disappear. In China, the elimination of criminal gangs and local fiefdoms—which had provided the Communist Party with safe havens during the revolutionary struggle—deprived opponents of means to resist attacks by the central state. At the start of the twenty-first century, China had a much weaker civil society than did many countries with similarly high levels of economic development. In Vietnam, the destruction of the landowning class and the weakening of the Catholic Church eliminated potential sources of opposition to communist rule.[177] By the 1960s, all independent sources of power outside the state had been crushed, leaving opponents without a mass base.[178] As we shall see in the cases of China and Iran, the destruction of alternative power centers does not inoculate regimes against large-scale protest; however, the absence of mobilizing structures makes it harder to sustain such mobilization.

In sum, we argue that in most revolutionary regimes, robust authoritarian institutions emerge out of a reactive sequence. Notwithstanding the initial weakness of many revolutionary governments, ideologically driven revolutionary elites launch radical initiatives that challenge power-ful domestic and international interests, resulting in civil war (Angola, Mexico, Mozambique, Nicaragua, Russia), external war (Afghanistan, Cambodia, China, Eritrea, Iran, Vietnam), or existential military threats (Albania, Cuba). Such conflict sometimes brings early regime collapse. But where regimes survive, counterrevolutionary conflict leads to the develop-ment of a cohesive elite, a strong and loyal military, and the destruction of alternative power centers. Because elite schisms, coups, and mass protest are three of the main sources of authoritarian breakdown, revolution and its aftermath effectively inoculate regimes against three leading causes of death.

We measure the three pillars of regime durability in the following way.[179] First, a cohesive elite is one in which defection to the opposition of high-level regime officials is rarely observed, even during periods of crisis.[180] When defections occur, few regime actors join them. Although intra-elite conflict may be extensive (and even violent), losers of factional battles and other dissident elites either close ranks or remain silent—rather than work against the regime—during crises.

Second, we separate the strength and loyalty of the coercive apparatus into its two component parts. A strong coercive apparatus is one in which the security sector—including the army, the police, intelligence agencies, and other specialized internal security agencies—is sufficiently large and effective to monitor dissent and thwart protest across the national terri-tory, down to the village and neighborhood levels. A loyal coercive appa-ratus is one that consistently supports the revolutionary regime, even during periods of crises. Loyal militaries are characterized by the absence (or near-total absence) of coup attempts or military rebellions aimed at changing the regime or removing its elite.

Third, in measuring the destruction of alternative centers of societal power, we distinguish between full and partial destruction. We score as full destruction cases in which all significant societal institutions, economic actors, and organized groups are either destroyed or emasculated and rendered dependent on the state. This was the case, for example, in com-munist revolutions such as in Russia, China, Vietnam, and Cuba. We score as cases of partial destruction those in which revolutionary governments destroy or emasculate some independent centers of societal power, but one or more societal institution survives and retains the capacity to mobi-lize against the regime. Examples include mosque networks in Algeria, the Catholic Church in Nicaragua, and trade unions in Bolivia. As we shall see, this difference can be consequential. Whereas revolutionary regimes that only partially destroy independent power centers often confront higher levels of societal contention (e.g., Bolivia in the early 1960s, Algeria in the early 1990s), in cases of full destruction, such as the Soviet Union, Cuba, and Vietnam, it is often extraordinarily difficult for opposition movements to establish themselves.

DIVERGENT PATHS

Although the revolutionary reactive sequence described above may be considered the ideal-typical trajectory of revolutionary regimes (figure 1.2), it is not the only one. Two other postrevolutionary paths generally lead to less durable authoritarianism. These paths are summarized in figure 1.3.

In the ideal-typical sequence, early radicalism triggers a revolutionary reactive sequence that leads to a robust authoritarian regime. However, the reactive sequence may be aborted in two ways, resulting in less stable regimes. First, early radicalism may trigger an external military reaction that brings violent defeat, thereby causing an *early death*. Nascent revolutionary regimes suffered such military defeats in four cases: Finland (1918),[181] Hungary (1919), Cambodia (1975–1979), and Afghanistan (1996–2001). In Cambodia, for example, the Khmer Rouge government recklessly provoked a war with Vietnam, which led to the regime's demise amid military defeat. In Afghanistan, the Taliban regime's refusal to break with al-Qaeda in the wake of the 2001 World Trade Center attacks led to a U.S. military intervention that ended the regime. Challenging powerful actors and states is a risky venture, and it sometimes has fatal consequences for regimes.

We have too few cases to generalize with any confidence about the conditions under which early radicalism leads to rapid regime collapse. However, such outcomes appear most likely in small, geopolitically vulnerable states. Each of the four cases of early death—Finland, Hungary, Cambodia, and Afghanistan—occurred in small states that were highly exposed to external intervention. In larger states (e.g., China, Iran, Russia), revolutionary governments are more likely to survive their early radicalism, allowing the reactive sequence we have theorized to unfold.

Second, revolutionary elites may prove *insufficiently* radical to trigger a full reactive sequence. This is the accommodationist path depicted in figure 1.3. In Algeria, Bolivia, and Guinea-Bissau, three borderline cases of revolution, ruling parties launched radical reform initiatives (if they did not, they would not be scored as revolutionary) but then scaled back or ceased many of these initiatives to avoid conflict with domestic interests or foreign powers. Because this more pragmatic approach threatened

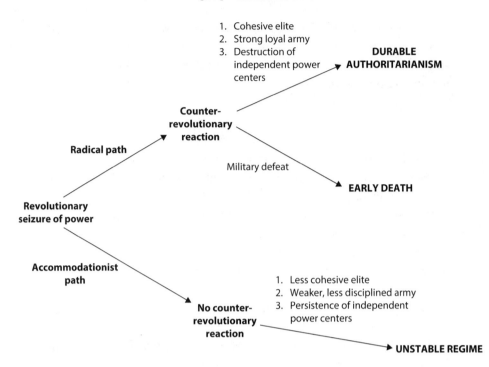

1. Cohesive elite
2. Strong loyal army
3. Destruction of independent power centers

DURABLE AUTHORITARIANISM

Counter-revolutionary reaction

Radical path

Military defeat

EARLY DEATH

Revolutionary seizure of power

Accommodationist path

No counter-revolutionary reaction

1. Less cohesive elite
2. Weaker, less disciplined army
3. Persistence of independent power centers

UNSTABLE REGIME

FIGURE 1.3: Three Revolutionary Regime Paths.

fewer interests at home and abroad, it provoked weaker counterrevolutionary reactions. Revolutionary governments that confiscate less property from powerful domestic and foreign actors, pursue less invasive cultural transformations, and avoid foreign policies that threaten the regional or geopolitical order are less likely to face strong counterrevolutionary resistance or external aggression. As a result, they tend to avoid the kind of destructive military conflict that threatened embryonic revolutionary regimes in Russia, Cuba, and Iran—and destroyed them in Afghanistan and Cambodia. Yet, precisely because they do not confront existential military threats, accommodationist governments build weaker regimes. They are less likely to develop cohesive elites or powerful garrison states, and they often lack the will or capacity to wipe out rivals and independent centers of power. In other words, they fail to develop the bases for long-run durability. The resulting regime is less stable because internal challenges and societal contestation are more frequent, more potent, and more likely to trigger a breakdown of the revolutionary regime.

Ultimately, then, where revolutionary elites were less extremist during the initial period, regimes avoided the counterrevolutionary reaction that either destroyed or fortified revolutionary regimes. Accommodation-ist governments tended to survive the early revolutionary period, but their regimes remained prone to both internal schism and opposition mobili-zation. In Bolivia, the Revolutionary Nationalist Movement (MNR) gov-ernment fell prey to a coup after just twelve years. In Guinea-Bissau, the regime suffered numerous coup attempts and finally collapsed in the face of military rebellion after twenty-five years. Although the Algerian regime survived, it was ridden by periodic crisis, including a palace coup and a series of debilitating schisms in the 1960s and massive protest, another palace coup, and a descent into civil war in the late 1980s and early 1990s.

What explains the choice between radical and accommodationist strat-egies? Leadership plays a role. Radical strategies are often undertaken by unusually strong-willed and risk-acceptant leaders who impose them over internal resistance and despite daunting odds. It is plausible to argue, for example, that strong-willed leaders such as Lenin and Stalin, Mao, Cas-tro, and Khomeini pushed through radical initiatives that their govern-ments might not otherwise have adopted. In Iran, for example, Khomeini's single-minded pursuit of an Islamic republic was critical to its founding, as the strategy was fiercely resisted by many of his revolutionary allies.[182] Likewise, the Vietnamese Communists' costly pursuit of revolution in South Vietnam—which provoked a massive U.S. military intervention—was driven by General Secretary Le Duan, whose "dogged persistence" enabled the "go for broke" strategy to prevail over the more cautious "North first" strategy advocated by other party leaders.[183] Finally, Castro's volun-tarism and "revolutionary messianism"[184] was likely decisive in steering Cuba's revolutionary government toward an "unequivocal, unwavering, and reckless" strategy of confrontation with the United States.[185] It is also plausible that different leaders in accommodationist cases might have pursued more radical strategies. For example, Guinea-Bissau's founding president, Luis Cabral, was more moderate than his Lusophone counter-parts in Angola and Mozambique, even though the Party for African Inde-pendence in Guinea and Cape Verde (PAIGC) was in a stronger military position than the Popular Movement for the Liberation of Angola (MPLA) in Angola or Frelimo in Mozambique.[186]

Beyond leadership, two factors appear consequential in shaping the choice between radicalism and accommodation. The first is ideology. Where revolutionary elites share a commitment to a well-defined revolu-tionary ideology prior to the seizure of power,[187] as was the case with the Bolsheviks in Russia, the Chinese, Vietnamese, and Cambodian Commu-nists, and Shiite leaders in Iran, they are more likely to adopt radical or risk-accepting strategies.[188] Shared ideological commitments—whether to Marxism, anti-imperialism, or religious fundamentalism—distort leaders' understanding of the world and induce the belief (frequently unwarranted) that radical strategies either are inevitable or will succeed in the end.[189]

Where revolutionary leaders lack a shared ideology, as in Algeria, Bolivia, Guinea-Bissau, and Mexico, pragmatic strategies are more likely to prevail. In such cases, pressure from below, in the form of worker or peasant mobilization, may lead nonideological revolutionaries to adopt radical strategies. This occurred in the aftermath of the Bolivian Revolution and at critical moments in revolutionary Mexico. However, whereas ideologically committed leaders in Russia, China, Vietnam, and Iran sustained radical strategies, often at great cost, pragmatists in Bolivia and Mexico abandoned them as soon as it was politically expedient to do so.

Second, foreign support facilitates the introduction of radical measures. Superpower patronage expands revolutionary governments' room to maneuver, giving the revolutionary elite greater confidence that they will be bailed out if their radical policies fail—or protected if their behavior triggers conflict. Cuba's radical foreign policy, for example, was made possible by Soviet support.[190] In Bolivia, by contrast, the absence of superpower support left the MNR government dependent on the United States, which encouraged accommodation.[191]

In sum, durable revolutionary regimes emerge out of a reactive sequence. Most of them are born weak. Revolutionary elites that do not build powerful party-armies and wipe out rivals during protracted guerrilla struggles (as in China and Vietnam) must do so after they seize power. Such postrevolutionary state- and party-building generally occurs only in response to an existential military threat. Radical measures undertaken by revolutionary governments, which create powerful domestic and external enemies, tend to generate such threats. These counterrevolutionary conflicts sometimes prove fatal, and they are sometimes insufficient to trigger a full-blown reactive sequence. But where revolutionary governments *survive* violent counterrevolutionary conflicts, as occurred in two-thirds of our cases, rapid state- and party-building and the destruction of independent power centers lay a solid foundation for durable authoritarianism.

Moderate strategies undertaken by revolutionaries thus have a paradoxical effect. Measures aimed at accommodating powerful domestic and international actors may help ensure regime survival in the short term, but they do little to inoculate the revolution against standard threats (elite schisms, coups) that imperil most authoritarian regimes.

Of course, social revolution is hardly the only source of robust authoritarian institutions. Scholars have identified several other phenomena that generate one or more of the pillars of durable authoritarianism described in this chapter. For example, as research by Dan Slater and others has shown, violent *counterrevolutionary* conflict may also enhance elite cohesion, strengthen ruling parties, and encourage the development of a powerful coercive apparatus.[192] Likewise, *political* revolution, in which successful insurgents build new armies but do not engage in radical social transformation, may give rise to relatively cohesive ruling parties and loyal militaries.[193] Finally, large-scale agrarian reform weakens a powerful alternative power center by destroying traditional landowning classes.[194] Yet, whereas counterrevolution, political revolution, and land reform strengthen one or two pillars of durable authoritarianism, social revolution strengthens *all three* of them. In other words, the revolutionary reactive sequence is not a unique source of authoritarian durability, but it is an especially potent one because it helps inoculate autocrats against *three* principal sources of regime breakdown: elite schism, coups, and societal mobilization.

THE ROLE OF THE INTERNATIONAL ENVIRONMENT

Regime trajectories are powerfully shaped by the international environment.[195] The geopolitics of the Cold War—and the emergence of the Soviet Union as a global superpower—weighed heavily on twentieth-century regime outcomes,[196] particularly those of revolutionary regimes. The Soviet Union inspired revolutionary movements across the globe, provided a model (Leninism) for organizing revolutionary regimes, and eventually became an important source of military and economic assistance for both aspiring revolutionary movements and existing revolutionary regimes. Either directly or through allies, the Soviets contributed to the success of revolutionary movements in Angola, Cambodia, China, Guinea-Bissau, Mozambique, and Nicaragua. Soviet bloc assistance also helped to shore up revolutionary regimes in Angola, Cuba, Mozambique, and Vietnam,[197] and in some cases, such as Cuba, it likely encouraged their radicalization. At the same time, Cold War polarization intensified the domestic and international reaction to revolutionary regimes,[198] which increased both the likelihood and the intensity of counterrevolutionary conflict. The heightened stakes and threat created by Cold War geopolitical competition appears to have strengthened regimes in Angola, Cuba, Mozambique, and Vietnam by enhancing elite cohesion. By contrast, regimes that were born after the Cold War, such as those in Eritrea and Rwanda, faced less polarized international environments and weaker external threats, which appears to have resulted in less cohesive elites.

Ultimately, however, the international environment is a secondary factor shaping revolutionary regime trajectories. In nine of our cases, including two of the most durable, Mexico and Russia, revolutionary regimes emerged either before or after the Cold War.[199] Four other revolutions (in Algeria, Bolivia, Cuba, and Iran) occurred during the Cold War but without Communist bloc assistance. Moreover, it is worth noting that among our revolutionary cases, the four leading beneficiaries of Soviet assistance (Angola, Cuba, Mozambique, and Vietnam) all survived for more than three decades after the Soviet collapse. Finally, revolutionary elites in post–Cold War Eritrea and Rwanda may be less cohesive than many of their Cold War counterparts, but as we show in the book's conclusion, reactive sequences in both countries nevertheless gave rise to durable autocracies. Robust revolutionary regimes, then, are not simply an artifact of the Cold War.

THE DURATION OF REVOLUTIONARY LEGACIES

Revolutionary legacies are enduring but not permanent. The pillars of authoritarianism degrade over time, albeit slowly and incompletely, eventually leaving regimes more vulnerable to breakdown. This process of decay was most evident in the cases of Mexico and the Soviet Union, the earliest and longest-lived regimes covered in this book.

The bases of revolutionary regime durability erode at different speeds and to varying degrees. Elite cohesion appears to degrade most rapidly. The siege mentality characteristic of most revolutionary regime elites tends to diminish as domestic and external threats subside. The process varies across cases. Where external threats persist for decades, as in Cuba, Iran, the Soviet Union, and Vietnam, cohesion erodes more slowly. Elite cohesion also weakens with generational change. The founding generation of revolutionary leaders tends to be more ideologically committed and wedded to a siege mentality, and the prestige of founding leaders such as Stalin, Mao, Josip Broz Tito, Castro, and Khomeini can have a powerful unifying effect even after the counterrevolutionary threat has disappeared. For example, Chinese veterans of the Long March in the 1930s (the "elders") almost universally viewed the 1989 Tiananmen Square protests in polarized, zero-sum terms and played a critical role in unifying the party leadership behind a repressive response.[200] The departure of this founding generation can thus be expected to yield a less cohesive elite.

As existential threats recede and the founding generation disappears, the nonmaterial bases of revolutionary elite cohesion weaken. Ambition and patronage replace ideology and perceived threat as the primary glue binding together regime elites,[201] gradually transforming revolutionary parties into the more run-of-the-mill ruling party machines theorized in the literature on parties and authoritarianism.[202] For example, ruling parties appear to grow more vulnerable to elite defection during crises,[203] which increases the importance of economic growth as a source of authoritarian stability.[204]

Even when the original bases of elite cohesion disappear, however, most revolutionary regimes continue to enjoy many of the advantages of institutionalized ruling parties. In the Soviet Union, China, Mexico, Vietnam, and Mozambique, for example, established formal and informal institutions governing collective decision-making, leadership selection, and succession helped regulate intraparty conflict and limit elite defection after the revolutionary generation had passed from the scene. In addition, decades of dominance often reinforce elite perceptions of ruling party hegemony, thereby discouraging defection.[205]

The coercive pillars of revolutionary regime durability appear to degrade more slowly and unevenly. For example, the size and effectiveness of the coercive apparatus appears largely unaffected by generational change. This is certainly the case in China, where the Communist regime not only retained its capacity to monitor and control dissent in the early twentieth century but in many respects—most notably, surveillance capacity—enhanced it.[206] Regimes in Vietnam and Cuba similarly retained vast repressive infrastructures—with a demonstrated capacity for low-intensity coercion—into the twenty-first century.

Institutionalized party-army linkages are also slow to change. Decades of party-army fusion help revolutionary regimes steer clear of self-reinforcing coup traps, in which each coup reinforces patterns of military intervention, thereby increasing the likelihood of future coups.[207] Most revolutionary regimes establish institutionalized patterns of civilian control that endure long after party-army fusion erodes and the armed forces professionalize.[208] Likewise, party penetration of the armed forces often persists, providing enduring mechanisms for political surveillance that reinforces political control. As a result, even after the revolutionary generation passed from the scene in Mexico, the Soviet Union, China, Vietnam, and Cuba, security forces remained strikingly subordinate to civilian authorities. Although many of the original sources of military loyalty, such as existential threat, overlapping leaderships, and the founding generation's "martial prestige,"[209] weaken or disappear over time, we observe little evidence of military disloyalty in aging revolutionary regimes.

One area in which revolutionary coercive capacity appears to erode over time is that of high-intensity coercion. With the passing of the revolutionary generation, the regime's capacity for high-intensity repression—such as the 1968 Tlatelolco massacre in Mexico, the 1989 Tiananmen Square crackdown in China, the 1992 anti-Islamist repression in Algeria, and the quelling of the 2009 Green Revolution protests in Iran—almost certainly diminishes. Whereas military officers from the founding generation tend to be ideologically committed, experienced with violence, and especially prestigious among rank-and-file soldiers, succeeding generations, which are made up of more ordinary professional soldiers with more limited revolutionary commitments, wartime experience, and prestige, may lack the confidence or "stomach" to fire on crowds or engage in other high-profile acts of repression. Such a generational change was evident, for example, in the Soviet Union in the late 1960s and the 1970s. According to an unpublished study by Liudmilla Alexeyeva and Valery Chalidze,[210] the use of high-intensity coercion against protests declined dramatically in the mid-1960s—after the founding generation of Soviet leaders had died off.[211] Partly as a result, Soviet leaders had difficulty motivating the armed services to crack down on protests in the late 1980s and early 1990s. The erosion of the capacity for high-intensity coercion may thus leave aging revolutionary regimes more vulnerable to large-scale opposition protest.

Finally, the state-society power asymmetries created by the destruction of independent power centers also degrade slowly, if at all. For example, in Mexico, a middle-income country in a region that witnessed the emergence of powerful democracy movements in the late 1970s and the 1980s, organized opposition remained weak as late as the 1990s.[212] In early twenty-first-century Cuba and Vietnam, opposition groups rarely mobilized more than a few dozen followers and were largely confined to the internet.[213] Eventually, independent social, economic, or cultural actors may (re)emerge (e.g., business associations in northern Mexico, nationalist organizations in Yugoslavia, the Church in Mexico and Yugoslavia). However, the speed and extent of this emergence varies. In wealthier countries with more open economies, such as late twentieth-century Mexico and Yugoslavia, the emergence of independent associations is likely to be more rapid. However, in countries with more extensive state controls (e.g., China, Vietnam), societal organizations have remained weak after decades of rapid economic development and show no signs of strengthening.

In sum, the pillars of revolutionary regime durability degrade over time, but they do so slowly and unevenly. Even though the initial sources of durability—an ideologically committed and prestigious founding elite facing an existential military threat—eventually disappear, undermining the bases of elite cohesion and high-intensity coercive capacity, other revolutionary legacies, such as vast coercive structures and extreme state-society power asymmetries, tend to endure long after counterrevolutionary threats fade and founding generations exit the stage.

Alternative Explanations

In the statistical analysis summarized above (and detailed in appendix I), we showed that revolutionary origins are strongly associated with authoritarian durability, even when we control for various other factors that have been shown to affect regime stability, such as economic performance, oil, and type of authoritarian regime.[214]

As in any observational study, we cannot know with certainty that we have controlled for all potential confounding explanations. It could be the case, for example, that revolutionary origins are endogenous to some other factor that is causing both social revolution and subsequent regime durability. Perhaps regime durability is a function not of revolutionary origins but rather of some antecedent condition that facilitates both revolution and robust authoritarian rule.

There are sound reasons, however, for treating social revolution as exogenous to authoritarian survival. Above all, the factors that are widely viewed as the principal causes of social revolution, namely, weak or collapsing states, defeat in war, and neopatrimonial or sultanistic rule, which hollows out state institutions,[215] are all conditions that undermine, rather than enhance, authoritarian durability. Social revolutions are always accompanied by a weakening or collapse of the state.[216] It is virtually impossible for revolutionary outsiders to seize power and initiate a transformation of the social order unless the armed forces of the old regime have been fundamentally weakened.[217] As Jack Goldstone notes,[218] "It is now a truism, but worth restating, that fiscally and militarily sound states that enjoy the support of united elites are largely invulnerable to revolution from below."

Indeed, nearly all the regimes examined in this book emerged out of weak or collapsed states. In Algeria, Angola, Guinea-Bissau, Mozambique, and Vietnam, colonial powers had undermined indigenous authority structures and failed to build (or, in the case of Algeria, sustain) an effective central state. In Afghanistan, Albania, Cambodia, China, Finland, Hungary,

Mexico, Russia, and Yugoslavia, civil or external war gutted the state before revolutionaries took power. In Cuba and Nicaragua, neopatrimonial states collapsed when dictators fled. In Iran and Rwanda, where preexisting states were more robust, the coercive apparatus disintegrated when leaders left power. In turn, state collapse makes it considerably harder to build a durable autocracy. It is highly unlikely, then, that durable authoritarianism would have emerged in our cases in the absence of social revolution. Until scholars identify a plausible factor that explains both social revolution and authoritarian durability, we remain skeptical that endogeneity is a problem for our analysis.

There exist other alternative explanations for revolutionary regime durability, however. These include *institutionalist* explanations, which focus on the role of communist or totalitarian institutions, and *society-centered* explanations, which focus on how redistributive policies or sociocultural transformation may build durable support for revolutionary regimes.

COMMUNIST INSTITUTIONS

Given that a majority (eleven of twenty) of our cases may be characterized as communist,[219] it could be that communist (or totalitarian) institutions, rather than revolutionary origins, are the primary source of regime durability. Indeed, an earlier literature argued that communist regimes' extensive state penetration and control of society, as well as ruling party penetration of the state, largely eliminated opportunities for organized opposition or internal challenges, thereby making such regimes difficult to overthrow.[220] There are at least two problems with such arguments, however. First, they do not explain how robust communist institutions emerged in the first place. In most cases, the establishment of effective communist and Leninist institutions was made possible by conditions—war, state collapse, and counterrevolutionary conflict—that were produced by social revolution.[221] For example, it was China's revolutionary civil war—which destroyed most preexisting power structures—that enabled the Communist Party to create new authority structures that penetrated the countryside.[222] Second, the durability of noncommunist revolutionary regimes such as those in Eritrea, Iran, Mexico, and Rwanda provides further evidence that origins in social revolution, rather than communist institutions best explain revolutionary regime durability. Indeed, our statistical analysis shows that communist regimes that emerged out of social revolution, such as Russia, China, Cuba, and Vietnam, survived more than twice as long as those that were installed from the outside, such as most of the communist regimes in Eastern Europe (see appendix I).

SOCIETY-CENTERED EXPLANATIONS

Scholars have also offered what might be called "society-centered" explanations of revolutionary regime durability. Our theory is top-down and state-centric. Society enters the explanation only to the extent that revolutionaries destroy societal organizations and institutions that might otherwise mobilize opposition. Yet, as Eric Selbin writes, "Revolutions are fundamentally about people: they are created by people, led by people, fought and died for by people."[223] Thus, an alternative explanation for revolutionary regime durability might focus on the societal bases of support for the regime. For Selbin, popular support is an "essential condition for the survival of the social revolutionary process. . . . Without public support the revolution cannot be and will not be consolidated."[224]

Two society-centered approaches merit attention. One focuses on redistribution and popular support. Revolutions create numerous actors who benefit materially under the new system and may thus develop a stake in its survival. Beneficiaries of revolutionary transformation include peasants who profit from land reform and often support governments or regimes that carry such reforms.[225] Revolutionary change may also benefit a broader array of individuals who gain access to housing and other property redistributed after the revolution,[226] as well as lower-income peasants and workers who achieve social mobility through the party, the revolutionary army, or the state bureaucracy.

Most social revolutions also bring an expansion of social welfare benefits distributed to previously excluded groups. Some scholars have argued, for example, that communist regimes forged a "social contract" in which societies exchanged popular quiescence for secure jobs, health care and other services, subsidized housing, and access to basic consumer goods.[227] Such an approach has been used to explain the collapse of many communist regimes in the late 1980s, as severe shortages and mounting economic crisis undermined governments' capacity to deliver on their end of the social contract.[228] Likewise, the Islamic Republic of Iran used oil wealth to finance a "martyr's welfare state" that distributed health care and other benefits to large numbers of Iranians who had been excluded under the shah.[229] These distributive social policies—which brought notable improvements in infant mortality rates and female life expectancy—are said to have helped the regime retain considerable public support (or at least acquiescence), especially in rural areas.[230]

A second society-centered approach, seen in the work of Richard R. Fagen and Eric Selbin,[231] might be described as sociocultural. Rather than material benefits, this second approach focuses on cultural or popular attitudinal change. According to Selbin, revolutions succeed (and endure) when rank-and-file citizens come to "embrace the social revolutionary project."[232] Thus, the key to revolutionary durability is not elite cohesion or coercive capacity but rather cultural transformation and the emergence of a "new man." For Selbin, popular acquiescence "cannot be coerced; it must be voluntary."[233] Thus, successful revolutions win over "the people's soul," such that the bulk of the population "adopts the core of the social revolutionary project not just in words but in deeds."[234]

A sociocultural approach has been used to explain the success of revolutionary regimes in Cuba and Iran,[235] as well as the failure of the revolutionary regime in Bolivia.[236] In Iran, for example, the durability of the Islamic Republic has been attributed to the committed support of highly religious rural families and a "hardline element of the Iranian population."[237] The loss of support among such committed supporters can be regime threatening. In Bolshevik Russia, for example, Lenin's introduction of the New Economic Policy led tens of thousands of activists to destroy their party cards in protest.[238] One of the regime's core supporters, the Kronstadt navy, led a rebellion against the Bolsheviks' perceived betrayal of revolutionary goals.

Society-centered approaches are difficult to test, in large part because information about public opinion is often scarce or nonexistent. Without credible public opinion data, it is difficult to measure societal support for revolutionary regimes—and even more difficult to assess the degree to which individuals internalize revolutionary goals. However, both the material and sociocultural approaches generate some observable implications. If the material approach is correct, we should see evidence that the mobilization of popular support was critical to regime survival during crises. Moreover, revolutionary regimes should have difficulty surviving periods in which they face broad public discontent, for example, during economic crises in which they cannot deliver the goods. If the sociocultural approach is correct, we should find evidence that the support of ideologically committed citizens was critical to regime survival. Crucially, moreover, government efforts to abandon the revolutionary regime's original project or goals should generate demonstrable rank-and-file resistance.

As we show in the chapters that follow, evidence in support of society-centered approaches is thin. The centrality of popular support is called into question by the fact that many revolutionary regimes experienced periods of disastrous government performance in which public support almost certainly eroded—such as the Soviet Union in the early 1920s and the 1930s, Mexico in the late 1920s and early 1930s, China in the late 1950s,

Vietnam in the late 1970s, and Cuba and Mozambique in the late 1980s and early 1990s. Indeed, some regimes have survived despite clear evidence of discontent, such as overwhelming electoral defeat (Algeria in 1991–1992), mass protest (e.g., China in 1989, Iran in 2009 and 2019), and large-scale emigration (Cuba in 1980). Thus, although the absence of good public opinion data prevents us from entirely ruling out material distribution and popular support as an alternative explanation, the stability of revolutionary regimes despite wide variation in performance—and in some cases, periods of extreme scarcity—suggests that broad support bases are not necessary for regime survival.

Evidence in favor of the sociocultural approach is even thinner. In several of our cases, governments abandoned core revolutionary goals without triggering substantial rank-and-file resistance. Most dramatically, regimes in Angola, China, Mozambique, and Vietnam discarded socialism in the 1980s and 1990s without substantial internal resistance. Likewise, the Mexican PRI's moderation in the 1940s and 1950s and Tito's transition from Stalinism to a much softer "socialist self-management" in Yugoslavia did not generate serious crises. Overall, then, our cases generate little evidence that society-centered factors better explain revolutionary regime durability than the state-centered framework employed in this book.

Theoretical Implications

The arguments we develop in this book have several important implications for theoretical debates about authoritarianism and authoritarian durability.

RETHINKING AUTHORITARIAN INSTITUTIONS

Our study highlights the importance of moving beyond the design of authoritarian institutions and paying closer attention to their strength, and especially the origins of that strength.[239] Contemporary studies of authoritarianism rarely take into account either variation in the strength of authoritarian institutions or the sources of that variation.[240] Yet institutional origins may be highly consequential. As we show in this book, many of history's most durable party-based autocracies were founded in violent struggle.[241] Often, ruling parties are as much a product as a cause of authoritarian durability.[242] In many of our revolutionary cases, including Russia, ruling parties were initially weak and undisciplined. In Mexico and Cuba, ruling parties *did not even exist* during the early years of the revolution. Parties were created years later, *after* regimes had consolidated. Thus, it appears that robust ruling parties were largely endogenous to the process of revolutionary state-building triggered by revolutionary and counterrevolutionary wars.

REVOLUTIONARY ORIGINS AND MILITARY COUPS

Our research also has important implications for research on the causes of military coups. The literature on coups has identified various factors that increase the likelihood of coups, including weak institutions;[243] economic crises and other government performance failures;[244] and perceived threats to the army as an institution, often driven by civilian interference.[245] Sheena Chestnut Greitens has argued that autocrats face a trade-off between coup prevention and coercive capacity.[246] Thus, autocrats often undermine the capacity of their own security institutions—for example, by promoting political loyalists over military professionals and by fragmenting the military through the creation of multiple agencies with overlapping responsibilities—in order to reduce the likelihood of a coup.

Our study highlights the importance of military origins in shaping the likelihood of a coup.[247] Because they create their own armies that are tightly linked to the ruling party, revolutionary autocracies suffer substantially fewer military coup attempts than nonrevolutionary regimes.[248] Revolutionary regimes such as Albania, Cuba, Iran, Mexico, the Soviet Union, and Vietnam survived for decades without facing any serious coup attempts. Indeed, just four of twenty revolutionary regimes (Algeria, Bolivia, Guinea-Bissau, and Mexico) experienced successful coups, and only Bolivia and Guinea-Bissau suffered regime-ending (as opposed to palace) coups.

Revolutionary coup-proofing is, in large part, a product of political-military fusion. Militaries founded and staffed by revolutionaries are too closely tied to the ruling elite to overthrow that elite. Revolutionary elites are also able to penetrate the armed forces in ways that inhibit coups. And due to party-army fusion, revolutionary governments have no need to engage in other types of coup proofing, such as fragmentation and the promotion of loyalists over professionals, that can undermine military efficacy. Hence, revolutionary regimes do not face a stark trade-off between military capacity and coup prevention. They tend to develop security forces that are powerful enough to suppress challenges from below but nevertheless lack the autonomy to mount coups.

THE ROLE OF IDEOLOGY

Our study highlights the critical role that ideology can play in the creation of durable authoritarian regimes. Most of the classic theoretical discussions of revolution—going back to Marx—downplay or ignore the importance of ideology.[249] Skocpol famously argued that ideologies do not provide predictive "blueprints" for revolutionary outcomes.[250] Likewise, most contemporary studies of authoritarianism treat autocrats as narrowly defined power maximizers.[251] Because leaders "need to hold office in order to accomplish any goal,"[252] the logic of political survival, rather than ideology, is said to drive autocrats' policy and institutional choices.

Although power-maximizing assumptions are frequently useful in explaining the dynamics of authoritarian rule, the early behavior of revolutionary leaders—and, consequently, longer-term revolutionary regime trajectories—cannot be understood without reference to ideology. Because extreme state weakness tends to leave revolutionary elites vulnerable after the initial seizure of power, one might expect them to accommodate powerful interests to ensure their survival. Yet, as the case studies of Russia, China, Vietnam, Cuba, and Iran demonstrate, revolutionary leaders who are guided by strong ideological commitments are more likely to undertake the risk-accepting behavior that triggers the revolutionary reactive sequence explored in this book. Acting "secure in the 'knowledge' of long-term success,"[253] ideologues display an unusual "willingness to ... sacrifice their peace and security"[254] and are often willing to "persevere against great odds."[255] Ideology thus helps account for why revolutionaries engage in the kind of high-risk or extremist behavior that contributes (albeit unintentionally) to long-run regime stability. Standard power-seeking politicians would be too risk averse, and too shortsighted, to engage in the radical strategies that ultimately give rise to durable revolutionary regimes.

Structure of the Book

Revolutionary autocracies are among the world's most durable regimes. This book focuses on the sources of that durability. We argue that revolutionary origins trigger a reactive sequence that, if allowed to unfold, gives rise to three pillars of durability: cohesive elites, powerful and loyal coercive structures, and the destruction of independent centers of power in society—conditions that help to inoculate revolutionary regimes from the kinds of challenges (internal schisms, coups, mass protest) that commonly undermine authoritarian regimes. Paradoxically, it is risky (and even reckless) behavior that triggers the counterrevolutionary violence that, in turn, fuels effective state- and party-building. Sometimes these policies lead to regimes' early self-destruction (e.g., Cambodia). Where revolutionaries survive the violent conflicts that their radical strategies engender, however, they establish the bases for durable authoritarianism. Revolutionary governments that backtrack and seek to accommodate powerful interests ultimately build weaker regimes.

To make this argument, we draw on in-depth case studies of thirteen revolutionary regimes. We have chosen cases that maximize variation on both the independent and dependent variables. Thus, the cases range in tenure from just a few months (Hungary in 1919) to more than seven decades (China, Mexico, the USSR), with a few in between (Bolivia, Guinea-Bissau, Nicaragua). We examine cases in which revolutionary governments pursued both radical (Cuba, Iran, Vietnam) and accommodationist (Algeria, Bolivia) strategies. Our cases also vary in terms of region, world historical period, size, and geopolitical importance. This variation provides some leverage both in assessing competing theoretical approaches and in identifying the relative importance of the different causal mechanisms highlighted in figures 1.2 and 1.3. (Because our focus is on causal mechanisms, and because we demonstrate the importance of revolutionary origins in the statistical analysis [which covers all authoritarian regimes, revolutionary and nonrevolutionary, since 1900; see appendix I], the case analyses are limited primarily to revolutionary regimes.[256])

The case studies explore the impact of revolutionary origins on regime durability. Each case is evaluated in terms of the revolutionary reactive sequence theorized in this chapter. We ask to what extent revolutionary elites pursued radical strategies, whether and to what extent those strategies triggered counterrevolutionary reactions, and whether and how those counterrevolutionary reactions contributed to the emergence of the three pillars of durable authoritarianism described above. In assessing regime durability, the case analyses examine both *actual* crises, when regime elites face serious threats to their power, and *potential crises that are averted* (i.e., when conditions that pose threats to most autocracies, such as economic crisis, major policy failures, or the death of the founding leader, are present but do not lead to a regime challenge). We then evaluate the degree to which our hypothesized mechanisms contributed to regime stability or collapse: Did the regime elite close ranks, and is there evidence that this response was linked to the degree of counterrevolutionary threat?

Did the army remain loyal, including during episodes of high-intensity coercion, and is there evidence that party-army fusion helped to avert this outcome? Finally, did public discontent lead to sustained collective mobilization against the regime, and, if not, is there evidence that the prior destruction of alternative power centers or low-intensity coercion inhibited such mobilization?

In each case analysis, we contrast our theoretical approach with alternative explanations that center around antecedent conditions, the independent role of the ruling party and other institutions, and the role of societal factors. Overall, we find that revolutionary origins better explain regime durability than these alternative approaches do. However, we also find that as revolutionary legacies degrade over time, particularly with the death of the revolution's founding generation, both institutions and public support sometimes take on greater importance.

The chapters are organized as follows. Chapters 2–4 examine the evolution of classic revolutionary regimes in "classical revolutions": Russia, China, and Mexico. Russia (chapter 2) and China (chapter 3) provide clear illustrations of the ideal-typical revolutionary reactive sequence: early radicalism triggered a large-scale counterrevolutionary war that fostered the emergence of a highly cohesive ruling party, the construction of a powerful and loyal coercive apparatus, and the destruction of alternative power structures. These legacies allowed regimes to both avert potential regime crises and survive actual crises via high-intensity coercion (e.g., the Tiananmen protests in China in 1989). Mexico (chapter 4) is a case of what we call segmented radicalism. Although radical attacks on the Church triggered a three-year civil war, accommodationist policies toward the United States and foreign capital limited counterrevolutionary threat by preventing its internationalization. Thus, even though a cohesive party-state emerged after the (belated) formation of a ruling party in 1929, the Mexican regime never developed a powerful coercive apparatus and only partially destroyed independent centers of power. As a result, regime survival hinged, in part, on steady economic growth.

Chapter 5 explores how revolutionary origins shaped authoritarian trajectories in three archetypical national liberation regimes that emerged out of successful anticolonial struggles: Vietnam, Algeria, and Ghana. Vietnam followed the ideal-typical revolutionary path described above. A violent war against French colonial rule, followed by a long war against the United States, generated a cohesive ruling party, a powerful and loyal army, and the near-total destruction of alternative power centers—legacies that undergirded decades of regime stability. Algeria is a case of revolutionary accommodation. The National Liberation Front (FLN) came to power through violent struggle and built its own army, but it moderated many of its policies soon after ascending to power. In the absence of a counterrevolutionary threat, the FLN elite was less cohesive and independent societal power centers—especially Islamist associations and mosque networks—were not seriously weakened. Although the liberation regime survived for more than half a century, it was far less stable than that of Vietnam. Finally, nonrevolutionary Ghana failed to build a military with strong ties to the ruling party. As a result, the regime collapsed after less than a decade.

Chapters 6–8 explore the divergent trajectories summarized in figure 1.3. In chapter 6, we show how the ideal-typical revolutionary reactive sequence in Cuba and Iran led to the creation of powerful and cohesive regimes capable of surviving severe economic downturns and threats from the United States. Chapter 7 focuses on cases of early revolutionary failure. The Hungarian Soviet Republic (1919), the Khmer Rouge in Cambodia (1975–1979), and the Taliban in Afghanistan (1996–2001) each engaged in radical behavior after taking power, which led to their destruction in the wake of foreign invasion by more powerful states. Chapter 8 explores the consequences of accommodation. Although the PAIGC in Guinea-Bissau, the MNR in Bolivia, and the Sandinistas in Nicaragua meet our criteria for revolutionary regime, they adopted accommodationist strategies in an effort to avoid or (in the case of Nicaragua) end counterrevolutionary conflicts. As a result, they developed less cohesive party-states (in Guinea-Bissau and Bolivia) or failed to destroy independent power centers (Bolivia and Nicaragua), which limited the durability of the new regimes.

Finally, the conclusion reviews the evidence for our argument and then briefly examines the seven revolutionary cases not covered in the study. These additional cases provide further empirical support for the book's central arguments. But they also generate some new insights. For example, although revolutionary radicalism gave rise to durable autocracies in Eritrea and Rwanda, these two recent cases suggest that elite cohesion may be harder to sustain in the less polarized geopolitical environment of the post–Cold War era. We conclude by asking whether the era of social revolutions is over, making the case that although Marxist revolutions may be a thing of the past, revolutions themselves are likely to continue into the twenty-first century.

PART I

Classical Revolutions

CHAPTER TWO

The Revolutionary Origins of Soviet Durability

IN THE LATE EVENING OF OCTOBER 24, 1917, Vladimir Lenin stepped off a Petrograd city tram, took off a wig he had been wearing to disguise himself, walked into the Second Congress of Soviets,[1] and, a few hours later, proclaimed the creation of the world's first socialist state. The announcement created an uproar, not only among supporters of the old tsarist order but also among other socialists. While declaring power in the name of the Soviets, the Bolsheviks had excluded almost all other socialist parties—many of which had far greater popular support. Before storming out, a Jewish Socialist leader, Henryk Erlich, declared his hope that "leaving will make the madmen and criminals come to their senses."[2] Indeed, most observers expected the Bolsheviks to last no more than a few weeks.

Of course, the Bolsheviks never "came to their senses," Trotsky correctly predicted that the departing socialists were destined for the "dustbin of history," and the Soviet Union became one of the most durable authoritarian regimes in modern history. Not only did it endure for seventy-four years, but it survived multiple and severe crises, including large-scale popular unrest, an early succession struggle following the death of Lenin, Joseph Stalin's assault on the Soviet party-state, and foreign invasion.

The history of the Soviet Union demonstrates how weak revolutionary governments' seemingly irrational challenges to powerful domestic and international interests can generate a reactive sequence that results in durable authoritarian institutions. Lenin's effort to eliminate the ruling class and to attack the global capitalist order sparked a brutal civil war and decades of international isolation. The conflict led to the destruction of alternative sources of political power, fostered a cohesive ruling party, and motivated the construction of powerful and loyal security services. These legacies contributed to regime durability in the face of five major crises that confronted the Bolsheviks after the civil war: popular unrest and the Kronstadt naval mutiny in 1921; the succession battle following the death of Lenin, 1922–1929; collectivization in 1929–1933; the Great Terror of 1937–1938; and the Nazi invasion of 1941. The regime would then persist for another fifty years, in part because the party-state that emerged out of the revolution virtually eliminated all forms of opposition.

The argument presented here provides a better understanding of Soviet durability than standard institutional accounts do. Discussions of Soviet durability have generally focused either on the party and its role in promoting tight discipline within the leadership or on the role of totalitarian institutions in suppressing opposition.[3] However, such approaches are inadequate to explain the Soviet Union's extraordinary durability. First, party institutions played a less central role than is sometimes assumed. Although the Bolshevik Party was created years before the revolution, it became the disciplined top-down vanguard organization imagined by Lenin only *after* the Russian civil war. As we show below, party discipline was less the product of institutional rules and more the outgrowth of violent revolutionary struggle. Second, the near destruction of the party during the Great Terror of the 1930s had little effect on the regime's capacity to survive the Nazi invasion a few years later. Third, although it is certainly true that opposition was wiped out by totalitarian party-state institutions, revolutionary origins are critical to understanding how such institutions emerged in the first place.

The Revolutionary Seizure of Power

On the eve of revolution, Russia was a large, politically retrograde, and economically underdeveloped European power. Unlike its counterparts in the West, Russia retained an absolute monarchy with a compliant nobility and few formal checks on tsarist power. The Russian economy remained underdeveloped and dominated by large landed estates. Serfdom had been abolished only in 1861 and replaced not by commercial agriculture but by traditional patterns of collective ownership and grounded in subsistence farming.[4] Per capita income was only about a quarter that of the United Kingdom.[5] Peasants still used wooden plows, and in the Crimean War, wooden Russian naval vessels confronted ironclad British warships. Military defeat convinced the government to undertake industrialization. By the 1890s, Russia was experiencing rapid industrial growth. A small but significant working class emerged and grew increasingly radicalized in the face of brutal state repression.[6]

Marxist groups began to mobilize this new militant working class, creating the Russian Social-Democratic Workers' Party—modeled after the German Social Democratic Party—in 1898. Fissures immediately appeared, however, reflecting the dilemmas of making a Marxist revolution in an overwhelmingly peasant society. On the one side, the Menshevik faction adhered to the orthodox Marxist position that the socialist revolution could occur only *after* a bourgeois revolution.[7] On the other side, the Bolsheviks, led by Lenin, supported the immediate seizure of power, even at the risk of civil war.[8] Indeed, the Bolsheviks embraced war as an inevitable product of capitalist development.[9] Lenin also focused on the importance of a small, theoretically informed, and tightly disciplined conspiratorial organization—a view that he laid out in *What Is to Be Done?*, which was published in 1902. The Bolsheviks expected party members to be professional revolutionaries who had an intimate and technical knowledge of Marxism—a knowledge that was often considered more important than familiarity with practical revolutionary tactics.[10] The Mensheviks, by contrast, believed that party membership should be open to all workers regardless of their knowledge of the ins and outs of Marxism. The Mensheviks embraced gradualism, democratic procedure, and efforts to strengthen the working class. The Bolsheviks embraced radicalism, illegal party activity, and a desire for top-down leadership of the revolutionary movement by a small group of intellectuals.[11] Bolsheviks tended to attract activists—exemplified by Lenin—who were fanatical and possessed an "impatient street-fighting disposition."[12] They readily engaged in criminal activity—including a major bank heist in 1907 in Tiflis (now Tbilisi) assisted by a young activist named Stalin—to fund their activities.[13]

At the same time, the prerevolutionary Bolshevik Party differed markedly from Lenin's vision (and what the party would eventually become). Notwithstanding Lenin's obsession with party discipline, disobedience within the leadership was the norm.[14] Throughout the prerevolutionary period, Lenin was unable to gain Bolshevik cooperation on key issues.[15] Squabbles over intricate points of ideology dominated party life and were the basis for the most serious internal divisions before 1917.[16] For example, a heated controversy erupted in 1909 around competing conceptions of epistemology—a dispute that contributed to the defection of a major Bolshevik leader, Alexander Bogdanov.[17] Finally, while the whole point of a conspiratorial party was to guard against government infiltration, the tsarist police were able to install an agent, Roman Malinovsky, as Lenin's right-hand man.[18] As a result, the Bolsheviks were in complete disarray on the eve of the revolution.[19]

The revolution was sparked by Russia's entrance into World War I in 1914. The war was initially popular (only Lenin was crazy enough to oppose it from the beginning) but quickly went disastrously for Tsar Nicholas II. Russia suffered massive losses and quickly ran out of trained soldiers. Soldiers often lacked the most basic supplies. Thousands went into battle barefoot, hungry, and without winter coats or ammunition. Many were forced to retrieve rifles from fallen comrades and had to fight with bayonets attached to empty rifles. As a result, military discipline collapsed as soldiers increasingly fled the front.[20] The Russian army turned into a "vast revolutionary mob."[21] Insurrection was catalyzed by persistent food shortages. In late February 1917, women standing in line for bread in Petrograd triggered a wave of strikes and protests against the regime. Nicholas II, who was outside the city leading the war effort, ordered the military to crack down. However, the police and military resisted and began to go over to the protesters' side. The system quickly collapsed, and the tsar was forced to abdicate.

The February Revolution created a power vacuum that was initially filled by a provisional government consisting of unelected ex-tsarist bureaucrats. However, de facto control of the country quickly fell into the hands of spontaneously elected soviets (councils), which sprang up in workplaces across the country. The soviets were dominated by a variety of socialist parties, the largest of which were the Mensheviks and the peasant-based Socialist Revolutionaries (SRs).[22] At the time, the Bolsheviks were still marginal and enjoyed little popular support.

Both for ideological reasons and because they feared civil war, the Mensheviks and SRs chose to share power with the provisional government.[23] This system of dual power led to an almost complete breakdown of the old state. According to Order No. 1 issued by the Petrograd Soviet in March, soldiers would follow the orders of the provisional government only if they did not contradict the soviet's decrees. Simultaneously, the provisional government disbanded the old police and security services (Okhrana), creating new citizens' militias that were largely ineffective. "Chunk after chunk of imperial Russia broke off like an iceberg into the sea."[24]

The February Revolution also triggered fundamental changes in the countryside.[25] Disillusioned peasant soldiers returned to their villages, often with socialist ideas learned at the front.[26] Energized village assemblies and self-governing communes set about overturning the rural social structure dominated by large, absentee landlords. One eyewitness described how peasants in a village near Moscow assembled at a manor house and "the axes began to strike . . . they chopped out the windows, doors, and floors, smashed the mirrors, and divided up the pieces, and so on. At three o'clock in the afternoon [peasants] set light to the house."[27] There would be no return to the old order. By 1919, virtually all landed estates had been wiped out and agriculture was dominated by small peasant landholders.[28]

In the cities, the Bolsheviks expanded their support base because the provisional government insisted on remaining in the war against Germany. Although Bolshevik opposition to the war had initially been considered extreme, the war was now highly unpopular. Partly as a result, the Bolsheviks won a majority in the Petrograd Soviet and had significant presence in other Russian cities.

In October 1917, Lenin began pushing the Bolsheviks to seize power without the participation of other socialist parties. In Lenin's view, creating a coalition government would be tantamount to "harnessing to the Soviet cart the swan, the pike, and the crab, setting up a government incapable of working harmoniously, and of even moving from the spot."[29] Yet the Bolsheviks lacked discipline, and Lenin's decision was highly controversial.[30] Two top Bolsheviks, Lev Kamenev and Grigory Zinoviev, broke with the party and denounced the decision—"an indiscretion [that] would be regarded as treacherous by any party in similar circumstances."[31]

The revolution was delayed until late October because Leon Trotsky insisted that the Bolsheviks needed the cover of the Second All-Russian Congress of Soviets. On October 24 and 25, Red Guard paramilitaries, backed by Russia's Kronstadt navy, seized the state bank, the telephone exchange, and eventually the Winter Palace—presenting the Congress of Soviets with a fait accompli that forced it to accept Bolshevik rule. The Mensheviks and other moderate parties walked out of the congress, but they could not stop the Bolshevik seizure of power. Masses of rank-and-file soldiers joined the Bolsheviks, while officers either disappeared or joined the emerging counterrevolution.[32]

In subsequent Constituent Assembly elections, the Bolsheviks were defeated by the SRs, which elected Victor Chernov as chairman when the assembly met in January 1918. But none of this mattered. A day after the assembly opened, pro-Bolshevik guards shut it down. Though popular, the SRs were too disorganized to defend their power.

The new revolutionary government was strikingly weak.[33] Lenin and Trotsky had momentarily outwitted the provisional government and other socialist parties but still only "commanded a few tables and ratty couches."[34] With the exception of the capital and a few other cities, Russia remained outside Bolshevik control. The former Russian Empire was quickly divided into thirty different governments, twenty-nine of which opposed Lenin's government.[35] Furthermore, in response to the Bolshevik seizure of power, the tsarist bureaucracy immediately went on strike, thus depriving the Bolsheviks of an effective state apparatus.

The Bolsheviks also lacked anything close to a disciplined army. The recently formed Red Guards, who attacked the Winter Palace in October 1917, consisted of improvised groupings who often fled at the sight of blood.[36] The first government crisis resulted from Red Guards' ingestion of a vast amount of wine stored beneath the Winter Palace. The initial days of Bolshevik rule were marked by a large-scale drunken bacchanalia on the streets of Petrograd. At the same time, many Red Guards conceived of themselves as the embodiment of revolutionary consciousness and thus felt justified to ignore central directives they disagreed with.[37]

Finally, the Bolsheviks faced substantial competition for power. The Mensheviks and the SRs opposed the new government.[38] The Bolsheviks also met with opposition from powerful remnants of the old regime, including a fragmented but still substantial tsarist army, remnants of the tsarist bureaucracy, landowners, the royal family, and the Orthodox Church, which retained a significant capacity to mobilize ethnic Russians.[39] At that point, almost no one expected the regime to last.

In the face of such daunting challenges, the Bolsheviks did not flinch. Instead, they launched an assault on the domestic and world capitalist order. The revolutionary government declared an end to private property, issuing decrees confiscating the possessions and land of the gentry, the Church, and the royal family.[40] By December 1917, the government halted all bond payments and stock dividends.[41] Within months, it had nationalized all banks.[42] Lenin called on workers to "loot the looters" by taking over factories and attacking members of the upper class.[43] Aristocrats and bourgeoisie became "former people" stripped of their belongings by criminals and party activists alike. The upper classes suffered spontaneous mob attacks that were later institutionalized into the Bolshevik Red Terror.[44] In one case, about fifty middle-class military cadets were tied up, taken to a metal factory, and thrown, one by one, into the blast furnace.[45]

Suddenly, the social structure was turned upside down. The houses of the wealthy were confiscated. Committees consisting of former servants and old house porters were given authority to divide up and allocate living quarters between their former masters and the poor.[46] Representatives of the old order—aristocrats, factory directors, stockbrokers, lawyers, former priests and tsarist officials—were rounded up and forced to do menial labor such as collecting trash and removing snow from streets while former laborers stood by and watched. These practices satisfied a widespread desire for social revenge.[47]

Bolshevik policies also reverberated outside Russia's borders. The decision to cease bond payments and close banks generated powerful adversaries among foreign lenders.[48] The new government abandoned Russia's wartime allies. The Bolsheviks exited the war and repudiated Russia's debts, causing "shock waves" in the international financial system and cutting Russia off from external lending.[49] The government also nationalized British- and French-owned factories.[50] Lenin transformed Russia into a pariah state, refusing to make even the most minor concession to Western powers whom he saw as irrevocably hostile.[51] In Lenin's famous mixed metaphor, the Soviet state became an "an oasis in the middle of the raging imperialist sea."[52]

Such incendiary behavior sparked a reaction—indeed it was *intended* to provoke a fight. Lenin and other Bolsheviks were attracted by the prospect of civil war—viewing violence as a "midwife" of the new order.[53] Attacks on global capitalism and old regime elites led to a formidable counterrevolution that in turn necessitated the creation of powerful and loyal security services, a cohesive ruling party, and the destruction of alternative sources of power. These legacies would form the bases of Soviet survival for the next seventy years.

Counterrevolution and the Origins of the Soviet Party-State

The Soviet republic is besieged by the enemy. It must be a single armed camp.

—VLADIMIR LENIN, JULY 9, 1919[54]

Five days after the Bolshevik Revolution on October 30, General Mikhail Alekseyev, the tsar's chief of staff, fled with a group of his supporters to Novocherkassk in the Don region to make an alliance with Don Cossacks, traditional defenders of the old regime.[55] He was followed by a long line of old regime supporters humiliated and stripped of their power and possessions—aristocrats, generals, military officers, bankers, businessmen, professors, lawyers—who came to southern Russia to seek safety and mount a challenge to the new order.[56] The new Volunteer Army was created by bringing together remnants of the tsarist army with Cossack units led by General Anton Denikin. This was very much an upper-class army. Of the 3,000 people who originally enlisted, only about a dozen were rank-and-file soldiers.[57] The relatively small army initially included 36 generals and nearly 200 colonels.[58]

Another anti-Bolshevik front was created by SRs who escaped Petrograd after the closure of the Constituent Assembly and joined forces with a 35,000-strong Czechoslovak legion to form the Committee of Members of the Constituent Assembly (Komuch) in Samara. Komuch seized the cities of Ufa and Simbirsk, Lenin's birthplace.[59] A string of anti-Bolshevik governments appeared throughout southern and eastern Russia, including the left-wing Provisional Government of Autonomous Siberia in Vladivostok, the liberal Provisional Regional Government of the Urals in Ekaterinburg, and the right-wing Provisional Siberian Government in Omsk.[60] This disparate group of die-hard monarchists, radical Socialists, tsarist officers, and liberal reformers was loosely referred to as the Whites. The Whites were supported by more than 50,000 Allied troops from the United States, Canada, Japan, France, and Great Britain.[61] The revolutionary government also confronted nationalist rebellions in the Baltics, Ukraine, the Caucasus, and central Asia. Less than a year after the Bolsheviks had seized power, nationalist and White forces had reduced Soviet Russia to the size of the medieval Muscovite state.[62]

In the summer of 1918, the Left SRs, an SR faction that had initially supported the revolution, grew disenchanted with Bolshevik policies and led an uprising in Moscow. In July, they assassinated the German ambassador (in an effort to undermine Russian-German peace talks); abducted Feliks Dzerzhinsky, the head of the recently created secret police (Cheka); and briefly seized Moscow's Central Telegraph.[63] In August, the head of the Petrograd Cheka was assassinated by a former tsarist military cadet. That month, a Left SR activist shot Lenin three times, nearly killing him. "Everything was crumbling," Trotsky lamented.[64]

These threats were further amplified—in the minds of Bolshevik leaders—by Marxist ideology. For the Bolsheviks, socialist revolution meant the literal destruction of the old ruling classes. It was assumed that these groups would do everything in their power to destroy the new order—a belief that became self-fulfilling.[65] The Bolsheviks also believed that capitalist powers would "spare no expense" to destroy the world's first and only socialist state—a view that was reinforced by the Allied intervention.[66] Fears of "capitalist encirclement" encouraged extreme brutality against all opposition.[67] The civil war was not simply a military conflict decided on the battlefield but a total war in which each side was threatened by annihilation.[68]

These existential challenges motivated the construction of a powerful party-state. Counterrevolutionary threats transformed the Bolshevik Party from a loosely structured organization into a more centralized and disciplined institution.[69] Military conflict made unity a supreme value—lest foreign enemies take advantage of divisions. The life-or-death character of the struggle convinced many local party officials to abandon demands for autonomy and seek greater subordination to the center.[70] Although local conflicts did not disappear, lower-level leaders readily submitted to extreme centralization in the face of existential threats from White forces.[71] Fear of counterrevolution combined to foster an intense, militarized, and almost mystical commitment to party discipline.[72]

The war also motivated the construction of powerful coercive structures. At the time of the revolution, the Bolsheviks, like most socialists at the time, assumed that the creation of a classless society would eliminate the need for a state and a standing army. However, the counterrevolution soon forced them to focus on building an effective military. The central problem was not just recruiting soldiers but creating a disciplined, professionalized force. The unruly and heavy-drinking Red Guards had been sufficient to seize a weakly defended Winter Palace but were thoroughly inadequate against the well-trained Volunteer Army.[73] Trotsky, whose only military experience consisted of a stint as a war correspondent in the Balkan Wars, took on the task of creating a professional, disciplined army.[74] He quickly realized that expertise was required and took the controversial decision to recruit 22,000 ex-tsarist officers to help lead the war effort.[75] Despite their suspect backgrounds, these officers provided critical expertise in building a disciplined military and carrying out effective military campaigns.[76]

At the same time, creating an army from scratch allowed the Bolsheviks to install political commissars and party cells throughout the military hierarchy. The party's involvement in military affairs blurred the distinction between party and military work.[77] Party involvement also appears to have strengthened military discipline.[78] Beginning in 1918, the party became the "backbone of the Red Army's organizational skeleton."[79] Party penetration of the military acted as a check on the loyalty of ex-tsarist military officers and is credited with bolstering the morale and cohesion of the Red Army, which was critical to the Bolsheviks' victory.[80] By the end of 1919, the two-million-strong Red Army had become a relatively disciplined force with a functioning chain of command,[81] a sharp contrast to the White forces, which descended into warlordism and brigandage.[82]

While the party became an integral part of the military, the Bolshevik Party was itself militarized by the influx of a tougher, less educated, and more obedient generation of military cadres.[83] The party enrolled entire platoons at a time, creating a substantial core of party members, who were used to obeying order and cared far less about the ideological debates that had consumed the party before 1917.[84] More intellectual and independent-minded cadres were thus quickly overwhelmed by new members imbued with military values.[85] For this new generation, the Bolshevik Party was, above all, a military organization and an armed defender of the revolution.[86]

The civil war's most enduring legacy—which lasted into the twenty-first century—was the creation of an effective political police. Faced with striking tsarist state bureaucrats in late 1917, Lenin called for the creation of the Cheka to combat the strike "by the most energetic revolutionary measures."[87] As the military threat posed by White forces mounted in 1918 and 1919, the size and scope of the Cheka expanded dramatically.[88] Later renamed the KGB, the Cheka would become one of the largest and most powerful security forces in modern history, with officials stationed in all major social, economic, and government institutions, and informants in virtually every apartment block in the country.[89]

The Cheka built upon what were initially spontaneous acts of mass violence to institute the Red Terror. The Terror targeted the aristocracy and clergy, as well as the "bourgeoisie"—a term that was loosely applied to anyone who might oppose the regime.[90] The Cheka also engaged in widespread hostage taking in order to compel the rich to pay taxes to the new regime. In the summer of 1918, the Left SR uprising and an assassination attempt on Lenin triggered a major upswing in government violence. The Red Army newspaper declared that "from now on, the hymn of the working class will be a hymn of hate and revenge."[91] Over the course of the civil war, the Cheka shot tens of thousands of people in basements, courtyards, and empty fields on the outskirts of towns.[92] As many as 100,000 people may have been killed in the Red Terror, far more than the number of people killed by the tsarist regime in the century before the revolution.[93]

Created by the party leadership, the Cheka was thoroughly loyal to the new regime.[94] Unlike many other security forces in history (including the Red Army), the Cheka recruited its personnel from outside preexisting coercive structures.[95] Many were drawn from the ranks of the party.[96] Security officials viewed themselves as the loyal servants of the party, or, in Dzerzhinsky's words, the "fighting arm of the Party."[97] The Cheka leadership was highly ideological,[98] and it was imbued with high esprit de corps linked to their role as defenders of the revolution.[99]

Partly as a result of this successful institution-building, the Bolsheviks gained the decisive advantage in the war by 1919. Although the Whites were sometimes larger and better armed, disunity undermined their cause.[100] Unlike the Bolsheviks, who were unified around a single ideology, the Whites encompassed SRs, liberal reformers, and die-hard monarchists.[101] Lacking anything resembling a common program or a political organization, they were constantly beset by infighting. Unable to garner sustained support from Western Allies exhausted by World War I, the Whites were constantly short of guns and money. Finally, the prominence of leaders opposed to land redistribution cost the Whites peasant support. As a result, the Red Army was able to mobilize a substantial number of peasants who feared losing their land.[102] The Whites suffered massive defections, and by early 1920, the Reds outnumbered them three to one.[103] Finally, in November 1920, General Piotr Wrangel, the last in a line of White military leaders, led an evacuation of forces from Crimea into exile. By the end of the year, the Reds had defeated virtually all armed forces in the country.

Victory came at enormous cost. As part of its effort to ensure adequate food supply for the cities, the new regime introduced a brutal system of rationing and state control over food that became known as War Communism. The party dispatched armed brigades to the countryside in a "battle for grain" that ended up costing hundreds of thousands of lives in famine.[104] Between 1914 and 1921, agricultural output declined by 57 percent and industrial output by as much as 85 percent.[105] Overall, as many as 1.2 million people died during the war, in addition to an estimated seven million civilian deaths from famine and disease.[106]

One consequence of this violence was the destruction of virtually all organized political alternatives. By 1920, the royal family was dead and the entire ruling class had been stripped of its resources and either killed or sent into exile.[107] White forces were defeated and their remnants forced abroad. The Church was also weakened (albeit not destroyed) by Cheka harassment.[108]

Finally, the civil war allowed the Bolshevik government to systematically destroy other socialist parties, including the SRs, which initially commanded greater popular support than the Bolsheviks.[109] Although socialists were tolerated to a greater degree than other parties,[110] the Bolsheviks sidelined them during the war. Thus, the Left SRs were "hounded out of all local organs to which they had secured election."[111] By July 1918, the new regime had shut down the Social Democratic press in its entirety.[112] By the early 1920s, neither the Mensheviks nor the SRs had an effective presence in the country, leaving the Bolsheviks as the "sole masters of the Soviet state."[113]

The Soviet Party-State Complex

In the decades after the civil war, the Soviet Union underwent enormous social and political transformations—including rapid industrialization and the creation of a centrally planned economy. Nevertheless, even *before* these major changes, the civil war had generated the central bulwarks of Soviet durability: a highly cohesive ruling party, a powerful and loyal coercive apparatus, and the destruction of all alternative centers of power.

First, the civil war fostered an increasingly disciplined ruling party that was grounded in a deeply ingrained siege mentality.[114] As evidenced in the discussion below, unity emerged less out of institutionalized rules and much more from deep fears that divisions would endanger the social revolution that activists had worked so hard to achieve.[115] Fears for survival, as well as the influx of military personnel into the party, created a large and powerful constituency for top-down centralization that would facilitate party cohesion. After three years of violent, ideological struggle, the Bolsheviks were far closer to the ideal presented by Lenin in *What Is to Be Done?* than they were in 1917. The war made Lenin's party "Leninist."

Certainly, the civil war did not put an end to factionalism. Between 1918 and 1921, several open factions (the Left Communists, the Democratic Centralists, and the Workers' Opposition) engaged in public debates over party policy, including peace with Germany, and trade union autonomy.[116] Yet factions tended to be elite affairs and were generally met with indifference by most party members, who feared that schisms would create openings for counterrevolution.[117] Most importantly, despite the presence of such factions, no top leaders would entertain leaving or splitting the party. Three years of brutal conflict against both internal and external enemies created an increasingly disciplined ruling party with a "hysterical concern for unity."[118]

The war also strengthened the party organization. At the start of the conflict, the party operated in just two rooms with a five-person staff; it was so small that its secretary, Iakov Sverdlov, was said to carry around the party archive in his head.[119] The party grew considerably over the course of the civil war.[120] During the conflict, moreover, the demands of survival encouraged the creation of new centralized institutions that would survive the entire life span of the party, including the Politburo, which would remain the effective center of Soviet power until 1990.[121] The central party apparatus expanded dramatically. Although the organization was still somewhat underdeveloped,[122] it institutionalized over the course of the war. The party's role in governing also increased significantly. Between 1919 and 1921, the party gradually became the principal institution of the regime.[123]

Second, the war led directly to the creation of a large, powerful and loyal coercive apparatus. In the immediate aftermath of the war, the army and the Cheka suffered losses of funding and personnel.[124] Even after reductions in personnel, however, both forces remained large. The security services retained a substantial 125,000 employees in the mid-1920s.[125] Despite some efforts to rein in Chekist abuse, the services continued to operate largely as before.[126] Long after the immediate impetus for the Cheka disappeared, the Cheka in its various subsequent guises—GPU, OGPU, NKVD, MGB, MVD, and finally KGB—retained its core strength and significant authority that it had gained during the war.[127] Although few Bolsheviks had envisioned the creation of anything like the Cheka before 1917, the civil war motivated the institutionalization of a vast, loyal, and "ever-effective"[128] security apparatus that would remain a central pillar of the Soviet regime until its collapse.

The creation of military and security forces from scratch dramatically reduced the likelihood of a coup, in part because of extensive penetration by party cells and political commissars but also because the army shared the party's revolutionary goals.[129] Created and thoroughly penetrated by the party, the army arguably lacked the autonomy to carry out a coup. Indeed, the Soviet Union would not experience a *single* coup attempt for seventy years prior to regime breakdown in 1991. Likewise, the internal security services were, by all accounts, extraordinarily disciplined.[130] Even at the height of the Great Terror in the 1930s, when the security services were responsible for hundreds of thousands of deaths and even ended up purging themselves, the secret police remained strictly subordinate to central party leadership.[131] Remarkably, and in contrast to Adolf Hitler, Stalin did not suffer any assassination attempts, despite several disastrous policy initiatives and his direct assaults on the core interests of the military and security services.

Third, by the end of the civil war, all organized opposition was "either exhausted and prostrate or pulverized."[132] The aristocrats, the royal family, and remnants of the tsarist army were either dead or in exile. The Church was badly weakened. And peasants, who played such a central role in the 1917 revolution, lacked any organization at all. Socialist parties that had once rivaled the Bolsheviks were either obliterated or sidelined.

Dzerzhinsky, the head of the Cheka, boasted, "Our enemies—where are they now? They have long been cast into the realm of the shadows."[133]

Revolutionary Regime Durability

The idea of counterrevolution was the gift that kept on giving.

—STEPHEN KOTKIN[134]

In the years following the end of the civil war, the Bolsheviks would face five significant crises that threatened regime survival: the large-scale peasant and military rebellions of 1921, the death of Lenin in 1924, collectivization and famine in 1929–1932, the Great Terror (1936–1938), and the Nazi invasion in 1941. Some of these (popular rebellions, the death of Lenin, the Nazi invasion) were largely exogenous. Others—collectivization, famine, and the Great Terror—were endogenous to the revolution.

Three legacies of the civil war were critical to the regime's durability during its first decades in power. First, a potent siege mentality and the nearly constant expectation of war greatly facilitated the leadership's efforts to maintain unity and discipline—and also encouraged the regime to engage in rapid industrialization and terror. Second, regime durability was bolstered by the exceptionally large, effective, and loyal security apparatus that emerged during the civil war. Third, the absence of alternative centers of societal power deprived the opposition of the ability to translate widespread discontent into an effective challenge. Indeed, the Soviet Union confronted virtually no organized opposition until the late 1980s.

KRONSTADT AND PEASANT REBELLIONS, 1920–1921

By late 1920, the Bolsheviks had vanquished the White armies and driven out the Western enemies from Soviet territory. Yet the civil war had left the country in ruins and the party isolated from its own population. War Communism and the Red Terror deeply alienated large sections of both the urban and the rural populations.[135] In particular, the forcible requisition of grain by the state had created widespread discontent and starvation. These measures contributed to a severe famine concentrated in the Volga region, which resulted in up to five million deaths in 1921–1922.[136]

In response to such conditions, Russia erupted into rebellion shortly after the final defeat of White forces in 1920.[137] Sometimes organized by surviving SR leaders and wielding slogans such as "Soviet power without the Bolsheviks," peasant armies in the southwest and other parts of the country fought Bolshevik leaders and seized control over parts of the countryside in late 1920 and early 1921.[138] In early 1921, whole provinces operated outside the regime's control.[139] Soviet leaders in Minsk and Smolensk were forced to evacuate in the face of incoming peasant armies.[140] Rebels nearly overran Petrograd and temporarily blocked the Trans-Siberian Railroad linking western Russia to Siberia.[141] By March 1921, Soviet power no longer existed in much of the countryside, while Moscow, Petrograd, and other cities were hit by a wave of strikes.[142]

Most momentously, in early 1921, the Soviet regime was rocked by a rebellion of the Kronstadt navy, based just outside Petrograd. The Kronstadt sailors had been among the first to support the Bolsheviks in 1917 and became symbols of Bolshevik power. A blank shot from the Kronstadt battleship *Aurora* had signaled the start of the October Revolution in 1917. Yet three years of war, starvation, and repression had generated widespread discontent, which bubbled forth after the defeat of the White armies. Half of the Kronstadt Bolsheviks burned their party cards.[143]

Rejection of Bolshevik power by the symbols of the October Revolution generated a serious identity crisis for the regime. Kronstadt by itself was too small to threaten Bolshevik rule. Yet given widespread discontent, the uprising could plausibly have sparked a much broader-based rebellion against the Bolsheviks.[144] Widespread popular discontent and the soldiers' impeccable revolutionary credentials might also have convinced Bolshevik leaders to back them and generated fatal splits in the regime.

Two products of the civil war helped the Bolsheviks to beat back these popular challenges: an intense siege mentality and a powerful, war-hardened coercive apparatus. First, three years of civil war had generated a powerful fear of counterrevolution in the Soviet leadership.[145] A "White scare" gripped the party rank and file.[146] Given the regime's international and domestic isolation, one did not have to be a Bolshevik fanatic to believe that the rebellion threatened to create an opening to counterrevolutionary forces abroad. Indeed, many soldiers saw the rebellion as a "betrayal" of the revolution. They supported the Bolshevik leadership because their fear of White restoration exceeded their opposition to Bolshevism.[147]

Lenin capitalized on the Kronstadt rebellion to push forward a ban on party factions at the Tenth Party Congress.[148] Although the ban was widely ignored, it symbolized the party's obsession with unity. Some Bolshevik leaders correctly predicted that such stringent demands for unity opened the door to abuse. However, there was universal agreement that such problems were outweighed by the danger that dissension within the party would create openings for counterrevolution.[149]

Second, the war had also left the regime with a battle-hardened and disciplined army and political police. The Bolsheviks were able to put down the Kronstadt rebellion by relying on 35,000–100,000 troops led by the war hero and commander Mikhail Tukhachevsky.[150] Marching across the frozen waters, troops overwhelmed the increasingly isolated rebels, and the revolt was put down at the end of March 1921. By the end of the year, the military and the Cheka had squashed the most important peasant rebellions.[151] Although these actions alienated many international socialists,[152] they saved the regime.

At the same time, intense dissatisfaction and economic dislocation generated by War Communism convinced Lenin to soften the regime's stance toward peasants and private commerce. The New Economic Policy (NEP), which was inaugurated in 1921 at the Tenth Party Congress, called for the replacement of grain requisitioning with a tax in kind that gave peasants freedom to sell surplus after paying the tax. As a result of NEP, commercial activity returned to the cities and the economy began to grow. Nevertheless, just three years after the civil war, the regime was beset with another crisis caused by the death of its founding leader.

LENIN'S DEATH

Incapacitated by a stroke in 1922, Lenin died on January 21, 1924. His passing created a dangerous situation for the regime and left the leadership in panic as reports came in from the countryside that peasants were preparing to revolt.[153] Although large-scale revolts never materialized, the party was left open to internal conflict as it decided who would lead the Bolsheviks next. Stalin, the commissar of nationalities, had been appointed by Lenin as general secretary of the party in 1922 and would ultimately replace Lenin.[154] However, the choice of Stalin was hardly a foregone conclusion. The post of general secretary, which was created just months before Lenin's health forced him to leave the scene,[155] was not viewed as an especially powerful position.

Indeed, most observers at the time assumed that Lenin would be succeeded by Trotsky, a brilliant orator and Marxist theoretician who had organized the Bolshevik takeover in early October 1917 while Lenin was in exile and led the military struggle during the civil war.[156] Outside of Lenin, no one was more publicly associated with the revolution than Trotsky. Trotsky's prospects were further enhanced by Lenin's deathbed statement, known as Lenin's Last Testament, which explicitly called for Stalin's removal from the position of general secretary.[157] Shortly before his death,

Lenin wrote Trotsky to encourage him to oppose Stalin.[158] Trotsky, who hated Stalin passionately, should not have needed any encouragement.

In fact, although Trotsky would later become a virulent critic of Stalin, he "scrupulously observed party discipline" and remained stunningly passive during the critical early stages of the succession struggle.[159] Forswearing the campaign against Stalin that Lenin had encouraged him to lead,[160] Trotsky refused to make public his opposition to Stalin and pledged loyalty to the alliance of Stalin, Zinoviev, and Kamenev that excluded him. Abiding by party discipline and avoiding open opposition, Trotsky publicly denied the existence of Lenin's Testament.[161] At the critical Twelfth Party Congress in 1923, he declared his "unshaken" loyalty to the leadership triumvirate of Stalin, Kamenev, and Zinoviev.[162] At the Thirteenth Party Congress a year later, Trotsky again refrained from seizing the mantle of opposition but instead declared that "the Party is always right."[163] At Central Committee meetings, Trotsky could be seen ignoring the proceedings and reading French novels—provocative perhaps, but not an open challenge to the party leadership.

When Trotsky did finally challenge Stalin, he did so in a halfhearted fashion. In 1925, the Stalin-Kamenev-Zinoviev triumvirate crumbled and Trotsky joined Zinoviev and Kamenev in the United Opposition against Stalin. At a party plenum in 1926, the small group of oppositionists vainly tried to use reasoned argument to bring members of the Central Committee to their side but were met with accusations that the group was illegally conspiring to overthrow the party. Dzerzhinsky threatened the opposition with "fresh gunpowder."[164] In an act of desperation, opposition supporters staged a series of demonstrations in factory party cell meetings, only to quickly repudiate this act as a violation of party discipline and renounce future factional activity.[165]

Indeed, throughout the succession struggle, Trotsky, Kamenev, and Zinoviev remained committed opponents of party factionalism.[166] Any sign of dissent was seen by party members as posing an existential threat to the revolution. This made it difficult for the United Opposition to mount a serious bid for power. Thus, a rally at a train station to protest the deportation of a Trotsky ally in 1927 terrified the majority of party members, who worried that public displays of intraparty dissent could be used by counterrevolutionary forces to threaten Bolshevik power.[167] In Stalin's words, "Now was the time to close the ranks in the face of common danger."[168]

The United Opposition was doomed. After Trotsky and Zinoviev were expelled from the Central Committee, they made a last-ditch effort to rally opposition to Stalin on November 7 before being kicked out of the party. Both Zinoviev and Kamenev renounced factionalism and submitted to Stalin.[169] At the Fifteenth Party Congress in late 1927, Kamenev declared that factionalism must be stopped before it led to the creation of a second party. The only option was "to submit completely and fully to the Party."[170] Trotsky was exiled to Kazakhstan in 1928 and expelled from the country in 1929. In exile, he would become famous for his denunciations of Stalin. But his passivity and commitment to party discipline had cost him the opportunity to defeat Stalin when he had the chance.

After the fall of Kamenev, Zinoviev, and Trotsky, the Right Opposition, led by Nikolai Bukharin, emerged in reaction to Stalin's growing opposition to NEP (see below). Like the oppositions before it, the Right Opposition was hemmed in by its commitment to party unity and refused to take its opposition public—a decision that Robert V. Daniels calls a "major blunder."[171] After being sidelined by Stalin, the defeated leaders of the Right Opposition published a full confession of their errors and committed to "a decisive struggle against all deviations from the general line."[172] By mid-1929, open factionalism within the party had disappeared.[173] Stalin had emerged as the single dominant figure in the regime.

The failure of the opposition—including Trotsky's seemingly inexplicable bouts of passivity—have mostly been explained in terms of failed leadership, including Trotsky's overconfidence and imperious attitude toward "lesser lights" in the party.[174] Yet it is hard to understand why such highly experienced revolutionaries—with decades of experience in intraparty battles—would suddenly become so irresolute. What could explain this sudden onset of incompetence?

To a significant extent, these failures reflected the dilemmas faced by a party opposition opposed to the very idea of party opposition.[175] Trotsky and the other oppositionists had repeatedly expressed strong support for punishing dissent in the party and in fact presented themselves as guardians of party unity.[176] They vociferously defended the ban on factions passed at the Tenth Party Congress.[177] Despite their hatred of Stalin, all the dissidents precluded a priori the possibility of creating a second party to challenge Stalin.[178] As a result, their efforts were always shrouded in secrecy lest they be called out for violating the very values they repeatedly championed.[179]

In a context of genuine fear of counterrevolution, it was also nearly impossible for intraparty opposition to garner support from within the party or from international socialists. The United Opposition was backed by a "tiny minority" of the party elite.[180] Potential supporters, including international Communists who knew Trotsky well, and Lenin's widow, Nadezhda Krupskaya, who had a rocky relationship with Stalin,[181] gave scant support to the opposition. The moment was "too serious to create a schism" and threatened the victory of Communism in Russia.[182]

In sum, Stalin's victory in the succession battle was not simply the product of his wiliness, his control over the party apparatus, or the failures of opposition leadership but was also rooted in the regime's international isolation and fears of counterrevolution, which discouraged any opposition that might split the party and destroy the revolution. Fear of counterrevolution and devotion to party unity created an important first mover advantage in internal conflict. Once Lenin had given Stalin the top job, even powerful figures faced enormous challenges opposing Stalin without seeming to split the party and threaten its defeat.[183] In a context of pervasive and existential threats of counterrevolution, even the slightest hint of organized opposition to Stalin was met with charges of counterrevolution that could quickly lead to the demise of the world's first socialist revolution.[184]

COLLECTIVIZATION AND FAMINE, 1929–1933

Stalin's victory would usher the Soviet Union into a period of social and political upheaval often described as Russia's "second revolution." Carrying out a policy of collectivization (the transfer of peasant-owned land to the state), the regime conquered the country's peasantry and helped transform Russia from an overwhelmingly rural country into an industrial power—at the cost of unimaginable suffering, death, and social dislocation. Revolutionary origins created the impetus, the means, and the opportunity to implement this profound social transformation. Fear of invasion by capitalist powers fostered an urgent need for rapid industrialization to build up the military. The regime's powerful coercive apparatus was essential to subdue the countryside, which nearly erupted into civil war. Finally, the destruction of alternative sources of societal power meant that there were no forces to mobilize the massive discontent created by Stalin's assault on Soviet society.

Collectivization emerged out of mounting international tensions and fear of foreign invasion. In the late 1920s, Soviet leaders became persuaded that war was on the horizon. In Poland in 1926, Marshal Józef Piłsudski, who had defeated Soviet armies during the civil war, came to power in a coup, generating worries that Poland would unite with other central European states into an anti-Bolshevik front.[185] Then, in May 1927, the

British broke off diplomatic relations in response to Soviet involvement in a general strike.[186] A month later, the Soviet ambassador to Poland, who had participated in the killings of the Romanovs, was shot by a young monarchist in Warsaw. These events convinced party leaders that the Soviet Union was about to be attacked.[187] Memories of Western intervention during the civil war were still fresh. Tensions confirmed the leaders' Marxist beliefs that war with capitalist states was inevitable.[188] According to Viacheslav Molotov, Stalin's second-in-command, "War was looming on the horizon."[189] Russia was increasingly under siege.[190]

Party leaders became alarmed by the slow pace of industrialization. Ten years after the revolution, Russia remained an overwhelmingly agrarian economy with limited arms production capacity. This left the regime vulnerable to both capitalist powers and a potentially hostile peasantry. Given that capitalist bankers could not be expected to finance communist development,[191] grain exports were one of the only sources of foreign exchange available. Without peasant cooperation, the Bolshevik regime would be unable to industrialize or feed the urban working class. In effect, the countryside held the new regime hostage.[192]

An overwhelmingly urban party, the Bolsheviks barely penetrated the countryside, where 80 percent of Russia's population lived.[193] Conservative institutions such as the Church maintained an active presence in many villages. Peasants also appeared to be increasingly hostile to the regime.[194] Police reports told of peasants rejecting Soviet currency and resigning from the Pioneers and Komsomol youth organizations.[195] In late 1927, the government faced mounting difficulties procuring grain, leading to fears that the regime would be unable to feed the cities and the Red Army.[196] Peasants thus came to be viewed as an imminent threat to Bolshevik survival.

The war scare, perceived peasant hostility, and food shortages provoked a serious debate within the party over whether to continue NEP, which had given peasants substantial autonomy over production and distribution.[197] In 1928, Stalin began to press for an end to NEP and the introduction of much more coercive measures to fund industrialization.[198] In his view, maintaining NEP would put "the brakes on industrialization" by reducing the amount of grain available for export, thereby limiting the foreign exchange available for industrial construction projects.[199]

The forced seizure and export of grain promised to both squash the peasants and help finance a massive industrialization program and military buildup, as well as generate a grain reserve to feed the army.[200] The industrialization of the 1930s would have an important military component, permitting the dramatic expansion of the armed forces from 586,000 in 1927 to 1,433,000 a decade later.[201]

Collectivization transformed Soviet society at a rate that had few historical precedents.[202] The urban population nearly doubled in size, from 18 to 32 percent.[203] The government instituted a system of centralized economic planning that would set out five-year targets for production of virtually all goods and services, starting with the First Five-Year Plan of 1928–1933. The goals set for industrialization and other areas were unrealistic, and reporting was filled with inaccuracies, making it difficult to assess exactly what was achieved. However, scholarly estimates suggest that industrial production increased by 80 percent in six years.[204] Such industrialization efforts would provide a critical base for military production during World War II.[205]

These socioeconomic changes were made by possible by a violent assault on the peasantry. The regime expropriated the property of peasants and forced them into state-controlled collective farms, where the government hoped to access grain.[206] Thousands of urban workers were sent to the countryside to help in the transformation. Attacks focused on the elimination of the so-called kulaks—a term denoting wealthy peasants that was broadly applied to all perceived opponents of the regime. "Dekulakization" involved the deportation of over two million peasants to remote locations in Siberia and elsewhere. Many were sent to the Gulag, a system of forced labor camps that came to symbolize Stalinist repression. Hundreds of thousands of people died in transport.[207] These policies also involved a broad attack on the peasants' culture and way of life.[208] Collectivization was combined with a violent assault on what remained of the Church. By late 1930, roughly 80 percent of village churches had been closed.[209]

These attacks generated a major crisis for the regime in the countryside.[210] Collectivization unified the overwhelming majority of peasants and provoked the bloodiest and most prolonged resistance to the Bolshevik regime since the civil war.[211] The countryside was engulfed in violence, including arson, and lynching of local officials.[212] In 1929, there were more than 3,200 terrorist attacks on Soviet civil servants.[213] In 1930, there were more than 13,000 riots, with over two million participants.[214]

Despite their numbers, however, peasant rebels faced impossible odds in battling the regime. First, the destruction of alternative power centers during the civil war—most notably, the peasant-based SRs—meant that there was no national political force to channel the intense peasant discontent and spontaneous uprisings into an effective national challenge to the revolutionary government.[215]

Second, the civil war bequeathed the Soviet Union with a powerful security apparatus. Given both the scale of repression and the violence it provoked, it seems unlikely that the regime could have undertaken such a massive operation if it did not already possess a considerable coercive force. Indeed, the OGPU—the successor to the Cheka—played a central role in planning and implementing dekulakization.[216]

The civil war was an important precondition for collectivization. Many of the same groups of individuals were "at the heart" of violence during the civil war, collectivization, and, later, the state-led terror of the 1930s (see below).[217] As Andrea Graziosi has argued,[218] the experience in civil war fostered the creation of tight-knit, battle-hardened networks encompassing tens of thousands of cadres that carried out collectivization.

These operations also brought a dramatic expansion of the security service and encouraged the construction of a vast system of rural monitoring and control that provided a foundation for the totalitarian state.[219] In the early 1930s, the Soviet state began not just to target regime opponents but to track the population as a whole.[220]

All of this came at unimaginable human cost. By imposing massively unrealistic quotas on collective farms, collectivization contributed to a man-made famine in grain-producing areas of Ukraine, the North Caucasus, and Kazakhstan. Millions of people starved to death in one of the worst humanitarian catastrophes in modern history.[221]

In sum, the Soviet Union's origins in violent revolutionary struggle help explain why such a radical policy as collectivization was undertaken and how it was successfully implemented. "Capitalist encirclement" and perceived threats of invasion generated by Lenin's attack on the global capitalist system provided a critical rationale for Stalin's policies.[222] By creating a powerful and loyal security service and destroying alternative power centers, the civil war made it possible for the regime to subdue such a large section of the country and carry out one of the most dramatic social transformations in modern history.

THE GREAT TERROR, 1937–1938

On December 1, 1934, Leonid Nikolayev, a mentally unstable, unemployed former functionary walked into the Leningrad party headquarters concealing a gun. Angered by his expulsion from the party months earlier, Nikolayev shot and killed Sergei Kirov, the Leningrad Party chief and close confidant of Stalin.[223] The assassination of such a high-level official would have alarmed leaders of any autocracy, but in the Soviet context it provided the prelude to the unprecedented and brutal Great Terror aimed at the very foundations of the Soviet party-state. Since 1917, the government had been focused on eliminating counterrevolutionary threats from the aristocracy, the bourgeoisie, capitalist states, and the peasantry. Now, it suddenly became obsessed with finding and exterminating enemies *within* the party-state. In the process, the Bolsheviks nearly committed suicide.[224] The Great Terror resulted in roughly 2.5 million arrests and over 800,000 killings in 1937–1938.[225] During this period, Soviet authorities executed more than 1,000 people every day.[226] While most of those killed were common citizens, a substantial portion were longtime supporters of Stalin and "old Bolsheviks" who had worked with Lenin to found the Soviet state.[227] There had not been anything like it since the Jacobins consumed themselves in the French Reign of Terror in 1794. The Soviet Union's origins in revolutionary civil war explain both why such a terror was possible and why the regime survived such a major attack on the core institutions of the Bolshevik regime.

The Kirov assassination took place in a hostile international environment. In the late 1920s, the Bolsheviks had seen foreign threats that in fact barely existed. But in the early 1930s, they were as real as they possibly could be. In Europe, the rabidly anticommunist Nazis seized power in 1933 and fascism began to take hold in countries throughout Europe. The raison d'être of these regimes was the destruction of communism. In July 1936, a military coup against the Spanish Second Republic sparked a brutal civil war that quickly turned into a proxy war between Communists and Fascists. And throughout all of this, Trotsky, exiled in Mexico, was gaining international fame by excoriating Stalin.

Such challenges were amplified in the minds of Bolshevik leaders by a worldview grounded in fears of capitalist encirclement. The Bolsheviks had come to power amid foreign intervention and were convinced that they could lose it at any moment through the combined efforts of foreign and domestic forces.[228] For Bolshevik leaders, there was no obvious distinction between international conflicts and domestic politics. The civil war experience had already primed Soviet leaders to expect imminent invasion.[229]

Fears of invasion were reinforced by concern that external enemies might draw on the support of the vast number of victims of Soviet policies.[230] The Bolsheviks had designated millions of people as "class enemies"—former tsarist officials, ex-priests, traders, bankers, better-off peasants, and random folk unlucky enough to be caught up in the machine of repression.[231] Furthermore, the Bolshevik Party had been purged so many times amid the upheaval of collectivization and famine that in many regions the number of former Communists outnumbered party members.[232] It was feared that such individuals would rise up against the Soviet Union if it were invaded. Indeed, the term "fifth column"—invented during the Spanish Civil War—was constantly on the lips of Soviet leaders during this period.[233] As war with fascist states appeared increasingly inevitable, panic took hold among the Bolshevik elite.[234]

Stalin used these tensions to attack his former rivals. Between 1936 and 1938, he orchestrated three widely publicized show trials in which top Bolshevik leaders—including Zinoviev, Kamenev, and Bukharin—were accused of working with Trotsky in a variety of outlandish plots to kill Stalin and Lenin and undermine the Soviet Union.

Then, in 1937, Stalin carried out a major assault on the foundations of Bolshevik rule. Under Stalin's direction, Nikolai Yezhov, a rising star in the NKVD (security services), delivered a report at a party plenum titled "Lessons of the Wrecking, Diversion, and Espionage of Japanese-German-Trotskyite Agents."[235] Yezhov, who would soon take over the NKVD and personify the Great Terror, attacked the party and security apparatus for insufficient vigilance against Trotskyites and other foreign enemies. A month later the head of the NKVD, Genrikh Yagoda, and his eighteen deputies were expelled from the party and subsequently shot. Yagoda was accused of being a German agent and plotting to assassinate the party leadership by throwing grenades into the special Politburo cinema room.[236] Ominously, Yezhov had begun removing local NKVD officials who had long protected party leaders in their areas.[237]

On June 11, the Soviet press announced that the most senior officials in the Red Army, including the civil war hero Tukhachevsky, had been arrested for treason. In an entirely fabricated accusation "corroborated" by a blood-stained confession, the government accused him of secretly working with Nazis to overthrow Stalin and ensure the Soviet Union's defeat in an upcoming war.[238] In subsequent months, Lev Mekhlis, the new head of the political division of the army, traveled across the country ordering arrests and executions.[239] The army's command and control structure was decimated. The overwhelming share of the military's high command was wiped out, including 3 of 5 marshals, 13 of 15 generals, 8 of 9 admirals, and 154 of 186 division generals.[240] Two-thirds of the 767 commanders above the rank of major general were imprisoned or executed.[241] The NKVD was also hit hard. Over the course of the Terror, nearly 10 percent of its ranks were arrested for "counterrevolution."[242] Successive heads of the NKVD, Yagoda, and Yezhov and nearly all of their deputies were soon massacred.[243]

The lists of those caught up in the Great Terror expanded exponentially as arrested officials denounced others, who, in turn, denounced still others.[244] As a result, the Terror engulfed vast swaths of the party *nomenklatura*. After midnight, elite apartment blocks across Moscow resounded with the sounds of NKVD officers banging on doors and wailing children and spouses. Politburo members suffered near-constant humiliation and threat of purge and were powerless to halt attacks on family members and close associates.[245] Stalin could remove, arrest, or execute them at any time.[246] For example, the aids of Molotov, Stalin's longtime protégé, were rounded up one by one.[247] Eventually, Molotov's wife was arrested. By 1939, the Great Terror had removed five of seventeen Politburo members, 71 percent of the Central Committee, over half of the delegates to the Seventeenth Party Congress in 1934, and about 80 percent of the Komsomol Central Committee.[248] Over the course of a year, the party's Central Committee consistently voted unanimously to expel its own members. "No party member was immune."[249] Even Stalin's *own family* was affected by the purge, including in-laws with whom he was close.[250]

The Terror decimated the party apparatus. High-ranking Politburo emissaries were sent to purge provincial leaderships and whip up local party committees to denounce their leaders.[251] Yezhov claimed that thirteen anti-Soviet organizations were operating across the country and that each provincial party organization was awash in Polish and German spies.[252] Ultimately, about 80 percent of regional and district party secretaries were purged.[253] The mass removal of party officials contributed to a breakdown of party authority in factories and other institutions as leaders became afraid to issue any orders that might somehow be perceived as sabotage. Underlings took advantage of the situation to disobey orders and threaten denunciation.[254]

The Terror was not an actual regime crisis in that it did not seriously threaten regime survival. But this is itself puzzling. A similar self-inflicted purge of revolutionary elites during Robespierre's Reign of Terror led to the fall of the Jacobins in 1794. In that case, members of the French National Convention, fearing for their survival, united against Robespierre.[255] As in France, Stalin's victims were hardly powerless. They included the most senior members of the Bolshevik elite and influential actors in all parts of the party-state.

Nonetheless, Stalin carried out his assault on the party apparatus in the face of virtually no resistance. There were no serious efforts to challenge Stalin in the 1930s.[256] The security services not only eliminated all domestic organized opposition but infiltrated and neutralized a wide range of anti-Soviet émigré groups abroad.[257] And despite Stalin's extraordinarily violent assault on the military and the security services (and maniacal search for plots), there is no evidence of any coup plot among spies or officers.[258]

How did the regime survive such a large-scale self-immolation? Why did the party actively cooperate in its own demolition?[259] One reason is that justifications for the Terror fit the Bolshevik worldview that emerged out of the revolution. Even though the regime had objectively wiped out all organized domestic opposition by the mid-1930s, officials' lived experience and worldview made Stalin's conspiracy theories potentially believable.[260] Perceived threats to the revolution provided a powerful motivation for party leaders to remain united.[261] As in France, the Terror was facilitated by fears of counterrevolutionary forces abroad.

However, the Bolsheviks possessed a stronger party and coercive apparatus than the Jacobins. The Jacobins launched their terror soon after taking power, when they were still weak. A loose collection of clubs rather than a disciplined party, the Jacobins relied on the highly factionalized Committee on Public Safety to carry out the Terror, and they had not eliminated other sources of opposition.[262] By contrast, the Bolsheviks had already survived the revolutionary reactive sequence and created a disciplined ruling party, hardened during years of conflict, in which it was exceptionally difficult for cadres to challenge the leadership.[263] The Bolsheviks were also backed by powerful security forces, which dramatically raised the costs of defection. It was obviously risky for any official to resist the Terror.

But why did the security services themselves go along when so many of their ranks were decimated by the Terror? The NKVD was reliably obedient to the party leadership even when the NKVD was itself under attack.[264] No top-level official and only a few mid-level officials defected under Stalin.[265] The military also does not appear to have responded to Stalin's unprecedented attack on its corporate interests. There were no coup attempts or serious plots to kill him.[266] Scholars of civil-military relations have long argued that coups occur in response to threats to the military's autonomy and core interests.[267] Surely, the physical extermination of almost the entire military leadership warranted *some* kind of response.[268]

To understand why the security forces were so passive, it is useful to compare Stalin's fate with that of Hitler, who confronted a serious coup conspiracy in 1938 and at least five assassination or coup plots by members of the military.[269] The different behavior of the Soviet and the German armed forces may be traced to the fact that Nazi seizure of power did not take place amid state collapse. The Wehrmacht, unlike the Red Army, preexisted the Nazi regime. Hitler consolidated power not by destroying the old army and creating his own but by gaining the acquiescence of the existing armed forces. Dominated by an aristocracy with weak ties to Hitler, the Wehrmacht retained considerable autonomy. Indeed, Winfred Heinemann shows that the July 1944 assassination attempt against Hitler mobilized military networks that preexisted the Nazi seizure of power. [270] By contrast, the SS, which *was* created by the Nazis, never seriously challenged Nazi power.

In the Soviet Union, the party's creation of the military and the security services made it easier for Stalin to infiltrate these organizations with party stalwarts. Both organizations were dominated by officials deeply embedded in Bolshevik notions of party discipline and lacked the kind of preexisting, autonomous networks that facilitated military challenges in Germany. For Soviet officials, the notion of a coup was anathema.[271] Simultaneously, intense levels of surveillance and risks of being denounced made conspiring virtually impossible. Even low-level officials felt they were under constant and intense scrutiny.[272]

In sum, the combination of a siege mentality, intense party discipline, and a powerful and loyal security force explains why the Soviet regime did not collapse despite the potential strains created by the Terror. Traditions of party discipline increased the costs of defection while the all-pervasive political police made it nearly impossible to organize any alternative to the existing regime.

THE NAZI INVASION

Any other government which had suffered such losses of territory as we did would not have stood the test and would have collapsed.

—JOSEPH STALIN[273]

Four years after Stalin gutted the Soviet military and nearly destroyed the Bolshevik Party, the USSR was forced to go to war with one of the most powerful armies in the world. In 1939, Stalin had kept the Nazis at bay by entering into a peace agreement—the Molotov-Ribbentrop Pact—that made arrangements for trade and divided up Poland and the Baltics between the two powers. However, Nazi ideology and German victories in Western Europe convinced Hitler to invade the Soviet Union. In the spring and early summer of 1941, intelligence reports poured into Moscow that Germany was preparing a major assault. Nonetheless, Stalin was convinced that the time had already passed for Hitler to make a successful attack before winter (which indeed it had), and he refused to allow Soviet troops to prepare for the invasion.[274] Against the advice of his generals, Stalin tried to avoid any action that might be seen as an abrogation of the Molotov-Ribbentrop Pact.[275] Confident that an attack would not occur, Stalin also took apart existing defense fortifications in the east and put forces too far forward—leaving the Soviet army defenseless in the rear.[276] Combined with Stalin's devasting purges of the army in 1937,[277] such tactical errors left the Soviet Union woefully unprepared for what happened next.

On June 22, 1941, the Soviet regime suffered one of the worst crises faced by any revolutionary regime discussed in this book. Overwhelmed by invading German armies, the Soviet Union ceded vast tracts of territory as whole armies lost contact with their commanders. In large parts of the country, the Red Army disintegrated into groups of fugitives seeking to escape the German onslaught.[278] According to Nikita Khrushchev, who was stationed in Ukraine at the time, soldiers were forced to fight with pikes and swords for lack of any other weaponry.[279] By December, more than two million Soviet lives had been lost and three million soldiers had been taken prisoner.[280] Because the Germans had cut communications lines before the invasion, leaders in Moscow had few means to contact Russian troops, creating a vacuum of authority on the front that was exacerbated by a panicked and confused Stalin.[281] Rather than taking immediate charge, Stalin had his protégé Molotov announce war with Germany on the radio. After several days of dithering, Stalin retreated to his dacha, apparently at a loss of what to do. The party leadership was left in the lurch. The Soviet Union appeared to be on the cusp of collapse.[282]

The Soviet Union's ultimate victory in World War II was driven by a number of factors unrelated to its revolutionary origins, including Western lend-lease aid, Russian military leadership, the vastness of Russian territory, and Hitler's strategic errors.[283] Although such factors were indeed critical, they cannot account for the regime's survival during the initial, catastrophic weeks and months of the conflict before Western assistance had become available.[284]

The early weeks of the crisis presented two potential sources of regime instability and breakdown. First, we might have expected the collapse of Soviet state authority at the front to trigger large-scale popular uprisings by the millions of citizens suffering from Soviet rule.[285] As discussed above, this is precisely what Soviet leaders feared would happen. Indeed, wartime state collapse or foreign invasion contributed to revolution in nine of the cases covered in this book.[286] Most notably, disastrous per-formance in war had led to the Russian Revolution barely two decades earlier. Now, however, the situation was different. In 1917, the central state did not reach deep into the countryside and peasants retained self-governing institutions.[287] However, the Soviet destruction of alterna-tive power centers limited any opposition movement's ability to seize the opportunity presented by the early military failure.[288] By the early 1940s, the Bolsheviks had eliminated all pockets of peasant self-organization and other autonomous power centers, leaving the population defenseless. Fur-thermore, while the state collapsed on the front lines, it remained cohesive in the rear, hindering efforts to mobilize discontent. Combined with the destruction of alternative power structures, the development of powerful coercive forces helped dampen any popular mobilization that might have arisen during the first weeks of the war.[289] The NKVD remained loyal and powerful even during the worst periods of crisis.[290]

Second, Stalin's disastrous meddling in military affairs and demon-strable show of weakness in the war's early days might have been expected to provoke a coup attempt.[291] Certainly, Stalin's behavior in the late 1930s had earned him no friends among top-level officials, who never knew if they would return home after a day at the office. However, as discussed above, the creation of coercive agencies from scratch reduced the auton-omy of both the military and the NKVD, which made it harder for power ministries to challenge Stalin's rule. Furthermore, over the course of the 1920s and 1930s, Stalin had used fear of counterrevolution and foreign invasion to eliminate all other prominent leaders in the party and security forces who were not directly beholden to Stalin. As a result, there were far fewer potential leaders of high stature to challenge Stalin than there might have been otherwise.

Although some scholars have argued that popular support for the regime contributed to the Soviet victory,[292] such an explanation has a hard time accounting for regime survival in the early stages of the conflict. Support for the regime among certain parts of the population does not explain why the millions of *other* citizens who suffered so severely under Stalin did not rebel. The passivity of so many victims of collectivization and the Great Terror can be explained by the regime's highly effective coer-cive apparatus, which had eliminated all independent centers of power and infiltrated virtually every nook and cranny of Soviet society.[293]

Finally, the Soviet war effort was bolstered by rapid industrialization, which had been stimulated by "capitalist encirclement" and the war scare of the 1920s and 1930s. As discussed above, huge investments had already been made to create the industrial base for large-scale arms production. By the late 1930s, the USSR had built a relatively effective economic planning system that was well suited to the demands of war and had in fact been created precisely to defend the country against invasion.[294] Collectivization had created large grain reserves and the administrative mechanisms to control production and supply.[295] This allowed the government to double the size of the army between 1939 and 1941 and rapidly build new armament plants in 1941 and 1942.[296] By the time of the war, the Soviet Union could produce more than 25,000 tanks and 18,000 fighter planes—three to four times more than Germany (although often of poor quality).[297] Such production efforts allowed the Soviet Union to survive the war until additional Western assistance became available.[298]

The Soviet defeat of German forces at Stalingrad in early 1943 dramatically changed the tide of the war. In 1943 and 1944, the Red Army pushed German forces to the Soviet border and began to march into Eastern Europe. On May 9, 1945, Germany surrendered, leaving the Soviet Union as the dominant military force in Poland, Bulgaria, Czechoslovakia, Romania, Hungary, and eastern Germany. In the end, the war resulted in far more Soviet deaths—27 million—than in any other country in the world.[299]

In sum, revolutionary transformation and the civil war created powerful legacies—a siege mentality and quasi-religious devotion to unity, a strong and loyal coercive apparatus, and the destruction of alternative power centers—that facilitated regime survival in the face of some of the most severe crises faced by any authoritarian regime in the twentieth century. In the process of responding to counterrevolutionary challenges both during and after the civil war, the government erected the building blocks of a powerful totalitarian state that would sideline opposition for decades to come.

The Persistence of Soviet Power, 1953–1985

Russia's victory in World War II, the death of Stalin a few years later, and the emergence of a new postrevolutionary generation of leaders who had not cut their teeth in the civil war brought profound changes to the system. The revolutionary siege mentality that had gripped the leadership in the regime's early decades diminished substantially as the Soviet Union no longer confronted immediate, existential threats to its survival. The civil war was now a distant memory, and the defeat of the Nazis became the centerpiece of Soviet propaganda. The Cold War between the USSR and the United States generated important challenges, including a high-stakes battle over the fate of Germany and occasional dangerous confrontations such as the Cuban missile crisis. But the Soviet Union was now a global superpower whose very existence was no longer in question.[300] At the same time, key revolutionary legacies endured, including a highly cohesive ruling party, the absence of alternative power structures, and an extensive and loyal coercive apparatus. Partly as a result, the system would not confront *any* real opposition challenges for another thirty-five years.

In the initial postwar years, little changed. Stalin retained total control and continued prewar repression and terror. In an echo of 1937, hundreds of officials in Leningrad were exiled, executed, or imprisoned on trumped-up criminal charges in the 1948 Leningrad Affair. The Gulags grew to include a gargantuan 2.75 million prisoners and became economically unsustainable.[301] On January 13, 1953, the official party newspaper, *Pravda*, reported the arrest of nine doctors in connection with a supposed "Doctors' Plot" to kill Stalin and other Soviet leaders. Another large-scale purge appeared to be in the offing.

But all of this came to a sudden halt when Stalin was found semiconscious on the floor of his bedroom on March 1, 1953, following an apparent stroke. Rather than calling for a doctor, his guards moved Stalin to a couch and phoned government leaders, who waited hours before bringing in medical assistance. (Such negligence was probably less an effort to kill Stalin than a response to the dangers of taking initiative in Stalin's Russia.) Stalin died on March 5.

Stalin's death threw the system into disarray. Since 1930, the regime had been under Stalin's complete personal control. Major questions of state had been decided at long, alcohol-infused midnight feasts organized by Stalin at his dacha rather than at party Politburo meetings.[302] The political police also gained unprecedented power.[303] Since 1939, the party had had only a single congress. It was initially unclear that the party would fill the power vacuum left by Stalin's departure.[304] The two most powerful figures were the head of the security services, Lavrenty Beria, and the chairman of the Council of Ministers, Georgy Malenkov. Khrushchev, whom most regarded as a country bumpkin, was appointed the top party official.[305] De facto power was in the hands of Beria, who in an effort to win support, began to dismantle the terror system.[306] Within three weeks, more than a million prisoners of the Gulag were released.[307] Given Beria's control over the powerful security services, however, party leaders were rightly terrified of him, and Khrushchev plotted with other top leaders to oust him at a meeting of the government on June 26. Marshal

Georgy Zhukov, who led Soviet military forces in World War II, arrested Beria. Fearing that he would run away, they removed his belt and cut off his pant buttons.[308] Several months later, he was executed.

Khrushchev then used his control over the party machine to build a base of support in key regions of Moscow, Leningrad, and Ukraine.[309] By late 1954, Khrushchev was considered the top leader of the country. As in the 1920s, the party again came out on top. Although it had been sidelined by Stalin, it still possessed a large, disciplined apparatus and enormous symbolic power within the system. Once in control, Khrushchev began a radical program of de-Stalinization—announced dramatically in his "Secret Speech" made at the party's Twentieth Congress in February 1956.[310] Khrushchev denounced Stalin's "cult of personality" and rehabilitated thousands of cadres who had been caught up in the Terror. Soviet policies relaxed significantly. The government focused less on eliminating internal class enemies and reducing consumption to pay for rapid industrialization and more on maintaining stability and increasing production of consumer goods.[311] The annual rate of housing construction nearly doubled between 1956 and 1965. More than 100 million people moved into new apartments.[312]

The Soviet "thaw" of the 1950s grew out of increasing leadership confidence in the Soviet Union's permanence.[313] The willingness of so many people to fight and die on the regime's behalf encouraged a belief that it could survive a relaxation of repression. Leaders no longer saw themselves as under siege from pervasive counterrevolutionary threats.[314] Policies also reflected an increased confidence on the international stage. As a great power, the USSR did not face an imminent threat of extinction. This was eventually reflected in a shift in foreign policy. The new leadership de-emphasized the inevitability of war with the West—a core belief of the founding revolutionary elite. At the Twentieth Party Congress, Khrushchev promoted the policy of "peaceful coexistence" with the West.[315]

Finally, the end of the terror was made possible by the fact that the regime had already built a vast and effective totalitarian state. The Soviet party-state now reached into all aspects of peoples' lives. Where people lived, where they worked, whether they went to university, what they consumed, and where they bought goods and how much they paid were all directly controlled by the party (renamed the Communist Party of the Soviet Union [CPSU] in 1952). The party penetrated every public institution in the country with cells that monitored activities in each education institution, factory, office, collective farm, and military unit with three or more party members.[316] A *nomenklatura* system—a list of personnel deemed politically reliable by party leaders to hold positions of authority—gave the party critical leverage over elites throughout society. *Nomenkla-tura* positions included a wide range of jobs—from the chair of an academic university department to factory director, to state administrator. This system allowed party leaders to dismiss any director, appoint a new director, and instantaneously change the social status of any official.[317] As Milan Svolik has argued,[318] the CPSU enhanced regime durability by giving officials at all levels a stable source of career advancement and thus a long-term stake in party dominance.

The party also controlled numerous "transmission belt" organizations, including trade unions and youth groups. All forms of independent organization—even chess clubs or other nonpolitical forms of association—were banned. Any type of independent political initiative was heavily discouraged. Thus, when a thirteen-year-old Marina Morozova, a friend of one of the authors, gathered four of her friends to protest American nuclear weapons in front of the U.S. embassy in Moscow in 1978, the endeavor was met with intense suspicion by Soviet authorities. After the girls marched to Red Square, they were taken in for interrogation and a KGB officer explained to the girls: "Today, you are organizing a protest against the United States. But tomorrow you could protest against the party!"

The system was enormously effective. The regime confronted virtually no organized opposition until the late 1980s. In the thirty years after Stalin's death in 1953, there were only forty-five nonstate mass actions (including riots at sports events) of 1,000 or more participants.[319] Resistance to the regime consisted almost entirely of small groups of marginal dissident intellectuals totaling no more than a few thousand citizens out of a population of over 200 million.[320] This system of control would have been virtually impossible to create in the absence of violent social transformation that tore up existing social structures outside party control and enabled the construction of a vast and loyal coercive apparatus.

At the same time that the party-state sidelined outside opposition, it also began to constrain the top leadership. The increased institutional power of the CPSU was most strikingly signaled by the ouster of Khrushchev in 1964—an event that Khrushchev himself referred to as "a victory for the Party."[321] In the early 1960s, Khrushchev began to make major policy decisions without regard to the interests of the party apparatus. New party statutes created term limits in the Central Committee and the Presidium (Politburo), which were intended to be applied to everyone but Khrushchev and a few other leaders at the very top.[322] Such changes were seen as a direct attack on the prerogatives and power of the party organization. These moves, combined with Khrushchev's sharp reduction of military spending, erratic behavior, and unilateral decision-making, antagonized officials at all levels and sparked a conspiracy led by former Khrushchev allies, including the head of the Central Committee, Leonid Brezhnev.[323] After a year of plotting, Brezhnev took power in a bloodless transition in October 1964.

Brezhnev largely maintained Khrushchev's domestic and international policies. The leadership viewed the Soviet Union as in the stage of "Developed Socialism" in which the transition to Communism was supposed to be highly gradual and devoid of class conflict.[324] He also invested heavily in détente with the West. Although the regime never completely abandoned the revolutionary project of struggle against capitalism, it focused less on fomenting revolt in more powerful states and instead developed a "revolutionary imperial paradigm," which entailed control over weaker states in Eastern Europe and support for pro-Soviet movements in the Third World.[325]

The transition from Khrushchev to Brezhnev also marked a reduction in killings of protesters.[326] Mass shootings virtually disappeared.[327] Although the regime continued to prohibit all opposition, responses to dissent grew more flexible and subtle. The KGB shifted its focus from large-scale repression to information gathering and analysis.[328] Rather than arresting and shooting large numbers of potential opposition as in the Stalinist period, the KGB used access to university entrance and other incentives to preempt protest activity.

The gradual demise of the revolutionary paradigm and the increased sense of security was almost certainly facilitated by the emergence of a new postrevolutionary generation in the 1950s. As figure 2.1 shows, the system's relaxation occurred roughly at the same time in the 1950s and 1960s that the civil war generation began to leave the scene. Increasingly, the leadership was dominated by a young group of officials—including Brezhnev, Andrei Gromyko, and Alexei Kosygin—who had been teenagers during the civil war, had experienced rapid career advancement during the Great Terror, and had been heavily influenced by their experiences in World War II, when the Soviet Union was emerging as a global power.[329] These officials had at best vague memories of the civil war or a time when the Soviet Union was an isolated socialist regime besieged by counterrevolutionary capitalist and fascist powers.[330]

At the same time, the rise of Brezhnev ushered in an era of deadening stability. In power until 1982, Brezhnev was, above all, committed to preserving the status quo.[331] An organization man, Brezhnev worked

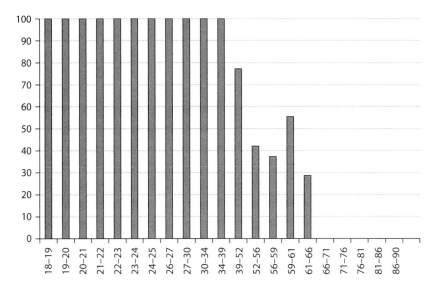

FIGURE 2.1: Share of Politburo from the Revolutionary Generation
(Politburo Members Who Were at Least Twenty Years Old in 1918).

hard to keep each faction of the party-state happy. He increased military spending and mostly avoided unilateral decision-making.[332] Although he removed about half of all regional leaders during his initial years in power, he subsequently did little to challenge regional officials—tolerating or even encouraging corruption and taking a hands-off policy to leadership.[333] No longer facing any serious internal challenges, Brezhnev substantially reduced turnover of party and state elites at both the central and the local levels.[334] Under this policy of "trust in cadres," officials became virtually unremovable.[335] A whole generation of younger, more dynamic leaders, including Mikhail Gorbachev, had to bide their time while an increasingly senile group of officials retained control. By the 1980s, the average age of Politburo members was over seventy.[336]

Reform and Regime Collapse, 1985–1991

In the mid-1980s, the Soviet Union was—by any measure—a stable authoritarian regime. Although there were signs of malaise, including slow economic growth and shortages, there were no signs of crisis. The CPSU exhibited no open or serious conflicts at the top and few if any cases of outright insubordination within the party. Virtually no organized opposition existed.

At the same time, the disappearance of the revolutionary siege mentality deprived the CPSU of the critical sources of cohesion that had facilitated regime survival during the first decades of Soviet power. By the 1970s and 1980s, ideology and fear of counterrevolution no longer acted as a glue holding the system together. Instead, cynicism and corruption became rampant.[337]

This pervasive cynicism and loss of revolutionary ethos left the regime more vulnerable to crisis than it had been in previous decades. While the system appeared secure, officials had no reason to defect from the party. They could be confident that loyalty would be rewarded with advancement and material enrichment.[338] However, because loyalty to the system could not be rewarded if the system itself collapsed, such officials were prone to waver in the face of serious challenges that threw the regime's fate into question.

Just such a crisis was generated from the top between 1987 and 1990, when Gorbachev dismantled the Soviet Union's system of social and political control. Gorbachev's policies of glasnost (openness) opened the party to public criticism. Dissidents such as Andrei Sakharov were released from prison. Then, during the critical Nineteenth Party Conference in the summer of 1988, Gorbachev—in his words—severed "the umbilical cord tying [the party] to the command-administrative system."[339] Under pressure from Gorbachev and party reformers, the conference agreed to a radical restructuring of the Central Committee and a sharp reduction in the party's control over the economy.[340] The conference also took the momentous step of approving the introduction of multicandidate elections and creating a bicameral legislature intended to sideline the party as the main center of power. Gorbachev began transferring property from the Communist Party to the state and ceased to rely on the party to implement key policies.[341] The Politburo, which had long been the center of power, was reduced to an advisory committee.[342] In 1990, the party's "leading role" was formally abolished.[343]

Catalyzed by Gorbachev's weakening of top-down controls, powerful nationalist movements emerged in the late 1980s, which fundamentally challenged Soviet power. Benefiting from dramatically reduced efforts to curtail dissent, protests exploded in Armenia, Azerbaijan, Georgia, Moldova, Russia, and Ukraine. Ethnonationalism became the main vehicle for liberalizing demands.[344] In almost all these states, nationalist demands were backed by factions in the CPSU, which were willing to do anything to hang on to power.

These forces were empowered by open elections to subnational legislatures in 1990. Anticommunist forces won power in Armenia, Moldova, and the Baltic states. Most momentously, in June 1990, the reformist party leader Boris Yeltsin was elected as chairman of the Russian republic legislature. The Russian legislature declared political sovereignty and the preeminence of Russian legislation over all-union laws. Russia's avowed sovereignty forced the hand of other republics. In the summer of 1991, Gorbachev and nine republican leaders met and negotiated a new union treaty.

In response to this turn of events, hard-liners in the Soviet government attempted to seize power. On August 18–19, they detained Gorbachev at his dacha in Crimea and declared martial law. Tanks rolled into Moscow and independent newspapers and electronic media controlled by the Russian republic were banned. However, with the Soviet Union in crisis, the party, which had previously shown remarkable unity in the face of serious challenges, now disintegrated. Many party elites either openly opposed the coup or took a wait-and-see approach. Yeltsin immediately declared his opposition to the coup and occupied the Russian legislature ("White House") in Moscow.

The leadership of the party-state also lacked the cohesion and self-confidence to carry out large-scale violence to put down the moderately sized protests that emerged in response to the coup attempt. Having long ago abandoned the use of large-scale repression, leaders were ill prepared to engage in significant violence to save the system. In the end, both indecisive leadership and a breakdown in central state control doomed the coup to failure. After Gorbachev refused to support the declaration of emergency, Defense Minister Dmitry Yazov admitted that they had no plan as to what to do next.[345] Throughout the coup attempt, security officials, beset by bureaucratic caution, waited to see who would come out on top.[346] On the nights of August 19 and 20, the military, the police, and the KGB surrounded the White House but failed to carry out an assault. Officers waited to be pushed to attack by a leadership unwilling to push them.[347] The police and the Alpha unit of the KGB refused to participate in the assault.[348] In the face of this insubordination, Yazov, who had been the coup leader most committed to the use of force, was forced to call off the attack at the last minute. Fearing arrest, Interior Minister Boris Pugo committed suicide.

The failed coup effectively destroyed what was left of the Soviet system. Gorbachev resigned as general secretary of the CPSU and urged the Central Committee to dissolve itself. Yeltsin transferred all party property to the

[82]   CHAPTER 2

Russian state and banned the CPSU. On December 8, Yeltsin, Stanislau Shushkevich of Belarus, and Leonid Kravchuk of Ukraine met in a forest in Belarus to formally dissolve the Soviet Union.

Conclusion

This analysis has argued that Soviet durability in the face of multiple and serious crises can be traced to the regime's origins in social revolution. Radical efforts to remake the domestic and global order provoked serious domestic conflict and international isolation. Three years of brutal civil war fostered a deeply ingrained siege mentality that put the regime on a nearly constant war footing. Fear of domestic counterrevolution and foreign invasion encouraged a "hysterical concern for unity,"[349] which made it nearly impossible for internal opponents to mount a serious challenge. The war also gave rise to a powerful and loyal political police that quashed all opposition and remained a pillar of the dictatorship for the next seventy years. Finally, the war destroyed key threats to Bolshevik power: the royal family, the landlord class, and competing socialist parties. This legacy allowed the regime to survive large-scale rebellion and an early succession struggle in the 1920s. It also gave Stalin the tools to carry out massive purges of the Soviet elite without suffering the fate of the Jacobins. The creation of a new revolutionary army meant that Stalin faced no resistance from the military despite his gutting of the military high command. The legacies of revolution also allowed the regime to survive the initial, disastrous weeks of the Nazi invasion in 1941.

Much of this legacy persisted decades after World War II. Soviet leaders confronted virtually no organized opposition; the party and a loyal coercive apparatus remained key pillars of regime stability. Yet the glue holding the regime together—a fear of counterrevolution from within and abroad—disappeared in the Brezhnev era. As a result, Soviet power became relatively brittle in the face of challenges that emerged during perestroika.

A focus on revolutionary origins provides a better understanding of Soviet regime durability than alternative approaches do. Some scholars have focused on the importance of public opinion, arguing that support for the Soviet system was an important factor in the Soviet Union's victory over Germany in World War II.[350] As argued above, such a perspective cannot explain why Stalin did not suffer a coup after the disastrous opening weeks of the war. Nor can it account for the Bolsheviks' survival during the Kronstadt crisis or amid collectivization and the Great Terror, during which the government carried out large-scale assaults on Soviet society.

Although totalitarian institutions served as the most important source of stability in the post-Stalin era, the postrevolutionary generation of leaders focused more attention on public support. Thus, concern for popular opinion was likely behind leaders' heavy investment in housing, consumer goods, and social welfare policies in the 1950s and 1960s.[351] In turn, the Soviet collapse was driven, in part, by widespread public discontent generated by shortages and mounting economic crisis.[352]

The chapter found mixed evidence for perspectives rooted in political institutions. Given the centrality of the CPSU, the Soviet case at first glance appears to confirm an extensive literature on the importance of ruling parties to regime durability. Indeed, all Soviet leaders arose out of the party apparatus—including Stalin and Khrushchev, who faced serious challengers based in the army and the security services. By the 1920s, the party had become a powerful and well-institutionalized organization. Developed party institutions likely explain why the Bolsheviks survived the Great Terror while the weakly organized Jacobins collapsed after the French Reign of Terror. At the same time, such an approach does not explain why the party was so strong. Indeed, despite Lenin's efforts to create a vanguard party in 1903, a serious party organization emerged only after revolutionary war nearly twenty years later. Even then, institutional rules were frequently ignored. While top leaders such as Trotsky limited their challenges to the party leadership, such behavior was rooted less in institutional rules than in fear of counterrevolution. Finally, the regime survived its most severe crisis—the Nazi invasion—just after Stalin had decimated and sidelined the party. Thus, although party institutions help account for Soviet durability, the evidence suggests that legacies of violent struggle provide a more comprehensive explanation.

Another institutionalist approach comes from an older literature on totalitarianism.[353] Extensive state penetration and control of society, as well as the party's infiltration of the state, virtually eliminated opportunities for organized opposition or internal challenges. However, such a perspective does not explain how the totalitarian system was created in the first place. As this chapter has shown, the construction of the totalitarian state—including a powerful coercive apparatus and the destruction of independent societal power centers—was a direct product of the revolutionary war and violent counterrevolutionary conflict.

Finally, it is worth considering whether something about the conditions in Russia would have made stable authoritarianism likely even in the absence of social revolution. Indeed, the prerevolutionary Romanov dynasty survived for 400 years, and Vladimir Putin consolidated stable authoritarianism in the early twenty-first century. Because we cannot rerun history, it is impossible to fully discount this perspective. However, as this chapter has shown, the features of Soviet rule that made the system durable were fundamentally novel.[354] The Soviet state radically transformed Russian society—eliminating classes and transforming Russia from an agricultural society into an industrial one. The CPSU had no counterpart in the tsarist regime. While the Soviet political police borrowed some techniques from its predecessor, the tsarist Okhrana, the Cheka was built almost entirely from new personnel and engaged in a level of violence and social control without equivalence in the tsarist period.[355] The party-state, which ultimately penetrated every aspect of life in the Soviet Union, was a fundamentally new type of authoritarian power. As we have shown, this system emerged out of an identifiable reactive sequence—one that would be repeated in other twentieth-century revolutions. We turn to these other cases in the chapters that follow.

CHAPTER THREE

The Revolutionary Origins of Chinese Authoritarian Durability

THE PEOPLE'S REPUBLIC OF CHINA (PRC) is one of the most durable authoritarian regimes in the modern era. Explanations of the regime's strength have focused on the party's "adaptive" responses to changes in the world,[1] as well the extraordinary economic growth that followed the economic reforms of the 1980s and 1990s.[2] Although China's economic transformation was indeed remarkable,[3] an exclusive focus on recent history ignores the fact that for these reforms to succeed, the Chinese Communists had to *first* create a modern, unified state and then survive crippling crises in the 1950s, 1960s, and 1980s.

Given its contemporary status as a global military and economic power, it is easy to forget that just a few generations ago, China was a weak state comparable to contemporary Afghanistan. Once a great empire, China declined precipitously in the nineteenth century under the Qing dynasty. During the "one hundred years of humiliation" (1849–1949), the country was wracked by rebellions and civil wars and carved up by British, French, Japanese, and American colonial powers. Following the collapse of the monarchy in 1911, competing warlords, imperial powers, criminal gangs, and secret societies dominated the country. Even after the Communists united China, drove out the imperialists, and seized power in 1949, they confronted major crises that could have destroyed the regime: an unprecedented famine during the Great Leap Forward, near civil war during the Cultural Revolution, and massive protest amid widespread communist collapse in 1989.

We argue that the emergence of a powerful state and autocracy in China was driven by a revolutionary reactive sequence. Demands for radical social transformation during the Great Revolution of 1925–1927 triggered a decades-long civil war, which fostered elite cohesion, gave rise to a powerful and loyal military,[4] and obliterated organized alternatives to Communist rule, clearing the way for totalitarian rule. These revolutionary legacies allowed the regime to survive challenges that would have sunk weaker regimes. First, the prior destruction of alternative centers of power and tight party-army fusion prevented the emergence of any significant internal or external opposition in the face of unprecedented famine during the Great Leap Forward. Second, the existence of a powerful but loyal military allowed the regime to endure the Cultural Revolution, during which Mao Zedong openly encouraged armed factional conflict—behavior that has triggered coups in many other autocracies. Third, the combination of a cohesive party elite and weak civil society allowed the regime to survive the Tiananmen protests at a time when communism was collapsing across Eurasia. Although the death of revolutionary veterans in the 1990s deprived the regime of an elite with the informal authority to impose unity amid crisis, key revolutionary legacies remained intact, including a pervasive and powerful coercive apparatus and a relatively disorganized civil society. Combined with China's successful economic transformation, such legacies provide a durable basis for regime survival.

The Revolutionary Reactive Sequence and the Rise of Durable Authoritarianism

China's dramatic transformation into a powerful, centralized state in the middle of the twentieth century was the product of a long and bloody conflict between a *political* revolutionary movement led by Chiang Kai-shek and the Nationalist Kuomintang (KMT) and a *social* revolutionary movement led by Mao and the Communist Party. The two revolutionary parties led armed movements to free China from the grips of imperialist and warlord power. However, they held contrasting visions of revolution. On the one hand, Chiang and the KMT sought to unite China by leaving existing social structures intact and negotiating with warlords to incorporate their armies into a rapidly expanding military force capable of quickly building a national state. The KMT succeeded in unifying most of China between 1927 and 1949. However, this success came at the cost of widespread corruption and an extraordinarily weak state. On the other hand, Mao and the Communist Party pursued a riskier—and arguably less rational—approach to revolution. Rather than working with land-lords and other existing structures, the party sought to destroy them—efforts that very nearly resulted in its annihilation in the 1930s. However, this approach generated a revolutionary reactive sequence that ultimately resulted in a powerful and centralized Chinese state that, for the first time in China's 5,000-year history, reached into every community, workplace, and family.

After the fall of the Qing dynasty in 1911, the first efforts to create a modern Chinese state were undertaken by the charismatic Nationalist leader Sun Yat-sen and his KMT party. The KMT overwhelmingly won competitive legislative elections held in 1912.[5] However, this victory meant little in the face of growing warlord influence. Power in early twentieth-century China was in the hands of a diverse and dense underbrush of secret societies, criminal gangs, gentry, and warlords that operated auton-omously of the central state.[6] The 200 or so warlords who dominated China were a motley crew that included Zhang Zongchang, known as the "Dog Meat General" for a betting game he enjoyed, and Feng Yuxiang, the "Christian General" who was said to baptize his troops with a fire hose.[7] Criminal gangs such as the infamous Green Gang in Shanghai dominated significant portions of the country.[8]

Sun and the KMT built an initial base in the southern city of Canton (Guangzhou) in 1920 with the hope of eventually extending their power to the rest of the country.[9] His vision of a powerful Chinese state free of foreign control attracted the support of educated elites from across China, who came to the city and helped the KMT to build key elements of a modern state, including a modern tax system and a military.[10] Sun and Chiang, the chief of the KMT army who succeeded Sun as head of the KMT after his death in 1925, relied on a pragmatic strategy to unify China. First, despite the KMT's opposition to class struggle and reliance on business support,[11] the party accepted the backing of the only major power willing to assist its anti-imperialist campaign: the fledgling Soviet Union.[12] Soviet leaders insisted that the KMT align with the tiny Soviet-controlled Chinese Communist Party (CCP), which had been formed in Shanghai in 1921. In return, the Soviets helped the Nationalists create the core of a modern army at the Whampoa military academy. Modeled on the Soviet Red Army, this new military was far more disciplined than the warlord-based forces it confronted.[13]

As professionalized as this new army was, however, its force of about 80,000 soldiers was too small to take on the warlords, who had up to a mil-lion troops at their disposal in the mid-1920s.[14] Thus, the KMT encouraged the defection of warlords to the Nationalist cause.[15] The KMT expanded the army by recruiting warlords such as Yan Xishan of Shanxi Province; Zhang Xueliang, the "Young Martial," in the northeast; and Feng Yuxiang, the "Christian General."[16] These "armed opportunists" provided military support but demanded substantial autonomy from the KMT leadership in return.[17] The KMT also welcomed into its ranks the sons of landed gentry and upper-class urban families, often making them army officers.[18]

This eclectic coalition of communist revolutionaries, commercial interests, and warlords enabled the KMT to build the National Revolutionary Army (NRA), a 100,000-strong force capable of unifying China under a single government.[19] Between 1926 and 1928, the KMT's loose coalition undertook the Northern Expedition, which aimed to establish centralized KMT rule by taking over warlord-controlled areas.[20] By co-opting rather than challenging warlords such as Feng, the KMT avoided many costly battles and rapidly expanded its territorial presence with relatively few troops.[21] In two years, the Northern Expedition created a national government uniting Beijing in the north and Guangzhou in the south. The government was robust enough to unify China and survive for twenty years in a very hostile international environment.

However, the KMT's coalition of diverse and contradictory interests contained the seeds of instability. Above all, the Soviet-imposed United Front between the Nationalists and the Communist Party was virtually doomed to failure. Although both parties were anti-imperialist, the similarities ended there.[22] Whereas the KMT sought to create a modern capitalist economy and had strong support in the commercial class and landowning elite, the Communists sought a social revolution that ended capitalism and attacked landowners. In the words of Harold R. Isaacs, the alliance forced the KMT and the CCP "to ride two horses pulling in opposite directions."[23]

In the mid-1920s, this contradiction exploded into violent conflict, marking the onset of decades of civil war. Between 1925 and 1927, the CCP helped to lead the Great Revolution, a series of large-scale strikes and protests that initially targeted foreign businesses.[24] The urban labor movement, which had been building strength since 1923, burst forth on May 30, 1925, after British troops fired on a Communist-led protest in Shanghai.[25] The British attack sparked a wave of strikes and boycotts against foreign businesses in Shanghai, Guangzhou, Hong Kong, and other cities.[26] Initially, the KMT and Chinese businesses supported the strikes because they targeted imperial interests and weakened warlords opposed to the KMT.[27]

But tensions with the Chinese commercial community quickly escalated into a wave of reaction, as the boycott of British trade hurt profits. Armed picketers began detaining Chinese business owners and confiscating the goods of those who did not go along with the boycott.[28] In the countryside, strike committees caused heavy damage to rice merchants and fomented conflict with the rural establishment, causing alarm among landowners.[29]

The Northern Expedition deepened tensions between the KMT and the Communists. By weakening local power structures, KMT victories created opportunities for Communist activists to organize and promote unrest, which resulted in an unprecedented wave of worker mobilization.[30] A diversity of new labor unions emerged in the wake of KMT military victories, and the labor movement grew exponentially in large parts of the south.[31]

By opening up much of the countryside to Communist political activity, the Northern Expedition polarized rural society and gave rise to mounting violence.[32] In the wake of KMT victories, local gentry often dissolved and were replaced by communist peasant associations led by poor farmers, who beat and killed "local bullies and bad gentry," looted Christian missions, seized the property of local landlords, and arrested local elites and paraded them through the streets with dunce caps.[33] These actions disrupted the local economic order, as peasants seized grain and blocked grain shipments outside their districts.[34] Witnessing these actions firsthand, Mao, then a rural Communist organizer, famously celebrated this violence in his "Hunan Report," proclaiming, "A revolution is not a dinner party. . . . Without using the greatest force, the peasants cannot possibly overthrow the deep-rooted authority of the landlords which has lasted for a thousand years. . . . [I]t is necessary to create terror for a while."[35]

Such attacks on established interests in the countryside triggered a right-wing reaction among the KMT elite, particularly KMT military officials, most of whom were sons of landlords.[36] Rumors spread that the Communists would confiscate property and "communize" wives.[37]

A full-scale counterrevolution began in the wake of a strike wave in Shanghai, which would prove to be the high point of labor power. In late March 1927, a force of 800,000 workers, led in part by Zhou Enlai, brought Shanghai to a halt.[38] Workers took control of police stations and military posts throughout the city as police took off their uniforms.[39] Strike leaders expected the advancing KMT army to support them, which allowed Chiang to enter Shanghai with little resistance.[40] Yet urban mobilization had stoked a powerful counterrevolutionary fervor.[41] The upsurge in labor activism threatened the existing political and economic order. Merchant guilds and organized crime in Shanghai provided Chiang with financial support in the expectation that he would quash the Communists.[42]

Then, in the early dawn of April 12, 1927, residents of Shanghai's narrow, winding streets were awakened by shrill bugle calls—the signal for the city's notorious Green Gang to root out, arrest, or kill supporters of the Communist Party. Activists were dragged onto the street and shot, beheaded, or clubbed to death.[43] Similar purges took place across the country.[44] In late May, thousands of Communists were slaughtered, leaving the CCP at the point of destruction. Peasant associations disintegrated or were quashed by military force.[45] The party was forced underground and left with virtually no means to defend itself against KMT attacks.[46]

Chiang's counterrevolutionary repression marked a turning point in the revolutionary process. The Shanghai massacre permanently polarized relations between the CCP and the KMT,[47] forcing the Communists to change strategy. Until then, the CCP had modeled itself on the Bolsheviks, focusing on the mobilization of urban workers. Like the Bolsheviks in 1917, the CCP lacked a real military organization. However, the Shanghai massacre taught the party that it needed to create an army to win power. As Mao famously argued in August 1927, political power must "be obtained from the barrel of a gun."[48] That summer, the party created the new Red Army (later renamed the People's Liberation Army [PLA]), which would become the center of the revolutionary struggle for the next two decades.[49] Simultaneously, the party was forced to abandon China's urban centers and focus on the countryside. In stark contrast to the Bolsheviks, then, the CCP would have to rely almost exclusively on rural support.

The Communist Party would have disappeared into history's dustbin after the Shanghai massacre had the Chinese state not been so weak. Covered by a mere 2,000 miles of road in the 1920s, China included vast territories that were inaccessible to vehicular traffic.[50] As a result, the party was able to avoid destruction by disappearing into the hinterland and out of the KMT's reach.[51] By the late 1920s, party supporters had established about a dozen bases in remote mountainous provincial border regions. The party benefited from the networks of local gentry, warlords, criminal gangs, and secret societies outside the control of the KMT. Thus, in Shanghai in the 1920s, Anyuan in 1922–1923, the Jinggang Mountains in 1928–1929, and elsewhere, the CCP secured local protection by "burrowing deeply into the world of local strongmen and bandits."[52]

Communist survival was further facilitated by Chiang's decision to build the Chinese state by stitching together existing social and political forces—an approach that resulted in a weak and undisciplined government hierarchy dominated by "residual warlords."[53] The many warlords-turned-KMT officials who saturated the Nationalist power structure resisted efforts to streamline central control and eliminate corruption.[54] They also rejected attempts to create a Soviet-style military organization and refused to allow KMT political commissars into their armies.[55] As a result, the army was a ramshackle "jumble of armies" with an extremely weak command-and-control structure in which Chiang was merely "the most powerful warlord."[56] Chiang faced a near-constant threat of military rebellion and was in fact briefly kidnapped by an allied warlord, Zhang Xue-liang, in 1936.[57] Such disorganization directly benefited the Communists, as units of the KMT army sometimes refused to engage the CCP in battle and even defected to the Communists.[58] It also allowed the Communists to avoid capture by bribing warlords during the Long March (see below).

In sum, the Great Revolution and its aftermath provide a clear illustration of the revolutionary reactive sequence. Large-scale urban and rural mobilization, fomented by a radicalized CCP, terrified the bourgeoisie, landowning elites, and KMT conservatives and sparked counterrevolutionary war. As a result, the CCP, like the Bolsheviks a decade earlier, was forced to build an army from scratch and engage in a violent struggle that would profoundly shape the character of the movement and, eventually, the regime.

VIOLENT CONFLICT AND THE PILLARS OF DURABLE AUTHORITARIANISM

The Communist Party's decimation in Shanghai marked the beginning of a military conflict that would continue virtually without pause until the conclusion of the Korean War in 1953. Violent conflict had three long-term effects. First, it created a cohesive ruling party. As in Russia, China's nominally Leninist party only became unified after extended revolutionary struggle. War fostered the emergence of a tight-knit core of leaders loyal to Mao, while failure on the battlefield eliminated or discredited competing contenders for power within the party. In addition, as in Russia, violent struggle fostered an intense two-front siege mentality rooted in fear of enemies both from within and abroad. Existential threats bolstered efforts by Mao to impose unity, purge the party of dissenters, and centralize power in his hands.

Second, armed conflict generated a strong and loyal army. The war with Japan and the 1946–1949 civil war gave rise to a large and effective military that would facilitate the consolidation of state power in the 1950s. Party-army fusion made it nearly impossible for the military to make an independent play for power. Thus, while the military would occupy a central role in politics after 1949, it always remained subordinate to the dominant factions within the party.

Third, war and radical social transformation facilitated the destruction of major centers of power, including the KMT military and warlords, as well as the dense network of lower-level gentry and secret societies that had long dominated local power structures. As a result, the CCP emerged in the early 1950s facing no alternative power centers, which gave the new regime enormous room for maneuver. Enhanced state power and its unprecedented penetration deep into Chinese society created the necessary conditions for totalitarian rule.

Revolutionary Struggle and the Emergence of a Cohesive Party-Army Complex, 1927–1936

The Shanghai massacre left the CCP fragmented and disorganized.[59] In addition to various underground forces in some cities such as Shanghai, the party survived as a collection of isolated base areas in remote parts of the country that operated with little party oversight.[60]

The situation was made worse by the fact that the party was tightly controlled by Moscow. The Soviet Union's repeated interventions forced the surviving remnants of the party leadership in Shanghai (the "Comintern faction") to carry out policies that made little sense on the ground.[61] There existed a vast gulf between the CCP's political leadership and military leaders in the base areas. Regional leaders with independent power bases, including Mao (who would not assume the party leadership until 1935), clashed repeatedly with party representatives in Shanghai and frequently ignored party commands.[62] Directives to move troops, attack particular cities, or consult with party leadership were often disregarded by local leaders.

During the first years of the conflict, the CCP's military efforts also suffered from a severe lack of discipline. Troops were a mishmash of experienced soldiers, secret society members, and bandits more intent on plundering than fighting.[63] In one of the first rebellions, the 1927 Autumn Harvest uprising, peasants lacked basic weapons training and often deserted or refused to fight.[64] As a result, the revolt failed.[65]

However, years of armed struggle fostered the developments of a more powerful and disciplined military.[66] Disasters such as the Autumn Harvest uprising convinced Mao and his close military ally, Zhu De, to make active efforts to foster military discipline. Considerable attention was paid to political education designed to bring soldiers together around a common mission.[67] Mobile military schools accompanied units wherever they traveled.[68] Soldiers were taught the "three disciplines" and the "eight points of attention," which emphasized the need to obey orders, treat the population with respect, and avoid plunder.[69] The party also increased the number of political commissars.[70] By the early 1930s, the Red Army had grown considerably more disciplined.

More than any particular teachings or formal institutions, however, the creation of a loyal military was the product of the CCP's dramatic struggle for survival during the Long March. In the early 1930s, Chiang Kai-shek, drawing on the advice of German officials, established an effective blockade of the Communists' main base in Jiangxi Province, which nearly destroyed the party.[71] The party leadership, consisting of a troika of Bo Gu, Zhou Enlai, and Soviet adviser Otto Braun, decided in October 1934 to embark on a march to avoid defeat and capture. They initially brought with them vast amounts of heavy equipment (including an X-ray machine that had to be tossed into the Xiang River mid-battle) and suffered devastating losses.[72] By late December, the Red Army had been halved, mostly due to desertion.[73]

Yet the KMT's attempts to trap and destroy the Communists were thwarted by the KMT's rapacious warlord allies, who frequently ignored Chiang's entreaties to crack down on the CCP. Communists evaded destruction by lugging trunks of Mexican silver dollars provided by Moscow to bribe warlords to let the marchers pass. Many warlords preferred to retain their strength rather than lose troops in battle. In fact, the party's initial withdrawal from its Jiangxi base in 1934 was made possible by a secret negotiation with NRA general (and leader of the Guangdong military faction) Chen Jitang, which allowed the Red Army to travel through his territory without engagement.[74]

The party was also able to escape the clutches of the KMT because of Mao's flexible and unpredictable military maneuvers, which led the marchers on a circuitous route through China roughly resembling a cursive "G." For just over a year, the party marched 6,000 miles across twenty-four large rivers, eleven provinces, dangerous swampland, and five mountain passes shod in slippers and straw sandals.[75] Of the 87,000 soldiers who departed Jiangxi in October 1934, between 5,000 and 10,000 made it to the city of Yan'an in Shaanxi Province, where the CCP established a permanent base.[76]

The Long March helped unify the CCP in several ways. First, the survival of a small band of leaders in the face of unimaginable adversity created strong bonds of trust.[77] Veterans of the Long March dominated the party and possessed a strong corporate identity until their deaths in the 1990s.

Second, the Long March also fostered party unity by eliminating Mao's most serious rivals.[78] Sidelined when the Long March began, Mao skillfully used a series of military defeats to maneuver his way into the party leadership.[79] Early catastrophes such as a disastrous crossing of the Xiang River in November discredited the Moscow-backed troika of Bo, Braun, and Zhou.[80] Mao, one of the only leaders not associated with these early debacles, replaced the troika and became the de facto leader of the party in March 1935.[81]

But intraparty conflict persisted. Mao was challenged by Zhang Guotao, a founding member of the party who headed a Communist base in the north.[82] When Mao's forces met up with Zhang's army in June 1935, toward the end of the Long March, Zhang was considered the more powerful leader.[83] In September, they each claimed to represent the legitimate Communist Party, resulting in a crisis that "brought the Red Army to the brink of disaster."[84] However, the dispute was resolved on the battlefield. By late October 1935, Zhang had lost tens of thousands of men to the KMT in a failed effort to capture Chengdu.[85] Then, in the fall of 1936, Zhang's Fourth Front army was nearly annihilated, leaving Mao at the top of the party hierarchy. Mao would face no serious challenges to his supremacy until his death in 1976.[86]

Third, the Long March strengthened party-army ties. The rise to power of Mao, who had risen to prominence on the battlefield, meant that power in the CCP was no longer in the hands of officials far removed from the armed struggle.[87] Those leading the military operations and the party were now one. In 1935, Mao required that party leaders take military posts at the front.[88] Partly as a result, nearly all of the founding leaders of China's revolutionary regime had substantial military experience (including Deng Xiaoping, whose role in the 1946–1949 civil war gave him solid military credentials).[89] In fact, most of the population was unable to distinguish the party from the army. The army *was* the party.[90]

Party-army fusion increased military loyalty and reduced the chances of coup by enhancing the informal authority of top political leaders. It also diminished the corporate identity of the military. This blurring of the party and the military that developed during the long struggle for power made it much harder for the military to conceive of its interests as separate from those of the party. The military's threat to the revolution had been virtually eliminated because "the military had *become* the revolution."[91]

Party Cohesion and State-Building during the War with Japan, 1937–1945

After settling in Yan'an after the Long March, the CCP was more unified. However, the revolutionary movement was still small and geographically fragmented.[92] Reduced to around 10,000 underfed, ill-equipped soldiers after the Long March, the Red Army was in no position to challenge the KMT. Furthermore, Japan's invasion of China in 1937 and the resulting eight-year war created an additional threat to the Communists' survival. Blockaded by about 500,000 KMT troops and suffering from periodic Japanese bombing campaigns,[93] Yan'an was a "precarious haven" in the late 1930s and early 1940s.[94] The CCP was gripped by fear of infiltration.[95]

Like his counterparts in the Soviet Union, Mao used this siege mentality to promote an almost religious devotion to party unity.[96] Confronted with a constant threat of infiltration by KMT forces and Japanese forces, the party created a variety of agencies—including the Social Affairs Department—that targeted clandestine activity and enemies of the regime.[97] By July 1943, more than 1,000 "enemy agents" had been detained in a sweeping anti-espionage campaign.[98]

This set the stage for the Yan'an Rectification Campaign of 1942–1943—a program of education and self-criticism that strengthened party cohesion and fostered an increasing cultlike atmosphere around Mao. The campaign gradually developed into an extensive purge encompassing about 30,000 cadres.[99] Intellectuals and artists critical of the party were subjected to intense "struggle sessions" in which hundreds of participants hurled verbal and physical abuse at victims for days on end.[100] The atmosphere of extreme military threat made it easy for Mao to justify the Rectification Campaign.[101] Policy disagreements became tantamount to treason, and internal critics were repeatedly excoriated as traitors.[102] Although far less violent than Stalin's purges, the operation helped to deter any dissent within the party, imposing an intense discipline and conformity that persisted long after the party came to power.[103]

The war with Japan also dramatically strengthened Communist military and political power.[104] Although the war left the CCP vulnerable to Japanese attack, it allowed the party to attract external assistance and gave the Communists critical breathing room from the larger and more serious KMT assaults—just at the point when the Nationalists had been in a position to eliminate the party.[105] While Chiang Kai-shek remained committed to the destruction of the Communists, numerous domestic groups—and later the United States—pressured Chiang to cooperate with the

Communists. Most notably, Zhang Xueliang, one of the KMT's "residual war-lords," kidnapped Chiang in late 1936 until he agreed to cooperate with the Communists in fighting Japan.[106] As a result, Chiang was forced to redirect much of his military away from the battle with the Communists—and even provide the Communists some material assistance to help fight the Japanese.[107] The Communists also benefited from Soviet military assistance.[108]

In the end, the war against the Japanese transformed the Communists from a small regional force into a serious contender for national power.[109] The Red Army expanded from a force of just 30,000 in 1937 to one encompassing 900,000 troops plus a militia of up to two million in 1945.[110] Communist territorial expansion during the war meant that, by 1945, the number of peasants in Communist territories increased from about 1.5 million to 90 million—approximately one-fifth of China's population.[111] Party membership increased from about 40,000 in 1937 to 2.7 million in 1945.[112] The Communists began to engage in state-building, creating their own currency and financing government-like structures through a system of taxation.[113] More broadly, the war generated public support for the CCP as a patriotic force battling a foreign aggressor.[114]

State-Building and the Destruction of Alternative Power Centers, 1946–1949

Notwithstanding U.S. and Soviet pressure to unite in the wake of Japan's surrender in 1945, the KMT and the CCP descended into a three-year civil war beginning in 1946.[115] At the start of the conflict, few expected the Communists to defeat the more powerful Nationalist army. However, the KMT was fractured and riddled with corruption and indiscipline.[116] Foreign aid was often diverted and never made it to the troops.[117] Chiang Kai-shek's decision to build the army by grafting together a variety of warlord fiefdoms allowed him to unify China relatively quickly, but it also generated a state that was weak and vulnerable to attack from the more disciplined Communists.

The civil war forced the CCP to build a powerful state apparatus. Confronting a much larger and better-equipped army, the Communists were motivated to develop reliable mechanisms to extract (often forcibly) enormous supplies of horses, men, provisions, and military equipment.[118] Guerrilla warfare may have allowed the CCP to survive near destruction in the 1930s. However, it was conventional warfare—based on military conscription—that made it possible for the CCP to seize power in 1949.[119] The PLA expanded dramatically between 1945 and 1949.[120] The CCP was forced to mobilize the entire population under its control, which resulted in a near total militarization of areas held by the party.[121] In this way, the CCP lay the foundation for a "vast, militarized bureaucracy that excelled at extracting sacrifice from subject populations and party cadres alike."[122]

Revolutionary civil war also facilitated the destruction of alternative centers of power. As noted above, much of early twentieth-century China was inhabited by a dense underbrush of international and localized power structures: local gentry, foreign and domestic churches, warlords, criminal gangs, secret societies, and clan networks. Such structures provided a critical haven for both bandits and political opposition.

However, war and CCP efforts to radically transform Chinese society weakened these competing power centers. The war against invading Japanese forces wiped out much of the state and social structure that had existed before 1937. By 1945, the "structures of society and government barely existed" in large parts of the country.[123] The many local elites who collaborated with the Japanese became targets of revenge attacks, weakening their hold on power.[124] The civil war also motivated the CCP to annihilate the KMT and to take on bandits and other societal groups that had once provided protection but now hindered the war effort.[125] The destruction of these forces left an opening for the CCP to establish new local and regional power structures.[126]

In addition, the scale of social transformation increased dramatically during the civil war. *Fanshen* (to turn over), a radical vision of social change pushed by Mao,[127] took hold among the Communists, driving the adoption of radical land reform in CCP-controlled areas in 1946 and 1947.[128] The move toward more severe measures culminated in the October 1947 Outline Agrarian Law, which eliminated the land ownership rights of all landlords, ancestral halls, schools, temples, and monasteries.[129] The party leadership instigated a series of political campaigns and a revolutionary terror targeting old elites.[130] Violence "became the essential catalyst of change."[131] Struggle sessions involving entire communities were orchestrated against the local rich and powerful.[132] Activists attacked whole families and seized their property—digging up graves to confiscate hidden wealth.[133] The upheaval "swept like a whirlwind through the villages," shattering the old landlord tenant system beyond recognition.[134] Poor and landless peasants rose up to replace the old gentry elite.[135] In some contested areas, the party moderated its demands in order to preserve alliances with wealthy groups.[136] However, once Chiang's armies withdrew and CCP victory became more certain, the party relaunched land reform campaigns. In the northeast, the party undertook "Sweep the courtyard" campaigns that revived struggle meetings and land confiscations.[137] An avalanche of red terror swept the countryside as activists from one village were used to attack enemies from nearby villages suspected of protecting kin from elite class backgrounds.[138]

Such measures intensified the revolutionary reactive sequence. Confronted with an existential threat, large landowners had no choice but to either support the KMT and fight the Communists or go into exile.[139] This, in turn, encouraged the CCP to wipe out the landowners.[140] In the end, *fanshen* dramatically weakened alternative power centers that might otherwise have competed with the CCP and had the effect of clearing the way for an unprecedented expansion of state power.[141]

The Korean War and the Destruction of Alternative Power Centers

In October 1949, the Chinese Communists took power—forcing Chiang Kai-shek to escape with much of his army to nearby Taiwan. In power, the CCP did not moderate its policies. Mao, who saw war with the United States as inevitable, refused to even *consider* granting Western powers diplomatic recognition because he assumed that Western embassies would provide a toehold for counterrevolutionary forces.[142] In 1948–1949, the regime held the American diplomat Angus Ward and twenty-one staff members under house arrest for a year on charges of espionage.[143]

The revolutionary government's hostility toward the West triggered a mass exodus of foreign actors that had long exercised power in China. All foreign assets and property were frozen or confiscated.[144] A massive flow of refugees abandoned the mainland.[145] Virtually all foreigners were forced to leave the country, while tourism and contacts with overseas Chinese ended.[146] Under heavy pressure from the new authorities, foreign businesses deserted China.[147] Foreign missionaries and other churches were shut down; by 1953, almost all of them had left.[148] Foreign interests that had permeated China since the late nineteenth century suddenly disappeared without a trace.

Viewing China as a "new type of international actor" that would "break with the existing principles and codes of behavior in international relations,"[149] Mao sent three million Chinese troops to fight against the United States in Korea in 1950.[150] The Korean conflict, which resulted in about a million deaths,[151] intensified the regime's siege mentality. U.S. intervention in Korea inspired hopes among KMT leaders that the CCP might be defeated, which encouraged intensive KMT-sponsored sabotage operations aimed at the new regime.[152] The war created a very real threat of counterrevolution, backed by the world's leading superpower and unseen enemies at home.[153]

In challenging the domestic and international order, China generated endemic external threats that heightened the regime's siege mentality and motivated the destruction of autonomous sources of power. Fears of invasion by Taiwan and the United States created an urgent necessity to root out potential enemies.[154] The Korean War inspired the "three antis" targeting corrupt cadres, as well as the "five antis" against the bourgeoisie.[155] In early 1950, the CCP launched a campaign to eliminate "counterrevolutionaries"—a term that included everyone from old KMT leaders to popular local leaders, bandits, religious sects, and priests.[156] The campaign targeted urban secret societies, criminal gangs, and religious sects with the capacity to challenge the regime.[157] The government shut down temples, shrines, monasteries, and other religious institutions.[158] In the end, the campaign wiped out almost all organized resistance and annihilated the remnants of Nationalist underground networks.[159] By May 1951, more than 2.5 million "reactionaries" had been arrested, and 710,000 were executed, according to the regime's own estimates.[160] Millions of people were killed in the various campaigns undertaken during the regime's first three years of existence.[161]

Many of the campaigns of the 1950s would likely have been carried out even in the absence of war. Nevertheless, the Korean War and other international threats generated a powerful rationale for eliminating potential enemies and implementing radical social change.[162] Indeed, although the leadership had initially signaled that land reform would be gradual, Beijing demanded more radical measures and an intensification of rural class struggle following China's entrance into the Korean conflict.[163] By the end of the campaign, about 20 million people had been classified as landlords and more than 40 percent of land had changed ownership.[164] By 1952, nearly one million landlords and their families had been killed.[165] As a result, the Chinese gentry was displaced by a new rural elite of young peasant activists embedded in the CCP.[166] Thus, revolutionary war and radical social transformation resulted in the elimination of important centers of power that might have otherwise acted as a brake on Communist rule after 1999.

Revolutionary conflict was critical to the creation of China's totalitarian system. The destruction of traditional local authority structures permitted the expansion and penetration of Communist power into parts of society that had never been subject to direct central control.[167] Party officials and "committees of the poor" spent weeks in each village classifying every family into particular social classes.[168] Combined with war, land reform made room for the CCP to create a pervasive and disciplined new political authority.[169] In particular, the conflictual "settling accounts" and land confiscation in the 1940s uncovered vast stores of hitherto hidden wealth. Seeking the fruits of *fanshen*, poor peasants and party cadres used struggle sessions and other measures to identify where local luminaries had buried money and other valuables.[170]

In urban areas, revolutionary transformation resulted in the creation of a system of *danwei* (workplace units) in which nearly all urban residents were embedded until the reform era of the 1990s. The *danwei* provided work and housing, as well as access to a wide range of other social goods, from food to vacation spots. It was also an effective mechanism of surveillance by the party-state.

In sum, whereas China entered the twentieth century with one of the world's weakest states, the long reactive sequence generated the three pillars of durable authoritarianism. First, revolutionary war fostered the creation of a tight-knit group of party elites. By sparking an intense two-front siege mentality, revolutionary conflict provided a powerful rationale for purging enemies and centralizing party power. Second, extended conflict motivated the creation of a powerful, highly disciplined, and loyal armed services. The length and brutality of the conflict encouraged the rise of political leaders with close ties to the military, eliminating the sharp divisions between party and military that had plagued the CCP in the late 1920s and early 1930s. Third, war and radical social transformation resulted in the annihilation of key alternative centers of power in Chinese society. The departure of foreign businesses and missionaries, the defeat of the KMT, and the elimination of local strongmen, secret societies, sects, and other informal power structures left the CCP without serious challengers in the mid-1950s and created room for totalitarian state structures that reached into every part of society.

Revolutionary Regime Durability after 1949

China's revolutionary regime proved strikingly durable. After 1949, the CCP confronted three major challenges: a massive famine during the Great Leap Forward; the Cultural Revolution, which brought the country to the brink of civil war; and the 1989 Tiananmen protests. As we see below, the legacies of revolution allowed the government to eliminate opposition before it could emerge in the Great Leap Forward and the Cultural Revolution and to rapidly suppress serious challenges that arose in 1989.

THE GREAT LEAP FORWARD

The Great Leap Forward (1958–1960) is widely regarded as one of the greatest catastrophes in modern human history. Revolutionary zeal produced a man-made famine that cost about 30 million lives.[171] Flush from its revolutionary triumph and inspired by Soviet successes, the CCP attempted to transform China into an industrial power by sheer force of will.[172] Motivated by Khrushchev's promise to overtake the United States in fifteen years, Mao declared that China would catch up with the United Kingdom in steel production in fifteen years.[173] Mao then called for a radical increase in production targets in March 1958,[174] and three months later at a meeting held at Mao's pool in Zhongnanhai, he declared that China would overtake British steel production in just *two* years.[175] No major party leader dared question him. CCP leader Chen Boda announced that under the new conditions of socialism, one day was equivalent to twenty years.[176] Ignoring "bourgeois" experts, Mao pushed provincial leaders to divert tens of millions of laborers away from agriculture toward vast, ill-conceived irrigation projects.[177] By early 1958, one in six Chinese was digging earth, often for projects that proved useless.[178] Planning was essentially abandoned and replaced by a "frenzied process of drawing up new plans, raising targets, and then doing it all over again."[179]

In mid-1958, the government decided to increase steel production by relying on small "backyard" steel furnaces.[180] Rather than build large steel mills, the government promoted the idea of "industry in every county."[181] By the fall of 1958, an estimated 10 percent of China's population was mobilized to produce steel in hundreds of thousands of small furnaces, often by melting down household utensils and agricultural equipment.[182] In the end, the campaign led to extraordinary levels of waste and the production of vast amounts of unusable steel.[183] At the same time, farmers were pressured to introduce counterproductive agricultural techniques (many of them borrowed from the Soviet Union) such as "close planting" and deep planting of grain, which led to a massive waste of resources.[184] Homes and other buildings made of mud brick were torn down for use as fertilizer.[185]

During this period, landholdings were rapidly collectivized as the country was organized into communes.[186] Private land ownership was virtually eliminated by the end of 1958,[187] as more than 90 percent of rural

households were forced into 23,397 communes.[188] Peasants were forced
to give up nearly all of their private possessions.[189] As part of a utopian
effort to introduce communism and eliminate the nuclear family, communal kitchens were introduced.[190] Families were forbidden to cook at home
and often forced to walk for miles to reach the nearest dining hall. Communes rapidly found themselves unable to meet promised guarantees of
food and other necessities as incentives to work disappeared.[191] Yet Mao,
inspired by falsified reports of production gains, worried that *too much*
food would be produced and therefore encouraged a reduction of land to
be used for food production in late 1958.[192]

These measures brought extraordinary misery to China.[193] The diversion of labor to irrigation projects and steel production contributed to
dramatic declines in food production.[194] Crops were often left to rot in
the fields as peasants busied themselves making steel.[195] Cadres, under
tremendous pressure to fulfill unrealistic production targets, engaged in
requisition of grain that, as in Soviet collectivization, resembled a military
campaign against the peasants.[196] Even in the midst of massive famine,
millions of tons of grain were exported abroad.[197] "Seldom has the willful
pursuit of an ideal led to such devastating results."[198]

The disastrous consequences of the Great Leap Forward caused significant, albeit subterranean, divisions within the party's senior leadership.[199] Yet Mao had already gained uncontested dominance in the early
1940s.[200] He was able to use the party's strong discipline, which had
developed in the late 1930s, to impose unity within the top ranks.[201] As
a result, no one from the upper reaches of the party opposed the Great
Leap Forward when it was introduced in early 1958, and top party officials reliably carried out the program, despite having expressed serious
(and well-founded) concerns about such "rash" development policies in
1956 and 1957.[202]

Accounts of the Great Leap Forward tend to focus on Mao's moti-
vations in pushing for such measures and the scale of the disaster that
resulted.[203] Yet it is also worth emphasizing the sheer mobilizational
capacity required by this campaign. Although figures were widely falsified,[204] the party demonstrated an unquestionable ability to motivate vast
numbers of peasants to engage in activity that contradicted their short-
term interests, such as ignoring food production in favor of utopian efforts
to build dams and produce steel.[205] "Snatching grain from the mouths of
starving peasants was no easy matter."[206]

To carry out this ambitious program, the central leadership drew on
15 million party members tied together by a militarized organization that

had developed over twenty years of violent struggle.[207] Implementation of the campaign was enforced by enormous "inspection contingents" of party activists sent to the villages in the summer and fall of 1958.[208] Party activists relied on struggle sessions and other techniques developed during the revolution to ensure compliance.[209] In addition, the army devoted more than 59 million manpower days to industrial and agricultural projects in 1958 and assisting in transport for the backyard furnaces.[210]

These disastrous policies might have been expected to generate opposition. However, decades of revolutionary civil war and three years of postrevolutionary conflict in Korea had helped to eliminate any serious challenges to party power.[211] Furthermore, unlike in the 1920s and 1930s, there was no vast network of secret societies, criminal gangs, and local power structures in which opposition could hide. And even if such opposition *had* emerged, it would have confronted a well-equipped army, with more than four million troops, which had penetrated every corner of the country.[212]

Arguably, the greatest potential threat came from the military. The Great Leap Forward represented the kind of massive policy failure that has frequently triggered military intervention in other cases.[213] Many PLA officers opposed army involvement in nonmilitary activities to support the Great Leap Forward.[214] Moreover, Mao directly threatened the military's prerogatives by organizing popular militias in the wake of increasing tensions with Taiwan in 1958—the kind of intervention that has brought about coups in other countries. The militias created the "specter of peasant hordes lugging rifles and even swords and spears into battle" that was "anathema to some officers."[215] To make matters worse, the government ordered the military to train and supply the militias with precious military equipment.[216] Mao appears to have feared a coup during this period.[217] Indeed, the 1965 coup in Indonesia was in part a reaction to Sukarno's plans to distribute small arms to workers and peasants.[218]

The most serious civil-military tensions arose during the Lushan conference in the summer of 1959. The defense minister, General Peng Dehuai, was concerned about the impact of the Great Leap Forward and sought to discuss his views with Mao privately during the conference. Finding Mao asleep, Peng left Mao a letter that praised the "great achievements" of the Great Leap Forward but criticized key aspects of the campaign, including communal kitchens, the "winds of exaggeration," and the militias, which Peng feared would weaken the PLA.[219] Peng appeared to have no desire to confront Mao and sought only to encourage him to continue policies the chairman had already initiated.[220] Yet Mao found the

letter intolerable and immediately had it copied and distributed to participants in the conference. Mao then launched a frontal attack on Peng.[221]

Peng was one of the most celebrated and senior generals in China.
He joined the party in 1928, helped lead military efforts during the war
against Japan, had been a member of the Politburo since 1936, and commanded Chinese forces in the Korean War. Given his status, as well as
widespread discontent in both the military and the party, we might have
expected regime elites to rise to his defense. However, almost none of
Peng's colleagues in the military uttered a word in his favor.[222] The fusion
between party and military made it difficult for the military to act autono-
mously against the party, even in a context of crisis when the military's
core interests were under threat. Given Mao's enormous military prestige
and authority, no one dared to challenge him, leaving Peng isolated.[223]

In sum, the PRC's capacity to both undertake and survive the Great
Leap Forward was a direct product of decades of violent revolutionary struggle. The creation of a large and disciplined party-state and the
destruction of alternative centers of power allowed the party to rapidly implement radical policies and to prevent any serious challenges to
emerge in reaction to the resulting crisis. Simultaneously, the tight fusion
of party and military structures deprived the military of the autonomy
necessary to challenge the new regime.

THE CULTURAL REVOLUTION

Let everything collapse, that's the best thing that could happen.

—MAO ZEDONG, AUGUST 1966[224]

The Cultural Revolution (1966–1976) triggered the most serious crisis that
the regime confronted since taking power.[225] It was unique in that the
primary threat to regime survival came not from external enemies, military coup plotters, or societal protest but rather from the very top.[226] In
1966 and 1967, Mao actively fomented the destruction of a robust party-
state forty years in the making—a move that created a massive power vacuum and nearly plunged China into civil war.[227] The regime's capacity to
survive the crisis is in part explained by revolutionary legacies that gave
regime leaders access to an effective *and* loyal military. The military was
powerful enough to restore the country to order but insufficiently autonomous to use this power to challenge the regime itself.

The Cultural Revolution began in the context of Mao's dissatisfaction over the revisionist direction of economic policy after the Great Leap

Forward.[228] In May 1966, Mao encouraged the activation of the Central Cultural Revolution Group (CCRG) led by Chen Boda; Mao's wife, Jiang Qing; Kang Sheng; and other radical supporters of Mao.[229] In May and June, student Red Guards at elite universities began attacking professors and administrators for bourgeois elitist and counterrevolutionary behavior. That summer, groups of Red Guards led a "Red Terror," destroying cultural artifacts and attacking and breaking into homes of well-off families.[230] While giving no clear instructions, Mao encouraged the Red Guard movement, calling on students to "bombard the headquarters" and appearing at a massive Red Guard rally on Tiananmen Square on August 18.[231] Everyone in China except for Mao became vulnerable to attack.[232] The Red Guard movement spread throughout the country, and by late 1966, it had entered factories and military academies.[233]

Critically, Mao felt that the mass movement could be unleashed only by taking apart the central party apparatus itself.[234] Thus, Mao ousted party leader Liu Shaoqi, Deng Xiaoping, and other top leaders, many of whom were veterans from the Long March.[235] In mid-1966, the party's Central Committee was decimated by purges and ceased to function.[236] Mao cut the party off from the military,[237] and the Secretariat was pulled apart while the Organization Department of the party was stripped bare.[238] Party structures in the capital and throughout the country eventually ceased to function.[239] Leaders in many parts of the country were paraded through the streets in dunce caps.[240]

With the party largely absent, there was little Mao or anyone else could do to limit factional struggles within the leadership.[241] All of this was exacerbated by the fact that power was handed to an erratic, fractious, and inexperienced group led by Mao's wife, a former movie actress.[242]

China descended into chaos.[243] Key levers of totalitarian power, including state controls over travel and urban residency, broke down.[244] Between 70 and 90 percent of cadres from the central ministries were sent into the countryside—depriving the central government of any means to govern the country.[245] In many areas, state authority collapsed.[246] A wave of power seizures swept local party organizations in Shanghai and elsewhere, and armed conflicts erupted in cities across China.[247] Major cities became ungovernable.[248]

The PLA, the only coherent state institution left intact,[249] was also a target of politicized attacks.[250] Radicals demanded that PLA leaders be subject to struggle sessions.[251] On July 18, 1967, Mao, fearing PLA support for right-wing factions, called for the arming of leftist students and workers, letting loose a "great chaos" that brought the country to the brink of civil war.[252] Chaos spread throughout the country. In at least one instance, prisoners in the Chinese gulag successfully seized weapons.[253] Arming students transformed factional battles that had earlier been fought with improvised weapons into serious military engagements.[254]

The breakdown of state and party power posed a serious threat to regime survival. Jing Huang argues that uncontrolled factional strife within the top leadership threatened Mao's power.[255] It is easy to imagine how such chaos, in a context of severe economic crisis, might have generated significant opposition challenges or a military coup.

Several factors contributed to the PRC's survival, however. First, because Mao threw support back to the party in 1970–1971, just a few years after destroying it, the party apparatus was able to quickly reestablish its authority.[256] Second, regime survival was facilitated by the fact that decades of violent revolutionary conflict had already destroyed any well-organized alternative to the CCP. Opposition forces simply lacked the capacity to take advantage of the political opportunity created by the Cultural Revolution.

Third and most importantly, the PLA, the "Great Wall" of Chinese Communism,[257] was able to restore order and put down incipient challenges. Thus, in the fall of 1967, Mao stepped back from the precipice, encouraging the PLA to restore order and ordering the arrest and disgrace of activists involved in attacks on the armed forces.[258] From late 1967 until 1971, the military played a central role in putting down rebellions across the country.[259] Rebel forces were violently suppressed in an "orgy of repression,"[260] and by 1968 the Red Guards had mostly been disbanded.[261] Military-led work teams were brought in to retake control of universities.[262] Nearly a million cadres were purged.[263] Ultimately, most of those who had taken up Mao's call to rebel against authority were repressed.[264]

By the Ninth Party Congress in 1969, the military was the most powerful institution in China, and Marshal Lin Biao was designated as Mao's successor.[265] The military became the top administrative and political power in China's provinces.[266] Military tensions and border skirmishes with the Soviet Union in 1969 further empowered the military.[267] Fearing a surprise Soviet invasion, Lin ordered the military to prepare for imminent war.[268]

Of course, all of this could have provoked the military to seize power from Mao. The Cultural Revolution was arguably a "perfect storm" for a military coup. Conditions widely seen as conducive to coups—weak and divided civilian authorities, the failure of civilian authorities to deal with problems facing the country, military involvement in domestic security, and attacks on military interests—*all* existed in China between 1966 and 1970.[269] Indeed, Mao's explicit appeals to violence and calls for rebel attacks on army officials appalled PLA officers and created severe tension in the military leadership.[270] In early 1967, top military commanders openly clashed with the CCRG in what became known as the February Countercurrent.[271] Then, in Wuhan in July 1967, local military commanders briefly took a top CCRG leader hostage before being subdued and taken to Beijing.[272] Amid these tensions, Mao and other leaders repeatedly expressed fears of a coup.[273] In particular, Lin Biao's central role in putting down the Wuhan rebellion and ability to mobilize troops in response to Soviet threats appears to have spooked Mao.[274] Most bizarrely, Lin, whose succession to the party chairmanship had been written into the constitution, was killed along with his family in September 1971 after their plane crashed in Mongolia on the way to the Soviet Union. According to the official Chinese version of events, Lin was trying to escape after a coup plot concocted by his son, Lin Liguo, was uncovered by the authorities.[275]

Ultimately, however, the regime confronted no successful coups or even serious coup *attempts*. The Wuhan uprising was a strictly regional rebellion that was quickly put down.[276] Furthermore, although the "Lin Biao affair" remains one of the enduring mysteries of modern Chinese history, two important points are clear. First, while there might have been a coup *plot*, it never was *actually attempted*. Lin Biao and his son died not while trying to overthrow the regime but while escaping the country. Second, even if Lin's son or Lin Biao himself *did* contrive to oust Mao, they were not supported by any other senior military officials.[277] Indeed, the military's increased power from 1969 to 1971 was driven by Mao himself rather than the military establishment.[278] The generals brought into the party at the Ninth Congress were all linked to Mao rather than to Lin Biao.[279] Overall then, tight bonds forged between civilian and military leaders during decades of armed revolutionary struggle generated a high degree of army loyalty even in the face of severe attacks on the military's autonomy.

The combination of military intervention and subordination to the party was again demonstrated after Mao died of a heart attack on September 9, 1976. During Mao's final years, he had supported the rise of ardent backers of the Cultural Revolution known as the Gang of Four.[280] Within a month of Mao's death, the four were arrested in what Roderick MacFarquhar and Michael Schoenhals call a "military coup,"[281] which ultimately brought Deng Xiaoping to power. However, the term "military

coup" is misleading. Although the removal of the Gang of Four was organized by the military, it was initiated and led by the top *party* official at the
time, Mao's designated successor Hua Guofeng.[282] Hua had supported the
Cultural Revolution but grew alienated from Jiang Qing and feared ouster
by the Gang of Four if he did not act.[283] Hua was backed by elder veterans
of the Long March, including Ye Jianying, Li Xiannan, and Mao's former
bodyguard, Wang Dongxing.[284]

In sum, revolutionary legacies provided the regime with the tools to
survive Mao's self-inflicted crisis during the Cultural Revolution. After dismantling significant chunks of the Chinese party-state and bringing China
to the brink of civil war, Mao was able to rely on an effective and loyal
military force to bring the regime back from the precipice. After Mao's
death, the military remained loyal to the CCP faction backed by Long
March veterans. The unmatched authority of this generation would again
be decisive a decade later in the Tiananmen crisis.

THE TIANANMEN CRISIS

The third major crisis to confront the PRC was sparked by massive demonstrations in Tiananmen Square and other cities that rocked China from
April to June 1989. Involving hundreds of thousands of mostly student
protesters, the Tiananmen crisis split the party and exposed important
weaknesses in the regime. With communism beginning to collapse in
Eastern Europe, many observers assumed that the PRC was also on the
verge of breakdown.[285] Ultimately, however, revolutionary "elders"—
veterans of the Long March—imposed unity on the party and pushed
through a crackdown that ended the threat.

The Tiananmen protests were in large part the outgrowth of reforms
undertaken by Deng Xiaoping, who ascended to power a few years after
the arrest of the Gang of Four. Hua Guofeng, Mao's designated successor,
was gradually sidelined by Deng, who had greater support among the revolutionary veterans who controlled the party.[286] Indeed, power in the 1980s
was held by eight senior veterans of the Long March, known variously
as the "elders," "octogenarians," or "immortals." Led by Deng, the elders
mostly did not hold formal positions of authority but nevertheless functioned as a kind of "final court of appeals" in the regime.[287] The formal party
leadership, including General Secretaries Hu Yaobang (1982–1987) and
Zhao Ziyang (1987–1989), was drawn mostly from younger generations.[288]

After taking power, Deng introduced transformational market reforms.
He allowed enterprises to retain a greater share of their profits and created

Special Economic Zones to attract foreign investment.[289] Gradually, market mechanisms crowded out central planning. The number and size of private businesses, joint ventures, and foreign firms exploded.[290] As the economy grew, living standards rose dramatically as families across China gained access to TV sets, refrigerators, and other consumer goods. At the same time, state controls over intellectual activities, art, and private life were loosened relative to the Mao era.[291] By the late 1980s, Deng had transformed the PRC from an ideological, revolutionary regime to a performance-based authoritarian regime.[292]

Economic reform and prosperity generated new challenges, however. Inflation, widespread corruption among party cadres, and unmet expectations—especially among students—gave rise to mounting discontent and, eventually, regime-threatening protest.[293] Protest erupted in April 1989, shortly after the death Hu Yaobang, a reformist party leader who had been ousted by Deng for his lax response to student protest in 1987. Protesting students demanded an end to corruption and Hu's rehabilitation. Demonstrations spread to twenty cities, and students in Beijing organized an autonomous union and began to boycott classes.[294] While the reformist party secretary Zhao Ziyang was in North Korea, party leaders published an editorial in the *People's Daily* attacking the protests as an antiparty revolt that should be suppressed. The editorial backfired, however, as protests spread. Upon his return to China, Zhao embraced the protesters and their demands for a revision of the April 26 editorial.[295]

The crisis deepened when protesters announced a hunger strike on May 13.[296] Within a few days, there were over 3,000 students participating in the strike and hundreds of thousands supporting them in demonstrations. Bolstered by favorable coverage in state media, the strike generated public sympathy and garnered widespread support from within the regime.[297] Notably, independent civil society organizations played a less important role in supporting the strike than official groups such as the Communist Youth League and CCP-controlled unions, which provided financing, transportation, food, and communications equipment.[298]

Debates on how to respond to the protests split the upper echelons of the party. On May 16, an emergency Politburo meeting lasted well into the night but was inconclusive.[299] Another meeting was then held at Deng's house on May 17. Only when several elders intervened was the decision made to impose martial law.[300]

Yet the initial efforts to impose martial law exposed severe weaknesses in the regime as ferocious opposition in the capital and throughout the country emerged to block troops from restoring order.[301] Protesters prevented troops from entering the center of Beijing.[302] Many officers—including the commander of the Thirty-Eighth Group Army—opposed the crackdown.[303] On May 20, eight retired generals sent Deng a declaration opposing martial law.[304] Official state media failed to unambiguously support martial law.[305] All of this, combined with widespread public support for the protests, make it conceivable that the demonstrations could have led to a regime change.

Ultimately, however, the regime was able to quash the rebellion. The group of eight elders or "immortals" was able to unify the party and mobilize sufficient support within the military to suppress the protests. As a major military leader during the revolutionary war, Deng in particular had enormous authority within the army. The elders as a whole had the informal status necessary to convince competing factions within the party to back violent suppression of the protests.[306] For example, the elders persuaded Vice Premier Wan Li, who had initially supported Zhao and the students, to reverse course and "hew to the line of the elders."[307]

The elders were unified by a polarizing zero-sum conception of political opposition that was rooted in their experience in the revolutionary struggle. In contrast to many younger leaders, Deng and other elders saw student actions as an existential threat to the regime "that could even lead to war."[308] One of the elders, Yang Shangkun, justified a crackdown, asserting, "There is no way for us to retreat. To retreat means our downfall. To retreat means the downfall of the People's Republic of China and the restoration of capitalism."[309] Such views motivated leadership unification around an uncompromising, hard-line response to the protests.[310]

Thus, after concluding that the younger leaders were unable to manage the crisis, the elders united around a decision to violently suppress the protests.[311] In a crackdown on the night of June 3–4, military forces cleared the square, killing hundreds of protesters.[312] Although this action initially sparked protest throughout the country, the regime successfully quelled unrest by the end of June.[313] Speaking on TV shortly after the crackdown, Deng expressed no remorse, leading a minute of silence to honor soldiers killed in the protests.[314]

Finally, the failure of the protests was also a product of the weakness of civil society that resulted from years of revolutionary war and social transformation described above.[315] Indeed, while the protests were large and widespread, they lacked leadership and coordination.[316] Student activists were not members of political organizations, "but part of crowds with changing leaders and loosely affiliated participants."[317] They often failed to coordinate on strategy,[318] and they had little capacity to absorb the assistance provided to them.[319] While even well-organized protests would probably have been squashed by a unified party leadership, such disorganization further undermined the students' cause.

In the end, the continued dominance of the revolutionary elders made a crackdown virtually inevitable. In this sense, the CCP was far better equipped to withstand the challenges from below than the Soviet Communist Party was in the late 1980s, where revolutionary struggle was a distant historical memory.

The suppression of protests initially put reform at risk. Many of the elders who had been so critical to regime survival were also deeply opposed to capitalism and worked to slow Deng's efforts to foster rapid capitalist growth.[320] However, Deng was convinced that high growth was essential if China was to avoid the fate of communist regimes collapsing across the globe in 1989. In 1992, Deng mobilized support for reform in a tour of southern provinces and successfully reversed efforts to back away from reform.[321] China would never be the same.

After the Revolution

After Tiananmen, the PRC completed a head-spinning transformation from one of the world's most radical communist regimes to its most dynamic center of capitalist growth. In the early 1990s, centralized planning disappeared with a "whimper, barely noticed."[322] Private entrepreneurs were allowed into the party, and by the 2000s they had become one of its "most important bases of support."[323] Party leaders actively encouraged members to "jump in the sea" of private business and "take the lead in getting rich."[324] By 2018, the private sector accounted for over 60 percent of China's GDP and 80 percent of employment.[325] With high growth rates linked in leaders' minds to regime survival, the CCP's interests were increasingly considered synonymous with those of capital.[326]

This far-reaching transformation was accompanied by the departure of the revolutionary generation. Age-based retirement requirements had already resulted in the exit of about 65 percent of revolutionary veterans by the late 1980s.[327] Shortly before retiring in the early 1990s, Deng also eliminated lifetime appointments for top leadership positions. The elders from the Long March gave up all formal and informal party control.[328] Jiang Zemin, who joined the party in the 1950s, became general secretary. He was succeeded in 2002 by Hu Jintao, who had joined the party in the 1960s. In 2012, Xi Jinping became the first general secretary not chosen by Deng since the early 1980s. Increasingly, state power was rooted in leaders' formal positions rather than informal authority gained in the revolution-ary struggle.[329]

The party transformed from a revolutionary into a ruling party. It abandoned revolutionary campaigns, class conflict, and ideological indoc-trination and focused instead on maintaining economic growth and social stability.[330] Ideology was reduced to a "post hoc rationalization device,"[331] as the party leadership grew increasingly technocratic.[332] Deng's maxim that "it doesn't matter whether a cat is black or white, as long as it catches mice" now defined the CCP's approach to governance. The government paid unprecedented attention to public opinion, combining the delivery of economic growth and improved living standards with nationalist appeals aimed at attracting youth.[333]

This shift toward more traditional authoritarianism diminished elite cohesion. Lacking the battlefield experience of the revolutionary genera-tion, CCP leaders no longer possessed informal authority over the mili-tary.[334] Civil-military relations became increasingly bifurcated.[335] Accord-ing to David Lampton, the military was an independent actor during the transitions from Jiang to Hu in 2002 and Hu to Xi in 2012.[336] In 2012, rumors (almost certainly false) even circulated that a supporter of Xi's main rival, Bo Xilai, had attempted a coup.[337]

Most strikingly, factionalism and corruption became rife at the turn of the century. Corruption among high-level officials reached "alarming pro-portions" in the post-Tiananmen era.[338] Scholars began to refer to China as "predatory," "lawless," "crony capitalist," and "crony communist."[339] The increase in corruption and the declining role of ideology were attended by a significant increase in opportunism in the party. Compared to those who joined in the first decades after the revolution, people who became party members after 1992 were more than twice as likely to say they did so to advance their careers and half as likely to say they did so to support communism.[340]

Several scholars have argued that corruption exacerbated factional-ism by generating resentment among those who lost out in battles over spoils.[341] Comparing the Communist Party to the KMT in the 1930s, Andrew G. Walder suggested that the scale of corruption allowed party officials to function as independent actors drawing on resources outside the state.[342] Public battles for leadership reached a dramatic high point in 2012 when Bo Xilai was arrested and put on trial for trying to cover up his wife's murder of an English businessman, Neil Heywood.[343] Such inci-dents convinced some observers that the regime was in crisis. Minxen Pei and Walder, for example, argued that the CCP was losing organizational coherence and was in "late-stage decay."[344] In response to corruption and factionalism, Xi carried out a large and sustained anticorruption drive that netted hundreds of thousands of officials in every part of the country and regime hierarchy.[345]

Others suggested that China's stunning economic development sowed the seeds of regime change. Due to remarkable and sustained growth, China transformed from a lower-income country in 1995 into an upper-middle-income country by 2010.[346] Bicycle-filled streets and the decaying low-rise remnants of prerevolutionary infrastructure were replaced by a plethora of new roads and skyscrapers and the most modern high-speed transport in the world. By lifting millions of people out of poverty, creating a large middle class, and generating a powerful group of business actors, economic development had the potential to undermine regime stability. Indeed, in the 1990s and 2000s, many authors predicted that economic development would facilitate democratization in the early twenty-first century.[347] Similar increases in levels of economic development had helped democratize South Korea and Taiwan in the late twentieth century. Drawing parallels with South Korea in 1988, some even expected the Chinese government to liberalize in response to the increased international attention that came with the Beijing Olympics in 2008.[348]

However, it soon became clear that democratization was not imminent. In the run-up to the 2008 Olympics, the government carried out a systematic attack on dissent.[349] The regime became even more closed in the 2010s under Xi, who cracked down harshly on *any* organized political opposition and built the Great Firewall that deprived the population of easy access to Google and a host of major Western media.[350]

In the face of China's clear failure to democratize, optimistic predictions of development-driven democratization were replaced in the 2010s by discussions of a "mismatch" between China's highly developed economy on the one hand and its lack of democracy on the other.[351] David Shambaugh argued that China was "trying to create a modern economy with a pre-modern political system."[352] If the regime did not become more inclusive, he argued, it would continue to "atrophy" and ultimately collapse. Continued political closure would lead to the CCP's "protracted political decline" and potentially generate divisions in the party and the military.[353] According to Carl Minzner, the regime's refusal to undertake political reform would lead to a "steady spiral of elite infighting, economic decline, ideological polarization, and rising social unrest—all under an atrophying, paranoid, and increasingly fragile authoritarian regime."[354]

The early twenty-first century provided some evidence of the dynamics described in these accounts. Most strikingly, there was a significant increase in mass actions—from 8,700 in 1993, to 87,000 in 2005, to

172,000—an average of 461 protests per day—in 2014.[355] Strikes and other types of labor unrest grew much more widespread in the 2010s.[356] The government also confronted protests in Tibet, Xinjiang, and Hong Kong.

Despite these challenges, however, the PRC retained significant sources of strength. For one, the regime benefited from exceptionally high growth rates for more than a generation. China's economy grew at an average rate of 9.4 percent a year between 1978 and 2019, resulting in a thirteenfold expansion, *in real terms*, of its GDP. This growth has generated more regime acquiescence than resistance. As Bruce Dickson has shown,[357] entrepreneurs, having made considerable money under the existing system, tend to have a strong stake in regime continuity. Thus far, Chinese capitalists have shown little support for democracy.[358]

At the same time, the persistence of key revolutionary legacies, such as a powerful coercive apparatus and the absence of alternative centers of societal power, provided regime leaders with both room for error and the tools to resist political change. The regime maintained a nearly unrivaled capacity to preempt challenges from below. China had the largest army in the world, with a large and well-developed paramilitary, the People's Armed Police, whose main purpose was to maintain domestic order.[359] It also maintained extensive party and state structures that penetrated society at all levels, including party cells in both foreign and domestic businesses.[360] Block captains, villager small groups, autonomous development committees, and party cells were "deeply embedded in local social networks" and served as the "state's eyes and ears on the street, collecting gossip and intimate information on individual behavior."[361] In urban areas, the government drew on a "grid management" system that divided cities into smaller cells responsible for their populations.[362] This pervasive presence allowed state actors to collect fine-grained information on potential opponents.[363]

The party-state's penetration of the economy helped the party gain the cooperation of technology enterprises in the surveillance and control of society. Major technology entrepreneurs held formal positions in the regime and, along with other companies, allowed the Chinese Ministry of Public Security to install "network security officers" at key sites and firms.[364] Drawing on the cooperation of high-tech firms, the Xi government crafted an electronic "social credit" system to monitor individuals' behavior—building on the *dang'an*, or dossier system, created after the revolution.[365]

Such controls reinforced opposition weakness. Protests and strikes were localized and almost entirely nonpolitical.[366] In the early twenty-first century, China had one of the weakest civil societies in the world—weaker than in far less developed countries such as Libya, Sudan, and Tajikistan.[367] Unlike South Korea and Taiwan in the run-up to democratization, China lacked any form of organized opposition.

Conclusion

Given China's economic and military power, its authoritarian durability might not seem like much of a mystery. But it was not always this way. The country began the twentieth century with one of the world's weakest states—one dominated by foreign powers and warlords. Few observers would have predicted that China would survive as a single state, much less one of the most durable regimes in modern history. China's emergence as a global power was made possible not just by the Deng-era economic reforms but also by the extraordinarily risky actions of Chinese communists, which triggered a reactive sequence that nearly destroyed the CCP but eventually gave rise to a powerful and cohesive party-state. The adaptation and reform of the late twentieth century would not have been possible had the revolutionary regime not first built a centralized state and survived the crises of the 1950s and 1960s. Even today, revolutionary legacies inhibit the emergence of organized opposition despite decades of economic development.

If antecedent conditions and economic reform cannot explain durability, what about institutional factors, such as the PRC's Leninist and totalitarian institutions? Although such institutions almost certainly strengthened the regime, they are hardly sufficient to explain its survival. Created by the Comintern in the 1920s, the CCP was initially weak. The party's leadership in Shanghai barely had contact with, much less controlled, communist fiefdoms in the hinterland. The system of political commissars created in the late 1920s failed to prevent repeated military disobedience. It was only after the Long March and war with Japan that a cohesive party-army emerged. And only after the 1946–1949 civil war did the central government begin to penetrate society sufficiently to fashion a totalitarian regime capable of surviving the Great Leap Forward, the Cultural Revolution, and the Tiananmen crisis. Furthermore, the authority of the party elders, which was critical to regime survival in 1989, emerged out of their role in the revolutionary struggle rather than their formal positions.

The durability of China's revolutionary regime also cannot be explained by support from below. Although it is certainly true that the CCP successfully built public support during the reform era, such an explanation cannot account for the regime's survival during decades of economic catastrophe and political crisis under Mao. Ideological commitment also lacks plausibility as an explanation, because it cannot explain how the regime abandoned communism in the late twentieth century with hardly a peep from supporters of the old system.

Instead, durable authoritarian institutions emerged out of a revolutionary reactive sequence. Attacks on core interests of the Chinese upper class in the 1920s and 1930s helped spark two decades of civil war, out of which emerged a highly cohesive ruling party, a strong and loyal military, and virtually no organized alternatives to the Communist party-state. Despite the CCP's abandonment of its original revolutionary ideology, the powerful party-state it created remains firmly intact.

CHAPTER FOUR

The Durability of Mexico's Revolutionary Regime

AMID HEATED DEBATE at Mexico's Constitutional Convention in Querétaro in December 1916, the revolutionary general Álvaro Obregón, who had lost his right arm in battle a year earlier, rose to the podium and proclaimed: "May men mutilate themselves . . . for [their] principles, but may they never mutilate [their] principles."[1] Obregón would help push through "the most radical constitution the world had yet seen,"[2] inaugurating the first social revolution in the modern era. The new constitution paved the way for a far-reaching land reform and an unprecedented attack on the Catholic Church, which triggered a three-year civil war that killed as many as 100,000 people—including Obregón himself, at the hands of a Catholic assassin.[3]

Despite his proclamation at the convention, however, Obregón had few principles to mutilate. Obregón and other Mexican revolutionary leaders were no Bolsheviks. They lacked a party or a shared ideology,[4] and their radical initiatives were often tempered by pragmatism and accommodation. The Mexican Revolution was *segmented*: radical in some areas but accommodationist in others. As a result, the reactive sequence played out differently than in Russia and China. Although attacks on the Church triggered a violent counterrevolutionary reaction, the Mexican Revolution never seriously challenged the capitalist system or the geopolitical order. The regime never faced the kind of sustained existential counterrevolutionary threats seen in China, Russia, Vietnam, Cuba, or Iran.

Segmented radicalism produced a somewhat distinct regime trajectory from those in Russia and China. Like these other cases, the Mexican Revolution and its aftermath gave rise to key pillars of durable authoritarianism.

Revolutionary leaders built their own army, which was tightly wedded to the regime, and powerful prerevolutionary actors were either destroyed (the old army, landowners) or badly weakened (the Church). These legacies lay a foundation for regime stability. After a counterrevolutionary war and an intra-elite conflict induced regime leaders to build a ruling party in 1929, there were no coups and few elite defections. The weakening of independent power centers left little space for opposition organization, which weakened anti-regime forces for decades. When opposition mobilization occurred, as in the case of the 1968 Mexico City protests, regime elites could rely on the army to carry out high-intensity coercion.

Nevertheless, the Mexican Revolution only partially transformed state-society relations. In the absence of a prolonged counterrevolutionary threat, the regime never developed a powerful coercive apparatus or vast totalitarian controls; nor did it eliminate the private sector or wipe out associational life. Thus, although revolutionary legacies were critical to the durability of Mexican authoritarianism, the regime's long-run stability is partially attributable to other factors, particularly decades of steady economic growth.[5]

The Revolutionary Seizure of Power

Conditions were not propitious for durable authoritarianism on the eve of the Mexican Revolution. Mexico had been plagued by state weakness and regime instability for most of the nineteenth century. For decades after independence in 1821, the state failed to establish control over the national territory and was often fiscally insolvent.[6] State weakness brought a series of foreign invasions and civil wars. Mexico lost half of its territory to invading U.S. forces in 1846–1848, collapsed into civil war in 1858–1860, and was occupied and ruled by France between 1863 and 1865.[7] Political regimes were unstable: there were forty-five different governments between 1821 and 1871.[8] Although the state strengthened somewhat under the long dictatorship of Porfirio Díaz (1876–1911),[9] Díaz's rule relied more on personal loyalties than an effective state, and corruption and coup-proofing measures weakened the coercive apparatus in the regime's later years.[10] By 1910, the state's coercive agencies were "rotten to the marrow," and they quickly collapsed in the face of a relatively modest uprising.[11] Given this level of state and regime fragility, it is difficult to argue that the bases of durable authoritarian rule existed prior to the revolution.

The Mexican Revolution unfolded in fits and starts. It began in 1910, when Díaz, facing a surprising electoral challenge from liberal

politician Francisco Madero, jailed Madero and thousands of his followers.[12] Although Díaz was reelected without opposition, Madero subsequently escaped from house arrest and launched an insurrection. In a
context of deep rural discontent rooted in the large-scale displacement of
peasants during the Díaz dictatorship,[13] what began as a narrow political uprising transformed into a mass rebellion.[14] Armed revolts broke out
across Mexico, including Francisco (Pancho) Villa's rebellion in the north
and a peasant-based insurrection led by Emiliano Zapata in the south. By
early 1911, the Federal Army was being routed by diverse armies that, combined, fielded nearly three times as many combatants as the army itself.[15]
The May 1911 Treaty of Juarez brought Díaz's departure and exile, and
in October, Madero was elected president. As he departed for exile, Díaz
declared, "Madero has unleashed a tiger; let us see if he can control him."[16]

The uprising against Díaz did not bring a social revolution. The
Federal Army and local state authorities (mayors, judges, police chiefs)
remained in place,[17] and Madero, a moderate who "plainly distrusted revolutionaries,"[18] never pursued radical change.[19] Governing with much of
the old elite, Madero continued Díaz's laissez-faire economic policies and
eschewed land reform, the principal demand of his erstwhile Zapatista
allies.[20] When peasants began to mobilize and seize land, Madero, pressured by landowners, turned to the Federal Army to disarm them.[21]

But the old status quo proved unsustainable. The 1910 insurrection had
triggered a social awakening, as a "new egalitarianism . . . seemed to infect
society," giving rise to a surge in societal contention.[22] In November 1911,
the Zapatistas rebelled against the Madero government, accusing it of
"bloody treason."[23] Agrarian revolts erupted in Morelos, Puebla, Guerrero, Tlaxcala, and elsewhere,[24] triggering calls for a crackdown by landowners and conservative ancien régime elites.[25] Madero, a true liberal,
could stomach neither the radical redistribution demanded by his peasant
allies nor the repression demanded by landowners.[26] Paralyzed, the government was overcome by social conflict. Peasant uprisings spread across
southern Mexico, and strikes and urban riots erupted in the cities.[27] As
Madero lost the capacity to maintain order, conservative forces conspired
to overthrow him. In February 1913, army forces led by General Victoriano
Huerta, backed by landowners, clerics, conservative politicians, and U.S.
ambassador Lane Wilson, toppled (and killed) Madero and established a
reactionary dictatorship.[28]

The 1913 coup accelerated the revolutionary process. Unambiguously
counterrevolutionary, the Huerta government destroyed Madero's nascent
democracy and brutally repressed his supporters.[29] The repression

backfired. The coup—and especially Madero's killing—shocked Mexicans and radicalized revolutionary forces.[30] Armed rebellions emerged on various fronts, including Zapatista forces in Morelos, Pancho Villa's army in the north, and the Constitutionalist Army led by Coahuila governor Venustiano Carranza.[31] Mexico plunged into a civil war that killed more than 200,000 people.[32] The war "chewed up the Federal Army,"[33] and by the time Huerta fled in July 1914, the Mexican state had collapsed.[34]

Huerta's fall did not end the war, however. Because the revolutionary movement was divided into the three armies, the Constitutionalists, the peasant-based Zapatistas, and Villa's Division of the North, Mexico descended into a bloody "war of the winners."[35] What began as a political revolution transformed into a social revolution.[36] As Mexico collapsed into anarchy, "wealth became punishable by death. Factories, mines, haciendas, and whole villages were ravaged. Railroads were dismantled. Libraries, schools, and great works of art were burned."[37] The army and police disintegrated, and prerevolutionary bureaucracies, judicial authorities, and local political bosses were swept away.[38] As an observer put it, the old state was "completely smashed."[39] By 1917, "the army was new, as was almost all the bureaucracy. So were the schools, newspapers, and pride in the fatherland."[40]

The civil war also transformed Mexico's class structure. The conflict destroyed the old elite and created a new one that "derived from markedly inferior social origins."[41] By 1915, large landowners had lost power. "Most languished in prison or exile. As a class they hardly even existed."[42] Landowner flight and peasant land seizures brought a de facto agrarian reform.[43] Long-standing rural caste barriers and "habits of 'obedience'" broke down.[44] The historian John Womack Jr. describes a scene in Morelos in 1916, in which the widow of a landowner seeks assistance from a Constitutionalist general in protecting her property and is told, "Oh lady, that is of the past. That is all over."[45]

Finally, the civil war enabled the eventual winners, the Constitutionalists, to defeat rival armies.[46] The Constitutionalists routed Villa's army in 1915, reducing it to a handful of small guerrilla bands.[47] (Villa himself was assassinated in 1923.) The Constitutionalists both co-opted and defeated the Zapatistas, reducing them to 2,000 troops by 1918 and killing Zapata in 1919.[48]

The Incipient Regime: A Revolution without a Party

The revolutionary seizure of power was completed when Constitutionalist forces installed Carranza as de facto leader in 1916, wrote a new constitution, and orchestrated Carranza's presidential election in March 1917.

Like their counterparts in Russia and China, Mexican revolutionaries built their own state, including their own army. The old Federal Army was disbanded and replaced by the Constitutionalist Army. The entire prerevolutionary officer corps was purged, and the new army leadership was filled exclusively by revolutionary combatants.[49] The Constitutionalists also purged the remaining state bureaucracy and packed it with revolutionaries.[50] Thus, the coercive apparatus was thoroughly penetrated and controlled by the revolutionary elite.[51] As in Russia and China, revolutionary state-building lay a foundation for what would ultimately be a loyal and disciplined military.

However, Mexico's embryonic regime differed from those in Russia and China in two important ways. First, it institutionalized multiparty electoral competition. Democratic elections had been a central demand of the 1910 uprising, and the 1917 constitution was nominally liberal democratic. Thus, revolutionary Mexico would be *electoral authoritarian*—a regime characterized by regular elections that, though neither free nor fair, remained at least nominally open to contestation by nonrevolutionary parties.[52] Moreover, because "no reelection" had been a central plank of the original rebellion, the 1917 constitution limited presidents to a single term; thus, the revolutionary elite was forced to choose a new leader every four (and, later, every six) years.

Second, Mexico's revolutionary elite lacked a ruling party. The revolutionary forces never unified under a single leadership, but rather remained a loose oligarchy of "revolutionary generals," or political-military leaders whose skills on the battlefield and capacity to mobilize peasants had vaulted them into the upper ranks of the Constitutionalist Army.[53] After the seizure of power, many of these revolutionary generals established themselves as de facto local authorities.[54] Some of them built local party machines and served as state governor, whereas others joined the new revolutionary army, serving as regional zone commanders. Because they were experienced in violence and maintained peasant followings that could be mobilized to fight, the revolutionary generals—or revolutionary caciques—were essential pillars of the new regime.[55] During the 1920s, they played a critical role in establishing order,[56] defeating regime challengers, and mobilizing grassroots support for national governments.[57] Initially, however, no party structure existed to ensure cooperation or discipline among them.

At the national level, the revolutionary elite was organized into multiple, competing, and short-lived parties.[58] The Constitutionalist Liberal Party (PLC), which dominated elections in 1917 and 1918,[59] was little more than a "booster club" for President Carranza.[60] Carranza soon abandoned the party, and it fell into oblivion.[61] The PLC coexisted with three other pro-revolutionary parties: the National Cooperative Party, the Mexican Labor Party (PLM), and the National Agrarian Party (PNA). These parties coexisted with dozens of smaller regional parties led by local revolutionary caciques.[62] Carranza's successors, Presidents Álvaro Obregón (1920–1924) and Plutarco Calles (1924–1928), governed with uneasy coalitions of national and regional parties.[63]

The lack of a ruling party undermined regime cohesion. In the absence of partisan coordination and control, the new army remained a loose amalgam of revolutionary generals, many of whom maintained their own militias.[64] Such a structure would prove fractious—and prone to rebellion.[65] As we shall see, the new regime was plagued by "Hobbesian" internal conflict between 1917 and 1929.[66] Each presidential succession during this period was accompanied by an armed rebellion.[67]

The Revolutionary Reactive Sequence

Mexico's early revolutionary period (1917–1929) was marked by segmented radicalism. Revolutionary governments launched a radical assault on the Church, but they did not pursue the kind of far-reaching socioeconomic transformation seen in most communist revolutions. Although radical anticlericalism triggered a violent counterrevolutionary reaction (the Cristero War), the Mexican regime never confronted the kind of sustained counterrevolutionary threat seen in Russia and China. In the absence of large-scale counterrevolutionary conflict, the primary threat to regime stability was rebellion from within.[68] Ultimately, the reactive sequence in Mexico produced a cohesive party-state complex with a smaller coercive apparatus that weakened, but did not fully destroy, alternative centers of societal power.

SEGMENTED RADICALISM

The Mexican regime was radical in some areas but accommodationist in others. The founding revolutionary elite was far less radical than the Bolsheviks or the Chinese Communists. None of the revolution's founding leaders were Marxists, and most lacked a coherent ideology.[69] Indeed, Carranza once declared, "I was never a revolutionary, nor am I, nor will I ever be."[70] Although many revolutionary generals called themselves socialist,[71] most of them opposed large-scale expropriation or state ownership of the economy.[72] Indeed, the bulk of the revolutionary elite was broadly committed to private ownership and capitalist development.[73] In terms of foreign policy, the Constitutionalists were "fervent nationalists,"[74] but their nationalism was tempered by geopolitical realism. Given the United States' regional hegemony (U.S. troops invaded Cuba, the Dominican Republic, Haiti, Nicaragua, and Panama in the years preceding or immediately after the Mexican Revolution), Mexico's revolutionary elite agreed that provoking a military conflict with the United States would be an act of "suicide."[75] Thus, few Constitutionalists envisioned the kind of radical foreign policies adopted by revolutionaries in Russia, Cuba, or Iran.

Mexican revolutionaries were unambiguously radical in one area: anticlericalism.[76] In a society that was 99 percent Catholic,[77] the Mexican revolutionary elite was militantly secular and openly atheist; no president publicly recognized a belief in God until 1939.[78] Because the Church had been an ally of the ancien régime,[79] and because many Catholic leaders backed Huerta's coup,[80] Constitutionalist leaders viewed the Church as an "enemy of the revolution."[81] One even declared that "God is the counter-revolution."[82] Thus, revolutionary leaders converged around the radical goal of wiping out religion. During the war, the revolutionaries seized Church properties and arrested, expelled, and occasionally executed priests.[83] In power, some of them sought to destroy the Church and replace it with a "new, revolutionary, civil religion."[84]

Despite their moderate orientation on socioeconomic issues, Mexico's revolutionary leaders were radicalized by the civil war.[85] To defeat Villa's and Zapata's armies, the Constitutionalists mobilized workers and especially peasants, which required an embrace of labor rights and land redistribution.[86] In need of peasant support, Carranza, a longtime opponent of land reform,[87] issued an agrarian reform decree in January 1915, declaring, "Today the social revolution begins."[88] This dynamic, in which the imperatives of military survival led revolutionary leaders to mobilize peasants, which, in turn, required programmatic radicalization, has been described by the historian Alan Knight as the "logic of the revolution."[89]

This revolutionary logic was made manifest in the 1916–1917 constitution-writing process. President Carranza was a liberal with little taste for revolutionary change.[90] He intended for the Constitutional Convention to produce a standard liberal charter, and he submitted a draft modeled on Mexico's (liberal) 1857 constitution.[91] Nevertheless, the convention saw the emergence of a radical faction—known as "Jacobins"—led by revolutionary generals who had built alliances with peasants during the war.[92] The Jacobins were zealously anticlerical and sympathetic to radical socioeconomic reform.[93] Although they were a minority, they enjoyed the support of General Obregón, whose status as the Constitutionalists' top military commander gave him enormous influence.[94] Obregón and other revolutionary generals viewed radical measures as a means of building the mass support needed to consolidate power.[95] A coalition of Jacobins and Obregónistas thus pushed through a series of radical amendments, producing what has been described as the most radical constitution in the world up to that date.[96]

The 1917 constitution was radical in several senses. It imposed dramatic new restrictions on property rights. Article 27 granted the state ownership of all subsoil and subsurface minerals and empowered the state to expropriate private property. These measures, which were virtually unprecedented at the time, paved the way for sweeping agrarian reform.[97] They also "fundamentally altered the rules of the game for foreign investment," permitting the nationalization of the oil industry.[98] The new constitution also enshrined a set of social rights, including labor rights, that were unprecedented at the time.[99] Finally, the constitution lay the bases for an "aggressively anti-Catholic state."[100] It banned parochial primary education, declared all Church property "national" property; empowered governments to severely restrict Church activity, including the number of priests in any given territory; and banned all forms of religious political activity.[101] Clergy were prohibited from voting, criticizing the government or any laws, and even holding religious ceremonies in public.[102] In effect, the constitution left the Church without legal status or the resources it needed to carry out basic functions.[103]

Although the 1917 constitution was never rigorously enforced, it proved highly consequential. Even if it was largely an exercise in "paper radicalism,"[104] writing the radical clauses into the constitution both legitimized and legalized the subsequent adoption of radical policy initiatives, first by local and state governments and eventually by national leaders.[105]

EARLY REVOLUTIONARY GOVERNMENTS:
BETWEEN RADICALISM AND ACCOMMODATION

The governments of Presidents Carranza, Obregón, and Calles combined elements of radicalism and accommodation. With the exception of Calles's assault on the Church, radical initiatives were frequently tempered or scaled back when they threatened powerful interests. Consequently, counterrevolutionary reactions were modest. The absence of a sustained counterrevolutionary threat, together with the absence of a ruling party, undermined elite cohesion. Indeed, the Mexican regime was riven with internal conflict between 1917 and 1929. In 1920, 1923, 1927, and 1929, conflict over presidential succession generated a violent schism, as a faction of the revolutionary elite took up arms against the government.

The Carranza Government (1917–1920)

The Carranza government was, in most respects, moderate. A classical liberal for whom private property was "sacred,"[106] Carranza refused to enforce most of the radical clauses in the 1917 constitution, including the anticlerical ones.[107] Carranza's orthodox economic policies, crackdown down on unions, and aversion to redistribution led scholars to describe his government as "conservative."[108] Indeed, not only did the government ignore peasant demands for land, but it even helped landowners regain properties lost during the war.[109]

Carranza's foreign policy was more radical.[110] The Carranza government briefly sought to spread "revolutionary nationalism" across Latin America, promoting an anti-imperialist "Carranza Doctrine" in opposition to the U.S. Monroe Doctrine.[111] It also engaged in unprecedented efforts to regulate foreign capital. Carranza rejected U.S. demands to repeal Article 27 of the new constitution, which asserted national ownership of subsoil and subsurface minerals,[112] and in 1918, he threatened to enforce it by exchanging foreign oil companies' property titles for concessions.[113]

Carranza confronted counterrevolutionary reactions on several fronts. Several counterrevolutionary insurgencies—led by elements of the old Federal Army—emerged between 1916 and 1920. The largest of these, the 3,000-man National Reorganizer Army, was launched by Porfirio Díaz's nephew, Félix Díaz, in 1917.[114] Díaz's rebellion mobilized Porfirista generals, government officials, landowners, clerics, and other backers of the old regime in a campaign to restore the Federal Army and the 1857 constitution.[115] A second insurgency, led by Manuel Peláez and backed by landowners and oil interests, emerged in Veracruz.[116] Neither of these insurgencies seriously threatened the regime, however,[117] and both had collapsed by 1920.[118]

Carranza also faced hostility from the U.S. government, which rejected the 1917 constitution as a threat to American citizens' property rights.[119] When Carranza announced plans to replace foreign oil companies' property titles with concessions, American oil interests lobbied for military intervention.[120] U.S. officials attacked the Carranza government as "Bolshevist," and numerous American politicians and business leaders called for its overthrow.[121] The U.S. consul general in Mexico described the situation as "an abscess which cries for a lancet," and in late 1919, the two countries appeared to be on the brink of war.[122]

The revolution did not trigger a war, however. Occasional threats notwithstanding, the U.S. government's overall response to the revolution was closer to ambivalence than outright hostility.[123] Ultimately, the greatest threat to Carranza came from within.

Carranza fell prey to a succession crisis in 1920. Obregón, a revolutionary war hero backed by unions, peasant movements, and numerous revolutionary generals, was widely viewed as Carranza's natural successor.[124] Carranza's attempt to impose a weak civilian successor, reportedly violating a prior agreement with Obregón,[125] triggered a massive rebellion that included the bulk of the revolutionary army and most of the remaining Zapatista forces.[126] In what would be Mexico's last successful coup,[127] Carranza was overthrown and eventually killed in April 1920, paving the way for Obregón's election. The uprising made it clear that power lay in the hands of the revolutionary generals.[128] It also demonstrated the political and military importance of agrarian movements, with which Obregón had forged strong alliances.[129]

The Obregón Government (1920–1924)

The revolution stabilized under Obregón. A "fanatically pragmatic president,"[130] Obregón pursued accommodation.[131] He adopted a cautious economic program and worked to improve relations with the United States, primarily through concessions to foreign oil interests.[132] In 1923, U.S. and Mexican officials negotiated the Bucareli Agreement, in which Mexico agreed not to apply Article 27 of the constitution to preexisting property titles. In exchange, the United States formally recognized the revolutionary government.[133]

Yet Obregón also took steps to redistribute land. Carranza had abandoned his civil war promise of land reform,[134] and, as a result, large landowners and their estates survived into the 1920s.[135] However, peasant mobilization made this status quo difficult to sustain. Having played a major role in the revolution, agrarian movements were a "fact of revolutionary life that had to be reckoned with."[136] Radical peasant leagues—many of them armed—proliferated, terrifying landowners and local political bosses.[137]

Convinced that peasant support was critical to regime survival,[138] Obregón forged alliances with Zapatista and other agrarian movements.[139] He brought Zapatista leaders into his government, placing them in charge of agrarian reform,[140] and reinitiated land redistribution, providing more than one million hectares—nine times more than Carranza—to 133,000 peasant families.[141] The Obregón government also oversaw a peasant organizational "boom," as peasant-based agrarian leagues, often led by revolutionary generals, emerged in states like Campeche, Jalisco, Michoacán, Puebla, Tabasco, Tamaulipas, Veracruz, and Yucatán.[142] A handful of states, including Veracruz, Tabasco, and Yucatán, became "laboratories of revolution" in the early 1920s, as local governments backed by agrarian movements experimented with far-reaching land reform and other radical measures.[143]

Land reform triggered some counterrevolutionary violence. Many large landowners and their estates (known as haciendas) survived the revolutionary war.[144] In parts of the country, they financed local paramilitary forces, called White Guards, which terrorized peasant leaders and agrarian activists.[145] However, the White Guards remained a localized phenomenon. Weakened by the revolutionary war,[146] and without influence over the new army, landowners' capacity to organize violent resistance was limited.[147]

Again, the primary threats to regime stability came from within. In 1923, Obregón's imposition of Calles as his successor triggered a rebellion led by revolutionary general Adolfo de la Huerta, an erstwhile ally and presidential aspirant.[148] Backed by landowners and nearly half the army,[149] the de la Huerta rebellion "literally split the revolutionary group in two."[150] Obregón was forced to rely on large-scale peasant mobilization to defeat it.[151]

The Calles Government (1924–1928)

The Calles presidency was more radical than its predecessors. Calles "boldly challenged both the Catholics and the gringos."[152] A 1925 law requiring foreign oil companies to exchange their property titles for concessions triggered a hostile reaction from the United States.[153] Calles also actively opposed the 1926 U.S. military intervention in Nicaragua, sending arms to Cesar Augusto Sandino's guerrilla army.[154] American officials, viewing Calles's behavior as a challenge to the U.S. sphere of influence,[155] spoke darkly of "Soviet Mexico" and attacked Calles as "the Stalin of Mexico."[156] Indeed, U.S. ambassador James Sheffield, backed by oil companies and Catholic groups, lobbied the White House to overthrow him.[157] By early 1927, Mexican leaders feared a U.S. invasion.[158] With U.S. Marines mobilized off the coast, war seemed a real possibility.[159] Indeed, Calles told his top officials to prepare a retreat to the interior and ordered military commanders to be ready to set fire to the oil fields.[160]

Ultimately, however, Calles reverted to accommodation. In 1927, the government backed off the petroleum law and U.S-Mexican relations subsequently thawed.[161] By 1928, Calles could declare that for the first time since the revolution, Mexico faced no external threat.[162]

Calles's most radical policies came in the cultural sphere. Whereas his predecessors had largely ignored the constitution's anticlerical provisions,[163] Calles enforced them "with religious zeal."[164] According to one biographer, Calles's "hatred of the church was so deep that it defied structuralist explanations."[165] Yet the Church also posed a threat.[166] With a network of educational, religious, and charitable agencies that extended into every corner of the country, the Church remained a powerful actor.[167] Catholic activism expanded in the early 1920s, as the Church began to organize workers and peasants and lay organizations such as the Mexican Catholic Youth Association and the National League for the Defense of Religious Freedom built large activist bases and began to mobilize.[168] At the same time, Archbishops José Mora y Del Rio and Francisco Orozco y Jimenez spoke out forcefully against the revolutionary regime.[169] When Calles took office in 1924, then, the Church was the regime's principal opponent.[170]

The Calles government mounted an extraordinary attack on the Church. After a failed effort to create a schismatic Mexican Apostolic Church,[171] Calles issued a series of decrees in 1926 aimed at enforcing the constitution's anticlerical provisions.[172] Under the so-called Calles Laws, the government expelled 200 priests and closed more than 100 Catholic schools and dozens of churches and convents.[173] State governments, under orders to "enforce the constitution at all costs," imposed strict limits on the number of priests allowed in their territory, often arresting or expelling priests.[174]

Calles's attacks triggered a strong Catholic reaction. In early 1925, Catholic activists created the 800,000-member National League for the Defense of Religious Freedom (known as the League), which led a massive petition drive calling for constitutional reform.[175] In early 1926, Archbishop Mora y del Rio called on Mexicans to oppose the revolutionary government and the constitution.[176] The government responded by expelling Mora y del Rio and 200 foreign priests and closing dozens of churches, monasteries, convents, and Catholic schools.[177] The July 1926 Calles Laws brought a definitive rupture with the Church.[178] Perceiving its very survival to be at stake, the Church suspended religious services, effectively going on strike.[179] The League and other Catholic groups organized a general strike—including a school and a tax boycott—and a series of protests, which led to the arrest of many of their leaders.[180] The conflict soon escalated into violence. In late 1926 and early 1927, a massive peasant uprising erupted in Mexico's central lowlands, or Bajío region, plunging Mexico into a civil war known as the Cristero War.[181]

An unambiguously counterrevolutionary movement,[182] the Cristeros posed the most serious challenge to the regime since the revolution.[183] Although the Church hierarchy did not support the rebellion, many local priests collaborated with it,[184] and Catholic lay organizations such as the League and the Mexican Catholic Youth Association provided arms, money, and men.[185] By 1928, the Cristero rebellion had grown into a major insurgency, with 50,000–60,000 rebels operating in twelve states.[186] Mexico descended into a three-year civil war that killed between 70,000 and 100,000 people.[187]

The Cristero War decimated the army, killing 50,000 soldiers and triggering tens of thousands of desertions, and forced the government to mobilize 25,000 peasant militia members to defeat the rebels.[188] The war also consumed nearly half of Mexico's national budget,[189] and it triggered a regime-threatening crisis when president-elect Obregón was assassinated by a Catholic militant in July 1928. By the time the government and the Church negotiated an accord in June 1929, under which the Church would cease political activity but resume spiritual and cultural activities,[190] the regime stood "on the brink of catastrophe."[191]

The regime crisis was exacerbated by internal conflict. The 1928 presidential succession triggered yet another violent schism. Obregón, the revolution's most prominent living figure, orchestrated a constitutional reform to allow for his reelection in 1928. The move divided the regime elite, leading to an abortive rebellion led by revolutionary generals Francisco Serrano and Arnulfo Gomez in 1927.[192] The government quelled the rebellion and Obregón was reelected, unopposed in July 1928. Just sixteen days after his reelection, however, he was assassinated.[193] Obregón's killing threw the regime into "the deepest internal crisis that the ruling elite had suffered during the revolutionary period."[194] Revolutionary leaders feared a regime collapse or civil war.[195]

BELATED PARTY-BUILDING AND THE FORGING OF ELITE COHESION

The crisis of the late 1920s, particularly the Cristero War, convinced the revolutionary elite to close ranks around a single party.[196] Fearing the mobilizational power of the Church, and facing the prospect of civil war in the wake of Obregón's assassination, the revolutionary elite forged a Hobbesian consensus.[197] In September 1928, Calles convened a meeting of thirty revolutionary generals, in which he called on them to set aside their immediate presidential ambitions and cooperate in the formation of a new ruling party, the National Revolutionary Party (PNR).[198] The party's founding convention was held in March 1929, led by an organizing committee composed of revolutionary generals.[199]

The construction of Mexico's long ruling party is often characterized as an elite project, created by a farsighted autocrat with the goal of reducing internal conflict.[200] That is (at best) only part of the story, however. Successful party-building, as well as the strength of the party that emerged after 1929, was rooted in the revolution and the revolutionary reactive sequence. First, as Mariano Sánchez Talanquer shows, a major impetus for party-building was the Cristero War, a core component of the revolutionary reactive sequence. Intra-elite conflict alone was not sufficient to induce party-building. The regime had been plagued by internal conflict since 1917, and there were numerous party-building initiatives in the 1920s, including Obregón's National Revolutionary Confederation in 1922;[201] Calles's effort to unite the PLM, the PNA, and smaller pro-regime parties into a single revolutionary bloc in 1924;[202] and Obregón supporters' 1926 effort to unite local parties and revolutionary bosses into an alliance of socialist parties.[203] All of these earlier initiatives came to naught.[204]

The Cristero War "provided a definitive impetus for party formation."[205] The war convinced the revolutionary elite that Catholic mobilization posed an existential threat and that a ruling party was therefore necessary to "protect the Revolution."[206] As Luis León, the PNR's first general secretary, put it during the founding party convention, "We have come here . . . to shout out to the reactionaries that we . . . are united [in] a single front, and that all their efforts will shatter against our revolutionary unity."[207] Another revolutionary general, Gonzalo Santos, declared, "We don't want another drop of blood in our fatherland . . . but that's not what the clerical reaction wants. . . . The moment of tolerance and ambiguity has passed. United we will combat the old *cristeros* and the new *cristeros*." In a clear reference to the Cristero War, Santos added that the PNR was being "formed on the crater of a volcano."[208]

Second, the PNR was not merely an elite party, but rather a mass party built upon local revolutionary organizations. Revolutionary forces engaged in local party-building activity throughout the 1920s, as revolutionary generals turned state governor or regional commander used alliances with unions and peasant leagues to build grassroots party machines.[209] An example is the Socialist Party of Yucatán, which become the Socialist Party of the Southeast (PSS). Revolutionary leader Felipe Carrillo, who served as governor of Yucatán between 1922 and 1924, organized dozens of peasant-based resistance leagues, with more than 60,000 members.[210] The leagues "served as syndicates, mutual aid societies, and community-level branch offices," transforming the PSS into a mass party.[211] Likewise, Tabasco governor Tomas Garrido built the Radical Socialist Party of Tabasco (PRST) into a mass organization based on peasant, worker, and women's leagues and the paramilitary Youth Bloc (Red Shirts).[212] Using state resources to coerce workers and peasants into joining mass organizations, Garrido built a disciplined machine that allowed him to dominate Tabasco politics for fifteen years.[213] In Tamaulipas, revolutionary general turned governor Emilio Portes Gil forged alliances with peasant agrarian leagues and transformed the Border Socialist Party into one of the best-organized parties in the country.[214] Well-organized socialist parties also emerged in Campeche, Chiapas, and Tlaxcala.[215]

Backed by Calles, the PNR's founders worked to unite these local revolutionary organizations into a single party.[216] PNR organizers traveled across the country, recruiting local revolutionary caciques and their parties to join the new ruling party.[217] Most of them did.[218] Thus, powerful state machines such as the PSS, the PRST, the Border Socialist Party of Tamaulipas, and the Confederation of Socialist Parties of Oaxaca affiliated with the PNR, becoming official party branches.[219] Overall, 148 revolutionary parties joined the new ruling party.[220] The PNR was thus born a "federation of revolutionary generals,"[221] most of whom maintained their own local machines and peasant bases.[222] This gave the party a mass character. The PNR was a "political octopus" that quickly "managed to extend its tentacles into every municipality in the country."[223] By the November 1929 election campaign, it had branches in all 5,000 of the country's municipalities.[224]

Calles and his allies did not, therefore, build a ruling party from scratch. Rather, "the groundwork was already well established" by a vast network of organizations that emerged out of the revolution.[225] Revolutionary legacies facilitated party-building in two ways. First, the revolution provided the building blocks of the new organization. The PNR was built upon "organizations born out of almost two decades of social mobilization."[226] The revolutionary generals who forged alliances with peasants during the civil war and transformed them into grassroots organizations—whether "socialist" party organizations, agrarian leagues, or patronage-based machines—in the 1920s served as the pillars of the new party. Although these local machines were often personalistic, many of them were led by experienced cadres with large (and loyal) popular constituencies.[227]

Second, a shared revolutionary identity enhanced ruling party cohesion. In creating the PNR, Calles promoted the notion of a single "revolutionary family" that encompassed everyone from Madero and Carranza to Villa and Zapata to Obregón and Calles. The "revolutionary family" was a revisionist artifact that ignored the fact that these leaders "had fought and, in some cases, even killed one another."[228] Nevertheless, it tapped into a set of existing identities, symbols, and shared experiences that emerged out of the revolutionary wars.[229] Thus, the "rhetoric and shared experience of the revolution became the foundation of the . . . PNR."[230]

Internal resistance to the PNR failed. In March 1929, during the PNR's founding convention, General José Escobar led what would be the regime's last major internal rebellion. With the PNR's future still uncertain, Escobar mobilized disgruntled Obregón supporters in the army and Congress in opposition to the new party.[231] About a third of the army joined the rebellion.[232] The regime elite closed ranks, however, and the rebels were easily defeated.[233] Ultimately, the 1929 rebellion strengthened the emerging party-state because it allowed Calles to purge the army of officers who opposed the PNR[234] and taught revolutionary politicians that the party was there to stay.[235]

That lesson began to sink in during the 1929 presidential election. Calles's embrace of Pascual Ortiz Rubio as the PNR candidate triggered resistance among revolutionary generals, many of whom preferred Aaron Saenz.[236] Although Saenz and his allies reportedly planned to abandon the party, they ultimately concluded that defection was "useless" and then closed ranks amid the Escobar rebellion.[237] The only major defector in 1929 was José Vasconcelos, a prominent progressive intellectual who became the presidential candidate of the Anti-Reelectionist Party.[238] Vasconcelos enjoyed urban middle-class support,[239] but with the revolutionary elite inside the PNR, he lacked a mass base. After Ortiz Rubio overwhelmingly won an unfair election,[240] Vasconcelos called for protest, but in the absence of party or army support, his calls fell on deaf ears.[241] Vasconcelos fled the country, anticipating an uprising that never came.[242]

By the early 1930s, the PNR had established such a dominant position that "no presidential candidacy seemed viable outside of it."[243] Various revolutionary generals sought the PNR's presidential nomination in 1934, but they closed ranks behind the eventual nominee, Lázaro Cárdenas—a "testament to the incipient strength of the PNR machine."[244]

Ruling party consolidation was completed under President Cárdenas (1934–1940). Although the PNR had built a strong territorial organization, its ties to unions and peasant movements were weak.[245] Cárdenas strengthened these ties. For one, he consolidated the party's peasant base. Under Cárdenas, the PNR sponsored the formation of peasant leagues across Mexico, using land distribution as an inducement for membership.[246] Thirty-two peasant leagues were formed, and in 1938, they were incorporated into the National Peasant Confederation (CNC), a mass peasant organization with close ties to the state.[247] Cárdenas also mobilized unions, sponsoring (and co-opting) the Mexican Workers Confederation (CTM).[248] In 1938, Cárdenas linked the ruling party to the CNC and the CTM through the creation of organized labor and peasant sectors. The party was renamed the Mexican Revolutionary Party (PRM) and, later, the Institutional Revolutionary Party (PRI). The CNC and the CTM became central pillars of the party, co-opting peasant and labor movements and delivering members' votes during elections.[249] With the incorporation of the labor and the peasant sectors, ruling party membership more than quadrupled, from fewer than one million to more than four million.[250] In effect, the PRM grafted mass labor and peasant organizations onto the PNR's preexisting territorial structure, transforming itself into a "true mass party."[251]

In sum, although Mexico's ruling party was built more than a decade after the seizure of power, its formation was intimately linked to the regime's revolutionary origins. The counterrevolutionary Cristero war encouraged a diverse array of revolutionary generals to support the creation of a single ruling party. In turn, the building blocks of the new ruling party were dozens of local organizations that emerged out of the revolutionary war. Finally, party cohesion was enhanced by a broad revolutionary identity (the "revolutionary family").

The establishment of a single revolutionary party had important knock-on effects for the emerging party-state. It enhanced state cohesion, particularly within the coercive apparatus.[252] Whereas intra-elite conflict had undermined military cohesion between 1917 and 1929, the emergence of a strong ruling party transformed the army into a cohesive and disciplined organization.[253] There were no more coup attempts after 1929. As Vicente Fuentes Díaz observed, "It is not a coincidence that the last military rebellion was . . . at the same time that the party was born."[254] After 1929, then, the Mexican regime possessed a cohesive party-state comparable to those in Russia and China.

There was one major difference, however. Whereas existential military threats in Russia, China, and other revolutionary cases led to a dramatic expansion of the coercive apparatus, in Mexico, where the counterrevolution was more limited and the threat of internal rebellion greater, revolutionary governments worked to *reduce* the size of the military. The Constitutionalist Army had swelled to more than 150,000 troops between 1915 and 1920, and in 1921 it consumed more than half the national budget.[255] In the absence of a cohesive party, schisms among revolutionary generals posed a constant threat of rebellion.[256] Thus, Obregón—who led one rebellion in 1920 and confronted another in 1923—reduced the size of the army to around 70,000.[257] Military spending fell from 61 percent of the national budget to 35 percent.[258] Although military spending increased during the Cristero War, it declined steadily thereafter, falling to 21 percent of the budget in 1935.[259] By the mid-1930s, Mexico had one of the smallest armies, per capita, of any authoritarian regime in the world.[260]

This outcome was almost certainly rooted in the fact that Mexico's revolutionary elite faced only modest counterrevolutionary threats and never fought an external war. Although U.S.-Mexican relations were conflictual during the revolution's first decade, the United States did not pose a sustained existential military threat. With brief exceptions in 1918–1919 and 1927, the threat of war with the United States was remote. That threat, moreover, faded in the 1930s and disappeared entirely with the coming of World War II.[261] In the absence of sustained domestic or external military threat, Mexico's revolutionary elite had little incentive to build a garrison state.

THE WEAKENING OF INDEPENDENT POWER CENTERS

Revolutionary war and counterrevolutionary conflict also weakened independent power centers, albeit to a lesser degree than in Russia and China. By 1920, the most powerful classes and institutions sustaining the old regime were either destroyed or incapacitated. The old Federal Army was eliminated and replaced by one that was more autonomous of traditional elites.[262] As Roderic A. Camp has shown, revolutionary army officers had few social ties to economic and other conservative elites.[263]

The rural oligarchy was also destroyed. Large landowners were weakened by the revolutionary war,[264] but they survived into the 1930s, resisting land reform through both the National Chamber of Agriculture (CNA) and the paramilitary White Guards.[265] Without the army, however, the weakened landowning class could not defend itself. The Cárdenas government's land reform (discussed below) brought the quick destruction of both the CNA and the White Guards.[266] By 1940, the landed elite and the hacienda system had been eliminated.[267]

A third pillar of the old regime, the Church, was politically neutralized. The Church took a beating during the 1920s and early 1930s, particularly during the 1926–1929 Cristero War. More than 90 percent of priests were displaced during the Cristero War, and dozens of priests were killed.[268] Under the 1929 accord that ended the war, the Church ceased all political activity in exchange for the freedom to carry out its spiritual and cultural work.[269] Not only did the Church abandon the political arena, but it also stifled opposition activities by local clergy and Catholic lay associations.[270]

State repression persisted after the Cristero War. Government forces killed an estimated 5,000 former Cristeros, including most of their important leaders, during the early 1930s.[271] At the same time, state governments heavily restricted the number of priests allowed in their territory.[272] Some 264 churches were closed between 1932 and 1934.[273] By 1935, there were only 375 open churches and 305 legally registered priests in Mexico.[274] Only five of thirty-four bishops were still in their diocese; hundreds of priests had either fled or were in hiding.[275] Overall, the number of priests working in Mexico declined from one per 1,600 Catholic parishioners under Díaz to one per 5,000 in the 1930s.[276] Such a defeat and subjugation of the Church had few parallels in Latin American history.

The destruction or sidelining of prerevolutionary power centers—army, landed oligarchy, and Church—had important consequences for the new regime. Without an army or police force, without control over land and peasants, and largely without the symbolic power of the Church, reactionary forces' ability to mobilize opposition to the revolution was dramatically reduced.

Two other societal actors—labor and peasant movements—were co-opted by the revolutionary regime. Peasants, who were highly mobilized in the 1910s and 1920s, were co-opted into the CNC and the PRM/PRI during the 1930s.[277] Land reform dramatically increased peasants' dependence on the state, which "rendered [them] politically ineffective."[278] The labor movement was similarly co-opted. The Regional Confederation of Mexican Workers, the dominant labor confederation in the 1920s, was linked to the state from its founding until it divided and weakened in the late 1920s and the 1930s.[279] Cárdenas mobilized the bulk of the labor movement into the CTM and incorporated it into the ruling party.[280] The unions grew dependent on state and party resources, which limited their capacity to challenge the regime.[281]

Revolutionary Legacies: The Mexican Party-State

The party-state complex that emerged in the 1930s was powerfully shaped by the segmented radicalism of the revolution's foundational period. The revolutionary reactive sequence bequeathed three legacies that contributed to durable authoritarianism: a cohesive ruling party; a loyal and disciplined coercive apparatus, and a weak opposition. At the same time, due to the more limited nature of the reactive sequence, and in particular the absence of a sustained existential threat, party cohesion never took on the quasi-religious character observed in Russia and China, the coercive apparatus remained small, and independent power centers never entirely disappeared.

A COHESIVE RULING PARTY

Mexico's ruling party—renamed the PRI in 1946—was highly cohesive. The creation of a single revolutionary party ended the "Hobbesian war of all against all" that had characterized the regime elite between 1917 and 1929.[282] The PNR established a monopoly over the revolutionary label, which helped to consolidate a single partisan identity and subculture. During its early decades, the PRI was marked by a "distinct cohesion and esprit de corps."[283] As the notion of a single "revolutionary family" took hold during and immediately after the Cristero War, the "us" versus "them" distinction that had been muddied by fratricidal conflict during the 1920s came into sharper view.[284] After 1929, there was a "clear line that separated those who fought . . . in the revolution from those who did not, or from those who fought on the wrong side."[285]

The PRI's monopoly over the revolutionary identity raised the cost of defection. Once the PRI became the sole legitimate representative of the revolution, politicians who opposed it could be "tarred with the brush of political treason."[286] Party loyalty became analogous to patriotism,[287] and politicians who broke with the PRI were dismissed as "traitors."[288] Appeals to "revolutionary loyalty" remained effective for decades.[289] Even revolutionary bigwigs were vulnerable to charges of "betraying the revolution" when they defected.[290]

After 1929, then, Mexico's ruling party became a "broad church outside of which there was no political salvation."[291] Losers in intra-elite power struggles learned that defection "risked entering a political wasteland"[292] and that their most viable strategy was to "bite their tongues and, however grudgingly, endorse the winner."[293] Although revolutionary generals broke away and ran as opposition presidential candidates in 1940 (Juan Almazán) and 1952 (Miguel Henríquez), these defections "bore scant fruit," as few regime elites were willing to join them.[294] By 1952, then, it was clear that the costs of defecting and opposing the PRI were "too high for any plausible candidate to bear."[295] Indeed, the party suffered no significant defections between 1952 and 1987.[296]

At the same time, in the absence of a shared ideology or a persistent existential threat, PRI cadres lacked the kind of zealous devotion to unity observed in Russia and China. Instead, ruling party cohesion was reinforced by the PRI's electoral dominance and monopoly over patronage resources,[297] as well as a set of strong informal institutions to manage intraparty competition and succession. The most important of these was the *dedazo*, an informal mechanism by which presidents unilaterally chose their successor—from among cabinet members, who could not publicly seek the nomination—and then retired from political life.[298]

PARTY-ARMY FUSION AND MILITARY LOYALTY

The post-1929 regime was also characterized by a cohesive and disciplined coercive apparatus.[299] This cohesion was rooted in a fusion of political and military elites that emerged out of the revolution.[300] As noted above, the regime was founded by a loose collection of "revolutionary generals,"[301] or leaders who served as military commanders during the war and then "straddled two careers, one in the army and another in politics," after 1917.[302] During the 1920s, revolutionary generals established themselves as de facto state- and regional-level power brokers across Mexico.[303]

Although the absence of a party left the generals prone to internal conflict during the 1920s, the formation of the PNR gave rise to a cohesive party-army complex. Initially, party-army fusion was near total.[304] Revolutionary generals such as Calles, Cárdenas, Joaquín Amaro, Juan Almazán, and Saturnino Cedillo dominated both the PNR and the government during the 1930s.[305] Every Mexican president elected during the 1920s and 1930s—Obregón, Calles, Ortiz Rubio, Cárdenas, and Manuel Avila Camacho—was a revolutionary general.[306] In the early and mid-1930s, the PNR leadership, most important cabinet posts, and half the governorships were held by revolutionary generals.[307] Although military influence began to erode in the 1940s, revolutionary veterans controlled the presidency and at least 40 percent of governorships through 1946, held the PRI presidency through 1964, and served as defense secretary through 1976.[308]

The military was, in turn, thoroughly revolutionary. The army was commanded and staffed by revolutionary veterans into the 1960s.[309] A revolutionary background was essential to promotion up the ranks; revolutionary veterans ascended more quickly and monopolized the top command positions.[310] Through the early 1960s, all generalships were reserved exclusively for revolutionary veterans, and the powerful zone commanders were almost exclusively revolutionary veterans.[311] Party-army fusion produced a loyal and disciplined coercive apparatus. As Camp has argued, shared "guerrilla roots" generated a "set of shared values between civilian and military leadership."[312] Military commanders viewed themselves as "guardians of the Revolution."[313] This revolutionary commitment was made manifest during the Cristero War. Rebel leaders tried to convince army commanders to turn on the unpopular Calles government, but "the army, a creation of the revolution . . . had no sympathy for the Cristeros."[314]

Party-army fusion generated a striking degree of military discipline.[315] The armed forces were "fiercely loyal" to the government after 1929.[316] In stark contrast to the rest of Latin America, Mexico became a "model of civil-military tranquility,"[317] marked by the absence of any coups—or even coup attempts.[318] The Mexican army became one of the most disciplined armies in the developing world.[319] Officers almost never spoke out against the government.[320] Only one active-duty general was found to have worked for the opposition between 1952 and 2000—and the military brought him up on charges.[321]

A MODEST COERCIVE APPARATUS

Although Mexico's military cohesion rivaled that of other revolutionary regimes, its coercive apparatus was considerably smaller. Because revolutionary leaders faced only modest external and counterrevolutionary threats, their incentives to invest in domestic and external security were weaker than those in most of the cases examined in this book. Thus, early Constitutionalist governments scaled back, rather than expanded, Mexico's security forces.[322] The army was reduced to a modest 50,000 troops after World War II.[323] Mexico became "one of the most lightly armed nations in the world,"[324] with only 0.1 percent of its population under arms in 1966.[325] Among Latin American states, only Costa Rica, which had no army, had a smaller percentage of its population under arms.[326] Likewise, defense spending fell from half the national budget in the early 1920s to a mere 8 percent in the mid-1950s.[327] As a percentage of GDP,

Mexican defense spending was among the lowest in Latin America in the 1960s and 1970s;[328] in 1976, it was lower than in Costa Rica, which had no standing army.[329]

The Mexican Revolution also failed to develop a police state.[330] Unlike Russia, early revolutionary governments did not invest in a powerful intelligence agency or political police.[331] The intelligence service, created in 1918, was weak and underfunded.[332] It initially had no office space, and as late as 1932, it had only fifteen full-time agents.[333] Although the intelligence service expanded during the Cold War,[334] it nevertheless remained a small agency with few full-time spies and limited information-processing capacity.[335]

Overall, Mexico's small but disciplined security forces proved effective at quelling episodic strikes and student, peasant, and postelection protests, as well as embryonic guerrilla movements.[336] They also proved capable, on occasion, of high-intensity repression.[337] However, it is less clear whether the coercive apparatus had the capacity to suppress large-scale and sustained opposition mobilization of the kind that emerged in China in 1989 or Iran in 2009.[338] Due to the weakening of independent centers of societal power, however, this capacity was never seriously tested.

A WEAKENED (BUT NOT DESTROYED) CIVIL SOCIETY

Finally, Mexico's reactive sequence weakened independent power centers but did not eliminate them as in Russia and China. The destruction of the landed oligarchy and the political emasculation of the Church, together with the co-optation of labor and peasant movements, weakened the bases for opposition. The pillars of political conservatism were decimated. Without the resources of landowners or the votes of peasants, the bases of conservative party-building were absent. The Church remained on the political sidelines for more than half a century. Church leaders rarely criticized the government, kept their distance from political parties, and clamped down on oppositionist Catholic lay associations.[339]

This behavior stood in sharp contrast to other countries in Latin America, where the Church played a decisive role in twentieth-century politics, supporting conservative coups (e.g., Venezuela 1948, Guatemala 1954, Argentina 1955), helping found Christian Democratic parties (e.g., Chile, El Salvador, Guatemala), and, later in the century, sponsoring antiauthoritarian social movements (e.g., Brazil, El Salvador, Nicaragua, and Peru in the late 1970s).

Business was also weak. The industrial sector was embryonic at the time of the revolution; it represented only 12.5 percent of Mexico's GDP in

1908 and declined during the war.[340] Industrialization brought a dramatic expansion of the business sector in the 1930s and 1940s.[341] Unlike labor and peasant movements, the private sector remained outside the ruling party coalition.[342] However, under Mexico's state-led industrialization model, many businesses depended on state concessions, licenses, subsidies, and other protections, which gave the PRI a plethora of tools with which to reward friendly businesses and punish unfriendly ones. Consequently, many business leaders readily cooperated with the government in exchange for particularistic benefits.[343] Thus, the bulk of the industrial sector maintained friendly relations with the government.[344] Indeed, after 1940, most industrialists adhered to an informal pact in which they could expect a friendly business climate and access to the state as long they stayed out of politics.[345]

Simultaneously, the PRI's co-optation of labor and peasant organizations left little space for left-wing or populist movements.[346] Because the leading peasant and labor organizations were "creatures of the state,"[347] popular sector groups had "no effective intermediaries."[348] As a result, there were "few organizations to represent the discontented."[349] Levels of peasant protest were relatively low after 1940,[350] and efforts to organize independent peasant organizations, such as that of the Independent Peasant Central in the early 1960s, failed.[351] The labor movement was similarly co-opted.[352] By the early 1950s, "there was no hope left of creating a united, independent, combative labor movement."[353] Efforts to create independent labor confederations, such as that led by Vicente Lombardo in the late 1940s, were thwarted by the PRI-state,[354] and levels of labor protest remained low through the 1980s.[355]

At the same time, the destruction of independent power centers was less thoroughgoing than in Russia and China. Importantly, the revolutionary government maintained a capitalist economy that, though heavily regulated, permitted widespread private ownership.[356] Although large landowners were wiped out and key sectors of the economy—including oil, railroads, electricity, telecommunications, and parts of the financial system—were nationalized,[357] much of the private sector, including the vast bulk of industry and commerce, was left intact.[358]

Capitalists retained some autonomy. A prominent example is the Monterrey Group, which encompassed some 200 entrepreneurial families in the northern state of Nuevo Leon and controlled about a quarter of Mexico's industrial production.[359] The Monterrey Group emerged as an important center of conservative opposition.[360] In 1929, it created the Employers Confederation of the Mexican Republic (COPARMEX), which, unlike other Mexican business associations, was "fiercely autonomous" and often openly antigovernment.[361] The Monterrey Group was a minority sector within the industrialist class, and prior to 1982, its efforts to mobilize business opposition were unsuccessful.[362] Through the early 1980s, then, the private sector was "an economic giant and a political dwarf."[363] However, industrialists remained a latent source of opposition. As we shall see, Mexico's capitalist development produced a large private sector with considerable resources, which would eventually be used to challenge the PRI.

The Church also remained a potential source of opposition. Although it carefully avoided politics after 1929, the Church maintained a vast network of priests, lay activists, and civic associations, which gave it considerable, if latent, mobilizational capacity. Whenever the Church decided to flex its muscles in the political arena, it had the potential to be a formidable actor.

More generally, Mexico's revolutionary regime never entirely closed off associational space. Thus, notwithstanding the PRI's extraordinary success in co-opting society,[364] associational life persisted. Among the largest associations were lay Catholic organizations such as the National Sinarquista Union (UNS), which had as many as 500,000 members in the late 1930s.[365] There were also pockets of middle-class activism, mostly notably among university students. As we shall see, the late 1960s saw the emergence of an independent and radical student movement that organized massive antigovernment protests in 1968.[366]

Even if the weakening of independent power centers was less complete than in Russia and China, however, it was nevertheless highly consequential. The revolution and its aftermath created an enduring power asymmetry between the PRI and its opponents. The PRI-state "acquired an exceptional degree of power relative to the rest of society,"[367] whereas its opponents, devoid of organized constituencies and starved of resources, remained "unorganized and silent."[368] Beginning in the 1940s, few, if any, sociopolitical actors could challenge the PRI.[369] Indeed, Mexican intelligence agencies recognized during the 1940s and 1950s that the regime faced "no real threats."[370]

The power asymmetries generated by the revolution were seen in the repeated failure of efforts to build viable right- and left-wing opposition. With economic elites and the Church on the political sidelines, and with peasants mobilized by the PRI, the bases for conservative opposition were weak. Numerous right-wing parties and movements emerged in the 1930s, including the Anti-Reelectionist Party, the Anti-Communist Revolutionary Party, and the Social Democratic Party, as well as quasi-fascist movements like the Sinarquistas and the Mexican Revolutionary Action (or Gold Shirts).[371] Yet these movements proved "numerically and financially weak,"[372] and nearly all of them collapsed within a few years.[373]

The only significant right-wing party to emerge was the National Action Party (PAN), which was founded by a coalition of Catholic activists and liberal professionals and businessmen in 1939.[374] Although the PAN survived throughout the 1940–1982 period, it was never more than a "small party of notables."[375] Despite the PAN's Catholic activist base, the Church hierarchy kept the party at arm's length,[376] and despite the PAN's pro-business platform, it received little support from industrialists.[377] The absence of Church or business support left the PAN with a fragile organization and meager financing.[378] Prior to the 1980s, the party could rely on only a "core of spirited and enthusiastic activists."[379] Unable to field candidates across the country,[380] the PAN was no more than a political "gadfly,"[381] never winning more than 14 percent of the presidential vote between 1940 and 1982.

At the other end of the ideological spectrum, the PRI's co-optation of peasants and unions "locked up" much of the Left's natural base, leaving little space for left-of-center parties and social movements.[382] Left-wing parties failed repeatedly after 1917.[383] The Mexican Communist Party (PCM, created in 1919) was pushed out of the labor movement in the 1930s, leaving it with a tiny base.[384] Never more than 30,000 members,[385] the PCM lost legal registration in 1946 and was "on the brink of extinction" by the 1950s.[386] The only other left party of significance during the 1940–1982 period was the Popular Party (PP) (later renamed the Popular Socialist Party), which was created by prominent leftists Narciso Bassols and Vicente Lombardo in 1948. The PP gained little union support, however,[387] and it managed to win only 2 percent of the vote in the 1952 election.[388]

In sum, the Mexican Revolution and its aftermath produced a cohesive party-state and weakened independent centers of societal power. However, the revolutionary elite neither developed a Soviet-style police state nor destroyed all independent power centers. Consequently, although the vast power asymmetry between the PRI-state and society was a major source of regime durability, the regime was arguably less robust—and more dependent on economic growth—than those in Russia and China.

Crisis and Regime Survival, 1929–1982

Mexico's revolutionary regime was one of the longest-lived in modern history, surviving for eighty-five years. The party-state that emerged out of the early revolutionary period proved sufficiently robust to survive the Great Depression, the intense polarization and conservative reaction triggered by the Cárdenas reforms of the late 1930s, and the Cold War polarization of the 1960s and early 1970s. In each of these periods, the party-army complex remained loyal and disciplined, helping the regime avoid the kind of coups or elite schisms that undermined other Latin American regimes during these periods—and permitting a high-intensity crackdown on a massive student protest movement in 1968. Regime stability was also rooted in the weakening of independent societal power centers. The destruction of the landowning elite, the sidelining of the Church, and the co-optation of labor and peasant movements limited the bases for societal organization, which weakened opposition forces—on both the right and the left—for decades.

As this chapter has shown, however, segmented radicalism gave rise to a weaker party-state complex than in Russia and China. As a result, revolutionary legacies alone are insufficient to explain the Mexican regime's extraordinary longevity. Arguably, the Mexican regime was less severely tested than those in Russia and China. Although this outcome was partly a product of the state-societal power asymmetries described above, it was also a product of economic growth.[389] Between 1933 and 1981, the Mexican economy grew at an average rate of more than 6 percent a year—one of the highest growth rates in Latin America.[390] At no point between 1940 and 1981 did the annual growth rate fall below 3.3 percent.[391] Steady growth helped to limit the societal challenges facing the Mexican regime, which, given its modest coercive capacity, may have been critical. Without a steady flow of resources to co-opt low-income constituencies and much of civil society,[392] it is likely that PRI governments would have faced greater opposition. It is not clear that the regime possessed the coercive capacity to thwart such challenges.

ECONOMIC CRISIS, POLARIZATION, AND REGIME SURVIVAL IN THE 1930S

Mexico in the 1930s was marked by economic crisis, radical reform, and extreme polarization—conditions that led to military coups across much of Latin America. President Pascual Ortiz Rubio (1930–1932), the first president elected under the PRN, inherited a profound crisis.[393] Not only did the Cristero War and Obregón's assassination shake the foundations of the regime, but the economy was in a freefall. Mexico's GDP contracted by 31 percent between 1927 and 1932 and by 16 percent in 1932 alone.[394] The economic crisis eroded public support for the government and triggered a sharp increase in popular mobilization and protest.[395] The number of strikes increased by more than twentyfold in the early 1930s,[396] and with land reform stalled, radical agrarian movements such as the National Peasant League emerged and began to mobilize against the government.[397]

The economic crisis triggered a series of political crises for the embryonic PNR. Backed by Calles, who remained the power behind the throne, Ortiz Rubio governed conservatively, resisting calls from PNR radicals (known as Reds) for land reform and other redistributive measures.[398] Unpopular and isolated, Ortiz Rubio was forced to resign the presidency in September 1932.[399] His successor, Abelardo Rodriguez, moved left, accelerating the agrarian reform, establishing Mexico's first minimum wage, and launching the radical Socialist Education program (described below).[400]

The PNR's radicalization continued during the presidency of Lázaro Cárdenas (1934–1940). A committed socialist, Cárdenas was far more ideological than his predecessors.[401] However, his radicalism was also driven by political imperatives. Cárdenas faced conservative opposition from Calles, who remained the dominant force in the PNR.[402] To overcome Calles's opposition, Cárdenas forged alliances with radical labor and agrarian movements, which demanded "genuinely radical" redistribution.[403] Thus, the Cárdenas government turned to the left, and the revolution briefly "began to transcend 'bourgeois' limits."[404] Cárdenas strengthened unions, dramatically raised workers' incomes, and carried out several major nationalizations, including the railroads in 1937 and the oil industry in 1938.[405]

Cárdenas's most radical policies, however, came in the area of land reform.[406] The Cárdenas government distributed 18 million hectares of land, nearly double the amount of land distributed by all previous revolutionary governments combined.[407] More than 800,000 peasant families gained access to land.[408] Much of the land was organized into communal lands, or *ejidos*, which by law could not be bought or sold. By 1940, 47 percent of Mexico's farmland was organized into *ejidos*.[409] Thus, the government sought to "reorder the life of rural society," turning the *ejido* into the primary mode of production in the countryside.[410]

The Cárdenas period thus marked the culmination of an agrarian reform that was announced in 1915 and legalized in the 1917 constitution, but which had been implemented slowly and intermittently before 1934. Ultimately, more than 50 million hectares of land were distributed to 2.2 million families between 1915 and 1965,[411] covering more land and people than any other agrarian reform in Latin America except Cuba.[412] The reform completed the transformation of the rural class structure that began in 1910. The landowning class, already weakened by two decades of revolution, was wiped out, and the centuries-old hacienda system was finally put to rest.[413]

Mexican revolutionaries also resumed their attacks on the Church in the 1930s. In what has been called a "veritable cultural revolution,"[414] hundreds of churches were destroyed or closed; hundreds of priests were attacked, jailed, or deported; and Catholics were purged from public schools and bureaucracies between 1930 and 1936.[415] In 1932, laws restricting the number of priests were tightened, bringing a new wave of expulsions.[416] By 1935, all priests had been expelled from sixteen states, and five or fewer remained in a half dozen others.[417] State governments attacked the Church with "unprecedented zeal,"[418] launching "de-Christianization" campaigns aimed at erasing Catholic traditions and symbols from society.[419] In some states, towns and streets named after Catholic saints were renamed, religious festivals were replaced with "patriotic festivals" and "cultural Sundays," and religious holidays were removed from school calendars.[420] Tabasco governor Tomas Garrido led a "campaign against God" in which books and songs mentioning God were banned, crosses were removed from graveyards, use of the term *adios* (to God) was prohibited, and priests were encouraged to marry;[421] some state governments sought to replace Sunday masses with "Red Sundays"[422] and to replace Catholic baptisms and wedding ceremonies with "socialist" ones.[423]

In 1933–1934, the Rodriguez government launched a radical "socialist education" campaign. Article 3 of the constitution, which mandated secular education, had not previously been enforced with rigor, but in 1931, Education Secretary Narciso Bassols, a Marxist, "decided to put some teeth into the law."[424] A 1934 constitutional reform explicitly required that all education must be secular and "socialist."[425] School textbooks were redesigned in line with these goals; reading lists distributed by the Education Ministry included works by Marx, Engels, and Lenin.[426] Schools were charged with transforming Mexican culture and creating "new revolutionary citizens."[427]

The radicalization of the revolution triggered a strong conservative reaction. The government's Socialist Education program triggered another armed Catholic rebellion in 1935. Although the *Segunda Cristiada* (or second Cristero uprising) was far smaller than the first, as many as 300 teachers were killed by terrorists.[428] Cárdenas's redistributive reforms also triggered a fierce reaction.[429] Much of the economic elite, especially Monterrey industrialists, viewed Cárdenas as a dangerous threat,[430] and much of the middle class grew fearful that Cárdenas "had placed their nation on the road to communism."[431] Moreover, Cárdenas's nationalization of the oil sector generated intense resistance from the United States and Britain.[432]

By 1938, Cárdenas confronted a "vast reservoir of opposition,"[433] including new counterrevolutionary movements such as the UNS, a quasi-fascist organization created in 1937.[434] Appealing to Catholic activists opposed to the Socialist Education program and peasants opposed to the *ejido* system,[435] the Sinarquistas grew rapidly in the late 1930s, mobilizing half a million members.[436]

Such crises frequently led to coups in twentieth-century Latin America. Indeed, the Great Depression and the rise of fascism triggered coups across Latin America in the 1930s. Outside of Mexico, thirteen of eighteen countries in the region experienced one or more military coups during the decade.[437] Moreover, nearly all of the governments that initiated redistributive reforms in mid-twentieth-century Latin America were toppled by military coups—including Peru and Venezuela in 1948, Guatemala in 1954, Argentina in 1955, the Dominican Republic in 1963, Brazil in 1964, and Chile in 1973.

Yet the Mexican regime avoided a coup. Party-army fusion was critical to this outcome. Unlike many other Latin American countries, where conservative forces held considerable sway over the military, the Mexican army was built and led by revolutionaries and thus "beholden to the . . . Revolutionary state."[438] Indeed, Cárdenas himself was a leading revolutionary general. As Knight put it, army leaders "might not care for *Cardenista* radicalism, but Cárdenas was one of their own."[439]

Military cohesion could be seen during two critical moments. One was an abortive rebellion in 1938, led by revolutionary cacique Saturnino Cedillo. Cedillo became as a leading figure on the right during Cárdenas's presidency, and in 1938, he launched a rebellion backed by landowners, oil executives, and fascist Gold Shirts.[440] However, Cedillo found few supporters in the army or the ruling party.[441] Without military support, Cedillo had to rely on his own private militia,[442] turning the uprising into "more of a regional political rebellion than a serious military event."[443] The rebellion was easily quelled.[444]

The 1940 presidential election also generated fear of rebellion. The ruling party faced a hostile electorate in 1940,[445] and its candidate, Manuel Avila Camacho, was unpopular.[446] In this context, revolutionary general Juan Almazán abandoned the party to run as a right-wing opposition candidate. Almazán was backed by Monterrey industrialists, landowners, parts of the Church, the Sinarquistas, the PAN and other right-wing parties, and much of the middle class.[447] As a prominent revolutionary general, moreover, he had numerous friends and sympathizers among the regime elite, including in the army.[448]

Almazán's candidacy thus posed a serious threat.[449] According to former president Emilio Portes Gil, even President Cárdenas believed Almazán would win.[450] To prevent such an outcome, the government engaged in massive fraud.[451] Almazán supporters mobilized in protest.[452] Many called for armed rebellion, and Almazán reportedly considered such a move.[453] Despite considerable rank-and-file military discontent, however, the army closed ranks behind the government.[454] Without military allies, Almazán abandoned any plans for rebellion and left the country.[455] His political movement quickly collapsed.[456]

COHESION, COERCION, AND REGIME SURVIVAL
AMID COLD WAR POLARIZATION

Between 1940 and 1982, a period in which Cold War polarization, popular mobilization, and conservative reaction led to at least one regime breakdown in *every other country* in Latin America, Mexico's authoritarian regime remained stable. The PRI won thirteen consecutive national elections between 1940 and 1979, always capturing at least 70 percent of the vote.[457]

Several factors contributed to regime stability after 1940. First, as noted above, steady economic growth allowed the PRI to co-opt potential rivals and finance an effective clientelist machine.[458] Second, PRI governments moderated, abandoning the radical policies of the Cárdenas era, which blunted opposition from business and the Church.[459] Third, World War II weakened extreme right-wing opposition and brought improved relations with the United States.[460] U.S. governments consistently supported the regime after 1940, reducing external pressure to a minimum.[461]

However, regime stability was also a product of two revolutionary legacies: a cohesive party-state and weak independent power centers.

The party-state proved remarkably cohesive. Whereas every other country in Latin America experienced at least one coup or successful armed uprising between 1940 and 1980, Mexico suffered no coups and *no coup attempts*.[462] As one scholar observed in the 1980s, "Nothing suggests that Mexico's military elites have offered any serious consideration to administering a military coup for forty years."[463]

Likewise, the PRI suffered few significant defections after 1940.[464] On the few occasions when leaders defected, they found few allies within the regime and wound up in the political wilderness. For example, when ex-foreign minister Ezequiel Padilla defected and challenged PRI candidate Miguel Aleman for the presidency in 1946, he gained almost no support from within the party.[465] Although Padilla denounced the election results as fraudulent, he was too politically isolated to challenge them. The PRI simply "overwhelmed . . . Padilla. No bloodshed, no threats of rebellion, no trouble."[466]

The Aleman administration's (1946–1952) conservative policies triggered some defections on the left. Most importantly, Miguel Henríquez, a revolutionary general with ties to the PRI's Cárdenista wing,[467] challenged PRI candidate Adolfo Ruiz Cortines in the 1952 election. Henríquez ran as a "true revolutionary," triggering fears that ex-president Cárdenas would endorse him.[468] However, Cárdenas and other party leaders closed ranks behind Ruiz Cortines,[469] who won overwhelmingly. Although the (likely fraudulent) results triggered protest and rumors of an armed rebellion,[470] the army remained loyal, no uprising occurred, and the Henriquista movement quickly collapsed.[471]

The PRI suffered no further elite defections between 1952 and 1987—a remarkable record of cohesion.[472] Party discipline extended to the legislature, at times reaching Soviet levels.[473] In 1941, for example, 100 percent of the bills proposed by the president were approved unanimously by the ruling party in Congress.[474]

Second, the regime confronted little societal opposition after 1940. In striking contrast to other industrializing countries in the region, such as Argentina, Brazil, Chile, and Uruguay, opposition forces in Mexico were persistently weak throughout the mid and even late twentieth century. With business and the Church on the political sidelines and labor and peasant movements co-opted, opposition movements languished. Opposition parties never won more than 17 percent of the national vote between 1940 and 1979, failing to capture even a single governorship.[475] Although fraud and coercion contributed to these results, analyses of the Mexican regime highlight the centrality of PRI hegemony and opposition weakness.[476] In other words, the PRI's electoral dominance was rooted more in long-term power asymmetries than in fraud or repression.[477]

Outside the electoral arena, the co-option of labor and peasant movements left little space for organized social movements.[478] Levels of strike activity and peasant protest were unusually low in the 1940–1982 period,[479] and opposition protest movements were small, episodic, and easily contained.[480]

Likewise, whereas significant guerrilla movements emerged in Colombia and Venezuela in the early 1960s and in Argentina, Brazil, and Uruguay in the late 1960s and early 1970s, insurgencies consistently failed to take hold in Mexico.[481] According to Sergio Aguayo Quezada, twenty-nine different guerrilla organizations emerged in the 1960s and early 1970s.[482] None of them established a mass base, however, and as a result, they never posed a threat to the regime.[483]

When societal challenges did appear, the security forces could be relied upon to crack down on them.[484] When the army was periodically called upon to quell strikes, peasant protest, postelection protests, and embryonic guerrilla movements, it did so effectively, even when it required high-intensity coercion.[485] For example, when a railway workers' strike threatened to paralyze the country in 1958–1959, the army occupied the railroads and the railway workers' union halls, raided workers' homes and forced them back to work, and launched a "nationwide dragnet" in which thousands of striking railway workers were jailed.[486] The strike was broken within two weeks.[487]

The robustness of the Mexican regime was made manifest during the 1960s, when the Cuban Revolution inspired new radical movements and guerrilla organizations across Latin America. The 1960s and early 1970s were thus a period of heightened polarization and popular mobilization, which undermined regime stability across the region.[488] Indeed, a striking two-thirds of Latin American states experienced regime-ending coups between 1963 and 1973.[489]

Although Mexico was not immune to polarization and crisis during this period, what is striking is that the regime survived those crises.[490] The Cuban Revolution threatened to divide the PRI.[491] For example, it inspired the formation of the National Liberation Movement (MNR), a left-wing PRI faction that gained the support of ex-president Cárdenas in the early 1960s.[492] The MNR's emergence triggered fears of a schism,[493] and, indeed, communist and other leftist groups encouraged the MNR to defect and compete against the PRI in the 1964 election.[494] Cárdenas and other left-leaning Priistas refused to defect, however, and no schism occurred.[495]

The PRI government responded to radical contention with effective repression. Prominent regime opponents were either imprisoned (union leader Demetrio Vallejo) or killed (e.g., peasant leader Ruben Jaramillo).[496] Security forces quelled peasant protest in Coahuila, Guerrero Oaxaca, and Veracruz; the 1964 "milk riots" in Puebla; student protests in Morelia (1966) and Hermosillo (1967); and postelection protests in Merida (1967).[497] They also systematically crushed leftist guerrillas.[498] Guerrilla groups such as the Party of the Poor, the Revolutionary Action Movement, and the September 23 League were all "repressed before they could gain a foothold."[499]

The most serious challenge during the 1960s, however, was the radical student protest movement that erupted in July 1968 and culminated in the October 2, 1968, Tlatelolco massacre. The largest social movement to emerge outside of the PRI-state since 1940,[500] the student protests mushroomed over the summer, threatening to embarrass the government as it hosted the 1968 Olympic Games in October. In August, between 300,000 and 500,000 protesters marched on the Zócalo, Mexico City's central plaza, "shaking the system to its foundations."[501]

Unlike other countries that experienced waves of popular mobilization during this period, including Argentina, Brazil, Chile, and Uruguay, there was no coup in Mexico. The PRI government responded to the protest with high-intensity repression. In September, President Gustavo Díaz Ordaz ordered the army to occupy the National Autonomous University, the principal hub of the student movement.[502] Hundreds of students were arrested.[503] On October 2, ten days before the Olympics began, more than 10,000 protesters gathered in the Plaza of Three Cultures in the Tlatelolco section of Mexico City, chanting slogans like "We don't want Olympics. We want revolution!" The plaza was surrounded by security forces, who were ordered to open fire on the students. According to eyewitness reports, helicopters fired green flares into the air, after which members of the army's Olympia Battalion moved on the crowd and began to fire—as "though somebody had pushed a button."[504] Between 200 and 325 people were killed and at least 2,000 arrested.[505]

Although both the exact death toll and the responsibility for ordering the repression remain disputed,[506] one fact is clear: the security forces complied swiftly and effectively with civilian orders to engage in high-intensity repression.[507] Even though the repression would badly tarnish the army's public image,[508] the Tlatelolco massacre was implemented "with complete and unquestioning loyalty."[509] Moreover, with the exception of the writer Octavio Paz, who resigned as ambassador to India, no one in the PRI government criticized the repression or defected in response to it.[510]

High-intensity repression continued into the early 1970s. In June 1971, army and paramilitary agents launched another wave of repression against leftist student movements in June 1971, killing more than 100 people,[511] and in 1973, the army launched a "scorched earth" campaign against guerrillas in Guerrero in which hundreds of people were killed.[512]

The repression succeeded. The student movement collapsed after the Tlatelolco massacre,[513] and the radical Left was effectively wiped out by the early 1970s.[514] Although the repression is said to have eroded the PRI's legitimacy,[515] the regime nevertheless stabilized and survived for three additional decades. Indeed, of the fourteen non-democracies that existed in Latin America in 1968, only those in Mexico and Cuba—both revolutionary—survived through the end of the century.

Regime Weakening and Breakdown, 1982–2000

The PRI regime weakened during the 1980s, gradually democratized during the 1990s, and finally ended in 2000 with the election of PAN presidential candidate Vicente Fox. Several factors account for the regime's eventual demise. First, the revolutionary generation passed from the scene. The influence of revolutionary veterans waned during the 1950s and 1960s.[516] Although President Lopez Mateos (1958–1964) held regular Revolutionary Unity breakfasts with revolutionary veterans, the veterans, who were described by one scholar as "spent cartridges of the revolution,"[517] exerted little influence.[518] By the 1970s, the revolutionary generation was gone. It was replaced, at the top, by a technocratic elite.[519] The rest of the party, however, operated like a traditional machine.[520] The PRI had long functioned like a patronage-based machine, but through the 1950s and into the 1960s, cohesion had been reinforced by revolutionary identities and a group of powerful revolutionary generals.[521] Beginning in the 1970s, however, the PRI relied almost exclusively on the distribution of material benefits,[522] which left the ruling party vulnerable to economic crisis.

Economic crisis is the second factor that weakened the regime. After more than four decades of steady economic growth, the Mexican economy fell into crisis in 1982. Real GDP declined by 0.1 percent a year between 1982 and 1988, and real wages plummeted.[523] Moreover, the 1982 debt crisis compelled the government of Miguel de la Madrid (1982–1988) to adopt painful austerity measures, which eroded public support, especially among the urban poor.[524] Eventually, the government launched a process of economic liberalization, which undermined the PRI's alliances with labor and peasants[525] and its patronage bases.[526] Thus, if government performance contributed to regime survival between 1940 and 1982, helping to compensate for a relatively modest party-state complex, after 1982 that substitute pillar was removed.

A third factor that undermined the regime was the persistence of independent centers of societal power. Unlike in Russia and China, where such centers were largely wiped out, in Mexico, the Church and the private sector, though politically sidelined, continued to function. Indeed, industrialization had given rise to a larger and wealthier bourgeoise than had existed before the revolution. Business entered the political arena during the presidency of Luis Echeverría (1970–1976), creating the Business Coordinating Council (CCE) to oppose Echeverría's statist economic policies.[527] The private sector's reentry into politics was accelerated by President José Lopez Portillo's 1982 bank nationalization,[528] which ruptured the long-established pact between the PRI and the private sector.[529] The CCE and COPARMEX began to openly oppose the regime,[530] and for the first time, prominent business leaders began to invest in the PAN, joining the party, providing it with unprecedented finance, and often running as candidates.[531] As a result, what had long been a mere protest party evolved, over the course of the 1980s and 1990s, into a well-financed organization capable of competing with the PRI.[532]

The Church also reentered politics, providing a platform for Mexicans to express discontent.[533] In the mid-1980s, for example, Church leaders provided moral and logistical support to civic protests against fraudulent elections in Chihuahua and other northern states.[534] The Church also lent resources and legitimacy to emerging indigenous movements in Chiapas, Oaxaca, Veracruz, and other states.[535]

Finally, by the late twentieth century, economic development had given rise to a vibrant civil society, including an extensive network of human rights and pro-democracy nongovernmental organizations and vibrant urban social movements.[536] By the late 1980s, then, the regime faced more organized opposition than at any time since the 1920s.[537]

Economic crisis and an emergent civil society conspired to weaken the regime in the 1980s. After decades in the political wilderness, the PAN emerged as a viable contender in the north; the PAN challenged the PRI in several state and local elections, and when the PRI resorted to fraud, the Panistas, backed by Church, business, and other civic groups, often organized large-scale protest.[538]

An even greater challenge came from within. The PRI's turn toward market-oriented economic policies gave rise to a dissenting center-left faction, the Democratic Current, which was led by Cuauhtémoc Cárdenas, son of former president Lázaro Cárdenas.[539] In 1987, when it was clear that the PRI would choose market-oriented economist Carlos Salinas as its candidate in the July 1988 presidential election, Cárdenas and his allies defected and formed what would become the Party of the Democratic Revolution (PRD).[540] Cárdenas emerged as a potent electoral challenger, attacking the PRI from a left-of-center and pro-democratic position.[541] The PRI was forced to engage in massive election-day fraud.[542] When Salinas was declared the winner (following a "computer crash" and a three-day delay) with 50.7 percent of the vote, Cárdenas led a series of massive protests, which continued, off and on, through September 1988.[543] Although Salinas survived the crisis for several reasons, including opposition division and strong U.S. support, his ability to ride out weeks of mass protest hinged crucially on military cohesion.[544] The army remained thoroughly aligned with the PRI,[545] and even at the peak of the protests, its support for the government never wavered.[546] Indeed, despite evidence of considerable rank-and-file military support for Cárdenas, not a single officer broke with the government.[547]

Although the PRI remained in power for another twelve years, it never reestablished the hegemony it exercised between 1929 and 1982. With the emergence of viable opposition parties on the left (the PRD) and the right (the PAN), Mexico evolved from de facto single-party rule into competitive authoritarianism.[548] Under domestic pressure and growing international scrutiny as it pursued the North American Free Trade Agreement, the Salinas government undertook a series of reforms to clean up the electoral system.[549] Thus, the 1994 presidential election—won by PRI candidate Ernesto Zedillo—was clean if not fair.[550] Yet the regime continued to weaken. In January 1994, an armed uprising led by the indigenous-based Zapatista National Liberation Army damaged the PRI's image at home and abroad. Although the rebellion was small and quickly neutralized by the army,[551] it called international attention to Mexico's democratic deficits and the PRI's increasingly anachronistic rule.[552] Later that year, a currency crisis plunged Mexico into recession, eroding public support and thus delivering the "final blows to PRI hegemony."[553] In 1996, a weakened President Zedillo negotiated a set of electoral reforms that leveled the playing field, which paved the way for the PRI's defeat in 2000.[554]

Conclusion

Mexico's regime trajectory was shaped by the fact that the revolution was less extreme than those in Russia and China. Although the revolutionary elite attacked landowners and the Church, it often accommodated powerful foreign and domestic interests. Such segmented radicalism generated a more limited counterrevolutionary reaction than in Russia and China.

The result was a regime with most, but not all, of the pillars of durable authoritarianism. Mexico's revolutionary war and the counterrevolutionary Cristero War gave rise to a loyal army and a cohesive ruling party, but the regime never developed powerful (much less totalitarian) coercive structures, and independent centers of power were weakened but not systematically destroyed.

For this reason, the PRI was forced to cultivate public support to a greater degree than the Bolsheviks or the Chinese Communists. Thus, where Soviet and Chinese land reform programs were heavily shaped by ideology, Mexico's land reform was driven by the need to win peasant support. Moreover, long-term regime survival in Mexico hinged more on economic performance than it did in Russia or China. An expanding economy gave the PRI the resources to sustain a broad coalition that included organized labor, peasants, and many domestic industrialists;[555] it financed a robust patronage machine capable of buying off potential defectors.[556] Growth provided the mass support that, together with an effective clientelist machine, facilitated overwhelming electoral victories, which helped deter elite defection and raise the cost of opposition.[557]

However, economic growth and redistribution alone cannot explain the longevity of the PRI regime. The regime survived several crises, including the Great Depression, the extreme polarization of the 1930s, the protest and repression of 1968, and the 1982 debt crisis. It was forced to commit massive electoral fraud in 1940 and 1988. Through all of this, the party-state remained strikingly cohesive. Mexico was the only country in Latin America to not suffer a coup or a successful armed rebellion between 1929 and 2000. Not only did the army remain loyal during crises, but it carried out orders to engage in high-intensity repression. Thus, although economic growth undoubtably contributed to regime stability, the foundations of regime durability—a cohesive party-state and more than sixty years of opposition weakness—were products of social revolution.

Party institutions, which helped to maintain elite cohesion and to mobilize popular support, provide an alternative explanation for regime survival. Indeed, cohesion increased substantially after the party was established in 1929. Yet party formation was itself endogenous to the revolution. It was created in response to counterrevolutionary violence and built upon grassroots organizations that emerged from the revolutionary war. Party formation, by itself, cannot account for the absence of coups after 1920, nor can it explain why societal opposition was so weak for so long. These pillars of durable authoritarianism are best explained by the regime's revolutionary origins.

PART II

National Liberation Regimes

CHAPTER FIVE

Regime Origins and Diverging Paths in Vietnam, Algeria, and Ghana

THE END OF WORLD WAR II gave rise to dozens of new states. The collapse of European empires, changing international norms, and the mobilization of vast numbers of colonial subjects during two world wars spurred powerful new nationalist challenges to colonial rule.[1] Between 1945 and 1965, the number of independent states nearly doubled, from 64 to 125.

Many of the regimes that emerged out of colonial rule called themselves revolutionary. In countries as diverse as Algeria, Burma, Ghana, Guinea-Conakry, Guyana, Indonesia, Mali, Mozambique, Niger, South Yemen, Tanzania, Vietnam, and Zambia, the nationalist movements that led the anticolonial struggle embraced the causes of socialism and Third World liberation. Many of them borrowed the institutional architecture of Leninism, including single-party rule.[2]

Behind the Leninist architecture and revolutionary discourse, however, liberation regimes were quite diverse. Although most postcolonial governments were nationalist, few of them were revolutionary. Indeed, only five of forty-eight authoritarian regimes that emerged from colonial rule between 1945 and 1989 meet our criteria for social revolution: Algeria, Angola, Guinea-Bissau, Mozambique, and Vietnam. In most cases, independence was achieved via nonviolent means, colonial states remained largely intact after independence, and new nationalist governments did not seek to radically transform their societies.[3]

This variation had important consequences for regime stability. Consistent with our theory, all five liberation regimes born of social revolution survived for at least twenty-five years, and, as of 2021, all but one (Guinea-Bissau) remained in power after forty-six years or more. Nonrevolutionary cases, by contrast, exhibit greater variation. Although a few nonrevolutionary postcolonial autocracies (e.g., Botswana, Tanzania, Malaysia) endured for decades, a majority (twenty-two of forty-three) survived for fewer than twenty years, and eleven of them collapsed after less than a decade—nearly all due to military coups. Overall, the annual breakdown rate of revolutionary liberation regimes is 0.4 percent, compared to 2.6 percent for nonrevolutionary liberation regimes.[4]

This variation is rooted, to a significant extent, in regime origins. In most postcolonial revolutions, violent seizures of power and radical efforts at societal transformation triggered a reactive sequence that generated powerful party-states and weakened independent power centers. By contrast, regimes that emerged out of nonrevolutionary independence movements were less likely to develop cohesive parties and loyal militaries, which left them more vulnerable to breakdown.

This chapter examines the impact of revolutionary origins through a comparison of three archetypical national liberation regimes: Vietnam, Algeria, and Ghana. The Vietnamese Communist Party (VCP), the National Liberation Front (FLN) in Algeria, and the Convention People's Party (CPP) in Ghana led anticolonial struggles during the 1950s, earning impeccable nationalist credentials. Ho Chi Minh, Ahmed Ben Bella, and Kwame Nkrumah became internationally prominent anticolonial leaders, and all three of them proclaimed their governments to be revolutionary and socialist.

However, the three regimes followed markedly different trajectories. Vietnam closely approximates our ideal-typical path of social revolution. The VCP came to power in 1954 after a brutal eight-year war against France. In power, the revolutionaries built a new state, including a new army, and launched a range of radical initiatives, including a bold effort to bring revolution to South Vietnam. Prolonged wars—first against France, then against the United States—gave rise to a cohesive ruling party and a powerful and loyal coercive apparatus. It also allowed the communists to wipe out political rivals and independent power centers, which limited the mobilization capacity of regime opponents. The result was a vast power asymmetry between the revolutionary party-state and society, which provided the bases for more than sixty years of regime stability.

Algeria is a case of revolutionary accommodation, which gave rise to a less stable (albeit long-lived) regime. Like the Vietnamese Communists, the FLN came to power in 1962 after a violent eight-year struggle against France. The revolutionary elite created its own army, which developed into a cohesive institution with a strong stake in the regime. Yet, whereas the VCP was unambiguously radical, the FLN adopted an accommodationist strategy. The party oversaw a radical transformation of property relations, but because much of the property was taken from European settlers who had fled the country, these policies triggered little counterrevolutionary reaction. At the same time, the FLN government's cooperative relationship with France helped to prevent the emergence of an external threat. In the absence of counterrevolution, the FLN never closed ranks or destroyed independent power centers. This left the regime vulnerable to both internal conflict and societal opposition. Although army cohesion facilitated a successful crackdown on Islamist opposition in the 1990s, the regime remained considerably more vulnerable than its Vietnamese counterpart.

The Ghanaian case, by contrast, was nonrevolutionary. Ghana gained independence peacefully in 1957, and the CPP government accommodated British interests and retained much of the colonial state, including the army. In the absence of violent conflict, the regime never developed the kind of cohesive party-state observed in revolutionary cases. As a result, the Nkrumah government was vulnerable to threats from within, especially from an army it neither created nor fully controlled. The regime fell prey to a coup after less than a decade.

VIETNAM

Vietnam is a case of a successful armed liberation movement that triggered prolonged military conflict, which lay the bases for durable authoritarian. The Viet Minh's liberation war against France gave rise to a powerful and cohesive party-state. The communist government's pursuit of revolution in South Vietnam triggered a second war, this time against the United States, which reinforced elite cohesion and further developed the regime's coercive capacity. The wars also destroyed independent power centers, giving rise to a state-society power imbalance that endured for decades. These features enabled the revolutionary regime to survive a severe economic crisis, the loss of Soviet patronage, and the global crisis of communism.

The Revolutionary Seizure of Power: A Two-Stage Revolution

Prerevolutionary Vietnam possessed few conditions favorable to durable authoritarianism. The precolonial state was weak and decentralized, which facilitated the French conquest in the mid-nineteenth century.[5]

State institutions were further weakened by colonial rule.[6] The French broke Vietnam up into protectorates, dismantled precolonial administrative structures, and weakened the monarchy and traditional local authorities.[7] By the 1940s, the precolonial state had been dismembered "to the point where, like Humpty Dumpty, it could not be put back together again."[8] As a result, much of Vietnam was effectively stateless during World War II.[9] It is difficult, then, to identify conditions in prerevolutionary Vietnam that would predict durable authoritarianism in the absence of a social revolution.[10]

The revolutionary seizure of power in Vietnam occurred in two stages: the short-lived August 1945 revolution and the protracted liberation struggle that culminated in the 1954 revolution. The events of 1945 constituted a *political* revolution, not a social one, but it nevertheless triggered a reactive sequence that gave rise to a powerful and cohesive party-state by 1954.

THE 1945 REVOLUTION

The August 1945 revolution was a historical accident. Vietnam's anticolonial movement, led by the nationalist Viet Nam Quoc Dan Dang (VNQDD) and Ho Chi Minh's Indochinese Communist Party (ICP), had been badly weakened by French repression.[11] World War II created an opening, however, as Japan's occupation of Indochina loosened colonial controls and opened space for organizing in the countryside.[12] In 1941, ICP leaders created a nationalist front called the Viet Minh, which launched a guerrilla struggle in 1944.[13]

Two events in 1945 catapulted the embryonic Viet Minh into power. First, in March, Japanese forces abolished the colonial state, disarmed and imprisoned French troops, and installed Nguyen dynasty heir Bao Dai as a puppet emperor.[14] The disappearance of French forces created a vacuum of authority in the countryside, which Japanese forces did not fill, allowing the Viet Minh to expand.[15] Second, Japan's August 1945 surrender in World War II threw Vietnam into anarchy.[16] Formal authority fell to Bao Dai, but his government had no army, no revenue, and no rural presence.[17] With French forces in disarray and allied U.S. and British forces not yet on the scene, the Viet Minh was the only viable political organization in the country.[18] Seizing the moment, ICP leaders launched an uprising.[19] They met no resistance from Japanese troops or the hapless Bao Dai government.[20] On August 19, 1945, Viet Minh troops entered Hanoi, having fired only "a few symbolic revolver shots."[21] Bao Dai abdicated shortly thereafter, and on September 2, Ho Chi Minh declared independence. The 1945 revolution was thus remarkably easy. Amid the collapse of the colonial state and the Japanese retreat, power "simply fell into Viet Minh hands."[22]

The Viet Minh government was weak. The ICP was small, with only 5,000 members,[23] and the new army was "miniscule."[24] The new government had no military presence in the south, and it was so ill equipped that cadets in the military academy used wooden rifles.[25] Finally, the Ho government was isolated internationally, failing to gain recognition or support from either the Allies or the USSR.[26]

The Ho Chi Minh government responded to this vulnerability with accommodation. Although it abolished the 1,000-year-old monarchy,[27] it left much of the colonial bureaucracy intact and made no real effort to overturn the existing socioeconomic order.[28] There were few expropriations, and the commanding heights of the economy, including the Bank of Indochina, remined in private—mostly foreign—hands.[29] The government also eschewed agrarian reform, leaving landowners' power intact.[30] Finally, Ho adopted a pragmatic foreign policy, embracing the Allied cause and allowing France to maintain its investments and 15,000 troops in Vietnam.[31]

Moderation achieved little, however. Vietnam was soon invaded on multiple fronts. British troops arrived in Saigon in September 1945, and British and French forces soon controlled most of South Vietnam.[32] French forces arrived in the north in November 1946 and forced the Viet Minh out of Hanoi by year's end.[33] France reestablished de facto colonial rule, naming Emperor Bao Dai as head of a figurehead government.[34] Forced back into the countryside, the Viet Minh resumed its guerrilla war.

THE 1946–1954 REVOLUTIONARY WAR

The 1946–1954 liberation war transformed the Viet Minh into a powerful party-army. The war was brutal: an estimated 500,000 Vietnamese were killed, while French forces suffered 75,000–95,000 deaths.[35] Yet the war dramatically strengthened revolutionary forces. The ICP underwent a "phenomenal expansion."[36] The party mobilized peasants on an unprecedented scale, expanding from 20,000 members in 1946 to more than 500,000 in the early 1950s.[37]

The Viet Minh also built a powerful army. Military threats from China and France had forced the Viet Minh government to rapidly build up its military.[38] Under the leadership of Vo Nguyen Giap, the embryonic People's Army of Vietnam (PAVN) grew from 5,000 soldiers in August 1945 to 40,000–60,000 by late 1946.[39] The Viet Minh also organized tens of thousands of young men into "self-defense patrols."[40] By the time the war began in earnest in December 1946, the PAVN had as many as 100,000 people under arms.[41]

The liberation war transformed the PAVN into a potent military force.[42] Within two years, Viet Minh forces had mobilized 250,000 troops and were fighting the French to a stalemate.[43] By 1949, the PAVN "possessed a seasoned officer corps and battle-hardened battalions moving toward regiment and division-size formations."[44] China's 1949 revolution accelerated the PAVN's growth by providing safe territory, arms, and training.[45] The PAVN expanded from 32 regular battalions in 1948 to 117 in 1951.[46] The Viet Minh took on state-like functions, governing 7,000 villages, taxing landowners, and operating schools for nearly a million children in liberated zones.[47]

By 1953, the Viet Minh had reached military parity with French forces.[48] According to French intelligence estimates, the PAVN had 125,000 well-trained soldiers in 1953, which, when added to 200,000 village militias and 75,000 regional troops, meant that the Viet Minh had as many as 400,000 combatants under arms.[49] The Viet Minh's May 1954 victory at Dien Bien Phu, which has been described as "one of the greatest defeats ever suffered by a colonial power,"[50] delivered the death blow to French rule.[51] Bao Dai's army disintegrated,[52] paving the way for Communist control of North Vietnam following the July 1954 Geneva Accords.

The revolutionary war also enabled the Viet Minh to destroy rival organizations that could have posed a threat to its rule. The ICP faced a plethora of rivals in 1945. In the north, it competed with nationalist groups like the VNQDD and Dong Minh Hoi;[53] in the south, it confronted the nationalist Dai Viet party, a well-organized Trotskyite movement,[54] and, most importantly, three powerful political-religious "sects": the Cao Dai, a 500,000-member religious movement with a 7,000-man army and "state-like ambitions";[55] the Hoa Hao, led by the mystic Hunyh Phu So, which built a 300,000-member following in western Cochinchina;[56] and the Binh Xuyen, a mafia-like organization that controlled gambling operations and the local police in Saigon.[57] Collaboration with the Japanese enabled the sects to build powerful militias and carve out autonomous enclaves in several southern provinces.[58]

The arrival of French troops in September 1945 provided a justification for the ICP to wage war on its political rivals.[59] The Viet Minh quickly set up "traitor elimination committees" and "secret investigation squads"[60] and launched a terror campaign in which an estimated 5,000 "enemies of the revolution" were killed.[61] Dozens of nationalist, Trotskyite, Catholic, and sect leaders were assassinated between 1945 and 1947.[62] In the south, the Trotskyites were wiped out.[63] More than 200 Hoa Hao cadres, including founding leader Hunyh Phu So, were assassinated.[64] In the north, Viet Minh forces waged a brutal campaign against the nationalist VNQDD, which retained a degree of popular support.[65] Hundreds and possibly thousands of VNQDD cadres were arrested or executed, and by late 1946, most nationalists had fled to China or were in hiding.[66] By 1947, all rival nationalist groups had been vanquished in the north,[67] which allowed the communists to monopolize the resistance to French rule.[68]

The Reactive Sequence: Radicalism, War, and Revolutionary State-Building

Vietnam's revolutionary regime was born out of the 1954 Geneva Accords, which partitioned the country into North and South. The Viet Minh had expected to rule all of Vietnam,[69] but Russia's and China's acquiescence to partition forced it to accept "socialism in half-a-country."[70]

Unlike the stillborn 1945 regime, the Democratic Republic of Vietnam was born strong. The liberation war transformed the ICP—now the VCP—into a powerful mass organization, with 500,000 members and branches that reached into every corner of the country.[71]

The VCP was also highly cohesive. The party's founding generation, which included Ho, Giap, Pham Van Dong, Truong Chinh, Le Duan, Pham Hong, Nguyen Chi Tranh, Le Thanh Nghi, and Le Duc Tho, was a "tight-knit group" that was "hardened by the struggle against French colonialism."[72] The liberation war generated a "deep sense of party solidarity"[73] and a "formidable sense of discipline"[74] among party leaders.[75] Cohesion was reinforced by Ho Chi Minh, whose prestige allowed him to serve as a "kind of unique umpire," whose decisions were accepted by all factions.[76]

The new regime also emerged from the liberation war with a powerful coercive apparatus.[77] By the time the PAVN became North Vietnam's regular army in 1954, it was a prestigious and battle-tested institution with 350,000–400,000 experienced soldiers.[78]

The PAVN was also highly disciplined. It was commanded exclusively by Viet Minh guerrilla veterans who, having fought together for decades, shared a "common sense of psychological identification."[79] Moreover, the PAVNs extraordinary victory over the French endowed army commanders with considerable prestige, which brought "unquestioned loyalty" from the rank and file.[80]

Party and army were fused.[81] All the PAVN's founding generals had been party members since the 1930s.[82] Thus, they were "not military leaders so much as . . . uniformed party leaders."[83] Party and military roles were "blurred,"[84] as army commanders shuttled "back and forth between PAVN and civilian duties."[85] For example, Vo Nguyen Giap, Vietnam's top military commander, was a high-ranking Politburo member and served as deputy prime minister.[86]

The VCP reinforced partisan control by establishing a dual command structure in which party agents were integrated into the military hierarchy—down to the "lowest echelon units."[87] The Central Military Party Committee, directly controlled by the Politburo, oversaw military decision-making, effectively fusing civilian and military commands.[88] Political commissars—equipped with their own security forces—operated within each brigade, battalion, platoon, and squadron.[89] Party cells (*chi bo*) operated in intelligence agencies, armaments plants, and military courts.[90]

Finally, the VCP confronted few domestic rivals when it took power in 1954. The Viet Minh's "campaign of demolition" during the war had cleared the terrain of political challengers, so by the time communists returned to power, "all opposing organizations . . . were in ruins."[91]

Independent power centers were weak. The monarchy had been emasculated by the French and abolished by the Viet Minh in 1945.[92] French domination of the colonial economy had crowded out Vietnamese capitalists, leaving behind an underdeveloped bourgeoisie.[93] Many landowners fled during the war, which diminished their collective power.[94]

Religious institutions were also weak. Buddhist associations had little history of political activism and were "enfeebled" by the French.[95] The Catholic Church could have posed a more serious threat. Although it represented only 10 percent of the population, the Church was well endowed and had boomed under French rule.[96] Most Catholic leaders were stridently anticommunist,[97] and a few powerful bishops had established armed enclaves during the liberation war.[98] Nevertheless, the Church was weakened by the massive exodus of Catholics in the aftermath of partition. Some 600,000 Catholics—nearly half the Catholic population—fled to South Vietnam in 1954.[99] A majority of bishops and two-thirds of the country's priests abandoned the country.[100] The exodus cleared a "vast reservoir of potential anti-communist subversive elements" from North Vietnam.[101]

Overall, then, the balance of societal forces heavily favored the revolutionary elite. The destruction of independent power centers during the liberation war left the VCP in a near-hegemonic position. By 1954, there was "no organized force to give articulation to protests and demands" in North Vietnam.[102]

EARLY RADICALISM

The post-1954 government was radical. VCP leaders were ideologues;[103] they considered it a "self-appointed duty" to "overturn the old social order" and create a "new Vietnamese man."[104] The communist government launched a series of measures aimed at overturning the social order.[105] One was a far-reaching land reform, which began in late 1953.[106] The reform redistributed more than 800,000 hectares of land (out of about two million hectares under cultivation) to 2.1 million families, or more than half the peasant workforce.[107] The reform "leveled the structure of land ownership," leaving poor peasants and landlords with "nearly equivalent standards of living."[108] Landowners suffered a "catastrophic loss," effectively disappearing as a class.[109] Agriculture was eventually collectivized; by 1968, 90 percent of peasant families were in cooperatives.[110]

The VCP used land reform to provoke a "class war" in the countryside.[111] Land reform cadres, "armed with ideological zeal and determined to build the brave new world," were sent to more than 15,000 villages with a mandate to overturn centuries-old power structures.[112] Cadres classified families by their class position, ranging from "friends" to "enemies" and "traitors."[113] Those considered "exploiters" were purged from positions of authority and often imprisoned or killed.[114] At the same time, poor peasants were mobilized as *cot can* (backbone elements) and given positions of authority.[115] Landowners lost their land, power, and status; thousands of them were killed and tens of thousands imprisoned.[116] Land reform cadres also attacked local party structures, declaring them infiltrated by landlords.[117] The process descended into a chaotic witch hunt, in which anyone who was not a poor peasant—including party officials—could be denounced as a "landlord" and purged.[118] Local party structures were ripped apart.[119] Estimates of the number of deaths range as high as 50,000, although most scholars place the figure between 5,000 and 15,000.[120]

The brainchild of VCP general secretary Truong Chinh, a committed Maoist,[121] the land reform undermined regime legitimacy,[122] decimated the party organization (which lost nearly half its members),[123] and triggered massive peasant resistance. In late 1956, a large-scale peasant uprising broke out in Nghe An, a heavily Catholic province, where churches were stripped of their property, leaving many unable to function.[124] It took the army a month to restore order.[125] Between 1,000 and 5,000 peasants were killed, and thousands of others were deported or sent to reeducation camps.[126] The crisis led to Truong Chinh's removal as general secretary, and Ho was forced to publicly apologize and launch a rectification campaign.[127] Nevertheless, the land reform achieved the VCP's goal of destroying the landowning class and eliminating potential sources of opposition.[128]

The revolutionary government also radically restructured the economy. Inspired by China's Great Leap Forward, the VCP launched a radical socialist turn in 1958.[129] Private firms were expropriated and most peasants were forced from private farms onto cooperatives.[130] By 1965, private industry had been eliminated and the state controlled more than 90 percent of agriculture.[131] Although the rapid transition to socialism imposed heavy costs on both peasants and capitalists, neither group had the capacity to put up much resistance.

The communists also dramatically transformed cultural life. Most religious associations, lineage halls, and spirit shrines were disbanded or placed under state control.[132] State officials took over the officiating of weddings, funerals, and death anniversaries.[133] Many traditional religious practices disappeared from public view.[134] The regime also stripped the Catholic Church of most of its property, closed parochial schools, and expelled non-Vietnamese clergy.[135] The crackdown generated some resistance, but by 1954 neither the Buddhists nor the Catholic Church had the capacity to mobilize much opposition.[136]

The VCP's most radical initiative, however, was its pursuit of a revolutionary war in the south. The VCP had expected the regime in the south to collapse quickly.[137] When it did not, a faction led by Le Duan pushed the party to support revolutionary efforts to overthrow it.[138] Through 1957, North Vietnam was restrained by the Soviet Union, which was committed to peaceful coexistence with the West.[139] VCP leaders criticized the Soviet position,[140] however, and in January 1959, the party decided to launch a guerrilla war in the south, resulting in the creation of the NLF.[141] The initiative was extraordinarily bold, because it was opposed by the United States, the Soviet Union, and China.[142]

COUNTERREVOLUTIONARY REACTION:
THE AMERICAN WAR

The NLF's early success—by 1962, it controlled roughly half of South Vietnam—ushered in a mounting U.S. military presence.[143] The U.S.-led counterinsurgency made it clear that promoting revolution in the south could bring a costly war against the world's leading military power.[144] Nevertheless, Le Duan and his allies advanced a "go for broke" strategy aimed at creating a "bigger war."[145] They did so in the belief that Western capitalism and imperialism were in decline, and that Vietnam could accelerate that decline.[146] Several party leaders, including General Giap, resisted Le Duan's strategy in favor of a "North First" approach aimed at consolidating the revolution at home.[147] However, Le Duan pursued the "go for broke" strategy with "dogged persistence."[148]

The "go for broke" strategy provoked a massive U.S. intervention. The Americanization of the war—the number of U.S. troops increased from 16,000 in 1963 to more than 500,000 in 1967—blunted the NLF advance, resulting in a costly stalemate.[149] A massive U.S. aerial bombing campaign killed more than 50,000 people, forced an evacuation of major cities, and destroyed much of North Vietnam's industry, dramatically setting back development.[150]

Despite these costs, however, the VCP maintained the "go for broke" strategy. In January 1968, it launched the Tet Offensive, a "risky strategy with little chance of success."[151] The offensive, which aimed to seize major cities across South Vietnam, was a military failure.[152] North Vietnamese forces suffered 40,000 deaths, and the NLF was decimated.[153] Nevertheless, the offensive demoralized the United States, ultimately contributing to its decision to pull out of Vietnam.[154]

Following a third "go for broke" offensive (the Spring Offensive) in 1972, Vietnam and the United States negotiated the Paris Peace Accords.[155] South Vietnamese forces weakened dramatically following the U.S exit, shifting the tide dramatically in the communists' favor.[156] In early 1975, the South Vietnamese army disintegrated amid a final Spring Offensive,[157] and in April 1975, it dissolved, as soldiers dropped their weapons, shed their uniforms, and fled.[158] The South Vietnamese state collapsed, opening the door for a rapid communist-led reunification in 1976.[159]

PARTY- AND STATE-BUILDING

The American war was extraordinarily costly for Vietnam. More than a million North Vietnamese were killed,[160] and much of the country's industry and infrastructure was destroyed.[161]

Yet the war also strengthened the regime in important ways. For one, it reinforced elite cohesion. The party remained on "war footing" for more than three decades.[162] The external threat generated a siege mentality and a strong sense of discipline,[163] which compelled internal critics to close ranks rather than defect.[164] Thus, even though the VCP was "wracked with dissention" over the 1964 Sino-Soviet split (with some leaders seeking to abandon the USSR for China) and the war in the south (Le Duan's

"go for broke" strategy versus Giap's "North First" approach),[165] it suffered no schisms. Party leaders fell "quickly into line" once decisions were
made,[166] and those who lost out in power struggles, including powerful
figures like General Giap, remained in the leadership. Likewise, the death
of founding leader Ho Chi Minh in 1969 did not trigger internal conflict or
defection.[167] Unlike postcolonial Algeria (see below), then, the VCP leadership remained remarkably stable.[168] There were no schisms or high-
level defections between 1954 and 1975.[169] Indeed, save for two deaths,
the entire thirteen-member Politburo of 1960—and nearly the entire 1951
Central Committee—remained intact in 1975.[170]

The war also facilitated state-building.[171] When the VCP took power in
1954, the colonial state was disintegrating.[172] State capacity increased dramatically over the next two decades. Tax capacity increased significantly,[173]
as did the state's capacity to penetrate, mobilize, and control society. During the 1950s and 1960s, the VCP institutionalized mass conscription, carried out large-scale population transfers, developed a national system of
household registration, equipped the population with identification cards,
and implemented an effective rationing system.[174]

Three decades of war also gave rise to a powerful "garrison state."[175]
Facing the threat of U.S. invasion, the government armed and trained
village militias across the country, creating "combat villages."[176] The
PAVN grew from 250,000 troops in 1965 to 650,000 in 1975, as the entire
population of young men was mobilized for war.[177] By the late 1960s,
North Vietnam was spending a greater share of its GDP on the military
(25 percent) than any other state in the world.[178] Army effectiveness also
increased.[179] The PAVN emerged from the war "numerically formidable
and battle-hardened."[180]

The war also strengthened the internal security apparatus. The public security agency (Cong an) developed a vast network of agents and
informers that penetrated "every corner of society."[181] These included
neighborhood "block captains," factory-level "vigilance committees," and
"hardcore" citizens in rural hamlets who served as "eyes and ears" for the
government.[182]

The war also reinforced military cohesion and loyalty.[183] Decades of
existential threat generated a bunker mentality that muted dissent within
the army's ranks.[184] Thus, although Giap and other generals opposed
the strategy of ramping up the war in the south, they fell in line after Ho
announced the party's decision.[185] And although the mounting costs of
war fueled public discontent in the late 1960s and early 1970s, triggering
fears of possible military unrest,[186] there were no hints of rebellion in the

armed forces.[187] Indeed, studies carried out by the Rand Corporation during this period concluded that PAVN morale remained high.[188]

Finally, the war accelerated the destruction of independent power centers. In the north, as noted above, the associational landscape was already
barren before the war. In South Vietnam, where pluralism was initially
greater, two developments undermined independent power centers. First,
the Ngo Dinh Diem government attacked and weakened the sects, the
most powerful anticommunist organizations in the south.[189] Second, the
war weakened South Vietnam's rural elite. Land reform—first by Diem
and later by NLF guerrillas—drove most large landowners out of the country,[190] and NLF assassinations of as many as 20,000 local officials wiped
out an entire class of village notables.[191] By the time the VCP gained control of South Vietnam, then, centers of societal opposition were weak.[192]

The Party-State Complex

By unification in 1976, then, three decades of war had produced the regime
legacies predicted by our theory: a powerful and cohesive party-state complex and the destruction of independent centers of societal power.

First, unified Vietnam was governed by a strong ruling party. The VCP
emerged from the war with a powerful grassroots organization. Party
membership tripled, from 500,000 in 1954 to more than 1.5 million in
1976.[193] The number of party cells also tripled, and by the 1980s the VCP
had 40,000 branches operating in every corner of the country.[194] The
party was "ubiquitous, its cadres and members found everywhere."[195]

The VCP was also cohesive. Its leadership was still dominated by the
generation of revolutionaries who created the party in the 1930s and led
the liberation struggle against France. This founding generation was characterized by a high degree of cohesion.[196] One scholar described it as a
"cult of solidarity."[197] The wars against France and the United States gave
rise to an enduring "siege mentality,"[198] which discouraged defection even
in the face of intense power struggles and policy disagreements.[199]

Second, the regime had a powerful coercive apparatus. Vietnam
emerged from the revolutionary wars with a "military machine . . . of mon-
strous size."[200] With more than a million regular soldiers and another 1.6
million paramilitary and regional force troops,[201] the Vietnamese armed
forces were the third largest in the world in the 1980s.[202]

The regime also boasted a vast internal security apparatus. Vietnam
became a police state.[203] The Cong an emerged from the war as a highly
effective instrument of control, with a vast capacity for low-intensity

coercion.[204] With as many as one million agents, many of whom had extensive wartime experience,[205] the security services penetrated Vietnam "down to the smallest alley."[206] Informants operated in workplaces, classrooms, and neighborhoods.[207] Every neighborhood was overseen by a state or party "warden," who met regularly with each family.[208] Agents kept tabs on every active dissident in the country, monitoring mail, phones, and later email.[209]

The security forces were remarkably cohesive. The PAVN was led by revolutionary veterans "whose loyalty was never suspect."[210] Nearly all top military officers were lifelong party cadres and members of the party's Central Committee.[211] This fusion of party and army helped to coup-proof the regime. Because military commanders were proven revolutionaries and active party leaders, the party "had little need to worry about the loyalties of the military leadership."[212]

Third, the VCP faced a barren associational landscape after 1975. The landowning class was extinct in the north and nearly so in the south.[213] Industrial and commercial interests in the south were weakened by emigration and quickly succumbed to nationalization.[214] Old regime elements attempted armed resistance but failed to establish a foothold and were quickly reduced to the status of "émigré opposition," seeking to orchestrate uprisings from abroad.[215] Religious organizations were also weak.[216] Buddhist organizations, which had long been politically feeble, were easily subordinated.[217] The Catholic Church remained staunchly anticommunist,[218] but due to Catholicism's minority status, it could not serve as a mobilizing structure for a broad opposition movement.[219] Indeed, the Church put up little resistance after unification, limiting itself to spiritual activities.[220] The sects, which had been weakened by the Diem government, were quickly shackled.[221]

In the aftermath of unification, then, there existed few autonomous organizations or institutions that could serve as bases for opposition mobilization.[222] As a result, Vietnamese society was marked by "remarkable placidity" for decades.[223]

Regime Durability, 1975–2020

The Vietnamese regime proved extraordinarily durable after 1975. Despite a series of crises and periods of widespread public discontent, there were virtually no ruling party defections and no military rebellions. Moreover, despite a loosening of totalitarian controls and more than three decades of economic opening, persistent state-society power asymmetries limited anti-regime mobilization, confining opposition groups primarily to the internet.

THE POSTUNIFICATION CRISIS

Vietnam fell into severe economic crisis soon after unification. Overoptimistic after its military victory in 1975, the VCP initiated a radical transformation in the south.[224] For example, it launched an ambitious effort to transform South Vietnamese culture and create a "new man."[225] The school system was shut down until teachers could be reeducated, and "cultural army units" were set up in each neighborhood to wipe out "neocolonial culture."[226] At least 300,000 people were sent to reeducation camps, and hundreds of thousands of others were relocated or arrested.[227]

The VCP also attempted a rapid transition to socialism.[228] In 1978, the government abolished private commerce, nationalized all industry, and began to force peasants into cooperatives.[229] Between 30,000 and 50,000 businesses—many of them Chinese owned—were confiscated.[230] The government also attempted to relocate more than a million southerners to New Economic Zones, mostly in the countryside, where they would work in state enterprises and cooperatives.[231] The results were disastrous. Hundreds of thousands of ethnic Chinese fled the country, badly disrupting the economy.[232] The New Economic Zones and the agricultural cooperatives were failures.[233] Production collapsed, plunging Vietnam into an unprecedented economic crisis.[234] Public discontent soared, throwing the regime's survival into question.[235]

The crisis was exacerbated by renewed military conflict. Vietnam plunged back into war soon after reunification. Facing mounting aggression by the Chinese-backed Khmer Rouge, Vietnam sent 180,000 into Cambodia in December 1978, beginning an eleven-year occupation.[236] Described by one scholar as "Hanoi's Vietnam,"[237] the war took 25,000–50,000 Vietnamese lives and further undermined the country's crisis-ridden economy.[238]

The invasion of Cambodia triggered a brief war with China. Sino-Vietnamese relations had deteriorated rapidly after 1975, as China, concerned about the power of a unified Vietnam, withdrew its long-standing support, pushing Vietnam firmly into the Soviet orbit.[239] Seeking to "teach Vietnam a lesson" after the Cambodia invasion,[240] China sent 100,000 troops across the border in February 1979, advancing forty miles into Vietnam (and carrying out a massive bombing raid) before pulling back.[241] Although the PAVN successfully resisted the incursion, Vietnam suffered as many as 50,000 casualties and widespread destruction along the border.[242]

The crises of the late 1970s and early 1980s posed a serious threat to the VCP.[243] Indeed, both the U.S. and Chinese governments expected the regime to collapse.[244] It did not. Although this outcome can be explained, in part, by massive Soviet assistance,[245] three revolutionary legacies of revolution were arguably critical to regime survival. First, party leaders remained united.[246] The regime suffered only one significant defection: pro-China Politburo member Hoang Van Hoan, who was removed from the leadership and later fled to China.[247] Second, military loyalty and discipline remained intact.[248] Despite considerable rank-and-file hardship, low pay, and plummeting morale in Cambodia, the PAVN experienced virtually no open dissent or insubordination in the late 1970s and early 1980s.[249] Third, widespread public discontent failed to generate organized opposition.[250] Although there were small outbreaks of religious and ethnic protest in the south, they never posed a serious threat to the regime.[251]

THE CRISIS OF COMMUNISM AND THE
PASSING OF THE FOUNDING GENERATION

The Vietnamese regime confronted three fundamental challenges during the 1980s and early 1990s. One was generational. The death of longtime VCP general secretary Le Duan (in 1986) and Prime Minister Pham Hong (in 1988) marked the demise of the legendary "Dien Bien Phu generation," which had led the struggle against France and founded the revolutionary regime.[252]

The global collapse of communism posed another challenge. The demise of the Soviet Union, which provided more than a billion dollars a year in military and economic assistance (about 40 percent of the national budget) during the early 1980s, eliminated a vital source of external support.[253]

The Soviet withdrawal and a mounting economic crisis convinced VCP leaders to abandon socialism for a market economy.[254] Following a period of limited reform in the early 1980s, new party leader Nguyen Van Linh launched a far-reaching economic reform program (Doi Moi) in 1986. Central planning was eliminated, prices were freed, small-scale private enterprise and individual landholdings were permitted, and the economy was opened to foreign investment.[255] By 1989, Vietnam could be described as a market economy.[256]

Finally, the wave of democratization in Eastern Europe generated pressure for political reform. The regime had begun to liberalize in 1986, releasing many political prisoners, loosening media restrictions (permitting the spread of "unlicensed" newspapers);[257] relaxing controls on religion, especially Buddhist spiritual activities;[258] and permitting independent associations as long as they steered clear of politics and did not criticize the government.[259] Beginning in 1989, however, the party faced unprecedented calls for democratization. Most prominently, Politburo member Tran Xuan Bach, a rising star who was viewed as a possible future party leader, praised the process of democratization in Eastern Europe and called for similar reforms in Vietnam.[260] Bui Tin, a war hero and deputy editor of the party newspaper, also called for democratic reform.[261]

Unwilling to abandon single-party rule, VCP leaders closed ranks in defense of the status quo. Tran Xuan Bach was removed from the Politburo, Bui Tin was expelled from the party and exiled, prominent democracy advocates were arrested, and the government cracked down on emerging independent media.[262]

By any measure, the VCP succeeded in navigating the transformations of the 1980s and 1990s. The party suffered no schisms or defections, and although market reforms reportedly triggered opposition among army officials,[263] there were no military rebellions.[264] Finally, unlike Eastern Europe and even China, the VCP faced no significant pro-democracy mobilization in the 1980s and 1990s.[265] The few dissident organizations that emerged, such as the Club of Former Resistance Fighters, a group of southern revolutionary veterans that tepidly pushed for political reform in the late 1980s, were easily silenced.[266] Ultimately, then, the Third Wave of democratization hit Vietnam "without much force."[267]

The regime survived for several reasons. First, the effects of generational change were mitigated by the fact that "second generation" leaders were *also* revolutionary war veterans, nearly all of whom had played prominent roles in the American war.[268] A second factor contributing to regime stability was persistence of a vast state-society power asymmetry. The regime maintained an extensive apparatus with a high capacity for low-intensity coercion.[269] Cong an agents continued to operate in every corner of the country, tracking, harassing, blacklisting, and occasionally arresting dissidents, which helped the government nip emerging protest movements in the bud.[270] At the same time, society's capacity to mobilize remained low. Although there is evidence of broad public discontent in the 1980s,[271] regime opponents lacked mobilizational structures.[272] Unlike in Third Wave democratizers such as South Korea and Taiwan, no student protest movement or independent labor movement emerged, which limited dissidents' capacity to broaden their support bases.[273]

Opposition was thus confined to "isolated pockets" and never threatened the regime.[274]

A third reason why the regime survived was economic growth. Vietnam's economy grew at an annual rate of 7 percent between 1985 and 1995.[275] During the critical 1991–1995 period, when the Soviet Union collapsed and many of its client states fell into crisis, the economy expanded 8 percent a year.[276] Rapid economic growth helped to dampen public discontent and generated resources that could be used to buy off potential regime critics.

THE REVOLUTIONARY REGIME IN
THE TWENTY-FIRST CENTURY

The Vietnamese regime underwent a far-reaching transformation in the early twenty-first century. Beginning in the late 1990s, the VCP's second-generation leadership was replaced by younger, more technocratic figures who had not played a leading role in the revolutionary wars.[277] By 2011, the country's leadership "troika"—Party General Secretary Nguyen Phu Trong, President Truong Tan Sang, and Prime Minister Nguyen Tan Dung—were all too young to have fought in the liberation war or to have held leadership positions in the American war.[278] Moreover, the middle ranks of the party and government were increasingly filled with Western-trained cadres who were born after the war.[279] Likewise, in the army, revolutionary veterans were replaced by younger Vietnamese who lacked the same commitment to the party and the revolution.[280] The final passing of the revolutionary generation was marked by the death of General Giap, aged 101, in 2013.

By the early twenty-first century, then, VCP leaders were no longer bound together by revolutionary struggle or an existential military threat.[281] Instead, the VCP evolved into a more traditional ruling party machine, bound together by the spoils of office.[282] Rent seeking replaced a siege mentality as the primary source of cohesion.[283] This transformation left the regime more vulnerable to elite schisms and likely weakened its capacity for high-intensity coercion.

Nevertheless, the regime remained stable. Between 2012 and 2015, the party was ridden with factional conflict between Prime Minister Nguyen Tan Dung and a more conservative faction led by VCP general secretary Nguyen Phu Trong, which culminated in Dung's removal from power.[284] Although several of Dung's allies lost their cabinet positions, his defeat did not trigger any ruling party defections.[285]

Regime opposition remained weak. Notwithstanding a proliferation of civil society organizations,[286] pro-democracy consistently failed to take hold. In 2006, a group of 118 dissidents—known as Bloc 8406—launched a campaign for civil liberties and democratic elections.[287] By late 2006, the movement had 2,000 supporters and, modeling itself on Burma's opposition, worked with Buddhist groups to create the Alliance for Democracy and Human Rights.[288] In 2007, however, the government cracked down, arresting dozens of Bloc 8406 members and intimidating others though home raids, firings, and blacklisting.[289] Bloc 8406 was decimated and the Alliance for Democracy and Human Rights was "stillborn."[290]

Other pro-democracy initiatives emerged in the 2010s, as rapidly expanding internet access opened new avenues for opposition activity.[291] In 2013, a group of prominent ex-party officials, veterans, and intellectuals known as Group 72 organized an online petition—signed by 15,000 people—calling for the adoption of a Western-style constitution.[292] However, pro-democracy activities were "confined to the digital space."[293] Party leaders ignored the petition, and over the next few years, dozens of bloggers were arrested, deported, or subjected to attacks by government-sponsored thugs.[294]

The regime's continued stability was rooted, in part, in economic growth. Vietnam's GDP grew at an average annual rate of nearly 7 percent between 2000 and 2018.[295] The poverty rate, which had been 75 percent in the mid-1980s, fell to just 6 percent in 2014.[296] As democratization in South Korea and Taiwan made clear, however, economic growth is no guarantee of regime survival. In Vietnam, persistent state-society power asymmetries continued to favor regime stability.[297] Despite its upper-middle-income status, Vietnam had a weaker civil society than Burundi, Gambia, Tajikistan, and Yemen in the early twenty-first century.[298] In the face of persistent low-intensity coercion,[299] dissident groups remained small, "compartmentalized,"[300] and mostly confined to the internet,[301] leaving regime opponents without the "unity, organization, or strength to challenge the party-state."[302]

In sum, Vietnam's postcolonial regime was revolutionary. The VCP ascended to power via armed struggle, built its own army, and launched a series of radical initiatives—including support for revolution in South Vietnam—that plunged it into a costly war with the United States. Three decades of war gave rise to a powerful and cohesive party-state complex and destroyed all independent centers of social, economic, and cultural power. The result was a regime that has endured for nearly seventy years, despite a traumatic unification, the passing of the founding generation, and the global crisis of communism.

ALGERIA

At first glance, the Algerian case parallels that of Vietnam. Like the Viet Minh, the FLN fought a bloody eight-year war against French rule and, upon seizing power, established an authoritarian regime that endured for decades. However, the Algerian regime was never as consolidated as its Vietnamese counterpart. It experienced debilitating internal conflict and societal opposition, and its survival likely hinged on conditions—such as oil—that were unrelated to its revolutionary origins. This diverging regime trajectory, we argue, was rooted in early accommodation. Because FLN policies did not threaten powerful domestic or international interests, they generated little counterrevolutionary reaction. In the absence of an existential military threat, the Algerian regime never developed the cohesion or coercive capacity observed in Vietnam, nor did it wipe out independent power centers. As a result, state-society power asymmetries were less pronounced, and the regime eventually confronted a massive Islamist opposition movement. Although a cohesive army managed to thwart the challenge, the regime remained more vulnerable—and more dependent on favorable economic and geopolitical conditions—than in Vietnam.

The Revolutionary Seizure of Power

Antecedent conditions for durable authoritarianism in Algeria were mixed. On the one hand, the FLN inherited a weak state. Precolonial Algeria lacked a centralized state,[303] and its traditional elites and institutions were largely wiped out by French rule.[304] The colonial state, which was built to serve European settlers,[305] largely collapsed at independence. On the other hand, Algeria possessed mineral resources. Oil and gas exports accounted for nearly half of Algeria's GDP in the 1980s.[306] Although the oil sector was still underdeveloped at independence,[307] and although even peak mineral rents were probably not sufficient to ensure regime stability,[308] oil provided Algerian governments with resources—to co-opt rivals and finance the coercive apparatus—that were not available to ruling elites in Vietnam and Ghana.

Like Vietnam, Algeria is a case of a successful armed liberation movement against French rule. The 1954–1962 anticolonial struggle, which was fiercely resisted by France, was one of the longest and bloodiest in history.[309] Estimates of the number of Algerians killed during the war range from 250,000 to more than a million.[310]

French resistance to independence was rooted in Algeria's status as a settler colony. Nearly a million Europeans lived in the colony in 1954, occupying nearly three million hectares of land.[311] French governments thus maintained a strong stake in the colony, which made the independence struggle far more difficult.

Algeria's nationalist movement emerged in the 1930s but took off after 1945, when brutal French repression convinced many activists that armed struggle was the only viable path to independence.[312] In the late 1940s, a group of young radical nationalists—including Ahmed Ben Bella—abandoned the nonviolent anticolonial movement and founded what would become the FLN.[313]

The FLN launched an armed insurgency in late 1954. It grew rapidly, earning broad support among the Muslim population.[314] Most rival organizations, including the Communist Party, the liberal Democratic Union of the Algerian Manifesto, and the Association of Algerian Muslim Ulama, joined the FLN-led struggle.[315] By late 1956, the FLN had more than 20,000 fighters and had developed a mass organization with cells operating across Algeria.[316] Its armed wing, the National Liberation Army (ALN), was organized into six local military zones, or *wilayas*, each led by one of the FLN's founding chiefs.[317] FLN guerrilla activity peaked in 1956–1957, when the organization launched a large-scale urban terror campaign.[318]

The FLN's trajectory diverged markedly from that of the Viet Minh, however. For one, the movement was far less cohesive.[319] Rather than a Leninist party with a coherent ideology, the FLN was a "loose-jointed" collection of Marxists, nationalists, liberals, and religious conservatives whose leaders never developed a shared ideology beyond nationalism.[320] Perhaps most importantly, whereas the Viet Minh fused its political and military leaderships, the contingencies of Algeria's liberation war divided the movement into an "external delegation," led by Ahmed Ben Bella, which spent most of its time abroad, and the *wilaya* leaders fighting in Algeria.[321] The lines of communication between the external leaders and the *wilayas* were weak,[322] and they largely disintegrated after October 1956, when Ben Bella and other external leaders were arrested in Europe and imprisoned for the rest of the war. Efforts to rebuild a unified civil-military command were undercut by French repression.[323] The French launched a massive counterinsurgency in 1956, raising their troop presence from 50,000 (in 1954) to nearly half a million and unleashing a massive wave of killing, arrests, and forced relocation.[324] The crackdown culminated in the 1957 Battle of Algiers, which French forces won overwhelmingly.[325]

The French counterinsurgency devastated the FLN. The movement's grassroots organization was destroyed and its underground cell network "dismantled so completely that Algiers became free of terrorism for at least two years."[326] Many top FLN leaders were either killed or forced to flee Algeria.[327] By 1958, all top FLN leaders were outside the country.[328] With the FLN leadership decimated, power in the movement fell to the ALN and the *wilaya* fighters.[329] Although exiled FLN leaders created the Provisional Government of the Algerian Republic (GPRA), they exercised little influence on the ground.[330] By the late 1950s, real power lay in the hands of the ALN and its commander, Houari Boumedienne.[331]

France very nearly won the war. In late 1957, French forces completed a 200-mile electric fence between Algeria and Tunisia, called the Morice Line, which prevented ALN forces from operating across the border.[332] ALN commanders and the vast bulk (35,000–40,000) of their troops were trapped in Tunisia for the remainder of the war, stranding about 15,000 poorly equipped *wilaya* fighters in Algeria.[333] The *wilayas* were decimated by French forces,[334] ending any hope of a guerrilla victory.[335]

If France won the military battles, however, it lost the political and diplomatic ones.[336] Reports of French brutality eroded support for the war at home and, crucially, undermined France's international standing.[337] By 1957, France was clearly "losing the diplomatic argument."[338] FLN leaders thus focused on "internationalizing" the conflict.[339] In December 1960, the UN General Assembly voted to recognize Algeria's right to independence.[340] In March 1962, facing mounting domestic and external pressure, French president Charles de Gaulle signed the Evian Accords, under which Algeria would gain independence in July 1962 in exchange for assurances of a continued French economic and military presence and protection for European settlers.[341] Despite losing the war, the FLN had achieved a "diplomatic revolution."[342]

The Evian Accords set the stage for a chaotic seizure of power. The transition effectively began in late 1961, when the Secret Army Organization (OAS), a terrorist body created by European settlers, launched a violent campaign aimed at derailing independence and establishing a South Africa–like settler state.[343] In what was essentially a preemptive counterrevolutionary war, the OAS's "scorched earth" campaign included attacks on schools, public buildings, factories, and oil facilities; the assassination of French officials; and a "truly mind-boggling" number of killings of Algerian Muslims.[344] Although French authorities put down the rebellion by spring 1962, the OAS did considerable damage:

1,000 Europeans and an even larger number of Muslim Algerians were massacred.[345]

The OAS's counterrevolutionary campaign accelerated another important development: the exodus of the settler population. Spooked by the 1961–1962 violence, Europeans fled Algeria en masse.[346] By late 1962, more than 800,000 Europeans—nearly 90 percent of the settler population—had left the country.[347] Because the settlers constituted the bulk of the capitalist class, including nearly all the leading industrialists and agricultural producers, the Algerian economy collapsed.[348] And because Europeans made up 90–95 percent of public administrators, their departure decimated the colonial state.[349] Public order evaporated, and tax collection and public service delivery virtually ceased.[350] The FLN would thus have to rebuild the state "virtually from scratch."[351]

Finally, whereas the Vietnamese Communists ascended to power in 1954 with a cohesive party-army complex, the FLN took power in a state of fragmentation and chaos.[352] The Provisional Government, led by Benyoussef Benkhedda, had negotiated the Evian Accords and expected to head the transition. However, the Tunisia-based ALN and Ben Bella's external delegation—recently released from prison—rejected both the pact and the Provisional Government's authority.[353] The *wilaya* leaders in Algeria, who were cut off from both sides, became local warlord-like figures.[354]

At independence, then, the liberation movement was fragmented into four distinct contenders for power: the Provisional Government, the FLN external delegation, the ALN, and the *wilayas*.[355] The Provisional Government claimed to be the legitimate government.[356] However, Ben Bella created a parallel Politburo backed by the powerful ALN, which marched on Algiers from the Tunisian border.[357] Ultimately, the ALN imposed the Ben Bella–led Politburo as the country's leadership.[358] When some of the *wilayas* refused to accept the new leadership, the ALN moved against them, plunging the country into a two-week civil war.[359] The *wilaya* fighters were no match for the 130,000-strong army, and by September 1962, the ALN had established control over the national territory, allowing Ben Bella, their handpicked ally, to become Algeria's founding leader.[360] In 1963, Ben Bella oversaw the promulgation of a new constitution enshrining the FLN as the only legal party, after which he was elected president.

The Army-Party Complex

Algeria's postcolonial regime differed markedly from those in both Ghana and Vietnam. Like Vietnam, the regime rested on the foundation of an army that was founded by the revolutionary elite and was deeply committed to the revolutionary project. Yet, whereas Vietnam's party-state was dominated by the VCP, Algeria's was dominated by the army.

The ruling party was strikingly weak.[361] With its organization decimated by French repression, the FLN "barely existed" at independence.[362] The FLN also lacked cohesion.[363] The physical separation of FLN elites during the war—with the external delegation imprisoned in Europe, the Provisional Government in exile, army commanders stuck in Tunisia, and the orphaned *wilayas* in Algeria—gave rise to a "segmented" movement with no common authority, organizational structure, or decision-making rules.[364] Unlike the Vietnamese Communists, then, FLN leaders shared no common wartime experience, identity, or ideology. The party also lacked a single leader—like Ho or Mao—whose authority spanned the entire movement. Thus, although the FLN had been "loosely unified" during the liberation war,[365] it entered independence with multiple and competing leaderships.[366]

The liberation army—renamed the People's National Army (ANP) after independence—was considerably stronger. Unlike in Ghana (see below), the new army was an indigenous institution that was forged by guerrilla leaders amid violent struggle. Founded as a 2,500-man guerrilla army in 1954, the ALN evolved into a disciplined force with 20,000 soldiers by 1956.[367] Although the Morice Line forced the ALN to the sidelines beginning in 1957, army chief Houari Boumedienne built it into a professionalized army, with an "iron discipline" enforced by "shadowy secret police."[368]

The ANP's guerrilla origins fostered a high level of cohesion and discipline.[369] Boumedienne and other ANP commanders all fought in the liberation war in Algeria between 1954 and 1957.[370] Shared revolutionary origins generated a "strong esprit de corps" and "almost Spartan" discipline.[371] They also endowed ANP commanders with considerable authority.[372] This cohesion generated a capacity for high-intensity coercion that would endure into the twenty-first century.[373]

The army-party complex that emerged in Algeria was, therefore, quite distinct from other revolutionary cases. The physical separation of ALN, *wilaya*, and civilian FLN leaders during the war prevented the kind of party-army fusion observed in Vietnam. Although army commanders developed a strong revolutionary identity, most of them were not active in—or deeply committed to—the party. Army officers were nominal FLN members, but their partisan ties were superficial. In practice, the FLN's presence in the armed forces was minimal.

Unlike most revolutionary regimes, moreover, the army was the dominant partner in Algeria.[374] Thus, whereas the Vietnamese army was tightly controlled by the VCP, in Algeria the army held the reins of power.[375]

Army commanders acted as "puppet masters";[376] they handpicked civilian governments and "more or less directed" them from behind the scenes.[377] Thus, although the FLN was formally constructed as a Leninist-style vanguard party, in reality it was a "rearguard party" whose responsibilities were largely ceremonial.[378]

Notwithstanding these differences, the Algerian regime shared some important characteristics with its Vietnamese counterpart. Like Vietnam's liberation war, Algeria's gave rise to a cohesive clique, or "revolutionary family."[379] Participation in the liberation struggle became an "essential pre-requisite to assuming the highest offices of state"; indeed every president and army chief (through 2019) was a revolutionary veteran.[380] The difference was that in Algeria, the army, not the party, was the principal representative of the revolutionary family.

The FLN did not confront significant rivals or independent power centers in 1962. Most rival political organizations joined the FLN during the liberation war.[381] The only remaining rival nationalist organization, the Algerian National Movement (MNA), was destroyed by FLN terror.[382] The FLN slaughtered hundreds of MNA cadres between 1955 and 1957,[383] using the "dramatic exigencies of the national liberation struggle" to justify its violence.[384]

Independent power centers were also weak. The most powerful landowners and capitalists were European settlers, nearly all of whom fled the country.[385] Both the indigenous landowning class and the local bourgeoisie were miniscule.[386] The commanding heights of the economy—including the oil sector—were foreign owned.

Two cultural communities were politically marginal in the early 1960s but would eventually take on greater importance. One was the Berbers, a non-Arab, secular-leaning, and broadly Francophile minority (about 20 percent of the population) that was concentrated in Kabylia.[387] The other community, Islam, was larger and potentially more influential. Islamist groups such as the Association of Algerian Muslim Ulama played only a secondary role in the independence struggle.[388] Most ulama leaders supported the postcolonial government, although their political influence was limited.[389]

THE REVOLUTIONARY REACTIVE SEQUENCE: ACCOMMODATION AND LIMITED REACTION

The FLN government was less radical than most of the revolutionary governments examined in this book. Although the Ben Bella government undertook some radical domestic and foreign initiatives, many of these initiatives did not threaten powerful actors. Moreover, in key areas, such as relations with France, the government adopted accommodationist positions. As a result, the FLN government did not confront a significant counterrevolutionary reaction.

THE FLN GOVERNMENT: "EASY" RADICALISM

The FLN was far less radical than the Vietnamese Communists. A broad front that included Marxists, liberals, and religious conservatives, it never developed a coherent program beyond nationalism.[390] Ben Bella and his allies, who gained control of the party in 1962, represented the party's radical wing.[391] A "romantic revolutionary" who surrounded himself with Marxist advisers, Ben Bella sought to replicate the Cuban model.[392] He initially rejected the Evian Accords and declared his intention to drive European settlers out.[393] The FLN's 1962 Tripoli program, which was written by Ben Bella's allies, included commitments to land reform, widespread nationalization, and a planned economy.[394] As president, Ben Bella declared Algeria "socialist" and aspired to transform it into a revolutionary "pilot state" that other governments could replicate.[395]

The revolutionary government oversaw a far-reaching redistribution of property and wealth. This redistribution was facilitated by the exodus of European settlers, who constituted the bulk of Algeria's large property owners before 1962.[396] In the wake of the settlers' departure, more than a million hectares of abandoned land and about 1,000 abandoned businesses were spontaneously occupied by Algerians.[397] Many farms and factories were occupied by their workers.[398] In March 1963, the government formalized the de facto property transfer with a decree expropriating 16,000 farms covering 800,000 hectares, as well as 200,000 private homes, 450 private industrial firms, and hundreds of commercial enterprises— nearly all of which had been European owned.[399] Referring to the settlers, Ben Bella declared, "Out with them, and good riddance. . . . If that's contrary to the Evian Accords, I don't give two hoots."[400] Later that year, all remaining French firms were nationalized.[401] This massive transfer of property, which prevented the settlers' return and removed much of the economy from the private sector, may have been the most revolutionary feature of the Algerian revolution.[402]

Equally ambitious—at least in principle—was the March 1963 decree creating a system of worker control of newly expropriated farms and enterprises (autogestion).[403] Borrowing from socialist Yugoslavia, the Ben Bella government created a "self-management" sector that encompassed

1,000 industrial and commercial enterprises and between 1.2 million and 1.5 million hectares of farmland, or about 13 percent of Algeria's cultivable land.[404] Enterprises in this sector would be run by elected workers' councils, albeit with state oversight.[405] The system was designed by Ben Bella's leftist advisers, many of whom were committed to building socialism.[406] Autogestion became the centerpiece of Ben Bella's domestic program, positioning Algeria as a "laboratory of Third World socialism."[407]

Notwithstanding Ben Bella's socialist discourse, however, the Algerian reforms were far less radical than those in Cuba or Vietnam. Expropriations were limited mainly to farms and businesses that had been abandoned by fleeing settlers—and thus did not threaten many powerful interests.[408] Beyond these "easy" expropriations, Ben Bella, who was wary of attacking Algerian landowners, undertook little land reform.[409] Although Ben Bella's successor, Boumedienne, launched a land reform in the 1970s, seeking to eliminate large landholdings and reorganize rural society into cooperatives and "socialist villages,"[410] most of the redistributed land was state owned,[411] and many landowners successfully lobbied state officials to keep their properties.[412] Ultimately, only about 10 percent of private land was expropriated, and most indigenous landowners were untouched.[413] The autogestion system also proved less radical in practice, as self-management committees quickly fell under the control of the Ministry of National Economy.[414]

The FLN's foreign policy was also more bark than bite. On the one hand, the Ben Bella government adopted a radical policy of anti-imperialism and Third Worldism.[415] Ben Bella sought to transform Algeria into a "Mecca of revolution,"[416] supporting armed liberation movements across Africa.[417] Algiers became an "entrepôt of subversion," hosting guerrillas from all over the world.[418] The Ben Bella government supported radical opposition groups in neighboring Morocco and Tunisia,[419] and it antagonized the United States by providing asylum for Black Panthers and publicly embracing the Cuban Revolution.[420]

Ultimately, however, the FLN's foreign policy stopped short of provoking a serious conflict with the West.[421] Because the United States was a vital source of food aid and an important market for oil exports,[422] the Ben Bella government often "put pragmatism before revolutionary principles" in dealing with the Americans.[423] Indeed, behind the scenes, Ben Bella was often "decidedly conciliatory" toward the United States.[424] During the 1962 Cuban missile crisis, for example, he worked with the John F. Kennedy administration to prevent the Soviets from obtaining an African refueling stop for an air bridge to Cuba—even as Algeria's state media condemned the U.S. blockade.[425]

The FLN government was even more accommodationist toward France. Algeria and France maintained cooperative relations after 1962.[426] France was Algeria's leading commercial partner in the 1960s, accounting for 70 percent of its trade and most of its foreign investment, as well as massive—and critical—economic assistance.[427] Many French nationals continued to work in the postcolonial state.[428] Although the nationalization of French properties generated occasional conflict,[429] the FLN was usually willing to make concessions in order to sustain French cooperation.[430] For example, after France reduced aid in the wake of the 1963 nationalizations, Ben Bella worked to salvage bilateral relations by ensuring continued French access to hydrocarbon resources and turning a blind eye to French nuclear tests in the desert.[431]

In sum, although the FLN government oversaw a massive transfer of property and supported liberation movements abroad, it was far more accommodationist than the VCP. Ben Bella maintained a cooperative relationship with France, and property redistribution rarely threatened powerful interests. When policies generated resistance, as in the case of land reform, the government often backed off, avoiding the violence that accompanied land reform in Vietnam. For these reasons, Algeria has been described as a "revolution of form without substance."[432]

A LIMITED COUNTERREVOLUTIONARY REACTION

A striking feature of the Algerian case is the near absence of a counterrevolutionary reaction. This outcome was due, in part, to the fact that the revolution's principal victims, European settlers, fled en masse before the FLN took power. Although the OAS's 1961–1962 terrorist campaign may be understood as a preemptive counterrevolutionary reaction, it paradoxically triggered a European exodus that wiped out the settler community. Because the bulk of the FLN's redistribution involved the transfer of abandoned properties, these measures triggered little reaction. Likewise, because the government was reluctant to forcibly expropriate indigenous landowners,[433] the 1971 land reform generated "few upheavals."[434]

The FLN also faced little resistance on the international front. Although Ben Bella's support for revolutionary movements abroad generated consternation in the West, Western governments made no serious effort to overthrow the regime.[435] As a result, the FLN faced no significant military threat.[436] Even at the height of Algerian foreign policy radicalism in 1963, U.S. trade and food assistance continued and bilateral relations were described as "normal if not overly cordial."[437]

Likewise, the FLN government faced no serious threat from France. Ben Bella's decision to maintain French advisers, military bases, and trade and investment ties facilitated a cooperative bilateral relationship.[438] Even when the FLN government threatened French interests, French governments responded with "patience and moderation."[439] Cooperation never broke down, and at no point did Algeria face a threat of French aggression.[440]

Algeria's relationship with France thus contrasts sharply with U.S.-Cuban relations during the 1960s (chapter 6). Whereas U.S. governments responded to the Castro government's radical nationalism with hostility, generating an enduring existential threat, France's mild response to Ben Bella's nationalism, together with Ben Bella's pragmatic efforts to maintain bilateral cooperation, eliminated any potential external threat. Indeed, the Algerian regime grew highly dependent on France, which imposed constraints on its behavior.[441] As Arslan Humbaraci put it, close ties to France "opened up various possibilities for Algeria. . . . The one thing it could not lead to [was] a socialist revolution."[442]

Algerian radicalism may have contributed to an October 1963 border war with Morocco.[443] The Moroccan monarchy feared revolutionary diffusion from Algeria, and the FLN supported Morocco's leftist opposition.[444] However, the Moroccan invasion was driven primarily by a long-standing territorial dispute.[445] Moreover, Ben Bella resisted calls from leftist advisers to widen the war into an "anti-imperialist" war for the "greater Maghrib," which might have triggered external intervention.[446] Indeed, when Cuba sent troops as a gesture of revolutionary solidarity, Ben Bella, under pressure from Egypt, backed off and negotiated a cease-fire.[447] Again, then, when radicalism threatened violent conflict, the FLN government chose accommodation.

The absence of counterrevolution had important regime consequences. Crucially, it meant that the ruling elite never developed the level of cohesion seen in Vietnam and other revolutionary regimes. The FLN had been held together by the "imperatives of war" between 1954 and 1962,[448] but in the absence of a counterrevolutionary threat, elite cohesion "evaporated."[449] Whereas ruling parties in Vietnam, China, Russia, and elsewhere closed ranks amid early crises, Algeria's revolutionary government, lacking an external threat, began to "consume its own."[450]

Indeed, Ben Bella's presidency was destroyed by intra-elite conflict. Ben Bella excluded much of the revolutionary elite from positions of power.[451] Only three of the FLN's six surviving "historical chiefs," Ben Bella, Mohamed Khider, and Rabah Bitat, were included in the Politburo, which led the other three chiefs—Hocine Ait Ahmed, Mohamed Boudiaf, and Krim Belkacem—to move into opposition. Boudiaf was arrested, while Ahmed created the Front of Socialist Forces and launched an armed rebellion in Kabylia.[452] More schisms followed. Khider ran afoul of Ben Bella in 1963 when, as FLN general secretary, he sought to strengthen the ruling party.[453] By year's end, both he and Bitat were in exile.[454] By late 1963, then, nearly the entire founding leadership had defected. Of the FLN's six living historical chiefs, three were in exile (Bitat, Khider, Krim), one was in prison (Boudiaf), and one was leading armed resistance (Ahmed).[455] Only Ben Bella remained. In July 1964, Boudiaf, Khider, Ahmed, and prominent *wilaya* leaders formed the National Committee for the Defense of the Revolution, which launched a failed uprising.[456]

Eventually, Ben Bella turned on army chief Houari Boumedienne, purging his allies from the cabinet and announcing the creation of a "people's militia," which threatened the army's coercive monopoly.[457] The army could not be easily shoved aside, however, and in June 1965, it removed Ben Bella, replacing him with the Revolutionary Council, chaired by Boumedienne.[458]

Ben Bella's removal was a palace coup. Army leaders had placed Ben Bella in power in 1962 and viewed him as a "figurehead."[459] Rather than alter the character of the regime, then, the 1965 coup simply removed the "fig leaf" of civilian rule.[460] The FLN (though weakened) remained in the governing coalition, and, crucially, the new government was dominated by revolutionary veterans.[461] All twenty-six members of the new Revolutionary Council participated in the liberation struggle, twenty-four of them as armed fighters.[462]

Even if the 1965 coup did not constitute a regime change, however, it was a clear sign of crisis. Ben Bella's removal—and the extraordinary partisan infighting that preceded it—highlighted the FLN's lack of cohesion. Lacking an existential threat after independence, the ruling party quickly became a "house divided against itself."[463]

The absence of an existential military threat also inhibited the development of a powerful coercive apparatus. The army, which had grown to 125,000 soldiers in 1962, was reduced to a modest 50,000–60,000 by the mid-1960s.[464] Although the army developed an extensive intelligence system,[465] it languished in the absence of security threats.[466] Military spending—generally below 3 percent of GDP—was low by regional standards.[467] Thus, although the ANP was highly professionalized,[468] Algeria was not an especially militarized state.[469] Indeed, in terms of both size and budget, Algeria's military remained on par with that of neighboring Tunisia.[470]

Finally, the absence of an existential threat weakened incentives to assault independent centers of societal power. Although the FLN had employed terror to destroy rival nationalists during the liberation war,[471] it relied primarily on co-optation after independence.[472] Without a serious external threat, and without firm control over the military, the Ben Bella government had neither the will nor the capacity to launch a reign of terror.[473] Likewise, the Boumedienne government "went to great lengths to avoid the resort to physical coercion" against rivals,[474] seeking instead to co-opt them.[475]

In the absence of repression, independent associations persisted in postcolonial Algeria. Though nominally aligned with the FLN, the General Union of Algerian Workers retained a degree of autonomy that was unthinkable in Vietnam.[476] Berber associations, such as the Berber Cultural Movement, operated above ground, despite the fact that some Berber leaders backed armed insurgencies in the early 1960s.[477]

The most important center of societal power, however, was the Islamist movement. Islamists had backed the liberation war, but opposition to Ben Bella's secular leftism led some Muslim leaders to form a conservative association called Al Qiyam (Values) in 1964.[478] Although it focused primary on cultural issues, Al Qiyam served as a channel for the public opposition that Ben Bella was "unable to suppress."[479] The subsequent Boumedienne government exerted greater control over Islamist organizations, banning Al Qiyam, regulating mosque construction, and granting itself the authority to appoint imams and even oversee the content of sermons.[480] However, these measures were only loosely enforced, and Islamist activism continued through Al Qiyam successor groups.[481] Islamists evaded state controls over mosque construction, establishing so-called "free mosques," often in makeshift buildings.[482] During the 1970s, the government's reluctance to crack down on illicit mosques permitted the proliferation of free mosques, "private mosques" financed by local notables, and "peoples' mosques" built in shantytowns by grassroots religious groups.[483] These mosques would later serve as mobilizing structures for the Islamist opposition.[484]

In sum, the FLN government's mix of easy radicalism and accommodation generated a limited counterrevolutionary reaction. In the absence of an existential domestic or external threat, elite cohesion remained low, the coercive apparatus remained modest in size and scope, and the government had little incentive to attack independent power centers. As a result, state-society power asymmetries never approached those observed in Vietnam, which left the regime vulnerable to societal opposition.

Regime Survival amid Opposition Contestation, 1965–2020

The 1965 coup ushered in two decades of regime stability, most of it under Houari Boumedienne (1965–1978). Several things changed under Boumedienne. Elite cohesion increased, in part because formal and de facto power structures were now aligned. The army, which had operated behind the scenes, now took center stage, while the FLN was reduced to an "empty shell,"[485] operating out of a "small office inside an army facility."[486] Unlike Ben Bella, moreover, Boumedienne filled the government with revolutionary veterans, particularly army and *wilaya* commanders.[487] Thus, although the FLN's founding *political* leaders were marginalized, the post-1965 regime was dominated by a cohesive group of military officials.[488] At least partly as a result, elite defection declined.[489] Outside of a failed military revolt in 1967,[490] the regime faced few internal challenges under Boumedienne.[491]

Yet Algeria's post-1965 regime stability also had economic roots. Oil and gas revenue enabled Boumedienne to finance an ambitious state-led industrialization project, transforming Algeria into a "semi-rentier state."[492] The economy boomed, growing 7 percent a year between 1967 and 1978.[493] Oil revenue allowed the government to co-opt potential opponents, particularly among Islamists and the private sector.[494] As a result, the regime faced little societal opposition prior to the 1980s.

The only potential crisis during the Boumedienne period emerged in the wake of his sudden death in 1978. The unexpected succession triggered a power struggle within the FLN, with leftists backing Mohamed Saleh Yahiaoui and conservatives backing Abdelaziz Bouteflika.[495] With the FLN deadlocked, military leaders imposed Chadli Bendjedid, a long-time army officer and protégé of Boumedienne.[496] Again, then, the military selected the president.[497]

Although the Algerian regime survived for more than four decades after Boumedienne's death, it was far less stable than that in Vietnam. The regime was challenged by a mass uprising in the late 1980s, armed Islamist insurgencies in the early 1990s, and large-scale pro-democracy protests in 2019. The army was sufficiently cohesive to thwart the Islamist challenge, but as the revolutionary generation departed in the late 2010s, the regime grew increasingly vulnerable.

CRISIS AND REGIME SURVIVAL
AMID CIVIL WAR, 1988–1999

The Bendjedid presidency (1979–1992) was riddled with crisis. The regime faced mounting societal contention. In the late 1970s, for example, Berber associations began to mobilize against the government's Arab-language policies.[498] In 1980, repression of protests led by Berber activists in Kabylia triggered a wave of opposition mobilization known as the "Berber Spring,"[499] which ended nearly two decades of societal quiescence.[500]

The Islamist movement posed a greater challenge. The regime's tenuous co-optation of Islam unraveled in the 1970s.[501] Independent mosques proliferated, emerging in "every available space, in garages, apartments, schools, hospitals, and, of course, in shantytowns."[502] By the mid-1980s, there existed some 6,000 unofficial mosques, matching the number of official ones.[503] Islamist movements built upon this expanding mosque network.[504] The mosque campaign evolved into a grassroots movement with a strong presence in the universities and among the urban poor.[505] The Bendjedid government, whose priority was economic reform, initially tolerated the growth of Islamism.[506] By the time it began to crack down on independent mosques in 1986, "the genie was out of the bottle."[507]

The Islamist challenge was exacerbated by economic crisis. Falling oil prices triggered a deep economic slump beginning in 1986. Declining oil revenue generated a fiscal crisis, which forced the government to adopt International Monetary Fund–backed austerity measures.[508] The economy contracted in 1987 and 1988, driving the unemployment rate up to 25 percent.[509] Strike and protest levels rose sharply.[510]

In October 1988, massive riots broke out across Algeria, triggering the largest uprising since independence.[511] Although the so-called Black October riots began spontaneously and encompassed diverse groups, Islamist activists played a central role, seizing control of the streets in many neighborhoods.[512] The government responded with heavy repression, killing at least 200 people.[513]

When repression failed to quell the uprising, Bendjedid launched a surprise political opening. In 1989, the government ended single-party rule; legalized the dominant Islamist party, the Islamic Salvation Front (FIS); and called local and parliamentary elections for 1990 and 1991.[514]

The opening backfired. The FIS won a stunning victory in the 1990 local elections, capturing 54 percent of the vote and more than half of Algeria's municipalities, including Algiers.[515] As the FLN fell into disarray,[516] the FIS began to impose a new "moral order" in the localities it governed, closing bars and movie theaters, enforcing sex segregation in schools, and harassing women in Western dress.[517] It called for an Islamic state, adopting the slogan "No constitution and no laws. The only rule is the Koran and the law of God."[518]

With the June 1991 parliamentary elections on the horizon, regime elites clumsily fought back, seeking to tilt the playing field in the FLN's favor via heavy gerrymandering and a ban on campaigning in mosques.[519] The FIS responded with a general strike and a mass protest campaign aimed at toppling the regime.[520] Under pressure from military leaders, the government declared a state of emergency, postponed the election until December, and called in the army to quell protest.[521] The security forces jailed the FIS's top leaders, Abbassi Madani and Ali Belhadj, and killed or arrested hundreds of Islamist activists.[522] However, Bendjedid refused to ban the FIS or bar it from competing in the election.[523]

The first round of the December 1991 parliamentary elections produced another stunning result. The FIS won nearly 50 percent of the vote and captured 188 of 430 districts, compared to 15 for the FLN. This put the Islamists on pace to win an overwhelming majority in the second round.[524]

The FIS victory "shook the army to the core,"[525] and when Bendjedid refused to cancel the election, military leaders forced him out.[526] On January 11, 1992, Bendjedid handed power to a military-dominated High Council of State (HCE). Like the fall of Ben Bella, Bendjedid's removal was a palace coup. Although the FLN was temporarily pushed aside, the military clique that founded the regime remained entrenched in power.[527] The new HCE was filled with revolutionary veterans, including Mohamed Boudiaf, one of the FLN's "historic chiefs," and Ali Kafi, an underground resistance leader during the liberation war.[528] The real power on the HCE, however, was Major General Khaled Nezzar, a liberation war veteran who was among the military's top commanders.[529]

The military's primary goal was to destroy the FIS.[530] This was an extraordinarily risky venture. Built upon a network of 9,000 mosques and funded by Persian Gulf allies,[531] the FIS was now the largest political movement in Algeria, with several million members and a capacity to mobilize hundreds of thousands of people in the streets.[532] Moreover, having just won an electoral landslide, the FIS enjoyed far greater legitimacy than the military government. Thus, a crackdown appeared to be "suicidal."[533] The FIS was simply "too big" to repress.[534] Observers such as Edward G. Shirley, comparing the regime to the shah's Iran, declared it "doomed."[535]

Nevertheless, the army proved strikingly cohesive in the face of an existential threat.[536] In early 1992, it declared a state of siege and launched a nationwide crackdown aimed at demolishing the FIS.[537] The FIS was dissolved, top FIS leaders were imprisoned, and all Islamist political activities were banned; the army seized 8,000 FIS-controlled mosques, removing their imams.[538] The security forces launched a campaign of terror in which thousands of FIS supporters were arrested or killed.[539] During the first two months of 1992, between 6,000 and 10,000 suspected Islamist activists were rounded up and sent to remote prison camps in the Sahara.[540] By year's end, between 3,000 and 6,000 people had been killed.[541]

Unlike in China in 1989 or Iran in 2009 or 2019, the repression did not silence opposition. Rather, it gave rise to multiple Islamist guerrilla movements, plunging Algeria into a bloody civil war. Almost immediately after the coup, Islamists launched the Islamic Armed Movement and the Movement for an Islamic state, both of which had ties to the FIS.[542] A third group, the more radical and violent Armed Islamic Group (GIA), broke with the FIS over the latter's willingness to negotiate with the state.[543] The FIS initially resisted armed struggle but later created the Islamic Salvation Army (AIS) to avoid being outflanked by the GIA.[544] By the mid-1990s, the various insurgent groups had between 25,000 and 40,000 guerrillas.[545] The civil war raged on for more than five years, until the AIS negotiated a cease-fire in 1997 and the GIA was subsequently defeated.[546] The human cost was enormous: between 100,000 and 200,000 people were killed.[547]

The government ultimately prevailed for several reasons. For one, it enjoyed strong support from Western powers, particularly France and the United States, which viewed Algeria as an ally in the fight against Islamic terrorism.[548] Thus, Western governments offered economic, military, and diplomatic support, while turning a blind eye to human rights violations.[549] More important, however, was military cohesion, which was rooted in the regime's revolutionary origins. The army's counterinsurgency strategy required sustained high-intensity coercion.[550] The security forces had to kill thousands of people and seize control of thousands of mosques, expelling their clerics.[551] Such repression undermined the army's public legitimacy.[552] Yet the army "had shown repeatedly over the years it was both willing and able to use lethal force on a massive scale."[553] Indeed, despite rank-and-file sympathy for the FIS,[554] the army remained loyal and cohesive throughout the civil war.[555]

The regime's capacity for high-intensity repression was rooted in the fact that the security forces were controlled by liberation war veterans.[556] The group of generals that dominated the regime in the early and mid-1990s, including Khaled Nezzar, Abdelmalek Guenaizia, Mohamed Lamari, Liamine Zéroual, and Mohamed Mediene, "had fought hard, at great risk, for Algeria's independence"; they viewed the Islamist challenge as a "threat to all that they had fought for."[557] As William B. Quandt observed, "This was not like the Shah's regime, where the generals ran for their Swiss bank accounts as soon as it was clear that Ayatollah Khomeini was going to return. The Algerian generals were prepared to fight."[558] Revolutionary veterans such as Nezzar and Lamari maintained a position of implacable opposition to the Islamists.[559] Although the regime elite divided over strategy, with some officials (known as "conciliators") seeking a negotiated end to the war,[560] the army's top brass remained firmly in the hard-line camp (the "eradicators"), which sought an all-out military victory over the Islamists.[561] The eradicators remained dominant throughout the war, which facilitated a cohesive military response.[562]

In sum, the persistence of independent centers of societal power seriously threatened the Algerian regime in the 1980s and 1990s. The Islamist movement, whose growth was largely unchecked by the FLN government, provided the bases for a massive opposition challenge between 1988 and 1997. The level of societal contestation far exceeded anything seen in Vietnam. Regime survival hinged, in large part, on army cohesion. The army, which was still commanded by the revolutionary generation, united behind a brutal strategy of high-intensity coercion that allowed the government to prevail.

THE ALGERIAN REGIME IN THE TWENTY-FIRST CENTURY

The Algerian regime stabilized in the late 1990s, returning to nominally civilian rule. Multiparty elections continued, but the FIS was banned and Islamists heavily repressed.[563] In 1999, Abdelaziz Bouteflika, a revolutionary veteran who served as foreign minister under both Ben Bella and Boumedienne, was elected president. For nearly two decades, the government faced few challenges, as Bouteflika was reelected in 2004, 2009, and 2014, each time with more than 80 percent of the vote.

This stability had at least three sources. One was the strength of the coercive apparatus. The security forces remained in the hands of the revolutionary generation,[564] and they expanded dramatically during the civil war.[565] Security spending rose from 4 percent of total spending in 1990 to 13 percent in 1998 and remained above 10 percent throughout Bouteflika's presidency.[566] By 2012, Algeria's military budget was more than twice that of Morocco and Tunisia *combined*.[567] The army doubled in size, adding a well-trained 45,000-man counterinsurgency force.[568] The police force quadrupled,[569] and the state developed a larger and more effective intelligence apparatus.[570] By the early 2000s, then, Algerian state had about 500,000 people under arms.[571] The effectiveness of the security forces also increased as the civil war reinforced their cohesion and provided them with considerable experience in repression.[572]

A second source of regime stability, which was not related to its revolutionary origins, was strong international support, especially after the 2001 terrorist attacks in the United States.[573] Thus, whereas human rights abuses had triggered international rebuke in the 1990s, Algeria became a "useful and welcome ally" in the U.S.-led war on terrorism in the 2000s.[574] By linking Algeria's Islamist opposition to al-Qaeda, Bouteflika insulated the regime from external pressure and expanded its access to Western military and economic assistance.[575]

A third source of regime stability, also exogenous to revolutionary origins, was resource rents.[576] Thanks to soaring oil and gas prices, Algeria's hydrocarbon export revenues increased dramatically between 1999 and 2009, which provided the government with the resources to co-opt economic and military elites,[577] dampen working-class militancy,[578] and finance a vast expansion of the coercive apparatus.[579]

The Algerian regime had little difficulty riding out the Arab Spring. Algeria experienced a major wave of protest in January 2011.[580] Triggered by a hike in fuel prices, riots broke out in Oran and quickly spread to cities across the country.[581] The protests gave rise to the National Coordination for Democratic Change, which mobilized as many as 300,000 protesters in Algiers's May First Square.[582] Although social and economic conditions in Algeria broadly mirrored those in Tunisia,[583] however, the Algerian protests quickly petered out.[584] Explanations for this outcome point to the strength of the coercive apparatus;[585] increased social spending, financed by oil revenue;[586] and the demobilizing effects of the civil war.[587]

The regime grew vulnerable again, however, during Bouteflika's fourth term (2014–2019). Bouteflika was in poor health, falling oil prices led to a mounting fiscal crisis,[588] and, crucially, the regime had to contend with generational change. The upper ranks of the army were increasingly occupied by officers who were too young to have fought in the liberation war,[589] which likely made high-intensity repression more difficult.

The regime fell into crisis in February 2019, when the ailing Bouteflika's announcement that he would seek reelection triggered a massive protest movement known as the Hirak (Movement). By early March, between two and three million people were protesting in cities and towns across the country.[590] The army refused to engage in the kind of high-intensity repression needed to quell the protest, forcing Bouteflika to resign.[591] However, the military rejected demands for truly free and fair elections, and former prime minister Abdelmadjid Tebboune, a longtime FLN leader with close ties to the army, won the presidency.[592]

Although the regime survived Bouteflika's fall, the departure of the revolutionary generation may leave it vulnerable. Beginning in 2019, neither President Tebboune nor Army Chief of Staff Said Chengriha was a revolutionary veteran. This fact is likely to weaken army cohesion, making the kind of high-intensity repression undertaken in the 1990s more difficult to carry out in the future.

Algeria's revolutionary regime has survived for nearly as long as its counterpart in Vietnam. Unlike Vietnam, however, the Algerian regime has experienced two palace coups and considerable mass-based opposition. These diverging outcomes can be explained by early differences in the two countries' regime trajectories. Algeria is a borderline case of social revolution; the revolutionary government was more accommodationist than its counterpart in Vietnam. The result was a regime that was more robust than Ghana's but weaker than Vietnam's. The liberation war generated a cohesive military that was founded and led by revolutionary veterans. Army cohesion helped avoid a regime-ending coup like that which brought down Kwame Nkrumah (see below), and it enabled the government to deploy the sustained high-intensity coercion necessary to thwart mass opposition. However, Algeria's abortive reactive sequence reinforced ruling party weakness and permitted the survival of alternative power centers, particularly networks of independent mosques. Algeria thus never developed the vast state-society power asymmetries observed in Vietnam, which left the regime vulnerable to societal contestation. Ultimately, then, factors outside our theory, including oil rents and international support, may be necessary to explain regime longevity.

GHANA

Ghana (1957–1966) represents a stark contrast to both Vietnam and Algeria. Like the two previous cases, Ghana under Kwame Nkrumah was a national liberation regime that embraced the cause of Third World revolution. However, the regime was not revolutionary. The struggle for independence and the 1957 transfer of power were peaceful. The Nkrumah government inherited the colonial army rather than build a new one, and, as a result, party-army ties were weak. Moreover, the Nkrumah government's relatively moderate policies triggered no serious reaction. Without an existential threat, the ruling Convention Peoples Party (CPP) never developed a cohesive organization. This left Nkrumah vulnerable to challenges from within. Military commanders maintained an autonomous identity and only weak ties to the CPP. Thus, when Nkrumah began to threaten the army's corporate interests, he triggered a regime-ending coup.

A Nonrevolutionary Transfer of Power

Nkrumah came to power as the leader of the independence movement in Ghana. The independence movement began after World War II, when Ghana (known until 1957 as the Gold Coast) experienced a surge of mobilization for self-rule. African merchants and professionals created the United Gold Coast Convention (UGCC) to push for a greater role running the colony.[593] Nkrumah, a U.S-trained teacher and activist, was chosen to head the organization.[594] In 1949, however, Nkrumah abandoned the UGCC and formed the more radical CPP. Under the slogan of "Full self-government now," the CPP declared it would use all nonviolent means to achieve independence.[595] The CPP was a nationalist party, not a revolutionary one. Vague references to socialism notwithstanding, it lacked a clear ideology.[596] Nevertheless, British authorities feared communist infiltration,[597] and when Nkrumah attempted to organize a nationwide strike in early 1951, British authorities, believing the colony to be on the brink of revolution,[598] declared a state of emergency and arrested him.

This moment represented a critical juncture. Had the British continued to crack down, as the French did in Vietnam and Algeria, the CPP might have radicalized and initiated a violent revolutionary struggle.[599] Instead, the British offered the CPP a constitutional path to power: legislative elections to choose an African government, to be held in 1951.[600] Although the new government would be subject to veto by British authorities, the election was widely seen as a stepping-stone to independence.[601] Less than two years after its foundation, the CPP won nearly 90 percent of the vote and thirty-four of thirty-eight seats in the 1951 parliamentary election.[602] Nkrumah was released from prison and appointed "leader of government business" for the territory. With the queen's approval, he was designated prime minister of the colonial territory in 1952.[603]

As colonial prime minister, Nkrumah cooperated extensively with British authorities.[604] For example, he used his authority to convince farmers to accept painful British policies to destroy cocoa plants in order to combat the swollen shoot disease that was ruining the cocoa economy.[605] Nkrumah also publicly distanced himself from Moscow, suspending the general secretary of the CPP trade union in 1953 for making contacts with the Soviet-backed World Federation of Trade Unions.[606] In 1954, Nkrumah announced that anyone active in the Communist Party would be barred from the public administration.[607] Such behavior gained him the trust of British authorities.[608]

Crucially, Nkrumah and the CPP pursued independence through constitutional means.[609] Independence was achieved via the British legislative process. After the House of Commons approved the Ghana Independence Act in December 1956 and the queen approved the bill in February 1957, Ghana was granted independence effective March 6, 1957.[610] Hundreds of international dignitaries, including U.S. vice president Richard Nixon, attended the ceremonies.[611] On the day of independence, Nkrumah declared: "We part from the former Imperial Power, Great Britain, with the warmest feelings of friendship and goodwill. . . . [I]nstead of that feeling of bitterness which is often born of a colonial struggle, we enter on our independence in association with Great Britain and with good relations unimpaired."[612]

One consequence of the peaceful transfer of authority was that unlike Vietnam and Algeria, Ghana's colonial state remained largely unchanged.[613] The bureaucracy was dominated by officials without ties to the CPP.[614] The colonial army also remained intact. The Gold Coast Regiment of the Royal West African Frontier Force, which had been created and commanded by British authorities, became the Ghana Army.[615] Nkrumah retained the bulk of the colonial army's British officer corps through 1961. At independence, 184 of the Ghana Army's 211 commanding officers were British.[616]

Accommodation and Limited Reaction

Notwithstanding Nkrumah's rhetorical embrace of socialism and anti-imperialism, the CPP government was strikingly accommodationist. Nkrumah did little to challenge powerful domestic or international interests. British cooperation embedded the new government in a web of Western commercial, military, and diplomatic interests, which gave the new government a stake in maintaining good relations with the West— and thus encouraged moderation.[617] Thus, while Nkrumah declared his intention to build socialism,[618] he eschewed the nationalization of industry and imposed few restrictions on foreign economic activity.[619] To maintain the confidence of Western investors, Nkrumah retained numerous British advisers, maintained conservative macroeconomic policies, kept Ghana's foreign reserves in London rather than Accra; although the government nationalized some gold mines, it purchased only the least profitable ones.[620]

In dealing with domestic interests, the CPP government's strategy was "not conflict, but adaptation and accommodation."[621] Thus, although Nkrumah sidelined local chiefs who had been empowered under British rule,[622] he did so with the cooperation of British colonial authorities and, ultimately, with minimal coercion.[623]

In 1960, Nkrumah initiated a high-profile "lurch to the left."[624] He visited Eastern bloc countries and reached agreements with the Soviet Union on trade and economic and technical cooperation.[625] Nkrumah also made a halfhearted effort to create a state ideology and opened the Nkrumah Ideological Institute, which was to be a Communist bloc–style party school for the CPP.[626] However, these initiatives were soon abandoned.[627] Moreover, despite tepid attempts to promote the state-run sector of the economy, the private sector continued to dominate the economy and 90 percent of Ghana's trade continued to be with the West.[628]

Ghana's foreign policy was accommodationist. Nkrumah was a prominent Pan-Africanist and anticolonial leader who championed the cause of Third World liberation. He hosted the high-profile Conference of Independent African States in 1958 and provided African liberation movements with office space in Accra.[629] Nevertheless, Nkrumah was unwilling to seriously challenge Western interests for the sake of regional transformation. For example, Ghana resisted calls by the African National Congress to boycott South Africa.[630] Indeed, Nkrumah maintained cordial relations with the apartheid state, refusing to criticize South Africa at Commonwealth meetings.[631] Although Nkrumah eventually bowed to pressure and announced a boycott of South Africa in 1960,[632] the boycott was implemented in a limited and contradictory way.[633]

Nkrumah's most significant regional intervention occurred in 1960–1961, when Ghana sent troops to defend Patrice Lumumba, the elected left-wing leader of independent Congo, against Belgian-backed separatists.[634] Although the move caused tension with the United States,[635] Nkrumah worked within Western-dominated international institutions.[636] Thus, Ghanaian troops operated under the auspices of the UN and ultimately stood aside as Lumumba was assassinated.[637]

In sum, Nkrumah's Ghana was far from revolutionary. The CPP ascended to power peacefully and maintained, rather than transformed, the colonial state. In power, Nkrumah sought to remain in the good graces of Western powers and established economic interests. As a result, his government provoked no violent domestic or international reaction.

A Weak Party-State Complex

Ghana's postcolonial party-state was weak. Having cooperated with, rather than fought against, British authorities, the CPP was never forced to build a strong and cohesive organization during the anticolonial struggle.[638] Indeed, the party suffered a series of defections in the run-up to independence.[639] The CPP's political dominance at independence was rooted less in its organizational strength than in the weakness of its political rivals.[640] Little changed after 1957. Without the bonds of trust forged during violent struggle or the siege mentality generated by military threat, the CPP evolved into a loosely organized machine that housed a diversity of competing interests.[641]

In the absence of revolution, moreover, Nkrumah had neither the opportunity nor good reason to create a new partisan army. The army, inherited from colonial rule, was small and underfunded.[642] Spooked by recent coups in Pakistan, Burma, Thailand, and Iraq, Nkrumah initially maintained an arm's-length relationship to the military.[643] He retained the bulk of the British officer corps,[644] expecting to gradually Africanize the army command over the course of a decade. Hence, CPP-army ties were weak. Without party-army fusion or a "revolutionary family" binding the military to the CPP, army leaders had little stake in the regime's survival. Indeed, because the military preexisted Nkrumah's ascent to power, it possessed an autonomous identity, which was reinforced by officers' education at Britain's Sandhurst and Eaton Hall military academies.[645] Thus, whatever camaraderie, shared trust, or sense of common purpose existed among the army officer corps, it was unconnected to the CPP. Such bonds would eventually facilitate efforts to orchestrate a coup.[646]

At the same time, Nkrumah confronted only limited challenges from society. Postcolonial civil society was weak. Thus, notwithstanding periodic strikes by railway and mine workers, the government largely co-opted trade unions.[647] Opposition parties were easily quashed. The anti-CPP Northern People's Party and National Liberation Movement, which won seats in the 1954 and 1956 elections, quickly collapsed in the face of repression. In 1958, leaders of the last remaining opposition, the United Party, were arrested for allegedly plotting Nkrumah's assassination.[648] United Party leader Kofi Busia went into exile. A 1964 referendum—with 99.9 percent of the vote officially in favor—abolished the opposition and established single-party rule.

Regime Collapse

Paradoxically, the transition to single-party rule weakened the regime. The CPP was left without a purpose, "rusted,"[649] and in "a state of sad confusion."[650] Party committees stopped meeting, and the party structure began to disappear across the country.[651] CPP discipline remained low, as some members maintained ties to the opposition.[652] This weakness left the regime vulnerable to internal challenges.[653]

The greatest threat was posed by the army. Nkrumah began to intervene more actively in military affairs in the early 1960s. Embarrassed that Africa's first independent military was dominated by white officers, Nkrumah abruptly dismissed British officers in September 1961, replacing them with Ghanaian officials.[654] However, the CPP's dearth of ties to military officials—including African ones—limited his ability to monitor or control the armed forces.[655] Efforts to infiltrate the army with informers failed,[656] and Nkrumah suffered assassination and coup attempts in 1962 and 1965.[657]

Threatened by the military, Nkrumah tried to politicize it. He circulated plans to introduce political commissars into the army, and beginning in 1963, officers were invited to join the CPP.[658] The government also sought to introduce ideological training for military officers.[659] However, these measures were quickly abandoned in the face of intense opposition by military leaders.[660]

Nkrumah next tried to protect himself by creating parallel armed forces directly subordinate to him. With Soviet assistance, he created the Presidential Guard in the wake of an August 1962 assassination attempt.[661] Within three years, the 1,100-man Guard was better armed than the army,[662] and many observers expected it to displace the army.[663] At the same time, Nkrumah fired leading army officials—such as Major General Stephen J. A. Otu and Lieutenant General Joseph Arthur Ankrah—who criticized the Guard or were suspected of disloyalty.[664]

The creation of the Presidential Guard and the firing of Otu and Ankrah generated intense hostility within the army.[665] Military officials grew fearful that the army would be replaced by pro-Nkrumah militias,[666] which generated support for a coup.[667] Paradoxically, then, measures aimed at thwarting a military coup ended up encouraging one.[668]

On the night of February 23, 1966, while Nkrumah was in Asia seeking to negotiate peace between the United States and Vietnam, a group of officers led by Lieutenant Colonel Emmanuel K. Kotoka—who had joined the colonial army in 1947 and attended Eaton Hall military academy—seized power. The coup was backed by the vast bulk of the military elite.[669] Pro-regime organizations dissolved, seemingly into thin air,[670] and the Presidential Guard, showing little desire to fight, was quickly immobilized.[671] Guard leaders may have been CPP members, but party membership meant little.[672] The CPP suffered sudden and large-scale defection.[673] Even those traveling with Nkrumah in Asia distanced themselves from the president.[674]

The coup was precipitated by a range of proximate causes, including economic crisis,[675] military underfunding,[676] the use of the army to put down domestic unrest,[677] officers' fear of dismissal,[678] and inspiration from recent coups in Africa and the Middle East.[679] Yet such factors were present in most of the cases covered in this book. That they triggered a regime-changing coup in Ghana may be attributed to the fact that the Ghanaian military was wholly autonomous of the ruling party. Army commanders were socialized in British military institutions,[680] and weak party penetration deprived the government of information about military officers' loyalties to the coup.[681] Finally, the absence of the kind of polarization and external military threat seen in most revolutionary cases lowered the stakes of regime change. Few actors in the army had much to lose if Nkrumah fell.[682]

Conclusion

This chapter has highlighted how the distinct origins of postcolonial liberation regimes shaped their durability. In Vietnam, violent revolutionary conflict destroyed alternative power centers and gave rise to a powerful and cohesive party-state. At the other extreme, Nkrumah's peaceful, non-revolutionary ascent to power in Ghana deprived the postcolonial regime of a cohesive party and a loyal military. Algeria is a mixed case. Although the regime emerged out of violent struggle, and although revolutionary leaders built their own army, the FLN government was more accommodationist than its counterpart in Vietnam, which resulted in a limited counterrevolutionary reaction and a weaker party-state. Although the Algerian regime survived for decades, it experienced considerable instability.

PART III

Explaining Variation in Revolutionary Outcomes

THIS BOOK FOCUSES PRINCIPALLY on the question of why most revolutionary regimes are so durable. As chapter 5 showed, however, revolutionary autocracies vary in their durability. The next three chapters explore the sources of this variation. Our theoretical framework, presented in chapter 1, is summarized in figure III.1. We argue that early choices about how much to challenge powerful domestic and foreign interests placed revolutionary regimes on diverging trajectories. In all cases, the power vacuum created by the collapse of preexisting state structures opens up a rare window for revolutionaries to seize power and initiate radical change. Nevertheless, developments during this window vary, producing three distinct paths. In the ideal-typical path (chapter 6), which is illustrated by two classic Third World revolutions, Cuba and Iran, early radicalism triggered a violent counterrevolutionary reaction, often backed by foreign powers. The resulting conflict posed an existential military threat, which embryonic revolutionary regimes survived. Conflict, in turn, reinforced elite cohesion, encouraged the development of a powerful coercive apparatus, and facilitated the destruction of rival organizations and societal power centers. This process of state-building laid the foundation for durable authoritarian rule.

A second path, examined in chapter 7, is early death. In Hungary (1919), Cambodia (1975–1979), and Afghanistan (1996–2001), revolutionary elites initiated radical projects, which triggered violent conflict. However, in part because they had seized power in relatively small and geopolitically vulnerable states, revolutionaries provoked wars that quickly destroyed their nascent regimes. In Cambodia, the Khmer Rouge's ethnic cleansing and attacks on Vietnam triggered a regime-ending foreign invasion. Likewise, aggressive behavior by the Hungarian Soviet Republic in 1919 and the Taliban in 2001 contributed to external intervention, military defeat, and regime collapse.

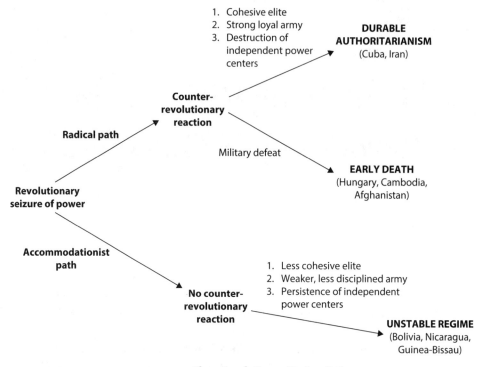

1. Cohesive elite
2. Strong loyal army
3. Destruction of independent power centers

DURABLE AUTHORITARIANISM
(Cuba, Iran)

Counter-revolutionary reaction

Radical path

Military defeat

EARLY DEATH
(Hungary, Cambodia, Afghanistan)

Revolutionary seizure of power

Accommodationist path

1. Less cohesive elite
2. Weaker, less disciplined army
3. Persistence of independent power centers

No counter-revolutionary reaction

UNSTABLE REGIME
(Bolivia, Nicaragua, Guinea-Bissau)

FIGURE III.1: Three Revolutionary Regime Paths.

A third path, examined in chapter 8, is accommodation. In Bolivia, Nicaragua, and Guinea-Bissau, revolutionary elites launched ambitious efforts to transform society. Unlike most revolutionary cases, however, the Revolutionary Nationalist Movement (Bolivia), the Sandinista National Liberation Front (Nicaragua), and the African Independence Party of Guinea and Cape Verde (Guinea-Bissau) tempered radical initiatives in an effort to limit the scope or intensity of the counterrevolutionary reaction. These are, in effect, borderline cases. Early policy measures were sufficiently radical to meet our criteria for revolution, but those measures were later accompanied by steps to limit conflict with powerful domestic or external interests. By averting or (in the case of Nicaragua) ending counterrevolutionary conflict, all three regimes avoided the early death observed in Afghanistan and Cambodia. However, accommodation inhibited the kind of state-building that lay a foundation for durable authoritarianism in Cuba and Iran. Thus, regimes in Bolivia, Nicaragua, and Guinea-Bissau built weaker party-states (Bolivia, Guinea-Bissau) and remained more prone to internal conflict (Bolivia, Guinea-Bissau) and societal opposition (Bolivia, Nicaragua). All three regimes broke down within twenty-five years.

CHAPTER SIX

Radicalism and Durability

CUBA AND IRAN

CUBA (1959–) AND IRAN (1979–) were among the most consequential revolutions of the second half of the twentieth century. They produced starkly different regimes. One was communist, with a Leninist one-party system, while the other was a conservative theocracy. Yet both cases closely approximate the ideal-typical reactive sequence presented in this book. Both revolutions took place amid the collapse of neopatrimonial or sultanistic regimes.[1] In both cases, revolutionary governments radically transformed their societies at home while seeking to promote revolution abroad. These challenges to domestic and geopolitical power structures provoked violent counterrevolutionary movements, which resulted in prolonged existential military threats. In the face of these threats, revolutionary elites in both countries closed ranks in defense of the regime, built powerful and loyal security forces, and wiped out alternative centers of societal power, creating a state-society power asymmetry that endured for decades.

CUBA

Cuba conforms closely to the ideal-typical path of revolutionary regime consolidation. Under the leadership of Fidel Castro, the revolutionary government launched an audacious strategy of societal transformation and internationalism, which triggered a powerful counterrevolutionary reaction, including domestic insurgencies and a U.S.-backed invasion. Having built its own army, the regime survived. Moreover, the prolonged counterrevolutionary threat reinforced elite cohesion, led to a dramatic expansion of the coercive apparatus, and accelerated the destruction of independent power centers. As a result, a regime that was born weak developed into one of the most robust in the hemisphere—one capable of surviving the collapse of the Soviet Union, severe economic crisis, and the death of Castro.

The Revolutionary Seizure of Power

Antecedent conditions in Cuba did not favor durable authoritarianism. The country had been plagued by state weakness and regime instability since independence in 1902. Early governments' reliance on U.S. intervention to maintain order inhibited the development of an effective coercive apparatus, which resulted in frequent armed insurrections.[2] State weakness was a persistent source of regime instability. All of Cuba's prerevolutionary autocracies collapsed in less than a decade, and on three occasions (1906, 1933, and 1958), they broke down because the security forces either collapsed or refused to combat an opposition uprising.[3] Overall, six Cuban governments fell prey to insurrections or coups between 1902 and 1959. Absent a social revolution, then, there was little reason to expect the emergence of a durable authoritarian regime in 1959.

The Cuban Revolution occurred in a context of state weakness. The dictatorship of Fulgencio Batista, which emerged out of a 1952 military coup, was a classic neopatrimonial regime.[4] Batista plundered the state and packed the armed forces with cronies and loyalists, leaving them poorly trained, ill equipped, and plagued by conspiracies.[5] Led by a "demoralized gaggle of corrupt, cruel, and lazy officers,"[6] Cuba's security forces had "little stomach for combat."[7]

Several insurgent groups emerged to challenge Batista in the 1950s. The most successful of these was the July 26 Movement, which was led by Fidel Castro and his brother Raúl. Fidel Castro rose to prominence when he led a failed assault on the Moncada military barracks on July 26, 1953. He later created the July 26 Movement, and in December 1956, the group launched an insurrection. Eighty-two rebels sailed from Mexico to Cuba by boat, the sixty-foot-long *Granma*, hoping to time their landing with a planned urban insurrection. The insurrection never materialized, and the rebels were nearly wiped out.[8] Eighteen survivors, including Fidel and Raúl Castro and Ernesto "Che" Guevara, regrouped in the Sierra Maestra and launched an improvised guerrilla campaign, carrying out a series of hit-and-run attacks on security forces in early 1957.[9] The government's heavy-handed response[10] boosted the rebels' public image and established Castro as a "larger than life" figure.[11] Despite numbering fewer than 300, the rebels gained control of most of the Sierra Maestra and Oriente Province in 1957 and early 1958.[12]

Castro pursued a maximalist strategy. In October 1957, when a broad coalition of opposition parties came together to sign the Pact of Miami, which called for Batista's resignation, the formation of a provisional government, and a return to Cuba's liberal democratic 1940 constitution, Castro rejected the pact (because it would have preserved Batista's army), preferring to go it alone.[13]

A strategy of going it alone with 300 ill-equipped fighters faced daunting odds. However, three factors worked in Castro's favor. First, opposition efforts to negotiate a peaceful transition failed, as Batista stubbornly clung to power.[14] The closure of reform alternatives undermined the moderate opposition and led a growing number of politicians, professionals, and business leaders to throw their support to the armed opposition.[15] It also cost Batista the support of the U.S. government, which suspended arms shipments in March 1958.[16]

Second, two rivals for leadership of the revolutionary movement, the Revolutionary Directorate (DR) and the urban underground resistance led by Frank País, both of which were larger and better organized than Castro's guerrillas,[17] were weakened by repression.[18] The DR's failed March 1957 attack on the presidential palace triggered a wave of repression that wiped out its leadership, including founder José Antonio Echeverría.[19] The urban resistance was weakened by the death of its talented leader, País, in July 1957, and by a failed general strike in April 1958.[20] Thus, whereas Castro's leadership of Cuba's revolutionary movement was initially contested by two urban rivals, by 1958, the July 26 Movement was dominant.[21]

Third, the guerrillas benefited from the ineffectiveness of the armed forces. In May 1958, the Batista government launched a major military offensive, sending fourteen army divisions, with 10,000 troops, into the mountains to combat the rebels.[22] The offensive failed badly, as the army suffered a series of humiliating defeats.[23] In ten weeks, the army lost 10 percent of its troops to desertion, death, and capture.[24] Entire units deserted or disintegrated.[25] By late July, the offensive had collapsed, as the army "simply ceased to fight."[26] In the end, 400 guerrillas held off 10,000 government troops,[27] revealing the rot in Batista's neopatrimonial state.

The failed summer offensive marked the beginning of the end for Batista. As the economy deteriorated and the dictatorship weakened, politicians and businessmen flocked to the rebels' side.[28] In July 1958, opposition leaders from across the political spectrum gathered in Caracas and recognized Castro as the "commander in chief of the revolutionary forces" and the July 26 Movement as the "main arm of the revolution."[29]

Castro's seizure of power on January 1, 1959, was not really a military victory.[30] Numbering only 2,000–3,000 guerrillas in December 1958, just before Batista's fall,[31] the July 26 Movement fought few significant battles.[32] Rather, Batista's forces simply collapsed, as small rebel victories triggered an avalanche of desertions.[33] The army "refus[ed], unit by unit, to fight the guerrillas,"[34] allowing the rebels to occupy towns without firing a shot.[35] By December, Batista's forces had "all but dissolved. Demoralized army detachments . . . had begun to lay down their arms, stay in their barracks, or join the swelling ranks of the rebels."[36]

Batista fled Cuba on December 31, 1958. Top army and police officials left with him.[37] Across the country, local commanders abandoned their posts, allowing advancing rebel troops to seize cities, towns, and command posts without resistance; police officers disappeared from the streets, plunging Cuba into anarchy.[38] Rebel militias quickly filled the power vacuum, seizing army barracks, police stations, government offices, and television and radio stations.[39]

When General Eulogio Cantillo attempted to form a provisional junta on January 1, 1959,[40] he discovered that he had no one left to command. All police precincts had surrendered, and the remaining soldiers in Cuba's largest military base, Camp Columbia, had stopped fighting.[41] In desperation, Cantillo handed the army command to General Ramón M. Barquín, a dissident officer who had been jailed under Batista.[42] Barquín sought to orchestrate a transition that preserved the armed forces,[43] but Castro insisted on total surrender.[44] With revolutionary militias seizing police stations and government offices across the country, Barquín, lamenting that he had inherited a "dead army,"[45] turned Camp Columbia over to rebel commander Camilo Cienfuegos.[46]

The revolutionaries initially installed a moderate government composed mainly of liberal professionals. Provisional President Manuel Urrutia was a prominent judge, Prime Minister José Miró Cardona was president of the Havana Bar Association, and Finance Minister Rufo López Fresquet was a mainstream economist.[47] Real power, however, lay in the hands of Castro and the rebel army.[48] Although he would not become president until 1976, Castro was "head of everything" from the beginning.[49] He "established a personal hold over the Cuban masses such as no Latin American leader had ever had. Not even [Juan] Peron at his peak had been so obviously and so universally loved."[50]

Castro completed the destruction of the old state, disbanding the old army, the police, and the intelligence services.[51] At least 550 army and police officers were executed, and thousands of others were jailed or exiled.[52] The new Revolutionary Armed Forces (FAR) was created out of the guerrilla army and staffed entirely by revolutionaries.[53] Prerevolutionary army officers were barred, and the new army's national, provincial, and even local commands were filled by trusted guerrilla veterans.[54] The National Revolutionary Police was also created from scratch,[55] and it, too, was commanded exclusively by members of the July 26 Movement.[56] The revolutionaries also purged the state bureaucracy and the judiciary, and many judicial functions were taken over by "revolutionary tribunals."[57]

The Revolutionary Reactive Sequence

Cuba's revolutionary regime was born weak. Unlike in China and Vietnam, where the communists built powerful armies and won prolonged revolutionary wars, the July 26 Movement was a ragtag guerrilla group that had seized power amid the collapse of the Batista state. The FAR had only 5,000 troops in early 1959—barely a tenth the size of Batista's army.[58] The revolutionaries also lacked a party. The July 26 Movement was a "tiny group of heroic youths,"[59] with no real organization.[60] Castro discouraged efforts to transform the guerrilla movement into a ruling party, preferring to rely on charismatic authority,[61] and, as a result, it soon disappeared.[62]

Although the new regime was institutionally weak, it was undergirded by a cohesive revolutionary elite. Nearly all the leaders who built and directed the revolutionary state were July 26 Movement members with roots in the guerrilla struggle.[63] Many of them participated in the 1956 *Granma* expedition and nearly all of them fought in the Sierra Maestra. These founding revolutionaries became what Jorge I. Domínguez called "civic soldiers," or revolutionaries whose "civilian and military roles were fused."[64] Their shared guerrilla experience gave rise to a "remarkable esprit de corps" and intense loyalty to Castro and the revolution.[65] Civic soldiers occupied all top positions in the state. Fidel Castro was the undisputed leader, Raúl Castro commanded the armed forces, Ramiro Valdes ran the intelligence agency, and Efigenio Ameijeiras led the National Revolutionary Police.

The revolutionary elite faced multiple rivals and threats in 1959.[66] On the left, although Fidel Castro quickly subordinated the DR,[67] he had to contend with the well-organized and Soviet-backed Popular Socialist Party (PSP). The PSP was a latecomer to the insurgency and contributed little to Batista's overthrow (Castro liked to say that PSP leaders "hid under the bed"),[68] but it was the strongest left-wing party in Cuba.[69]

Although most prerevolutionary parties, interest groups, and media outlets weakened under Batista or in the wake of his fall,[70] a few influential actors remained. One was the Catholic Church. The Cuban Church was a primarily middle- and upper-middle-class institution, with fewer than 700 priests and little presence in the countryside or the Afro-Cuban community.[71] Nevertheless, it remained Cuba's most important social institution.[72] It ran hundreds of parishes and schools and sponsored trade unions and important student associations.[73]

The new government also confronted a large private sector that included cattle ranchers, sugar and tobacco planters, sugar mill owners, and industrialists. The power of Cuban capitalists was limited by the extensive penetration of U.S. capital, and it was further eroded by emigration in 1959.[74] However, economic elites were well connected to the United States,[75] and the existence of well-endowed associations such as the National Association of Cattle Ranchers, the National Mill Owners' Association, the Colonos (Sugar Planters) association, the National Association of Industrialists, and the Chamber of Commerce gave them a capacity for collective action that few other societal actors possessed.[76]

The greatest counterrevolutionary threat, however, came from abroad. In 1958, U.S. private investment in Cuba amounted to about $1 billion, the highest level per capita in Latin America.[77] Americans owned more than 90 percent of Cuba's electricity and telecommunications sectors, most of the hotel and casino industries, about a third of the sugar industry, much of the financial sector, half the railroads, two of three oil refineries, the entire mining sector, and more than three million acres of the best farmland.[78] This meant that any effort to expropriate or redistribute wealth would directly affect American economic interests, which was almost certain to trigger a strong reaction by the United States.[79]

EARLY RADICALISM

The Cuban regime was strikingly radical. The Castro government undertook a "massive restructuring of the social and political order,"[80] and it did so with "astonishing speed."[81] As Richard R. Fagen observed, "Few nations have ever undergone such massive transformations in so short a time."[82]

Although Castro had never been very ideological,[83] and although the July 26 Movement's original program was "humanist," rather than socialist,[84] several factors radicalized the government. First, given Cuba's extensive economic ties to the United States, even modest redistribution or economic nationalism was likely to trigger U.S. hostility.[85] This tendency was exacerbated by the Cold War. Indeed, the U.S.-backed overthrow of the reformist Arbenz government in Guatemala five years before the Cuban Revolution appears to have taught Castro that a moderate reform strategy was futile.[86] In addition, the availability of Soviet support enhanced the viability of a radical strategy. Massive Soviet assistance allowed the regime to survive a U.S. trade embargo and helped deter U.S. aggression. Beginning in 1960, then, Soviet protection allowed the Castro government to pursue high-risk strategies that would otherwise have brought almost certain collapse. Finally, Castro had a radical mind-set. As one biographer put it, he was "determin[ed] to make radical, structural social and economic changes in Cuba."[87] Moreover, he was willing to engage in risk-accepting behavior to achieve them.[88]

The Castro government's radical turn began with a May 1959 land reform law. The law subjected all farms over 1,343 hectares and most farms over 403 hectares to expropriation and prohibited foreign ownership of sugar plantations.[89] Expropriated land would be distributed to the tenants who worked it.[90] More than six million acres of land—many of them owned by Americans—were seized by early 1960.[91]

The May 1959 land reform marked a turning point in the regime's relationship with moderates, the private sector, and the United States.[92] Half the cabinet resigned, and in July, President Urrutia resigned and was replaced by leftist Osvaldo Dorticós.[93] The land reform was a "bombshell" for landowners.[94] One shocked sugar planter called it a "dagger in the heart."[95] The conservative *Diario de la Marina*, considered a mouthpiece of the sugar industry, launched a campaign against communism.[96] The Church also opposed the reform.[97] Bishops began to warn against Soviet communism, and in November 1959, Church leaders mobilized more than a million Catholics in downtown Havana in a show of strength.[98]

Finally, the U.S. government, which had initially adopted a conciliatory position toward Castro,[99] reacted to the land reform with hostility.[100] By late 1959, the Eisenhower administration had drawn up covert plans to overthrow Castro and was aiding counterrevolutionary groups in the Escambray Mountains.[101] In March 1960, Eisenhower authorized the CIA to organize and train Cuban exiles for an invasion.[102] Castro appears to have learned of these activities in May.[103]

By early 1960, then, Castro faced a dilemma. The hostile domestic and international response to the 1959 reforms made it clear that radicalism would trigger a confrontation with the United States.[104] Because the United States was Cuba's leading trade partner, accounting for two-thirds of its exports,[105] a rupture with the United States would have devastating economic consequences. To avoid a costly conflict with the world's leading military and economic power, the revolutionary government would have to moderate.

But Castro doubled down. Taking a "bold risk,"[106] the government radicalized in early 1960, canceling elections and closing independent media.[107] In June, the government nationalized Cuba's oil refineries, expropriating Texaco, Shell, and Standard Oil.[108] In August, Castro announced the expropriation of about $2 billion in U.S.-owned properties, including thirty-six sugar mills, the Cuban Telephone Company, and the Cuban Electric power company.[109] In October, the government nationalized 382 industrial and commercial enterprises, including banks, sugar mills, textile mills, rum distilleries, department stores, and cinemas.[110] Later that month, it nationalized 166 U.S.-owned companies, including remaining hotels and insurance companies and properties owned by Coca-Cola, General Electric, International Harvester, Sears Roebuck, and Woolworth.[111] By late 1960, all but very small businesses had been nationalized, more than 80 percent of industry was in state hands, and the state's share of agricultural production exceeded that in Bulgaria, Hungary, and Poland.[112] Cuba thus underwent an extraordinarily rapid transition to socialism, doing "in 18 months what the Chinese did in 7 years."[113]

The Castro government also aggressively pursued an alliance with the Soviet Union, a bold move in the United States' geopolitical backyard.[114] At first, the Soviets did not take the Cuban Revolution seriously (Khrushchev viewed Castro as a "romantic"[115]), establishing diplomatic relations, followed by agreements on sugar purchases and petroleum shipments, only in early 1960.[116] As conflict with the United States escalated, however, Castro desperately sought out Soviet protection. In April 1961, he declared Cuba to be "socialist."[117] Although Americans viewed Castro's declaration as an act of provocation, in reality it was "addressed to the Soviet Union," in an effort to secure its protection.[118]

Finally, the Castro government adopted a radical foreign policy.[119] Viewing Cuba as "the new Mecca of revolution in the Americas," Castro promoted insurgencies across the region—and beyond.[120] In 1959, Cuba backed unsuccessful uprisings in the Dominican Republic, Nicaragua, and Panama, and by the early 1960s, it was supporting guerrillas in Argentina, Colombia, Guatemala, Nicaragua, Peru, Venezuela, and elsewhere.[121] Thus, Castro gave Cuba "not only a national revolution but an international civil war."[122]

Castro's efforts to export revolution were costly, as they antagonized the United States, generated tension with the Soviet Union (which frowned on such efforts), and destroyed Cuba's relations with other Latin American governments.[123] Although these initiatives were almost certainly rooted in Castro's radicalism, or "revolutionary messianism,"[124] they were ultimately made possible by Soviet support.[125] Without the Soviet Union's protective umbrella, Castro's messianic foreign policy might have had ruinous consequences for the new regime.

COUNTERREVOLUTIONARY REACTION

The radicalization of the Cuban Revolution triggered a violent counterrevolutionary reaction. The first armed rebellions, led mainly by members of Batista's security forces, appeared in 1959.[126] Several larger rebellions broke out in 1960, principally in the Escambray Mountains.[127] Led by farmers who had lost land or feared losing it,[128] groups such as the National Liberation Army, the Second Front of Escambray, and the White Rose mobilized hundreds of combatants, transforming Escambray into a "center of serious conflict."[129] Backed by Catholic groups and the CIA,[130] insurgencies spread across Cuba in 1960 and 1961,[131] plunging the country into civil war.[132] As many as 179 counterrevolutionary groups operated in Cuba between 1959 and 1965, with somewhere between 1,000 and 8,000 individuals under arms.[133] Even if we take lower-end estimates, the number of rebels exceeded that of Castro's guerrillas in late 1958. Likewise, even conservative estimates of 2,000–2,500 combat deaths between 1959 and 1965 match the number of people killed during the anti-Batista uprising.[134] The counterrevolution did an estimated $1 billion in damage.[135] Between October 1960 and April 1961, rebels carried out 110 bombings, destroyed 300,000 tons of sugar, burned forty-two tobacco warehouses, and derailed six trains.[136]

The United States posed an even greater threat. The expropriation of American property generated intense U.S. hostility.[137] In July 1960, the Eisenhower administration suspended Cuban sugar imports, and in October, it imposed a full-scale trade embargo.[138] At the same time, U.S. officials began to plot Castro's overthrow.[139] As early as the spring of 1960, the CIA was organizing and training Cuban exiles for an armed invasion.[140]

U.S. counterrevolutionary efforts peaked with the Bay of Pigs invasion. On April 17, 1961, 1,400 Cuban exiles, organized, trained, armed, and supplied by the U.S. government and accompanied by U.S.-supplied B-26 bombers, invaded Cuba.[141] The Castro government reacted quickly, mobilizing 20,000 troops, as well as militia forces, to repel the invasion.[142] Within seventy-two hours, the revolutionary army had surrounded and defeated the invading force, capturing or killing nearly all of them.[143] Unwilling to deploy U.S. forces, the Kennedy administration cut bait,[144] handing Castro a "total, dizzying triumph."[145] As Kennedy later put it,

"Castro ought to be grateful to us. He gave us a kick in the ass and it made him stronger than ever."[146]

The Bay of Pigs invasion helped consolidate the regime.[147] The revolutionary elite closed ranks and moved swiftly to wipe out domestic opposition.[148] Police detained everyone "remotely suspected of hostility to the government," to "smash all chances that the opposition . . . might have to assist the invasion."[149] As many as 100,000 people were arrested.[150] When the jails filled up, detainees were herded into sports arenas, theaters, stables and corrals, and other makeshift prisons.[151] The vast majority of underground activists were arrested,[152] effectively "liquidating" any remaining potential for counterrevolutionary activity.[153]

The Bay of Pigs fiasco did not end U.S. efforts to topple the regime. In November 1961, the Kennedy administration launched Operation Mongoose, which authorized U.S. agencies to covertly sponsor acts of sabotage, violence, and even assassination in Cuba.[154] Thus, the Kennedy administration armed and financed dozens of Florida-based terrorist groups that attacked oil refineries, electricity plants, sugar mills, industrial plants, maritime facilities, railroads, and other targets.[155] U.S. officials were also behind numerous efforts to assassinate Castro.[156]

Although these efforts failed, they convinced the revolutionary elite that the regime was in grave danger. Cuban leaders lived in constant fear of a U.S. invasion in the aftermath of the Bay of Pigs fiasco.[157] The threat led Castro to aggressively seek Soviet military protection, even declaring himself a "Marxist-Leninist" in November 1961.[158] Indeed, Soviet military support increased markedly after the Bay of Pigs invasion.[159] This support included massive conventional military assistance, the deployment of Soviet troops and advisers, and, most controversially, the installation of nuclear missiles on the island.[160]

The introduction of Soviet missiles was an extraordinary gamble for Castro.[161] Indeed, the October 1962 missile crisis "almost brought about the destruction of his country."[162] The crisis forced the government to mobilize the entire population to prepare for an invasion.[163] Yet Castro maintained a hard-line position, revealing a greater willingness than his Soviet allies to risk a nuclear conflict.[164]

The counterrevolutionary threat diminished after the missile crisis. The United States abandoned invasion plans,[165] and although CIA operations and support for exile activities continued,[166] they slowed after Kennedy's death and "sputtered to a halt" as the U.S. attention turned to Vietnam.[167] By 1965, all domestic insurgencies had been defeated.[168]

Although exile-based terrorist attacks continued through the 1970s,[169] they posed little threat to the regime.

The 1959–1965 counterrevolutionary war strengthened the regime in several ways. For one, it reinforced elite cohesion. The regime confronted a clear existential threat. A U.S. invasion "was daily expected" in the early 1960s,[170] generating a "paranoiac fear" among the revolutionary elite.[171] Operating in this "quasi-war status,"[172] the revolutionaries felt compelled to close ranks.[173] Internal critics were effectively "trapped," as any opposition was seen as "tantamount to inviting intervention by the United States," which transformed dissidents into "tactical allies of the counterrevolution."[174] According to Carlos Franqui, a July 26 Movement activist who later went into exile, "The great struggle of the day was between the revolution and the USA." In such a context, opposition was "unthinkable."[175]

It merits note that the revolutionary elite remained cohesive without a ruling party. Between 1959 and 1961, Castro ruled without a party, governing with a group of trusted veterans from the Sierra Maestra.[176] In July 1961, under pressure from the Soviet Union,[177] Castro announced that the July 26 Movement and the pro-Soviet PSP would be fused into the Integrated Revolutionary Organization (ORI), and he appointed PSP leader Aníbal Escalante to organize the party.[178] Escalante "took his job seriously,"[179] building a Soviet-style ruling party and packing its leadership with PSP cadres.[180] When the party asserted some independence, however, Castro turned on it, complaining that ORI leaders had created "a straightjacket, a yoke" and dismissing the new party as a "pile of garbage."[181] In March 1962, Castro "tore the lid off the organization," purging its entire leadership.[182] Castro replaced the ORI with the Unified Party of the Socialist Revolution (PURS), which his biographer described as his "own, special, Castroite Communist Party."[183] But the PURS existed only on paper, and in 1965 it was replaced by the Cuban Communist Party (PCC).

The counterrevolutionary war also strengthened Cuba's coercive apparatus. The revolutionary army had at most 3,000 soldiers in early 1959,[184] and Castro initially planned for a small army of about 16,000.[185] However, the mounting counterrevolutionary threat forced Castro to change course.[186] By 1960, the revolutionary government was "fighting for its life,"[187] which convinced Castro and his allies that "arming to the teeth [was] necessary if the revolution and its leaders were going to survive."[188]

The government responded by building a garrison state,[189] with armed forces that were "sufficiently large to contemplate real deterrence of a superpower."[190] By early 1961, the army had 32,000 troops, with an additional 300,000 people in armed militias.[191] The expansion of the security forces accelerated after the Bay of Pigs invasion, as Castro "could now more than justify the deployment of major resources to an internal and external threat that had finally shown its teeth."[192] The army more than quadrupled in size, reaching 130,000 by late 1961 and 300,000 in 1964.[193] Military spending increased from 2 percent of GDP under Batista to 8 percent in 1962.[194] Cuba became "the most heavily armed country in Latin America."[195]

The regime also built a vast intelligence apparatus.[196] The government began to develop its intelligence capacity in 1960 in response to proliferating counterrevolutionary groups,[197] and by the time of the Bay of Pigs invasion, the Interior Ministry's embryonic intelligence network was able to thoroughly dismantle the underground opposition.[198] The government also created Committees for the Defense of the Revolution (CDRs), a neighborhood-level surveillance system that served as an "adjunct to the internal security apparatus."[199] The CDRs' chief purpose was surveillance and repression.[200] Founded under the slogan "Sweep the worms from the cities," CDRs rounded up tens of thousands of suspects during the Bay of Pigs invasion.[201] The CDRs expanded dramatically after the invasion; by 1962, there were 100,000 of them.[202] According to counterrevolutionary leader Rafael Quintero, the CDRs "were everywhere, all over the place . . . [and] became very strong. In fact, they totally destroyed the underground."[203]

Finally, the counterrevolutionary war accelerated the destruction of independent power centers. The counterrevolutionary threat, particularly the Bay of Pigs invasion, allowed the government to "cast a wide net for 'enemies.'"[204] One such enemy was the Church. With 200 churches and 212 religious schools, radio and television stations, and allied lay associations such as the Catholic University Group, the Young Catholic Students, and the Young Catholic Workers,[205] the Church was the only national institution that remained outside the government's control.[206] Given its strong upper-class ties,[207] the Church inevitably became an "institutional base" for conservatives seeking to resist the revolutionary onslaught.[208]

Indeed, Church leaders were at the forefront of opposition. In November 1959, Church leaders mobilized more than a million Catholics in downtown Havana for the National Catholic Conference, which, though nominally apolitical, took an oppositional tone, with participants chanting "Down with communism!"[209] In 1960, Church leaders launched a national campaign against communism.[210] They threatened to suspend services, as the Mexican Church had done in the 1920s.[211] At the same time, the Catholic University became a "center of opposition and conspiracy,"[212] and students from the Catholic University Group actively collaborated with the armed counterrevolutionary movement.[213]

The government began to repress the Church in late 1960, closing Catholic television and radio programs.[214] However, the crackdown escalated after the Bay of Pigs invasion, with which many Catholic activists collaborated.[215] When the invasion began, militias occupied churches, often suspending masses.[216] All bishops and most priests were arrested, and Cardinal Manuel Arteaga y Betancourt was forced to take refuge in the Argentine embassy for more than a year.[217]

The government used the April 1961 invasion to justify an all-out assault on the Church. Attacking the Catholic hierarchy as the "fifth column of the counterrevolution,"[218] Castro expropriated Church properties, shut down the Catholic University, dissolved Catholic organizations, and closed all Catholic schools.[219] In July, more than 100 priests, including Archbishop Enrique Pérez Serantes, were arrested, and following a September 1961 protest led by Bishop Eduardo Boza, 335 priests, including Boza, were expelled from the country.[220]

The repression "broke the back of Church resistance,"[221] destroying its counterrevolutionary potential.[222] With the departure of more than 450 priests, the number of clergy in Cuba fell by more than 70 percent.[223] The number of inhabitants per priest increased from 6,601 in 1959 to 35,400 in 1968, by far the highest ratio in Latin America.[224] Decimated by repression, the Church surrendered,[225] abandoning opposition for a "modus vivendi" in which it could engage in limited spiritual activities so long as it avoided politics or criticism of the government.[226] The Church was thus "reduced to liturgical practices."[227] By 1963, it had ceased to be a threat.[228]

The counterrevolutionary war also wiped out the landowning class. The 1959 land reform eliminated only large estates, and remaining middle farmers and ranchers provided a base for counterrevolutionary movements in the early 1960s.[229] Amid these persistent counterrevolutionary threats, the government launched another, more far-reaching land reform in 1963. The second reform expropriated all private holdings over 167 hectares,[230] which effectively eliminated landowners as a class.[231]

Likewise, the urban industrialist class was eliminated "in less than three years."[232] Because Cuban industry was so closely tied to the United

States, the U.S. military threat encouraged a rapid socialization of the economy in order to "prevent the Cuban private sector from collaborating with the United States."[233] Thus, most large- and medium-size businesses were nationalized in the late 1960s and early 1961.[234] By late 1961, the urban bourgeoisie had been destroyed.[235]

Counterrevolutionary forces were also weakened by mass emigration. Much of Cuba's socioeconomic and political elite fled to the United States after 1959. More than 200,000 Cubans left the country between 1960 and 1963, with most of them settling in Miami.[236] By the 1970s, more than 500,000 Cubans—nearly 10 percent of the population—had emigrated.[237]

The exodus of much of the prerevolutionary elite thinned the ranks of the opposition, limiting its capacity to challenge the regime.[238] Although the exile-based opposition remained active into the 1980s, transforming Miami into the "capital of the counterrevolution,"[239] it did not seriously threaten the regime.[240] The revolution thus "exported its political opposition," leaving behind "a more politically pliable population."[241]

By 1965, then, the revolution had consolidated. Counterrevolutionary movements had been defeated, U.S. invasion plans had been shelved, and the organizational bases for opposition had been destroyed. By the mid-1960s, there were "no truly associational interest groups" left in Cuba.[242] Regime consolidation could be attributed, in large part, to the Bay of Pigs invasion. As ex-counterrevolutionary leader Rafael Quintero put it, the revolution "started with the Bay of Pigs, because that's when Castro consolidated his power; that's when he was able to eliminate the underground resistance; that's when the Soviets started arriving."[243]

In sum, Castro's early radicalism triggered a powerful U.S.-backed counterrevolutionary reaction. The revolutionary elite responded to the counterrevolutionary threat by closing ranks, building a powerful security apparatus, assaulting independent power centers, and forging a close alliance with the Soviet Union—steps that would prove critical to the regime's long-run survival.

Revolutionary Legacies: A Durable Party-State

The regime that emerged from the counterrevolutionary conflict was considerably stronger than it had been in 1959. The regime rested upon a powerful party-state complex. Although the PCC was largely inactive until 1975, Cuba was nevertheless governed by a cohesive group of revolutionary veterans, most of whom had fought in the Sierra Maestra. The PCC was wedded to a powerful and disciplined coercive apparatus. At the same time, potential centers of societal resistance were virtually nonexistent.

ELITE COHESION AMID BELATED PARTY-BUILDING

Cuba's revolutionary elite was highly cohesive after 1965. Although this cohesion permitted the construction of a powerful ruling party, it was not generated by that party. Two distinctive characteristics of Cuba's revolutionary elite merit note. First, it was dominated by Castro. Revolutionary Cuba was a near-ideal-typical case of charismatic leadership.[244] Castro was the regime's primary source of legitimacy and popular support. He, not the PCC, was the linchpin holding the elite together.[245] Castro "overwhelmed" the party-state; once he made a decision, "neither the FAR nor the PCC could stop him."[246]

A second—related—characteristic was ruling party weakness. Although the PCC was founded in 1965, it "barely functioned" until 1975.[247] It lacked a program, its Central Committee rarely met, and it never held a congress.[248] Castro ignored it, instead ruling in an "institutional void."[249] As of the late 1960s, there was "no evidence that the Party Central Committee . . . made any decisions on its own."[250] The PCC strengthened in the 1970s,[251] adopting features of the Soviet Leninist model such as regular party congresses, a functioning Central Committee, a mass organization with cells in every corner of the country, and a "slightly more collective . . . leadership."[252] Nevertheless, Castro's unquestioned dominance over the party would persist until he retired in 2008.[253]

Notwithstanding the ruling party's weakness, Cuba's revolutionary elite remained highly cohesive. Nearly all top party positions were filled by loyal guerrilla veterans.[254] The PCC's founding leadership in 1965 was, in effect, a reincarnation of the July 26 Movement.[255] Six of the eight members of the new Politburo were commanders during the guerrilla war, and 70 of the 100 Central Committee members belonged to the July 26 Movement or fought in the rebel army.[256] These leaders were imbued with a "guerrilla mentality"[257] and a "remarkable esprit de corps."[258]

The PCC leadership would prove highly cohesive.[259] All eight original 1965 Politburo members and more than three-quarters of the original Central Committee members retained their posts in 1975.[260] As Herbert L. Matthews observed, nearly all the July 26 Movement's founding members were with Castro two decades later, serving as "leaders of his revolution, members of his government, his communist party, and his armed forces."[261]

A POWERFUL AND DISCIPLINED
COERCIVE APPARATUS

The regime also had a powerful coercive apparatus. By the mid-1960s, Cuba had developed a "more sophisticated . . . range of security services than had been seen in probably any Latin American government to date."[262] As noted above, the counterrevolutionary threat and the specter of U.S. invasion led the Castro government to invest heavily in domestic and external security.[263] Military spending—about 10 percent of government expenditures in the 1960s and 1970s—exceeded that of every other country in Latin America.[264] The army expanded to 300,000—ten times larger than Batista's army.[265] Thanks to Soviet assistance, moreover, the army was well trained, armed, and equipped.[266] By the mid-1960s, then, the U.S. State Department had concluded that Cuba had "the most powerful military establishment in Latin America."[267]

Ronald Reagan's presidency triggered further militarization in the 1980s.[268] Fearing that Cuba could not rely on the Soviet Union in the event of a U.S. attack, the government created the 800,000-strong Territorial Militia Troops, a Vietnam-style program aimed at raising the cost of a U.S. invasion.[269] By the mid-1980s, Cuba was one of the most militarized societies on earth, able to mobilize as many as two million people—20 percent of the population—for national defense.[270]

The FAR was also effective. Cuban security forces defeated counterrevolutionary insurgencies between 1959 and 1965,[271] thwarted the Bay of Pigs invasion, and were "probably sufficient to deter an invasion" in the 1970s.[272] In 1976, 20,000 Cuban troops confronted and pushed back the South African military in Angola.[273] By the 1970s, then, Cuba had one of the most developed armed forces in the world, with a "professional combat capacity that far exceeded what might be expected of a relatively small island nation."[274]

The regime also developed an "omnipresent" internal security apparatus,[275] at the heart of which was the General Direction of Intelligence (DGI, also known as the G-2). A highly effective secret police,[276] the DGI operated a vast network of trained agents, supplemented by as many as three million informants.[277] At the same time, neighborhood CDRs functioned as a "street by street spy system."[278] By 1965, there were 102,000 CDRs—with more than two million members—operating across Cuba.[279] Widespread surveillance and an extensive rationing system allowed the Cuban state to establish unprecedented societal control, which facilitated low-intensity coercion.[280] By the 1980s, Cuba had one of the most effective intelligence systems on earth. Former CIA analyst Brian Latell rated the Cuban intelligence system one of the five or six best in the world.[281]

PARTY-ARMY FUSION AND MILITARY COHESION

The revolutionary security forces were tightly wedded to the ruling party. The Cuban regime was characterized by near-total party-army fusion.[282] Cuba's civilian and military elites were "inextricably linked."[283] The FAR emerged directly out of the guerrilla army, and nearly all its leaders were veterans of the Sierra Maestra.[284] The commanders of the army (Raúl Castro) and the domestic security apparatus (Ramiro Valdes) were members of the original *Granma* expedition.[285] Indeed, revolutionary veterans permeated the entire military hierarchy. In 1968, all Cuban army captains were ex-guerrillas.[286] This fusion persisted into the 1980s.[287] As Rafael Fermoselle's biographies of Cuban military officials show, nearly all the army's top generals in the mid-1980s had fought against Batista.[288]

Military leaders also played a major role in the party leadership. When the PCC was founded in 1965, six of eight Politburo members were former revolutionary commanders, and five of eight were active military officers.[289] A striking 69 percent of Central Committee members held a military title, and 58 percent were active members of the military.[290] In 1975, more than 60 percent of Central Committee members had military backgrounds—a degree of party-army fusion that exceeded that of China and the Soviet Union.[291]

The PCC did not establish a Soviet-style commissar system.[292] Although political officers and party cells operated in each military unit, party operatives were recruited from within the army, appointed by army officers, and answered to the army command.[293] This arrangement had no discernible impact on army loyalty, however. Because the army command was fused with the revolutionary elite, military officers could do political work as reliably as party operatives.

Party-army fusion brought a striking degree of military loyalty.[294] Army officers "saw themselves primarily as revolutionaries."[295] As William M. Leo-Grande observed, there was "no real issue of civilian control over the armed forces" because "those who held administrative control *were* the armed forces."[296] Indeed, Cuba experienced virtually no civil-military conflict after 1959.[297] With the single exception of Huber Matos, a regional commander who was removed and arrested after criticizing Castro's radicalization in October 1959,[298] the loyalty of the armed forces was never in doubt.[299] Indeed, there was not a single coup attempt between 1959 and 2021.[300]

WEAK CENTERS OF SOCIETAL POWER

Finally, independent centers of societal power were largely wiped out by 1965. Beyond family-owned farms and businesses, the private sector was extinct. Land reform eliminated the landowning class, and the nationalizations and emigration of the early 1960s reduced the bourgeoisie to "barbers and beauticians."[301]

The Church was badly weakened. By the early 1960s, the Cuban Church was "institutionally the weakest in all of Latin America."[302] It was stripped of most of its property, including all schools and media outlets, and it lost three-quarters of its priests to expulsion and exile.[303] Church attendance plummeted.[304] Thus, the Church was left with "virtually no role in Cuban society."[305] After 1962, the Catholic hierarchy was politically silent.[306] Church leaders never criticized the regime and eventually began to publicly endorse government positions.[307] By the 1970s, Domínguez observed that Church leaders "criticize the government less than the government criticizes itself."[308]

By the late 1960s, then, most regime opponents had been "killed, jailed, or neutralized in one way or another,"[309] and independent associational life had been stamped out.[310] Thus, opposition mobilization was hindered not only by state repression but also by the "absence of institutional mechanisms . . . in which to develop political activity."[311]

In sum, the three pillars of durable authoritarianism were established in Cuba by 1965. The regime was led by a cohesive elite (though not a strong party), which was fused to a powerful and disciplined coercive apparatus. Independent centers of societal power had been wiped out by repression and exile, creating a state-societal power asymmetry that would endure for decades. Although Cuba would rely heavily on Soviet military and economic assistance in the years that followed, it is clear that the revolution was "internally secure . . . well before the Soviets committed themselves."[312]

Crisis and Regime Durability, 1965–2020

Cuba's revolutionary regime endured for more than sixty years, demonstrating a "remarkable capacity to survive under difficult circumstances."[313] Unlike Mexico, the Cuban regime did not benefit from economic growth. Cuba's per capita GDP declined during the 1960s, grew modestly in the 1970s and 1980s, and then declined again in the 1990s.[314] In 1999, per capita GDP was at roughly the same level as it was at the end of the Batista dictatorship.[315]

To be sure, the regime benefited from massive Soviet support. The USSR provided an estimated $65 billion in economic subsidies and at least $13.4 billion in military assistance between 1960 and 1990.[316] Military assistance was critical to building up Cuba's armed forces,[317] and billions of dollars in Soviet trade subsidies made the regime "immune to the laws of bankruptcy."[318] By the 1980s, Soviet economic assistance reached $4–$6 billion a year, covering more than half the Cuban budget.[319] Without this assistance, the revolution might have failed.[320]

Yet the fact that the regime survived for more than three decades *after* the collapse of the Soviet Union suggests that the domestic bases for regime stability were strong. These bases were provided by three revolutionary legacies. The first was an unusually cohesive elite. The PCC leadership was dominated by revolutionary veterans, or *historicos*, into the twenty-first century.[321] Described by Herbert L. Matthews as a "cohesive, blindly loyal group,"[322] the *historicos* were characterized by a marked "tendency . . . to close ranks in defense of the revolution."[323] Indeed, Cuba's ruling elite suffered remarkably few schisms.[324] Through the mid-1980s, not a single member of the founding PCC leadership defected.[325] All the original Politburo members remained except for President Dorticós, who died, and Fauro Chomon, who was demoted to the Central Committee.[326] Although the PCC grew more factionalized in the 1980s and 1990s,[327] there were no high-level defections through the early twenty-first century.[328]

Second, the regime was characterized by extraordinary military cohesion and loyalty. Like the PCC, the army and internal security hierarchies were dominated by revolutionary veterans into the twenty-first century.[329] By all accounts, the armed forces remained disciplined and loyal throughout the 1965–2020 period—a strikingly unusual outcome in Latin America.[330]

Third, the combination of a powerful security apparatus and the destruction of independent power centers created a vast and enduring power asymmetry between the regime and its opponents. Thus, even during periods of widespread public discontent, such as the late 1960s and the early and mid-1990s, dissidents lacked the organizational resources to mobilize opposition. This allowed the Castro government to make major policy mistakes and "each time survive to continue making unwise decisions."[331]

THE "HERESY" PERIOD, 1965–1970

The first serious crisis faced by the revolutionary regime after consolidation was of its own making. Between 1965 and 1970, the Castro government pursued radical domestic and foreign policies that threw Cuba's economy into turmoil and threatened its alliance with the Soviet Union. In what has been described as the revolution's "heresy" period,[332] Castro abandoned Soviet-style orthodoxy in favor of utopian ideas associated with Che Guevara.[333] Thus, the government sought to eliminate material exchange and build an economy based on moral incentives.[334] Budgets, taxation, payments, and virtually all links between production and remuneration would be eliminated.[335] Indeed, Castro declared his intention to eliminate money altogether.[336]

The transition to "communism" would be accompanied by the emergence of a "new man," whose behavior would be guided by "moral," rather than material, incentives.[337] In line with these objectives, the government mobilized tens of thousands of Cubans for volunteer labor; volunteer work accounted for 8–12 percent of all labor in 1967 and 1968.[338]

The shift to a "moral economy" was accompanied by the March 1968 Revolutionary Offensive, in which about 57,000 small businesses—including all grocery stores, restaurants, cafés, laundries, garages, and even fruit stands—were expropriated, wiping out the last vestiges of private ownership.[339] Almost overnight, Cuba became "the most socialized economy in the world."[340] In defending these measures, Castro declared that the revolution had "not been sufficiently radical" and that "we will not create a socialist consciousness . . . with the mentality of shopkeepers."[341] Although the Revolutionary Offensive generated domestic resistance and was criticized by Soviet officials,[342] the government accepted these risks. As President Dorticós told Polish intellectual K. S. Karol, Cuban leaders "have our little heresy."[343]

The Cubans also broke with Soviet foreign policy. Despite Soviet opposition, the Castro government continued its "unbending" support for guerrilla movements in Latin America and elsewhere in the mid- and late 1960s.[344] By 1968, Castro was "becoming almost intolerable" to the Soviets.[345]

The utopian turn proved catastrophic.[346] Moral incentives failed; absenteeism soared, reaching 50 percent in some places,[347] while productivity plummeted,[348] throwing Cuba into a serious economic crisis.[349] By 1968, Castro was in "deep trouble."[350] Cuban-Soviet relations had reached a breaking point, and exasperated Soviet leaders threatened to cut off Cuba's oil supply.[351] At home, "everything seemed to be coming apart."[352]

Castro responded by doubling down. Although he tempered his foreign policy in line with Soviet demands,[353] he launched another utopian economic scheme: the 10-million-ton sugar harvest. The campaign to harvest 10 million tons of sugar in 1970 was a political Hail Mary pass.[354] Cuba had never harvested more than 7.2 million tons of sugar, and in the mid-1960s the harvest had ranged between 4 and 5 million tons.[355] Castro's target of 10 million tons was thus utopian.[356] Nevertheless, he bet the regime's legitimacy on the harvest, calling it a "yardstick by which to judge the capacity of the Revolution"[357] and declaring that even a 9.999-million-ton harvest would be a "moral defeat."[358] "Virtually all national resources" were diverted into the campaign.[359] Two-thirds of the army were mobilized,[360] and an estimated 1.2 million workers—many of them "volunteers"—were redeployed, at great cost, from other sectors of the economy.[361] Yet the campaign only achieved 8.5 million tons—a "colossal failure."[362]

The failure of the sugar campaign dealt an unprecedented blow to the regime's legitimacy.[363] As Castro declared, "Our enemies say we are faced with difficulties, and in fact our enemies are right."[364]

Yet these failures did not seriously threaten the regime. Despite widespread discontent, there were no regime defections.[365] At the height of the conflict with the Soviet Union, an intraparty crisis—known as the "microfaction" crisis—erupted when a group of ex-PSP leaders with ties to Moscow attempted to challenge Castro, apparently with Soviet support.[366] About three dozen (mostly ex-PSP) cadres were arrested.[367] Importantly, however, none of the dissidents were high-level party leaders, revealing that if Soviet officials conspired against Castro, they "found few, if any, proxies within the PCC to challenge [him]."[368] Likewise, Castro faced no challenge from the military.[369] Even in the wake of the disastrous sugar campaign, there were no signs of military rebellion.[370] Finally, the destruction of independent power centers made it difficult to translate public discontent into organized opposition. Thus, even though the Castro government faced a severe legitimacy crisis, "no opposition existed that could present a viable new alternative."[371]

THE CRISIS OF COMMUNISM AND THE SOVIET COLLAPSE, 1986–1995

The regime was relatively stable between 1970 and the mid-1980s. Although Reagan's ascent to the presidency triggered renewed fears of U.S. intervention,[372] the renewed threat ultimately strengthened the regime by reinforcing a siege mentality among the revolutionary elite.[373]

Beginning in the mid-1980s, however, the regime faced a series of mounting challenges. For one, the economy ground to a halt, generating widespread discontent.[374] Yet, whereas communists in the Soviet Union, China, and Vietnam pursued market-oriented reforms in the late 1980s, Castro responded to the crisis by rejecting markets in favor of a return to "consciousness" and volunteer work.[375] Declaring that Cuba's past errors had come from mimicking the Soviet Union,[376] Castro rejected perestroika in favor of rectification, which combined orthodox communism and elements of the "moral economy" approach of the 1960s.[377] Thus, the government abolished farmers markets and other private economic activities that had been permitted in the 1970s[378] and mobilized 400,000 workers—14 percent of the workforce—into volunteer "microbrigades" to work in agriculture and the construction of housing, health clinics, and day care centers.[379]

Rectification triggered a level of internal dissent not seen since the late 1960s.[380] Most notably, General Arnoldo Ochoa, a decorated and popular military officer who reportedly sympathized with Soviet reformer Mikhail Gorbachev, came to be viewed as a potential threat.[381] Although Ochoa never actually rebelled, plotted, or even spoke out against the government, he and several allies were purged from the armed forces in June 1989, arrested for drug trafficking, and executed the following month.[382] Given Ochoa's stature and popularity, his execution "would have been inconceivable in most Latin American countries,"[383] and there is evidence that it triggered discontent within the army.[384] However, no military rebellion ensued.[385]

The Ochoa case was just the beginning of the crisis, however. Beginning in 1990, the collapse of the Soviet Union generated an external shock the likes of which few regimes have survived. Soviet subsidies had kept the Cuban economy afloat in the 1980s, covering more than half the government budget.[386] Without Soviet support, observers noted, the Cuban economy "would simply collapse."[387]

That is precisely what happened. The Soviet Union's demise threw the regime into an unprecedented crisis.[388] Cuba's economy contracted by 25 percent in 1991 and between 35 and 50 percent between 1989 and 1993.[389] Cubans' purchasing power fell by 70 percent, and fuel and energy supplies nearly evaporated.[390] In late 1991, Castro acknowledged that Cubans faced "the most difficult period in [our] history."[391]

Nevertheless, Castro refused to adopt either market-oriented economic reforms, as in China and Vietnam, or liberalizing political reforms, as in Eastern Europe.[392] He declared, "Capitalist reforms? Never! Everybody must know that the revolution won't retreat even one millimeter on this. . . . We are not going to 'privatize' absolutely anything."[393] Instead, the government hunkered down, inaugurating the "Special Period" of peacetime austerity, marked by extensive rationing and a dramatic reduction in public consumption.[394] Blackouts became routine, and fuel was so scarce that the government was forced to import half a million bicycles from China, with Castro telling Cubans, "We are entering the bicycle era."[395] For the first time since 1959, the government was unable to provide basic foodstuffs.[396] By 1993, most Cubans had been largely without meat or dairy products for two years.[397]

The economic collapse posed a major challenge. Public discontent soared,[398] and dozens of dissident groups emerged.[399] Even the long-silent Church called for an end to single-party rule in 1993.[400] Government officials feared a "social explosion,"[401] and, indeed, there were unprecedented street riots in 1993 and 1994.[402] The largest of these was the August 1994 *Habanazo*, in which 3,000 protesters destroyed stores, threw stones and bottles, and chanted "Down with Fidel!" at the main esplanade (Malecon) in central Havana.[403]

The 1990–1994 crisis led many observers to believe the regime was on its last legs. A CIA working group on Cuba concluded that the odds of Castro's falling were better than 50–50.[404] Longtime observer Andres Oppenheimer published a book titled *Castro's Final Hour*, and influential scholars characterized the revolution as being in its "last days."[405]

Yet the regime survived. There are three main reasons for this outcome, all of which are linked to the regime's revolutionary origins. First, the ruling elite remained cohesive.[406] The PCC leadership was still dominated by the founding revolutionary generation.[407] In 1991, fourteen of twenty-five Politburo members were veterans of the revolutionary struggle.[408] United by a "siege mentality,"[409] the regime elite again closed ranks. There were no schisms or defections.

Second, the armed forces remained loyal.[410] The Soviet collapse brought severe shortages in supplies and other resources, which generated considerable rank-and-file discontent within the armed forces.[411] As Richard L. Millet observed, "If the FAR were a traditional Latin American military institution, such a situation would seem to invite a coup."[412] However, such an outcome was "never in the cards."[413] Like the party, the armed forces were still commanded by first-generation revolutionaries with deep loyalties to the regime.[414] Indeed, there is no evidence of army disloyalty during the Special Period.[415]

Third, the persistence of vast state-society power asymmetries made it difficult to translate societal discontent into anti-regime mobilization. Due to the absence of autonomous associations or institutions capable of sustaining collective action, organized opposition never grew beyond a few dozen small dissident groups.[416] No protest ever mobilized more than 3,000 people.[417] The feared "social explosion" never materialized. As Enrique A. Baloyra observed, the population's seeming passivity was rooted in both the regime's repressive capacity and the weakness of independent power centers:

> There are practically no autonomous intermediary institutions in Cuban society. In Cuba, there is no [Catholic] Church that can mobilize the masses as was the case in Poland . . . an independent labor movement such as Solidarnosc is nowhere in sight. . . . Cuban dissidents and intellectuals have been unable to come together into anything comparable to Charter 77. . . .
>
> Absent institutional sanctuaries and social spaces . . . the atomization that characterizes Stalinist forms of political control has been singularly effective in preventing the development of horizontal solidarities that normally precede the crystallization of organized forms of public protest.[418]

The limited societal contestation that *did* emerge in the early 1990s was easily contained via low-intensity coercion. The government deployed CDRs and "rapid-reaction brigades" to nip protest in the bud.[419] Dissidents were monitored, harassed, fired from their jobs, and, in some cases, arrested and imprisoned.[420] Effective low-intensity repression thus deterred collective mobilization, making a mass uprising "improbable."[421]

CASTRO'S DEATH AND LEADERSHIP SUCCESSION, 2008–2021

The regime stabilized in the second half of the 1990s. The Cuban economy recovered somewhat,[422] and the government undertook modest economic reforms, including the legalization of small-scale private economic activities.[423] The loosening of totalitarian controls permitted the emergence of a "proto civil society."[424] Small dissident groups emerged, such as Concilio Cubano, the Cuban Human Rights Committee, the National Commission for Human Rights and Reconciliation, the Harmony Movement, and the Varela Project.[425] These groups remained small and scattered,[426] however, which allowed the regime to rely on low-intensity coercion—surveillance, harassment, and occasional arrests—to keep them in check.[427] An example is the Varela Project, which was created by prominent dissident Oswaldo Payá in 1998.[428] In 2002, the Varela Project collected 11,000 signatures calling for a referendum on free elections and civil liberties.[429] This was too much for Castro, and in March 2003, twenty-one Varela Project leaders and more than fifty other dissidents were imprisoned.[430] The organization never recovered.[431]

The most serious regime challenge in the early 2000s was posed by succession. In 2006, illness forced Castro to take leave of the presidency, and in 2008 he formally retired (he died in 2016). He was succeeded by his brother, Vice President Raúl Castro. Fidel's departure was widely expected to trigger a regime crisis. When news of it broke, Miami's Little Havana neighborhood exploded in anticipatory celebration.[432] U.S. assistant secretary of state for Western Hemispheric Affairs Thomas Shannon declared that dictatorships "are like helicopters. There are single fail point mechanisms. When a rotor comes off a helicopter, it crashes. When a supreme leader disappears from an authoritarian regime, the authoritarian regime flounders."[433] Yet the succession was uneventful. There were no protests,[434] no stirring in the military, and "no fissures . . . in the leadership."[435]

Raúl Castro presided over the departure of the revolutionary generation. Between 2010 and 2013, much of the old guard leadership was replaced.[436] In 2018, Raúl Castro stepped down from the presidency. His successor, Vice President Miguel Díaz-Canel, was born after the revolution. Castro stepped down as first secretary of the Communist Party in 2021. Although the succession occurred without serious incident, the passing of the revolutionary generation poses a significant challenge. Unlike China and Vietnam, Cuba has not achieved sustained economic growth. The regime faced unprecedented protest in mid-2021. Although the protests were put down with relative ease, the regime's capacity to sustain elite cohesion and, if necessary, engage in high-intensity repression is open to question.

The Cuban case largely conforms to our ideal-typical path of revolutionary regime consolidation. Radical domestic and foreign policies triggered counterrevolutionary rebellions, a U.S-backed invasion, and a persistent U.S. military threat. In response, the "civic soldiers" that surrounded Fidel Castro crystalized into a cohesive civilian and military elite that built a vast security apparatus and wiped out independent centers of societal power. The result was a vast state-societal power asymmetry that endured for more than a half a century, allowing the regime to survive its own misguided policies, the collapse of the Soviet Union, and Castro's death.

Alternative explanations cannot explain this regime durability. First, the fact that no prerevolutionary autocracy had ever endured for more than a decade before 1959 limits the plausibility of claims that there existed conditions for durable authoritarianism absent a revolution. Second, the Cuban regime survived for many years without a real party. Although the PCC eventually became an institutionalized ruling party, the fact that it was founded and led for decades by a stable network of revolutionary veterans suggests that party strength was rooted in the revolution. Third, the widespread discontent generated by the economic crisis of the 1980s and 1990s belies claims that mass support undergirded regime stability. Instead, it was the authoritarian pillars that emerged out of the revolutionary reactive sequence—a cohesive elite, a powerful and loyal security, and the destruction of associational life—that best explain the durability of Cuba's revolutionary regime.

IRAN

Like the Castro government, Iran's revolutionary government was born weak but immediately attacked everything around it. The Islamic Republic of Iran (IRI) emerged in 1979 out of a ramshackle coalition of secular nationalists, communists, and clerics that barely controlled the country. But rather than seeking to shore up domestic and international support, Ayatollah Ruhollah Khomeini imposed clerical rule, fomented revolution abroad, and supported the seizure of hostages in the U.S. embassy. The revolutionary government became a major sponsor of terrorism in the Middle East and eventually launched a program of nuclear armament. No other revolutionary regime examined in this book has been so internationally isolated for so long.

At the same time, unlike most revolutionary autocracies, the IRI lacked almost *any* Leninist institutions. Instead, the regime was constructed in a way that seemed to encourage intra-elite conflict. Not only was there no ruling party for most of its existence, but the IRI held regular, semi-competitive elections, which encouraged factions to flourish.[437]

Despite these challenges, however, the IRI endured for more than forty years, surviving a costly eight-year war with Iraq, the death of its founding leader, a massive protest movement in 2009, and debilitating sanctions and popular unrest in the 2010s. And even though factionalism was more open and intense than in most revolutionary cases, regime insiders remained almost entirely loyal to clerical rule.

As in Cuba, this durability was rooted in a revolutionary reactive sequence. Khomeini's radical challenges to the domestic and international order generated a violent insurgency and war with Iraq, which reinforced elite cohesion and motivated the development of a powerful and loyal coercive apparatus and the destruction of virtually all organized alternatives. The revolutionary reactive sequence produced a formidable "deep state" capable of putting down popular threats, as well as a regime elite that, though riven by factionalism, almost entirely avoided outright opposition.

The Revolutionary Seizure of Power

Like Cuba, the Iranian revolution emerged out of a sultanistic dictatorship. The Pahlavi dynasty was founded in 1925 by Reza Khan, a commander of the Persian Cossack brigade who declared himself king. Due to his Axis sympathies, Reza was ousted by the British in 1941 and replaced by his son, Mohammad Reza Pahlavi. The second Pahlavi monarch was initially weak and constrained by an elected Majlis (parliament). In the early 1950s, the Majlis produced a nationalist government led by Mohammad Mosaddegh, whose National Front tapped into the growing opposition to British control over Iran's natural resources.[438] After Mosaddegh sought to nationalize Iranian oil, a U.S.- and British-backed coup toppled Mosaddegh, forced the National Front underground, and established the shah firmly in power.[439]

Taking advantage of greater access to oil revenue, the shah dramatically expanded his personal power after 1954.[440] Increasingly, the line between public resources and the shah's personal finances was blurred. Corruption was rampant.[441] The shah soon began to exercise an extraordinary degree of personal control over the armed services. He forbade military chiefs from communicating with each other and packed the armed services with cronies. The shah's explicit permission was required for all appointments and arms purchases, and even to move troops from one barrack to another.[442] As a result, the military was highly fragmented. With U.S. and British support, the shah also built a large, well-funded, and effective security apparatus under his direct control—the SAVAK.[443]

The shah used his power to eliminate checks on his rule. Opposition parties were banned, and in 1963, a set of sweeping reforms—the so-called White Revolution—expropriated the landholdings of the powerful "Thousand Families," effectively eliminating landowners as an independent social class.[444] After that, very little organized opposition remained.

The Pahlavi regime enjoyed decades of stability. Thanks to a combination of steady economic growth, oil revenue, U.S. support, and a powerful security apparatus, Iran appeared to be a beacon of stability through the mid-1970s.[445] As late as mid-1978, the CIA concluded that Iran was "not in a revolutionary or even a pre-revolutionary situation."[446]

The shah was vulnerable, however. Because the regime was sustained in large part by the security forces, oil revenue, and the United States, the shah did not need to build a broad domestic support coalition.[447] Personal rule allowed him to govern in a manner that was at odds with leading interests, public opinion, and the prevailing culture. His government trampled on property rights and, in the 1970s, arrested thousands of shopkeepers in an effort to control inflation.[448] In addition, the shah's support for Israel[449] and open disregard for religious traditions generated fierce opposition among the country's Shiite clerics.[450]

One high-ranking cleric in particular, Ayatollah Khomeini, emerged as a prominent critic of the regime after the White Revolution threatened the autonomy and power of the Shiite clergy.[451] Following an uprising in June 1963 supported by radical clerics, Khomeini was exiled to Turkey and then Iraq.[452] However, his stature only grew. In a context in which all other opposition had been either co-opted or locked away, Khomeini's clear and uncompromising opposition attracted broad popular support from a wide range of both secular and religious opponents of the shah.[453]

In exile, Khomeini developed and diffused a set of radical new ideas. He wrote several books arguing that clerics should directly rule Iran according to religious doctrine. His ideas of clerical rule—Velayat-e Faqih (Rule of the Jurist)—marked a sharp break from traditional Shiite beliefs, which held that clerics should remain outside secular power structures.[454] Before Khomeini, the terms "Islamic" and "Republic" had never been put together.[455] Such views were opposed by most Shiite clergy, both in Iran and across the Middle East.[456] Yet the exiled Khomeini would eventually become a unifying figure for the opposition—and his radical ideas would eventually transform the region's politics.

Khomeini's influence was reinforced by a dramatic growth in religious institutions during the 1960s and 1970s.[457] By the 1970s, there were 9,000 mosques and 180,000 mullahs in Iran.[458] In Tehran alone, there existed 12,300 religious associations. Even so, the demand for clerics often outstripped supply, leading to the development of a vast market for religious tapes and cassettes—which helped to diffuse Khomeini's message.[459] Although mosques cooperated with the regime for most of the shah's tenure, their autonomy and societal penetration gave them vast revolutionary potential.

The shah's regime thus faced a diversity of opponents, including leftists, secular nationalists, merchants, and religious conservatives. These groups were united in their antipathy toward the regime. They were also bound by nationalism. Due to the shah's close ties to the West, he was widely viewed as a lackey of the United States. Finally, the exiled Khomeini emerged as a powerful unifying figure for regime opponents, including leftists and secular nationalists—many of whom did not take his plans for clerical rule seriously because they viewed religion as a "dying force."[460]

The shah's vulnerability was exacerbated by the regime's sultanistic character. By hollowing out and personalizing state institutions, the shah created a regime that was brittle and thoroughly dependent on his leadership. When he faltered, so, too, did the regime.

The 1979 revolution was rooted in a series of contingent events and missteps by the shah. On the external front, the election of Jimmy Carter brought pressure for reform, generating fears that the United States was no longer fully committed to the shah's survival.[461] At home, a government-sponsored editorial in 1978 calling Khomeini a British agent, together with a tragic fire at the Cinema Rex theater in the city of Abadan, triggered waves of protest that increasingly threatened the shah's hold on power.[462] Protesters gained the support of *bazaari* shopkeepers and a growing number of mosques; by mid-1978, large-scale protest had erupted across Iran.[463]

The shah's inconsistent response to these protests—brutal repression, followed by concessions—further fueled anti-regime mobilization.[464] On September 8, 1978, known as Black Friday, the shah declared martial law and troops massacred eighty-eight protesters. The shah followed this repression with mixed signals, arresting thirteen loyalists to appease protesters (effectively telling supporters that loyalty to the shah would be punished) but also appointing a military commander as prime minister to enforce martial law. On December 10 and 11, millions of Iranians took to the streets across the country to call for the shah's departure and Khomeini's return. A month later, the shah left the country, never to return—triggering state collapse.

On February 1, 1979, Khomeini's Air France flight from Paris set down in a country that not only lacked a government but increasingly had no state. Because control over the military had been so thoroughly personalized under the shah, the armed forces could not rule—or even maintain order—in his absence. As a result, they were paralyzed and grew increasingly demoralized.[465] State power evaporated.[466] Between 5 and 10 percent of the army's soldiers had deserted their posts by the time Khomeini returned from exile.[467] On February 9, 800 air force technicians and mechanics from the Doshan Tappeh Air Force Base defected to Khomeini.[468] Loyalist Imperial Guards attacked the air base in response, but over "three glorious days," leftist and religious militias—the Islamist-Marxist Mojahedin-e-Khalq (MK) and the Marxist-Leninist People's Fadai—battled and defeated the Imperial Guards, seized weapons, and distributed them to mosques and community centers.[469] These events triggered a wave of arms seizures across the country, as well as mass defections from all ranks in the army. The Iranian state disintegrated. Whole units surrendered, and on February 11, the Supreme Council of the Armed Forces declared neutrality, thereby sealing the fate of the shah's regime.[470]

Revolutionary forces quickly set out to disable what remained of the coercive apparatus. Viewing the military as a bastion of U.S. imperialism that had "the Shah in its blood,"[471] Khomeini and his allies grew obsessed with purging it.[472] Revolutionary tribunals were set up, and on February 15, four high-ranking generals were executed on the roof of the revolutionary headquarters, a former girls' elementary school. Hundreds of other military officials were executed in the weeks that followed.[473] In July, the discovery of a shah loyalist's plot to bomb Khomeini's home led to executions of 144 officers and the purge of 4,500 military personnel.[474] By September 1980, 12,000 soldiers had been discharged.[475] The army's officer corps shrank by as much as 60 percent.[476] By 1980, the Iranian army had been reduced nearly in half, from 285,000 to 150,000 troops.[477] Within a few years, the state bureaucracy was radically transformed, and the Pahlavi elite almost entirely replaced.[478]

The Revolutionary Reactive Sequence

Like Cuba's, Iran's revolutionary regime was born weak. The new government was "a conglomerate of contradictory forces united only in their rejection of the shah's regime."[479] It included secular nationalists, communists, and clerics. Although Khomeini was very popular, he had not been in the country since 1964 and lacked anything remotely like the kind of organization needed to establish order.[480] He could not even find enough trusted allies to fill the newly created Council of the Islamic Republic.[481] Prime Minister Mehdi Bazargan, a secular nationalist, had little influence. As in Russia in early 1917, formal power was vested in a provisional government, but real authority lay in the hands of a disorderly collection of revolutionary leaders and ill-defined councils. Amid the power vacuum created by the dissolution of the old regime, a hodgepodge of militias and 1,500 revolutionary *komitehs* (committees) emerged to establish order.[482]

Despite the precariousness and diversity of his coalition, Khomeini initiated a radical campaign to transform Iranian society and establish clerical rule. He declared divorce illegal, banned alcohol, shut down discos and bars, restricted foreign travel, and attacked women's rights, revoking many shah-era gender equality reforms and eventually making it illegal for women to appear in public without a head covering.[483] Harsh penalties were imposed for insulting clerics or denigrating Islam.[484] Universities were shut down for three years to cleanse them of Western influence.[485] On April 1, a referendum was held in which Iranians could choose to either maintain the monarchy or create an Islamic republic. With the choice framed so starkly, the Islamic Republic won overwhelmingly.[486]

Most importantly, Khomeini and his allies unilaterally designed a new constitution that allowed for semi-free elections for a president and a legislature (Majlis) but gave ultimate power to a supreme leader, or faqih. The Council of Guardians, which included six experts in Islamic law appointed by the faqih, approved candidates for the Majlis, the presidency, and the Assembly of Experts, who were in turn responsible for appointing the faqih. The popularly elected president was in charge of the government but subordinate to the supreme leader. This effort to institutionalize clerical rule triggered resistance from erstwhile leftist allies, as well as from prominent religious moderates such as Ayatollah Mohammad Kazem Shariatmadari.[487]

Khomeini also boldly confronted the United States. On November 4, 1979, in what Khomeini called "Iran's second revolution," radical students seized the U.S. embassy in Tehran, taking more than fifty hostages.[488] The action generated international outrage, and the hapless Prime Minister Bazargan resigned after failing to stop it.[489] The ensuing 444-day crisis left Iran isolated and cost the government $12 billion in assets held abroad.[490] With a single stroke, Iran became a global pariah.

Although seizing American hostages was extraordinarily risky, the ensuing conflict temporarily unified many of the regime's disparate forces at a critical moment in the transition.[491] With Iran under siege from the United States and much of the world, and with foreign agents believed to be everywhere,[492] many nationalists and leftists were put on the defensive. The Communist Tudeh Party set aside its opposition to clerical rule and closed ranks behind the regime. Khomeini was able to shut down debate on the constitution. In this context of intense international threat, opposition to the new constitution was equated with treason.[493] The new constitution was approved in December 1980.

But unity was short-lived. The imposition of clerical rule generated intense opposition, including a major counterrevolutionary insurgency. The leftist MK militia, an ally in the struggle against the shah, launched a wave of assassinations in 1981, including Prime Minister Javad Bahonar and Iran's second president, Ali Rejai.[494] On June 27, 1981, future supreme leader Ali Khamenei suffered a bomb attack during a sermon, which incapacitated his right arm. A day later, another bomb struck the headquarters of the pro-government Islamic Republican Party (IRP), killing seventy-three officials, including Chief Justice Seyyed Beheshti.[495] Hundreds of government officials were killed during this period.[496] Leftist guerrilla groups briefly seized the city of Amol in early 1982.[497] Armed rebellions also broke out in Tabriz, Kurdistan, and Khuzestan,[498] nearly plunging Iran into civil war.[499] The stakes were further heightened after the Majlis impeached President Abolhassan Bani-Sadr. Bani-Sadr responded by aligning with the MK and seeking to incite a popular uprising against the clerics.[500] This would be virtually the only direct challenge to clerical rule by a major regime insider for more than four decades.

In response to this violent resistance, the revolutionary government launched a massive terror campaign that eliminated virtually all organized opposition.[501] At least 3,000 people, and perhaps as many as 8,000, were executed between 1981 and 1983.[502] The MK was forced into exile. The Communist Tudeh Party was banned and repressed, and all other political groups were destroyed or forced underground.[503]

Critically, the conflict also gave the government an excuse to quash the many influential Shiite leaders who opposed clerical rule. Prominent moderate clerics were assaulted by pro-government thugs and effectively silenced.[504]

Violent conflict gave rise to a powerful and loyal security apparatus. Unlike most revolutionary cases, Iran's prerevolutionary army survived the revolution. However, it was purged, downsized, and significantly downgraded in importance.[505] Simultaneously, the revolutionary government created two new and more powerful security forces from scratch. One was the Islamic Revolutionary Guard Corps (IRGC). Created from revolutionary guerrilla units battling loyalist army units in February 1979,[506] the IRGC became the most important security force in the country,[507] dwarfing the power of the army. The other new security force was the Basij. Created in late 1979, the Basij was intended to be a "20-million-man militia" to defend the revolution against internal and external enemies.[508]

The IRGC and the Basij were commanded by revolutionary ideologues with close ties to the supreme leader.[509] These ties fostered an intense commitment to the regime and its survival.[510] The capacity to crack down on dissent was considered a prerequisite for promotion in the IRGC.[511] Leaders were expected to act regardless of public opinion.[512] Viewing themselves as religious organizations and the source (and judge) of revolutionary purity in Iran,[513] the Basij and the IRGC demonstrated extraordinary loyalty to the supreme leader.[514] Efforts by moderate factions to assert control over the security forces under President Bani-Sadr and Seyyed Mohammad Khatami failed.[515]

Counterrevolutionary conflict led to a dramatic increase in the size, scope, and capacity of the IRGC and the Basij. The IRGC began as an underfunded and ill-trained group of guerrilla fighters.[516] However, the Khomeini government relied heavily on the IRGC to put down attacks by the MK and other armed rivals in the early 1980s,[517] and, as a result, it quickly developed into one of the most powerful—and best-funded—institutions in Iran.[518] The IRGC expanded from about 4,000 troops in May 1979 to 25,000 in September 1980.[519] The Guard's central role in the counterinsurgency led it to rapidly develop its intelligence capacity and expand its presence in urban areas.[520] For its part, the Basij played a major role in defeating leftist guerrillas and suppressing communist revolts in northern Iran.[521]

The revolutionary regime also plunged into external conflict in the 1980s. The 1979 hostage crisis made an enemy of the United States, and relations with the Soviet Union deteriorated after Iran banned the Tudeh Party and subjected its members to Stalinist-style show trials in 1983.[522] The regime also generated tension in the Middle East. Khomeini called on the Iraqi public to rise up against Saddam Hussein and appealed for an Islamic revolution throughout the Persian Gulf.[523] Such moves triggered hostility among most Arab states.[524] Iran became a major sponsor of terrorism in the region. In response to Israel's invasion of Lebanon in 1982, Iranian officials created the Hezbollah,[525] which organized the deadly 1983 bombing of American and French military barracks in Beirut.[526] In 1987, Iran laid antiship mines in the Persian Gulf, which deepened tension with the United States. Finally, in 1989, Khomeini issued a decree calling for the death of Salman Rushdie for his book *The Satanic Verses*, which brought international outrage and the end of diplomatic relations with Great Britain.[527] In the words of one IRGC commander, Iran went to "war against the whole world."[528]

The regime's most consequential external conflict was the 1980–1988 war with Iraq.[529] The revolution dramatically increased tensions between the two states. Khomeini's discourse threatened the Iraqi government.[530] He called on Shiites to rise up against Hussein and threatened to invade following the assassination of a Shiite cleric in Iraq in April 1980.[531] More importantly, however, the revolution created a window of opportunity for

Hussein to weaken a long-standing geopolitical rival.[532] Not only had the revolution and subsequent purges weakened the Iranian army, but Iran's international isolation meant that Iraq would enjoy the support of the United States and the Persian Gulf States.[533] Indeed, at the start of the war, the military balance favored Iraq.[534]

The war began in September 1980, when 45,000 Iraqi troops crossed into Iran. The Khomeini government's initial reaction seemed to confirm Hussein's hopes. Preoccupied with domestic counterinsurgencies, Iran's military forces initially failed to notice the incursion, allowing Iraqi troops to advance rapidly into Iranian territory.[535] However, several factors, including Iran's larger size, better-trained air force, and early support from Israel helped the IRI survive, regroup, and eventually turn the tide.[536]

Ideology also played a role. Iran's clerical elite viewed the war as a religious war, which almost certainly helped sustain the regime in the face of initial losses.[537] Furthermore, Iran's depleted military capacity was partially compensated by the Khomeini government's ability to mobilize large numbers of highly motivated volunteers from the Basij, who utilized human wave techniques to cross minefields and reach Iraqi positions.[538] Although such techniques were costly, they assisted the military's defensive campaign in the war's early stages.[539]

By June 1982, Iraq had withdrawn to the border. By this point, domestic insurgencies had been defeated and rivals forced underground or into exile.[540] Thus, the revolutionary regime could be considered consolidated. Rather than ending the war, however, Iran marched into Iraq in the hope of spreading the Islamic revolution.[541] Because Iraq could turn to the United States and the Persian Gulf States for assistance,[542] Iranian forces were stymied, and the war dragged on for an additional six years.

Although the war imposed enormous costs on Iran, it strengthened the regime's coercive structure, particularly the IRGC and the Basij.[543] The IRGC grew from about 25,000 troops in 1980 to 450,000 late in the war,[544] before stabilizing at about 150,000 in the 1990s.[545] The IRGC developed considerable military efficacy during the Iraq war.[546] The war also imbued the Guard with enormous prestige,[547] which, together with lavish resources, allowed it to attract the best recruits.[548] By the end of the conflict, the influence of the Guard had expanded into the cabinet and the media.[549] The war also strengthened the Basij. At its peak in 1986, the Basij mobilized about 100,000 volunteers on the front lines.[550] The Basij became "an omnipresent feature of life" in many Iranian cities.[551]

As in China, Russia, and Vietnam, the experience of war fostered an enduring siege mentality; commanders of both the IRGC and the Basij organizations viewed themselves as being in a "constant state of war" and confronting an imminent and existential threat from abroad.[552]

Finally, the war against Iraq justified the suppression of remaining opposition forces, which were viewed as treasonous "fifth columnists."[553] In particular, the government obliterated the last remnants of the MK, which had survived in Iraq and made a quixotic attempt to invade Iran in 1988. The severely undertrained and ill-equipped surviving remnants of the MK were bombed out of existence. Then, in a move that shocked many inside and outside the regime, the government massacred at least 4,000 MK supporters who had been languishing in Iranian prisons.[554]

A Nonparty Deep State

Iran's revolutionary reactive sequence transformed the IRI from a loose coalition of disparate groups into a powerful authoritarian regime. Violent, ideologically driven conflict fostered an intense siege mentality, destroyed alternative centers of power, and bequeathed the regime with effective, ideologically committed, and loyal security services.[555]

First, the revolution and its violent aftermath wiped out organized threats to the regime. The shah had already destroyed the landowning class.[556] The prerevolutionary army remained intact, but, as noted above, it was badly weakened by the revolution and subsequent purges and downsizing.[557] Second, the regime established "political ideological departments" within the army to indoctrinate and vet the loyalty of candidates for promotion.[558] By 1986, such "religious commissars" were operating in every branch of the army.[559] State agents were posted in universities, which were perceived as vulnerable to foreign influence.[560] Thus, while some prerevolutionary institutions survived the revolution, they were heavily infiltrated by the new regime.

Finally, as noted above, counterrevolutionary conflict and the Iran-Iraq War decimated potential rivals, including the MK, the Communist Party, and the remnants of the National Front. Military conflict was also used to justify the sidelining of prominent religious moderates such as Ayatollah Shariatmadari.[561] After the revolution, the clerical establishment was subjected to "an unprecedented level of politicization and control."[562] The Special Court for the Clergy was created in 1987 to prevent "deviance," which led to the arrest of hundreds of clerics.[563] The Basij also formed a special brigade to monitor clerics across the country.[564] These measures seriously weakened the power of nonconformist clergy.[565] Thus, the IRI emerged from the Iraq war with few organized challengers.

At the same time, the clerical establishment retained a substantial degree of autonomy from the government.[566] Due in part to donations from followers, clergy maintained some financial independence, which enabled them to at times criticize government policies and even resist government dictates.[567] In the early 1990s, for example, despite intense government pressure, the clerical establishment in Qom refused to grant Khamenei the important religious title of *marja*—a status that was initially required to become supreme leader.[568] Although the clerical establishment never mobilized against the regime between 1979 and 2021, independent religious authorities remained a latent source of opposition that had no equivalent in Cuba.

The IRI also lacked the institutional architecture of most durable revolutionary regimes. Importantly, the IRI did not have a ruling party. Although the IRP functioned as a ruling party during the early 1980s,[569] Khomeini disbanded it (ironically, on the grounds that it was a source of factionalism) in 1987.[570] The absence of a ruling party to regulate elite conflict, together with the existence of regular semi-competitive elections, resulted in higher levels of open elite conflict than in Cuba and most other revolutionary cases.[571] Regime officials fought viciously over policy and public office, and a few major figures, including the prestigious cleric Hussein-Ali Montazeri, fell out with the supreme leader and were sidelined (see below).

However, this conflict obscured a relatively high degree of unity among the regime elite. Although reformist politicians like Seyyed Mohammad Khatami in the 1990s and Mir Hussein Mousavi in 2009 were backed by Iranian voters who opposed the regime (which arguably created incentives for oppositionist behavior), they themselves never opposed the IRI or sought its overthrow. Indeed, with few exceptions, reformist elites remained committed to the preservation of clerical rule, even after losing out to conservatives.[572] As we show below, this reluctance to move into outright opposition critically undermined efforts to overthrow the IRI. Thus, although Iran is a more ambiguous case than Cuba, the systematic failure of regime leaders to defect to the opposition suggests a strikingly cohesive elite.

Crucially, moreover, the regime's real power center—the "deep state" controlled by the supreme leader and backed by the IRGC and the Basij—was unambiguously cohesive and loyal.[573] The IRGC and the Basij were inseparably linked to the supreme leader. They recruited heavily from poor and religious families that were committed to clerical rule.[574] Nearly all studies of the Guard highlight its leaders' deep commitment to a dogmatic conception of Islam.[575] Ideology enhanced cohesion by heightening perceptions of an existential threat from outside forces.[576] The raison d'être of the revolutionary armed forces was to defend the revolution.[577] Discipline was reinforced by the Supreme Directorate of Ideological and Political Affairs, which embedded officials in each Guard unit to monitor members' political reliability.[578] Due to this combination of ideological commitment and state infiltration, the IRGC was "fanatically loyal to Khomeini."[579] There is no evidence that the Guard ever seriously challenged the supreme leader.[580] Overall, the IRGC was one of the regime's "most well-organized and disciplined bases of support."[581] As Khomeini put it, "If there was no IRGC, there would be no country."[582]

Despite a degree of openness and competition among the political elite, these hard-line elements retained a near-monopoly control over the security services, which gave them a decisive advantage in power struggles.[583] As we shall see, this nonparty "deep state" was critical to regime survival in the three decades after the Iraq war.

Regime Survival amid Multiple Crises

The IRI confronted three major challenges in the decades that followed the war in Iraq. First, Khomeini's death in 1989 and the lack of a clear successor generated a potential crisis. Second, the end of the war opened up a chasm between popular reformists on one side and hard-liners in the faqih and the revolutionary armed forces on the other. This rift simmered in the 1990s and exploded in a massive 2009 protest movement that nearly brought down the regime. Third, international sanctions crippled the economy in the 2010s and contributed to another wave of protests beginning in 2017. Several revolutionary legacies helped the regime survive these crises. For one, the cohesion of both the deep state and the broader political elite facilitated a smooth succession in 1989. In addition, the destruction of alternative power centers deprived the opposition of the capacity to translate popular support into a serious regime challenge. Efforts to draw on the support of reformist factions within the regime were hampered by insiders' unwillingness to oppose clerical rule.[584] Finally, loyal and effective security forces consistently beat back mass-based challenges.

KHOMEINI'S DEATH AND LEADERSHIP SUCCESSION

Khomeini's death in June 1989 posed a serious problem for the regime.[585] Indeed, the CIA predicted a "better than even chance" that the regime would face "serious instability" after Khomeini died.[586] Not only was

Khomeini a uniquely charismatic figure, but few individuals possessed the formal qualifications to replace him. The position of faqih, or supreme leader, had been created especially for Khomeini, and it was explicitly designated for a cleric who had received the high status of *marja* among Shiite clergy.[587] This was not some minor technical requirement. The IRI's legitimacy rested on the unquestioned religious authority of the supreme leader.

However, the only plausible cleric with a claim to *marja* status was Montazeri, who had been Khomeini's designated successor but fell out with Khomeini in the late 1980s over opposition to the massacre of MK prisoners in 1988. As a result, Khomeini sidelined Montazeri and told close associates (but did not write down) that he wanted Khamenei, a close ally, to succeed him.[588]

But there was a problem. Although Khamenei was a powerful insider, he was *not* a *marja*; in fact, he was considered a "religious lightweight" by much of the clerical establishment.[589] To allow Khamenei to become supreme leader, top regime officials decided to change the constitution. But they had not completed the process when Khomeini died. With no legitimate successor in place, the founding leader's death generated fear of a power vacuum at a time of mounting international isolation and threat.[590] Indeed, following Eric Selbin,[591] any attempt to impose a leader without the proper religious qualifications might have been expected to generate dissent among the regime's base of true believers.

However, the transition went smoothly. Montazeri, despite his earlier status as designated successor, considerable religious qualifications, and significant support network, instructed his supporters to accept his dismissal and quietly left the public eye.[592] The Assembly of Experts chose Khamenei as successor a day after Khomeini's death, even though the move was unconstitutional at the time (the constitution was then quickly amended).[593] Montazeri did not openly challenge Khamenei's selection but instead sent him a congratulatory letter.[594] As in Russia after Lenin's death, the regime faced too serious a threat from abroad for any high-level official to consider defying the new leader.

THE RISE OF REFORMISTS AND THE
2009 GREEN REVOLUTION

After the Iraq war ended, revolutionary vigilance became more difficult to sustain, and Iranians grew tired of social controls and economic austerity.[595] Simultaneously, the existence of semi-competitive elections created incentives for reformist appeals. The result was a growing divide between reformists, many of whom enjoyed broad public support, and the hard-line faqih and the Revolutionary Guard.[596] Although reformists did not openly challenge clerical rule, they called for greater political freedom, a relaxation of social controls, and the enforcement of constitutional limits on the power of the faqih.[597] Conservatives resisted these reforms.[598]

It was not an equal fight. Backed by Khamenei and the deep state,[599] conservatives used their control over the coercive apparatus to strengthen themselves and reinforce the new Islamic social order.[600] The Basij in particular became "a bulwark against the spread of cultural liberalization."[601] During the 1990s, it played an active role in moral policing as part of the Office for Vivification of the Propagation of Virtue and Prohibition of Vice, which enforced restrictions on immodest dress, mixed-gender parties, and the possession of alcohol and illicit books and films.[602]

Conservative forces were strengthened by President Akbar Rafsanjani, who directed postwar reconstruction projects to the IRGC, transforming it into one of the best-endowed organizations in the country.[603] The IRGC's access to resources attracted opportunists who were less committed to the organization's hard-line mission.[604] However, the IRGC leadership continued to be dominated by revolutionary veterans, and the institution remained unambiguously loyal to the supreme leader. Cases of high-level disobedience were virtually nonexistent.[605]

This gave rise to a dynamic in which reformist politicians would capitalize on public discontent to win elections but then find themselves stymied by powerful conservative forces in the state. In 1997, former culture minister Seyyed Mohammad Khatami, a reformist, won the presidency with a stunning 69 percent of the vote. Khatami captured the support of the many Iranians who were "visibly angry with the ruling clerical oligarchs."[606] His election brought optimistic predictions of a "second revolution" and "the dawn of an Islamic democracy."[607]

However, Khatami's reform efforts immediately ran into the wall of the IRI's deep state. Despite the new president's popular support, he "had neither the authority nor the independence" to do anything without the consent of Khamenei, who was backed by the security apparatus.[608] Thus, shortly after Khatami took power, the security forces shut down several reformist publications.[609] In April 1998, the reformist mayor of Tehran, Gholamhossein Karbaschi, was tried on false corruption charges, imprisoned, and barred from politics for ten years.[610] Numerous dissident writers and nationalists were the victims of murders that were later tied to the security services.[611] After the reformist paper *Salam* was shut down in mid-1999, thousands of students took to the streets in cities across Iran but were quickly suppressed by Islamic vigilantes and Basij militias.[612]

In 2000, reformists won 215 of 290 seats in parliamentary elections, and in 2001, Khatami was reelected with an extraordinary 76 percent of the vote. But again, none of this really mattered. Continued attacks on the reformist media, including multiple newspaper closures, crippled it.[613] Khatami lacked the power to defend his reformist allies.[614] His efforts to install reformists in the security forces were rebuffed by Khamenei.[615] As a result, large-scale human rights abuses persisted. Thus, Khatami's presidency "started with a deafening roar and ended in an unceremonious whisper."[616] Overwhelming popular opposition to the dominant hardliners did little to destabilize the regime.

Regime stability was not only rooted in deep state repression, however. It was also driven by the *loyalty of the reformers themselves.* Although some reformist politicians skirted close to opposition in the late 1990s and 2009, regime insiders almost never opposed clerical rule.[617] The leading reformer, Khatami, for example, refused to challenge the supreme leader.[618] As president, he maintained "unconditional loyalty" to Khamenei and denounced reformist calls to change the constitution as "tantamount" to "treason."[619] When pro-reform protests began to grow in 1999, Khatami accused the protesters of having "evil aims" and "attacking the foundations of the regime."[620] Speaking on state television, the president denounced the protests as "demagogic, provocative, socially divisive, and a threat to national security."[621] Later, when numerous reformist publications were shuttered in 2000, Khatami appealed for calm rather than fomenting opposition.[622] Seeking to avoid unrest and preserve the ruling Islamic establishment he "believed in," Khatami repeatedly retreated in the face of conservative opposition to democratic reforms.[623]

Khatami's refusal to confront the regime drove opposition forces to despair and created a significant obstacle to opposition mobilization.[624] Thus, the quick suppression of student protests in 1999 was almost certainly facilitated by Khatami's harsh condemnation of their activities, which left activists feeling "tricked" and "confused and abandoned."[625] Students could be heard shouting, "Khatami, Khatami, where are you? Your students have been killed."[626] By the end of his second term, prominent supporters of reform began to turn against Khatami. Frustrated by Khatami's passivity, the Iranian human rights activist Shirin Ebadi called on Khatami to resign in early 2004.[627] Widespread demoralization may have contributed to the 2005 victory of the archconservative mayor of Tehran, Mahmoud Ahmadinejad, in the presidential election.[628]

The success of Ahmadinejad represented a remarkable electoral turn-around for conservatives, who often had difficulties at the ballot box. However, their triumph did not silence opposition for long. Ahmadinejad's public support eroded amid a weakening economy,[629] and in 2009, former prime minister Mir Hussein Mousavi ran against him on a reformist platform. Mousavi's open style and sharp exchanges with Ahmadinejad in televised debates generated a wave of enthusiasm. Heavy turnout encouraged expectations of a Mousavi victory.[630] However, the vote appears to have been manipulated, and Ahmadinejad officially "won" with 63 percent of the vote.[631] The response was a "tsunami of protest" that became known as the Green Revolution.[632] In "the most serious internal challenge to the stability of the IRI since its foundation,"[633] more than a million protesters took to the streets in Tehran. Demonstrations soon spread to more than twenty cities.[634] Chants of "Death to the dictator!" could be heard from windows at night.[635] Protests continued over the course of the summer, drawing support from regime elites. Several senior clerics backed Mousavi, and ex-president Rafsanjani, the chair of the Assembly of Experts, criticized the election (though he did not openly question the results).[636] Nearly two-thirds of the legislature refused to attend Ahmadinejad's inauguration.[637]

The government initially panicked.[638] Given the size of the protests and Mousavi's insider status, one might have expected the security forces to abandon the incumbent, as militaries did in Serbia in 2000, Ukraine in 2004, and Egypt in 2011. Indeed, numerous rank-and-file Basij deserted their assignments during the protests.[639] However, the regime's most powerful actors remained steadfast in their support for Ahmadinejad and showed little hesitation in cracking down.[640] Although some Interior Ministry officials initially backed Mousavi, the IRGC stood behind Khamenei and played a leading role in quashing the protests.[641]

Despite widespread domestic and international condemnation, the security services hit the opposition hard.[642] At least seventy-two people were killed and thousands of others were beaten, often in their homes in the dead of night.[643] In the run up to the inauguration, the regime executed a number of previously imprisoned dissidents, apparently as a message to other critics.[644] The government made little effort to hide repression, instead holding high-profile show trials in which opposition leaders were forced to make public confessions.[645] The government was also unafraid to attack family members of key regime elites, including those of Mousavi and Rafsanjani.[646] Pro-government thugs even attacked Mousavi himself.[647]

Protest continued throughout the fall of 2009, especially on public holidays.[648] On Ashura Day (December 27), tens of thousands of protesters took to the streets in Tehran and at least ten other cities. The government again responded with repression,[649] resulting in one of the bloodiest confrontations since the uprisings began.[650] In early 2010, the regime unleashed "an epidemic of arrests,"[651] while numerous opposition activists were sentenced to death.[652] By early 2010, the regime had worn the opposition out. The movement "retreated into a period of soul-searching and regrouping";[653] even the 2011 Arab Spring failed to rejuvenate it.

The loyalty of the IRGC and the Basij during the crisis may be traced, at least in part, to regime origins. The security forces' readiness to crack down on protesters was driven by a polarized "us–them" worldview that emerged from the revolution.[654] For many IRGC officials, the protesters represented a direct challenge, not merely to their power and prerogatives but also to the revolution—views that were hardened by years of battling insurgencies and Iraqi forces.[655] These officials viewed the protest movement as an "existential threat" and an attack on the "revolution itself."[656] Political prisoners reported that security personnel "internalized the regime's propaganda line out of a solid ideological devotion to the regime as being the embodiment of God's will on earth."[657] This provided an ideological justification for crackdown that was unavailable to besieged governments in other contemporary autocracies such as Ukraine in 2004 and Egypt in 2011.

Crucially, moreover, the regime elite held together throughout the crisis. Although many leading politicians—including Rafsanjani—opposed Ahmadinejad and criticized the elections, very few of them crossed the line into outright opposition.[658] To be sure, Mousavi edged close to opposition. He became the focal point for regime opponents and criticized hard-liners—with whom Khamenei was closely associated—of distorting Islam.[659] But like Khatami, Mousavi proved to be a "reluctant standard bearer" for the opposition.[660] He never openly called for the overthrow of the IRI or the supreme leader and criticized Khamenei in the most oblique manner during the protests.[661] Moreover, Mousavi played little role in organizing or leading the uprisings.[662] Under intense pressure to avoid inciting protest, he called for a halt to protests a week after the election and urged supporters to remain loyal to the Islamic Republic.[663] Mousavi's Facebook page exhorted supporters to remain "faithful to the sacred system of the Islamic Republic" and to "use legal channels."[664] In fact, the leaders of the Green Revolution "never fundamentally disputed the Republic's legitimacy."[665]

Finally, the Green Revolution suffered from the prior destruction of independent power centers. Compared to the Algerian opposition, which used mosque networks as mobilizing structures, the Iranian opposition had less access to societal institutions. The security forces thus confronted an opposition that was in "organizational disarray" and that relied heavily on spontaneous online interaction.[666] Support from the *bazaaris* or the working class would have improved the movement's chances of success, but "repression and organizational weaknesses prevented either class from participating."[667] Instead, the movement relied on divisions within the regime elite, a strategy that was derailed by reformers' extreme reluctance to oppose the regime.

SANCTIONS AND POPULAR UNREST IN THE 2010S

Despite "relentless state persecution" after 2009,[668] reformist and opposition forces continued to attract broad popular support. Thus, when Ahmadinejad's second term ended in 2013, Iranians again elected a moderate, Hassan Rouhani, as president. But faced with opposition from the deep state, Rouhani had little impact on the regime.[669]

Nevertheless, the IRI confronted a new round of protest in the late 2010s, driven by a deepening economic crisis. Years of lax enforcement of international sanctions came to an end after Iranian efforts to build a nuclear weapon were uncovered in the early 2000s.[670] The United States successfully lobbied for stricter sanctions, which began to cripple Iran's economy in the late 2000s and early 2010s.[671] The breadth of the new sanctions' regime—encompassing banking and business transactions, insurance, and shipping—made it difficult for Iran to operate in the global economy.[672] More than a billion dollars of Iranian assets were frozen.[673] The United States also imposed "secondary sanctions" on businesses with dealings in Iran, which triggered a wave of disinvestment.[674] Iran was deprived of access to SWIFT banking services, which made it harder to secure payments for oil exports.[675] Crude oil exports declined from 2.5 million to 243,000 barrels a day between 2011 and 2019.[676] Iran's GDP contracted by 20 percent in the early 2010s.[677] Although a 2015 deal with the Obama administration led to a softening of sanctions in exchange for regulation of Iran's nuclear program, the United States withdrew from the agreement in 2018, reimposing sanctions.[678] Between 2017 and 2019, Iran lost at least $50 billion in oil revenue and its economy contracted by 13 percent.[679]

The economic crisis generated widespread discontent.[680] In December 2017, protests erupted in Iran's second-largest city, Mashhad, and quickly spread to more than two dozen towns. Protesters shouted, "Death to the dictator!," burned pictures of Khamenei, and attacked a police station in Qahdarijan.[681] Protest flared up again in June 2018, reaching nearly every province in the country.[682] The most serious demonstrations erupted in November 2019 after the government announced steep increases in gas prices. Tens of thousands of protesters took to the streets in 100 cities across the country, ransacking banks and stores.[683] According to the Interior Ministry, protesters set fire to more than 140 government sites, hundreds of banks, dozens of petrol stations, and fifty security bases.[684] Protesters calling for the death of the supreme leader seized control of the historic town of Mahshahr.[685] Much of the unrest occurred in low-income neighborhoods that had historically supported the regime.[686]

The uprising shocked the regime leadership, especially after reports emerged that protesters had destroyed a statue of Ayatollah Khomeini.[687] Within twenty-four hours, internet access was almost entirely shut down. Many cities and neighborhoods became security zones, with police searching door-to-door looking for dissidents.[688] Police shot and killed protesters on the street and indiscriminately fired into crowds.[689] Estimates of those killed range from several hundred to 1,500.[690] Whatever the figure, state killing was far greater than the during the Green Revolution.[691] Sidelined reformers such as Khatami denounced the crackdown[692] but, once again, stopped short of calling for the overthrow of clerical rule.[693] Within two weeks, the protests were crushed. While the regime edged toward instability in the late 2010s, the clerical establishment was able to quickly and systematically suppress all challenges that emerged—in stark contrast to unstable cases such as Algeria, where it took about a decade for the government to defeat opposition threats at the end of the Cold War (see chapter 5).

In sum, nearly ten years of economic crisis in Iran failed to bring down the regime for two reasons. First, the destruction of most alternative power centers meant that although regime opponents enjoyed broad public support, they lacked the organizational infrastructure to "coordinate discontent" and translate it into an effective regime challenge.[694] Second, and perhaps most importantly, the security forces remained loyal and willing to repress.[695]

Despite intense external pressure and widespread public discontent, Iran's revolutionary regime endured for more than four decades. The

IRI underwent a smooth leadership succession in 1989 and successfully suppressed popular threats in 2009 and 2019. Such durability is surprising when one considers the fragility of the regime that emerged in 1979. Khomeini had virtually no organization on the ground when he returned to Iran after fifteen years in exile. Rather than accommodating powerful domestic and international interests, however, he imposed clerical rule, supported the takeover of the American embassy, and called for revolution throughout the Persian Gulf. These measures triggered a domestic insurgency and a war with Iraq. The conflicts reinforced cohesion, motivated the destruction of alternative centers of societal power, and gave rise to a powerful and loyal coercive apparatus. Revolutionary polarization created a rationale for repression that is absent in most autocracies. As a result, neither the faqih nor the security forces hesitated to engage in high-intensity repression. The security forces, moreover, never once rose up against the regime.

Less evidence exists for competing approaches. For one, the IRI's durability might be explained by antecedent conditions. After all, the shah's regime developed a powerful apparatus and survived for decades. However, the shah's neopatrimonial state disintegrated after his fall, forcing the revolutionaries to thoroughly rebuild the military and state bureaucracy. Indeed, the most important foundations of regime durability—the IRGC and the Basij—were entirely new agencies that emerged out of revolutionary conflict.

Another alternative explanation focuses on oil.[696] Oil is said to enhance authoritarian durability by financing a vast coercive apparatus and providing autocrats with ample resources to buy off potential opponents and limit popular discontent.[697] Indeed, the IRI used oil wealth to finance a "martyr's welfare state" that distributed health care and other benefits to many Iranians who had been excluded under the shah.[698] These social policies are said to have helped the regime retain considerable public support (or at least acquiescence), especially in rural areas.[699]

Yet there are reasons to doubt that oil is the main source of durability. For one, the IRI persisted even after sanctions had largely deprived it of oil revenue. At best, then, oil revenue explains durability only for a portion of the IRI's tenure. Moreover, although oil rents helped finance Iran's vast security apparatus, the existence of such rents does not explain why the Revolutionary Guard never attempted to the overthrow the supreme leader. The IRGC clearly developed a material stake in retaining power.[700] However, it could have seized a greater share of the pie for itself—and did not.

Similarly, the impact of oil-financed social programs on public support for the regime is not clear. Kevan Harris argues that social welfare programs actually empowered many of the Iranians who supported reformists in elections in the 1990s and 2000s. [701] He notes that oil-fueled welfare state expansion in the 1970s and 1990s "ended with the two most contentious mobilization upsurges in the country's modern history," the 1979 revolution and the 2009 protest movement, concluding that "if welfare is a bribe by the state, then it is not a very effective one."[702] Finally, our statistical analysis of all autocracies since 1900 shows that revolutionary origins predict regime durability even when we control for access to natural resource wealth.[703] Thus, although oil may have heightened the IRI's resilience, we are skeptical that it provides a better explanation than revolutionary origins.

Some evidence also exists for the sociocultural approach. The IRI's durability could be rooted in the committed support of religious rural families and other "hard-line element[s] of the Iranian population."[704] Indeed, strong rural support for the regime's ideology may have helped it survive the 2009 crisis.[705] At best, however, such support provides only a partial explanation. As this chapter has shown, regime survival hinged on repression in the 2000s and 2010s.

More generally, widespread support for reformist politicians and frequent public displays of mass opposition belie the claim that regime durability rested on public support. Available public surveys suggest limited public support for religious social controls.[706] Overall, the supreme leader has relied more on brute force and nonelected authorities than on popular support to hold on to power.[707]

A final alternative approach focuses on institutions. The absence of a ruling party, combined with regular elections, gave rise to intense intra-elite conflict.[708] Ultimately, however, strikingly few regime elites defected. Indeed, reformist politicians remained almost entirely loyal to clerical rule despite electoral incentives to tap into anti-regime sentiment. This surprising degree of elite cohesion is rooted in the IRI's revolutionary origins.

Conclusion

Cuba and Iran conform closely to the ideal-typical path to revolutionary durability. In both cases, weak revolutionary governments aggressively challenged powerful domestic and international interests. Early radicalism triggered violent counterrevolutionary conflict and decades of international hostility, which gave rise to cohesive regimes backed by loyal and powerful security services. As a result, both regimes were able to survive the passing of charismatic founding leaders and broad public discontent caused by sanctions and economic crisis. Regime stability was reinforced by the destruction of organized alternatives, which inhibited popular mobilization.

The Cuban and Iranian cases illustrate the limitations of Leninist institutions as an explanation of the durability of revolutionary regimes. In Cuba, Castro ruled without a real party until the mid-1970s. The Iranian regime was not even remotely Leninist; the ruling party was abandoned in the 1980s, and authority was held by a confusing collection of competing agencies. However, the absence of Leninist institutions did not undermine regime durability in either case. Instead, regimes were sustained by powerful states made cohesive by violent, polarizing revolutionary struggle.

CHAPTER SEVEN

Radical Failures

EARLY DEATHS OF THE HUNGARIAN
SOVIET REPUBLIC, THE KHMER
ROUGE, AND THE TALIBAN

IN MOST REVOLUTIONARY AUTOCRACIES, radical efforts at societal transformation triggered revolutionary reactive sequences that fostered durable
authoritarianism. In some cases, however, radical revolutionaries were
destroyed by the counterrevolutionary wars they provoked. This chapter
examines the three revolutionary regimes in our sample that died young—
all at the hands of foreign enemies. Despite their distinct historical backgrounds, regional contexts, and ideologies, the Hungarian Soviet Republic
(1919), the Khmer Rouge (1975–1979), and the Taliban (1996–2001) followed similar trajectories. In each case, radical initiatives by revolutionary
governments in small and vulnerable states generated military conflicts
that destroyed embryonic regimes.

We argue that the early death of revolutionary regimes was rooted in a
combination of radical behavior and geopolitical vulnerability. Like their
successful revolutionary counterparts, leaders in Hungary, Cambodia,
and Afghanistan challenged the core interests of powerful domestic and
international actors. However, unlike Russia, China, Vietnam, and Iran,
which were relatively large states that became regional powers, Hungary,
Cambodia, and Afghanistan were relatively small states that were prone
to intervention by powerful neighbors. Hungary, a country of eight million people, was surrounded on three sides by hostile powers, which left it
exposed to foreign aggression. Likewise, Cambodia and Afghanistan were
peripheral states that had been buffeted by Cold War proxy conflicts. Such
vulnerability increased the likelihood that radical revolutionary regimes

would be wiped out before the reactive sequence could strengthen them. Thus, after Béla Kun and the Communist Party attacked Hungary's dominant classes, invaded Czechoslovakia, and declared war on Romania, the regime was toppled by foreign armies after only 133 days in power. Similarly, the Khmer Rouge regime collapsed after it invaded neighboring Vietnam, and the Taliban regime was defeated after its leaders facilitated an extremist terrorist attack on the United States.

THE HUNGARIAN SOVIET REPUBLIC

Established in 1919, two years after the Russian Revolution and just months after Hungary's defeat in World War I, the Hungarian Soviet Republic was radical. It attacked the interests of peasants, property owners, and the Church; invaded two of its neighbors (Czechoslovakia and Romania); and attempted to foment a putsch in a third (Austria). As in other radical cases, these measures triggered counterrevolutionary conflict. Yet, unlike radical governments in Russia, Cuba, and Iran, Hungary's revolutionaries did not survive this conflict. Amid a rebellion of aristocrats and old regime military officers, the regime collapsed—after barely four months in power—in the face of an invasion by French-backed Romanian troops.

THE REVOLUTIONARY SEIZURE OF POWER

The Hungarian Soviet Republic emerged out of the collapse of the Austro-Hungarian Empire. As the armies of the empire and other Central powers faced defeat in World War I, Hungary declared independence in October 1918. Count Mihály Károlyi, in alliance with the moderate Social Democratic Party,[1] seized nominal power. However, the new government never fully controlled the national territory; Hungary was regarded as the "spoils of war" by Entente powers,[2] and about half of its territory was occupied by Serb, Czech, and Romanian troops.[3] Under economic blockade from European powers, the country was deprived of critical economic resources,[4] and it faced constant threat of foreign invasion.[5] Yielding to pressure from Entente powers, Károlyi ordered all Hungarian troops to disarm.[6] Partly as a result, military discipline collapsed and the country was beset by food riots.[7] The state's coercive capacity eroded, plunging Hungary into anarchy. As in Russia in 1917, many rank-and-file army units and local administrations and much of the country's economic production were under the control of spontaneously organized councils and trade unions.[8] "Everyone commanded but no one obeyed."[9]

Into this breach stepped Béla Kun and the Hungarian Communist Party (HCP). Kun was one of many Hungarians who took part in the Russian Revolution after they were stranded in Russia as prisoners during World War I.[10] Kun was active in revolutionary politics in the Siberian city of Tomsk (where he had been imprisoned), met Lenin in Petrograd, and built friendships with various Bolshevik luminaries, including Lenin's wife, Nadezhda Krupskaya.[11] By 1918, he had become one of the most prominent foreign Socialists in Petrograd.[12] Kun helped create the HCP in Moscow on November 4, 1918, and then founded the party on Hungarian soil after returning home at the end of the month.[13]

Kun and the HCP were quite radical. Sponsored and controlled by the Soviet government, the HCP modeled itself on the Bolsheviks and was gripped by a "messianic" ideology.[14] Like the Bolsheviks, the Hungarian Communists supported an immediate transition to socialism, the seizure of private property, and the elimination of the bourgeoisie.[15] Unlike many socialists, including Lenin, Kun also opposed the distribution of landed estates to peasants because, in his view, it would promote the development of private property.[16] Instead, Kun maintained a "dogmatic" commitment to state ownership of the land.[17]

Mimicking Bolshevik strategies, Kun fomented instability to discredit the ruling Social Democrats.[18] He mobilized antigovernment protest, attacked anticommunist newspapers, organized and armed radical workers, and incited military rebellion.[19] Inspired by the recent Bolshevik Revolution, Hungarian workers spontaneously seized factories, and army and police refused to take orders from superiors. The army was transformed into an "armed mob,"[20] and "detachments of drunken soldiers roamed the streets."[21]

In February 1919, Kun was arrested after attempting to seize the headquarters of the Social Democratic newspaper.[22] He became a cause célèbre when reports emerged that he had been badly beaten by prison guards. Tens of thousands of people protested.[23] The Soldiers' Council, which controlled the military, threw its support behind the Communists, as did the police and the National Guard.[24] In much of the country, but particularly the capital, government authority vanished.[25]

Feeling powerless to stop the process of radicalization, and under growing pressure from their radical wing,[26] Social Democratic leaders began to negotiate with the imprisoned Kun. In mid-March, the Social Democrats and the Communists forged an alliance called the Pact of Union.[27] Soon afterward, the chief of the Allied Military Mission in Hungary delivered an ultimatum to President Károlyi to surrender more Hungarian territory to Romania. Károlyi, whose government had bet heavily on friendly relations with the Entente powers,[28] chose to resign instead. He handed power to the Social Democrats, unaware of their pact with the Communists.[29]

The Hungarian Soviet Republic thus began its ill-fated tenure. Sándor Garbai, a Social Democrat, formally became president. It was clear to all, however, that real power in the new government lay with Kun, who was appointed foreign minister. (In accounts of this period, Garbai's name is barely mentioned.)[30] Kun's de facto power was rooted in the desperate hope that he would be able to use his ties to Lenin and the Bolsheviks to attract Russian support against Entente powers.[31] Given Hungary's extreme international isolation, many in the governing coalition saw the Soviet Union as Hungary's last hope. It was also widely expected that revolution would soon spread across Europe.[32] Thus, despite being the only communist in the government, Kun clearly defined its policies.[33]

The Hungarian Soviet Republic was born weak. Although the Social Democrats and Communists attempted to create a unified party, they nevertheless remained divided, with the moderate Social Democrats in control of the party apparatus and the more radical communists, led by Kun, controlling the government.[34] Notwithstanding their influence, the communists were organizationally weak.[35] They lacked enough cadres to fill ministries,[36] had little influence in the trade unions or among peasants,[37] and could not control the revolutionary workers' and soldiers' councils that spontaneously emerged in late 1918 and early 1919.[38]

The revolutionary government also had limited coercive capacity. The Hungarian Red Army, which was created out of the remnants of the Royal Hungarian Army,[39] "existed in name only."[40] It was badly undersupplied, and its troops "panicked at the first sound of artillery fire."[41] Discipline and cohesion were low, in part because Kun eliminated all military ranks.[42] Thus, despite the HCP's installation of commissars in spring 1919, the regime faced two coup attempts that summer, and military officials betrayed the government and informed Entente forces of the republic's plans to invade Romania in July.[43]

The revolutionary government confronted an array of threats, both domestic and external.[44] Although the exodus of thousands of aristocrats and military officers to Austria left conservative forces in disarray,[45] the new government met resistance from the Catholic Church, old regime holdovers in the state bureaucracy, and anticommunist secret societies created by Hungarian officers.[46]

Most importantly, Hungary's revolutionary government was internationally isolated. The new regime was opposed by the major Western powers, as well as by neighboring Austria, Czechoslovakia, and Romania. Crucially, moreover, the revolutionary government received only rhetorical support from Russia, which was too consumed with civil war (see chapter 2) to deliver on promises of military assistance.[47]

THE ABORTED REACTIVE SEQUENCE:
RADICALISM AND REGIME COLLAPSE

Despite the regime's clear weakness, Kun attempted a "great leap forward to communism."[48] Thus, the government nationalized all factories employing more than twenty people, as well as all banks, insurance companies, theaters, barbershops, retail shops, wholesale trade, and apartment buildings. Large bank deposits and jewelry were confiscated.[49] Wealthy citizens had their artworks appropriated and put on public display.[50] Racetracks—considered an aristocratic pastime—were ploughed under. Interest payments ceased. Private houses were nationalized; apartments were sequestered and divided. Families were entitled to no more than three rooms.[51] Communist activists known as the "Lenin Boys" attacked aristocrats and former bourgeois politicians and raided wealthy homes at night, taking hostages in order to extract tax payments.[52] They also desecrated churches, harassed priests, burned crucifixes, and shut down monasteries.[53] These measures turned the social order upside down. In the words of one eyewitness: "Before long, the stately and silent mansions were echoing with the cries of barefooted little ragamuffins, while in the spacious halls the costly rugs were trodden by dirty, hob-nailed boots and the silken wallhangings were begrimed with the smoke of the miserable little emergency stoves on which proletarian families cooked their dinners."[54]

At the same time, the government attacked the core interests of peasants, who had taken advantage of state collapse to seize large estates in late 1918 and early 1919.[55] Kun considered Lenin's decision to distribute land to peasants to be an "unnecessary compromise."[56] Instead, the government transferred all land directly to the state.[57] Many of the new state farms retained the hated estate managers that ran them before the revolution.[58] As a result, peasants were transformed from "natural allies" into "objective enemies."[59] In the spring and summer, spontaneous uprisings erupted in western Hungary.[60] While these were easily put down, peasant refusal to accept the regime's currency and relinquish their crops severely undermined the government.[61]

Finally, despite the country's extraordinary external vulnerability, Kun sought to transform Hungary into a center of global communist revolution.[62] Thus, the revolutionary government sent precious gold reserves to the revolutionary Sparticists in Germany and transformed its embassy in Vienna into the headquarters of a revolutionary insurrection against Austria.[63] After attempting to spark an Austrian insurrection in June, Hungarian militants sent by the government were expelled from the country.[64] That month, Hungarian troops invaded Czechoslovakia and set up the short-lived Slovak Soviet Republic in the town of Eperjes (Prešov).[65] In July, Hungary declared war on Romania.[66]

Such measures triggered counterrevolutionary movements at home and abroad. Almost immediately taking power, the Hungarian regime confronted a broad counterrevolutionary coalition consisting of hostile peasants, aristocrats, dispossessed middle sectors, and Catholic clergy.[67] Passive peasant resistance brought widespread food shortages.[68] In June, aristocratic military officers, humiliated by having their medals stripped off by agitated crowds and lower-ranking soldiers, gathered in the French-occupied city of Szeged to create a counterrevolutionary Hungarian national army. The army was led by Nicolaus von Horthy, former admiral of the Austro-Hungarian fleet.[69] Initial efforts met with failure. Thus, an antigovernment insurrection at the end of June was put down after twenty hours of fighting in Budapest.[70] However, rebellions persisted. In July, the government confronted insurrections in the cities of Kalocsa, Solt, and Dunapataj and in the Ludovika Military Academy in Budapest.[71]

The regime finally collapsed in mid-1919 in the face of foreign intervention. The government confronted increasing opposition from France, the United States, and other Western countries intent on preventing the spread of communism in the center of Europe.[72] After the republic declared war on Romania, the Royal Romanian Army, backed by France, marched on Budapest.[73] The Hungarian Red Army collapsed, and on August 1, Kun escaped to Austria.[74] Admiral Horthy seized power and set up a right-wing dictatorship.

In sum, the Hungarian Soviet Republic demonstrates the risks of radical social revolution in small and geopolitically vulnerable states. Under international occupation, Hungary was probably the most internationally vulnerable state among those examined in this chapter. But such weakness did not discourage the embryonic revolutionary government from challenging the geopolitical order. The government's dogmatic adherence to communist orthodoxy and aggressive efforts to foment world revolution provoked a powerful counterrevolution that destroyed the regime long before it could consolidate.[75]

THE KHMER ROUGE

Like the Hungarian Soviet Republic, the Khmer Rouge was destroyed by its own radicalism fewer than four years after taking power. The regime killed a quarter of Cambodia's population in the process of turning the country into "one great labor camp."[76] Efforts at radical societal transformation fostered cohesion and siege mentality within the party, a relatively loyal military, and the destruction of all organized alternatives within the country. At the same time, radical purges reminiscent of Jacobin France gutted the state and external belligerence provoked an invasion by Vietnam that quickly toppled the regime.

THE REVOLUTIONARY SEIZURE OF POWER

Cambodia's revolutionary movement emerged out of the regional Indochinese Communist Party, which was dominated by the Vietnamese Communists.[77] When the 1954 Geneva Accords granted Cambodia independence from French rule, the communists were suppressed by the postcolonial government led by Prince Norodom Sihanouk. About 1,000 activists fled to North Vietnam, while others remained in Cambodia.[78] Among those who remained was Saloth Sâr, later known as Pol Pot. The French-educated son of a rich peasant family, Pol Pot had been introduced to communism in Paris in the early 1950s when he joined the French Communist Party on the eve of Stalin's death.[79]

In 1960, the Cambodian Communist Party (CPK) broke away from the Indochinese Communist Party, although the party continued to receive assistance from Vietnam.[80] The communists suffered extraordinary repression, and in 1963, they took refuge, under Pol Pot's leadership, in the dense jungles of northern Cambodia.[81] This impenetrable area, known as the *maquis* (bush), both protected and transformed the CPK. Living among impoverished subsistence farmers, party leaders had almost no contact with the outside world for more than a decade. External communication, which was undertaken by messengers on foot or elephants, occurred with a month's delay.[82] One of Pol Pot's few trips abroad was to China in 1967, at the height of the Cultural Revolution.

The Khmer Rouge's peculiar antiurban communism emerged out of this period of isolation.[83] The movement's ideology was grounded in the utopian idea that rural poverty, self-sufficiency, and the elimination of foreign ideas would create a pure, uncorrupted society.[84] Although Khmer Rouge leaders embraced Marxist denunciations of capitalism and imperialism, they rejected the working class and all things urban.[85] In a stunning departure from Marxism, their central goal became the destruction of urban society. Indeed, the party systematically excluded factory workers after 1965.[86] Khmer Rouge leaders also rejected expertise and were intensely anti-intellectual.[87] For them, salvation lay not in education but in physical labor. The movement also attacked the nuclear family, seeking to integrate all individuals into centralized state-controlled cooperatives. Like the Taliban, the Khmer Rouge severely restricted public displays of affection, adultery, and all forms of entertainment, including sports.[88] The whole enterprise had the feel of a doomsday cult rather than a political party.

Finally, the Khmer Rouge was intensely xenophobic, extolling the glories of "Kampuchea's race."[89] According to Ben Kiernan,[90] race was more important than class for the CPK. Despite receiving years of support from North Vietnam, CPK leaders were intensely anti-Vietnamese, seeking to expel Vietnamese from the country.[91] Such views were in part a reaction to Vietnam's historical dominance in the region. Many communist activists chafed at perceived attitudes of superiority among their Vietnamese sponsors.

The CPK came to power via violent struggle. Lacking an army, the CPK avoided armed struggle through the mid-1960s.[92] This changed following a 1967 peasant uprising in the Samlaut area.[93] Assuming the CPK was behind the revolt, the Sihanouk government bombed the CPK's jungle bases, which pushed the party toward violence.[94] In the wake of the bombing, the Khmer Rouge pulled together a few thousand ill-trained and underequipped soldiers and formed a guerrilla army.[95] According to Pol Pot, the CPK was forced to wage war "with empty hands."[96]

The trajectory of the Khmer Rouge's guerrilla war was fundamentally altered by a 1970 military coup against Prince Sihanouk, led by the army chief of staff, Lon Nol. The North Vietnamese Communists, the CPK's main patron, had previously opposed military operations against Sihanouk because they depended on his cooperation in their war against South Vietnam. With Lon Nol's seizure of power, however, Cambodia allied with the United States against North Vietnam. Suddenly, the interests of the Cambodian and Vietnamese communists were aligned.

In March 1970, Vietnam launched a major attack on Cambodia, overwhelming Lon Nol's small, poorly trained army.[97] Although the North Vietnamese bore the brunt of the fighting, the Khmer Rouge built a relatively disciplined (albeit poorly equipped) fighting force of about 40,000 troops.[98] The force survived by capturing weapons and buying material from corrupt Lon Nol officials. It also benefited from training provided by returning Cambodian communists who had escaped to Vietnam in the 1950s. By 1972, the Khmer Rouge army was strong enough to fight on its own even after the Vietnamese troops withdrew.[99] A defector at the time wrote of the movement's "iron discipline."[100]

The Khmer Rouge seized power in 1975 amid the collapse of Cambodian state institutions. Lon Nol presided over a failing state. Although his government received more than a billion dollars in U.S. assistance,[101] much of the aid was siphoned off or wasted.[102] After just a few days' training at the Phnom Penh golf course, many soldiers went into battle armed with sticks and wearing sandals, blue jeans, and remnants of old French colonial uniforms.[103] Many went unpaid for months.[104] Partly as a result, by late 1973, the Khmer Rouge controlled more than two-thirds of the country.[105]

At the same time, extensive aerial bombing by the United States—aimed at North Vietnamese bases in Cambodia—shattered the country's already weak infrastructure. President Nixon authorized two massive bombing operations, Operation Menu (1969–1970) and Operation Freedom Deal (1973), which delivered three times the tonnage dropped on Japan during World War II and killed about half a million Cambodians.[106] The widespread destruction of roads and villages left the landscape unrecognizable.[107] The bombing triggered a large-scale exodus from many villages,[108] and village authority structures were torn asunder—a fact that would facilitate the CPK's subsequent efforts to create a new social order.[109]

In January 1973, a U.S.–North Vietnamese peace agreement largely ended direct U.S. involvement in the region's wars. Despite encouragement from North Vietnam, the Khmer Rouge boycotted the peace talks in the expectation that it could win a military victory. At that point, Vietnam largely abandoned Cambodia,[110] leaving the Khmer Rouge to fight against Lon Nol on its own.

During this period, the Khmer Rouge began to implement its radical utopian vision in parts of the country it controlled. The guerrillas organized populations into fortresslike rural cooperatives that functioned as militarized work camps. All property was seized for the war effort. Contact with the outside world was forbidden. Schools, markets, and religious institutions were closed. All shops and restaurants were shut. Money was abolished and travel eliminated. The Khmer Rouge forbade bright clothes, jewelry, and other forms of decoration. All residents were required to wear black clothing.[111] The communists also imposed puritanical codes of sexual conduct. Flirting was strongly discouraged. "Gaiety was suspect."[112] Even the mildest dissent was severely punished. Those suspected of opposition were often dragged away at night and disappeared. "Dread and fear enveloped many of the cooperatives."[113] At the same time, travel restrictions and limited communication with the outside world meant that outsiders were largely unaware of the conditions in these communities.[114] Few Cambodians had a clue of what was about to hit them.

The Khmer Rouge's disciplined army of 60,000–70,000 defeated Lon Nol's ill-trained and demoralized army of 200,000,[115] and on April 17, 1975, the communists seized the capital, Phnom Penh. The old regime quickly dissolved, as thousands of soldiers shed their uniforms and fled.[116] Old regime officials who remained in Cambodia "were butchered like common livestock."[117] The Khmer Rouge incorporated no soldiers from the old regime, killing them instead. All personnel from the old army were told to strip off their uniforms on the spot and were loaded into trucks, taken to the countryside, and shot.[118] Within weeks, the Khmer Rouge had wiped out virtually all organized opposition.[119]

THE ABORTIVE REACTIVE SEQUENCE:
RADICALISM AND REGIME COLLAPSE

Cambodia's revolutionary regime was born weak, with too few soldiers to control the country and too few trained personnel to govern it.[120] The CPK was small, with only 14,000 members in 1975,[121] and it lacked *any* organized support in the cities. The communists also lacked a unified military structure.[122] Because of severe limits on communication, military commanders had functioned with near total independence during the war.[123] As a result, the regime was born in April 1975 with six separate military and party command structures in six different zones of the country.[124] Phnom Penh was initially divided among five different zonal command units, and skirmishes broke out between different units jockeying for control.[125] A nominally unified army only emerged three months after the seizure of power,[126] and it would take about a year for the regime to create a functioning state apparatus.[127]

Despite its weakness, however, the Khmer Rouge launched an unprecedented effort at radical social change the moment it entered the capital. Fearing that urban businessmen, merchants, intellectuals, and remnants of the old bureaucracy would unite to destroy the new order, the government first moved to eliminate urban life *as such*.[128] The CPK evacuated all inhabitants of Phnom Penh, which had a population of over a million at the time. Everyone, including hospital patients, was forced to abandon the city. People were stripped of most of their possessions, and soldiers piled up air conditioners, refrigerators, bicycles, and other goods on the street or collected them into makeshift warehouses.[129] Between 10,000 and 20,000 people died in the evacuation of Phnom Penh.[130] Similar evacuations took place in all large cities in the country.[131] About half the Cambodian population found itself on the road.[132] Cities became ghost towns, inhabited only by a few government officials. Even the few foreign communist diplomats permitted to remain in Phnom Penh were forbidden to go much beyond their tightly guarded compounds.[133] Pigs and cattle roamed the empty streets of the capital.[134]

The evacuations plunged Cambodia into chaos, creating an "inferno of revolutionary change."[135] Money was abolished.[136] Within a year, the regime had shut down markets and confiscated virtually all private property.[137] Buddhist pagodas, libraries, and schools were destroyed and monks defrocked and murdered.[138] Kiernan estimates that less than 5 percent of the country's monks were still alive when the regime collapsed in 1979.[139] The Khmer Rouge also shut Cambodia off from the rest of the world, severing relations with all but a few countries.[140] The government cut almost all telephone and telegraph lines, eliminated international mail, and mined the country's borders.[141]

In the months that followed, the regime introduced a brutal caste system.[142] Former urban residents—"new people"—were classified as second-class citizens and forced to undertake hard labor in rural areas. "New people" were "last on the distribution lists, first on the execution lists."[143] Thousands of them died of starvation and disease as a result. By contrast, poor peasants were classified as "base people" and given priority access to food and medical care. They were initially allowed to grow their own food and were punished lightly for infractions.[144]

The regime extended the cooperative system created in 1973 to the whole country. Within two years, agriculture was fully collectivized.[145] Residents slept in gender-segregated barracks, worked without pay, and ate in communal dining halls.[146] The institution of the family disappeared, as parents were forced to give up children over seven years old to work in the fields.[147] Babies were often abandoned because there was no one to care for them.[148] Married couples were forced to live apart except for a few days a month.[149] Schools, churches, and hospitals were closed.[150] Books and other forms of writing disappeared. Leisure time was eliminated and replaced by political education.[151] Basketball courts and other sports facilities were dug up and converted into gardens.[152] Even foraging was outlawed.[153]

The Khmer Rouge's radicalism stunned even their allies in Communist China. When the Chinese premier, Zhou Enlai, warned CPK leaders of the dangers of moving too quickly toward communism, they responded with "an incredulous and superior smile."[154]

As in China's Great Leap Forward, the CPK government was dismissive of formal training and scientific knowledge.[155] Expertise was so devalued that many skilled workers tried to pass as unskilled laborers to avoid political reprisal.[156] Regime propaganda proclaimed that "to build dams, all you need is a political education."[157] Enterprises and government institutions were staffed by children and young teens, who were considered more pliable and obedient.[158] For example, a majority of workers and managers at a major oil refinery were children aged eight to fifteen.[159]

All of this produced disastrous results. New dams were built without spillways in order to save time. As a result, the dams burst during heavy rains, drowning hundreds of villagers.[160] Mismanagement and the diversion of labor to large-scale dam-building and irrigation projects led to a dramatic decline in food production and starvation.[161] Famine broke out in 1976 and 1977, resulting in hundreds of thousands of deaths.[162]

The Khmer Rouge also engaged in massive repression aimed at an array of perceived enemies: anyone connected with the former government or foreign officials, professionals and intellectuals, and a broad range of ethnic minorities including Vietnamese, Chinese, Thai, Muslims, and Buddhist monks. Ultimately, an estimated 20–25 percent of Cambodia's population died under Pol Pot's rule.[163]

Despite the devastating consequences of Khmer Rouge rule and the widespread discontent it generated,[164] the revolutionary regime faced relatively little domestic resistance.[165] In part, this was due to the near-total destruction of alternative centers of societal power. The war, the American bombing campaign, and the chaos created by large-scale population transfers eliminated not only remnants of the old order but also all organized opposition.[166]

However, the CPK also built a robust, if embryonic, party-state. The ruling party was highly cohesive. Years of physical isolation in the *maquis*, followed by years of war, left Khmer Rouge leaders "obsessed with the threat of enemies."[167] The result was an extraordinary level of internal discipline. For example, although Pol Pot had effectively led the CPK since the early 1960s, the Khmer Rouge was able to hide this fact from virtually everyone—including the CIA—until several years *after* the seizure of power. Even the extraordinarily effective Vietnamese Communists repeatedly failed in their efforts to infiltrate the CPK leadership.[168] Despite a series of crises, then, the Khmer Rouge leadership suffered few defections. All surviving members of the Standing Committee, the party's highest leadership body, remained loyal—even following the party back underground after it was toppled in 1979.[169]

The CPK also developed a decentralized but effective coercive apparatus.[170] The military, which was responsible for both domestic and external security,[171] remained highly fragmented.[172] In order to remove a regional commander, the government had to mobilize a commander from another zone to mount a military-style attack, referred to as a "regional coup."[173] Such fragmentation likely contributed to regional rebellions in 1976 and 1978.[174] At the same time, the central military apparatus and zonal commanders were loyal and disciplined.[175] CPK orders were always obeyed.[176] For example, despite his closeness to Vietnamese-trained colleagues, Eastern Zone military commander So Phim carried out orders by Pol Pot to execute them.[177] Indeed, notwithstanding Pol Pot's disastrous policies, there do not appear to have been any high-level coup attempts against him.[178] Although regime propaganda described numerous conspiracies, Foreign Minister Ieng Sary later acknowledged that these accusations were concocted to justify repression.[179] Many military officers defected to Vietnam, often in response to purges (see below), but most of these were junior officials.[180]

Despite its catastrophic rule, then, the Khmer Rouge faced only limited domestic challenges. Resistance was limited to isolated revolts.[181] Instead, Cambodians responded primarily by trying to flee the country. Tens of thousands of refugees crossed into Vietnam and other neighboring countries in 1976 and 1977.[182]

Ultimately, the revolutionary regime destroyed itself by purging its state apparatus and, above all, by provoking an invasion by Vietnam. The Pol Pot government carried out a series of brutal purges of regime elites—reminiscent of Jacobin France in 1794 and the Soviet Union in the 1930s—that left the state and the regime in disarray on the eve of the Vietnamese invasion. In a speech to party cadres in late 1976, Pol Pot warned that "ugly microbes" were infecting the revolution and needed to be expunged.[183] People were arrested for even the most subtle deviation from regime dictates.[184] The purge quickly took on a life of its own, as party members were encouraged to denounce one another and confessions, extracted under torture, revealed more supposedly counterrevolutionary elements. Thousands of high-level officials were taken to the

Tuol Sleng death camp, tortured, forced to write extensive confessions, and then killed. Virtually every one of the 12,000–20,000 prisoners who entered Tuol Sleng were killed.[185] The pace of executions increased over time. In the spring of 1977, the regime liquidated more than 1,000 people a month.[186] By July 1978, half of the party's Central Committee, five of the thirteen highest-ranking officials, and a majority of regional secretaries had been killed.[187]

The regime would likely have survived these purges had it not been invaded by Vietnam. The Khmer Rouge had long been driven by an intense hostility toward its more powerful neighbor. In the early and mid-1970s, the party eliminated hundreds of Hanoi-trained cadres—"Vietnamese in Khmer bodies"—who had fled Vietnam in the 1950s and returned to battle Lon Nol.[188] By 1975, all Vietnamese advisers had been pushed out and Cambodians who had spent time in Vietnam eliminated. In mid-1977, the government issued a directive to kill people of Vietnamese ancestry.[189] Some 100,000 Vietnamese fled the country; by 1979, the Vietnamese community in Cambodia had been eradicated.[190]

The CPK also began military assaults on Vietnam, which it viewed as a stalking horse for the USSR and an existential threat to the regime.[191] Just months after seizing power, the Khmer Rouge sent troops to the border, with the apparent intention of capturing parts of southern Vietnam and creating "Lower Cambodia."[192] In early 1977, the Khmer army conducted border raids into Vietnam, claiming control over parts of the Mekong Delta along Cambodia's southern border.[193] In September of that year, the Cambodian army overran six Vietnamese villages in Dong Thap Province and advanced about ten kilometers into Tay Ninh Province.[194] The Vietnamese government was initially restrained in its response,[195] presenting the CPK with a peace proposal in February 1978. When Pol Pot refused to even receive the proposal, however, the Vietnamese leadership concluded it would have to invade.[196]

Just as the CPK was provoking Vietnam and preparing for a "holy war" against its former patron,[197] Pol Pot launched a massive purge of commanders in eastern Cambodia, on the Vietnamese border. Fearing traitors, Pol Pot had disarmed several Eastern Zone units in early 1977,[198] and in 1978, he dispatched Southwest and Central Zone commanders to carry out a full-scale purge of the Eastern Zone Command structure—the very commanders who were responsible for thwarting a Vietnamese invasion.[199] By late April, 400 Eastern Zone officials were locked up in the Tuol Sleng death camp.[200] When the army's top Eastern Zone commander, So Phim, was targeted, he escaped into a forest north of Phnom Penh and then shot himself.[201] The purge sparked a major rebellion among surviving Eastern Zone units,[202] which was brutally put down; by late July, at least 10,000 people were dead and 60,000 local villagers were dislocated.[203] Just months before the Vietnamese invasion, then, Cambodia's military infrastructure near the border was torn apart. Local authority structures were in disarray, as each commune and district became divided against itself.[204] Pol Pot also purged key central government officials, including Vorn Vet, who was arrested and sent to Tuol Sleng just hours after being placed in charge of military supplies on the Vietnamese border.[205]

On December 24, 1978, Vietnam invaded Cambodia. Although China provided the Khmer Rouge with substantial economic and military assistance,[206] it did not intervene to thwart the attack. As a result, the Khmer Rouge quickly collapsed. Badly weakened by purges, the Cambodian forces fell apart and put up almost no resistance.[207] On January 7, 1979, Vietnamese forces entered Phnom Penh and installed a pro-Vietnamese government—the Kampuchean United Front for National Salvation—whose core consisted of lower-tier Khmer Rouge officials who had fled Cambodia during the purges.[208]

In sum, the Khmer Rouge came to power in a geopolitically vulnerable state that had been the site of a major Cold War conflict on the edges of the Vietnam War and launched a radical challenge to the domestic and regional order but was wiped out by counterrevolution.[209] The Khmer Rouge arguably began in a stronger position than did the revolutionary governments in Hungary and Afghanistan. It had a cohesive ruling party and a loyal (albeit decentralized) military, and it faced no political rivals or alternative power centers. Indeed, despite the CPK's catastrophic assault on Cambodian society, it confronted almost no domestic reaction. Ultimately, however, the regime committed suicide by invading Vietnam in the wake of massive purges that gutted the state.[210] Thus, the reactive sequence destroyed a regime that, like the French Jacobins in 1794, was already weakened by internal purges.

THE TALIBAN

The Taliban regime in Afghanistan (1996–2001) was also destroyed by its own radicalism. After seizing national power in 1996, the Taliban imposed Sharia law and facilitated a massive terrorist attack on the world's most powerful country. As in most other cases examined in this book, ideologically driven radicalism triggered counterrevolutionary reactions at home and abroad. Although the Taliban remained cohesive, the 2001 U.S. invasion—a reaction to Taliban radicalism—destroyed the regime before it could create an effective army or consolidate control over the country. In 2021, however, it would return to power.

THE REVOLUTIONARY SEIZURE OF POWER

The Taliban seized power in a context of extreme state weakness.[211] Afghanistan is a mountainous, ethnically diverse country with a state that has rarely reached much beyond the capital. The country was historically dominated by a moderate form of Islam embedded in traditional authority structures.[212] The December 1979 Soviet intervention changed all that. As Soviet military forces occupied the country to prop up a Marxist client government, the United States, Pakistan, and Saudi Arabia financed an anti-Soviet Mujahideen dominated by radical Islamists.[213] Pakistani military dictator Muhammad Zia-ul-Haq funded ethnic Pashtun Islamist forces under the leadership of Gulbuddin Hekmatyar, systematically sidelining moderate and royalist forces.[214] Pakistan and Saudi Arabia also encouraged the incursion of Arab Islamists into the conflict. By the time Soviet forces withdrew in 1989, 4,000 Arab fighters remained in Afghanistan.[215] There now existed more than 30,000 religious schools in and around Afghanistan, mostly dominated by a radical, Saudi-inspired curriculum.[216]

The Soviet exit and eventual collapse of the Soviet-backed regime in 1992 left Afghanistan in chaos.[217] The war gutted the traditional authority structures that had long held the country together, and no new central power structure emerged to replace them.[218] The Mujahideen had never operated under a single command,[219] and the Soviet withdrawal intensified the conflict between factions led by Hekmatyar in the east and Ahmad Massoud and Burhanuddin Rabbani in the north.

Afghanistan descended into violent chaos. By 1992, there were more personal weapons in Afghanistan than in India and Pakistan combined.[220] Warlords robbed merchants and kidnapped children as sex slaves.[221] There were multiple, competing currencies,[222] and Afghanistan rivaled Colombia and Burma as a source of heroin.[223] For local economic actors, the extraordinary number of impromptu roadblocks set up by local gangs on the main highways to extort money made trade nearly impossible.[224]

The absence of any force capable of maintaining order created an opening for the rise of radical alternatives.[225] The Taliban ("students of Islam") emerged out of a small group of supporters and veterans of the

Mujahideen around a one-eyed schoolteacher, Mullah Mohammed Omar, who became famous for coming to the aid of victims of warlord attacks in the small village of Sangesar in Kandahar Province in southern Afghanistan.[226] Like the Khmer Rouge, the Taliban was an extraordinarily radical movement that had been isolated from the modern world before coming to power. A former junior commander in the Mujahideen, Omar was "cut off, religiously and politically" and showed a "stunning ignorance of world affairs."[227] He apparently had never ridden in an airplane, slept in a hotel, or watched a satellite movie, and he had never been openly photographed.[228] He almost never left Kandahar, even after the Taliban took power.[229] Although most Taliban leaders were Mujahideen veterans,[230] many rank-and-file soldiers were young men who came from refugee camps and had spent little time in Afghan society. They possessed almost no knowledge of the country's complex tribal and ethnic makeup or the traditions that had grounded most citizens before the war.[231]

Many Taliban supporters were schooled in madrassas near Peshawar and in refugee camps, which taught a Saudi-influenced, conservative form of Islam.[232] The movement's ideology was grounded in Deobandism, a radical branch of Islam that had emerged out of India and was taught in madrassas along the Afghan-Pakistani border.[233] It posited that Muslims should live exactly as the followers of Prophet Mohammed did 1,400 years ago. Followers compiled long lists of rules to eliminate modern intrusions from society.[234] Many proponents of Deobandism took extreme positions on gender separation and female education and employment, and like the Wahhabi movement in Saudi Arabia, they exhibited an intense distaste for decoration or music.[235]

The astonishingly rapid rise of the Taliban, from a tiny group of lightly armed religious students in 1994 to Afghanistan's dominant political force in 1996, can be attributed to a combination of external backing, support from local businesses interests, and, above all, extreme state weakness.[236] Mullah Omar's reputation for confronting warlords gained the attention of the trucking mafia, which was heavily affected by the myriad roadblocks inhibiting trade. With assistance from trucking groups, 200 Taliban fighters won control of Spin Boldak, a trading hub on the border with Pakistan.[237] In the process, they seized the Pasha Arms Depot, which held 18,000 Kalashnikovs, dozens of artillery pieces, rockets, numerous vehicles, and vast quantities of ammunition that the Pakistani government had dumped across the border following the 1988 Afghan-Pakistani peace accords.[238] It was more than enough to equip a small army. Within forty-eight hours, the Taliban conquered Kandahar and shut down roadblocks, freeing up trade.[239] Although local warlords recognized the Taliban as a threat, they were too disorganized to respond effectively.[240]

The Taliban's early successes attracted the support of ethnic Pashtun political groups, as well as thousands of volunteers from madrassas across Afghanistan.[241] They also brought in support from the business community, including the transport magnate Hashmat Ghani Ahmadzai, as well as warlords such as President Rabbani (1992–1996), and Ismail Khan of Herat.[242] The royalist Karzai family, which included future president Hamid Karzai, donated $50,000 and a cache of weapons.[243] Most importantly, the Taliban's early victories convinced Pakistan to throw its support behind the Taliban rather than Hekmatyar. The Taliban would later receive considerable support from Saudi Arabia and the Pakistani Inter-Services Intelligence (ISI) agency.[244]

External support was critical to the Taliban's seizure of national power.[245] Facing a fragmented opposition, the Taliban rapidly won control of twelve of thirty-one Afghan provinces.[246] It captured Hekmatyar's headquarters in Wardak Province in early 1995 and seized Herat, Afghanistan's third-largest city, by the end of the year.[247] Then, in September 1996, following a ten-month siege, Taliban forces captured the capital.[248] Upon its arrival, the Taliban detained the last pro-Soviet leader, Mohammad Najibullah. He was beaten to death, castrated, and strung up in the center of the city.[249] Although the Taliban never controlled the entire national territory, it would eventually rule about 90 percent of Afghanistan.[250]

THE ABORTIVE REACTIVE SEQUENCE: RADICALISM AND REGIME COLLAPSE

Like the Hungarian Soviet Republic and the Khmer Rouge, the Taliban regime was born weak. The new government lacked a political party[251] or a modern state bureaucracy. The Taliban had insufficient cadres to control most of the country outside the major population centers.[252] Like the Chinese Nationalists in the 1920s, it gained control of many cities not through military conquest but by bribing warlords of uncertain loyalties.[253] In power, the Taliban relied on a loose network of religious authorities (ulama) to manage much of the country and depended heavily on foreign aid agencies to provide services.[254] State-building was hindered by the fact that the Taliban was ideologically opposed to the existence of a salaried state bureaucracy.[255] Thus, after taking power, the Taliban emptied out much of the state, and several ministries "ceased to function."[256]

Throughout the 1996–2001 period, the Taliban competed for control over much of the country with Massoud's Northern Alliance. Even in areas under its nominal control, moreover, its influence was limited. In the late 1990s, for example, Osama bin Laden—then under Taliban protection—avoided traveling in parts of the north for fear of capture.[257]

The Taliban also lacked an effective coercive apparatus. Its armed forces were fragmented and lacked a clear hierarchical structure; family members regularly rotated in and out of service at the front.[258] They were also poorly equipped, with the army relying heavily on pickup trucks[259] and ex-communist and former jihadi mercenaries hired to drive tanks, pilot airplanes, and carry out other specialized tasks.[260] Most soldiers did not receive regular pay.[261] Much of the fighting was done by armed Pashtun militias that "reflagged" themselves as Taliban.[262]

Despite this weakness, the Taliban immediately imposed Sharia law.[263] Building on earlier gender restrictions in place during the Mujahideen era, the Taliban required women to wear the burqa, shut down all girls' schools, and banned all women from the workplace, including about 50,000 widows who provided the only support for hundreds of thousands of children.[264] Given the prevalence of women in many parts of the state bureaucracy, this measure gutted the state, especially in the health care and education sectors.[265] Some 8,000 women were expelled from Kabul University. Women were forbidden to leave their homes without male accompaniment and were barred from washing clothes in the river.[266] Backed by a religious police (Amr bil-Maroof wa Nahi An il-Munkir), the government outlawed an extraordinarily large number of goods and activities, including marbles, cigarettes, kite flying, Western-style haircuts, homing pigeons, dancing, and singing.[267] Televisions were smashed. Individuals caught carrying audio- or videocassettes were beaten. Shops were punished for displaying fashion magazines. Soccer was initially banned.[268] The regime declared that toothpaste should be abandoned in favor of the natural root favored by the Prophet.[269]

The Taliban also provoked sectarian conflict with the Shia Muslim Hazara community. After taking control of Mazar-i-Sharif, Afghanistan's fourth-largest city, in the summer of 1998, the Taliban slaughtered 5,000–6,000 Hazaras over the course of two days.[270]

The Taliban's radicalism triggered powerful domestic and international reactions. At home, the regime faced armed opposition led by the Northern Alliance. At the same time, the revolutionary government's human rights abuses and attacks on women generated widespread international backlash.[271] The Taliban became a "pariah movement."[272]

Yet the Taliban's highly ideological top leaders unified and radical-ized in the face of mounting threats.[273] They refused to bend to interna-tional criticism, declaring the regime's treatment of women to be accor-dance with "God's law."[274] Indeed, following military setbacks, the Taliban tightened its gender policies in order to sustain internal morale.[275] In March 2001, the regime destroyed large Buddha statues in Bamiyan in cen-tral Afghanistan—a move apparently designed to generate international outrage.[276]

Most consequentially, the Taliban forged alliances with important Arab radicals, including Osama bin Laden.[277] Bin Laden, who had been active in the Mujahideen in the 1980s, came to Afghanistan in 1996 from Sudan, where he had been exiled by Saudi Arabia for his criticism of the royal family.[278] He built a close relationship with Omar, marrying one of his daughters.[279] Drawing on a fortune of more than $250 million, he set up camps—such as the Darunta camp near Jalalabad—that trained about 1,000 militants and aimed to develop chemical weapons.[280] Backed by about 2,000 supporters, bin Laden provided considerable support to the Taliban, financing construction projects and aiding the Taliban's assault on the north in 1997 and 1998.[281] By the late 1990s, al-Qaeda provided between 30 and 40 percent of the Taliban's military forces.[282]

In exchange, al-Qaeda used Afghanistan as a base for terrorist activi-ties. In February 1998, bin Laden issued a fatwa on behalf of the Interna-tional Islamic Front for Jihad against Jews and Crusaders, which sanctioned the killing of Americans and Jews everywhere.[283] In August of that year, al-Qaeda bombed the U.S. embassies in Kenya and Tanzania, killing more than 200 people, and in October 2000, it attacked the USS *Cole*, killing seventeen U.S. soldiers.[284] In response, U.S. cruise missiles targeted an al-Qaeda base in Khost, Afghanistan, and the United Nations (UN) Secu-rity Council imposed sanctions against individuals and entities associated with al-Qaeda and the Taliban.[285]

The Taliban came under enormous pressure to surrender bin Laden. Omar remained firm, however. In response to appeals by Prince Turki bin Abdullah Al Saud, the director of the Saudi Arabia General Intelligence Directorate, Omar called bin Laden "a courageous, valiant Muslim" and refused to hand him over.[286] Turki then withdrew the Saudi ambassador from Afghanistan.[287] Similar efforts by Pakistan were rebuffed.[288]

The regime's support for Arab jihadists and efforts to impose Sharia law alienated the Taliban from its early supporters and generated wide-spread opposition among Afghanistan's traditional and urban educated populations.[289] For example, the Karzai family went into opposition and campaigned for the return of King Mohammed Zahir Shah, who lived in exile in Italy. In response, men on motorcycles assassinated the Karzai patriarch as he walked home from mosque.[290]

As in Cambodia, however, domestic resistance alone was insufficient to oust the Taliban.[291] The Northern Alliance was weak and underequipped, with limited access to weapons and only a few barely functioning helicopters that could scarcely cross Afghanistan's many mountain passes.[292] Massoud's assassination by two al-Qaeda agents on September 9, 2001 further weakened the movement. Given the near defeat of the Northern Alliance and the absence of other viable opposition groups, it is plausible that the Taliban would have eventually consolidated control over the country absent U.S. intervention in late 2001.

Ultimately, the Taliban, like the Khmer Rouge, was felled by a more powerful invading army. Following the death of moderate Taliban leader Rabbani of cancer in early 2001, the Taliban further radicalized.[293] The government closed foreign hospitals, banned the internet, shut down the UN World Food Program, and required that Afghan Hindus wear yellow badges.[294] A week before the September 11, 2001, attacks, the Taliban issued a list of banned items that included objects made of human hair, sound recording devices and audiocassettes, all instruments producing music, chessboards, billiard tables, playing cards, masks, nail polish, firecrackers, centipedes, lobsters, all statues of animate beings, and neckties.[295]

On September 11, al-Qaeda killed nearly 3,000 people in attacks on the World Trade Center in New York City. No Afghans were directly involved in the attacks, and it is likely that Taliban leaders did not know about the attacks beforehand.[296] However, the Taliban had protected al-Qaeda. Furthermore, the mastermind behind the 9/11 operation, Mohamed Atta, was trained in Afghanistan, where he coordinated and planned the attacks with bin Laden.[297]

The attacks led directly to the collapse of the Taliban regime. Although an effort was made to convince Omar to surrender bin Laden, negotiating with Omar was like "banging one's head against the wall," and Omar refused.[298] On October 7, the United States launched the military invasion Operation Enduring Freedom, and by mid-November, the Taliban had been routed from Kabul.[299] In December 2001, the Taliban formally surrendered, and U.S.-backed Hamid Karzai was inaugurated as president on December 22, formally ending Taliban rule. The Taliban "ceased to exist as a physical entity."[300]

However, like the Viet Minh after its defeat in 1946 (see chapter 5), the Taliban regrouped, continued to fight, and eventually regained power.

Benefiting from growing resentment over abuse by U.S. soldiers and U.S.-backed Afghan officials, as well as support from local mosques, the Taliban gradually rebuilt itself as a guerrilla movement in the years following the 2001 American invasion.[301] The movement remained highly ideological, continuing large-scale attacks on schools that did not abide by its proscription of female education.[302] The Taliban also remained cohesive: it suffered few enduring divisions, even after the deaths of Omar and his successor, Akhtar Mansour, in the mid-2010s.[303] Consisting of a loosely connected collection of small battle formations (*mahaz*) and *shura* councils in Afghanistan and Pakistan, the Taliban lacked the discipline or professionalization of the Viet Minh.[304] However, with assistance from Iran and from Pakistan's ISI, Taliban forces upgraded their organizational and military capacity in the early 2010s.[305] Drawing on nationalism, religious ideology, and extensive external assistance, the movement successfully recruited tens of thousands of young men to join its ranks and replace the thousands of activists killed in battle.[306] Most of the Taliban's 50,000–60,000 fighters fought without regular salaries.[307] By 2015, the Taliban had established an armed presence across the national territory.[308]

As in 1996, the Taliban's seizure of power was facilitated by the extreme weakness and eventual collapse of the Afghan state. When the U.S. government announced the withdrawal of American troops in the spring of 2021, the Afghan army disintegrated. The Taliban marched quickly to power, seizing Kabul on August 15.

The Taliban's early behavior in power suggested that it remained committed to radical transformation. Almost immediately, the new government began restricting women's right to work and access to education and recreation.[309] As of late 2021, however, it remained unclear whether the new regime would return to its radical foreign policy orientation, including support for international terrorist activities. That choice will very likely shape the longer-run trajectory of the regime.

In sum, as in Hungary and Cambodia, a combination of extreme radicalism and geopolitical vulnerability in Afghanistan led to rapid regime collapse. Like the Khmer Rouge, the Taliban nearly consolidated power at home but was ousted following an invasion by a far more powerful state.

Conclusion

This chapter examined three revolutionary regimes in geopolitically vulnerable states that suffered quick deaths—all due to external intervention. Radical efforts to create a new social order triggered a reactive sequence that was soon aborted. Powerful external threats gave rise to cohesive elites and loyal militaries in Cambodia and Afghanistan and led to the destruction of alternative centers of societal power in Cambodia. However, military intervention by foreign powers quashed the regimes before they could consolidate. Not only did these regimes experience early deaths, but their demise can be directly traced to the revolutionary reactive sequence. As the chapter makes clear, then, the survival of revolutionary regimes during their early stages is a contingent outcome, and when revolutionary governments pursue extremist policies, they may provoke fatal counter-revolutionary reactions.

At the same time, the outcome was not entirely contingent. Although our sample is too small to draw any definitive conclusions about the sources of early death, state size and military vulnerability seem important. Whereas Russia, China, Vietnam, and Iran were all large, regional powers, Hungary, Cambodia, and Afghanistan were relatively small states that were especially prone to foreign intervention.[310] Hungary had just emerged from defeat in World War I and was occupied by multiple European powers. Cambodia and Afghanistan had been the sites of destructive Cold War proxy conflicts. By contrast, revolutionary governments in bigger states had greater success in withstanding external attacks. Russia survived foreign intervention during its civil war; Iran persisted in the face of the Iraqi invasion in the 1980s; and China endured direct confrontation with the United States in Korea. In Iran and Russia especially, sheer territorial size gave revolutionary governments some breathing room to eventually recover.

A potential alternative explanation for the early demise of regimes in Hungary, Cambodia, and Afghanistan is that revolutionary governments in these countries were exceptionally radical. We are skeptical of this argument. For one, although the policies undertaken by Kun and Pol Pot were indeed extreme, they were arguably matched by Stalin in the 1930s, Mao in the 1950s and 1960s, and Castro in the 1960s. Like Hungary, Russia, Iran, and Cuba actively promoted revolution abroad. Moreover, whereas the strongest case for greater extremism comes in the area of domestic policy, all three regimes were destroyed by foreign invasion, not domestic opposition.

External vulnerability certainly does not make early death inevitable. Radical governments in Cuba (population 11 million) and Eritrea (population 3 million) survived the reactive sequence and built powerful autocracies. However, revolutionary elites in these cases had far less room for error than in China, the USSR, or Vietnam.

CHAPTER EIGHT

Accommodation
and Instability

BOLIVIA, NICARAGUA, AND GUINEA-BISSAU

CHAPTER 7 HIGHLIGHTED THE RISKS of initiating radical strategies in vulnerable states. In Hungary, Cambodia, and Afghanistan, radical measures triggered military conflicts that resulted in the quick death of revolutionary regimes. Yet moderation may also inhibit revolutionary consolidation. Where revolutionary governments tempered their early radicalism in order to accommodate powerful interests, regimes were less likely to develop the elite cohesion, powerful and loyal coercive structures, and state-societal power asymmetries that undergird long-run durability.

This chapter examines three revolutionary regimes—in Bolivia, Nicaragua, and Guinea-Bissau—that combined early radicalism with accommodationist strategies. These cases meet the book's criteria for social revolution in that governments emerged out of violent social revolution and initiated radical efforts to transform their societies. Unlike our ideal-typical cases, however, revolutionary elites in Bolivia, Nicaragua, and Guinea-Bissau—spooked by counterrevolutionary threats or restrained by pragmatic allies—moderated in an effort to limit the intensity of the counterrevolutionary reaction.

Efforts to accommodate powerful interests are quite rational from the perspective of leaders seeking to consolidate power in the near term. Governments that do not engage in radical redistribution, invasive cultural transformations, or aggressive foreign policies are less likely to confront existential counterrevolutionary threats. By tempering or aborting the revolutionary reactive sequence, however, accommodationist strategies inhibit longer-term regime consolidation. Precisely because they do not face a counterrevolutionary threat, accommodationist governments are less likely to fall into a siege mentality, build a disciplined party, or invest in a powerful garrison state, and they often lack the will and capacity to wipe out rival power centers. This leaves regimes more prone to schisms and coup conspiracies from within and opposition challenges from without. This accommodationist pattern was seen in Algeria in chapter 5. Because the National Liberation Front (FLN) government did not provoke a domestic counterrevolutionary movement or a serious external military conflict, it never developed a cohesive elite or destroyed rival power centers. As a result, the Algerian regime suffered far greater internal conflict and societal contestation than its counterpart in Vietnam.

This chapter examines the trajectories of accommodationist revolutionary regimes in Bolivia, Nicaragua, and Guinea-Bissau. In Bolivia, militant unions pushed the Revolutionary Nationalist Movement (MNR) government to nationalize the tin mines and initiate a far-reaching land reform. However, MNR leaders took steps to limit the scope of reform so as to avoid a major conflict with the United States. Absent a serious counterrevolutionary conflict, the MNR had no need to close ranks or assault rival power centers. These developments, together with the fateful decision to let the old army rebuild itself, contributed to the crisis and the coup that ended the regime in 1964.

In Guinea-Bissau, the Party for African Independence of Guinea and Cape Verde (PAIGC) split into radical and moderate factions. When it achieved independence, radicals expropriated colonial properties and aspired to create a centrally planned economy. However, moderates quickly reversed course, abandoning socialism and pursuing friendly relations with Portugal and the West. As a result, the regime confronted little counterrevolutionary reaction. In the absence of an existential threat, the PAIGC atrophied and latent elite divisions reemerged. The regime suffered a series of internal conflicts before falling prey to a military rebellion in 1999.

Nicaragua followed a somewhat different path. The Sandinista National Liberation Front's (FSLN) early radicalism triggered a costly counterrevolutionary war backed by the United States. As in Cuba, the existential threat posed by the counterrevolution gave rise to a cohesive elite and a powerful and disciplined coercive apparatus. However, the costs of the war, together with the dawn of the Gorbachev era in the Soviet Union, induced the Sandinistas to moderate. Ultimately, the FSLN's failure to destroy the private sector and the Catholic Church proved costly, as these actors played a major role in defeating the Sandinistas in elections.

BOLIVIA

Bolivia's April 1952 revolution gave rise to a dominant party regime that styled itself after the Mexican Institutional Revolutionary Party (PRI). The MNR government seized control of the tin mines and launched the most radical land reform in Latin America since the Mexican Revolution. Yet the Bolivian Revolution failed to consolidate. In 1964, President Victor Paz Estenssoro was overthrown in a regime-ending coup.

Why was Bolivia's revolutionary regime so short-lived? The 1952 revolution triggered little violent conflict,[1] in large part because the MNR pursued an accommodationist strategy. Although labor and peasant mobilization induced the revolutionary government to launch radical reforms in 1952 and 1953, MNR leaders were pragmatists. Believing that the regime could not survive without the United States' support, they tempered their reforms to win the confidence of the U.S. government. They succeeded, and the MNR confronted only a mild counterrevolutionary reaction. As a result, the regime never developed the pillars of durable authoritarianism. The MNR elite was not forced to close ranks, build a powerful coercive apparatus, or wipe out rival organizations or power centers—including the prerevolutionary army. What emerged was a weak regime. When faced with labor opposition, the MNR government turned to a military it did not control. And when elite schisms and mounting social protest weakened the government in 1964, the military put an end to the regime.

The Revolutionary Seizure of Power

The Bolivian Revolution occurred in a context of state weakness and regime instability. Bolivia's postcolonial state was strikingly weak.[2] The army routinely failed to maintain order or defend the national borders. Thus, Bolivia lost wars to Chile in 1879–1881, Brazil in 1899–1903, and Paraguay in 1932–1935,[3] and the country experienced 227 armed uprisings between 1925 and 1960.[4]

Prerevolutionary Bolivia was highly exclusionary. Power was concentrated in the hands of large landowners and tin barons, who constituted an oligarchy known as La Rosca.[5] The economy was based on tin exports,[6] and more than 80 percent of tin production was in the hands of the "Big Three" mining companies: Aramayo, Hochschild, and Patiño.[7] Rural society was "quasi-feudal."[8] In 1950, 4.5 percent of the population owned 70 percent of the farmland. The indigenous majority was subjected to a system of forced labor on landowners' estates (*pongueaje*).[9] Exploitation was so extreme that one U.S. ambassador described indigenous peasants as "slaves."[10] As late as 1950, two-thirds of Bolivians reportedly lived under *pongueaje*.[11]

The oligarchic order began to crumble in the 1930s, after Bolivia's defeat at the hands of Paraguay in the Chaco War.[12] The army was decimated, losing as many as 60,000 soldiers and effectively ceasing to be a viable repressive force.[13] Military defeat and the Depression also eroded the legitimacy of the traditional political elite.[14] The result was mounting instability, with five coups and a successful urban insurrection between 1935 and 1950.[15]

The 1930s and 1940s saw the emergence of new anti-oligarchic movements.[16] The Chaco War forced the army to mobilize indigenous workers and peasants, many of whom returned home armed and unwilling to accept the old status quo.[17] Labeled the Chaco generation, these veterans filled the ranks of the leftist Union Federation of Bolivian Mineworkers, nationalist army factions such as Razon de la Patria (RADEPA), and new leftist and nationalist parties, the largest of which was the MNR.[18]

Anti-oligarchic forces first seized power in 1936, when a nationalist coup gave rise to a short-lived experiment with "military socialism" (1936–1939).[19] In 1943, a RADEPA-led coup established a reformist military government led by Lieutenant Colonel Gualberto Villarroel, in alliance with the MNR.[20] The Villarroel government confronted strong U.S. opposition,[21] and in 1946, Villarroel was toppled—and hung from a lamppost—in a street uprising.[22] The MNR was banned and repressed in the conservative restoration that ensued.[23]

The MNR radicalized after 1946, abandoning its quasi-fascist platform for a left-leaning one and forging an alliance with the growing mine workers union.[24] After launching a series of failed insurrections between 1946 and 1951,[25] the MNR participated in elections in 1951. Running from exile, MNR presidential candidate Victor Paz Estenssoro pledged to nationalize the Big Three mining companies, which earned him the enmity of La Rosca.[26] Paz appears to have won, but the army canceled the election and installed a junta headed by General Hugo Ballivan—a move that closed off the legal path to power and, as Paz put it, "forced us to make a revolution."[27]

The 1952 revolution began as a coup conspiracy between the MNR and the head of the military police (*carabineros*), General Antonio Selene. On April 9, the MNR and about 2,000 *carabineros* launched an uprising, with the understanding that the army would back the rebels and that Selene would become president.[28] When the army remained loyal, however,

Selene gave up and sought asylum in the Chilean embassy.[29] The MNR and armed mine workers fought on, however, transforming the putsch into an urban insurrection.[30] Fighting broke out in cities across Bolivia, at which point the army began to disintegrate.[31] The army was filled with untrained conscripts,[32] many of whom had "dedicated themselves to realizing practice exercises for the military parade." Thus, the soldiers "could parade very well but they did not know how to fight."[33] Many deserted when the conflict began.[34] In La Paz, pro-government forces consisted of the 600-man presidential guard, 400 military academy cadets, and 240 poorly armed members of the Second Engineer Battalion.[35]

On April 10 and 11, rebel militias defeated the armed forces in La Paz, shattering them.[36] Army commander Humberto Torres and other top officers fled the country; others simply went home, leaving only a handful of soldiers in the barracks.[37] Defeated by a "ragtag force of civilian irregulars," the army surrendered on April 11.[38] Paz returned from exile to assume the presidency.[39]

By comparative standards, the MNR seizure of power was quick and easy.[40] It took only three days and resulted in 550–600 deaths.[41] MNR leaders were stunned by their victory. Indeed, Paz declared that "never in [their] boldest dreams" did they expect a full-blown revolution.[42]

The Reactive Sequence: Accommodation and Limited Reaction

The new regime was weak. For one, it lacked a cohesive elite. The MNR encompassed diverse and conflicting elements, including leftist union leaders such as Juan Lechín, an anticommunist faction led by Walter Guevara Arze, and a pragmatic center that included President Paz and Vice President Hernán Siles Zuazo.[43] These factions lacked a coherent ideology or a shared experience of violent struggle, which left the MNR prone to schism.[44]

Another source of weakness was the absence of an army. The prerevolutionary army collapsed in April 1952.[45] Senior officers were exiled or imprisoned, most rank-and-file soldiers deserted, and the military academy was closed.[46] Reportedly, all that remained of the army in mid-1952 were the band and the Engineer Corps.[47] Unlike other revolutionary cases, however, the MNR did not build a new army after seizing power. Instead, it relied on miners' militias and a shrunken police force to maintain order.[48] The old army was thus temporarily disabled but not permanently replaced.[49]

Counterrevolutionary forces were relatively weak. The oligarchy—
La Rosca—was weakened by the exodus of many landowners and tin
barons[50] and the disabling of the prerevolutionary army.[51] The Catholic
Church was small by Latin American standards. It was understaffed, with
only half as many priests, per capita, as the Mexican Church, and its influence over Bolivia's predominantly indigenous population was limited.[52]
Thus, unlike in Mexico and Nicaragua, the Church "simply did not matter
so much" in Bolivia.[53]

If traditional elites were weak, however, labor and peasant organizations were strong.[54] Mine workers unions played a decisive role in
the revolution.[55] Hundreds of new unions emerged in 1952, and they
came together in the leftist Bolivian Workers Central (COB).[56] The
COB's power was rooted in its control over the mines and the union militias.[57] The unions, not the government, ran the mining camps,[58] and the
20,000-strong miners' militias outnumbered the army and the police combined.[59] Although peasants played only a minor role in the April revolution, they mobilized in its aftermath.[60] Armed peasant unions proliferated
in 1952 and 1953.[61]

In sum, Bolivia's revolutionary regime was born weak. Lacking an
army and facing an array of independent social and political actors, the
new MNR government depended on autonomous worker and peasant
militias for its survival.

THE MNR IN POWER:
AN ACCOMMODATIONIST GOVERNMENT

The MNR was a "reluctant band of revolutionaries."[62] Founded in 1941 as a
nationalist party, its program was reformist and state capitalist, not socialist.[63] The early MNR did not even champion land reform,[64] but rather
modernization of the agricultural sector.[65] MNR leaders never contem-
plated breaking with the United States,"[66] and in stark contrast to other
revolutionary leaders, they largely eschewed violent social change.[67] As
Guevara Arze put it, "We want the Mexican Revolution without 10 years
of Pancho Villa."[68] The MNR had "no grand plan" for governing when Paz
ran for president in 1951.[69] Paz himself was a pragmatic politician with
"firmly conservative sensibilities."[70]

The MNR's moderation was reinforced by the geopolitical landscape.
Bolivia's economy depended on the United States.[71] The United States
consumed half of Bolivia's tin exports, which, in turn, accounted for
70 percent of the country's foreign exchange.[72] MNR leaders "recognized

that no Bolivian revolution could afford to alienate the United States,"[73] unless, as Paz joked, they found a way to ship tin to Europe "by submarine from Lake Titicaca."[74] Bolivia also depended heavily on U.S. aid, and MNR leaders were "willing to bend quite a bit in order to obtain it."[75]

Finally, unlike in the 1960s, when Soviet patronage helped the Cuban regime survive, the USSR was uninterested in Latin American client states in 1952,[76] which meant that Bolivia had few alternative allies outside the United States.[77] Thus, whereas Castro embraced Marxism-Leninism to secure the support of the Soviet Union, MNR leaders went to great lengths to "avoid the label of a communist-inspired regime"[78] in order to deny U.S. cold warriors any "fodder for red-baiting."[79] For example, during the 1952 May Day parade, the MNR banned red flags and forcibly expelled anyone wearing a red armband.[80]

Nevertheless, the MNR was radicalized by pressure from its labor and peasant allies.[81] Unlike the reformist MNR, the COB sought a "swift, thorough cleansing of the old order."[82] COB leaders demanded nationalization and worker control of the mines, land reform, and the army's replacement by worker militias.[83] The COBs power was rooted in its control over the mining camps and worker militias.[84] Because the MNR lacked an army and thus depended on the militias for its survival, it was forced to accept union demands that went well beyond its traditional program.[85] In effect, COB leaders told the MNR that "like it or not, there was going to be a revolution."[86]

The MNR adopted genuinely radical policies during the first Paz administration (1952–1956). Paz formed a "co-government" with the COB, appointing labor leaders to head the Labor, the Mining, and the Agriculture and Peasant Affairs Ministries.[87] The Paz government undertook two truly radical initiatives: the 1952 nationalization of tin mines and the 1953 land reform. These two measures were transformative in that they destroyed Bolivia's traditional economic elite. In both instances, however, the MNR government tempered its radicalism with measures aimed at maintaining a cooperative relationship with the United States.

Control over the tin mines had long been a source of conflict in Bolivia. The Big Three tin producers, which accounted for 80 percent of tin production and generated 95 percent of Bolivia's foreign exchange,[88] were considered untouchable.[89] Indeed, previous nationalist governments' efforts to reign them in were seen as responsible for the fall of those governments.[90] Fearing such an outcome, many of the MNR's advisers counseled against nationalization.[91] However, nationalization and worker control of the mines were core COB demands.[92] According to a

U.S. State Department report, Lechín "pounded the table for immediate, outright nationalization" during Paz's first cabinet meeting.[93] Union pressure proved impossible to resist, and in October 1953, Paz issued a decree nationalizing the 163 mines operated by the Big Three.[94] A state mining company, the Bolivian Mining Corporation (COMIBOL) was created, and a system of "worker control" (*control obrero*) was established in which unions gained two of seven seats on the COMIBOL directorate and each mine elected a worker control representative with veto power over the mine's operations.[95]

However, when the U.S. government rejected the nationalizations and threatened to discontinue tin purchases, the MNR government, dependent on American tin markets, moved quickly to mend relations with the United States.[96] Bolivia's ambassador to the United States, Victor Andrade, declared "time and time again" that the mining nationalization was a "special case," that the Big Three would be fully compensated, and that the MNR was committed to private property and foreign investment.[97] Indeed, the expropriations were limited to the Big Three, as hundreds of smaller mines were left in private hands.[98] Finally, in June 1953, the Paz government reached a compensation agreement with the Big Three, thereby rejecting the COB's demand for "nationalization without compensation."[99]

Land reform was similarly driven by pressure from below. Land reform was absent from the MNR's original program.[100] The MNR remained divided over the issue in 1952, and party leaders initially sought only a modest reform.[101] However, conditions on the ground compelled the MNR to radicalize. Rural Bolivia descended into a "state of upheaval" in 1952 and early 1953.[102] The countryside was "immersed in disorder," as peasants attacked landlords, ransacked estates, and seized land.[103] With peasants reportedly threatening to attack towns, civil war seemed like a "menacing possibility."[104] In August 1953, a "reluctant" MNR government approved a radical agrarian reform law.[105] Large estates, or *latifundias*, were abolished, and with them, *pongueaje* and other forced labor practices.[106] The landed oligarchy was destroyed.[107] The reform was extensive.[108] About 160,000 families, or 45 percent of Bolivian farm families, received land, a far higher percentage of beneficiaries than in Venezuela, Colombia, Chile, Costa Rica, or Peru.[109] Through 1980, only Cuba and Mexico—both revolutionary cases—had undertaken more far-reaching reforms in Latin America.[110]

However, Bolivia's land reform differed markedly from those of other revolutionary cases. For one, it was capitalist. Small- and medium-sized farms were protected, as were larger farms (up to 5,000 acres) that engaged in "modern" agricultural production.[111] Land was distributed in individual family-size plots; there were no state farms and few cooperatives.[112] The goal was not socialism but rather the breakup of quasi-feudal estates and the establishment of a more modern—and equitable—system of private ownership.[113] The Bolivian reforms also followed legal and bureaucratic procedure to a greater degree than in other revolutionary cases. Landowners were entitled to compensation and had multiple levels of appeal available to them.[114] This attention to legal niceties slowed land distribution,[115] which became a source of public discontent.[116]

In sum, although labor and peasant mobilization compelled the MNR government to launch far-reaching socioeconomic reforms, a combination of pragmatism and external dependence induced MNR leaders to soften their most radical initiatives. Thus, as Richard Patch observed at the time, the Bolivian Revolution "did not follow the rules. There was no class struggle. There was little loss of life. . . . There was no accession of the extremists, no reign of terror, no Thermidor."[117] This accommodationist strategy would powerfully shape the regime's long-term trajectory.

A LIMITED COUNTERREVOLUTIONARY REACTION

The 1952–1953 reforms triggered only a modest counterrevolutionary reaction. Conservative forces reacted with hostility. The Big Three mining companies hired lobbyists in Washington and pushed for a U.S. embargo on Bolivian exports.[118] Major newspapers, owned by members of La Rosca, also reacted with hostility.[119] Newspaper owner Demetrio Canelas accused the MNR of provoking "racial belligerence," replacing "a conscientious and cultivated citizenry of European extraction with an illiterate indigenous electorate," and "ruin[ing] the vital forces of the Bolivian economy."[120]

However, oligarchic resistance was ineffective, in part because the army that had long protected traditional elites was now disabled.[121] Counterrevolutionary rebellions thus lacked force.[122] In January 1953, for example, a rebellion backed by right-wing MNR leaders was easily put down by labor and peasant militias.[123] Likewise, the right-wing Falange Socialist Party, or Falange, which emerged as the primary representative of landowner, Catholic, and other counterrevolutionary interests,[124] organized a series of armed rebellions during the 1950s.[125] Without the army to back them, however, the rebellions floundered.[126]

Finally, the MNR faced little resistance from the United States.[127] In stark contrast to the United States' hostile response to the Cuban and the Nicaraguan Revolutions, the United States tolerated and eventually embraced the Bolivian regime.[128] There are two major reasons for this difference. First, the United States had only limited economic interests in Bolivia.[129] Few Americans owned land in Bolivia, and the tin barons had relatively few U.S. shareholders.[130] Unlike in other Latin American revolutions, then, the U.S.-based lobby for intervention in Bolivia was weak.[131] Second, the Paz government's accommodation and diplomacy convinced U.S. officials that the Bolivian Revolution did not pose a communist threat.[132]

U.S. officials initially had "deep misgivings" about the revolution.[133] Paz was distrusted by the U.S. establishment (where, incredibly, he was cast as both a Nazi and a communist),[134] and the Americans found COB leader Juan Lechín "horrifying."[135] However, State Department officials soon developed the view that Paz was not a communist but rather a Kerensky-like figure whose failure risked a more radical outcome.[136] Thus, the Truman administration offered the regime "grudging recognition."[137]

The October 1952 mine nationalization threatened this initial rapprochement. U.S. officials rejected the measure, suspending discussion of a new tin contract.[138] In March 1953, the newly inaugurated Eisenhower administration announced that it would no longer pursue a long-term tin contract.[139] Given that the tin crisis took place amid mounting Cold War tensions, it could have escalated into a regime-threatening rupture like that in Cuba. However, the conflict was quickly defused—due, in large part, to MNR accommodation. The Paz government ceased expropriations, eschewed plans to sell tin to the Eastern bloc, and, in June 1953, reached an agreement to compensate the Big Three.[140] In July, U.S. officials reciprocated, announcing a new one-year tin contract.[141] That month, President Eisenhower's brother Milton traveled to Bolivia, where he concluded that the MNR was an anticommunist ally worthy of U.S. support.[142] By late 1953, the Eisenhower administration had fully embraced the Paz government and begun to shower it with aid.[143] U.S. assistance more than doubled in 1954.[144] Overall, the United States provided more than $300 million in aid between 1953 and 1964, making Bolivia the leading per capita U.S. aid recipient in Latin America.[145] Indeed, U.S.-Bolivian relations "may have been closer than between any other two countries in the hemisphere."[146]

The MNR's accommodation effectively defused any counterrevolutionary reaction and locked Bolivia into a trajectory not unlike that of the FLN in Algeria (chapter 5). As we shall see, dependence on U.S. assistance encouraged policies—such as economic orthodoxy and a rebuilding of the army—that not only put the brakes on revolutionary change but also undermined regime consolidation.[147]

LIMITED STATE-BUILDING

In the absence of a strong counterrevolutionary reaction, the MNR government did little state-building. As noted above, the MNR did not build its own armed forces. No revolutionary army emerged from the April 1952 insurrection.[148] For more than a year, the old army lay dormant, while order was maintained by union militias.[149] The COB called for the army's abolition and replacement with worker militias.[150] However, Paz opted to preserve it, formally reconstituting it in July 1953.[151]

The military was substantially reformed. Paz purged nearly all top officers and about a quarter of the officer corps.[152] The military academy, which had been restricted to upper-class families, began to recruit officers from non-elite backgrounds.[153] The army was also downsized. Absent an external threat, MNR leaders were mainly concerned about challenges from the army, which had toppled half a dozen governments since 1930.[154] Thus, Paz slashed the army from 20,000 to 5000 troops,[155] reducing it to "something more like a palace guard."[156] The police force was also scaled back, leaving the security forces outmanned by worker militias.[157] Military spending fell from more than 20 percent of the budget in 1952 to 6.7 percent in 1957.[158] Officers' salaries were so low that they complained of living in rented garages and having to use their rations to feed their families.[159] Indeed, the army adopted such a low profile that many outside observers believed it had been destroyed.[160]

Although the MNR weakened the army, it failed to control it. The Bolivian Revolution produced no party-army fusion. Unlike in Mexico, Cuba, and Nicaragua, militias that defeated the Bolivian military in 1952 never formed part of the revolutionary state. Efforts to penetrate the reconstituted armed forces were ineffective. The Paz government packed the army command with allies, many of them RADEPA members who had been purged during the 1940s.[161] Paz declared the army to be partisan, renaming it the Army of the National Revolution.[162] Officers were required to take an oath of loyalty to the MNR and were pressured to join the ruling party.[163] Paz sought to solidify army loyalty by placing MNR "political instructors" in the military academy.[164]

However, these measures did little to bridge the gap between the MNR and the army leadership. Although many military commanders had nationalist sympathies, they were, first and foremost, career officers whose loyalties lay with the armed forces. Far from Mexico's revolution-ary generals or Cuba's revolutionary "civic soldiers," then, Bolivia's army commanders were lifelong military men who did not participate in the revolution or have a stake in its success.[165] For example, General Alfredo Ovando, whom Paz appointed to command the armed forces, joined the MNR but had no previous ties to the party.[166] Despite the military acad-emy's reorganization, moreover, most new officer recruits continued to be drawn from middle-class backgrounds, which meant that the army would continue to be "staffed by men from groups who were essentially hostile to the MNR."[167]

In this context, the MNR's efforts to politicize the army proved ineffec-tive. Party memberships and loyalty oaths were "paper phenomena,"[168] or pro forma activities that were not taken seriously by officers, who regarded them as a "requisite for service, nothing more."[169]

The MNR's efforts at partisan penetration were thus a far cry from those observed in other revolutionary cases. Not only did Paz leave pre-existing military institutions intact, but he left army leaders in charge of transforming them.[170] As a result, the army retained considerable institu-tional autonomy.[171]

THE SURVIVAL OF RIVAL POWER CENTERS

The modest nature of the counterrevolutionary reaction also limited the MNR's incentive to eliminate alternative power centers. The revolution did, of course, destroy traditional centers of economic power. The tin barons and the big landowners either fled the country or were weakened by nationalization and land reform.[172] By 1953, La Rosca had effectively ceased to exist.[173]

Beyond that, however, the MNR did little to weaken centers of societal power. Without a counterrevolutionary threat, the MNR never attempted a "root and branch elimination" of its rivals.[174] Prerevolutionary institu-tions and organizations were not destroyed, and political rivals were never killed and only rarely jailed or exiled.[175] The government also refrained from attacking the Church; indeed, it occasionally turned to Church lead-ers to mediate conflict.[176]

The MNR was also restrained in its treatment of the universities. The universities were bastions of upper-class conservativism,[177] and after 1952, they became centers of right-wing reaction.[178] Nevertheless, efforts to cur-tail university autonomy were quickly aborted.[179] In 1954, COB militias, claiming—with some foundation—that the universities were centers of counterrevolutionary activity, seized control of most campuses with the goal of transforming them into "popular universities."[180] Within a few months, however, the government backed down and returned the universities to their owners.[181] The universities remained centers of counterrevolutionary activity until the end of MNR rule.[182]

Repression of rival political organizations was also limited.[183] Although the counterrevolutionary Falange suffered some repression, mostly in the form of arrests,[184] it was never banned or forced underground.[185] Indeed, the Falange competed actively in the 1956 and 1960 elections, finishing second (with 14 percent of the vote) in 1956.

The MNR also failed to subordinate its union and peasant allies. Lacking an army, the MNR government had neither the capacity nor the will to disarm union and peasant militias. As a result, the miners unions remained in control of the mining camps and armed peasant *sindicatos* (unions) entrenched themselves in much of the countryside.[186]

In sum, the MNR's accommodationist strategy succeeded in preempting a counterrevolution, and, as a result, the Paz government never confronted an existential military threat. In the absence of such a threat, however, the revolutionary government had little incentive to build a powerful coercive apparatus or weaken alternative centers of societal power.

The Post-1956 Regime: Weak Authoritarian Pillars

When Paz's first presidential term ended in 1956, all counterrevolutionary threats had subsided. La Rosca was no more, the United States was an ally, and Falange rebellions had taken on "all the normalcy of a common cold."[187] By the time Hernán Siles Zuazo assumed the presidency in August, the mild reactive sequence triggered by the 1952 revolution was completed.

Yet the foundations of authoritarian rule were weak. For one, the regime elite lacked cohesion. The MNR remained prone to debilitating schisms.[188] As early as January 1953, right-wing MNR leaders backed an abortive coup.[189] As we shall see, the MNR "split and split again" in the 1950s and early 1960s,[190] ultimately contributing to regime collapse.

The regime also lacked a strong and loyal coercive apparatus. The 8,000-strong army was less than half its prerevolutionary size,[191] and it operated on a "starvation budget."[192] Moreover, unlike ruling parties in Mexico, Cuba, and Nicaragua, the MNR's ties to the army were weak.[193] Only four of twenty-four top army officers had strong MNR ties in the late 1950s,[194] and army chief Alfredo Ovando was not among them.[195]

Finally, the MNR government continued to confront rival social and political organizations, both on the right (the Falangists) and, more consequentially, on the left (the COB). Unlike in Mexico, where the PRI established tight control over workers and peasants, Bolivian unions remained "independent allies rather than loyal subordinates."[196] The 20,000-strong mine workers' militias were "probably the strongest military force in Bolivia,"[197] outmanning the army.[198] Peasant groups also remained autonomous.[199] Because the MNR-state never fully penetrated the national territory, swathes of the countryside fell under the de facto control of rural barons who controlled "their own personal armies" and "dispensed justice independently of the central government."[200]

In sum, despite the "formal façade" of single-party rule, revolutionary Bolivia was in fact quite pluralist.[201] Lacking an existential threat, the MNR never developed a cohesive elite, built a powerful coercive apparatus, or wiped out rival power centers. As a result, the vast power asymmetries that emerged out of revolutionary reactive sequences in China, Cuba, Mexico, Vietnam, and elsewhere never developed in Bolivia.

The Evolution and Breakdown of the Regime, 1956–1964

The foundations of the revolutionary regime began to erode during the presidency of Siles, who succeeded Paz in 1956. Siles inherited a severe economic crisis. Bolivia's per capita GDP declined by 20 percent between 1952 and 1957.[202] The economy also collapsed into hyperinflation, leading Siles to prioritize stabilization.[203] Given Bolivia's dependence on the United States (U.S. assistance covered 40 percent of the annual budget), MNR leaders saw little alternative but to turn to the Americans.[204] In late 1956, the government negotiated a draconian stabilization program—designed by U.S. economist George Eder—with the United States and the International Monetary Fund (IMF).[205] The Eder Plan included a 40 percent spending cut; the elimination of price controls and subsidies; trade, financial, and exchange rate liberalization; and a wage freeze.[206] In exchange, Bolivia received $25 million in U.S. and IMF assistance.[207] Effectively trapped by its ties to the United States, the MNR responded to the economic crisis by abandoning much of its original program.[208]

The Siles government's conservative turn triggered a series of developments that weakened the regime. Importantly, it disrupted the MNR's alliance with labor and the Left.[209] The unions strongly opposed the 1956–1957 stabilization program.[210] Strike activity increased, and the

COB called a general strike for July 1957.[211] Although Siles convinced COB leaders to call off the strike,[212] the stabilization plan undermined the MNR coalition. Vice President Nuflo Chávez, a COB member, resigned,[213] effectively ending "co-government."[214]

The 1956–1957 stabilization program thus "set Bolivia on a new path," on which the COB's revolutionary program had no place.[215] The stabilization fight also led MNR leaders to rethink the role of the armed forces. If the government were to continue its capitalist course, it would face labor resistance. In such a scenario, an army that was outmanned by workers' militias was undesirable. The Siles government thus made a fateful decision. It rebuilt the army, effectively "reactivate[ing] the Frankenstein monster."[216] Military spending increased from 6.7 percent of the budget in 1956 to 13.5 percent in 1962,[217] while the army grew from 8,000 to 12,000 troops.[218]

The MNR's conservative drift continued after Paz's return to the presidency in 1960. The 1960 succession triggered a schism in the ruling party. To regain the labor support in his pursuit of the MNR's presidential nomination, Paz named COB leader Juan Lechín as his vice presidential candidate (reportedly promising him the presidency in 1964).[219] The Paz-Lechín ticket led to the defection of minister of government (and MNR cofounder) Walter Guevara Arze.[220] Guevara Arze took much of the MNR's right wing with him.[221]

Paz's second term (1960–1964) was, in some ways, more successful than his first one. The economy grew briskly,[222] and Bolivia received $205 million in assistance as part of the Alliance for Progress.[223] Bolivia became the second leading per capita U.S. aid recipient in the world.[224]

Ties to the United States powerfully shaped the regime's trajectory in the early 1960s.[225] The Alliance for Progress called for a set of "modernizing" reforms—opening up to foreign investment, rationalizing the state-run mining sector—that placed Paz on a "collision course" with the unions.[226] In effect, the need for labor acquiescence encouraged Paz to continue Siles's effort to weaken the labor movement.[227]

The armed forces were central to those efforts.[228] Encouraged by U.S. officials, Paz strengthened the army, restoring its prerevolutionary role as the primary guarantor of domestic order.[229] Military spending rose from below 7 percent of the national budget in the mid-1950s to 17 percent in 1964.[230] The army expanded to 15,000 soldiers, overtaking the union militias.[231] The buildup was made possible by $12.4 million in U.S. military assistance.[232] Indeed, U.S. military aid was so extensive that Paraguay formally complained that it was disrupting the regional balance of power.[233] By 1964, the armed forces were once again the "arbiter of national political life."[234]

The regime began to unravel in 1961, when Paz launched the Triangular Plan, a U.S.-funded program to nationalize the mining sector, which included both layoffs and the dismantling of the worker control system through which the unions had exercised influence over production and employment decisions.[235] The Triangular Plan definitively ruptured the MNR-labor alliance.[236] A wave of strikes and protest began in 1962 and continued throughout 1963.[237] Emboldened by U.S. security assistance, Paz declared three states of siege to quell the unrest and eventually mobilized the army to break the strike.[238]

The regime might have survived labor opposition had the ruling party remained intact. However, the MNR suffered a series of schisms in 1964. The central conflict revolved around Paz's reelection. In 1962, Paz had pushed through a constitutional reform enabling him to seek reelection.[239] His candidacy faced internal opposition, however.[240] Lechín, whom Paz had reportedly promised the nomination,[241] enjoyed strong labor and left-wing support.[242] However, U.S. officials opposed Lechín's candidacy, reportedly threatening to withdraw aid if he were nominated.[243] With Lechín out of contention, Paz orchestrated his own renomination,[244] which shattered the MNR.[245] Lechín and much of the Left defected, forming the Revolutionary Party of the Nationalist Left (PRIN).[246] Ex-president Siles also moved into opposition.[247] By early 1964, then, three of the MNR's founding leaders—Guevara Arze, Lechín, and Siles—were in opposition. It was "almost literally one man against everyone."[248] Lechín's PRIN, Guevara Arze's Authentic Revolution Party, Siles, and the Falange all boycotted the 1964 election.[249] Running unopposed, Paz won with 98 percent of the vote.

In the wake of his reelection, Paz declared that the revolution had "institutionalized, following the Mexican precedent."[250] He was wrong. The aftermath of the election was "marked by riots, demonstrations, protests, and calculated violence,"[251] by both the labor Left and the counterrevolutionary Right. Mine workers launched a series of strikes and protests in mid-1964, culminating in the formation of a parallel "popular government" in August.[252] Teachers began a nationwide strike, and the Falange launched a guerrilla uprising in Santa Cruz.[253] In the fall, student riots erupted in several cities.[254] By September, the country was in a state of insurrection.[255] With the mines and schools closed and the streets of the capital in chaos, Paz declared a state of siege and ordered the army to seize the mining camps and repress student protests.[256] Yet army officers refused to repress.[257] By late 1964, most MNR leaders were "either actively plotting against Paz or passively hoping for an end to his rule."[258] Siles, Guevara Arze, Lechín, and the COB all lobbied for a coup.[259]

On November 3, 1964, Paz was toppled by a coup led by Generals Alfredo Ovando and Rene Barrientos. Both generals had taken the MNR loyalty oath, and Paz believed they would remain loyal—a miscalculation that he later described as his greatest mistake.[260]

When Paz fled the country, workers celebrated in the belief that Lechín would succeed him. Carrying Lechín on their shoulders, they chanted "Lechín to the palace!"[261] They were mistaken. The 1964 coup ended the revolutionary regime. Under General Barrientos, the MNR was purged from the state and replaced by an all-military cabinet.[262] MNR leaders were exiled, the COB was outlawed, and the labor movement was "smashed."[263] As the historian Luis Antezana Ergueta put it, the unions and the Left had "joined a counterrevolution that handed power to the ultra-Right; it was as if Mao . . . had returned power to Chiang Kai-shek."[264]

Two critical aspects of Bolivia's revolutionary reactive sequence contributed to the regime's early and inglorious demise. First, because the MNR's accommodationist strategy dampened the counterrevolutionary reaction, the regime never confronted an existential military threat. Consequently, it never developed a cohesive elite or destroyed rival organizations. MNR defectors such as Siles, Arze, and Lechín and autonomous social actors such as the mine workers union, peasant barons, and universities contributed directly to the 1964 governability crisis and coup. Second, the MNRs decision not to build its own army prevented the kind of party-army fusion that effectively coup-proofed regimes elsewhere. Ultimately, the combination of societal contention and an autonomous military left Bolivia's revolutionary government as vulnerable as other—nonrevolutionary—governments in Latin America.

NICARAGUA

The Nicaraguan case only partially fits our theory. The FSLN was more radical than the MNR, and it confronted a devastating counterrevolutionary war. As in other revolutions, the war gave rise to a cohesive elite and a powerful and loyal coercive apparatus. However, the Sandinistas refrained from destroying independent power centers, most notably the private sector and the Church, which prevented the development of extreme state-society power asymmetries. Moreover, because Nicaragua's counterrevolutionary war occurred at the end of the Cold War, the FSLN faced strong external pressure to moderate. Thus, the Church and the private sector survived, providing resources and legitimacy to the opposition. Accommodation also brought competitive elections, which created an opening for opposition groups to defeat the revolution at the ballot box.

The Revolutionary Seizure of Power

The Nicaraguan Revolution occurred amid the collapse of a sultanistic regime. Nicaragua had long been plagued by state weakness. The country was in a state of "nearly permanent civil war" during its first thirty-five years of independence,[265] and in 1855, an American mercenary named William Walker seized power for more than a year.[266] The United States occupied Nicaragua in 1909, transforming it into a virtual protectorate.[267] The Marines left in 1925 but returned in 1927 after a U.S.-sponsored constabulary collapsed amid a Liberal uprising.[268] U.S. diplomats brokered a peace between rival Conservative and Liberal forces, but dissident Liberals led by Cesar Augusto Sandino waged a guerrilla war until U.S. forces left for good in 1933.[269] Before departing, U.S. forces created the 2,000-man National Guard (GN) and placed it under the command of Anastasio Somoza García.[270] Control over the GN transformed Somoza into a de facto strongman, and in 1936, he seized power in a coup.[271]

The 1936 coup ushered in forty-three years of sultanistic rule,[272] beginning with the dictatorship of Somoza García, continuing after his 1956 assassination under the joint rule of his sons Luis (who became president) and Anastasio (who controlled the GN), and culminating, following Luis Somoza Debayle's 1967 death, in the personal rule of Anastasio Somoza Debayle. The Somocista state was thoroughly neopatrimonial.[273] Anastasio Somoza García became the largest landowner in Nicaragua, with fifty-one cattle ranches, forty-six coffee farms, and eight sugar plantations.[274] His son Anastasio accumulated more than $500 million in wealth and 20 percent of Nicaragua's farmland.[275] The GN became Anastasio Somoza Debayle's "private militia."[276] Its hierarchy was packed with family members and loyalists. During the 1970s, for example, the GN's main infantry force, the Third Battalion, was led by Somoza's half-brother, while the Basic Infantry Training School, a 2,000-man elite force, was run by Somoza's son.[277] Loyalty to Somoza was the key to ascent in the GN's upper ranks.[278]

The Somoza regime was stable into the 1970s. Steady economic growth allowed the Somozas to generously fund the GN[279] and co-opt opposition politicians, industrialists, and even the Catholic Church.[280] The Somozas also enjoyed consistent U.S. support, as they deftly positioned Nicaragua as a loyal Cold War ally.[281]

The road to revolution was thus long and difficult. The FSLN was created in 1961 by Carlos Fonseca, Tomás Borge, and a handful of other radicals who took to the mountains seeking to replicate Castro's success in Cuba.[282] They failed and were nearly wiped out.[283] After the failure of a second insurrection in 1967, the FSLN was militarily dormant for seven years,[284] posing no more than an "occasional inconvenience" to Somoza.[285]

The political tide began to turn in 1972, when Somoza's inept response to a massive earthquake in Managua revealed the depths of the regime's corruption.[286] Somoza and his cronies pocketed international relief funds and seized the lion's share of reconstruction contracts.[287]

Opposition soon emerged on several fronts. For one, a group of industrialists moved into opposition, forming the Superior Private Enterprise Council (COSEP) and, in 1974, the Democratic Liberation Union.[288] The Church also turned against the regime,[289] and grassroots Catholic base communities became hubs of opposition activism.[290] Finally, the FSLN resurfaced in 1974, leading a spectacular raid on a Christmas party attended by much of the Managua elite.[291]

Somoza declared a state of siege in 1975, and the ensuing repression nearly wiped the FSLN out.[292] Fonseca was killed in 1976, and by 1977, the CIA estimated that the guerrillas were down to fifty fighters.[293] Moreover, the Sandinistas split into three rival factions: the rural Prolonged Popular War faction, led by founding leader Tomás Borge; the urban Proletarians, led by Jaime Wheelock; and the Insurrectionary, or Tercerista, faction, led by Daniel and Humberto Ortega.[294] As late as 1977, then, a guerrilla victory seemed like a "pipe dream."[295]

Two important changes occurred in 1977 and 1978, however. First, the Carter administration, ending years of unconditional U.S. support, suspended military and economic aid, forcing Somoza to ease repression.[296] Second, in January 1978, Pedro Joaquin Chamorro, editor of Nicaragua's leading newspaper, *La Prensa*, and the country's most prominent opposition figure, was assassinated by Somoza associates.[297] The assassination triggered broad societal opposition,[298] including a February 1978 uprising in Monimbó, Masaya, which took the GN two weeks to put down. Similar uprisings followed in other cities.[299]

The opposition divided into moderate and revolutionary camps. On the one hand, business groups and most opposition parties came together in May 1978 to form the Broad Opposition Front (FAO), which became the primary vehicle for nonrevolutionary opposition.[300] On the other hand, the revolutionary movement reemerged with force in August 1978, when an FSLN commando seized the National Palace, which housed the Congress. Although the Sandinistas had barely 500 fighters,[301] they tapped into a larger wave of urban popular mobilization, which was backed by progressive sectors of the Church.[302] In September 1978, the FSLN launched a nationwide offensive, overrunning GN stations in Managua and other cities.[303]

Alarmed by the FSLN's ascent, the Carter administration pressed Somoza to negotiate with the moderate FAO.[304] U.S. officials hoped that OAS-sponsored talks in October 1978 would bring Somoza's resignation and an interim government that preserved the GN, thereby forestalling a revolutionary outcome.[305] Somoza refused to step down, however, derailing the negotiations and discrediting the FAO.[306]

The revolutionary movement was strengthened by two developments in early 1979. First, the FSLN united. Pressured by Fidel Castro, the guerrillas formed a collegial leadership body, the National Directorate, composed of three representatives of each faction.[307] Second, despite mounting U.S. and domestic pressure, Somoza stubbornly clung to power.[308] Believing he could "ride the waves" of U.S. policy,[309] Somoza decided, as he put it, to "stick it out."[310]

Somoza's refusal to leave fatally weakened the nonrevolutionary opposition.[311] With the negotiated path foreclosed, a growing number of politicians, business leaders, and Church officials joined the revolutionary coalition.[312] By early 1979, the FSLN had more than 2,000 fighters and was seizing cities in the north.[313]

In May 1979, the FSLN launched a "final offensive," and by early July it controlled 80 percent of the country.[314] The GN "began coming apart one unit at a time"; as soldiers deserted and reserves refused call-ups, the Guard shrank from 14,000 to 10,000 troops.[315]

International efforts to prevent a revolutionary outcome failed.[316] U.S. officials sought to preserve the GN as a bulwark against revolution but were divided over how to do it.[317] National Security Adviser Zbigniew K. Brzezinski viewed military intervention as the only way to thwart a Sandinista victory; however, Secretary of State Cyrus Vance and other officials—spooked by Vietnam and distracted by other crises—rejected such a move.[318] Unwilling to intervene militarily, the United States sought to influence the transition "without using its hands."[319]

On July 11, the revolutionaries unveiled the National Reconstruction Junta, which included FSLN leader Daniel Ortega, Violeta Chamorro (widow of murdered opposition leader Pedro Joaquin Chamorro), businessman Alfonso Robelo, writer Sergio Ramírez, and leftist academic Moisés Hassán. Although Ortega was the lone guerrilla on the junta, Ramírez and Hassán were Sandinista allies.

By July 13, the FSLN controlled all roads to Managua.[320] Realizing the game was up, Somoza resigned on July 16, and early the next morning, Somoza, his family, and top GN commanders flew to Miami.[321] Congress named Francisco Urcuyo interim president.

The revolutionary outcome was assured when Urcuyo, who had been expected to hand power to the junta while leaving the GN intact, declared that he would remain in office until Somoza's term ended in 1981.[322] The FSLN responded by accelerating its march on Managua, which triggered the collapse of the state.[323] The GN decomposed. At 2:30 A.M. on July 18, U.S. defense attaché James McCoy was awakened by a phone call from GN officers, who had, in McCoy's words, "decided it was all over . . . and . . . were getting on planes to Honduras."[324] By 6:00 A.M., McCoy "concluded that the Guard no longer existed."[325] GN units disintegrated as soldiers abandoned their posts.[326] Even high-ranking officers "could be seen ripping off their uniforms and trying to melt into crowds"; officers went into exile, into hiding, or simply home.[327] The air force quit en masse.[328] A U.S. official visited air force headquarters and found "no one left but a woman burning documents."[329]

Reversing course, Urcuyo attempted to transfer power to the armed forces, but GN commander Francisco Mejia told him that "we are also leaving."[330] When Sandinista forces reached Managua on July 19, only the chief of the Managua transit police remained to surrender power.[331] The GN's collapse stunned the FSLN, creating, in the words of one Sandinista, a "better situation than we had imagined in our wildest dreams."[332]

The seizure of power in Nicaragua was far more difficult than in Bolivia or Cuba. The GN fought fiercely and with great brutality, forcing anti-Somoza forces to endure a "bloodbath."[333] At least 10,000 Nicaraguans were killed in the final months of the insurrection, and at least 30,000 were killed between 1977 and 1979.[334]

The Reactive Sequence

The FSLN victory destroyed the Somocista state. The GN was dissolved, and soldiers who did not flee the country were rounded up, given show trials, and imprisoned.[335] Seeking to maintain international support, the revolutionaries avoided acts of summary justice.[336] Thus, although

6,310 members of the old regime (mainly GN members) were imprisoned, there were no firing squads or reigns of terror.[337]

The FSLN rebuilt the armed forces from scratch.[338] The Sandinista Popular Army (EPS) and the Sandinista Police were founded and staffed by FSLN guerrillas.[339] All EPS commanders were ex-guerrilla leaders, and guerrilla units became EPS units.[340] Former GN members were systematically excluded.[341]

The new junta, which included prominent nonrevolutionaries Violeta Chamorro and Alfonso Robelo, announced a moderate program of political pluralism, a mixed economy, and a nonaligned foreign policy.[342] The new cabinet was majority non-Sandinista.[343] Real power, however, lay in the hands of the FSLN National Directorate.[344] From day one, the Sandinistas controlled "all things military."[345] The EPS was led by FSLN commander Humberto Ortega, while the Interior Ministry, which controlled the police and other internal security agencies, was occupied by FSLN leader Tomás Borge. According to Robelo, these appointments "were never discussed. They just happened."[346] The Sandinistas also postponed elections.[347] Army chief Humberto Ortega declared that there would be no "raffle to see who has power, because the people have the power through their vanguard, the [FSLN]."[348]

Although the Sandinistas dominated the revolutionary government, the regime itself was fragile. The revolutionary army was small, ill equipped, and poorly trained.[349] It initially had about 5,000 troops, expanding to 18,000 by late 1979.[350] The FSLN was small (1,500 members),[351] and it had spent much of the insurrectionary period "locked in internecine conflict."[352] Indeed, the party was so plagued by internal rivalries that the sociologist James Petras predicted it would quickly fragment like the Bolivian MNR.[353]

The revolutionary government confronted a range of potential enemies. Although Somocista forces—including the GN and Somoza's Nationalist Liberal Party—disappeared, other societal actors remained strong. One of these was the Church. Unlike in Cuba and Mexico, where the Church backed the old regime until the end, the Nicaraguan Church broke with Somoza and eventually backed the insurrection.[354] Indeed, Archbishop Miguel Obando y Bravo led a celebratory mass after Somoza's fall.[355] The Church split in the wake of the revolution, however; although a progressive wing backed the new regime, the Church hierarchy, which maintained close ties to the conservative establishment, adopted a more critical posture.[356]

The Church posed a potential threat to the new regime. More than 90 percent of Nicaraguans were Catholic,[357] and Archbishop Obando y Bravo was considered "the most popular man in Nicaragua."[358] The Church also maintained a formidable organizational infrastructure that included 178 parishes, a network of religious schools, and a popular radio station, Radio Católica.[359] The Church was highly influential;[360] indeed, it was considered virtually "untouchable."[361]

Capitalists also survived the revolution. The departure of Somoza, who owned more than 100 businesses,[362] and the heads of the two dominant financial groups, the Nicaraguan Bank of Industry and Commerce and the Bank of America, "delivered a heavy blow to the traditional bastions of economic power."[363] However, most private industrialists and retailers remained in Nicaragua—and they were well organized.[364] COSEP, which encompassed the industrial sector, the chamber of commerce, and major agricultural producers, emerged as an important political actor in the struggle against Somoza.[365] Although Nicaragua lacked a strong rural oligarchy,[366] it had vibrant private cotton, coffee, sugar, rice, and cattle ranching sectors, which were represented by the 6,000-member Union of Agricultural Producers.[367]

The private sector was closely linked to Nicaragua's largest newspaper, *La Prensa*.[368] Run by prominent opposition leader Pedro Joaquin Chamorro until his assassination in 1978 (after which it passed into the hands of Chamorro's widow, Violeta), *La Prensa*'s domestic and international prestige made it "almost as untouchable as the Church."[369]

Opposition parties were weak in the aftermath of the revolution. The traditional Conservatives were divided and discredited by decades of co-optation,[370] and other mainstream parties, such as the Independent Liberals, the Social Christians, and the Nicaraguan Democratic Movement, were small middle-class organizations.[371] As we shall see, however, opposition parties' ability to draw on private-sector and Church resources would greatly enhance their ability to contest for power.

EARLY RADICALISM

The FSLN government mixed radicalism and accommodation. The Sandinistas—particularly the dominant Tercerista faction—are generally viewed as pragmatists.[372] Rejecting what founding leader Carlos Fonseca called the "pseudo-Marxist gobbledygook" of orthodox communist parties,[373] FSLN leaders developed an eclectic worldview that blended Marxism, nationalism, and Christianity.[374] Nevertheless, the Sandinistas were wedded to a "Castroist" worldview.[375] The FSLN's founding was inspired by the Cuban Revolution,[376] and Sandinistas of all factions embraced the Cuban model.[377] According to former vice president Sergio Ramírez, the Sandinistas "wanted to assimilate the Cuban model in everything. . . . It was a blind form of trust."[378] Indeed, the Sandinistas' devotion to Castro was such that less than a week after Somoza's fall, the entire FSLN leadership traveled to Havana to celebrate.[379] This embrace of Castroism had a radicalizing effect. For FSLN leaders, revolution entailed "fundamentally remaking the structure of Nicaraguan society" and creating a "new man" and a "new woman."[380]

The FSLN confronted a challenging geopolitical environment, however.[381] The United States remained the dominant power in Central America, and the Soviet Union cared little about Nicaragua.[382] This created incentives for the Sandinistas to remain on good terms with Western governments. Even Castro counseled moderation, reportedly telling Sandinista leaders to "avoid the early mistakes we made in Cuba, the political rejection by the West, premature frontal attacks on the bourgeoisie, economic isolation."[383]

The Sandinistas only partially heeded Castro's advice. Driven by what army chief Humberto Ortega described as "youthful romanticism,"[384] the revolutionary government mixed elements of radicalism and accommodation.[385] Early economic policy was relatively pragmatic. Because Somoza and his cronies owned about 25 percent of the country's industry and more than 20 percent of the farmland,[386] their departure left hundreds of abandoned properties that could be expropriated without a fight. Thus, soon after seizing power, the Sandinistas ordered the expropriation of more than 300 properties owned by Somoza and his associates.[387] Moreover, because the owners of the largest financial groups also abandoned the country, bankrupting the financial system, the government could nationalize the banks without resistance.[388] Like the FLN in Algeria, then, the Sandinistas expropriated vast amounts of abandoned property, expanding the state's share of GDP from 15 percent in 1978 to 41 percent in 1980,[389] without triggering the kind of bourgeois resistance seen in Cuba.

The FSLN thus established a mixed, rather than a socialist, economy.[390] The state monopolized trade and nationalized banking, insurance, mining, and transportation.[391] However, nearly 60 percent of the economy—including 75 percent of industry and agriculture—remained in private hands.[392]

The revolutionary government was even more accommodationist in the cultural arena. The Sandinistas' alliance with progressive Catholics during the revolutionary struggle made an anti-Church orientation unthinkable.[393] Although a few Marxist hard-liners sought to disrupt traditional religious practices such as Christmas and the December 8 Purísima celebration,[394] the FSLN leadership adopted a more pragmatic position. As a December 1979 party document put it, "To confront a tradition of more than 1,979 years . . . would carry us into political conflicts and we would lose influence among our people. At the same time, it would feed the campaign that our enemies abroad are launching against our revolution."[395] The FSLN thus issued a series of public statements in 1979 and 1980 embracing Christianity and declaring an "inalienable right" to religious freedom.[396] Although FSLN-Church relations deteriorated after 1980, the Sandinistas never attacked the Church as an institution or threatened its vital interests.[397]

Nevertheless, Sandinista radicalism threatened powerful interests in two important areas. One was land reform. The 1981 Agrarian Reform Law permitted the expropriation of all idle or underutilized farmland over 750 acres in size.[398] Some 1.1 million acres of land were expropriated between 1981 and 1984.[399] The percentage of farmland in large private estates fell from roughly 40 percent in 1978 to 8 percent in 1988.[400] A 1986 law opened more land for expropriation, resulting in hundreds of additional expropriations.[401] Ultimately, the FSLN redistributed about 28 percent of Nicaraguan farmland, providing land to 43 percent of peasant families.[402]

Nicaragua's agrarian reform was milder than Cuba's. Most land remained in private hands,[403] and most small- and medium-sized farmers were exempted.[404] However, two aspects of the reform generated resistance. First, unlike Bolivia's legalistic land reform, the Sandinista reform was implemented in an arbitrary and politicized manner, and it was accompanied by a radical Marxian discourse that frightened many farmers.[405] Second, and again in contrast to Bolivia, most of the expropriated land was organized into state farms and cooperatives, rather than individual holdings.[406] Wedded to the Cuban model, Sandinista leaders were reluctant to distribute land to individuals because it ran counter to their long-term socialist goals.[407] This reluctance proved costly in that the creation of state farms and cooperatives "fundamentally disrupted the way of life" in the countryside, generating considerable rural opposition.[408]

The other area in which early radicalism proved consequential was foreign policy.[409] Sandinista leaders were wedded to an anti-imperialist worldview.[410] Most of them had grown up viscerally anti-American. As Daniel Ortega put it, "We were anti-Coca-Cola, anti-comic book, against everything, good and bad, represented by the United States, except baseball."[411] Given the history of U.S intervention in Nicaragua, FSLN leaders believed that they "had to be against the United States"[412] and that a Bolivian-style accommodation with the United States risked "the loss of our nationality."[413]

Foreign policy radicalism was manifested in two important ways. First, the FSLN embraced Cuban-style support for revolutionary movements abroad, particularly the Farabundi Martí Liberation Front (FMLN) in El Salvador.[414] Such "internationalism" risked a serious conflict with the United States. Yet it was core to the Sandinista identity. As National Directorate member Bayardo Arce put it, if the Sandinistas did not support the Salvadoran guerrillas, they would "cease being revolutionaries."[415] The Sandinistas initially agreed to U.S. demands not to ship arms to the FMLN.[416] However, Reagan's victory in November 1980 appeared to confirm their belief in the inevitability of U.S. aggression, and so as the FMLN prepared its January 1981 final offensive, the Nicaraguans "opened the floodgates."[417] The move, which Humberto Ortega later attributed to "internationalist romanticism,"[418] proved costly, as the CIA's discovery of the arms shipments in January 1981 gave the incoming Reagan administration an "ideal pretext" for launching the Contra war.[419]

Second, the Sandinistas' anti-imperialist worldview cast conflict with the United States as inevitable,[420] which led them to forego opportunities for the kind of negotiated accommodation observed in Bolivia. As Ramírez put it, FSLN leaders "decided that this was a fight to the death against imperialism. This fate was already written and could not be avoided."[421] Such "biblical fatalism" discouraged the FSLN from taking U.S. diplomatic initiatives seriously.[422] This was especially manifest in 1981, when U.S. assistant secretary of state for inter-American affairs Thomas Enders offered the Sandinistas peace if they abandoned their support for the FMLN, tempered their relationship with Cuba, and limited the size of the armed forces to 15,000 troops.[423] The Sandinistas did not take the offer seriously, a move they would later regret.[424] Junta leader Daniel Ortega told Enders that the Sandinistas would "defend our revolution by force of arms, even if we are crushed."[425] The talks failed, after which the United States stepped up support for the Contras.[426] Years later, when FSLN leader Bayardo Arce was asked if the Sandinistas regretted their response to Enders, he replied, "We made our decision based on principles. It was not a matter of cold analysis, or else the choice might have been different.

Remember what the climate was at the time. We were still in a wartime mentality."[427]

In sum, the FSLN government combined radicalism and accommodation between 1979 and 1981. Although the government maintained a mixed economy, legalized opposition, and left the Church and much of the private sector untouched, its radical orientation led to unpopular agrarian policies and a risky (and ill-timed) confrontation with the United States.

THE COUNTERREVOLUTIONARY REACTION

The Nicaraguan Revolution triggered an unusually strong counterrevolutionary reaction. This outcome was rooted, in large part, in historical timing and contingency. The United States initially responded to the revolution with moderation. Hoping to avoid replicating U.S. mistakes in Cuba, the Carter administration worked to "deny the Sandinistas an enemy" in 1979–1980, even sending $75 million in assistance.[428] Had Carter been reelected, the counterrevolutionary reaction might have been milder.

However, Reagan's ascent to the presidency heightened U.S. hostility toward Nicaragua. Operating under the belief—also drawn from the Cuban experience—that revolutionary regimes must be destroyed early, before they consolidate,[429] the Reagan administration launched a three-pronged "war of attrition" against the Sandinistas.[430] First, on the economic front, it withdrew all aid, pressured international agencies not to lend to Nicaragua, and, in 1985, imposed a full-scale trade embargo.[431] Second, the CIA and other U.S. agencies engaged in a series of clandestine attacks on Nicaraguan ports, bridges, communications centers, and oil tanks, the most notable of which was the 1983 mining of Nicaraguan harbors, as well as a series of military maneuvers aimed at generating fears of a U.S. invasion.[432] Although U.S. officials did not seriously consider an invasion, they sought to create the perception that one was imminent.[433] The goal, as then CIA director William Casey put it, was to "make the bastards sweat."[434]

The third and most important component of the U.S. strategy was support for armed counterrevolutionary forces, or Contras.[435] The Contras were initially a small group of former GN members who began organizing along the Honduran border soon after Somoza's overthrow.[436] They forged an alliance with northern peasant-based militia groups—known as Popular Anti-Somoza Militias—that had fought against Somoza but later turned against the FSLN.[437] The two forces created the Nicaraguan Democratic Front in 1981.[438]

The Contras grew rapidly, reaching 13,000–17,000 fighters by the mid-1980s.[439] This growth had both external and domestic causes. On the external front, the CIA began to support the Contras in 1981, providing $15 million in covert assistance.[440] The Contras received an additional $100 million in U.S. assistance over the next three years, and U.S. officials armed, supplied, and trained the emerging Contra army.[441] As Robert A. Pastor put it, the campaign was like a "prolonged Bay of Pigs operation."[442]

The Contra movement also had domestic roots, however.[443] The revolutionary government's early agrarian policies sowed the seeds of peasant rebellion. As noted above, the FSLN's radical discourse terrified many farmers.[444] Even small farmers "began to fear that the lands in which their lives were sewn would be suddenly taken away from them."[445] The FSLN's insistence on state farms and cooperatives was also deeply unpopular.[446] Moreover, the government's heavy-handed response to peasant resistance—harassing, threatening, arresting, and even killing peasants who were suspected of disloyalty—led entire rural communities to join the Contras.[447]

Nicaragua thus plunged into civil war in 1982. The six-year war took more than 29,000 lives and generated between $1.5 and $4 billion in damage.[448] It also badly eroded public support for the FSLN government.

Yet the Contra war also strengthened the regime. As in other revolutionary cases, the U.S.-led counterrevolutionary war generated an enduring perception of existential threat among the revolutionary elite.[449] The Reagan presidency triggered "near hysteria" among Sandinista leaders.[450] Reagan had called for the overthrow of the Nicaraguan regime,[451] and the U.S. military buildup in Honduras, increased U.S. military exercises in the region, and the 1983 invasion of Grenada convinced FSLN leaders that the United States posed an imminent and existential threat.[452]

The U.S. threat had predictable effects. For one, it reinforced elite cohesion.[453] The Sandinistas continued to be riven by personal and strategic differences,[454] but as former vice president Ramírez observed, the threat of U.S. aggression led them to close ranks "out of necessity."[455] FSLN leaders "developed acute senses of paranoia, never trusting anyone outside their own tightly knit group."[456]

The Contra war also expanded the regime's coercive capacity.[457] The Reagan administration's aggression reinforced the perception among Sandinista leaders that "the United States was out to destroy them, and their only route to survival lay . . . in strength."[458] Thus, the Sandinistas invested heavily in security and national defense.[459] By 1987, military spending constituted 62 percent of the national budget.[460] Initial plans for an army roughly the size of Somoza's GN were shelved in favor of "accelerated army-building."[461] The army expanded from 6,000 soldiers in 1979 to 46,000 in 1984 to 134,000 in 1986.[462] An additional 100,000 joined militias.[463] By the late 1980s, the Sandinistas had between 175,000 and 250,000 people under arms.[464] The Sandinistas also built a vast internal security system, developing a Cuban-trained secret police force that one opposition leader described as a "second army."[465] As Christopher Dickey observed, the Sandinistas developed a level of military power "the likes of which Central America had never seen. They were a match for any of Washington's allies in the area, and potentially for all of them combined. And by their lights they had to be."[466]

The military buildup was made possible by large-scale Cuban and Soviet assistance. Soviet bloc military assistance increased from $6 million in 1980 to $250 million in 1984 and reached $500 million a year in the late 1980s.[467]

Unlike other revolutionary regimes facing existential threats, however, the FSLN did not systematically assault independent centers of societal power. The Sandinistas had reason to worry about the loyalty of key domestic actors. Many small farmers were openly counterrevolutionary; nearly 40,000 of them took up arms in the 1980s.[468] COSEP and the main opposition parties—including the Conservatives, the Social Christians, and the Nicaraguan Democratic Movement—were financed and advised by the CIA,[469] and their leaders had close ties to the Contras. Finally, the Church refused to condemn the Contras,[470] and hard-liners such as Bishop Pablo Vega defended their "right to insurrection."[471] Even Archbishop Obando y Bravo "could not avoid a certain sympathy" for the Contras.[472]

Not surprisingly, then, the FSLN responded to the Contra war with repression. In March 1982, following the first Contra attacks on Nicaraguan soil, the government declared a state of emergency that suspended civil liberties.[473] Opposition parties, unions, business associations, human rights groups, and other associations were infiltrated by state security, denied permits for public meetings, harassed by pro-government mobs, and occasionally saw their leaders arrested or exiled.[474]

Yet the level of repression never approached that of Cuba. Unlike Castro after the Bay of Pigs, the FSLN never banned opposition parties or forced them underground. Indeed, opposition parties were allowed to participate in elections in 1984 (though most boycotted).[475] Likewise, the Sandinistas never attempted to wipe out the private sector. Although business leaders who criticized the government were sometimes expropriated or arrested,[476] COSEP remained legal and above ground, even at the height of the civil war.[477]

Similarly, the FSLN never attempted to destroy landowners as a class.[478] Unlike in Cuba, many large producers retained their land, and several leading landowning families emerged from the revolution unscathed.[479] Indeed, attacks on landowners were often more bark than bite. During one heated public meeting with big farmers, when the feared internal security chief, Lenin Cerna, lost his temper and declared, "You're all under arrest," one farmer shouted back, "Okay. Pick the cotton yourself!"[480] Finally, the Sandinistas, recognizing the failure of their early agrarian policies, distributed land to individual farmers beginning in 1982.[481] By 1988, 80 percent of farmland was in private hands.[482]

Finally, the FSLN never seriously threatened the Church. The government orchestrated occasional mob attacks on Church services, deported ten foreign priests, and ran smear campaigns against opposition bishops and priests.[483] However, the government never closed down Church institutions, expropriated Church property, or prohibited Church activities.[484] Archbishop Obando y Bravo was free to oppose the FSLN. Indeed, in 1985, he undertook a national tour that had the "atmosphere of an anti-Sandinista campaign tour."[485]

The FSLN's comparatively light treatment of civil society was driven by the geopolitical context. Soviet support for the regime was relatively modest.[486] Soviet leaders refused to send top-of-the-line weaponry and made it clear that they would not defend Nicaragua in the face of a U.S. invasion.[487] As Humberto Ortega observed, "Nicaragua isn't Cuba. It has no Soviet umbrella."[488] Without a Soviet umbrella, FSLN leaders turned to the diplomatic arena, seeking support among Western democracies in order to counter U.S. aggression. Winning this diplomatic war required accommodation. Because the Reagan administration used attacks on opposition parties, the private sector, the Church, and the media to justify its support for the Contras, the FSLN had powerful incentives to limit such attacks.

Briefly, at the height of the war, the Sandinistas repressed rival power centers with greater vigor. In early 1986, the Reagan administration asked Congress for $100 million in assistance to the Contras—a dramatic escalation of the conflict.[489] Domestic regime opponents lobbied on behalf of the bill.[490] Bishop Antonio Vega traveled to Washington and defended the Contras,[491] and *La Prensa* editor Jaime Chamorro penned a *Washington Post* op-ed supporting Contra aid.[492] When the bill passed in June 1986, the Sandinistas responded by closing *La Prensa* and expelling Bishop Vega and Radio Católica director Father Bismarck Carballo.[493] Opposition activity largely ceased, as many leading opposition figures opted for exile and the Contras.[494]

Unlike Cuba after the Bay of Pigs, however, the Sandinistas soon reversed course. By 1986, Nicaragua's war-torn economy had collapsed into a prolonged recession,[495] and the Soviet Union, now under Gorbachev, was sending signals that Nicaragua could not count on continued assistance.[496] These developments dramatically heightened the cost of isolation from the West.[497]

Within months of the mid-1986 crackdown, then, the FSLN returned to a strategy of accommodation. In September 1986, President Ortega met with Archbishop Obando y Bravo, giving rise to a new "modus vivendi" in which the Church enjoyed greater political latitude.[498] In 1987, Bishop Vega and Father Carballo returned to Nicaragua and Radio Católica returned to the airwaves.[499] *La Prensa* reopened in late 1987, and most independent radio programs were back on the air by 1988.[500] The FSLN also softened its approach to capitalists. "Broke, battered, and under pressure from foreign enemies," the government adopted more business-friendly policies beginning in 1987.[501] The number of expropriations declined markedly, ceasing altogether by 1989.[502]

In sum, the Contra war led FSLN leaders to close ranks and build up the coercive apparatus. However, signs of Soviet withdrawal and an incipient post–Cold War realignment induced the government to ease up repression beginning in late 1986. As a result, the Church, much of the private sector, and key independent media remained intact.

Revolutionary Legacies and the Emergent Regime

Sandinista forces turned the tide of the civil war in the mid-1980s.[503] By early 1988, the Contras had been "strategically defeated."[504] Peace talks led to a March 1988 cease-fire, which effectively ended the war. The regime that emerged in 1988 was a hybrid. On the one hand, the counterrevolutionary war produced a cohesive elite and a powerful and loyal coercive apparatus, much like revolutionary regimes in Cuba and elsewhere. On the other hand, the regime was multiparty and pluralist. The 1983 Political Parties Law legalized opposition,[505] competitive (though not fully democratic) elections were held in 1984,[506] and a formally liberal democratic constitution was promulgated in 1987.[507] Thus, although the post-1988 regime remained authoritarian, it was "a far cry from the party-state model envisioned in [1979]."[508]

A COHESIVE ELITE

Nicaragua's revolutionary elite was cohesive.[509] The FSLN leadership, or National Directorate, became a "tightly-knit group," marked by a "quasi-religious dedication."[510] Vice President Ramírez likened it to a "monastic order" in which members "take a vow of silence, suffer great privations, make sacrifices, and take a Christian-like vow to the death."[511]

Unlike the Bolivian MNR, the FSLN leadership remained intact throughout the revolutionary period, despite a devastating war, economic failure, and eventual electoral defeat. Notwithstanding important internal differences, there were no purges or defections in the National Directorate.[512] Thus, serious disagreement over whether to pursue Cuban-style socialism or accommodation never led to a schism.[513] The 1987 Central American peace talks triggered a "life-or-death debate" between President Ortega and hard-liners led by Borge—one so acute that Ortega traveled to Cuba to court Castro's support.[514] However, the hard-liners never dissented publicly.[515] Likewise, a long-standing rivalry between Borge and Ortega never split the party. When Ortega was selected over Borge, a founding FSLN leader, as the party's presidential candidate, Borge swallowed his frustration and closed ranks behind Ortega.[516] The only notable defection was that of Eden Pastora, a guerrilla hero who, despite his international fame, never held a high-ranking leadership post. Pastora expected numerous Sandinistas to follow him out of the party in 1981, but very few did.[517]

A POWERFUL AND LOYAL COERCIVE APPARATUS

The regime also developed a powerful and loyal coercive apparatus. The new armed forces were "by far the strongest ever seen in Central America,"[518] with nearly 250,000 people under arms.[519] The 134,000-strong EPS was easily the largest and best-equipped army in the region, with twice as many tanks and armored personnel carriers as the other Central American states combined.[520] Well trained and experienced in combat, the EPS was, by all accounts, a highly effective military force.[521]

The internal security apparatus was also highly developed. By the mid-1980s, the state security agency had more than 3,000 full-time agents—ten times the size of Somoza's secret police—and operated surveillance networks in every corner of the country.[522] In addition, 15,000 neighborhood-level Sandinista Defense Committees (CDS) engaged in domestic surveillance and counterinsurgency operations, serving as "eyes and ears of the revolution."[523] As the journalist Shirley Christian observed at the time, neighborhood CDS leaders "clearly know who is friendly to the revolution and who is not."[524]

The Sandinista security forces were loyal and disciplined.[525] The revolutionary regime was characterized by a near-total party-army fusion.[526] Sandinista guerrillas founded and staffed the army and the internal security services,[527] which meant that the FSLN and EPS hierarchies were effectively "merged as one single body."[528] Indeed, the EPS was commanded by President Ortega's brother, Humberto; all top army and police commanders were revolutionary veterans and high-ranking FSLN leaders; and 80–85 percent of army officers were active FSLN cadres.[529] Concerned about infiltration by ex-GN members and rival leftists, the Sandinistas carefully screened the EPS hierarchy.[530] High-level army promotions were based on officers' role in the guerrilla struggle,[531] and officers reportedly had to be Sandinista members to rise above the rank of captain.[532]

The FSLN also established partisan structures within the security forces,[533] including intermediate party committees, which commanded the EPS at the regional level, and FSLN base committees, which operated within all local military units.[534] Nicaragua's army and police were thus "explicitly Sandinista."[535] As Roberto J. Cajina put it, Sandinista influence in the army was "total. . . . The immense majority of officers were possessed by a genuine sense of mission that transcended the strictly military. They were defenders and guarantors of a revolutionary political project."[536] Due to this shared identity, the army was "very unlikely to stage a coup against [its] own government."[537]

Indeed, army loyalty was strikingly high. There were no coup attempts between 1979 and 1990.[538] Popular guerrilla commander Eden Pastora attempted to trigger an army rebellion in 1982, believing he enjoyed broad rank-and-file support, but his efforts "bore little fruit."[539]

THE PERSISTENCE OF
INDEPENDENT POWER CENTERS

Although Nicaragua's counterrevolutionary war gave rise to a cohesive elite and a powerful coercive apparatus, it did not destroy independent centers of societal power. For example, in stark contrast to revolutionary Mexico and Cuba, the Church in Nicaragua "flourished" under the Sandinistas.[540] The number of churches and parishioners *increased* between 1979 and 1988.[541] And whereas the Mexican and Cuban Churches steered clear of opposition politics, the Nicaraguan Church remained politically active and "viscerally anti-Sandinista."[542]

Private-sector associations also remained active. In 1985, COSEP maintained a membership of 9,304 businesses and encompassed both the chambers of commerce and industry and associations of cotton, rice, cattle, dairy, and coffee producers.[543] During the mid-1980s, at the height of the Contra war, COSEP emerged as the principal voice of political opposition.[544]

Private media also survived. Notwithstanding censorship, restrictions on newsprint, and periodic attacks on independent media,[545] *La Prensa* and Radio Católica remained both influential and militantly anti-Sandinista in the late 1980s.[546]

In sum, Nicaraguan's emergent revolutionary regime was stronger than Bolivia's because it had a more cohesive elite and a far more developed and disciplined coercive apparatus. Due to the survival of alternative power centers, however, an infrastructure of independent organizations remained in place, which left the regime vulnerable to opposition challenges.

Regime Breakdown via Democratization, 1987–1990

The revolutionary government won the civil war but was nevertheless devastated by it. Nicaragua suffered six consecutive years of recession between 1984 and 1990, and inflation reached 33,000 percent in 1988.[547] Years of war and military conscription badly eroded public support.[548] The regime was further buffeted by the withdrawal of Soviet aid beginning in early 1987.[549] Indeed, when President Ortega traveled to Moscow in 1987, Soviet leaders advised him to reconcile with the West.[550]

Economic crisis and the loss of Soviet patronage created incentives for accommodation.[551] Thus, in 1987, the Ortega government embraced the Esquipulas II Central America peace process. The August 1987 accords entailed major concessions, with the FSLN required to hold peace talks with the Contras, undertake political liberalization, and hold democratic elections in 1990.[552] With Soviet support fading, however, the FSLN viewed the accords as critical to boosting Nicaragua's international standing—and blunting U.S. aggression.[553]

Political liberalization began soon after Esquipulas II.[554] In February 1988, the government lifted the state of emergency. Opposition leaders returned from exile and prepared to contest the 1990 election. Although they suffered harassment and occasional repression,[555] the government's ability to crack down was constrained by intense international scrutiny.[556]

By 1989, opposition media "flourished free of censorship, and political dissidents were allowed to protest without interference."[557]

The revolutionary government held competitive elections in February 1990. Fourteen opposition parties united into the National Opposition Union (UNO) nominated Violeta Chamorro to run against Ortega. Both the FSLN and the opposition expected Ortega to win.[558] The Sandinistas were far better organized and financed,[559] and incumbent abuse of state resources and media tilted the playing field in their favor.[560]

Several factors worked against the FSLN, however. For one, the war and the economic crisis had eroded public support.[561] In addition, private-sector and Church support helped UNO compensate for its organizational weakness. COSEP contributed funding and extensive logistical support to the UNO campaign.[562] Although Church leaders were less openly partisan, they, too, lent Chamorro their support.[563] Church networks were mobilized to back UNO, especially in the countryside,[564] and Obando y Bravo—Nicaragua's most popular figure—endorsed Chamorro in his Sunday homilies.[565] Thus, although UNO could not even compete with the FSLN's massive infrastructure, business and Church support, together with U.S. assistance,[566] helped level the playing field.

Chamorro won the 1990 election with 55 percent of the vote, compared to 41 percent for Ortega. Under intense international pressure, the Sandinistas accepted defeat and ceded power,[567] bringing the revolution to a surprising end.

The Nicaraguan case highlights the importance of geopolitical context, historical timing, and contingency. The FSLN was more radical than the MNR, and it initially embarked on high-risk initiatives such as the export of revolution to El Salvador. However, it was considerably less radical than the Castro government. Were it not for Reagan's ascent to the presidency, the counterrevolutionary reaction might have been weaker. Like Cuba and other radical cases, Nicaragua's counterrevolution strengthened the regime, giving rise to a cohesive elite and a powerful coercive apparatus. However, Nicaragua diverged from the ideal-typical path in two ways. First, the Sandinistas did not destroy independent power centers. Second, because Nicaragua's counterrevolutionary war occurred at the end of the Cold War, the FSLN came under intense pressure to accommodate Western powers.

Like the MNR in Bolivia, the Sandinistas ultimately fell victim to an accommodationist strategy. Due to FSLN's failure to destroy or cripple independent power centers, the regime never developed the extreme state-society power asymmetries observed in Cuba and Iran. Although opposition parties were weak, they could turn to the private sector and the Church for resources, infrastructure, and legitimacy—support that was arguably essential to the Sandinistas' eventual defeat.

GUINEA-BISSAU

Guinea-Bissau under the PAIGC was an accommodationist revolutionary regime that experienced considerable instability before falling prey to a military rebellion. The PAIGC came to power through a violent independence struggle, transformed colonial state structures, and pursued radical social change. Within a year, however, the PAIGC halted many of its radical measures, ceased calling itself socialist, and improved relations with neighboring states, Portugal, and Western powers. Although such pragmatism helped prevent a counterrevolutionary reaction, the absence of an existential threat weakened incentives to build a cohesive party-state. Instead, it created a permissive environment in which ethnic cleavages that had not been salient during the independence war came to the fore, culminating in a palace coup in 1980. The regime then suffered repeated coup attempts and defections before falling to a military rebellion in 1999.

The Revolutionary Seizure of Power

Portuguese Guinea (Guinea-Bissau after 1974) was one of three colonies— together with Angola and Mozambique—that had been claimed by Portugal since the 1500s but effectively occupied only since the turn of the twentieth century.[568] Whereas Mozambique and especially Angola were relatively strategic colonies, Portuguese Guinea was a tiny outpost on the west coast of Africa that attracted few European settlers.[569] With a population of under one million, its primary economic value to the Portuguese lay in peanut farms that produced a source of vegetable oil.[570] Given the scarcity of economic opportunities, the colony attracted fewer settlers than Angola or Mozambique did.[571]

The PAIGC was founded in 1956 by Amilcar Cabral and a small group of mostly mixed-race, Portuguese-educated Guineans and Cape Verdeans. From the beginning, the PAIGC was ideologically diverse. Influenced by the Portuguese Communist Party (PCP), the party embraced socialism.[572] Several PAIGC leaders, including Vasco Cabral (no relation to Amilcar), were PCP members.[573] Like the MNR in Bolivia, however, dominant factions of the PAIGC were pragmatic.[574] Though influenced by the Marxist ideas that pervaded African networks in Portugal at the time, Amilcar Cabral never belonged to a Marxist party, and unlike his counterparts in Angola and Mozambique, he chose not to adopt Marxism-Leninism as his party's ideology.

The PAIGC initially focused on mobilizing urban workers against colonial rule in the hopes of encouraging a peaceful transition to independence.[575] The strategy failed, however, as dictator Antonio Salazar, bucking international trends, refused to cede Portugal's colonies. In 1959, Portuguese police massacred dozens of workers and activists involved in a PAIGC-backed strike at the Pidjiguiti docks in Bissau. Forced out of the cities by the ensuing repression, PAIGC leaders changed course and began to prepare for armed struggle.[576] Party leaders escaped into newly independent Guinea-Conakry, whose government allowed them to establish a guerrilla training camp.[577]

Conditions for guerrilla struggle were relatively propitious. The PAIGC procured weapons and advisers from Cuba and the Eastern bloc.[578] Thanks to Cabral's effective diplomacy, it also gained the support of neighboring Senegal and Guinea, whose governments refrained from backing rival independence movements.[579] Thus, unlike its counterparts in Angola and Mozambique, the PAIGC faced no significant internal rivals and could focus its fire on the Portuguese.

Most importantly, the PAIGC confronted a weak colonial state.[580] Portugal was by far the poorest imperial power in Africa, and Portuguese Guinea—with a population of under 800,000—was the least economically important of Portugal's colonies.[581] Although Portugal remained committed to preserving its empire until 1974, it built only a flimsy administrative structure in Portuguese Guinea and invested few resources into controlling the colony.[582] Portugal's international isolation—it was the only European power to retain major colonies in the late 1960s—also worked in the PAIGC's favor.[583]

At the outset of the independence campaign, the PAIGC drew heavily on the support of the Balanta population in the south. The Balanta dominated the ranks of the guerrilla army.[584] Initially, Balanta soldiers operated with little oversight and committed numerous abuses.[585] In early 1964, however, Cabral asserted greater political control over the guerrillas.[586] Several Balanta were executed for their violent attacks on civilians,[587] and fighters were integrated into the new 600-strong People's Revolutionary Armed Forces (FARP).[588]

Despite its small size and lack of arms and training, the PAIGC enjoyed striking success after launching armed operations in 1963.[589] By late 1964, the colony had been "cut in two" and the Portuguese had lost control of the border with Guinea-Conakry.[590] Fearing that the PAIGC's success would inspire guerrilla movements in more strategic Angola and Mozambique, the Portuguese brought in 20,000–25,000 troops to combat the now 5,000-strong rebel army.[591] However, colonial troop morale was low, and the Portuguese lacked the resources to maintain control over large sections of the territory.[592] Troops were concentrated in their garrisons along the major roads and virtually absent in the interior.[593] By the late 1960s, the PAIGC controlled 60 percent of the colony and had disrupted the activities of major Portuguese trading companies.[594]

The PAIGC built an embryonic state infrastructure during the anticolonial struggle, operating schools and hospitals in "liberated" territories and creating a network of People's Stores to distribute agricultural and other supplies.[595] These investments in infrastructure were part of a Maoist-like strategy to consolidate popular support on the ground.[596] There were some efforts at radical societal change in liberated areas. The PAIGC sought to collectivize agriculture and transform village-level power structures by bringing in young leaders from outside the traditional ruling families.[597] Nevertheless, state-building prior to the seizure of power was more limited than in China, Vietnam, or Yugoslavia.[598]

Although the PAIGC was considered the most successful anticolonial movement in Lusophone Africa,[599] it was never very strong. The party was unable to control large towns before 1974,[600] and despite its announced intentions, it never established its leadership in Portuguese Guinea itself, residing instead in neighboring Guinea-Conakry.[601] The guerrillas did not collect taxes until independence, drawing instead on foreign aid to finance its infrastructure of schools and hospitals.[602] The PAIGC also lacked the capacity to effectively screen new members, which left it prone to infiltration.[603]

Notwithstanding these limitations, the PAIGC achieved important military and diplomatic gains in the early 1970s, heightening the cost of Portuguese occupation.[604] With Soviet bloc assistance, the PAIGC beat back a Portuguese offensive in 1970 and eventually claimed control of 80 percent of the territory.[605] In 1972, Amilcar Cabral gained the blessing of Pope Paul VI and the support of the United Nations (UN).[606] That year, the PAIGC elected the National People's Assembly in liberated areas.[607] By 1973, Soviet surface-to-air missiles had enabled the FARP to weaken Portuguese control of the airspace. Thus, the PAIGC was widely perceived to be on the brink of military victory, mainly because the Portuguese lacked the resources to launch a sustained counteroffensive.[608]

After surviving a leadership crisis generated by the 1973 assassination of Amilcar Cabral (by a disgruntled PAIGC naval commander, with Portuguese support),[609] the PAIGC, now led by Cabral's half-brother, Luis Cabral, launched a final push for independence. On September 24, 1973, the National People's Assembly declared independence, a move that was backed by the UN General Assembly but not by Western powers.[610]

Final victory came by other means, however. In April 1974, a military coup in Portugal brought to power a new government that moved quickly to dismantle the colonial empire. Military activities ceased, and in September 1974, Portugal and the PAIGC negotiated a transfer of power.[611]

The Reactive Sequence: Accommodation and Limited Reaction

The PAIGC government was revolutionary. It dismantled the colonial state and upended preexisting authority structures. Traditional chiefships were abolished,[612] and the PAIGC government engaged in a violent "settling of accounts" against chiefs who had supported the colonial regime.[613] Early economic policy was radical. One of the National Assembly's first acts was to nationalize all land.[614] The revolutionary government took control over Portuguese trading companies, banks, and other property.[615] The powerful Portuguese conglomerate Casa Gouveia was seized.[616] Much of this property was transferred to government-run People's Stores, which were seen as "a state weapon against imperialism and local capitalists."[617] In the mid-1970s, People's Stores controlled 60 percent of trade in Guinea-Bissau.[618] Radicals such as Jose Araujo, Mario Cabral, and Vasco Cabral pushed a "relatively dogmatic ideological stance" on various fronts.[619] For example, Vasco Cabral, a former PCP member, called for the immediate establishment of a centrally planned economy.[620]

However, the PAIGC did not sustain a radical course. The new ruling party as a whole was less doctrinaire than other revolutionary movements of the period. Founding leader Amilcar Cabral had been known for his "boundless pragmatism,"[621] and the dominant leaders among the surviving revolutionary elite—President Luis Cabral, Prime Minister João Bernardo Vieira, and party head Aristides Pereira—were similarly pragmatic. Indeed, some regime insiders complained that the revolutionary government operated in an "ideological vacuum."[622]

Unlike revolutionary governments in Angola and Mozambique, then, the PAIGC quickly abandoned any radical pretensions in favor of efforts to attract broad domestic and international support.[623] Domestically, the Cabral government focused less on societal transformation than on constituency-building. Shortages generated by early radical policies convinced the PAIGC government to abandon efforts to build socialism.[624] Thus, the PAIGC's 1977 platform made no mention of socialism and declared the primacy of national unity over class conflict. Radicals within the regime soon grew disillusioned with this "right-wing course."[625]

Internationally, the revolutionary government established good relations with Portugal.[626] Luis Cabral became the first leader of a former Portuguese colony to visit Lisbon. He turned "non-alignment into a fine art," seeking "to attract as much aid and loans as possible from as many countries as possible, East and West and Arab."[627] Indeed, despite having received substantial Soviet bloc support during the independence struggle, the PAIGC distanced itself from the Soviet Union, instead obtaining most of its aid from the West, Saudi Arabia, and the right-wing dictatorship in Brazil.[628]

Finally, it is important to note that the PAIGC's early radicalism did not trigger the same degree of conflict observed in other postcolonial revolutionary regimes. Unlike Angola and Mozambique, for example, Guinea-Bissau lacked a large white settler population and did not border a settler state. Consequently, black rule threatened the interests of fewer powerful interests than it did in these other newly independent Lusophone states. In addition, Guinea-Bissau's private sector was weak from the outset. No sizable landowning class existed at independence, which meant that nationalization of the land was largely a formality.[629] As in Algeria, then, seemingly radical measures such as nationalization met with relatively little resistance.

The PAIGC's accommodationist orientation and the low cost of early radicalism helped prevent a counterrevolutionary reaction. The PAIGC government confronted little opposition—armed or otherwise—during the 1970s.[630] There were no serious insurgencies, and the PAIGC government encountered little hostility from Western powers. These dynamics contrasted sharply with developments in Angola and Mozambique, where radical domestic policies and support for insurgencies against white rule in Namibia, South Africa, and Rhodesia triggered major South African–backed insurgencies that threw both countries into bloody civil wars.[631] Thus, whereas regimes in Angola and Mozambique faced existential threats to their survival in the late 1970s, Guinea-Bissau was considered to be "one of the politically most peaceful and stable countries in Africa."[632]

A Weak Party-State Complex

Appearances can be deceiving, however. Although the PAIGC's accommo-dationist policies helped it stave off counterrevolutionary threats, they also contributed to the development of a relatively weak regime. The PAIGC *did* exhibit some elements of the ideal-typical revolutionary party-state. Above all, its creation of its own armed forces gave rise to considerable party-army fusion. During the liberation struggle, the PAIGC's military and political wings were indistinguishable. The PAIGC penetrated the military with political commissars, while army leaders were incorporated into the party leadership.[633]

Absent an existential threat, however, the PAIGC failed to build a strong state or maintain elite cohesion. Colonialism left Guinea-Bissau with a meager state infrastructure and few qualified personnel able to staff the new bureaucracy.[634] Years after independence, the central government still lacked representatives in many localities.[635] The army, which won independence mostly due to Portuguese impotence, also remained weak. During the independence war, the FARP had operated as a decentralized "tri-regional army," with soldiers often refusing to fight outside their home regions.[636] Facing no military threat, the PAIGC had little incentive to strengthen the army. As a result, the military remained small, in per capita terms, relative to other revolutionary cases.[637]

The ruling party was also weak. Like revolutionary movements in Russia, Cuba, Nicaragua, and elsewhere, the PAIGC did not develop a strong organization during the struggle for power. It failed to establish head-quarters in the colony, and its vulnerability to infiltration contributed to Amilcar Cabral's 1973 assassination.[638] Unlike our radical cases, however, the PAIGC grew weaker and less cohesive after taking power.[639] Veterans of the armed struggle retained considerable prestige,[640] but without the "ideological pressure of the struggle,"[641] the "old combatants" had little reason to close ranks.[642] Indeed, many PAIGC activists grew demoralized after the government discouraged anticolonial and anti-American state-ments in pursuit of Western aid.[643] As a result, the ruling party descended into inactivity and passivity; by the late 1970s, it was a "shell" of what it had been during the liberation struggle.[644]

At the same time, splits in the regime were exacerbated by divisions between lighter-skinned Cape Verdeans who held most of the top posi-tions and Balanta and other black natives of mainland Guinea-Bissau who dominated the military rank and file.[645] These divisions were hardly inevi-table. Ethnic tensions virtually disappeared in the late 1960s, when the

Portuguese posed an existential threat.[646] Portuguese efforts to foment ethnic differences failed,[647] and the PAIGC leadership remained unified throughout the independence struggle.

After independence, however, the absence of an existential threat created a permissive environment in which latent divisions undermined both elite cohesion and military loyalty. Although party-army fusion was relatively high, low cohesion within the PAIGC left the government vulnerable to military rebellion. President Luis Cabral, who played only a minor role in the military struggle, spending much of the war in Senegal as a PAIGC representative, lacked the strong military ties and prestige that Mao, Ho, Tito, Castro, and other revolutionary leaders enjoyed.[648] In the absence of an external threat to bind the revolutionary elite together, Cabral was vulnerable. Indeed, he confronted coup attempts in 1975 and 1978.[649]

Cabral's fall was rooted in a conflict with Prime Minister João "Nino" Vieira, a high-level army commander who had led the southern front during the liberation struggle. In 1979–1980, the government's inability to pay military salaries exacerbated tensions between Cabral and Vieira.[650] As in Ghana in the 1960s, coup fears convinced the president to take actions that, paradoxically, triggered military intervention. Cabral relieved Vieira of his military responsibilities in 1979, and, a year later, he announced constitutional changes that would have led to Vieira's removal as prime minister.[651] Vieira responded by mobilizing Balanta resentment against the lighter-skinned political leaders, securing overwhelming military support for a coup. On November 14, 1980, Cabral was arrested and forced into exile.

The coup did not put an end to the regime, however. Vieira was a high-ranking PAIGC leader, and his ascent to power temporarily strengthened the ruling party's standing.[652]

Regime Instability and Breakdown, 1980–1999

The absence of elite cohesion continued to undermine regime stability after 1980. Amid a deepening economic crisis, Vieira faced coup attempts in 1982, 1983, and 1985.[653] In the most important of these, in 1985, Vice President Paolo Correia and five senior military officials plotted to oust Vieira.[654] In response, Vieira launched a sustained attack on the Balanta elite, which generated conflict between the government and the Balanta.[655]

Like other African autocracies in the post–Cold War era,[656] Guinea-Bissau liberalized in the early 1990s. In 1991, the revolutionary government legalized other parties and agreed to hold multiparty elections.[657] A faction of PAIGC backbenchers, called the Group of 121, launched a campaign for greater democracy within the ruling party.[658] Many of them eventually abandoned the party. Prominent PAIGC leaders such as Rafael Barbosa Miranda, Victor Saud Maria, Victor Mandinga, Aristides Menezes, and Kumba Ialá defected, and Ialá became the main opposition candidate in the 1994 presidential election.[659] Vieira narrowly beat Ialá—with 52 percent of the vote—in a runoff, and PAIGC eked out a parliamentary majority.

The regime ultimately collapsed in the face of military rebellion. In the late 1990s, Guinea-Bissau fell into severe economic crisis. Food shortages heightened civil-military tensions, as many soldiers left their posts and returned to their villages in search of food.[660] In early 1998, Vieira suspended military chief of staff Ansumane Mané, accusing him of illegally selling weapons to rebels in Senegal. Mané responded by launching a military rebellion with considerable rank-and-file support. In May 1999, pro-government forces surrendered, and Vieira went into exile in Portugal, ending twenty-five years of PAIGC rule.[661] A new military junta organized presidential elections in 2000, which were won by Ialá.[662]

Like Bolivia, Guinea-Bissau illustrates the longer-term risks of accommodation. Unlike most of our ideal-typical revolutionary cases, the PAIGC was a coalition of pragmatic nationalists and radical Marxists in which the former were dominant.[663] The PAIGC's decision to moderate soon after taking power deprived the new regime of a salient raison d'être and motivation to build a powerful party-state. As a result, the PAIGC atrophied after independence. Absent a serious threat, party leaders had little incentive to overcome internal divisions. The result was a palace coup in 1980, large-scale defection in the 1990s, and a military rebellion in 1999 that ended the regime.

The impact of accommodation in Guinea-Bissau is evident in a comparison with Angola and Mozambique, where revolutionary regimes also emerged out of violent nationalist struggles against Portugal in the 1970s (see chapter 9). As noted above, radicalism by the Popular Movement for the Liberation of Angola (MPLA) and the Front for the Liberation of Mozambique (Frelimo) contributed to large-scale, foreign-backed insurgencies in both countries. This counterrevolutionary conflict strengthened both regimes. In Mozambique, Frelimo transformed from a factionalized party in the 1960s into one of the most cohesive parties in Africa.[664] This cohesion was critical to avoiding a military coup[665] and surviving the Soviet collapse and the transition to multiparty rule. In Angola, counterrevolutionary conflict helped transform the MPLA regime from a weak, fragmented regime into a powerful and cohesive party-state,[666] which has helped the regime endure for nearly half a century.

In sum, Guinea-Bissau illustrates both the advantages and the pitfalls of the accommodationist path. On the one hand, the quick reversal of radical policies allowed the PAIGC government to avoid the traumatic counterrevolutionary struggles confronted by its Lusophone counterparts. On the other hand, the ease of the initial transition led to the emergence of a weak and ultimately unstable regime.

Conclusion

Bolivia, Guinea-Bissau, and, to a lesser degree, Nicaragua conform to our theoretical framework in that revolutionary governments abandoned early radicalism for accommodationist strategies, which in Bolivia and Guinea-Bissau (but not Nicaragua) resulted in lower levels of elite cohesion, weaker party-state complexes, and, consequently, less durable regimes. In Nicaragua, the FSLN faced a powerful counterrevolutionary reaction and developed a powerful party-state complex but failed to destroy independent power centers, which ultimately undermined regime stability.

However, the cases also highlight some factors that lie outside our theory. One is timing and geopolitical context. For example, the fact that the MNR came to power in 1952, when Soviet patronage was not yet available, powerfully shaped its decision to accommodate U.S. interests. By the time the Soviets came around to offering $150 million and a "long coveted tin smelter" in 1960,[667] the MNR's ties to the United States were so extensive that the Paz government declined the offer.[668] Likewise, the rise of Gorbachev and the Soviet withdrawal created powerful incentives for the Sandinistas to move in the accommodationist direction in the late 1980s. Finally, Guinea-Bissau's geopolitical insignificance reduced the likelihood that the PAIGC would provoke a Western-backed insurgency.

Finally, the cases also highlight the role of historical contingency. For example, had Reagan not won the 1980 U.S. presidential election, the Sandinistas' mix of radicalism and accommodation might not have triggered a full-scale counterrevolutionary war. Whether such a path would have contributed to regime consolidation or simply given rise to a less cohesive regime—more like Bolivia than Cuba—is less clear.

CHAPTER NINE

Conclusion

REVOLUTIONARY REGIMES are among the world's most durable autocracies. They are also the most reckless. This is no coincidence. As this book has shown, revolutionary assaults on powerful domestic and foreign interests often trigger a reactive sequence that, over time, lays a foundation for authoritarian durability. Early radicalism generates violent and often regime-threatening counterrevolutionary conflict. Regimes that survive these conflicts tend to develop a cohesive elite and a powerful and loyal coercive apparatus capable of both systematic low-intensity repression and, when necessary, high-intensity crackdown. They also tend to weaken or destroy political rivals and alternative centers of societal power. These three characteristics—elite cohesion, a powerful and loyal coercive apparatus, and the absence of alternative power centers—are central pillars of durable authoritarian rule. Cohesive elites inhibit regime schisms; fused party and army leaderships reduce the likelihood of military coups; and the vast power asymmetry generated by a state with a highly developed coercive apparatus, on the one hand, and a society whose independent power centers have been emasculated, on the other, can inhibit opposition mobilization for decades. As a result, revolutionary regimes whose trajectories approximate this ideal-typical reactive sequence, such as the Soviet Union, China, Mexico, Vietnam, Cuba, and Iran, are among the most durable in modern history.

The book identified two alternative regime paths. In some cases, the violent conflict triggered by early radicalism destroyed embryonic revolutionary regimes, aborting the reactive sequence. Regimes in Hungary, Cambodia, and Afghanistan are cases of such early death, all via external military intervention. In other cases, revolutionary governments tempered radical initiatives in order to accommodate powerful domestic or international interests, thereby dampening the counterrevolutionary reaction. In the absence of sustained counterrevolutionary conflict, regimes failed to develop cohesive elites, invest in powerful coercive organizations, or dramatically weaken alternative power centers. The result was more vulnerable regimes that either died relatively young (Bolivia, Nicaragua) or survived for longer but suffered endemic instability (Algeria, Guinea-Bissau).

Assessing the Argument

The book's main argument can be broken down into three core claims. First, radical initiatives launched by revolutionary governments generate violent counterrevolutionary reactions, whereas accommodationist policies do not. Second, in regimes not destroyed by the initial counterrevolutionary reaction, the reactive sequence gives rise to three pillars of durable authoritarianism: a cohesive elite, a developed and loyal coercive apparatus, and the destruction of alternative centers of societal power. Third, revolutionary state-building—the construction of these three pillars—contributes to durable authoritarianism. The thirteen case studies elaborated in this book provide historical evidence supporting these three claims. Table 9.1 summarizes how our theory fared in each case.

RADICALISM AND COUNTERREVOLUTIONARY REACTION

We found considerable evidence of a link between early radicalism and the strength of counterrevolutionary reactions. Every revolutionary government that carried out radical policies confronted a violent counterrevolutionary reaction. In Hungary, Afghanistan, and Cambodia, these reactions wiped out nascent revolutionary regimes. In other cases, they posed a clear existential threat. In Russia, for example, the Bolsheviks' assault on property and preexisting social classes led supporters of the old regime to mobilize everything they had against them, and the revolutionary government's attacks on the international capitalist order led a coalition of Western powers to support these counterrevolutionary efforts. The Bolsheviks were only saved from destruction by the fact that Western states were too exhausted by World War I to invest heavily in their overthrow. In China, the Communist Party's attacks on capitalism and rural elites united merchants behind Chiang Kai-shek and triggered a twenty-two-year civil war that nearly wiped the Communists out. In Cuba, the Castro government's attacks on domestic and international capital brought decades of

Table 9.1 Scoring the Cases

| | Initial Policies | Counterrevolutionary Reaction | Three Pillars of Authoritarian Durability[1] | | | | Summary Score | Regime Duration |
| | | | Cohesion | Strong/Loyal Military | | Destruction of Independent Power Centers | | |
				Strong	Loyal			
China	Radical	Yes	Yes	Yes	Yes	Full	3/3	71+
Cuba	Radical	Yes	Yes	Yes	Yes	Full	3/3	62+
USSR	Radical	Yes	Yes	Yes	Yes	Full	3/3	74
Vietnam	Radical	Yes	Yes	Yes	Yes	Full	3/3	67+
Iran	Radical	Yes	Yes	Yes	Yes	Partial	2.5/3	42+
Mexico	Segmented[2]	Yes	Yes	No	Yes	Partial	2/3	85
Nicaragua	Radical, then accommodation	Yes	Yes	Yes	Yes	No	2/3	11
Algeria	Accommodation	No	No	No	Yes	Partial	1/3	59+
Bolivia	Accommodation	No	No	No	Yes[3]	No	.5/3	12
Guinea-Bissau	Accommodation	No	No	No	No	Partial	.5/3	25
Afghanistan	Radical	Yes/early death						5
Cambodia	Radical	Yes/early death						4
Hungary	Radical	Yes/early death						<1

[1] In accordance with our theoretical framework, the three pillars of authoritarianism are measured after the resolution of the initial counterrevolutionary conflict (the nature and dates of resolution of these conflicts in each case are provided in appendix II). In cases without counterrevolutionary conflict, we apply the criteria five years after regime formation. Early death cases (shaded) are not scored because their failure to survive the reactive sequence does not yield any theoretical predictions.

[2] Mexico is a case of accommodation in economic and foreign policy but radicalism with respect to the Catholic Church, which resulted in a civil war with Catholic peasants but a more limited counterrevolution in other areas.

[3] Loyalty is scored as high because there was only one quasi-military rebellion between 1952 and 1964. However, as chapter 8 shows, the MNR never gained control over the military and fell to a military coup in 1964.

U.S. hostility, including a U.S.-backed invasion that could have destroyed the regime. In Vietnam, the revolutionary government's efforts to subvert the regime in South Vietnam provoked a long and destructive war with the United States. In Iran, the move to create an Islamic state triggered a leftist insurgency and breakdown in the armed forces that encouraged an invasion by Iraq—backed by the United States and Persian Gulf monarchies—that nearly destroyed the regime.

By contrast, where revolutionary governments tempered their reforms, often in an effort to avoid conflict with the West, they faced weaker counterrevolutionary threats. In Algeria, the National Liberation Front (FLN) government's cooperative relationship with France reduced the prospect of foreign-backed efforts to oust the regime. In Guinea-Bissau, the Party for African Independence in Guinea and Cape Verde's (PAIGC) decision to loosen ties to the Soviet Union and improve relations with Portugal helped it avoid armed conflict and gain substantial Western assistance, and in Bolivia, the Revolutionary Nationalist Movement's (MNR) cautious approach to nationalization and land reform allowed it to maintain friendly relations with the United States.

Mexico and Nicaragua are mixed cases. Radicalism in Mexico was segmented, as the revolutionary elite engaged in a far-reaching attack on the Catholic Church but adopted accommodationist strategies toward foreign capital and the United States. The result was a narrower, but still significant, counterrevolutionary reaction. The revolutionary government did not confront serious external aggression, but its anticlerical initiatives provoked a three-year civil war (the Cristero War). In Nicaragua, the Sandinista government also combined radicalism and accommodation, but the Reagan administration's hard-line response led to a costly counterrevolutionary war.

COUNTERREVOLUTIONARY CONFLICT AND REVOLUTIONARY STATE-BUILDING

The case studies also provide evidence linking counterrevolutionary conflict to the construction of the three pillars of durable authoritarianism outlined above. First, in nearly all cases of counterrevolutionary conflict, existential military threats contributed to the emergence of an unusually cohesive regime elite. Thus, when Trotsky lost out to Stalin in the battle to succeed Lenin in Russia, he initially did everything he could to preserve party unity—despite his hatred of Stalin. Although Stalin confronted many internal rivals, none of them were willing to even consider defecting to the opposition, which was seen to threaten the revolutionary regime. Likewise, in Vietnam, decades of war against France and the United States generated a siege mentality and a military-style discipline that persisted into the late twentieth century. The Vietnamese Communist Party leadership did not suffer a single defection between 1954 and 1975. In Cuba, where the enduring threat posed by the United States led the revolutionary elite to close ranks around Castro, the regime elite suffered no significant defections for half a century. In China, shared experience in the 1934–1935 Long March generated an exceptionally cohesive group of leaders that dominated the party until the 1990s. Even in highly factionalized Iran, polarization and violent conflict generated by Khomeini's headlong plunge into clerical rule fostered a highly cohesive elite unwilling to challenge clerical rule.

Second, counterrevolutionary conflict encouraged the development of loyal and powerful armed forces that were closely wedded to the ruling party. In virtually all cases of counterrevolutionary conflict, revolutionary elites built new security forces from scratch, filling their ranks with trusted veterans from the liberation struggle. In China, Cuba, Mexico, Nicaragua, Russia, Vietnam, and, in a different way, Iran,[1] revolutionary state-building fused party and army leaderships and allowed revolutionary elites to infiltrate the armed forces from top to bottom. Such party-army fusion greatly enhanced military loyalty. Radical revolutionary regimes experienced virtually no coup attempts or no palace coups, even in the face of severe economic crises.

Counterrevolutionary conflict also strengthened regimes' coercive structures. In Russia, the civil war led to the construction of the largest and most powerful internal security force in modern history. In China, the civil war with the Kuomintang in the late 1940s motivated leaders to build a standing army with the capacity to confront the United States in the early 1950s. In Vietnam, war with the United States gave rise to the largest and most powerful army in the developing world, and in Cuba, the 1961 Bay of Pigs invasion led the Castro government to quadruple the size of the military and create a vast—and highly effective—intelligence apparatus.

Third, counterrevolutionary conflict led to the weakening or destruction of alternative centers of societal power. The Russian civil war destroyed the old monarchy, the tsarist army, the bourgeoisie, and the landowning classes, as well as rival socialist parties. Similarly, China's long civil war allowed the Communist Party to wipe out the dense network of gentry, secret societies, criminal gangs, and other forces that had dominated urban and village life for centuries. In Vietnam, wars against France and the United States allowed the Communists to wipe out rival nationalists and weaken landowners, the Catholic Church, and religious sects. In Cuba, the Bay of Pigs invasion and the specter of U.S. intervention created an opportunity for Castro to emasculate the Church and accelerate the destruction of the private sector. Finally, in Iran, counter-insurgency and war with Iraq in the early 1980s encouraged and enabled the revolutionary elite to smash Marxist insurgencies, ban the Communist Party, and sideline competing imams.

By contrast, accommodationist governments built weaker party-states. For one, ruling parties were less cohesive. In Algeria, the ruling FLN quickly splintered; within a year of independence, every living member of the party's founding elite other than President Ben Bella had moved into opposition. Likewise, in Bolivia, all the MNR's top leaders except President Paz had defected by the early 1960s, and in Guinea-Bissau, the ruling PAIGC divided along ethnic lines, culminating in a palace coup in 1980.

Accommodationist governments were also less likely to develop powerful and loyal coercive structures. Neither the MNR in Bolivia nor the PAIGC in Guinea-Bissau developed a large coercive apparatus. The Algerian military was also modest in size until the 1990s, when it confronted a major Islamist insurgency. Militaries were also less disciplined in accommodationist cases. Ruling parties in Algeria and Guinea-Bissau suffered palace coups within a decade of taking power.

Finally, where counterrevolutionary conflict was limited, alternative power centers were more likely to survive. In Algeria, for example, the FLN government lacked an incentive to eliminate autonomous networks of mosques and Islamic associations, while in Bolivia the MNR government left autonomous labor and peasant organizations intact.

The two mixed cases, Mexico and Nicaragua, were characterized by divergent outcomes. In Mexico, the revolutionary elite initially did not build a party, and, as a result, the regime suffered a series of debilitating schisms between 1917 and 1929. However, the Cristero War induced the revolutionary elite to close ranks behind President Calles's party-building effort, after which elite cohesion increased markedly. Party-army fusion helped ensure military loyalty. Mexico was the only country in Latin America to not suffer a single coup or successful armed uprising between 1929 and 2000. In the absence of a sustained military threat, however, the revolutionary elite did not develop a vast coercive apparatus or eliminate independent power centers.

In Nicaragua, the Sandinista National Liberation Front (FSLN) elite responded to a U.S.-backed counterrevolutionary war by closing ranks and building a powerful and loyal coercive apparatus. However, the prospect of international isolation in the face of a looming Soviet withdrawal led the Sandinistas to liberalize after 1986, leaving key societal power centers, including the Church and the private sector, intact.

The case studies thus provide ample evidence that counterrevolutionary conflict contributed to the development of three pillars of durable authoritarianism: a cohesive elite, a strong and loyal military, and the weakening or elimination of alternative centers of societal power. By contrast, limited counterrevolutionary conflicts allowed regimes to survive without closing ranks or investing seriously in state-building. As table 9.1 shows, most of the cases substantiate our theory.[2]

REVOLUTIONARY STATE-BUILDING AND REGIME DURABILITY

The chapters also examined the degree to which revolutionary state-building affected regime durability. We find considerable evidence of a link between the three pillars of authoritarian durability outlined above and regimes' capacity to survive (or preempt) crises. The impact of elite cohesion could be seen in the case studies. In Russia, for example, fear of counterrevolution united the Bolshevik elite in the face of massive peasant protests and rebellion by Kronstadt naval forces in 1921 and again after Lenin's death in 1924. The dearth of elite defections in the 1920s and 1930s meant that the massive discontent created by collectivization, famine, and terror did not translate into any serious regime challenge. Likewise, in Vietnam and Cuba, the absence of regime schisms in the wake of the Soviet collapse (or, in the Cuban case, amid the extraordinary economic crisis that followed it) left dissidents isolated and unable to mobilize societal discontent into the kind of robust opposition challenges seen in many Third Wave transitions. In Iran, factional conflict encouraged opponents of the Islamic Republic of Iran to back reformers over conservatives. However, reformers' unwillingness to openly oppose clerical rule demoralized opposition, deprived it of leadership, and made protest difficult to sustain.

Military loyalty was also critical to regime survival. For example, the Soviet military might have rebelled against Stalin during the Great Terror or in the wake of the disastrous first weeks of the Nazi invasion in 1941—but did not. In Mexico during the 1930s, when the revolutionary government was unpopular and faced a powerful right-wing reaction, the armed forces did not intervene as they did elsewhere in Latin America. Likewise, in the late 1960s and early 1970s, when polarization and the rise of radical leftist movements led to a wave of coups across Latin America, the Mexican military never intervened. In Cuba, despite considerable rank-and-file discontent over the 1989 execution of popular general Arnoldo Ochoa and the economic catastrophe of the early 1990s, the army never rebelled. Finally, Mao seemed to do everything he could to provoke a military coup during the Cultural Revolution—inciting armed factional conflict and encouraging politicized attacks on the military—but never faced a serious challenge to his rule.

Our chapters also provide evidence that the development of a powerful coercive apparatus contributed to regime survival. In the Soviet Union, powerful security services were central to the suppression of resistance to collectivization and of anti-Soviet dissent in the early weeks of the Nazi invasion. In China, military capacity reduced the potential for opposition protest in the wake of the Great Leap Forward and enabled the Communist government to effectively suppress protest in 1989. In Cuba, a powerful security apparatus helped prevent broad public discontent from generating large-scale protest in the 1990s. In Iran, coercive capacity allowed the regime to quickly put down mass protests in 2009 and 2019.

More generally, the vast power asymmetries created by the emergence of a powerful coercive apparatus, on the one hand, and the destruction of alternative centers of societal power, on the other, made it extraordinarily difficult to build and sustain anti-regime opposition movements. In the USSR, in the thirty years after Stalin's death, there were only forty-five nonstate mass actions (including riots at sporting events) with 1,000 or more participants.[3] For decades, anti-regime resistance was limited to small groups of dissident intellectuals totaling no more than a few thousand citizens (in a country of more 200 million).[4] Indeed, the Soviet Union saw sustained protest only in the late 1980s—*after* Gorbachev relaxed controls and the party-state began to unravel. In early twenty-first-century Cuba and Vietnam, opposition remained limited mainly to online groups with no more than a few hundred members. Even in Mexico, which never developed the kind of totalitarian controls seen in the Soviet Union, China, Vietnam, or Cuba, the Institutional Revolutionary Party (PRI) faced virtually no organized national opposition of any significance between 1940 and 1982. Despite comparable levels of modernization, the kind of antiauthoritarian mobilization that emerged in Argentina, Brazil, Chile, Peru, and Uruguay during the late 1970s and 1980s never materialized in Mexico.

Powerful coercive structures and the destruction of independent power centers did not, of course, eliminate opposition. In Mexico in 1968, China in 1989, and Iran in 2009 and 2019, large-scale protests seriously threatened regimes. However, regimes possessed the cohesion and coercive capacity to crack down forcefully on these protests, and the dearth of societal mobilizing structures and elite defections made it far more difficult for opponents to take advantage of these openings and sustain anti-regime mobilization in the face of repression. As a result, even large-scale protest movements could be quelled.

By contrast, where a more limited reactive sequence did not give rise to a powerful coercive apparatus or the destruction of independent power centers, regimes were more vulnerable to societal challenges. In Bolivia, where the MNR neither built its own army nor wiped out rival power centers, the Paz government was overwhelmed by strikes and protest before suffering a regime-ending coup in 1964. In Algeria, autonomous mosque networks provided the bases for a massive Islamist opposition challenge in the 1990s.

Table 9.1 summarizes the evidence linking the development of pillars of durable authoritarianism to revolutionary regime survival. Given that a variety of factors—including the geopolitical environment, economic boom and bust cycles, and the death of leaders—affect the duration of any given regime, one should hardly expect a perfect correlation between authoritarian pillars and regime duration. Nevertheless, the data are suggestive. Each of the four regimes that developed all three pillars of durable authoritarianism (and thus receive scores of 3 of 3 possible points) survived for sixty years or more. By contrast, regimes in Guinea-Bissau and Bolivia, which failed to develop any pillars of durable authoritarianism, survived for much shorter periods of time.[5]

Extending the Theory

This section extends the book's theoretical framework to the seven revolutionary regimes not covered in the case studies: Finland (1918), Albania (1944–1991), Yugoslavia (1945–1990), Angola (1975–), Mozambique (1975–), Eritrea (1993–), and Rwanda (1994–). These cases provide further evidence that revolutionary durability is grounded in the revolutionary reactive sequence described in this book. Only one case—the Finnish People's Deputation, which ascended to power in Helsinki in 1918—is a clear outlier. Although the Finnish People's Deputation was accommodationist,[6] it had the misfortune of coming to power during a world war in the immediate aftermath of the Bolshevik Revolution—a context that encouraged the anticommunist White general, Count Carl Mannerheim, to oust the regime with help from Germany after a mere seventy-five days.

The remaining six cases approximate the ideal-typical reactive sequence described in this book. In each case, a radical government triggered counterrevolutionary conflict, which—with the partial exception of Mozambique—gave rise to strong institutions and durable regimes. At the same time, these cases illustrate the importance of world historical time. The two post–Cold War revolutionary cases—the Rwandan Patriotic Front (RPF) and the Eritrean People's Liberation Front (EPLF)—suggest ways in which the revolutionary trajectories may be shaped by the international environment. Specifically, the RPF and the EPLF did not tap into global ideological rivalries or trigger superpower-sponsored conflicts and thus never developed the siege mentality and elite cohesion observed in other cases.

COLD WAR REVOLUTIONARY REGIMES

Four additional countries underwent social revolution during the Cold War. Yugoslavia and Albania experienced what Samuel Huntington called "Eastern" revolutions, in which the bulk of the reactive sequence played out before the seizure of power.[7] In each case, revolutionary conflict during World War II wiped out traditional elites and left communist regimes with powerful party-states and few significant domestic rivals. In Angola and Mozambique, revolutionaries came to power in violent anticolonial struggles. Both countries became sites of Cold War proxy battles that seriously threatened the new revolutionary regimes but also gave rise to robust authoritarian institutions.

Yugoslavia

The People's Republic of Yugoslavia (1945–1990) was surprisingly durable. The Yugoslav state was an extraordinarily precarious entity. Nonexistent before World War I, it was created in 1918 as a patchwork of Serb, Croat, and Slovenian territories that were orphaned following the collapse of the Austro-Hungarian and Ottoman Empires.[8] Strong nationalist movements persisted, however, particularly among Croats and Serbs. In the absence of a strong Yugoslav national identity, the new Kingdom of Yugoslavia was fragile, and it quickly collapsed in the wake of Germany's April 1941 invasion.[9] World War II gave rise to intense conflict—and genocidal violence—between nationalist Croat and Serb forces.[10] Thus, constructing a viable multinational state and regime in Yugoslavia after World II was a formidable task.

The communist People's Republic of Yugoslavia was founded by Josip Broz Tito's Partisan forces, which seized power in 1945 after defeating Nazi occupiers. Following the 1941 Nazi invasion, Tito and the Communist Party of Yugoslavia (KPJ)—backed by a few thousand Yugoslav veterans of the Spanish Civil War—launched a guerrilla war.[11] Described as "fanatic[al]," "reckless," and "more orthodoxly Marxist than Moscow,"[12] Tito and the Partisans soon entered into conflict with Stalin over their insistence on combining the fight against foreign occupation with "class struggle."[13] The Partisans attacked the remnants of the old monarchy, destroyed land records, and assaulted traditional authority structures.[14] Communist-led "proletarian brigades" were mobilized to uproot and assassinate local notables and replace them with young peasants who challenged the authority of family, clan, and other local power structures.[15] Crucially, moreover, the Partisans launched a war on Serbian Chetnik forces, which were pro-monarchist and closely tied to traditional elites.[16]

The Communists' pan-Yugoslav program allowed them to build support among the country's diverse nationalities,[17] which gave them a decisive advantage over the exclusively Serbian Chetniks.[18] Beginning with a guerrilla force of about 40,000 in 1941, Tito built a loyal, effective army that ultimately encompassed nearly a million troops.[19] Yugoslavia was one of the only countries in Europe to be largely liberated by its own forces during World War II.[20]

Like China and Vietnam, then, Yugoslavia's revolutionary regime was born in 1945 with a relatively robust party-state. Party cohesion, which was already high on the eve of the Axis invasion, was reinforced by the war.[21] The war also gave rise to a powerful security apparatus. With 800,000 troops at the end of World War II, Yugoslavia had the fourth-largest army in Europe.[22] The armed forces were "unswervingly loyal."[23] Built and commanded by the Partisans and infiltrated by a vast network of political commissars and security agents,[24] the Yugoslav army was a "thoroughly political organization."[25] The KPJ also developed an effective and disciplined internal security service. Created during the war, the Department for People's Protection (State Security Administration [UDBA] after 1946) functioned as an "extended arm of the party," and its agents penetrated deep into Yugoslav society.[26] By the late 1940s, Yugoslavia possessed "one of the most rigorous security systems in the world."[27]

Finally, the war created opportunities for the Communists to destroy key political rivals, including the monarchy, traditional elites, and nationalist

Chetnik forces.[28] At the end of the conflict, Partisan units massacred thousands of collaborators and right-wing Chetniks.[29] By the late 1940s, the government had wiped out most independent power centers, with the notable exception of the Catholic clergy (discussed below).[30]

Yugoslavia's revolutionary government was quite radical. Tito launched an "avalanche of economic and social reforms."[31] Described as "more Stalinist than Stalin," the Communists nationalized 90 percent of all enterprises, including all banks and the vast majority of industrial enterprises— moves that provoked outrage in the West.[32] All large private landholdings were eliminated.[33] The Communists expropriated four million acres of land, belonging mostly to the Catholic Church, banks, and German minorities. By 1947, the state sector accounted for 90 percent of production.[34]

The Tito government also abolished the monarchy and assaulted organized religion.[35] Although the Serbian Orthodox Church was relatively weak and easily co-opted,[36] the staunchly anticommunist Catholic Church, which had a strong presence in Croatia and Slovenia, posed a bigger threat. At the end of the war, hundreds of priests and nuns were killed, imprisoned, or forced to emigrate.[37] The KPJ removed religious symbols from public institutions, seized all church buildings and social facilities, and expropriated vast amounts of church land.[38] All prewar Catholic magazines and newspapers were shuttered.[39] When Croatian archbishop Alojzije Stepinac refused to break with Rome, he was arrested for collaboration with the Nazis and convicted in a public show trial.[40]

The Tito government also sought to weaken nationalist forces, which, given the region's history of interethnic conflict, posed a potential threat to regime stability.[41] Institutions such as the Croatian Cultural Society were banned; others, such as the century-old Matica Hrvatska organization, survived but were placed under the command of regime loyalists.[42]

The KPJ also adopted an aggressive foreign policy, seeking to transform Yugoslavia into a hub for communist expansion in southeastern Europe.[43] The new government provided assistance to communist insurgents in Greece,[44] declared Yugoslav sovereignty over the southern Austrian town of Carinthia,[45] and aided Albanian efforts to mine the Corfu Channel against British warships in 1946.[46] In May 1945, Yugoslav troops entered the disputed area of Trieste on the Italian border—a move that provoked threats of intervention from Truman and Churchill.[47]

Tito's behavior generated dangerous tensions with the West. There were more than 2,000 incidents on Yugoslavia's terrestrial and maritime borders in the first years after the war.[48] In August 1946, Yugoslav fighter planes downed two U.S. military aircraft, killing five airmen and bringing

East-West tensions to a boiling point.[49] When Soviet foreign minister Viacheslav Molotov complained to Yugoslav officials, asking, "Don't you realize they have the atomic bomb?" the response was, "They have the atomic bomb, but we have the Partisan one."[50]

Most consequentially, Tito challenged the Soviet Union's regional hegemony by seeking to create a federation of Balkan states (with Albania and Bulgaria) to counter the influence of both the West and the Soviet Union.[51] Tito's ambitions for regional leadership and, more generally, his insistence on autonomy from the Soviet Union infuriated Stalin, who ordered the international communist movement (Cominform) in 1948 to expel Yugoslavia and called on Yugoslav Communist Party members to oust Tito.[52] The Soviet leader grew obsessed with eliminating Tito, ordering his assassination, making plans to invade Yugoslavia, and encouraging dozens of trials of "Titoists" in Soviet satellite states.[53]

Stalin posed an extraordinary threat to Tito. Having just presided over the defeat of the Nazis, Stalin enjoyed both unmatched prestige and overwhelming military dominance in Eastern Europe. Moreover, it was widely taken for granted that any Communist Party member anywhere, but especially in the Communist bloc, would follow directives from Moscow.[54] The Soviets had trained many of Yugoslavia's top army and intelligence officials, and they had numerous agents operating in the Yugoslav party-state, including among Tito's bodyguards.[55] It was thus far from clear that Tito (who had himself been appointed to head the KPJ by Soviet authorities) would be able to retain control of the party or the coercive apparatus. Indeed, Stalin boasted that he could get rid of Tito by lifting his little finger.[56]

The Stalin-Tito split generated a serious regime crisis.[57] Stalin recruited a handful of senior Yugoslav officials, including army chief of staff Arso Jovanovich, Finance Minister Sretan Zhujovich, and the head of planning, Andrija Hebrang.[58] Yugoslavia was left with no allies outside the Communist bloc.[59] Thus, Stalin's turn against Tito plunged the regime into a world in which it "literally did not have a single friend."[60]

Yet the regime survived. The Soviet conspiracy collapsed in the face of a united party leadership and a powerful secret police.[61] Having fought together in World War II, the vast bulk of the Yugoslav party-state backed Tito.[62] The entire KPJ Central Committee, the army, and the police backed Tito throughout the crisis.[63] Hebrang and Zhujovich were purged before they could act, and Jovanovich, having failed to convince the army to rebel, was shot while attempting to flee to Romania.[64] The internal security service also remained loyal, thwarting Soviet efforts to assassinate Tito.

The Yugoslav regime was relatively stable from 1948 until Tito's death in 1980. Anti-regime opposition disappeared, and the party-state, dominated by revolutionary veterans who fought in the war,[65] remained cohesive. Following Yugoslavia's split with the USSR, the regime reconciled with the West, becoming a major recipient of Western economic and military assistance.[66] The economy boomed, growing at a pace of 6 percent a year for three decades.[67]

At the same time, the incomplete destruction of alternative centers of power created the potential for instability. In particular, both the Croatian Catholic Church and the Matica Hrvatska cultural association survived the revolution.[68] Although the Church was weakened and pushed to the political sidelines,[69] it successfully resisted government infiltration, and foreign funding allowed it to maintain a strong societal presence.[70] Matica Hrvatska and the Catholic Episcopate—together with strong nationalist sentiment in many republics—generated latent separatist threats to the regime.[71]

One such threat emerged in the late 1960s, with the wave of Croatian nationalism known as the Croatian Spring.[72] After censorship and controls over associational life were relaxed in 1966, Matica Hrvatska, which had been controlled by regime supporters, came to life, leading a controversial campaign to raise the status of the Croatian language.[73] Matica Hrvatska membership exploded, from about 2,000 in 1970 to 30,000 a year later, threatening the party's monopoly in the republic. The group's demands radicalized, to the point where it called for a separate Croatian military force.[74] Pushed by nationalists, Croatian party leaders sought greater autonomy from the center but quickly lost their grip over the republic.[75] For a time, Yugoslavia appeared vulnerable to breakup.

However, the party-state quickly reestablished control. When nationalist students at Zagreb University went on strike to demand greater Croatian sovereignty, Tito threw his weight behind a crackdown.[76] Backed by a "tightly knit" group of party and military officials who had led the Partisans during the war, Tito's intervention was "swift and final."[77] After meeting with Tito at his hunting retreat in Karadjordjevo, party leaders who had embraced nationalist demands resigned, and the crisis soon subsided.[78]

Revolutionary cohesion thus contributed to regime survival amid the 1948 Stalin-Tito conflict and the 1967–1971 Croatian Spring. In both instances, party-state cohesion was safeguarded by World War II veterans of the Partisan struggle. Led by Tito, this founding generation provided a critical bulwark against rising nationalism at both the federal and the republican levels.

The passing of the revolutionary generation—marked by Tito's death in May 1980—thus posed a major challenge.[79] The departure of the generation that had cut its political teeth during the Partisan struggle deprived the regime of a critical source of cohesion—just as a deteriorating economy eroded public support for the regime.[80] Facing a mounting legitimacy crisis in the 1980s, younger party leaders such as Slobodan Milosevic, who had only childhood memories of the war, abandoned Tito's project for nationalist appeals.[81] A mild-mannered technocrat who had never been particularly nationalistic,[82] Milosevic threw his support behind Serb nationalists in 1987—a move that encouraged a corresponding rise of nationalism in Croatia and other republics.[83] Tolerated by the state, nationalist organizations proliferated, and in 1990, competitive elections brought nationalists to power across Yugoslavia. In Croatia, dissident Franjo Tuđman, a Matica Hrvatska leader in the 1960s who enjoyed the strong support of the Catholic clergy,[84] swept to victory in 1990. Absent any serious countervailing force, nationalist movements quickly broke up the Yugoslav state, and the communist regime collapsed.

In sum, the revolutionary reactive sequence in Yugoslavia gave rise to a surprisingly robust regime. Despite the weakness of the prerevolutionary state and the strength of nationalist forces in Croatia and Serbia, the multinational communist regime established by Partisan forces after World War II endured for forty-five years—nearly three times the length of the average autocracy. Like Mexico, however, the Yugoslav case shows how the failure to eliminate alternative centers of societal power can sow the seeds of future crisis.

Albania

Albania's communist regime (1944–1991), led by the Albanian Party of Labor (APL), followed a more ideal-typical trajectory.[85] During World War II, the movement to liberate Albania included both the Communists, led by Enver Hoxha, and the Balli Kombetar (National Front), which was based in traditional village power structures.[86] As in Yugoslavia (and partly under the Partisans' influence), Hoxha refused to unite with the nationalists and instead fought a "two-pronged" war against the Balli Kombetar on one side and Germany on the other.[87]

The two-front war gave rise to a robust party-state. The Communist Party, which had been divided, evolved into a disciplined and ideological organization.[88] The communist army expanded to nearly seven times the size of the prewar royal army and developed into a disciplined organization capable of posing a serious challenge to the German occupiers.[89] Party and army were fused. The army was commanded by party leaders such as Hoxha and Mehmet Shehu and was honeycombed with party commissars.[90] By the war's end, the Communists had wiped out not only their nationalist rivals but also traditional elites that had dominated prewar Albania.[91]

The Communists seized power in late 1944, giving rise to one of the most radical revolutionary governments in the world.[92] The government jailed or killed old elites, seized property, and carried out a radical land reform that wiped out the landowning class.[93] All industry was nationalized. Hoxha declared Albania an atheist state, demolishing churches and mosques. The Hoxha government also adopted a radical foreign policy. In October 1946, for example, the government mined the Corfu Channel against British warships, despite the fact that the British had provided the Partisans with considerable assistance during the war.[94]

These actions triggered intense hostility from Western powers. Such threats were especially severe given Albania's vulnerability at the Western edge of the Communist bloc. External vulnerability deepened in 1948 when Albania broke with Yugoslavia, which had been an important ally and a source of aid during and immediately after World War II.[95] After the Stalin-Tito split, Hoxha split from Yugoslavia and executed the pro-Yugoslav party leader, Koci Xoxe.[96]

The break left Albania exposed. Indeed, in the late 1940s and early 1950s, U.S. and British intelligence officials viewed Albania as the weak link in the Communist bloc—and made preparations to overthrow the APL.[97] External threats gave rise to a siege mentality among the revolutionary elite. The ruling APL "resembled a sect," bound together by a common existential threat.[98] Albania became one the most militarized autocracies in the world, transforming itself into an armed camp.[99] The government built hundreds of thousands of bunkers, air-raid shelters, trenches, and other military fortifications throughout the country.[100] The secret police force (Sigimuri), which was created by the APL after the war, was staffed by combat veterans and was powerfully shaped by the wartime experience.[101]

Albania's revolutionary regime survived multiple challenges, including endemic food shortages and hostile relations with virtually every country in the world.[102] Hoxha's ability to survive the exit from Yugoslavia's influence can partly be attributed to Stalin's support. However, the Soviet Union was not in a position to back the regime militarily. Given the strong ties between the APL and Yugoslav Communists, one might have expected substantial defection among APL elites after the break with Tito. Nevertheless, the regime elite remained intact, in large part because Hoxha was backed by a group of revolutionary veterans who were "tested in battle and trusted for their political loyalty."[103]

External threats deepened after Albania broke with the Soviet Union, its most important ally, in response to Khrushchev's denunciation of Stalin at the Twentieth Party Congress in 1956.[104] The Twentieth Congress sent shockwaves throughout Eastern Europe, causing regime crises in East Germany, Poland, and Hungary. It also reverberated in Albania's communist establishment, leading to a brief conflagration at the Tirana party conference in April 1956. Unlike other Eastern European cases, however, Albania's Stalinist elite remained intact. After Hoxha appeared at the Tirana conference and attacked anti-Stalinist critics as "enemies," delegates sank into their seats and the conference was transformed into a ferocious trial against supposed antiparty conspirators.[105] Hoxha continued to defend Stalin's legacy,[106] responding to Khrushchev's threat to cut off aid by declaring that he and his compatriots would rather "eat grass" than yield to Soviet pressure.[107] After the 1960 Sino-Soviet split, Albania sided with China and severed relations with the Soviet Union—despite the fact that China offered little economic assistance.[108] Following China's rapprochement with the United States in the 1970s, Hoxha broke with China and Albania descended into near-complete international isolation.[109]

Despite terrible economic conditions, including widespread poverty and persistent food shortages, Albania's communist regime remained stable throughout the 1970s and 1980s. There were no coups, elite schisms, or serious societal challenges prior to regime collapse in 1992.[110]

Angola and Mozambique

Revolutionary reactive sequences also contributed to durable authoritarianism in Angola and Mozambique. Both the Popular Movement for the Liberation of Angola (MPLA) and the Front for the Liberation of Mozambique (Frelimo) came to power in armed struggles against Portuguese colonial rule. Subsequent efforts to transform domestic and regional power structures sparked decades-long counterrevolutionary wars that led to the development of cohesive autocracies backed by loyal militaries. Armed struggle fostered the creation of a powerful state and the destruction of alternative power centers in Angola but not in Mozambique, making the latter case less consistent with our theory. Nevertheless, regime durability can be clearly traced to a reactive sequence in both cases.

Angola. The MPLA regime was born weak. The anticolonial insurgency, which began in 1961, encompassed three rival armies: the Cuban-backed MPLA; the anticommunist National Liberation Front of Angola

(FNLA), led by Holden Roberto; and the National Union for the Total Independence of Angola (UNITA), which was created by Jonas Savimbi in 1966. The rebels failed to achieve a military victory and remained divided when the 1974 Portuguese coup opened the door to independence. In January 1975, with independence imminent, the three rebel armies agreed to form a transitional coalition government, create a unified army, and call elections for a legislative assembly. The agreement broke down, however, and when the Portuguese left in November, Angola was mired in civil war. The MPLA gained control of Luanda, the capital, and MPLA leader Agostinho Neto established the People's Republic of Angola—of which he became president—on November 11, 1975.

The MPLA government was vulnerable in the wake of independence. The MPLA was "practically spent as a fighting organization."[111] It controlled no more than an "archipelago of cities,"[112] and it confronted two rival armies that, by most counts, were larger than its own. The MPLA itself had long been divided, experiencing debilitating schisms in the early 1960s and again in the early 1970s.[113] In the regime's early years, the MPLA descended into severe internal conflict, as a radical faction—whose members were known as *fractionists*—led by former interior minister Nito Alves, challenged Neto's leadership, culminating in a bloody coup attempt that left thousands of people dead.[114]

Despite its early weakness, however, the MPLA—backed by Cuba and the Soviet Union—launched a set of radical domestic and foreign policy initiatives. Domestically, the state nationalized thousands of private farms and industrial firms (the vast majority of which were abandoned by Portuguese settlers who left the country at independence), as well as banking, trade, and the critical oil and diamond sectors.[115] It also launched a radical "villagization" process that uprooted peasants and transferred their land to communal control.[116] On the external front, the MPLA pursued a high-risk strategy of assisting the African National Congress (ANC) in South Africa and the Namibian independence movement, led by the South West Africa People's Organization (SWAPO).[117] As a result, Angola was quickly drawn into Cold War proxy battles with its neighbors. Zaire and the FNLA invaded from the north, and South Africa and UNITA attacked the new government from the south.[118] Although the FNLA was quickly defeated, the war with UNITA continued for decades, resulting in the death of as many as half a million people.[119]

Counterrevolutionary war helped transform Angola into a powerful and cohesive party-state.[120] Following the failed coup, President Neto carried out a wide-ranging purge of the MPLA. Party cohesion subsequently increased and remained high for the rest of the civil war.[121] The war also gave rise to a powerful coercive apparatus. In 1975, the MPLA created a secret police force, the Directorate of Information and Security of Angola, to combat the numerous counterrevolutionary threats.[122] Over the years, the regime built a large and powerful army.[123] By the 2000s, Angola's police, military, and paramilitary forces were the largest, per capita, in sub-Saharan Africa outside of (revolutionary) Eritrea.[124] The revolutionary army was tightly fused to the ruling party, via both overlapping leaderships and an extensive system of political commissars.[125] During the 1970s and into the 1980s, about half of the MPLA's Central Committee consisted of military personnel with guerrilla or civil war backgrounds.[126]

Finally, more than two decades of civil war enabled the MPLA to eliminate all organized opposition.[127] By the end of the war, rival organizations had been defeated and all potential sources of societal autonomy, including traditional authorities, had been weakened or co-opted by the state.[128]

The Angolan regime has now survived for nearly half a century. Not only did the MPLA defeat a major South African–backed insurgency, but it oversaw a smooth transition following President Neto's death in 1979 and, crucially, survived the Soviet collapse in the early 1990s. Although the MPLA renounced Marxism and adopted a nominally multiparty system following internationally brokered peace accords in 1994, the ruling party remained disciplined, cohesive, and in full control of the armed forces.[129] Unlike Nicaragua, multiparty elections posed little threat to the MPLA. Indeed, the regime confronted no serious domestic challenges in the two decades after the end of the war. Although mineral rents likely strengthened the MPLA's hand,[130] the power asymmetries created by a vast coercive apparatus and the destruction of independent power centers clearly undergirded the regime's stability into the twenty-first century.

Mozambique. The revolutionary regime in Mozambique followed a similar trajectory, although state-building was more limited. Frelimo was founded in Dar es Salaam in 1962 as a loosely structured and ideologically diverse nationalist movement. It launched a guerrilla struggle against Portuguese rule in 1964, and quickly sidelined rival groups to establish itself as Mozambique's predominant nationalist movement.[131] Initially, the guerrillas suffered from heavy infighting,[132] but they grew more cohesive and ideological after founding leader Eduard Mondlane was assassinated in 1969.[133] Violent conflict and the adoption of a Marxist ideology under new leader Samora Machel transformed Frelimo from a loosely organized, broad-based anticolonial movement into a disciplined, ideologically committed party.[134]

The revolutionary regime in Mozambique was born weak. Like the MPLA in Angola, Frelimo was unable to defeat the Portuguese on the battlefield but gained power in the wake of the 1974 Portuguese coup. Although the independence war gave rise to a cohesive ruling party and a guerrilla-based army that was tightly wedded to it, Frelimo initially had weak control over most of the country,[135] and it was backed by a small, undisciplined, and underfunded military.[136]

Despite this early weakness, however, the Frelimo government initiated a set of radical reforms aimed at building socialism and creating a "new man."[137] Widespread nationalization triggered an exodus of Portuguese professionals.[138] Abandoned settler farms were nationalized and transformed into Soviet-style state farms in an effort to bring about the "rapid proletarianization" of the peasantry. This project entailed uprooting peasants from their homes and forcibly relocating them into communal villages.[139] Frelimo also abolished the colonial-era *regulado* system of local governance, displacing traditional chiefs.[140] On the external front, the Frelimo government provided bases for both the ANC and Zimbabwe African National Union guerrillas.[141] These initiatives triggered a violent counterrevolutionary insurgency, the Mozambican National Resistance (Renamo), which was actively supported by Rhodesia and later South Africa.[142] The civil war lasted until 1992 and cost an estimated 800,000 lives.[143]

As in other cases, the counterrevolutionary war reinforced regime cohesion. The regime experienced no serious schisms or defections during the 1980s, despite major military defeats and severe economic hardship.[144] The army, which was created and commanded by Frelimo leaders and thoroughly penetrated by the party, remained loyal.[145] Ex-guerrilla commanders, known as the "historic generation" or "old fighters" (*antigos combatentes*), linked party and army and provided a critical source of regime cohesion.[146]

Unlike other cases (including Angola), however, Mozambique's coercive institutions remained relatively underdeveloped.[147] Moreover, although Frelimo survived the seventeen-year civil war, it was unable to wipe out Renamo and thus faced opposition in the aftermath of the 1992 peace accords and transition to multiparty rule.[148]

Although the Frelimo party-state was weaker than those in other revolutionary cases, the regime nevertheless survived through 2021. Indeed, the regime endured not only the severe economic and military crises of the 1980s but also the loss of Soviet patronage following the collapse of the USSR, Frelimo's abandonment of Marxism, and the transition to multiparty rule. Outside of a small failed mutiny by underpaid police and former guerrilla soldiers in late 1975, there were no significant coup attempts.[149]

The military restructuring mandated by the 1992 peace accords (in which Renamo officers were integrated into the army command) appears to have given rise to coup conspiracies among some army commanders. However, the plot was discovered by military intelligence and the coup never materialized.[150] Frelimo's extensive penetration of the army thus enabled it to preemptively thwart a military challenge.

Ruling party cohesion allowed Frelimo to reconsolidate power in the 1990s and 2000s. Despite holding only a narrow legislative majority after the 1994 election, iron-clad party discipline, reinforced by the predominance of the "historic generation," enabled Frelimo to dominate parliament, weaken electoral and other institutions created by the 1992 peace agreement, and establish political hegemony.[151]

POST–COLD WAR REVOLUTIONARY REGIMES

Two post–Cold War cases, the regimes led by the RPF in Rwanda and the EPLF in Eritrea, hue closely to the ideal-typical radical trajectory. However, they also illustrate the effect of world historic time. During the Cold War, revolutionary conflict tapped into highly salient ideological polarization and a superpower rivalry that heightened the stakes of conflict, fostering perceptions of existential threat and thus strengthening elite cohesion. To varying degrees in Albania, Angola, Cuba, Mozambique, Nicaragua, and Vietnam, alliances with the Communist bloc generated serious Western threats, which, in turn, reinforced elite cohesion. After the Cold War, the global stakes of conflict diminished, potentially weakening elite cohesion. Thus, in Rwanda and Eritrea, attacks on important domestic and international interests triggered substantial counterrevolutionary conflict, which, in turn, gave rise to powerful and loyal military forces. However, these conflicts were not linked to endemic Cold War ideological divisions that could sustain polarization after the defeat of counterrevolutionary forces. Partly as a result, it seems, elite cohesion was less robust. Because states were strong, however, leaders in Rwanda and Eritrea were able to quickly quell incipient challenges from former allies.

Rwanda

The RPF was founded in Uganda in 1987 by exiled opponents of autocrat Juvénal Habyarimana. In 1990, the RPF and its military wing, the Rwandan Patriotic Army (RPA), invaded Rwanda. In 1994, genocide by pro-government Hutu forces against the minority Tutsi population led to the breakdown of social order and the collapse of Rwanda's historically strong state institutions.[152] By late July 1994, the RPF had seized the capital and taken control of the country. RPF leader Paul Kagame became the country's de facto leader (though he was nominally vice president through 2000), and the RPA became the new army.

The Kagame government was revolutionary. Not only did it remake the state, but it launched a radical program of social and cultural engineering, seeking to create a "new Rwanda and a new Rwandan."[153] The RPF embraced an ideology that viewed Rwanda's Hutu-Tutsi divide as a foreign construct propagated by German and Belgian colonial powers.[154] Thus, the RPF government outlawed Hutu and Tutsi identities in favor of "Rwandinity."[155] A genocide ideology law criminalized ethnic identification and effectively banned any public discussion of ethnic identity.[156] Tens of thousands of Rwandans were forced into reeducation camps (*ingandos*), and the public education system was radically overhauled.[157]

The Kagame government confronted counterrevolutionary threats from old regime forces, which organized an insurgency in refugee camps in southwest Rwanda and neighboring Zaire (where President Mobutu Sese Seko provided critical assistance).[158] The Interahamwe paramilitary, which had already wiped out 75 percent of Rwanda's Tutsi population, plotted to "finish the work" of the genocide.[159] The insurgency carried out a campaign of anti-Tutsi pogroms, targeted assassinations of RPF officials, and attacks against RPA soldiers.[160]

The RPF government responded with a series of radical coercive measures, including large-scale villagization, in which hundreds of thousands of citizens were forcibly displaced from their homes and moved into centrally planned villages.[161] As many as 10,000 people reportedly died in these campaigns.[162] In 1996, the RPF invaded Zaire, helping to oust Mobutu and bring Laurent Kabila, an ally, to power in 1997.[163]

The reactive sequence in Rwanda dramatically strengthened the state, which had been decimated during the genocide.[164] Between 1994 and 2002, the size of the military more than doubled, from about 30,000 to 70,000 troops.[165] The RPF built an effective military from scratch. Party and army leaderships were tightly intertwined. Kagame emerged out of the guerrilla army, and his former guerrilla comrades came to dominate national politics.[166] RPF commissions operated in every army unit.[167] The RPF state reached deep into Rwandan society and was supported by a vast network of government "eyes and ears" in virtually every enterprise and organization.[168] The RPF tightly controlled the population,[169] creating an extensive Leninist party organization with parallel party structures at every level of the state.[170]

Counterrevolutionary conflict also contributed to the destruction of alternative power centers. By the early 2000s, the insurgency had been wiped out and opposition driven underground or into exile.[171] The Catholic Church, which had been a powerful economic and political force, was "beheaded" and substantially weakened.[172]

The RPF regime proved robust. It was never seriously challenged by opposition groups between 1994 and 2021, and it suffered no coup attempts.[173] Unlike other revolutionary regimes, however, the RPF suffered numerous high-level defections. Various RPF leaders were forced into exile after breaking with the Kagame leadership.[174] However, a highly effective security apparatus allowed Kagame to swiftly suppress dissidents, preventing these defections from triggering regime crises. Thus, in May 1998, Seth Sendashonga, a former interior minister who had defected in 1995, died after his car was fired upon in Nairobi, and on New Year's Day in 2014, Patrick Karegeya, the former head of external intelligence who had fled Rwanda after falling out with Kagame, was strangled to death in a Johannesburg hotel.[175]

In sum, Rwanda's revolutionary reactive sequence failed to generate sustained elite cohesion. However, it dramatically strengthened the state and wiped out alternative centers of power, which has permitted nearly three decades of stable authoritarian rule.

Eritrea

The EPLF followed a similar trajectory. It emerged in the early 1970s out of splinter groups from the Eritrean Liberation Front (ELF), which had led the fight for independence from Ethiopia since 1960.[176] Commanded by Isaias Afwerki, who had trained in China in the 1960s, the EPLF was grounded in an ideological commitment to abolish feudal land relations; overturn economic, gender, and other social hierarchies; and create "new Eritrean men and women."[177] Modeling itself on the Chinese communist experience in the 1940s, the EPLF carried out land reform and attempted to radically transform gender relations in the areas it controlled—moves that generated considerable local opposition.[178] Although the EPLF moderated its Marxist rhetoric in the late 1980s in an effort to attract Western support, these changes "were largely rhetorical," and the EPLF retained a strong commitment to radical transformation.[179]

In 1991, the EPLF seized control of Eritrea in the wake of the collapse of the Derg regime in Ethiopia (Eritrea gained formal independence in 1993). Afwerki became president. Whereas most movements of Marxist origin (including those in Ethiopia and Uganda) abandoned many of their radical goals after the end of the Cold War, the Afwerki government engaged in a serious effort to transform both Eritrean society and the regional order. Domestically, the government wiped out existing land tenure systems, eliminating peasants' property rights and transferring all land to the state.[180] These reforms dramatically altered peasants' lives and social organization.[181] The EPLF also sought to abolish the *enda*, the traditional extended family unit based on common descent from a shared ancestor.[182]

Internationally, the new government, seeing itself as a "regional revolutionary vanguard," engaged in armed conflict with every land neighbor.[183] Thus, the EPLF supported rebellions in eastern and southern Sudan and aided Islamist insurgents in Somalia—actions that led to United Nations sanctions in 2009.[184] Eritrea clashed with Yemen over the Hanish Islands and engaged in a military standoff with Djibouti.[185] Most importantly, in May 1998, Eritrea attacked Ethiopia, a country nearly five times its size, sending troops into the disputed border area of Badme.[186]

These aggressive measures triggered serious domestic and external conflict and isolated Eritrea from almost every country in the world.[187] The incursion into Ethiopia sparked one of the bloodiest conflicts in Africa after the Cold War. Ethiopia responded by launching an attack deep into Eritrean territory, including air attacks on the airport of the capital Asmara.[188] The war, which lasted until 2000, resulted in the loss of 19,000 Eritrean soldiers and 70,000–100,000 lives overall.[189] At the same time, Sudan responded to Eritrea's sponsorship of insurgencies by supporting the Eritrean Islamic Jihad Movement, which carried out raids in western Eritrea.[190]

These conflicts strengthened the Eritrean state, which had been weakened by the thirty-year war for independence.[191] The state developed extraordinary coercive capacity.[192] Amid the war with Ethiopia, the EPLF government conscripted everyone in nonessential occupations.[193] National service obligations, which were enforced by police raids on homes, workplaces, and social gatherings, became virtually indefinite,[194] leading some observers to compare it to slave labor.[195] Overall, the number of military personnel nearly quadrupled, from 55,000 in 1994 to 202,000 in 2000.[196] In the 2000s, Eritrea was the second most militarized country in the world, trailing only North Korea.[197]

The revolutionary party-state was also characterized by tight fusion and party control.[198] As in China in the 1940s and 1950s, there was no clear organizational distinction between the party and the military.[199] The EPLF maintained organizational cells at all levels of the military. Army and party personnel were closely monitored by a large security service, Halewa Sewra (Guardians of the Revolution).[200] Due in part to this fusion and penetration, the Eritrean military remained loyal and capable of high-intensity coercion,[201] despite severe resource scarcity and disastrous decisions such as the attack on Ethiopia. Over the course of three decades, there were only two attempted mutinies (in 1993 and 2013), and both were put down within a few hours.[202]

By the early 2000s, the EPLF regime had successfully wiped out or driven into exile all organized opposition, creating "one of the worst totalitarian regimes in the world."[203] The ELF had been defeated and destroyed in the early 1980s.[204] The only serious domestic challenge to emerge in the 1990s was the Sudanese-backed Eritrean Islamic Jihad Movement, but the group was eliminated by 2003.[205]

The EPLF regime has now survived for nearly three decades. As in Rwanda, the regime has suffered an unusual number of high-level defections. In the wake of the disastrous war with Ethiopia, a group of prominent EPLF officials—known as the "G15"—publicly criticized President Afwerki for "acting without restraint, even illegally" and calling for political reforms, including free and fair elections.[206] The group encompassed senior EPLF military and political officials, including EPLF cofounder Petros Solomon.[207] As in Rwanda, however, the government was able to quickly suppress internal dissent. Eleven of the fifteen dissidents were charged with treason, arrested, and never heard from again.[208] The others managed to escape into exile but remained quiet thereafter.[209] Like Rwanda, Eritrea demonstrates that while the end of the Cold War likely reduced elite cohesion, the revolutionary reactive sequence still generated highly durable regimes.

Table 9.2 summarizes the seven additional cases. As the table shows, the Finnish case, in which the regime was destroyed early on by a counterrevolutionary reaction despite accommodationist strategies, does not conform to our theory. In the other six cases, radical policies triggered counterrevolutionary reactions, which in all cases gave rise to at least two pillars of durable authoritarianism.[210] All six cases survived for at least forty years or remained intact at the time of this book's publication.

Summing Up the Evidence

A review of all twenty revolutionary regimes since 1900 largely confirms the theory presented in this book (see table 9.3). Although early radicalism led to the destruction of a few regimes, those that survived violent counterrevolutionary movements built powerful party-states that endured for decades, often despite multiple and severe crises. By contrast,

Table 9.2 Scoring the Additional Cases

		Counterrevolutionary Reaction	Three Pillars of Authoritarian Durability[1]					Summary Score	Regime Duration
	Initial Policies		Cohesion	Strong/Loyal Military		Destruction of Independent Power Centers			
				Strong	Loyal				
Albania	Radical	Yes	Yes	Yes	Yes	Full		3/3	47
Angola	Radical	Yes	Yes	Yes	Yes	Full		3/3	46+
Eritrea	Radical	Yes	No	Yes	Yes	Full		2/3	28+
Mozambique	Radical	Yes	Yes	No	Yes	Partial		2/3	46+
Rwanda	Radical	Yes	No	Yes	Yes	Full		2/3	27+
Yugoslavia	Radical	Yes	Yes	Yes	Yes	Partial		2.5/3	45
Finland	Accommodation	Yes/early death							<1

[1] In accordance with our theoretical framework, the three pillars of authoritarianism are measured after the resolution of the initial counterrevolutionary conflict (the nature and dates of resolution of these conflicts in each case are provided in appendix II). Early death cases (shaded) are not scored because their failure to survive the reactive sequence does not yield any theoretical predictions. For cases that experience no serious counterrevolutionary conflict, the three pillars are measured after the fifth year of regime foundation.

Table 9.3 Summarizing the Theory's Performance

Case	Hypothesis 1: Radicalism generates violent counterrevolutionary reaction; accommodation generates limited or no counterrevolutionary reaction	Hypothesis 2: Counterrevolutionary reaction brings early death or development of three pillars of durable authoritarianism;[1] cases without counterrevolutionary reaction do not develop such pillars	Hypothesis 3: The development of at least two pillars of durable authoritarianism contributes to regime durability; fewer than two pillars results in regime instability[2]	Case Conforms to Theory?
Afghanistan	Yes	Yes (early death)	Not Applicable	Fully
Albania	Yes	Yes	Yes	Fully
Algeria	Yes	Yes	Yes	Fully
Angola	Yes	Yes	Yes[3]	Fully
Bolivia	Yes	Yes	Yes	Fully
Cambodia	Yes	Yes (early death)	Not Applicable	Fully
China	Yes	Yes	Yes	Fully
Cuba	Yes	Yes	Yes	Fully
Eritrea	Yes	Mostly	Yes[3]	Mostly
Finland	No	Yes (early death)	Not Applicable	No
Guinea-Bissau	Yes	Yes	Yes	Fully
Hungary	Yes	Yes (early death)	Not Applicable	Fully
Iran	Yes	Mostly	Yes	Mostly
Mexico	Yes[4]	Yes[5]	Yes	Fully
Mozambique	Yes	Mostly	Yes	Mostly

(Continued)

Table 9.3 (*continued*)

Case	Hypothesis 1: Radicalism generates violent counterrevolutionary reaction; accommodation generates limited or no counterrevolutionary reaction	Hypothesis 2: Counterrevolutionary reaction brings early death or development of three pillars of durable authoritarianism;[1] cases without counterrevolutionary reaction do not develop such pillars	Hypothesis 3: The development of at least two pillars of durable authoritarianism contributes to regime durability; fewer than two pillars results in regime instability[2]	Case Conforms to Theory?
Nicaragua[6]	**Yes**[6]	Mostly	No	Partially
Rwanda	**Yes**	Mostly	Yes	Mostly
Soviet Union	**Yes**	**Yes**	Yes	**Fully**
Vietnam	**Yes**	**Yes**	Yes	**Fully**
Yugoslavia	**Yes**	**Mostly**	Yes	Mostly

Note: Dimensions that do not fully confirm to our argument are in bold.

[1] Radical cases that develop three pillars are considered fully consistent with the theory. Radical cases that develop two pillars are considered mostly consistent with the theory. Cases of accommodation that develop one or fewer pillars are considered consistent with the theory.

[2] We define durable regimes as those regimes that survive for at least twenty-five years without experiencing a palace coup or more than one serious national opposition challenge to regime survival. Unstable regimes are those that either collapse after fewer than twenty-five years or, during the first twenty-five years, experience a palace coup or more than one serious national opposition challenge to regime survival. In cases of counterrevolutionary conflict we apply the criteria to the period after the conflict has been resolved (as per our argument). In cases without counterrevolutionary conflict, we apply the criteria beginning five years after regime formation. See appendix II for full coding criteria and a list of the nature and dates of conflicts.

[3] At the time of publication, the regime was in power but had not quite survived twenty-five years since the resolution of the counterrevolutionary conflict, as predicted by our theory. See appendix II for full coding criteria. (At the same time, Eritrea had survived for nearly thirty years and Angola for more than forty-five years since regime founding.)

[4] Mexico's segmented radicalism, in which the revolutionary government attacked the Church but was accommodationist toward the United States and foreign capital, triggered a limited counterrevolutionary conflict (the Cristero War) in that it had no significant international component. This outcome is consistent with our theory.

[5] Because Mexico's limited counterrevolutionary conflict encompassed only peasants and the Catholic Church (and did not involve the United States or the urban private sector), the failure to develop a large coercive apparatus or destroy all independent power centers (thus giving rise to two, rather than three, pillars of durable authoritarianism) is consistent with our theory.

[6] Nicaragua's revolutionary government mixed elements of radicalism and accommodation, but we consider support for guerrillas in El Salvador and Cuban-style agrarian reform to be sufficiently radical to expect a counterrevolutionary reaction.

revolutionary regimes that adopted accommodationist strategies avoided counterrevolutionary reactions but created weaker and less stable regimes.

The cases provide evidence for each of the three hypotheses laid out in this book. First, the cases confirm that radical initiatives generate violent counterrevolutionary reactions that threaten regime survival, whereas more accommodationist policies do not. All fourteen radical cases and the two mixed cases (Nicaragua and Mexico) experienced a violent counterrevolutionary reaction. By contrast, only one of four accommodationist cases (Finland) generated serious counterrevolutionary conflict.

Second, the evidence suggests that if radical regimes survive the counterrevolutionary reaction, reactive sequences give rise to three pillars of durable authoritarianism. In eleven of fourteen radical revolutionary cases, regimes survived counterrevolutionary wars. All eleven developed at least two of three pillars; six established all three and five established at least two.[211] The two mixed cases, Mexico and Nicaragua, generated two of three pillars. By contrast, none of the accommodationist cases developed more than a single pillar.

Third, we find evidence that revolutionary state-building contributes to durable authoritarianism. As of 2021, regimes with all three authoritarian pillars have, on average, survived for sixty-nine years, whereas those with one or fewer pillars have survived, on average, for thirty-two years. If we exclude Algeria, which has survived for fifty-nine years despite weak authoritarian pillars, this latter number falls to fourteen years

Table 9.3 summarizes the overall fit between our theory and the twenty revolutionary regimes that emerged in the twentieth century. Overall, eighteen of the twenty cases fully or mostly conform to our theoretical framework. Thirteen cases are fully consistent with our theory, in that all our hypotheses are confirmed. In Afghanistan, Cambodia, and Hungary, early radicalism led to counterrevolutionary war and early death. In Albania, Angola, China, Cuba, Russia, and Vietnam, early radicalism led to counterrevolutionary conflict and the development of all three pillars of durable authoritarianism, which resulted in long-lived, durable regimes. In Mexico, segmented radicalism led to a more limited counterrevolutionary reaction and the development of two of three pillars—and the regime also proved stable. In Bolivia and Guinea-Bissau, accommodationist regimes did not face violent counterrevolutionary conflict, failed to build durable authoritarian institutions, and proved relatively short-lived. In Algeria, an accommodationist government confronted no significant counterrevolutionary reaction, which resulted in a less-cohesive elite, a less-developed coercive apparatus, and the survival of independent power centers, particularly mosques. Consistent with our theory, the Algerian regime suffered greater intra-elite conflict and societal opposition than is observed in the radical cases. Although the regime survived for six decades, this longevity is explained, to a considerable degree, by factors that were unrelated to revolutionary origins, such as oil resources and external support.

Five other cases mostly conform to our theory, in that at least two of three hypotheses are fully confirmed. In Eritrea and Rwanda, early radicalism triggered violent counterrevolutionary conflict, which led to the development of strong and loyal coercive apparatuses and the destruction of alternative power centers. However, elite cohesion was somewhat lower, perhaps due to the less polarized post–Cold War environment into which these regimes were born. Nevertheless, revolutionary state-building clearly contributed to regime durability in both cases. In Iran and Yugoslavia, the revolutionary reactive sequence generated powerful autocracies but failed to wipe out all alternative power centers. In Iran, counterrevolutionary conflict weakened or destroyed most independent power centers but left intact a relatively autonomous clerical establishment with latent capacity to challenge the regime. In Yugoslavia, the revolutionary party-state proved quite durable; however, the persistence of influential communal elites contributed to regime—and state—collapse at the end of the Cold War. Finally, in Mozambique, radicalism triggered a major counterrevolutionary war that, in line with our theory, gave rise to a cohesive party-state that survived for more than a generation. Contrary to our theory, however, Frelimo did not develop a powerful coercive apparatus or fully destroy independent power centers.

One case, Nicaragua, only partially conforms to our theoretical framework in that it developed two pillars of durable authoritarianism but collapsed after only eleven years. This outcome is largely attributable to geopolitical context. First, although the U.S.-sponsored civil war gave rise, as predicted, to a powerful party-state complex, the specter of international isolation encouraged the FSLN to limit attacks on the Church and the private sector. Second, due to the winding down of the Cold War and the looming Soviet withdrawal, the FSLN grew increasingly accommodationist over time, creating opportunities for regime opponents. The regime remained cohesive and militarily strong, but when international pressure induced the Sandinistas to hold clean elections in 1990, opposition forces, backed by business and the Church, were able to defeat them.

One case, Finland, fails entirely to conform to our theory. The Finnish People's Deputation suffered an early death at the hands of powerful counterrevolutionary forces despite adopting an accommodationist strategy.

Alternative Hypotheses

The book assessed our theoretical framework against three alternative sets of hypotheses: antecedent conditions, institutionalist approaches, and society-centered explanations. First, although we cannot irrefutably discount the possibility that *some* antecedent factor caused both revolutions and durable authoritarianism, our analysis of the cases provides virtually no evidence that this was, in fact, the case. In nearly all the cases covered in the book, the prerevolutionary period was characterized by extreme state weakness, which, by virtually all scholarly accounts, contributes to regime *fragility*, not durability. In Algeria, Eritrea, Vietnam, Guinea-Bissau, Mozambique, and Angola, colonial rule and decolonization left strikingly weak state institutions. In Afghanistan, Albania, Cambodia, Finland, and Yugoslavia, war decimated the central state. Prerevolutionary China, which lacked a national state and was controlled by competing warlords, was comparable to contemporary Afghanistan. In Cuba and Nicaragua, neopatrimonial rule hollowed out already weak states. In Russia, Mexico, Iran, and Rwanda, revolutionary regimes were preceded by stronger states and more durable autocracies. In Russia and Mexico, however, those states weakened in the early twentieth century and were then decimated by revolutionary civil wars. In Iran and Rwanda, states collapsed during the revolution. In all four of these cases, moreover, revolutionaries thoroughly remade the state. The regimes' most powerful institutions—the party and the KGB in Russia, the PRI and the army in Mexico, the clerical authorities and the Revolutionary Guard in Iran, and the RPF and the army in Rwanda—were created anew by revolutionary forces and had no ties to the old regime. Until scholars identify a factor that plausibly contributed to both revolution and authoritarian durability, we remain skeptical that antecedent factors explain the durability of modern revolutionary regimes.

The book also examined the role of institutions in explaining regime durability. The literature on totalitarianism offered an early institutionalist explanation of revolutionary regime durability.[212] Totalitarian institutions—characterized by an extensive party and terror apparatus, total state control of the economy, and a monopoly over communications—were said to inhibit societal opposition and thus enhance regime stability. However, effective totalitarian structures were not principally a product of institutional design.[213] Rather, as we show in this book, they were rooted in counterrevolutionary conflict. In Russia, China, Vietnam, Cuba, Yugoslavia, and arguably Eritrea, it was social revolution and revolutionary violence that enabled states to penetrate deep into society, and it was counterrevolutionary conflict that drove the expansion of the security apparatus and the destruction of pockets of societal autonomy.

More recent institutionalist approaches, which focus on the centrality of ruling parties, appear plausible. Most revolutionary regimes were governed by institutionalized parties, which Barbara Geddes and others argue help discourage defection by giving regime elites a stake in the regime's survival. In fact, institutions *did* sometimes shape outcomes in important ways. For example, the absence of a ruling party in Mexico in the 1920s almost certainly weakened elite cohesion.[214] Party institutions, moreover, often played a central role in sustaining revolutionary regimes after the demise of the founding generation. In the Soviet Union, China, Mexico, Vietnam, Mozambique, and Cuba, revolutionary origins and years of institutionalized hegemony gave rise to party institutions capable of shaping elite expectations in ways that Geddes, Jason Brownlee, Beatriz Magaloni, and other scholars theorize.

Overall, however, the case evidence suggests that party institutions played a secondary role in regime survival. Revolutionary origins—not party institutions—explain why regimes in Russia, China, Mexico, Vietnam, Algeria, Cuba, and Iran survived their most serious crises. In Iran, the top leadership bodies (the supreme leader and the Revolutionary Guard) remained strikingly cohesive between 1979 and 2021, even after the ruling party was dismantled in 1987. And although the absence of a ruling party and semi-free elections may have encouraged factionalism, political factions in Iran remained almost completely loyal to the regime—even during periods of severe economic crisis and large-scale anti-regime protest. In China during the Cultural Revolution and in Russia during the Great Terror, regimes survived even though ruling party organizations were decimated. In many cases, moreover, strong party institutions can be explained by revolutionary origins. In Cuba, for example, the Communist Party was not created until long after the revolutionary regime had consolidated. Finally, it is important to note that most of the cases *also* possessed cohesive and effective states. Thus, although parties often played a more independent role after the passing of the founding generation, their effect was almost certainly enhanced by the fact that they were embedded in strong (revolutionary) states.[215]

The chapters also examined the explanatory power of society-centered explanations. One variant of this approach might be characterized as sociocultural.[216] Eric Selbin, for example, argues that the successful consolidation of revolutionary regimes hinges on the degree to which citizens accept and internalize the revolutionary project.[217] There is, to be sure, evidence that rank-and-file revolutionary commitments mattered. For example, deeply religious rural supporters appear to have helped shore up Iran's Islamic Republic in the wake of the contested 2009 crisis, giving the regime elite confidence to crack down on urban protest.

In most cases, however, we found little evidence that mass ideological commitments contributed to revolutionary regime durability. For example, when the Kronstadt sailors—leading symbols of the Russian Revolution—rebelled against the Bolsheviks' betrayal of revolutionary ideals, party leaders closed ranks and the rebellion was quelled by loyal security forces. Importantly, moreover, several of the regimes examined in the book underwent far-reaching ideological transformations without triggering popular resistance. If a societal embrace of revolutionary ideology were critical to regime survival, then the regime's abandonment of that ideology should trigger grassroots resistance. Yet in Angola, China, Mozambique, and Vietnam, ruling parties abandoned socialism for capitalism without triggering such backlash. Finally, some revolutionary regimes, most notably those in Mexico and Algeria, endured for decades without a clear ideological project. Given the absence of ideology at the top, it is unlikely that mass ideological commitments contributed to regime durability in these cases.

Other society-centered approaches link revolutionary regime durability to support bases generated by redistributive measures.[218] Revolutionary regimes are thus said to be sustained by those who benefit materially from them. Although support coalitions—often constructed via land reform and, in a few cases (China, Vietnam), reinforced by economic growth—may contribute to regime stability,[219] we found considerable evidence that revolutionary regimes can survive *without* such support. Most revolutionary regimes survived periods of deep economic crisis (e.g., Mexico in the late 1920s and early 1930s, Vietnam in the late 1970s, Cuba and Mozambique in the late 1980s and early 1990s), extreme shortages (e.g., the USSR in the 1930s, Albania under Hoxha), and even mass starvation (e.g., the USSR in the early 1920s and early 1930s, China in the late 1950s), during which the distribution of material benefits was limited and popular support almost certainly plummeted. It is worth noting, moreover, that revolutionary leaders often built and sustained vast internal security apparatuses because they expected or feared large-scale popular opposition. Revolutionary governments that develop coercive apparatuses like those in the USSR, China, Vietnam, Cuba, and Iran were clearly unwilling to rely on popular support alone to retain power.

Finally, as scholars such as Theda Skocpol and Mark R. Beissinger have argued, revolutionary trajectories are affected by world historic time.[220]

Most of the social revolutions discussed in this book occurred during the Cold War. Marxist ideas, which dominated revolutionary politics in the twentieth century, provided activists with a lens through which to interpret the world, a blueprint for societal change, and the confidence that their efforts would succeed.[221] The Soviet Union became a model for revolutionary regimes and an important source of military and economic assistance.[222] The early successes of communist Russia, China, Vietnam, and Cuba inspired revolutionary leaders all over the world, and Soviet assistance—directly or through allies such as Cuba and Vietnam—contributed to the success of revolutionary movements in Cambodia, China, Guinea-Bissau, Angola, Mozambique, and Nicaragua. Finally, Cold War geopolitics often exacerbated and prolonged local conflicts, thereby enhancing the reactive sequence described in this book.[223]

There is some evidence, moreover, that the Soviet collapse and the end of the Cold War weakened the impetus for both social revolutionary change and counterrevolutionary reaction.[224] As foreign support for communist revolution dried up, many of the Marxist movements and leaders that emerged during the Cold War—including Yoweri Museveni in Uganda, Laurent Kabila in Zaire/Congo, SWAPO in Namibia, the Sudan People's Liberation Movement in South Sudan, and the Tigray People's Liberation Front (TPLF) in Ethiopia—abandoned efforts at radical social transformation when they came to power.[225] Even revolutionary regimes such as those in Rwanda and Eritrea exhibited lower levels of cohesion in the post–Cold War era.

The impact of the Cold War should not be exaggerated, however. Although assistance from Cold War allies contributed to revolutionary outcomes in some cases,[226] it cannot explain most twentieth-century social revolutions. In most cases, revolutions either occurred without substantial support from Cold War patrons (Albania, Algeria, Bolivia, Cuba, Iran) or took place before (Mexico, Russia) or after (Afghanistan, Eritrea, Rwanda) the Cold War. Importantly, moreover, external assistance at best only partially explains revolutionary regime durability. During the Cold War, China and Yugoslavia survived for many years without Soviet support, and tiny Albania persisted in the face of decades of Soviet and Yugoslav hostility and in the face of total international isolation after 1976. And while Cuba, Vietnam, Angola, and Mozambique all benefited from Soviet aid, each of these regimes persisted for more than three decades *after* Soviet support dried up. Furthermore, although the end of the Cold War may have reduced the cohesion of revolutionary Marxist regimes born after 1989, reactive sequences in Rwanda and Eritrea nevertheless still resulted in the construction of powerful autocratic states.

Finally, it is worth recalling that the Cold War was itself a product of revolution. The Cold War was grounded in intense ideological and geopolitical rivalry generated by the Russian Revolution, as well as the Soviet defeat of the Nazis, which was at least partly attributable to the revolutionary reactive sequence (see chapter 2).

Implications for the Study of Authoritarianism

Revolutionary regimes are rare, but their study nevertheless generates three important lessons for research on authoritarian durability. First, our analysis highlights the role of ideology in state- and regime-building. Most contemporary studies of authoritarianism treat autocrats as rational actors, narrowly defined in the sense that their behavior is driven by short-term power-maximizing goals.[227] Such assumptions are often useful in explaining the dynamics of authoritarian rule. However, the early behavior of revolutionary leaders—and, consequently, longer-term revolutionary regime trajectories—cannot be understood without reference to ideology. Although ideology may not provide a "blueprint" for revolutionary outcomes,[228] it nevertheless drives revolutionaries to undertake risky—even reckless—behavior that triggers the revolutionary reactive sequence described in this book. Because policies such as large-scale expropriation, introduction of Sharia law, or military assaults on powerful neighboring states seriously threaten revolutionaries' hold on power, they are difficult to understand in terms of the imperatives of political survival. Ideology thus helps explain why revolutionaries engage in the kind of risk-accepting behavior that contributes to long-run regime stability but puts their regimes—and themselves—at great risk in the short run.

Second, our study contributes to an emerging body of research on the nonmaterial bases of regime cohesion and durability.[229] In line with the work of Adrienne LeBas,[230] Dan Slater,[231] and others, we find that elite cohesion is often rooted in existential threats to group survival rather than institutions.[232] Although this book found some support for institutionalist explanations, the most important sources of elite cohesion were extra-institutional. Polarization, violent conflict, and existential military threats—conditions that were often generated by the revolutionary reactive sequence described in this book—can be a critical source of regime discipline.[233] In Russia, China, Vietnam, Cuba, Nicaragua, Iran, Mozambique, and elsewhere, fear of annihilation amid civil or external wars generated a powerful and often enduring incentive to close ranks. Existential military threat can create a siege mentality that discourages defection for decades. In such cases, leaders often remain in the fold even in the face of economic and other crises that have been shown to encourage schisms in nonrevolutionary regimes.[234] This book showed that where counterrevolutionary threats were limited, as in Algeria, Bolivia, and Guinea-Bissau, ruling parties often suffered debilitating schisms. And where existential threats faded over time, party institutions themselves often proved insufficient to prevent defection (e.g., Mexico, the USSR, and Yugoslavia in the late 1980s and early 1990s).

Existential threat is also an important source of elite cohesion in *nonrevolutionary* autocracies.[235] Slater, for example, has shown how radical insurgencies induced postcolonial elites in Malaysia, Singapore, and elsewhere to close ranks in counterrevolutionary "protection pacts" that served as the foundation for durable authoritarian rule. Such pacts, Slater argues, are most likely to emerge where "a wide range of elites perceive the danger to their property, privileges, and persons to be endemic and unmanageable."[236] In Malaysia and Singapore, as well as in comparable cases such as mid-twentieth-century Taiwan and Spain, counterrevolutionary elite cohesion laid a foundation for strikingly robust dictatorships.

Elite cohesion rooted in existential fear may also emerge in cases of ethnic conflict. Where minority ethnic groups control the state and ethnic elites perceive a loss of power to pose an existential threat, shared ethnicity can be a powerful source of regime cohesion. Such cohesion may explain the tenacity with which the Alawite-based government of Bashar al-Assad clung to power in Syria—despite a massive insurrection and near-total collapse of the state—in the early twenty-first century.[237] Another example is Togo, where a shared Kabye ethnicity—in a context of polarized conflict with the larger Ewe ethnic group—served as an important source of elite cohesion sustaining the long-lived Eyadéma regime. Fear of revenge for Gnassingbé Eyadéma's killing of Togo's first president, Sylvanus Olympio, an Ewe, fostered a sense of existential threat among the Kabye military leaders who sustained Eyadéma in power.[238] As a result, the government remained united in the face of large-scale opposition mobilization in the early 1990s, allowing the regime to engage in brutal acts of high-intensity repression.[239]

A third theoretical contribution lies in the realm of civil-military relations and the causes of military coups. Coups are a major cause of authoritarian breakdown.[240] Revolutionary regimes rarely suffer coups. A central characteristic of revolutionary regimes is that revolutionary elites build their own armies and internal security forces from scratch, staffing them with veterans from the liberation struggle and often penetrating them with partisan agents. As the chapters in this book showed, the fusion of revolutionary civilian and military elites helped ensure army loyalty under circumstances that are widely associated with military rebellion in other cases, such as periods of mass protest in which armies were called upon to engage in high-intensity coercion (e.g., Mexico in 1968, China in 1989, Iran in 2009); attacks on core military interests (e.g., Stalin's Great Terror, China's Cultural Revolution); severe economic crises that undermined army morale (e.g., Vietnam in the 1970s, Cuba in the 1990s); and major military defeats (e.g., the USSR in 1941). In both communist (China, the USSR, Vietnam, Cuba) and noncommunist (Mexico, Iran) states, revolutionary regimes survived for decades without suffering coups. By contrast, in Bolivia, which is the only one of our cases in which the revolutionary elite did not create a new army, the MNR fell prey to a coup after only twelve years.

The finding that militaries built from scratch are less prone to rebellion extends beyond revolutionary cases.[241] Take the case of Tanzania.[242] In power since independence in 1962, the Chama Cha Mapinduzi (CCM) (originally the Tanganyika African National Union [TANU]) regime is one of the world's longest-lived autocracies. The regime was not born of social revolution; TANU came to power via a peaceful decolonization process, not violent struggle. It did, however, build and tightly control its own army. While President Julius Nyerere initially left the colonial-era military intact, a 1964 mutiny enabled Nyerere to dissolve it and, in his words, "build an army almost from scratch."[243] In September 1964, the Nyerere government created the Tanzanian People's Defense Force (TPDF).[244] TANU controlled both recruitment into the army and officer promotions. The regime also established a system of political commissars,[245] and it operated a "pervasive network of informants in the military."[246]

Party-army fusion helps explain why, despite poor economic conditions, scarce resources, and low army morale, the TANU/CCM regime never suffered a successful coup. During the 1970s, the military was relatively quiescent in the face of the economic crisis generated by Nyerere's radical reforms. Although junior officers attempted a coup in 1983 amid a severe economic downturn, the plot was "easily put down" by army loyalists.[247] The TPDF has remained loyal to the regime ever since.

Where postcolonial elites did not create their own militaries and tie them to the new regime, regimes were more prone to coups. As chapter 5 showed, for example, Ghana's postcolonial regime collapsed in part because the Nkrumah government left the colonial-era military virtually intact. Military leaders had no stake in Nkrumah's survival and responded to the president's subsequent interference in military affairs by overthrowing him.

Finally, our research suggests that scholarship on authoritarian durability should take the state more seriously. Most of the world's robust authoritarian parties are embedded in strong states.[248] This outcome is by no means accidental. Authoritarian durability is enhanced where cohesive elites also possess the institutional capacity to repress opposition challenges and, crucially, inoculate themselves against coups. Autocrats are often said to face a trade-off between creating powerful coercive structures, which could potentially overthrow them, and coup-proofing, which often entails fragmenting the coercive apparatus and exposing the regime to threats from below.[249] Revolutionary regimes avoid this trade-off. Many of them build security forces that are powerful enough to suppress challenges from below but, because they are fused to the ruling party, lack the autonomy to carry out coups. This appears to be critical to long-term regime survival.

The Future of Social Revolution

Is the concept of social revolutions still relevant in the twenty-first century? With the demise of Marxism, one could plausibly conclude that social revolutions can be consigned to the history books.[250] The collapse of the Soviet Union—and with it, the disappearance of the Soviet model and Soviet bloc aid—brought the near extinction of Marxist revolutionary movements. Yet social revolution did not disappear. Indeed, the weakening of states across the global periphery in the wake of the Soviet collapse, as peripheral autocracies lost the patronage of rival superpowers, created more favorable conditions for revolution. Without superpower patronage, states in Afghanistan, Benin, Cambodia, Congo, Ethiopia, Haiti, Liberia, Madagascar, Rwanda, Sierra Leone, Somalia, and Yemen weakened or collapsed, giving rise to a mounting number of "failed states" and civil wars in parts of Asia and sub-Saharan Africa.[251] State collapse created a variety of new opportunities for revolutionary forces to seize power.

The breakdown of post–Cold War states created an opening for two types of revolutionary movements: the two "Marxist orphans," Eritrea and Rwanda, which were founded by guerrilla movements born during the Cold War, and radical Islamist movements such as the Taliban in Afghanistan and the Islamic State of Iraq and Syria (ISIS). Islamist movements arose primarily out of the anti-Soviet insurgency in Afghanistan in the 1980s. The insurgency produced tens of thousands of battle-hardened fighters inculcated with radical Islamic ideology in Saudi- and Pakistani-funded schools.[252] As we saw in chapter 7, these actors facilitated the rise of the Taliban amid state collapse in Afghanistan.[253]

Similarly, ISIS emerged in the wake of the U.S. invasion of Iraq, after American authorities dismantled the Iraqi military and systematically excluded former Ba'athists from power, creating a "black hole" of state authority characterized by lawlessness and widespread looting.[254] With assistance from former Ba'ath officials, Abu Musab al-Zarqawi, a Jordanian who had led a terrorist training camp in Afghanistan in the late 1990s, organized a series of suicide bombings aimed at foreign powers and Shiite authorities in Iraq.[255] In 2004, al-Zarqawi gained control of the Iraqi city of Ramadi and promptly banned female education and instituted a harsh moral code, outlawing smoking and Western-style fashion and haircuts.[256] ISIS expanded further in the wake of civil war in neighboring Syria.[257] In 2014, it seized the Syrian city of Raqqa and the Iraqi cities of Tikrit and Mosul, as well as gas and oil fields that generated about a billion dollars in annual revenue.[258] In June 2014, ISIS announced the creation of a caliphate claiming authority over all Muslims worldwide. It instituted harsh theocratic rule in the territories it controlled, as well as a genocide against the Yazidi minority.[259] It became internationally known for the release of graphic videos depicting the beheadings of American and other foreign captives. ISIS ultimately claimed control of a proto-state consisting of an "archipelago of provinces" in Syria and Iraq.[260]

The Taliban and ISIS cases offer two important lessons. First, Afghanistan and ISIS, together with the cases of Hungary and Cambodia (chapter 7), suggest that because revolutionary regimes are born weak, early and concerted international efforts to destroy them can be effective. Many twentieth-century revolutionary regimes survived long enough to consolidate because powerful states—due to military exhaustion after World War I, the struggle against fascism, or the geopolitical complexities of the Cold War—did not make a sustained, concerted effort to destroy them. By contrast, the military defeat of embryonic Islamist regimes in Afghanistan and Iraq was made possible by a broad-based international effort to defeat emergent revolutionary forces before they could build strong states and regimes.

As we argued in chapter 7, the Taliban's support for al-Qaeda generated widespread international outrage and led the United States to invade Afghanistan following the 9/11 attacks, which ended the regime in

December 2001. Likewise, ISIS's provocative attacks on American forces *and* the Russian-backed Assad government in Syria led to a serious and relatively united international response that destroyed the movement before it could consolidate state power. In mid-2014, a U.S.-led international force consisting of personnel from thirty countries carried out thousands of air attacks against ISIS. These actions were accompanied by Russian-led attacks on ISIS in Syria. In 2017, ISIS lost control over Mosul and Raqqa, and in March 2019, U.S. forces eliminated ISIS from its last territorial base in Baghuz, Syria.[261]

Second, the Taliban and ISIS cases demonstrate the persistent power of radical ideologies in the wake of Marxism's demise, especially in contexts of state collapse. Despite their military defeats, the Taliban and (to a lesser extent) ISIS continued to vie for power.[262] Indeed, the Taliban survived two decades of grinding war with the United States, using nationalism, religious ideology, and extensive support from Pakistan and Iran to build a fighting force capable of resisting the American-backed Afghan state.[263] When U.S. forces left Afghanistan in August 2021, the Taliban quickly recaptured power.

Thus, although the demise of Marxism will undoubtably change the character of future social revolutions, it does not mean the end of efforts to radically transform societies. In one form or another, radical ideologies will persist. As long as radical ideologies and weak states exist, so, too, will the possibility of social revolution. There will almost certainly be more revolutions in the twenty-first century. Whether they will give rise to durable autocracies remains to be seen.

Statistical Analysis of Revolutionary and Nonrevolutionary Regimes

TO TEST OUR HYPOTHESIS that social revolutions create durable regimes, we compare the survival of the eighteen revolutionary autocracies against that of all nonrevolutionary autocracies since 1900 (there are 355 authoritarian regimes in total).[1] We probe the robustness of the association between regime survival and revolutionary origins through a multivariate survival regression. We chose a semiparametric Cox model because it imposes minimal assumptions on the shape of the baseline hazards.

We estimate an equation of the form

$$h_i(t) = h_0(t)e^{\beta_1 R_i + \beta_2 X_i},$$

where the dependent variable $h_i(t)$ is the hazard for regime i at time t, R_i is a binary indicator that equals 1 if the regime was born of revolution, and 0 otherwise. X_i is a vector of economic, political, and demographic controls,

---

Excerpted from Jean Lachapelle, Steven Levitsky, Lucan Way, and Adam E. Casey, "Social Revolution and Authoritarian Durability," *World Politics* 72, no. 4 (2020).

1. Because our authoritarian regimes data set (in line with GWF and other data sets) excludes cases that collapsed before the end of the calendar year, we exclude Hungary and Finland from the analysis. Our main results hold when we include all twenty cases—including Finland and Hungary—that emerge out of social revolution. See figure AI.1, table AI.4, and figures AI.3, AI.4, and AI.5.The coding procedure is described in appendix II. Summary codings for every authoritarian regime since 1900 can be found in appendix III. Detailed coding justifications for each of these cases can be found at https://press.princeton .edu/books/revolution-and-dictatorship.

and $h_0(t)$ is a time-dependent baseline hazard shared by all regimes. We assess goodness of fit by performing likelihood ratio tests that compare the model including revolution to the nested model without revolution.

We control for several factors believed to predict authoritarian survival. The first is GDP per capita, which modernization theory posits as a source of democratization and thus authoritarian breakdown.[2] The second is GDP growth, which is said to enhance regime survival.[3] Moreover, revenue from oil and gas can lengthen authoritarian regimes' horizons by providing "free" resources for co-opting the opposition and funding security forces.[4] Finally, we control for total population to ensure that durability is not a function of the fact that many revolutionary regimes are large, regional powers (e.g., Russia, China). To ensure the exogeneity of our controls, we use the value of the covariate one year before the regime begins.[5]

We estimate regressions with and without stratifying the baseline hazards on previous authoritarian regime breakdowns within the same country. This method accounts for the possibility that previous breakdowns may influence future risks of breakdown.[6] Moreover, we estimate regressions with and without stratifying the baseline hazards by geographic region in order to account for the presence of region-specific time-invariant confounders.[7]

We also address the possibility that regime type might be driving the results (i.e., revolutions create party-based regimes, which scholars argue are very durable) by performing additional regressions that control for regime type (i.e., whether the regime is led by a party, the military, a monarch, or a personalist leader). Regime type is a posttreatment variable in these analyses (because revolutions produce strong parties), and therefore care should be taken in interpreting the results. These additional regressions do not estimate the causal effect of revolution on survival. Instead,

2. Lipset (1959).

3. See Haggard and Kaufman (1995: 267); Magaloni (2006: 44–64).

4. See Ross (2001); Geddes et al. (2014). Our measure of reliance on natural resources is log (per capita value of oil and gas production + 1) as provided by Ross and Mahdavi (2015). The data on per capita GDP (logged) and GDP growth are from the Maddison Project Database 2018, as provided by Coppedge et al. (2019). The data on population size are from the Correlates of War "National Material Capabilities" data set, version 5 (Singer 1988).

5. The results are the same when using country-year as the unit of observation and controlling for time-varying covariates (see tables AI.5 and AI.6).

6. Box-Steffensmeier et al. (2006).

7. The regions are defined by V-Dem's *e_regionpol* variable (Coppedge et al. 2019).

they estimate—under some strong ignorability assumptions[8]—the portion of the effect of revolution on durability that is not mediated by regime type, thus offering a stronger test of our theory that party institutions are an important yet insufficient explanation for the durability of authoritarian regimes. Party is a binary variable that takes the value 1 for all regimes that have a party component and 0 otherwise.[9] Military takes the value 1 if the regime type is a pure military and 0 otherwise. Monarchy takes the value 1 for monarchical regimes and 0 otherwise, and personalist takes the value 1 for all regimes that have a personalist component. Finally, we control for communism, which is another posttreatment variable. (Communism takes the value 1 if the regime was communist and 0 otherwise.) We add an indicator of foreign imposition of communism to account for the fact that several communist regimes were directly imposed by foreign powers and thus potentially bolstered by external intervention.[10] The *foreign installed communist* variable takes the value 1 if the communist regime was imposed by a foreign power and 0 otherwise. Table AI.1 shows the descriptive statistics for all variables.

Our data contain incomplete observations (see table AI.5). We deal with these by using multiple imputation.[11] We follow Lall and add level of democracy as measured by Polity IV[12] and the decade to the imputation model, as the rate of missingness is higher the more undemocratic a country is and the earlier the observation.[13] Twenty independent draws of the missing data were imputed using the Amelia II routine.[14] For each imputed data set, we used heteroscedasticity-consistent standard errors and we combined the results from the twenty analyses using Rubin's rules. Likelihood ratio tests were performed following Meng and Rubin.[15] To ensure the Cox model's proportionality assumption is met, we conducted diagnostic tests, which are available on request.

---

8. Acharya et al. (2016).

9. These include party-personalist (e.g., Cuba, 1959–), party-military (e.g., Burundi, 1966–1987), and party-personalist-military (e.g., Egypt, 1952–2011). The correlation between party and revolution is 0.345. See table AI.7.

10. While Czechoslovakia had a popular indigenous communist party, we code it as foreign imposed because communism was installed in a 1948 coup by security forces under the direct command of the Soviet Union.

11. Listwise deletion of incomplete observations yields similar results. See table AI.6.

12. Marshall et al. (2018).

13. Lall (2016).

14. King et al. (2001).

15. Meng and Rubin (1992).

Results

Column 1 in table AI.2 shows the baseline model controlling for revolution, GDP per capita, GDP per capita growth, and population size. Consistent with our hypothesis, the estimated coefficient for revolution is highly significant at the 0.001 level and large in absolute terms. Revolutionary origins are associated with a 72 percent reduction in the hazards (with a 95 percent confidence interval of 49–85 percent), which is indicated by the hazard ratio of $\exp(-1.282) = 0.28$. Moreover, the revolution variable significantly improves the model's fit, as shown by a likelihood ratio test that compares the models with and without revolution (shown in the bottom row). The test strongly rejects the null hypothesis of no improvement in the fit ($p < 0.001$).

Model 2 controls for oil and gas production. The coefficient estimate for oil has the expected sign (although it fails to achieve statistical significance). Including this control does not affect our results: the coefficient estimate for revolution remains negative and significant at 0.001. Model 3 stratifies the baseline hazards on geographic region to account for time-invariant region-specific confounders. When stratifying the hazard, the coefficient estimate for revolution becomes larger in absolute value (−1.671) and remains significant at 0.001. Model 4 stratifies the baseline hazards on the number of previous authoritarian breakdowns to account for the effect of a country's past history.[16] The coefficient estimate for revolution is −1.586 in model 4, which corresponds to a decrease of the hazard by 80 percent ($p < 0.001$).

Models 5 and 6 show that the association between revolutionary origins and durability is robust to conditioning on regime type. The coefficient estimate for revolution remains significant when conditioning on party, military, and personalistic or monarchical rule.[17] Revolutionary origins are associated with a 58 percent decrease in the hazards in model 5 (without stratification) and a 67 percent decrease in model 6 (with stratification on the number of previous breakdowns). Moreover, revolution explains variation in survival that is unaccounted for by regime type. Likelihood ratio tests that compare models with and without controlling for revolution reject the null hypothesis that conditioning on revolution does not

16. Box-Steffensmeier el al. (2006).

17. Party and monarchy are associated with a decrease of 64 percent and 81 percent, respectively, in the hazards (column 5). In contrast, military rule is associated with an increase in the hazards.

improve model fit (p=0.009 in model 5 and p=0.002 in model 6).[18] These results suggest that regime type, which has been the focus of an enormous amount of scholarly attention, provides an incomplete explanation for the survival of authoritarian regimes.

Models 7 and 8 show that the association between revolution and durability remains statistically significant when we condition on communism. Revolution is associated with a 62 percent decrease in the hazards in model 7 ($p<0.05$), and this association becomes stronger when accounting for foreign imposition of communism (model 8). Revolution is associated with a 70 percent decrease in the hazards when we also condition on the foreign imposition of communism.

Robustness

We conducted several robustness checks. First, we assessed the sensitivity of our results to different operationalizations of authoritarian regime spell. This addresses Lueders and Lust-Okar's concern that the findings in quantitative studies of authoritarian survival tend to be sensitive to the choice of regime data set.[19] To address this possibility, we replicated the analysis from table AI.2, model 2, using three alternative authoritarian data sets: the "Autocratic Breakdown and Regimes Transitions" data set by Geddes et al.,[20] the "Ruling Coalitions in Dictatorships, 1946–2008" data set by Svolik,[21] and the "Autocracies of the World 1950–2012" data set by Magaloni et al.[22] (we use table AI.2, model 2 as the benchmark throughout this section).

In addition, we replicated the analysis adding the two revolutionary governments that died in their infancy—Finland (1918) and Hungary (1919)—to our regimes data set. This expanded data set of 357 regimes omits the large numbers of nonrevolutionary authoritarian governments that lasted less than a year and thus offers a harder test of our hypothesis. Figure AI.1 plots the estimate for the effect of revolution along with 95 percent confidence intervals using the four alternative data sets. As

18. In additional analyses, we conducted a goodness of fit test that compares two nested models: one that controls for the GWF variables (party/personal/military/monarchy) and one that controls for both the GWF variables and revolution. An analysis of deviance test shows that the latter model (with revolution) fits the data significantly better than the former ($p<0.001$). In table AI.8, we show that results hold when bootstrapping the standard errors in Cox regressions and controlling for regime type and communism.

19. Lueders and Lust-Okar (2018).

20. Geddes et al. (2014).

21. Svolik (2012).

22. Magaloni et al. (2013).

[362] APPENDIX I

shown, the coefficient estimate remains negative and significant at 0.05 across all four analyses, indicating that the results are not sensitive to the choice of a regime data set.[23]

Second, given the small number of revolutionary regimes, one might worry that our results are driven by a few outlier cases that happen to be exceptionally durable for unexplained reasons. To address this possibility, we repeated the Cox regression analysis after discarding the six longest-lasting revolutionary regimes in our data set: Mexico (85 years), the USSR (74 years), China (> 66 years), Vietnam (> 61 years), Cuba (> 56 years), and Algeria (> 53 years). Discarding these observations should heavily bias the results against our hypothesis. Nevertheless, the estimated coefficient for revolution remains negative and significant at a 0.05 confidence level after removing these six regimes in the benchmark model. These results suggest that the findings are not driven by a few exceptional cases (see table AI.3).[24]

Third, to address potential issues arising from the fact that the number of revolutionary cases is small, we employ two data preprocessing methods in order to reduce model dependency.[25] The first one consists of reweighing observations in the control group using the covariate balancing propensity score (CBPS)[26] and estimating the average treatment effect on the treated (ATT). The second approach consists of applying exact matching on the coarsened data[27] and estimating a feasible sample average treatment effect on the treated (FSATT).[28] Because the two methods rely on different assumptions, employing both should increase confidence in the validity of the results.

For data preprocessing, we choose conditioning variables based on existing scholarship on revolutions. Scholars have argued that economic breakdown and war increase the risks of revolutions. We therefore consider GDP per capita, GDP growth, and militarized interstate conflict.[29] We also

23. In figures AI.3, AI.4, and AI.5, we also show that our findings are not sensitive to alternative codings of borderline cases such as South Yemen, North Korea, Zimbabwe, and Algeria, in addition to Hungary and Finland.

24. When conditioning on regime type, the results remain significant at $p < 0.05$ after removing the two longest-lasting regimes. In table AI.9, we show that the results are robust ($p < 0.05$) to stratifying the baseline hazards by country when using the specifications from models 1 and 2.

25. Ho et al. (2007).

26. Imai and Ratkovic (2014).

27. Iacus et al. (2012).

28. King et al. (2017).

29. Chorley ([1943] 1973); Gurr (1970); Skocpol (1979). The data on interstate war are

include the type of the previous regime (democracy, party, personalist, military, or monarchy) to account for the fact that personalistic rule might promote revolutions because the narrow support bases of such regimes and their repressive behaviors encourage unified opposition among a diverse range of interests and groups.[30] We used the Amelia routine to deal with missing observations (twenty imputations). For each imputed data set, we use heteroscedasticity-consistent standard errors[31] and compute final estimates using Rubin's rule.

Figure AI.2 presents measures of covariate balance between revolutionary and nonrevolutionary regimes. It shows, across all imputed data sets, the standardized mean differences before and after CBPS reweighting. Consistent with existing literature, places that are experiencing economic crisis, low development, war, and authoritarianism are at a higher risk of revolution, as shown by the relatively large absolute mean differences (> 0.1) for these variables. Reweighting observations using the CBPS greatly improves covariate balance (the absolute mean difference is below 0.1 for all variables across all imputation), indicating that the reweighting procedure was successful. Using these weights in a weighted Cox regression, we find that the average effect of revolution in the treated group is -1.286 ($p < 0.001$), which corresponds to a 72 percent decrease in the hazards.

Next, we employed coarsened exact matching.[32] We coarsened the covariates and removed units that could not be matched exactly on the coarsened scale in order to further reduce model dependency.[33] This procedure generated a new data set with seventy observations: twelve revolutionary and fifty-eight nonrevolutionary cases.[34] We estimate the feasible sample average treatment effect on the treated (FSATT) of revolution using weighted Cox regression.[35] The estimate for the average effect of revolution (within the sample of twelve revolutionary cases that could be matched to control observations) that we obtained from this procedure is -1.199 with $p < 0.001$.

from the Correlates of War "Inter-State War" data set, version 4.0 (Sarkees and Wayman 2010). We use the value of the covariates one year before the beginning of the regime.

30. See Goodwin (2001).

31. Morgan and Winship (2015: 242–243).

32. Iacus et al. (2012).

33. We also match on missing values.

34. The revolutionary cases are Albania 1944–1991, Algeria 1962–, Angola 1975–, Bolivia 1952–1964, China 1949–, Eritrea 1993–, Guinea-Bissau 1974–1999, Mexico 1915–2000, the USSR 1917–1991, Rwanda 1994–, Vietnam 1954–, and Yugoslavia 1945–1990.

35. King et al. (2017).

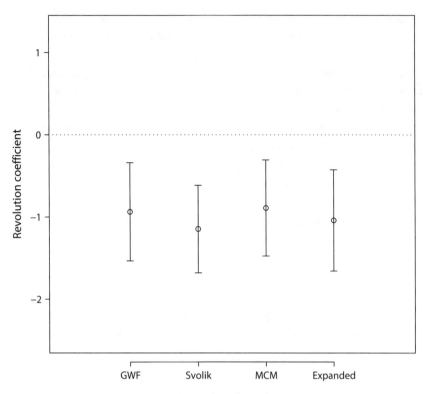

FIGURE AI.1: Cox Regressions Using Alternative Regime Data Sets.
Notes: The plot shows coefficient estimates and 95 percent intervals from Cox survival regressions using four alternative data sets of regime change: the "Autocratic Breakdown and Regimes Transitions" data set by Geddes et al. (2014) (GWF); the "Ruling Coalitions in Dictatorships, 1946–2008" data set by Svolik (2012); the "Autocracies of the World 1950–2012" data set by Magaloni et al. (2013) (MCM); and an expanded data set that includes Finland (1918) and Hungary (1919).

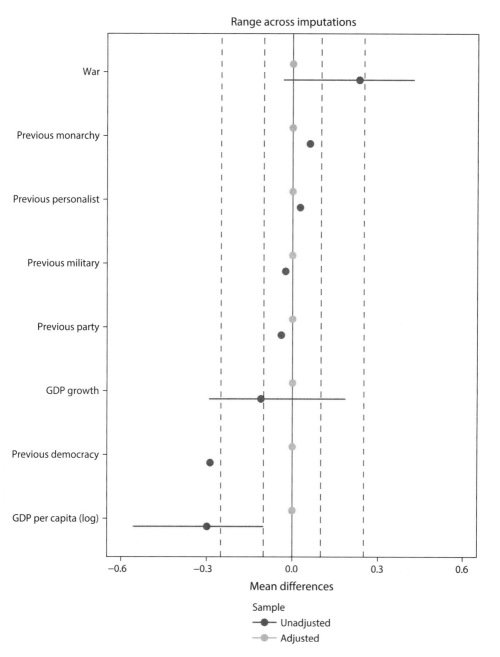

FIGURE AI.2: Covariate Balance before and after Adjustment.

NOTE TO FIGURES AI.3–AI.5: Sensitivity to alternative codings.

We redid the analysis after changing the codings for plausibly liminal cases. We generated thirty-one alternative data sets that correspond to all combinations of the following recodings: treating South Yemen (1967–1990) as revolutionary; treating Rwanda (1994–) as non-revolutionary; treating North Korea (1948–) as revolutionary; treating Zimbabwe (1980–) as revolutionary; treating the coup of 1992 as regime breakdown in Algeria; including revolutionary Finland and Hungary in the regime data set. Figures A.3, A.4, and A.5 show revolution coefficient estimates along with 90 percent (thick line) and 95 percent (narrow line) intervals from Cox regressions that use these thirty-one alternative data sets. Figure A.3 uses the benchmark model specification (table A.3, model 2); figure A.4 controls for regime type (table A.3, model 6); and figure A.5 controls for regime type and communism (table A.3, model 8). NK = North Korea, SY = South Yemen, RW = Rwanda, ZM = Zimbabwe, and HU/FI = Hungary and Finland. Thus the label NK + SY + RW indicates that North Korea, South Yemen, and Rwanda were recoded.

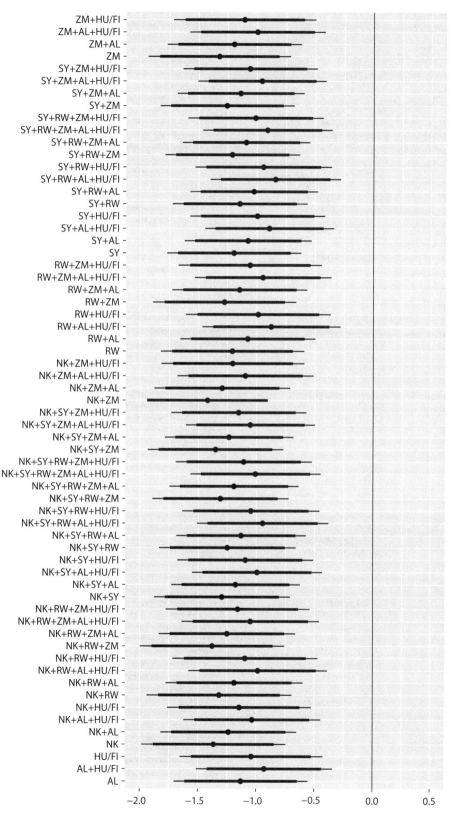

FIGURE AI.3: Cox Models, Alternative Codings, Benchmark Model Specification.

FIGURE AI.4: Cox Models, Alternative Codings, Controlling for Regime Type (Posttreatment).

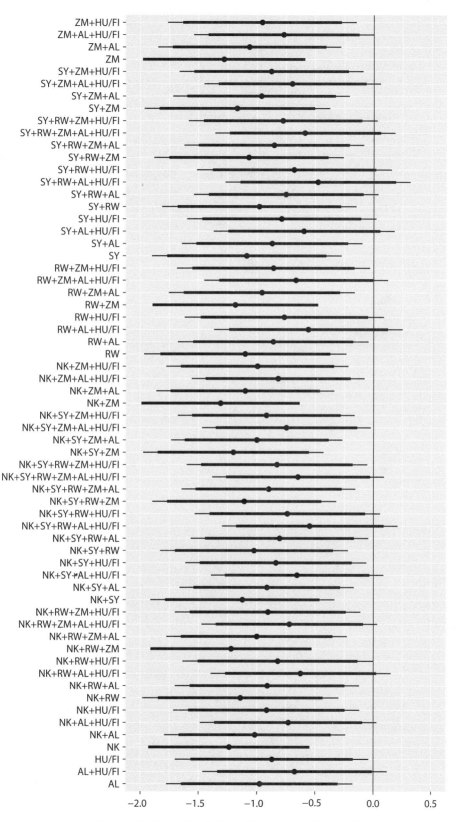

FIGURE AI.5: Cox Models, Alternative Codings, Controlling for Regime Type and Communism (posttreatment).

Table AI.1 Descriptive Statistics, 1900–2015

Statistic	N	Mean	St. Dev.	Min.	Pctl.(25)	Pctl.(75)	Max.
Revolution	355	0.05	0.22	0	0	0	1
Per capita GDP (log)	281	7.64	0.77	4.90	7.10	8.00	10.28
GDP growth (percent)	268	0.01	0.08	−0.31	−0.02	0.04	0.43
Population (log)	279	8.79	1.36	6.11	7.85	9.60	13.24
Oil and gas products per capita (log)	224	1.82	2.44	0.00	0.00	3.33	10.43
Party	355	0.25	0.43	0	0	0.5	1
Personalist	355	0.50	0.50	0	0	1	1
Military	355	0.19	0.40	0	0	0	1
Monarchy	355	0.06	0.23	0	0	0	1
Communist	355	0.07	0.26	0	0	0	1
Foreign-installed communist	355	0.03	0.17	0	0	0	1

Table AI.2 Cox Regressions of Authoritarian Regime Breakdown

	Nonstratified		Stratified		Controlling for regime type (posttreatment)		Controlling for communism (posttreatment)	
	(1)	(2)	(3)	(4)	(5)	(6)	(7)	(8)
Revolution	−1.282***	−1.260***	−1.671***	−1.586***	−0.878**	−1.103***	−0.955**	−1.204***
	(0.308)	(0.312)	(0.406)	(0.357)	(0.358)	(0.395)	(0.406)	(0.432)
Per capita GDP (log)	−0.079	0.001	−0.025	0.017	−0.125	−0.095	−0.104	−0.100
	(0.082)	(0.098)	(0.104)	(0.101)	(0.102)	(0.106)	(0.108)	(0.109)
GDP growth (%)	0.107	0.117	0.125	0.397	−0.074	−0.102	−0.021	0.018
	(0.771)	(0.775)	(0.839)	(0.844)	(0.786)	(0.853)	(0.844)	(0.852)
Population (log)	−0.045	−0.025	0.044	−0.009	−0.077	−0.055	−0.051	−0.052
	(0.062)	(0.065)	(0.065)	(0.060)	(0.061)	(0.060)	(0.062)	(0.062)
Oil and gas products per capita (log)		−0.048	−0.030	−0.061*	−0.001	−0.012	−0.014	−0.013
		(0.031)	(0.034)	(0.032)	(0.035)	(0.036)	(0.037)	(0.037)
Party					−1.018***	−0.989***	−0.872***	−0.821***
					(0.222)	(0.239)	(0.240)	(0.240)
Personalist					−0.195	−0.192	−0.198	−0.214
					(0.225)	(0.228)	(0.225)	(0.225)
Military					0.734***	0.660**	0.633**	0.631**
					(0.261)	(0.269)	(0.269)	(0.268)
Monarchy					−1.661***	−1.486***	−1.508***	−1.511***
					(0.404)	(0.399)	(0.404)	(0.405)
Communist							−0.607***	−0.207
							(0.205)	(0.240)
Foreign-installed communist								−0.851**
								(0.347)

(Continued)

Table A1.2 (*continued*)

	Nonstratified		Stratified		Controlling for regime type (posttreatment)		Controlling for communism (posttreatment)	
	(1)	(2)	(3)	(4)	(5)	(6)	(7)	(8)
Stratified by event number	*No*	*No*	*No*	*Yes*	*No*	*Yes*	*Yes*	*Yes*
N observations	355	355	355	355	355	355	355	355
N breakdowns	300	300	300	300	300	300	300	300
Multiple imputation	*Yes*	*Yes*	*Yes*	*Yes*	*Yes*	*Yes*	*Yes*	*Yes*
p-value of significance test:	0.000	0.000	0.000	0.000	0.009	0.002	0.010	0.003

* $p < 0.1$; ** $p < 0.05$; *** $p < 0.01$.

Notes: The unit of analysis is an authoritarian regime. Control variables are measured one year before the beginning of the regime. Models 3 and 4 stratify the baseline hazards by geographic region and the number of previous regime failures, respectively. The bottom row shows *p*-values of likelihood ratio tests under the null hypothesis that controlling for revolution does not improve the fit relative to the same model without controlling for revolution. Missing values were imputed using the Amelia routine (twenty imputations). We used heteroscedasticity-consistent standard errors for each analysis and combined the results using Rubin's rules. Likelihood ratio tests were performed following Meng and Rubin (1992).

Table AI.3 Robustness Tests, Cox Regressions after Discarding Longest-Surviving Revolutionary Regimes

a) Without regime-type controls

	N − 1 (1)	N − 2 (2)	N − 3 (3)	N − 4 (4)	N − 5 (5)	N − 6 (6)
Revolution	−1.254***	−1.283***	−1.180***	−1.043***	−0.885***	−0.762***
	(0.344)	(0.378)	(0.366)	(0.353)	(0.334)	(0.318)
Per capita GDP (log)	−0.001	−0.0003	−0.004	−0.006	0.003	0.001
	(0.097)	(0.096)	(0.096)	(0.096)	(0.097)	(0.096)
GDP growth (%)	0.124	0.135	0.153	0.179	0.181	0.203
	(0.770)	(0.770)	(0.765)	(0.763)	(0.759)	(0.753)
Population (log)	−0.026	−0.027	−0.021	−0.020	−0.021	−0.021
	(0.064)	(0.064)	(0.065)	(0.064)	(0.064)	(0.065)
Oil and gas products per capita (log)	−0.047	−0.047	−0.048	−0.049	−0.052*	−0.051
	(0.031)	(0.030)	(0.031)	(0.031)	(0.031)	(0.031)
Stratified by geographic region	*No*	*No*	*No*	*No*	*No*	*No*
Stratified by event number	*No*	*No*	*No*	*No*	*No*	*No*
N observations	354	353	352	351	350	349
N breakdowns	299	298	298	298	298	298
Multiple imputation	*Yes*	*Yes*	*Yes*	*Yes*	*Yes*	*Yes*
p-value of significance test:	0.000	0.000	0.000	0.001	0.007	0.026

b) With regime-type controls

	N − 1 (1)	N − 2 (2)	N − 3 (3)	N − 4 (4)	N − 5 (5)	N − 6 (6)
Revolution	−0.835**	−0.865**	−0.768*	−0.619	−0.482	−0.345
	(0.387)	(0.421)	(0.414)	(0.405)	(0.411)	(0.399)
Per capita GDP (log)	−0.127	−0.126	−0.130	−0.133	−0.122	−0.126
	(0.102)	(0.102)	(0.102)	(0.103)	(0.104)	(0.103)
GDP growth (%)	−0.070	−0.061	−0.032	0.009	0.025	0.061
	(0.783)	(0.785)	(0.784)	(0.783)	(0.778)	(0.776)
Population (log)	−0.079	−0.078	−0.072	−0.072	−0.073	−0.073
	(0.061)	(0.060)	(0.061)	(0.061)	(0.061)	(0.061)
Oil and gas products per capita (log)	−0.0004	−0.001	−0.002	−0.004	−0.008	−0.006
	(0.035)	(0.035)	(0.035)	(0.035)	(0.036)	(0.036)
Party	−1.015***	−1.031***	−1.032***	−1.031***	−1.007***	−1.005***
	(0.223)	(0.222)	(0.223)	(0.223)	(0.225)	(0.225)
Military	0.740***	0.723***	0.720***	0.722***	0.754***	0.756***
	(0.262)	(0.260)	(0.260)	(0.261)	(0.264)	(0.264)
Monarchy	−1.607***	−1.606***	−1.606***	−1.608***	−1.576***	−1.580***
	(0.397)	(0.388)	(0.389)	(0.390)	(0.393)	(0.393)

(*Continued*)

Table AI.3 (*continued*)

b) With regime-type controls

	N−1 (1)	N−2 (2)	N−3 (3)	N−4 (4)	N−5 (5)	N−6 (6)
Personalist	−0.191	−0.206	−0.207	−0.206	−0.168	−0.168
	(0.226)	(0.224)	(0.224)	(0.224)	(0.230)	(0.230)
Stratified by geographic region	No	No	No	No	No	No
Stratified by event number	No	No	No	No	No	No
N observations	354	353	352	351	350	349
N breakdowns	299	298	298	298	298	298
Multiple imputation	Yes	Yes	Yes	Yes	Yes	Yes
p-value of significance test:	0.017	0.016	0.033	0.094	0.209	0.382

* $p<0.1$; ** $p<0.05$; *** $p<0.01$.

Notes: An observation is an authoritarian regime. All variables except revolution are measured one year before regime onset. Model 1 shows results after discarding Mexico (1915–2000). Model 2 shows results after discarding Mexico and the USSR (1917–1991). Model 3 shows results after discarding Mexico, the USSR, and China (1949–). Model 4 shows results after discarding Mexico, the USSR, China, and Vietnam (1954–). Model 5 shows results after discarding Mexico, the USSR, China, Vietnam, and Cuba (1959–). Model 6 shows results after discarding Mexico, the USSR, China, Vietnam, Cuba, and Algeria (1962–). Results are shown without (*top*) and with (*bottom*) controls for regime type. Missing values were imputed using the Amelia routine (twenty imputations). We used heteroscedasticity-consistent standard errors for each analysis and combined the results using Rubin's rules.

Table AI.4 Robustness Tests, Cox Regressions after Including Finland (1918) and Hungary (1919)

	Nonstratified		Stratified		Controlling for regime type (posttreatment)		Controlling for communism (posttreatment)	
	(1)	(2)	(3)	(4)	(5)	(6)	(7)	(8)
Revolution	-1.064***	-1.041***	-1.387***	-1.290***	-0.657*	-0.798**	-0.666*	-0.870**
	(0.309)	(0.314)	(0.387)	(0.346)	(0.357)	(0.381)	(0.384)	(0.423)
Per capita GDP (log)	-0.076	0.008	-0.024	0.025	-0.115	-0.083	-0.091	-0.088
	(0.081)	(0.097)	(0.103)	(0.100)	(0.102)	(0.105)	(0.106)	(0.107)
GDP growth (%)	0.056	0.066	0.092	0.387	-0.116	-0.078	-0.019	0.014
	(0.759)	(0.764)	(0.826)	(0.825)	(0.778)	(0.835)	(0.826)	(0.833)
Population (log)	-0.052	-0.031	0.034	-0.016	-0.083	-0.061	-0.056	-0.057
	(0.062)	(0.065)	(0.065)	(0.060)	(0.061)	(0.060)	(0.061)	(0.061)
Oil and gas products per capita (log)		-0.050	-0.033	-0.062*	-0.005	-0.016	-0.019	-0.018
		(0.031)	(0.034)	(0.032)	(0.036)	(0.036)	(0.036)	(0.036)
Party					-1.000***	-0.973***	-0.875***	-0.828***
					(0.219)	(0.234)	(0.235)	(0.236)
Personalist					-0.190	-0.204	-0.208	-0.223
					(0.221)	(0.222)	(0.219)	(0.219)
Military					0.731***	0.644**	0.626**	0.625**
					(0.256)	(0.262)	(0.263)	(0.262)
Monarchy					-1.633***	-1.470***	-1.489***	-1.491***
					(0.398)	(0.393)	(0.397)	(0.398)
Foreign-installed communist								-0.741*
								(0.429)
Communist							-0.499**	-0.163
							(0.204)	(0.244)

(*Continued*)

Table AI.4 (*continued*)

	Nonstratified		Stratified		Controlling for regime type (posttreatment)		Controlling for communism (posttreatment)	
	(1)	(2)	(3)	(4)	(5)	(6)	(7)	(8)
Stratified by geographic region	*No*	*No*	*Yes*	*No*	*No*	*No*	*No*	*No*
Stratified by event number	*No*	*No*	*No*	*Yes*	*No*	*Yes*	*Yes*	*Yes*
N observations	357	357	357	357	357	357	357	357
N breakdowns	302	302	302	302	302	302	302	302
Multiple imputation	*Yes*	*Yes*	*Yes*	*Yes*	*Yes*	*Yes*	*Yes*	*Yes*
p-value of significance test:	0.000	0.000	0.000	0.000	0.040	0.018	0.057	0.021

* $p < 0.1$; ** $p < 0.05$; *** $p < 0.01$.

Notes: An observation is an authoritarian regime. Control variables are measured one year before the beginning of the regime. The analysis includes Finland (1918) and Hungary (1919). These cases do not enter the data set of authoritarian regimes because these governments were not in power on January 1. Missing values were imputed using the Amelia routine (twenty imputations). We used heteroscedasticity-consistent standard errors for each analysis and combined the results using Rubin's rules.

Table AI.5 Cox Regressions with Time-Varying Covariates, Multiple Imputation

	Nonstratified		Stratified		Controlling for regime type (posttreatment)		Controlling for communism (posttreatment)	
	(1)	(2)	(3)	(4)	(5)	(6)	(7)	(8)
Revolution	-1.399***	-1.355***	-1.715***	-1.651***	-0.932***	-1.165***	-1.017**	-1.255***
	(0.334)	(0.334)	(0.392)	(0.380)	(0.357)	(0.407)	(0.404)	(0.438)
Per capita GDP (log)	-0.119	-0.027	-0.053	-0.004	-0.125	-0.090	-0.103	-0.096
	(0.077)	(0.098)	(0.100)	(0.106)	(0.102)	(0.109)	(0.110)	(0.111)
GDP growth (%)	-2.029***	-2.070***	-1.874**	-2.387***	-2.176***	-2.541***	-2.548***	-2.540***
	(0.738)	(0.759)	(0.902)	(0.832)	(0.795)	(0.881)	(0.877)	(0.879)
Population (log)	0.019	0.039	0.110**	0.031	-0.054	-0.036	-0.033	-0.034
	(0.043)	(0.045)	(0.048)	(0.049)	(0.050)	(0.052)	(0.052)	(0.052)
Oil and gas products per capita (log)	-0.051*	-0.051*	-0.026	-0.064**	-0.014	-0.025	-0.026	-0.027
	(0.028)	(0.028)	(0.029)	(0.029)	(0.031)	(0.032)	(0.032)	(0.031)
Party					-0.990***	-0.949***	-0.826***	-0.774***
					(0.194)	(0.202)	(0.209)	(0.210)
Personalist					-0.184	-0.192	-0.198	-0.208
					(0.205)	(0.213)	(0.210)	(0.211)
Military					0.794***	0.710***	0.689***	0.693***
					(0.232)	(0.239)	(0.239)	(0.240)
Monarchy					-1.617***	-1.444***	-1.470***	-1.470***
					(0.357)	(0.349)	(0.347)	(0.348)
Foreign-installed communist								-0.846*
								(0.508)
Communist							-0.629**	-0.230
							(0.268)	(0.343)

Table AI.5 (*continued*)

	Nonstratified		Stratified		Controlling for regime type (posttreatment)		Controlling for communism (posttreatment)	
	(1)	(2)	(3)	(4)	(5)	(6)	(7)	(8)
Stratified by geographic region	*No*	*No*	*Yes*	*No*	*No*	*No*	*No*	*No*
Stratified by event number	*No*	*No*	*No*	*Yes*	*No*	*Yes*	*Yes*	*Yes*
N observations	5,723	5,723	5,723	5,723	5,723	5,723	5,723	5,723
N breakdowns	300	300	300	300	300	300	300	300
Multiple imputation	*Yes*	*Yes*	*Yes*	*Yes*	*Yes*	*Yes*	*Yes*	*Yes*
p-value of significance test:	0.000	0.000	0.000	0.000	0.006	0.002	0.008	0.003

* $p < 0.1$; ** $p < 0.05$; *** $p < 0.01$.

Notes: An observation is an authoritarian regime. Missing values were imputed using the Amelia routine (twenty imputations). We used heteroscedasticity-consistent standard errors for each analysis and combined the results using Rubin's rules. Likelihood ratio tests were performed following Meng and Rubin (1992).

Table AI.6 Cox Regressions with Time-Varying Covariates, Listwise Deletion

	Nonstratified		Stratified		Controlling for regime type (posttreatment)		Controlling for communism (posttreatment)	
	(1)	(2)	(3)	(4)	(5)	(6)	(7)	(8)
Revolution	−1.224***	−1.226***	−1.468***	−1.464***	−1.035**	−1.164***	−1.006**	−1.233***
	(0.334)	(0.340)	(0.394)	(0.386)	(0.418)	(0.420)	(0.423)	(0.463)
Per capita GDP (log)	−0.099	−0.120	−0.245**	−0.087	−0.289**	−0.205*	−0.214*	−0.207*
	(0.079)	(0.113)	(0.119)	(0.122)	(0.122)	(0.123)	(0.124)	(0.124)
GDP growth (%)	−1.882***	−1.483*	−1.037	−1.852**	−1.097	−2.126**	−2.158**	−2.145**
	(0.721)	(0.772)	(0.899)	(0.840)	(0.962)	(0.920)	(0.919)	(0.923)
Population (log)	0.016	0.072	0.104*	0.060	−0.011	−0.007	−0.004	−0.005
	(0.047)	(0.054)	(0.057)	(0.059)	(0.064)	(0.061)	(0.062)	(0.061)
Oil and gas products per capita (log)		−0.020	0.005	−0.037	0.004	−0.003	−0.005	−0.006
		(0.032)	(0.033)	(0.034)	(0.036)	(0.035)	(0.035)	(0.035)
Party					−0.906***	−0.821***	−0.683**	−0.646**
					(0.265)	(0.269)	(0.282)	(0.283)
Personalist					−0.353	−0.337	−0.321	−0.338
					(0.274)	(0.292)	(0.292)	(0.295)
Military					0.554*	0.658**	0.653**	0.647**
					(0.316)	(0.322)	(0.326)	(0.328)
Monarchy					−1.158**	−1.012**	−1.001**	−1.010**
					(0.559)	(0.424)	(0.421)	(0.421)
Communist							−0.610**	−0.222
							(0.307)	(0.399)
Foreign-installed communist								−0.781
								(0.558)

(*Continued*)

Table AI.6 (*continued*)

	Nonstratified		Stratified		Controlling for regime type (posttreatment)		Controlling for communism (posttreatment)	
	(1)	(2)	(3)	(4)	(5)	(6)	(7)	(8)
Stratified by geographic region	*No*	*No*	*Yes*	*No*	*No*	*No*	*No*	*No*
Stratified by event number	*No*	*No*	*No*	*Yes*	*Yes*	*Yes*	*Yes*	*Yes*
N observations	4,806	4,182	4,182	4,182	4,182	4,182	4,182	4,182
N breakdowns	257	220	220	220	220	220	220	220
Multiple imputation	*No*	*No*	*No*	*No*	*No*	*No*	*No*	*No*
p-value of significance test:	0.00	0.00	0.00	0.00	0.01	0.00	0.00	0.00

* $p < 0.1$; ** $p < 0.05$; *** $p < 0.01$.

Notes: An observation is a country-year. All variables are lagged one year. We used Listwise deletion to deal with missing observations.

Table AI.7 Correlation Table

	Rev.	GDP	Growth	Pop.	Oil/Gas	Party	Pers.	Mil.	Mon.	Communist	Foreign-installed communist
Rev.	1	-0.014	-0.059	-0.012	0.005	0.345	-0.155	-0.123	-0.021	0.218	-0.026
GDP	-0.014	1	0.176	0.251	0.599	-0.172	0.012	0.115	-0.094	-0.144	-0.162
Growth	-0.059	0.176	1	0.057	0.185	-0.055	-0.131	0.159	-0.023	-0.133	-0.061
Pop.	-0.012	0.251	0.057	1	0.399	-0.060	0.027	0.066	0.089	-0.046	-0.022
Oil/Gas	0.005	0.599	0.185	0.399	1	-0.076	0.106	-0.034	0.017	-0.072	-0.036
Party	0.345	-0.172	-0.055	-0.060	-0.076	1	-0.228	-0.295	-0.050	0.346	0.270
Pers.	-0.155	0.012	-0.131	0.027	0.106	-0.228	1	-0.661	-0.112	0.010	-0.051
Mil.	-0.123	0.115	0.159	0.066	-0.034	-0.295	-0.661	1	-0.065	-0.140	-0.080
Mon.	-0.021	-0.094	-0.023	0.089	0.017	-0.050	-0.112	-0.065	1	-0.024	-0.013
Communist	0.218	-0.144	-0.133	-0.046	-0.072	0.346	0.010	-0.140	-0.024	1	0.568
Foreign-installed communist	-0.026	-0.162	-0.061	-0.022	-0.036	0.270	-0.051	-0.080	-0.013	0.568	1

Notes: An observation is an authoritarian regime. *Rev.* denotes a revolutionary regime. *GDP* denotes per capita GDP (logged) (source: Maddison Project Database 2018, as provided by Coppedge et al. 2019), *Growth* denotes GDP growth. *Pop.* denotes logged size of the population (source: Correlates of War "National Material Capabilities" data set, version 5 [Singer 1988]). *Oil/Gas* denotes the log of per capita value of oil and gas production +1 (Ross and Mahdavi 2015). *Party* is a binary indicator of whether the regime has a party element. *Pers.* is a binary indicator of whether the regime has a personalistic element. *Mil.* is a binary indicator of whether the regime is a pure military regime. *Mon.* is a binary indicator of whether the regime is a monarchy. *Communist* is a binary indicator of communist regime from Svolik (2012). *Foreign-installed communist* denotes communist regimes installed by a foreign power.

Table AI.8 Cox Regressions with Bootstrapped Standard Errors

	(1)	(2)	(3)
Revolution	−0.998**	−0.849*	−1.062**
	(0.458)	(0.468)	(0.497)
Party	−1.012***	−0.903***	−0.874***
	(0.244)	(0.246)	(0.247)
Personalist	−0.209	−0.213	−0.228
	(0.238)	(0.240)	(0.242)
Military	0.655**	0.646**	0.640**
	(0.278)	(0.281)	(0.281)
Monarchy	−1.684**	−1.703***	−1.721***
	(0.446)	(0.455)	(0.459)
Communist		−0.533**	−0.174
		(0.213)	(0.285)
Foreign-installed communist			−0.700
			(0.538)
N observations	355	355	355
N breakdowns	300	300	300
Stratified by geographic region	*No*	*No*	*No*
Stratified by event number	*No*	*No*	*No*
p-value of significance test:	0.002	0.011	0.017

* $p < 0.1$; ** $p < 0.05$; *** $p < 0.01$.

Notes: An observation is an authoritarian regime. Standard errors were computed with the bootstrap (100,000 replicates).

Table AI.9 Robustness, Stratified Cox Regressions by Country

	(1)	(2)
Revolution	−1.539**	−1.538**
	(0.635)	(0.636)
Per capita GDP (log)	−0.017	−0.024
	(0.159)	(0.182)
GDP growth (%)	0.080	0.066
	(1.176)	(1.185)
Population (log)	0.074	0.074
	(0.097)	(0.100)
Oil and gas products per capita (log)		0.005
		(0.050)
Stratified by geographic region	*No*	*No*
Stratified by event number	*No*	*No*
N observations	355	355
N breakdowns	300	300
Multiple imputation	*Yes*	*Yes*
p-value of significance test:	0.004	0.004

* $p < 0.1$; ** $p < 0.05$; *** $p < 0.01$.

Notes: Baseline hazards are stratified by country. An observation is an authoritarian regime. Control variables are measured one year before the beginning of the regime. Missing values were imputed using the Amelia routine (twenty imputations). We used heteroscedasticity-consistent standard errors for each analysis and combined the results using Rubin's rules.

Operationalization of Major Variables

Revolutionary Autocracies

Revolutionary autocracies are political regimes that emerge out of social revolutions.[1] We define a social revolution as the violent overthrow of an existing regime from below, accompanied by mass mobilization and state collapse, which triggers a rapid transformation of the state and the existing social order.

1. *Violent, Irregular Seizure of Power*: Transfer of power that occurs outside of existing regime institutions and is accompanied by violence. This includes negotiated transitions that follow successful armed struggle.

2. *Regime Ruled by a Mass-Based Movement That Emerges outside the State*: This includes

- Guerrilla movements
- Political parties or movements that mobilize mass constituencies

It excludes

- All military factions
- Any government led by individuals or groups that held a high position in the old regime

3. *State Transformation*: Collapse of the preexisting coercive apparatus and creation of new armed forces.

1. For a detailed description of our coding of all 357 autocracies after 1900, see the codebook available at https://press.princeton.edu/books/revolution-and-dictatorship.

a. Armed forces are dissolved or incapacitated. The military is considered incapacitated when disruption of the chain of command, large-scale mutiny, and/or widespread rank-and-file desertion prevent it from operating as a coherent body.

b. Creation of new security forces that play a primary role in external defense and internal security or a far-reaching reconstruction of the existing security apparatus.

Examples:

- Large-scale purge of the prerevolutionary military command and replacement with revolutionary veterans
- Creation of new security forces that dominate preexisting armed forces

4. *Attempted Transformation of the Existing Social and/or Geopolitical Order*: By the end of the first year in power, top government officials embark on a radical transformation of the existing social and/or geopolitical order that seriously threatens the interests of other states or way of life of powerful domestic actors (e.g., landowners) or large groups in society (e.g., peasants, women).

Examples:

- Transformation of property rights: large-scale expropriation and redistribution of property (e.g., land reform)
- Transformation of the existing racial/ethnic order
- Radical cultural transformation, including efforts to weaken or destroy dominant religious institutions or impose radical change in laws governing social behavior (e.g., introduction of Sharia law)
- Serious challenge to the regional and/or geopolitical order

  - Support for efforts to overthrow foreign governments
  - Behavior that seriously threatens the economic or security interests of regional or global powers

Revolutionary Paths

RADICAL REVOLUTIONARY PATH

A case is scored as following a radical path when the revolutionary government initiates radical measures during its first year in power and sustains most of those measures beyond the first year.

ACCOMMODATIONIST REVOLUTIONARY PATH

A case is scored as following an accommodationist path when, within a year of having launched radical initiatives, the revolutionary government abandons or substantially scales back most or all of those initiatives.

Revolutionary Reactive Sequence

The revolutionary reactive sequence begins when the founding revolutionary government initiates policies aimed at radically transforming the domestic and/or international order, which then triggers a violent (domestic and/or external) counterrevolutionary reaction.

The reactive sequence ends when the principal counterrevolutionary conflict is resolved.

The revolutionary reactive sequence is coded in the following manner:

Afghanistan

Initial Radicalism: Introduction of Shariah law; formation of alliance with Arab radicals in 1996.[2]

Principal Counterrevolutionary Conflicts: Conflict with the Northern Alliance; military conflict with the United States.

Resolution of Counterrevolutionary Conflict: U.S. defeat of the Taliban in 2001.

Albania

Initial Radicalism: Seizure of property; initiation of a two-front war against the Balli Kombetar, representing the old social elite, and Germany in 1942–1943.[3]

Principal Counterrevolutionary Conflicts: Conflicts with the Balli Kombetar and Germany

Resolution of Counterrevolutionary Conflict: Communist defeat of Germany in 1944.

Algeria

No significant counterrevolutionary conflict.

2. Bearden (2001: 24–25); Coll (2004: 227; 2019: 68); Dorronsoro (2005: 304–305).

3. Hibbert (1991: 115); Fevziu (2016: 68). Vickers (2011: 149, 155). Italy occupied Albania in 1939 and was replaced by German forces following the fall of Mussolini in 1943.

Angola

Initial Radicalism: Villagization in 1975–1976;[4] support for the African National Congress in South Africa and the South West African People's Organization in Namibia in 1976.[5]

Principal Counterrevolutionary Conflicts: Conflict with the National Liberation Front of Angola and rebels from the National Union for the Total Independence of Angola (UNITA).

Resolution of Counterrevolutionary Conflict: Final defeat of the UNITA in 2002.[6]

Bolivia

No significant counterrevolutionary conflict.

Cambodia

Initial Radicalism: Emptying out of cities in 1975; mass killing of Vietnamese and border raids into Vietnam in 1977.[7]

Principal Counterrevolutionary Conflict: Conflict with Vietnam.

Resolution of Counterrevolutionary Conflict: Vietnamese defeat of the Khmer Rouge in 1979.

China

Initial Radicalism: Communist threats to business/landowning interests during the "Great Revolution" of 1925–1927.[8]

Principal Counterrevolutionary Conflict: Conflict with the Kuomintang (KMT).

Resolution of Counterrevolutionary Conflict: Victory over the KMT in 1949.

Cuba

Initial Radicalism: Land reform in May 1959; expropriations of American-owned properties in June–August 1960; support for revolutionary uprisings elsewhere in Latin America in 1959–1960.

4. T. Young (1988: 171, 175).
5. Washington (1984: 24); Somerville (1986: 51); Tvedten (1997: 38).
6. "Angolan Military Meets Unita Rebels," BBC News, March 16, 2002.
7. Chandler (1992: 3, 120, 141); E. Becker (1998: 242, 304–305); P. Short (2004: 372, 375); Kiernan (2008: 357–366).
8. Isaacs ([1938] 2010: 295); Meisner (1999: 23).

Principal Counterrevolutionary Conflicts: U.S.-backed counter-revolutionary insurgencies, beginning in 1959 and peaking with the Bay of Pigs invasion in April 1961.[9]

Resolution of Counterrevolutionary Conflict: Defeat of domestic insurgencies in 1965.[10]

Eritrea

Initial Radicalism: Eritrean attack on Sudan in 1994; Eritrean attack on the Ethiopian border in 1998.[11]

Principal Counterrevolutionary Conflicts: War with Ethiopia.

Resolution of Counterrevolutionary Conflict: Algiers Agreement between Ethiopia and Eritrea in 2000.

Finland

Initial Radicalism: Land reform; nationalization of factories and banks.[12]

Principal Counterrevolutionary Conflict: The German-backed Whites, led by General Count Carl Mannerheim, attacked the Finnish People's Deputation in January 1918.

Resolution of Counterrevolutionary Conflict: The defeat of the Finnish People's Deputation by the Whites in April 1918.[13]

Guinea-Bissau

No significant counterrevolutionary conflict.

Hungary

Initial Radicalism: Land reform; seizure of property; invasion of Czechoslovakia in June 1919; declaration of war on Romania in July 1919.[14]

---

9. Blight and Kornbluh (1998: 159); Farber (2006: 61, 135); Rasenberger (2011: 40, 55–56).

10. Escalante Font (2008); Etcheverry and Gutierrez Oceguera (2008).

11. Human Rights Watch (1998); Reid (2011: 193); Calchi Novati (2021: 16).

12. Tikka (2014: 98, 97); Upton (1980: 354, 359, 390).

13. Upton (1980); Engelstein (2018: 283). Counterrevolutionary conflict was a preemptive response motivated by the Russian Revolution that had occurred months earlier, rather than a reaction to specific policies of the Finnish revolutionary government.

14. Tőkés (1967: 167, 191, 205); McAdams (2017: 123).

Principal Counterrevolutionary Conflict: War with French-backed Romania.[15]

Resolution of Counterrevolutionary Conflict: Romanian defeat of the Hungarian Soviet Republic in August 1919.[16]

Iran

Initial Radicalism: Seizure of U.S. embassy in 1979; Khomeini calls for uprisings in Iraq and other Persian Gulf states; establishment of clerical rule in 1981.[17]

Principal Counterrevolutionary Conflicts: Counterinsurgency against Mojahedin-e-Khalq; Iraqi invasion in 1980.[18]

Resolution of Counterrevolutionary Conflict: End of the Iran-Iraq War in 1988.

Mexico

Initial Radicalism: Passage of the 1917 Constitution and the enforcement of radical anticlerical provisions beginning in 1925.

Principal Counterrevolutionary Conflict: The Cristero War, beginning in 1926.

Resolution of Counterrevolutionary Conflict: The 1929 accord, which ended the Cristero War.

Mozambique

Initial Radicalism: Initiation of villagization policies in 1976–1977;[19] provision of bases to Zimbabwe African National Union in 1976.[20]

Principal Counterrevolutionary Conflict: Civil war with the Mozambican National Resistance (Renamo).[21]

Resolution of Counterrevolutionary Conflict: Rome Peace Agreement in 1992, ending the civil war.

---

15. Borsányi (1993: 154).

16. Borsányi (1993: 154).

17. Bakhash (1990: 220); Alahmad and Keshavarzian (2010: 17); Ottolenghi (2011: 10); Axworthy (2013: 214).

18. CIA (1980); Kharsh (1990: 266); Robins (1990: 88); Moin (1999: 236); Axworthy (2013: 191); Razoux and Elliott (2015: 23–26).

19. Lorgen (2000: 175–176).

20. Reno (2011: 59–60).

21. Mozambican National Resistance.

Nicaragua

Initial Radicalism: Seizure of Somocista properties and banking system in 1979; support for guerrillas in El Salvador in 1980; land reform in 1981.
Principal Counterrevolutionary Conflict: U.S-backed Contra War beginning in 1981.
Resolution of Counterrevolutionary Conflict: Esquipulas II Peace Accords in August 1987, ending the U.S.-backed counterrevolutionary threat.[22]

Russia

Initial Radicalism: Attacks on bourgeoisie and confiscation of property;[23] cessation of alliance with the Entente powers; end to bond payments in 1917.[24]
Principal Counterrevolutionary Conflict: Civil war against the White Armies.
Resolution of Counterrevolutionary Conflict: Defeat of the main White Armies at the end of 1920.

Rwanda

Initial Radicalism: Initiation of a radical program of social and cultural engineering, seeking to create a "new Rwanda and a new Rwandan."[25]
Principal Counterrevolutionary Conflicts: Counterinsurgency against Interahamwe; war with Zaire/Congo in 1996.[26]
Resolution of Counterrevolutionary Conflict: End of the first Congo War between Rwanda and Congo in 1997.

Vietnam

Initial Radicalism: Land reform in 1953–1954; support for guerrillas in South Vietnam beginning in 1959.

22. Jarquin (2019: 202–250).
23. Service (1991: 269); Chuev (1993: 98); Engelstein (2018: 183, 188).
24. Mawdsley (2005b: 73); Kotkin (2014: 239).
25. Reyntjens (2004: 209, 204; 2013: 253).
26. Human Rights Watch (1999); Prunier (2009: 26, 56, 68, chap. 4); Roessler and Verhoeven (2016).

Principal Counterrevolutionary Conflict: War with the United States, especially beginning in 1965.
Resolution of Counterrevolutionary Conflict: The Paris Peace Accords in 1973, ending the U.S-Vietnam military conflict.

Yugoslavia

Initial Radicalism: Attacks on landowning elite; start of a two-front war between Chetniks and Germans in 1941.[27]
Principal Counterrevolutionary Conflicts: War with Chetniks and Germany.
Resolution of Counterrevolutionary Conflict: Defeat of Germany in 1945.

Three Pillars of Durable Authoritarianism

Our theory predicts that radical revolutionary regimes will have established the three pillars by the end of the revolutionary reactive sequence.

A COHESIVE ELITE

A cohesive elite exists where the defection of national-level government or party officials to the opposition is infrequent (no more than one per decade) and inconsequential, in that few other regime elites or cadres accompany them.

A STRONG AND LOYAL COERCIVE APPARATUS

1. *A Strong Coercive Apparatus*: A large, well-trained, and well-equipped internal security apparatus with a presence across the national territory; existence of specialized intelligence or internal security agencies with a demonstrated capacity to penetrate civil society and monitor and repress opposition activities at the village and neighborhood levels across the country.

2. *A Loyal Coercive Apparatus*: Military rebellions and coup attempts against the regime are highly infrequent (no more than one per decade).

---

27. Hoare (2011: 210).

DESTRUCTION OF ALTERNATIVE
CENTERS OF SOCIETAL POWER

Destruction or crippling of all institutions, organizations, and social classes that have the resources or legitimacy/symbolic power to mobilize significant opposition to the regime. This includes prerevolutionary armies, monarchies, traditional local authorities, landowners, industrialists, religious institutions and associations, rival political movements or parties, and independent labor, peasant, nationalist, ethnic, and other associations.

- *Full destruction*: revolutionary elite systematically assaults independent centers of societal power, leaving no actor in society with the capacity to mobilize substantial opposition to regime.
- *Partial destruction*: some independent power centers are weakened or destroyed, but at least one independent power center retains the capacity to mobilize against the regime.[28]
- *Nondestruction*: most or all independent power centers remain intact.

Regime Outcomes

EARLY DEATH

Cases of early death are those in which the ruling revolutionary party, coalition, or clique falls from power during the initial counterrevolutionary conflict.

DURABLE AUTHORITARIANISM

A regime is considered durable if it remains in power for at least twenty-five years and during this period,[29] it

1. does not experience a successful palace coup;[30]
2. does not confront recurrent (more than one) episodes of national opposition mobilization (successful or unsuccessful) that are widely viewed as threatening the regime's survival.

28. We score as partial destruction those cases in which revolutionary elites do not systematically assault alternative centers of societal power because societies lack such centers (or they are very weak) due to structural factors such as underdevelopment.

29. In accordance with our theory, in cases of counterrevolutionary conflict we apply the criteria to the period after the conflict has been resolved. In cases without counterrevolutionary conflict, we apply the criteria five years after regime formation.

30. A palace coup is defined as the replacement of leaders within the ruling group outside normal procedures.

UNSTABLE REGIME

A regime is considered unstable[31] if

1. The regime collapses after less than twenty-five years.
2. During the first twenty-five years, the regime experiences at least one of the following:

   - A successful palace coup.
   - Recurrent (more than one) episodes of national opposition mobilization that are widely viewed as threatening the regime's survival.

31. In accordance with our theory, in cases of counterrevolutionary conflict we apply the criteria to the period after the conflict has been resolved. In cases without counterrevolutionary conflict, we apply the criteria five years after regime formation.

Summary Coding for All Authoritarian Regimes, 1900–2015

Country	First Official Leader/Party	Years in Power	Reason for Exclusion
Afghanistan	A. Rahman	1919–1929	Within state
Afghanistan	Mohammed Nadir Shah	1929–1973	No social change
Afghanistan	Mohammed Daoud Khan	1973–1978	Within state
Afghanistan	Abdul Qadir, People's Democratic Party	1978–1992	Within state
Afghanistan	Mohammed Omar, Taliban	1996–2001	Revolution
Afghanistan	Hamid Karzai	2009–2014	Regular transfer
Albania	Hamed Zogu (King Zog I)	1925–1939	Within state
Albania	Enver Hoxha, Albanian Communist Party (ACP)	1944–1991	Revolution
Algeria	Ferhat Abbas, National Liberation Front (FLN)	1962–	Revolution
Angola	Agostinho Neto, Popular Movement for the Liberation of Angola (MPLA)	1975–	Revolution
Argentina	Jose Felix Uriburu	1930–1943	Within state
Argentina	Edelmiro Julian Farrell	1943–1946	Within state
Argentina	Juan Peron, Peronist Party	1951–1955	Regular transfer

For detailed explications of coding rules and justifications for each country coding, see https://press.princeton.edu/books/revolution-and-dictatorship.

Country	First Official Leader/Party	Years in Power	Reason for Exclusion
Argentina	Pedro Eugenio Aramburu	1955–1958	Within state
Argentina	Arturo Frondizi, Intransigent Radical Civic Union (UCRI)	1958–1966	Regular transfer
Argentina	Juan Carlos Ongania	1966–1973	Within state
Argentina	Jorge Rafael Videla	1976–1983	Within state
Armenia	Levon Ter-Petrosyan, Pan-Armenian National Movement	1994–1998	Regular transfer
Armenia	Robert Kocharian	1998–	Within state
Austria	Engelbert Dollfuss, Christian Social Party, Landbund, Heimwehr, Fatherland Front	1933–1938	Regular transfer
Azerbaijan	Ayaz Mutalibov	1991–1992	Within state
Azerbaijan	Heydar Aliyev, New Azerbaijan Party (YAP)	1993–	Within state
Bangladesh	Sheikh Mujibur Rahman, Bangladesh Awami League	1971–1975	No new state
Bangladesh	Sheikh Mujibur Rahman, Bangladesh Krishak Sramik Awami League	1975–1982	Within state
Bangladesh	Hussain Muhammad Ershad, Jatiya Party	1982–1990	Within state
Bangladesh	Iajuddin Ahmed	2007–2008	Within state
Bangladesh	Abdul Hamid, Bangladesh Awami League	2014–	Regular transfer
Belarus	Vyacheslav Kebich	1991–1994	Regular transfer
Belarus	Alexander Lukashenko	1994–	Regular transfer
Benin	Hubert Maga, Dahomeyan Democratic Rally (RDD)	1960–1963	Regular transfer
Benin	Christophe Soglo	1963–1965	Within state
Benin	Christophe Soglo	1965–1967	Within state
Benin	Maurice Kouandete	1967–1969	Within state
Benin	Paul-Emile de Souza	1969–1970	Within state
Benin	Mathieu Kerekou	1972–1990	Within state
Bolivia	Carlos Blanco Galindo	1930–1931	Within state
Bolivia	Daniel Salamanca Urey, Genuine Republican Party (PRG)	1931–1936	Regular transfer
Bolivia	David Toro	1936–1940	Within state
Bolivia	Enrique Penaranda, Concordance	1940–1943	Regular transfer

(*Continued*)

Country	First Official Leader/Party	Years in Power	Reason for Exclusion
Bolivia	Alfredo Ovando Candia	1969–1971	Within state
Bolivia	Hugo Banzer	1971–1979	Within state
Botswana	Seretse Khama, Botswana Democratic Party (BDP)	1966–	Regular transfer
Brazil	Getulio Vargas	1930–1945	Within state
Bulgaria	Kimon Georgiev, Bulgarian Communist Party	1944–1989	Foreign control
Burkina Faso	Maurice Yameogo, African Democratic Rally (RDA)	1960–1966	Regular transfer
Burkina Faso	Sangoula Lamizana	1966–1980	Within state
Burkina Faso	Saye Zerbo	1980–1982	Within state
Burkina Faso	Thomas Sankara	1982–1987	Within state
Burkina Faso	Blaise Compaore	1987–2014	Within state
Burundi	Mwambutsa IV	1962–1966	Within state
Burundi	Michel Micombero, Union for National Progress (UPRONA)	1966–1987	Within state
Burundi	Pierre Buyoya, Union for National Progress (UPRONA)	1987–1993	Within state
Burundi	Pierre Buyoya, Union for National Progress (UPRONA)	1996–2003	Within state
Burundi	Pierre Nkurunziza, National Council for the Defense of Democracy–Forces for the Defense of Democracy	2010–	Regular transfer
Cambodia	Norodom Sihanouk	1953–1970	Within state
Cambodia	Lon Nol, Sangkum / Khmer National Armed Forces (FANK)	1970–1975	Within state
Cambodia	Sihanouk, Khmer Rouge (CPK)	1975–1979	Revolution
Cambodia	Khmer People's Revolutionary Party	1979–	Foreign control
Cameroon	Ahmadou Ahidjo, Cameroonian Union (UC)	1960–1983	Within state
Cameroon	Paul Biya, Cameroon National Union (UNC)	1983–	Regular transfer
Central African Republic	David Dacko, Movement for the Social Evolution of Black Africa (MESAN)	1960–1965	Within state
Central African Republic	Jean-Bedel Bokassa	1966–1979	Within state
Central African Republic	David Dacko, Movement for the Social Evolution of Black Africa (MESAN)	1979–1981	No social change

Country	First Official Leader/Party	Years in Power	Reason for Exclusion
Central African Republic	Andre Kolingba	1981–1993	Within state
Central African Republic	Francois Bozize	2003–2013	Within state
Central African Republic	Michel Djotodia	2013–2014	Within state
Chad	Francois Tombalbaye, Chadian Progressive Party (PPT)	1960–1975	Regular transfer
Chad	Felix Malloum	1975–1979	Within state
Chad	Hissene Habre, Armed Forces of the North (FAN) / National Union for Independence and Revolution (UNIR)	1982–1990	No social change
Chad	Idriss Deby, Patriotic Salvation Movement (MPS)	1990–	No social change
Chile	Carlos Ibanez del Campo	1927–1931	Within state
Chile	Augusto Pinochet	1973–1989	Within state
China	Yuan Shih-Kai, Beiyang Clique	1912–1916	Within state
China	Chiang Kai-shek, Kuomintang (KMT)	1927–1949	No social change
China	Mao Zedong, Chinese Communist Party (CCP)	1949–	Revolution
Colombia	Laureano Gomez Castro, Conservative	1949–1953	Regular transfer
Colombia	Gustavo Rojas Pinilla	1953–1958	Within state
Congo Republic	Abbe Fulbert Youlou, Democratic Union for the Defence of African Interests (UDDIA)	1960–1963	Within state
Congo Republic	Alphonse Massamba-Debat, National Movement of the Revolution (MNR)	1963–1968	Within state
Congo Republic	Marien Ngouabi, Congolese Party of Labour (PCT)	1968–1991	Within state
Congo Republic	Denis Sassou-Nguesso, Congolese Party of Labour (PCT)	1997–	No social change
Costa Rica	Frederico Tinoco Granados, Peliquista	1917–1919	Within state
Costa Rica	Jose Figueres Ferrer	1948–1949	No social change
Cuba	Tomas Estrada Palma, Republican	1902–1906	Regular transfer

(Continued)

Country	First Official Leader/Party	Years in Power	Reason for Exclusion
Cuba	Jose Miguel Gomez, Liberal	1909–1933	Regular transfer
Cuba	Fulgencio Batista, Progressive Action	1933–1944	Within state
Cuba	Fulgencio Batista, Progressive Action	1952–1959	Within state
Cuba	Osvaldo Dorticós Torrado, July 26 Movement (M-26 July)	1959–	Revolution
Czechoslovakia	Klement Gottwald, Communist Party of Czechoslovakia (KSČ)	1948–1989	Foreign control
Democratic Republic of the Congo	Joseph-Desire Mobutu, Popular Movement of the Revolution	1960–1997	Within state
Democratic Republic of the Congo	Laurent Kabila, Alliances des Forces Democratiques pour la Liberation du Congo-Zaire (AFDL)	1997–	Foreign control
Dominican Republic	Horacio Vasquez, Red	1924–1930	Regular transfer
Dominican Republic	Rafael Trujillo, Confederation of Parties / Dominican Party (PD)	1930–1962	Within state
Dominican Republic	Elias Wessin y Wessin	1963–1965	Within state
Dominican Republic	Joaquin Balaguer, Social Christian Reformist Party (PRSC)	1966–1978	Regular transfer
Ecuador	Eloy Alfaro, Ecuadorian Radical Liberal Party	1906–1911	Within state
Ecuador	Isidro Ayora, Ecuadorian Radical Liberal Party	1925–1931	Within state
Ecuador	Jose Maria Velasco Ibarra	1934–1935	Regular transfer
Ecuador	Frederico Paez	1936–1937	Within state
Ecuador	Alberto Enriquez Gallo	1937–1938	Within state
Ecuador	Aurello Mosquera Navarez, Ecuadorian Radical Liberal Party	1938–1944	Regular transfer
Ecuador	Jose Maria Velasco Ibarra	1944–1947	Within state
Ecuador	Ramon Casto Jijon	1963–1966	Within state
Ecuador	Jose Maria Velasco Ibarra	1970–1972	Regular transfer
Ecuador	Guillermo Rodriguez Lara	1972–1979	Within state
Egypt	Fuad I	1922–1952	Within state
Egypt	Mohamed Naguib, Gamal Nasser, Liberation Rally	1952–2011	Within state
Egypt	Mohamed Hussein al-Tantawi / Supreme Council of the Armed Forces	2011–2012	Within state

Country	First Official Leader/Party	Years in Power	Reason for Exclusion
Egypt	Abdel Fattah el-Sisi	2013–	Within state
El Salvador	Maximiliano Hernandez Martinez, National Pro Patria Party	1931–1948	Within state
El Salvador	Oscar Osorio Hernandez, Revolutionary Party of Democratic Unification	1948–1982	Within state
El Salvador	Alvaro Alfredo Magana Borja, Democratic Action Party	1982–1994	Regular transfer
Eritrea	Isaias Afwerki, Eritrean People's Liberation Front (EPLF)	1993–	Revolution
Estonia	Konstantin Pats, Patriotic League	1934–1940	Regular transfer
Ethiopia	Mengistu Haile Mariam	1974–1991	Within state
Ethiopia	Meles Zenawi, Tigray People's Liberation Front (TPLF) / Ethiopian People's Revolutionary Democratic Front (EPRDR)	1991–	No social change
Finland	Kullervo Manner, Finnish People's Deputation	1918	Revolution
Gabon	Leon M'ba, Gabonese Democratic Party (PDF)	1960–	Within state
Gambia	Dawda Jawara, People's Progressive Party	1965–1994	Regular transfer
Gambia	Yahya Jammeh, Armed Forces Provisional Ruling Council	1994–	Within state
Georgia	Zviad Gamsakhurdia, Round Table–Free Georgia	1991–1992	Regular transfer
Georgia	Eduard Shevardnadze, Union of Citizens of Georgia	1992–2003	Within state
Germany	Adolf Hitler, National Socialist German Workers' Party (NSDAP)	1933–1945	Regular transfer
Germany, East	Wilhelm Pieck, Socialist Unity Party	1949–1990	Foreign control
Ghana	Kwame Nkrumah, Convention People's Party (CPP)	1960–1966	Regular transfer
Ghana	Joseph Arthur Ankrah, National Liberation Council	1966–1969	Within state
Ghana	Ignatius Kutu Acheampong, National Redemption Council	1972–1979	Within state
Ghana	Jerry Rawlings, Provisional National Defence Council	1981–2000	Within state

(*Continued*)

Country	First Official Leader/Party	Years in Power	Reason for Exclusion
Greece	Ioannis Metaxas, Freethinkers' Party	1936–1941	Regular transfer
Greece	Georgios Papadopoulos	1967–1974	Within state
Guatemala	Jose Maria Orellana, Liberal	1921–1930	Within state
Guatemala	Jorge Ubico, Progressive Liberal Party	1931–1944	Within state
Guatemala	Carlos Castillo Armas, National Liberation Movement	1954–1958	No new state
Guatemala	Miguel Ydigoras Fuentes, National Democratic Reconciliation Party (REDENCION)	1958–1963	Regular transfer
Guatemala	Enrique Peralta Azurdia, Institutional Democratic Party	1963–1966	Within state
Guatemala	Julio Cesar Mendez Montenegro, Revolutionary Party	1966–1970	Regular transfer
Guatemala	Carlos Manuel Arana Osorio, Institutional Democratic Party	1970–1985	Regular transfer
Guatemala	Vincio Cerezo, Guatemalan Christian Democracy	1985–1995	Regular transfer
Guinea	Ahmed Sekou Toure, Democratic Party of Guinea–African Democratic Party (PDG-RDA)	1958–1984	Regular transfer
Guinea	Lansana Conte, Unity and Progress Party (PUP)	1984–2008	Within state
Guinea	Moussa Dadis Camara	2008–2010	Within state
Guinea-Bissau	Luis Cabral, Party for African Independence in Guinea and Cape Verde (PAIGC)	1974–1999	Revolution
Guinea-Bissau	Kumba Ialá, Party for Social Renewal (PRS)	2002–2003	Regular transfer
Guinea-Bissau	Mamadu Ture Kuruma, People's Revolutionary Armed Forces (FARP)	2012–2014	Within state
Haiti	Pierre Nord Alexis	1902–1911	Within state
Haiti	Cincinnatus Leconte, National Party	1911–1914	Within state
Haiti	Joseph Davilmar Theodore	1914–1915	Within state
Haiti	Stenio Vincent	1934–1941	Regular transfer
Haiti	Elie Lescot, Liberal Party	1941–1946	Regular transfer
Haiti	Paul Magloire, Peasant Worker Movement	1950–1956	Within state
Haiti	Francois Duvalier, National Unity Party	1957–1986	Within state

Country	First Official Leader/Party	Years in Power	Reason for Exclusion
Haiti	Henri Namphy	1986–1988	Within state
Haiti	Prosper Avril	1988–1990	Within state
Haiti	Raoul Cedras	1991–1994	Within state
Haiti	Rene Preval, Fanmi Lavalas	1999–2004	Regular transfer
Honduras	Manuel Bonilla, National	1903–1907	Within state
Honduras	Miguel Davila, Liberal	1907–1911	Within state
Honduras	Manuel Bonilla, National	1912–1919	Regular transfer
Honduras	Rafael Lopez Gutierrez, Liberal	1920–1924	Within state
Honduras	Francisco Bueso, Liberal	1924–1929	Regular transfer
Honduras	Tiburcio Carias Andino, National	1933–1956	Regular transfer
Honduras	Oswaldo Lopez Arellano	1963–1971	Within state
Honduras	Oswaldo Lopez Arellano	1972–1981	Within state
Hungary	Mihály Károlyi, Party of Independence and '48 (F48P)	1918–1919	Regular transfer
Hungary	Sándor Garbai / Béla Kun, Hungarian Communist Party (HCP)	1919	Revolution
Hungary	Miklos Horthy	1919–1944	No social change
Hungary	Zoltan Tildy, Independent Smallholders, Agrarian Workers and Civic Party (FKGP)	1947–1990	Foreign control
Indonesia	Sukarno, Nationalist Party of Indonesia	1949–1966	No social change
Indonesia	Suharto, Golkar Party	1966–1999	Within state
Iran	Reza Pahlavi	1925–1979	Within state
Iran	Ruhollah Khomeini	1979–	Revolution
Iraq	Faysal II	1932–1958	Within state
Iraq	Abd al-Karim Kassem	1958–1963	Within state
Iraq	Abd al Salam Aref	1963–1968	Within state
Iraq	Ahmed Hassan al-Bakr, Iraqi Ba'ath	1968–1979	Within state
Iraq	Saddam Hussein, Iraqi Ba'ath	1979–2003	Regular transfer
Iraq	Jalal Talabani, Patriotic Union of Kurdistan	2010–	Regular transfer
Italy	Luigi Facta, Liberal Union / Italian Liberal Party	1922–1943	Regular transfer

(Continued)

Country	First Official Leader/Party	Years in Power	Reason for Exclusion
Ivory Coast	Felix Houphouet-Boigny, Democratic Party of Ivory Coast–African Democratic Rally (PDCI-RDA)	1960–1999	Regular transfer
Ivory Coast	Robert Guei	1999–2000	Within state
Ivory Coast	Laurent Gbagbo, Ivorian Popular Front (FPI)	2000–2011	Regular transfer
Japan	Saito Makoto	1932–1945	Within state
Jordan	Abdullah I bin Al-Hussein	1946–	Within state
Kazakhstan	Nursultan Nazarbayev, Communist Party of Kazakhstan (QKP)	1991–	Within state
Kenya	Jomo Kenyatta, Kenya African National Union	1963–2002	Regular transfer
Korea, North	Kim Il-sung, Workers' Party of North Korea	1948–	Foreign control
Korea, South	Syngman Rhee, National Association	1948–1960	Foreign control
Korea, South	Park Chung Hee	1961–1987	Within state
Kuwait	Mubarak al-Sabah	1961–	Within state
Kyrgyzstan	Askar Akayev	1991–2005	Within state
Kyrgyzstan	Kurmanbek Bakiyev	2005–2010	Within state
Laos	Phoumi Nosavan	1959–1960	Within state
Laos	Phoumi Nosavan	1960–1962	Within state
Laos	Souphanouvong	1975–	Foreign control
Latvia	Karlis Ulmanis	1934–1940	Within state
Lesotho	Leabua Jonathan, Basotho National Party	1970–1986	Regular transfer
Lesotho	Justin Metsing Lekhanya	1986–1993	Within state
Liberia	William Tubman, True Whig Party	1944–1980	Regular transfer
Liberia	Samuel Doe, National Democratic Party	1980–1990	Within state
Liberia	Charles Taylor, National Patriotic Party	1997–2003	No social change
Libya	Sayyid Idris	1951–1969	Foreign control
Libya	Muammar Qaddafi, Arab Socialist Union	1969–2011	Within state
Lithuania	Antanas Smetona	1926–1940	Within state
Madagascar	Philibert Tsiranana, Social Democratic Party of Madagascar (PSD)	1960–1972	Regular transfer
Madagascar	Gabriel Ramanantsoa	1972–1975	Within state

Country	First Official Leader/Party	Years in Power	Reason for Exclusion
Madagascar	Didier Ratsiraka, Association for the Rebirth of Madagascar (AREMA)	1975–1993	Regular transfer
Madagascar	Andry Rajoelina, Young Malagasies Determined (TGV)	2009–2013	No new state
Malawi	Hastings Banda, Malawi Congress Party	1964–1994	Regular transfer
Malaysia	Tunku Abdul Rahman, Alliance Party (UMNO)	1957–	Within state
Mali	Modibo Keita, Sudanese Union–African Democratic Rally (US-RDA)	1960–1968	Regular transfer
Mali	Moussa Traore, Democratic Union of the Malian People (UDPM)	1968–1991	Within state
Mali	Amadou Sanogo	2012–2013	Within state
Mauritania	Moktar Ould Daddah, Mauritanian Regroupment Party (PRM) / Mauritanian People's Party (PPM)	1960–1978	Within state
Mauritania	Mustafa Ould Salek	1978–2005	Within state
Mauritania	Ely Ould Mohamed Vall	2005–2007	Within state
Mauritania	Mohamed Ould Abdel Aziz	2008–	Within state
Mexico	Victoriano Huerta	1913–1914	Within state
Mexico	Venustiano Carranza, Liberal Constitutionalist Party	1915–2000	Revolution
Mongolia	Mongolian People's Party	1921–1993	Foreign control
Morocco	Mohammed ben Yusef	1956–	No new state
Mozambique	Samora Machel, Front for the Liberation of Mozambique (Frelimo)	1975–	Revolution
Myanmar	Ne Win, Burma Socialist Programme Party	1958–1960	Within state
Myanmar	Ne Win, Burma Socialist Programme Party	1962–1988	Within state
Myanmar	Saw Maung	1988–	Within state
Namibia	Sam Nujoma, South West Africa People's Organization (SWAPO)	1990–	No social change
Nepal	Tribhuvan Bir Bikram Shah	1951–1991	No new state
Nepal	Gyanendra Bir Bikram Shah	2002–2006	Regular transfer

(*Continued*)

Country	First Official Leader/Party	Years in Power	Reason for Exclusion
Nicaragua	Juan Bautista Sacasa, Liberal	1933–1936	Regular transfer
Nicaragua	Anastasio Somoza García, Nationalist Liberal Party (PLN)	1936–1979	Within state
Nicaragua	Daniel Ortega, Sandinista National Liberation Front (FSLN)	1979–1990	Revolution
Niger	Hamani Diori, Nigerien Progressive Party–African Democratic Rally (PPN-RDA)	1960–1974	Within state
Niger	Seyni Kountche	1974–1991	Within state
Niger	Ibrahim Bare Mainassara, National Union of Independents for Democratic Renewal (UNIRD) / Rally for Democracy and Progress (RDP-Jama'a)	1996–1999	Within state
Niger	Mamadou Tandja	2009–2010	Regular transfer
Niger	Salou Djibo	2010–2011	Within state
Nigeria	Yakubu Gowon	1966–1979	Within state
Nigeria	Muhammadu Buhari	1983–1993	Within state
Nigeria	Sani Abacha	1993–1999	Within state
Oman	Taimur bin Faisal	1920–	Within state
Pakistan	Muhammad Ali Jinnah, Pakistan Muslim League	1947–1958	Within state
Pakistan	Ayub Khan	1958–1971	Within state
Pakistan	Fazal Ilahi Chaudhry, Pakistan Peoples Party	1975–1977	Regular transfer
Pakistan	Muhammad Zia-ul-Haq	1977–1988	Within state
Pakistan	Pervez Musharraf	1999–2008	Within state
Panama	Juan Demostenes Arosemena, National Liberal Party	1936–1941	Regular transfer
Panama	Ricardo Adolfo de la Guardia Arango	1941–1945	Regular transfer
Panama	Arnulfo Arias, Panamenista Party	1949–1951	Within state
Panama	Jose Antonio Remon Cantera, National Patriotic Coalition	1953–1955	Regular transfer
Panama	Omar Torrijos	1968–1982	Within state
Panama	Manuel Noriega	1982–1989	Within state
Paraguay	Juan Antonio Ezcurra, National Republican Association–Colorado Party (ANR-PC)	1902–1904	Within state

Country	First Official Leader/Party	Years in Power	Reason for Exclusion
Paraguay	Albino Jara, Liberal	1908–1911	Within state
Paraguay	Eduardo Schaerer, Liberal	1912–1936	Within state
Paraguay	Rafael Franco	1936–1937	Within state
Paraguay	Ramon Paredes	1937–1939	Within state
Paraguay	Jose Felix Estigarribia, Liberal	1940–1948	Regular transfer
Paraguay	Juan Natalicio Gonzalez, National Republican Association–Colorado Party (ANR-PC)	1948–1954	Within state
Paraguay	Alfredo Stroessner, National Republican Association–Colorado Party (ANR-PC)	1954–1993	Within state
Peru	Oscar Benavides	1914–1915	Within state
Peru	Augusto Leguia, Reformist Democratic Party	1919–1930	Regular transfer
Peru	Luis Miguel Sanchez Cerres, Revolutionary Union	1930–1945	Within state
Peru	Manuel Odria	1948–1956	Within state
Peru	Ricardo Perez Godoy	1962–1963	Within state
Peru	Juan Velasco Alvarado	1968–1980	Within state
Peru	Alberto Fujimori, Fujimorism	1992–2000	Regular transfer
Philippines	Ferdinand Marcos	1972–1986	Regular transfer
Poland	Jozef Pildsudski	1926–1939	Within state
Poland	Boleslaw Bierut, Polish Workers' Party	1944–1989	Foreign control
Portugal	Sidonio Bernardino Cardoso da Silva Pais	1917–1918	Within state
Portugal	Antonio de Oliveira Salazar	1926–1974	Within state
Romania	Carol II	1938–1940	Within state
Romania	Ion Antonescu	1940–1944	Within state
Romania	Constantin Sanatescu	1944–1945	Within state
Romania	Petru Groza, Romanian Communist Party	1945–1989	Foreign control
Russia	Boris Yeltsin	1993–	Regular transfer
Russia	Vladimir Lenin, Bolshevik Party	1917–1991	Revolution
Rwanda	Gregoire Kayibanda, Parmehutu	1962–1973	Regular transfer

(Continued)

Country	First Official Leader/Party	Years in Power	Reason for Exclusion
Rwanda	Juvénal Habyarimana, National Republican Movement for Democracy and Development (MRND)	1973–1994	Within state
Rwanda	Pasteur Bizimungu, Rwandan Patriotic Front (RPF)	1994–	Revolution
Saudi Arabia	Ibn Saud	1927–	No social change
Senegal	Leopold Sedar Senghor, Socialist Party of Senegal (UPS)	1960–2000	Regular transfer
Sierra Leone	Andrew Juxon-Smith	1967–1968	Within state
Sierra Leone	John Amadu Bangura	1968–1992	Regular transfer
Sierra Leone	Valentine Strasser	1992–1996	Within state
Sierra Leone	Johnny Paul Koroma	1997–1998	Within state
Singapore	Lee Kuan Yew, People's Action Party	1965–	Regular transfer
Somalia	Siad Barre, Somali Revolutionary Socialist Party	1969–1991	Within state
South Africa	Louis Botha, South African Party	1910–1994	Regular transfer
South Sudan	Salva Kiir Mayardit, Sudan People's Liberation Movement (SPLM)	2011–	No social change
Spain	Miguel Primo de Rivera	1923–1930	Within state
Spain	Francisco Franco, National Movement	1939–1976	Within state
Sri Lanka	J. R. Jayewardene, United National Party	1978–1994	Regular transfer
Sri Lanka	Mahinda Rajapaksa, Sri Lanka Freedom Party	2010–	Regular transfer
Sudan	Ibrahim Abboud	1958–1964	Within state
Sudan	Jaafar Nimeiry, Sudanese Socialist Union	1969–1985	Within state
Sudan	Abdel Rahman Swar al-Dahab	1985–1986	Within state
Sudan	Hassan 'Abd Allah al-Turabi	1989–	Within state
Swaziland	Sobhuza II	1968–	Within state
Syria	Shukri al-Quwatli, National Bloc / National Party	1946–1947	Within state
Syria	Adib Shishakli, Syrian Social Nationalist Party	1949–1951	Within state
Syria	Adib Shishakli, Syrian Social Nationalist Party	1951–1954	Within state
Syria	Zahr al-Din	1962–1963	Within state

Country	First Official Leader/Party	Years in Power	Reason for Exclusion
Syria	Amin al-Hafiz, Ba'ath Party	1963–	Within state
Taiwan	Chiang Kai-shek, Kuomintang (KMT)	1949–2000	Within state
Tajikistan	Rahmon Nabiyev, Communist	1991–	Within state
Tanzania	Julius Nyerere, Tanganyika African National Union (TANU)	1964–	Regular transfer
Thailand	Phahonphonphayuhasena, Khana Ratsadon	1933–1944	Within state
Thailand	Khuang Aphaiwong	1944–1947	Regular transfer
Thailand	Plaek Phibun Songkhram, Conservative Party	1947–1957	Within state
Thailand	Sarit Thanarat	1957–1973	Within state
Thailand	Sangad Chalayu	1976–1988	Within state
Thailand	Suchinda Kraprayoon	1991–1992	Within state
Thailand	Sonthi Boonyaratglin	2006–2007	Within state
Thailand	Prayut Chan-o-cha	2014–	Within state
Togo	Sylvanus Olympio, Party of Togolese Unity (CUT)	1960–1963	Regular transfer
Togo	Gnassingbé Eyadéma	1963–	Within state
Tunisia	Habib Bourguiba, Neo-Destour	1956–2011	No social change
Turkey	Mustafa Kemal Ataturk, Republican People's Party	1923–1950	Within state
Turkey	Celal Bayar, Democrat Party	1957–1960	Regular transfer
Turkey	Cemal Gursel	1960–1961	Within state
Turkey	Kenan Evren	1980–1983	Within state
Turkmenistan	Saparmurat Niyazov, Communist Party of Turkmenistan	1991–	Within state
Uganda	Milton Obote, Uganda People's Congress	1966–1971	Regular transfer
Uganda	Idi Amin	1971–1979	Within state
Uganda	Paulo Muwanga, Uganda People's Congress (UNLF)	1980–1985	Regular transfer
Uganda	Yoweri Museveni, National Resistance Movement	1986–	No social change
Ukraine	Viktor Yanukovych, Party of Regions	2012–2014	Regular transfer
United Arab Emirates	Zayed bin Sultan Al Nahyan	1971–	Within state

(Continued)

Country	First Official Leader/Party	Years in Power	Reason for Exclusion
Uruguay	Gabriel Terra, Colorado	1933–1938	Regular transfer
Uruguay	Chiappe Posse	1973–1984	Within state
Uzbekistan	Islam Karimov, Communist Party of the Soviet Union	1991–	Within state
Venezuela	Juan Vicente Gomez	1908–1945	Within state
Venezuela	Carlos Delgado Chalbaud	1948–1958	Within state
Venezuela	Hugo Chavez, United Socialist Party	2005–	Regular transfer
Vietnam	Ho Chih Minh, Indochinese Communist Party (ICP)	1954–	Revolution
Vietnam, South	Ngo Dinh Diem, Can Lao	1954–1963	Within state
Vietnam, South	Duong Van Minh	1963–1975	Within state
Yemen	Yahya Muhammad Hamid ed-Din	1918–1962	No social change
Yemen	Abdullah al-Sallal	1962–1967	Within state
Yemen	Abdul Rahman Iryani	1967–1974	Within state
Yemen	Ibrahim al-Hamdi	1974–1978	Within state
Yemen	Ali Abdullah Saleh	1978–2012	Regular transfer
Yemen, South	Qahtan Muhammad al-Shaabi, National Liberation Front	1967–1990	No new state
Yugoslavia	Alexander Karadjordjevic	1929–1941	Regular transfer
Yugoslavia	Ivan Ribar, Communist Party of Yugoslavia (League of Communists of Yugoslavia)	1945–1990	Revolution
Yugoslavia (Serbia)	Slobodan Milosevic, Socialist Party of Serbia	1991–2000	Regular transfer
Zambia	Kenneth Kaunda, United National Independence Party (UNIP)	1967–1991	Regular transfer
Zambia	Frederick Chiluba, Movement for Multi-Party Democracy	1996–2011	Regular transfer
Zimbabwe	Canaan Banana, Zimbabwe African National Union	1980–	No new state

Chapter 1

1. Mawdsley (2005a: 100).
2. Overy (1997: 64); Glantz and House (2015: 45, 51); Khlevniuk (2015: 183).
3. Khlevniuk (2015: 206).
4. See Mikoian (1999: 391).
5. Quoted in Mawdsley (2005b: 44).
6. Levitsky and Way (2010).
7. These are China, Cuba, Laos, North Korea, and Vietnam. Laos and North Korea are ambiguous cases. Both were communist regimes that emerged out of violent conflict, but since the revolutionaries' ascent to power was heavily assisted by a foreign power (Vietnam in the case of Laos, the Soviet Union in the case of North Korea), we do not score them as revolutionary. Nevertheless, regime dynamics in these cases paralleled those of revolutionary cases.
8. See Lachapelle et al. (2020), excerpted in appendix I.
9. Lachapelle et al. (2020). Revolutionary autocracies survived an average of thirty-nine years. Nonrevolutionary autocracies survived fifteen years.
10. The annual rate of breakdown of revolutionary regimes is 1.28 percent, compared to 5.80 percent for nonrevolutionary regimes. See Lachapelle et al. (2020) and appendix I.
11. A log-rank test strongly rejects the null hypothesis of no difference in the hazards between revolutionary and nonrevolutionary regimes ($p < 0.001$).
12. See Lachapelle et al. (2020) and appendix I.
13. Skocpol (1979, 1988).
14. See Adelman (1985: 3–4); Gurr (1988); Skocpol (1988); and especially Walt (1996).
15. Walt (1996).
16. Walt (1996: 22–41).
17. Walt (1996: 1).
18. Weyland (2019).
19. We focus on revolutionary regimes that emerged after the onset of mass politics in the early twentieth century.
20. We borrow the term "reactive sequence" from James Mahoney (2001).
21. Mao (2003: 15).
22. This definition draws on Huntington (1968), Skocpol (1979), and Chalmers Johnson (1982).
23. Skocpol (1979).
24. See Huntington (1968: 264); also Gurr (1970) and Chalmers Johnson (1982).
25. Skocpol (1979: 4).
26. Chorley ([1943] 1973); Skocpol (1979).

27. Chorley ([1943] 1973: 186). Examples include the Red Army in Soviet Russia, the People's Liberation Army in China, the National Liberation Army in Yugoslavia, the People's Army of Vietnam, and the Revolutionary Armed Forces in Cuba.

28. Huntington (1968: 264); Chalmers Johnson (1982: 2); Selbin (1993: 11–12); Colgan (2012: 446).

29. See appendix II for the full coding criteria of revolutionary autocracies.

30. Trimberger (1978).

31. On the distinction between political and social revolutions, see Goodwin (2001: 9). In a few cases, such as South Yemen and Zimbabwe, regimes emerge out of violent struggle but do not radically transform the state. We do not consider such cases revolutionary.

32. Goodwin (2001: 256).

33. See Ash (1993) and Goodwin (2001: 260).

34. The fall of communism in Romania is not considered a case of revolution because the Romanian state remained intact and because the new government under Ion Iliescu, a former Communist official, did not engage in radical social transformation.

35. Postcommunist regimes also came to power via elections in the former Yugoslavia.

36. Although the Soviet state collapsed, nearly all post-Soviet states relied heavily on the Soviet-era security structures (Amy Knight 1996). Armenia and Croatia are exceptions, but in both cases new elites came to power via elections and did not engage in radical social transformation.

37. Schoenbaum (1966).

38. In Italy, for example, the Fascists took control with the support of the army and King Victor Emmanuel III (Bosworth 2002: 167–169). Similarly, the Nazi seizure of power was achieved through established procedure, and with the consent of German president Paul von Hindenburg, rather than through violent overthrow from below.

39. Goodwin (2001: 9–10); also Colgan (2012); Goldstone (2014: 10); Lee (2015: 12); Beissinger (2022).

40. Drawing on version 4.1 of the Archigos data set (see Goemans et al. 2009) and following the rules laid out by Geddes, Wright, and Frantz (see Geddes et al. 2014, 2018), we expanded this data set (which goes back only to 1945) and identified all authoritarian regimes from 1900 to 1945.

41. See Geddes et al. (2018). We also excluded all cases with a population under 500,000 at the time of regime transition, as well as those cases that are foreign-occupied (meaning that the army was directly controlled by a foreign power) at the time of transition.

42. More detailed explications of coding decisions with a full list of references for each country may be found online at https://press.princeton.edu/books/revolution -and-dictatorship.

43. Geddes et al. (2014, 2018) include only governments that were in power on January 1 of a particular year.

44. These were identified using version 4.1 of the Archigos data set (Goemans et al. 2009).

45. In line with Geddes et al. and other data sets (Magaloni 2008; Cheibub et al. 2010), these two cases are excluded—along with all other authoritarian governments that collapsed before the end of the calendar year—from the sample used in the quantitative analysis. To ensure that their exclusion does not affect our results, we include the two cases in the robustness tests (see appendix I).

46. Thus, 217 of the 219 leaders who came to power irregularly and survived less than a year (according to the Archigos data set) were nonrevolutionary.

47. Reyntjens (2013).

48. Tronvoll (1998: 481); Rock (2000: 224); Pool (2001: 188, 192); Kibreab (2009b: 41). By contrast, the Tigray People's Revolutionary Front in Ethiopia, which also came to power by violent struggle, did not engage in attempts at radical social transformation (J. Young 1997; Clapham 2017: 69).

49. The main exception is fascism, which is discussed above.

50. Skocpol (1979).

51. B. Moore (1966). The Bolivian and Mexican revolutions plausibly had such long-run democratizing consequences as well.

52. This definition of durability is similar to those offered by Svolik (2012) and Geddes et al. (2014). Also see Brownlee (2007) and Slater (2010).

53. Przeworski et al. (2000); Magaloni (2006); Reuter and Gandhi (2011).

54. See Ross (2001, 2012) and Morrison (2009). For a critique, see Haber and Menaldo (2011). For more nuanced arguments about the relationship between oil and regime outcomes, see B. Smith (2007) and Dunning (2008).

55. See Geddes (1999); Brownlee (2007); Gandhi and Przeworski (2007); Lust-Okar (2007); Gandhi (2008); Magaloni (2008); Blaydes (2010); and Svolik (2012). For a critique, see Pepinsky (2014).

56. Gandhi and Przeworski (2007); Blaydes (2010).

57. Gandhi and Przeworski (2007); Lust-Okar (2007); Gandhi (2008).

58. Geddes (1999); Brownlee (2007); Magaloni (2008); Svolik (2012).

59. See Geddes (1999); Magaloni (2006, 2008); Brownlee (2007); Gandhi (2008); Reuter and Gandhi (2011); Svolik (2012). For an earlier account, see Huntington (1968).

60. Geddes (1999: 129, 131); Brownlee (2007: 13, 215).

61. See O'Donnell and Schmitter (1986); Geddes (1999); Brownlee (2007).

62. B. Smith (2005). Also Huntington (1970: 6, 8); Levitsky and Way (2010, 2012); Slater (2010).

63. Andrew C. Janos (1970: 231–234) makes a similar point. Also Huntington (1968).

64. For a compelling argument along these lines, see Pepinsky (2014). Also Slater (2010).

65. See Lachapelle et al. (2020) and appendix I.

66. The annual failure rate of revolutionary party regimes is 1.35 percent, compared to 2.95 percent for party-based regimes without revolutionary origins ($p = 0.005$, log-rank test). See Lachapelle et al. (2020) and appendix I.

67. See B. Smith (2005, 2007); Pepinsky (2009); Slater (2010); Levitsky and Way (2012); Reuter (2017).

68. Huntington (1970: 13–14).

69. Huntington (1970: 14).

70. Huntington (1970: 14).

71. Chorley ([1943] 1973).

72. This literature is vast. Prominent work includes Edwards (1927); Brinton ([1938] 1965); Chorley ([1943] 1973); Chalmers Johnson (1966); B. Moore (1966); Huntington (1968); Wolf (1969); Gurr (1970); Dunn (1972); Goldfrank (1975, 1979); Paige (1975); S. Eisenstadt (1978); Tilly (1978); Skocpol (1979, 1982, 1994); Goldstone (1980, 1991, 2001); Dix (1983); Sewell (1985); Skocpol and Goodwin (1989); Farhi (1990); Goldstone et al. (1991); Wickham-Crowley (1992); Foran (1997, 2005); Halliday (1999); Goodwin (2001); and Lawson (2019). For an excellent review, see Goldstone (2001).

73. For reviews of these debates, see Skocpol (1979, 1994); Selbin (1993); Foran (1997, 2005); Goldstone (2001); and Goodwin (2001).

74. Skocpol (1979).

75. See Skocpol (1979, 1994); Goldstone (1980, 1991, 2001); Skocpol and Goodwin (1989); Farhi (1990); Selbin (1993); Foran (1997); Goodwin (2001).

76. Skocpol (1979, 1982, 1994); Goldstone (1980, 1991, 2001); Skocpol and Goodwin (1989); Goodwin (2001).

77. Selbin (1993).

78. See Eckstein (1976, 1982); Kelley and Klein (1981).

79. Chorley ([1943] 1973); Skocpol (1979, 1988); Gurr (1988); Farhi (1990); Foran and Goodwin (1993); Walt (1996); Becker and Goldstone (2005); Taylor and Botea (2008).

80. Chorley ([1943] 1973); Skocpol (1979, 1988); Gurr (1988); Carter et al. (2012).

81. Brinton ([1938] 1965: 176–204); Gurr (1988).

82. Walt (1996); Halliday (1999).

83. Huntington (1968: 270–335) and Skocpol (1979) are exceptions. Recent scholarship has shown how rebel victory in civil wars may enhance subsequent authoritarian stability (Lyons 2016a, 2016b; Toft 2016). However, most of the cases examined in this literature are nonrevolutionary. Slater (2010) and Slater and Smith (2016) examine how *counterrevolutionary* struggles contribute to authoritarian durability.

84. Huntingon (1968, 1970).

85. Mahoney (2001).

86. B. Smith (2005).

87. Slater (2010).

88. Mahoney (2001).

89. Huntington (1968: 270–273).

90. Quoted in Malley (1996: 76).

91. China in 1949 and Vietnam in 1954 are exceptions.

92. Hibbert (1991: 219).

93. Katzman (1993: 1).

94. LeoGrande (1978c).

95. Karol (1970: 456); A. Suárez (1971: 10).

96. Schapiro (1971: 174); Rabinowitch (1976); Fitzpatrick (1984: 112); Kotkin (2014: 192, 214).

97. Pettee (1938: 96).

98. On critical junctures in comparative regime studies, see Collier and Collier (1991); Mahoney (2001); Capoccia and Keleman (2007); Slater and Simmons (2010); Soifer (2012); Capoccia (2016).

99. Reid (1974: 8).

100. Mampilly (2011: 157); LeRiche and Arnold (2012: 145); Rolandsen and Daly (2016: 133–135).

101. Brinton ([1938] 1965: 255).

102. Kotkin (2014: 239).

103. Halperin (1972: 318–345).

104. Del Aguila (1984: 102–109).

105. Ideology is defined here as an explicitly articulated vision of the world rooted in eschatological or utopian expectations of a new society (S. Eisenstadt 1992: 25).

106. Brinton ([1938] 1965: 119).

107. S. Hanson (2010: 53); also Vu (2017).

108. On the Bolsheviks' ideological commitments, see Rees (2000: 446). On the ideological commitment of the Vietnamese Communists, see (Vu 2017). On China, see Pantsov and Levine (2012); on Iran, see Brumberg (2001).

109. Colburn (1986: 11).

110. Chorley ([1943] 1973: 185).

111. Chorley ([1943] 1973: 185); Skocpol (1988); Goldstone (1991: 427–428); Walt (1996).

112. See Brinton ([1938] 1965: 172); Huntington (1968: 269–270); Gurr (1988). As Jonathan R. Adelman (1985: 4) observes, the fate of revolutions is ultimately "determined on the battlefield."

113. Skocpol (1988); Walt (1996: 23–41).

114. Walt (1996: 342, 238–239).

115. These are Afghanistan, Albania, Angola, Cambodia, China, Cuba, Eritrea, Finland, Hungary, Iran, Mexico, Mozambique, Nicaragua, Russia, Rwanda, Vietnam, and Yugoslavia. In Albania, China, and Yugoslavia, the counterrevolutionary war occurred primarily before the seizure of national power.

116. Brinton ([1938] 1965: 232–255).

117. Sweig (2007: 55).

118. LeBas (2011: 44–47).

119. On the USSR, see Khlevniuk (2015) and Kotkin (2017); on China, see MacFarquhar and Schoenhals (2006).

120. P. Short (2004: 360).

121. O'Donnell and Schmitter (1986); Geddes (1999); Brownlee (2007).

122. Levitsky and Way (2010, 2012); Reuter and Gandhi (2011).

123. Quoted in Ihonvbere (1996: 70).

124. Daniels (1960: 186).

125. Daniels (1960: 402).

126. Pike (1978: 61–67).

127. Pérez (2015: 303–307).

128. Chorley ([1943] 1973: 186).

129. Iran (chapter 6) and Bolivia (chapter 8) are partial exceptions. Iran's revolutionaries heavily purged but did not eliminate the old military and built new and

more powerful coercive structures. In Bolivia, the revolutionary elite purged and temporarily deactivated the old army but did not build a new one.

130. Perlmutter and LeoGrande (1982: 782).
131. Perlmutter and LeoGrande (1982: 782).
132. Domínguez (1982a: 45–46).
133. LeoGrande (1978d: 279).
134. Turley (1977, 1982); Pike (1986a: 147, 181–188).
135. Turley (1988: 197).
136. Torigian (2016: 24).
137. Chorley ([1943] 1973: 149, 258).
138. Nordlinger (1977: 17).
139. Nordlinger (1977: 17).
140. Callahan (2005: 190).
141. Wilcox (1965: 144–145); Shah (2014: 86).
142. Huntington (1968: 311–313); Perlmutter (1977: 224).
143. Perlmutter (1977: 15, 206).
144. Hofheinz (1977: 299); emphasis added.
145. Cajina (1997: 125). This and all subsequent translations from the Spanish have been provided by the authors.
146. Katzman (1993: 23).
147. Adelman (1982) and Perlmutter and LeoGrande (1982) make similar arguments.
148. Svolik (2012: 5).
149. Finer (1962: 47, 79); Huntington (1968: 221); Nordlinger (1977: 49, 65, 75); Londregan and Poole (1990: 155).
150. Singh (2014: 7).
151. Singh's estimate of coups includes both military and nonmilitary coups.
152. Palace coups—coups led by regime leaders that did not change the regime or the ruling elite—occurred in Algeria in 1965 and 1992, and in Mexico in 1920. In Mexico, there were no successful uprisings after 1920.
153. The annual rate of coup attempts is 15.1 percentage points lower in revolutionary regimes compared to nonrevolutionary regimes ($p=0.029$). An average treatment effects analysis shows that revolutions reduced the annual rate of coup attempts by 9.8 percentage points ($p=0.004$). See Lachapelle et al. (2020).
154. Sumich and Honwana (2007: 15); Darch (2018: 114).
155. Svolik (2012).
156. Skocpol (1979: 161; 1988); Adelman (1985); Gurr (1988); Becker and Goldstone (2005); Carter et al. (2012).
157. Gurr (1988: 57); Skocpol (1988); Walt (1996); Carter et al. (2012).
158. Fall (1968: 130–168); Turley (1988: 195).
159. Klepak (2012: xiii).
160. Calculated from Correlates of War "National Material Capabilities" data set, version 5, https://correlatesofwar.org/data-sets/national-material-capabilities.
161. Magaloni (2006); Svolik (2012); Greitens (2016).
162. Levitsky and Way (2010: 57–59).
163. Amy Knight (1991: 765); Albats (1994: 23, 68); Pringle (2000: 196); Waller (2004: 336).
164. Joiner (1990: 1064).

165. Long (1981: 15).

166. Long (1981); Hayton (2010: 68–70); C. Thayer (2014: 136, 145–146).

167. Bellin (2012: 131–132).

168. Huntington (1968: 292–328) makes a similar argument.

169. Leggett (1986: 304).

170. Denitch (1976: 470, 473).

171. Buttinger (1967a: 408–412).

172. Pike (1978: 92).

173. Slater (2009).

174. Womack (1968); Alan Knight (1986b).

175. Denitch (1976: 470).

176. Selden (1971: 104); McDonald (1978: 5); Perry (1993, 2012).

177. Margolin (1999b: 568).

178. Post (1989a: 291); Post (1989c: 98).

179. See appendix II for complete coding rules.

180. Levitsky and Way (2010: 65).

181. As discussed in chapter 9, the Finnish case was less radical and more accommodationist than other revolutionary autocracies.

182. Moin (1999: 226).

183. L. Nguyen (2012: 89–91, 109–119).

184. Del Aguila (1984: 102).

185. Halperin (1972: 2). The behavior of foreign powers also matters. Whereas Charles de Gaulle's government in France was unusually tolerant of Ahmed Ben Bella's radical discourse in Algeria, which helped to prevent a counterrevolutionary conflict, U.S. administrations responded with hostility to Castro's radicalism, which helped to accelerate the conflict.

186. Unlike the MPLA and Frelimo, the PAIGC is widely seen as having been on the brink of military victory over the Portuguese when it gained independence in 1974. See MacQueen (1997: 42); Chabal (2003: 103); Reno (2011: 46).

187. According to Selbin (1993: 76), ideology "provides the believer with a picture of the world both as it is and as it should be."

188. S. Hanson (2010); Vu (2017).

189. S. Hanson (2010: 53); Vu (2017).

190. Gleijeses (2009: 72).

191. Blasier (1971b: 99); Burke and Malloy (1974: 52).

192. See Slater (2010); Slater and Smith (2016).

193. Examples include Uganda in 1985 and Ethiopia in 1991. See Lyons (2016a, 2016b) and Geddes et al. (2018).

194. Huntington (1968); Albertus (2015); Waldner (2017).

195. See Skocpol (1979); Vachudova (2005); Levitsky and Way (2006, 2010); Mainwaring and Pérez-Liñán (2013); Beissinger (2022).

196. Mainwaring and Pérez-Liñán (2013); Gunitsky (2017).

197. Casey (2020).

198. Weyland (2019).

199. These were Afghanistan, Albania, Eritrea, Finland, Hungary, Mexico, Russia, Rwanda, and Yugoslavia. Revolutionaries in Albania and Yugoslavia were initially Soviet allies and came to power just before the Cold War, but they did not receive

significant Soviet assistance prior to their emergence as powerful revolutionary parties. Albania received no Soviet assistance prior to coming to power in 1944 (Fischer 1999: 245). Similarly, the Yugoslav Partisans had already eliminated domestic rivals and established themselves as a powerful and disciplined movement before Soviet troops entered the country at the tail end of World War II (Barnett 2006: 57; Trifković 2016: 267, 169; Pirjevec 2018: 84).

200. Cheng (1990: 137); Vogel (2011: 650).

201. Jowitt (1992).

202. Geddes (1999); Magaloni (2006, 2008); Brownlee (2007); Svolik (2012).

203. Reuter and Gandhi (2011).

204. Magaloni (2006).

205. Magaloni (2006).

206. Economy (2018: 80); Wuthnow (2019).

207. Londregan and Poole (1990).

208. Algeria, where the army was always the dominant actor in the revolutionary coalition, is an exception.

209. Torigian (2016).

210. Alexeyeva and Chalidze (1985: 352).

211. We thank Mark R. Beissinger for providing us a copy of this study.

212. Bruhn (1997); K. Greene (2007).

213. On Cuba, see Fernández (2003) and Chaguaceda (2015). On Vietnam, see C. Thayer (2009a, 2009b, 2010) and Hayton (2010).

214. Lachapelle et al. (2020).

215. Chorley ([1943] 1973); Skocpol (1979); Skocpol and Goodwin (1989); Snyder (1992, 1998); Goldstone (2001); Goodwin (2001).

216. Skocpol (1979); Becker and Goldstone (2005).

217. Chorley ([1943] 1973: 108); Goldstone (1980, 1991, 2001); Skocpol (1982, 1994); Skocpol and Goodwin (1989); Farhi (1990); Selbin (1993); Goodwin (2001).

218. Goldstone (2001: 146).

219. Albania, Angola, Cambodia, China, Cuba, Finland, Hungary, Mozambique, Russia, Vietnam, and Yugoslavia (see Svolik 2012).

220. Selznick (1952); Friedrich and Brzezinski (1965).

221. In Eastern Europe, the establishment of these institutions was made possible by foreign imposition in the wake of World War II.

222. Westad (2003: 128); also Pepper (1999: 244, 277, 289); Walder (2015: 47, 49).

223. Selbin (2010: 14).

224. Selbin (1993: 33).

225. Huntington (1968: 376–378); Magaloni (2006); Waldner (2017).

226. Figes (2014: 528–529).

227. Breslauer (1978); Bialer (1980); Hauslohner (1987); Cook and Dimitrov (2017).

228. Cook and Dimitrov (2017: 9).

229. K. Harris (2017: 8–11, 15).

230. M. Milani (1994: 205); Alamdari (2005); Saeidi (2009); K. Harris (2017: 28).

231. See Fagen (1969) and Selbin (1993).

232. Selbin (1993: 13).

233. Selbin (1993: 33).

234. Selbin (1993: 20–21).

235. On Cuba, see Fagen (1969). On Iran, see Hashemi and Postel (2010); Daly (2012); Saha (2014); Barany (2019: 54).

236. Selbin (1993).

237. Hashemi and Postel (2010: xviii–xix); also Daly (2012); Saha (2014); Barany (2019: 54).

238. Figes (2014: 771); also Daniels (1960: 155); Chuev (1993: 122); Allen (2003: 49).

239. Huntington (1968). Also see Pepinsky (2014).

240. For similar critiques, see B. Smith (2005); Levitsky and Murillo (2009); Pepinsky (2014); and Brinks et al. (2019).

241. Also Huntington (1968, 1970); B. Smith (2005); Levitsky and Way (2012).

242. Pepinsky (2014).

243. See especially Huntington (1968: 196); also Finer (1962: 22); Zolberg (1968: 75); Nordlinger (1977: 93).

244. Nordlinger (1977: 64, 89–90); Londregan and Poole (1990); Luttwak (2016: 18).

245. Nordlinger (1977: 64–77).

246. Greitens (2016).

247. For an elaboration of this argument, see Way et al. (2019).

248. Way et al. (2019).

249. For reviews of this literature, see Goldstone (1980, 2001).

250. Skocpol (1979: 170).

251. See Geddes (1999); Bueno de Mesquita et al. (2005); Magaloni (2006); Gandhi (2008); Blaydes (2010); Levitsky and Way (2010); Svolik (2012). Slater (2009) is an exception.

252. Bueno de Mesquita et al. (2005: 7).

253. S. Hanson (2010: 53).

254. Brinton ([1938] 1965: 155).

255. Vu (2017: 1).

256. One exception is chapter 5, which examines the case of postcolonial Ghana, a case that provides an instructive contrast to revolutionary national liberation regimes in Algeria and Vietnam.

Chapter 2

1. The All-Russian Congress of Soviets was a quasi legislature that emerged during the revolution.

2. Quoted in Schapiro (1977: 67). Erlich was Lucan Way's step-great-grandfather.

3. Selznick (1952); Schapiro (1971); Svolik (2012).

4. Skocpol (1979: 129, 132).

5. Nafziger and Lindert (2013: 4).

6. Fitzpatrick (2008: 20).

7. This position may have been correct Marxism, but it was politically awkward because it suggested that in order to be victorious, the revolutionaries first had to wait for their opponents to win.

8. Service (1985: 134); Liebich (1997: 50).

9. Service (1985: 135).

10. The Bolsheviks, like many Russian revolutionaries at the time, "read the latest research on physics, psychiatry, and philosophy" (Service 1985: 175).

11. Daniels (1960: 12). Also Wolfe ([1948] 2001); Liebich (1997).

12. Rees (2000: 446); Kotkin (2014: 124).

13. Suny (2020: 365–368).

14. Wolfe ([1948] 2001: 247–251); Schapiro (1971: 107, 149); Service (1985: 6); Getty and Naumov (2010: 22); Kotkin (2014: 103).

15. Service (1985: 153, 135); Fitzpatrick (2008: 36). Lenin's allies "tended to elevate every difference into a matter of principle" (Wolfe [1948] 2001: 166); also Chuev (1993: 135).

16. Getty and Naumov (2010: 11).

17. Daniels (1960: 21).

18. Wolfe ([1948] 2001: 164); Schapiro (1971: 103); Service (1991: 49–50, 65, 63); Easter (2000: 31); Kotkin (2014: 117, 118, 132, 133, 154).

19. In 1910, just five or six active Bolshevik committees existed in imperial Russia (Kotkin 2014: 118). On the eve of the October Revolution, the party counted just four rural party organizations and 494 peasant members (Kotkin 2014: 426).

20. Figes (2014: 257–263).

21. Figes (2014: 263).

22. The SRs had emerged out of nineteenth-century radical movements that predated the Marxists.

23. Liebich (1997: 62).

24. Kotkin (2014: 180, 238).

25. Skocpol (1979).

26. von Hagen (1990: 17).

27. Quoted in Keep (1976: 212).

28. Chamberlin (1935: 257).

29. Quoted in Rigby (1979: 26).

30. Schapiro (1971: 174); Rabinowitch (1976); Fitzpatrick (1984: 112); Kotkin (2014: 192, 214).

31. Deutscher ([1954] 2003: 251).

32. Chorley ([1943] 1973: 148).

33. Mawdsley (2005b: 8–12).

34. Kotkin (2014: 228–229).

35. Lincoln (1999: 73).

36. Schapiro (1977: 236).

37. Benvenuti (1988: 78); von Hagen (1990: 53–54, 96); Figes (2014: 539, 565).

38. Service (1979: 88).

39. Leggett (1986: 361); Service (1995: 110).

40. Service (1991: 269); Chuev (1993: 98); Engelstein (2018: 183, 188).

41. Kotkin (2014: 239).

42. Mawdsley (2005b: 73).

43. Mawdsley (2005b: 72).

44. Figes (2014: 523, 525, 527); Engelstein (2018: 274).

45. Figes (2014: 526).

46. Figes (2014: 528–529).

47. Figes (2014: 529).

48. Mawdsley (2005b: 73).

49. Kotkin (2014: 239); also Mawdsley (2005b: 73).

50. Mawdsley (2005b: 46).

51. Overy (1997: 6); Kotkin (2014: 444–446).

52. Quoted in Overy (1997: 60).

53. Fitzpatrick (1984: 108; 1989: 388); also Suny (1972: 207–208); Holquist (2002: 166; 2003: 645).

54. Quoted in Mawdsley (2005b: 178).

55. Lincoln (1999: 80); Smele (2016: 34–35).

56. Holquist (2002); Engelstein (2018: 214).

57. Figes (2014: 560).

58. Lincoln (1999: 89).

59. Lincoln (1999: 101).

60. Lincoln (1999: 100–101); Smele (2016: 69).

61. Lincoln (1999: 181–187).

62. Lincoln (1999: 187).

63. Lincoln (1999: 142).

64. Lincoln (1999: 187).

65. Lauchlan (2013: 24–25).

66. Viacheslav Molotov, Stalin's right-hand man, quoted in Chuev (1993: 101).

67. Daniels (1960: 80); Fitzpatrick (1999: 19–24).

68. Lincoln (1999: 85).

69. Lewin (1989: 412); Graziosi (1996: 37); Suny (1998: 134). As Daniels wrote, "All shades of opinion within the Party realized the seriousness of the struggle with counter-revolution, and submitted to extreme centralization" (1960: 93).

70. Service (1979: 61). "The one goal that gripped everyone's imagination was the need to sustain an effective war effort" (Service 1979: 87; also Gill 1990: 60).

71. Daniels (1960: 93); Gill (1990: 60).

72. Daniels (1960: 304); Fitzpatrick (1999: 18).

73. von Hagen (1990: 50).

74. Lincoln (1999: 189).

75. Figes (2014: 591).

76. Swain (2014: 54); also von Hagen (1990); Mawdsley (2005b).

77. Fainsod (1958: 40).

78. Schapiro (1977: 244); Benvenuti (1988: 39, 53–55); von Hagen (1990: 125). For a different perspective, see Herspring (1996: 59, 71).

79. Benvenuti (1988: 39).

80. Schapiro (1977: 243); Benvenuti (1988); von Hagen (1990: 80–85, 113, 125). Colton (1979) argues that the commissars were *not* important in generating army loyalty.

81. Lincoln (1999: 197–198, 361–362).

82. von Hagen (1990: 125).

83. Schapiro (1971: 237); Fitzpatrick (1989).

84. Pethybridge (1974: 91); Benvenuti (1988: 214); Mawdsley (2005b: 180).

85. Lewin (1989: 412–413).

86. Holquist (2002: 173).

87. Leggett (1986: 16).

88. Pethybridge (1974: 94); Leggett (1986: 121).

89. Amy Knight (1991: 765); Albats (1994: 23, 68); Yasmann and Zubok (1998: 5); Pringle (2000: 196); Waller (2004: 336). KGB officials read every piece of international mail sent by Soviet citizens and conducted spot checks on domestic mail (Kalugin 1994: 298).

90. Engelstein (2018: 270).

91. Lincoln (1999: 159).

92. Figes (2014: 647).

93. Lincoln (1999: 384).

94. Pethybridge (1974: 95, 91); Leggett (1986); Boeva (2009: 41, 42).

95. Lauchlan (2013: 16). By contrast, the Nazi Gestapo and police in revolutionary France exhibited strong continuities with police in the regimes that preceded them (Lauchlan 2013: 16).

96. Party membership in the security services was higher than in other state agencies in the 1920s (Boeva 2009: 44).

97. Quoted in Shearer and Khaustov (2015: 2).

98. Leggett (1986: 114). Legget (1986: 114) argues that much of the violence perpetuated by the Cheka was not driven by "congenital cruelty" but rather "a single minded dedication to Lenin's doctrine of a merciless class war, in which the victory of the oppressed proletariat justified any and every means necessary for its attainment." Also Lauchlan (2013: 18–19).

99. Leggett (1986); Lauchlan (2013: 17).

100. Lewin (1989: 402, 406).

101. Lincoln (1999: 229).

102. Figes (2014: 668).

103. Osinsky and Eloranta (2014: 327).

104. Figes (2014: 612–619).

105. Wemheuer (2014: 8); also Allen (2003: 48–49).

106. Pethybridge (1974: 83); Lewin (1989: 404); Mawdsley (2005b: 3). Kotkin (2014: 332) cites figures of 700,000 Red deaths and over 130,000 White deaths. For a discussion of different estimates of civil war dead, see Mawdsley (2005b: 285).

107. The royal family was murdered in July 1918 by government officials who were terrified that Nicholas II might be liberated by White forces.

108. Service (1995: 109–110). Twenty-eight bishops and thousands of priests were killed during the war (Service 1995: 109).

109. Leggett (1986: 304).

110. Liebich (1997: 74). The Mensheviks and the Left SRs, for example, were initially allowed to operate legally and even participate in elections to Soviet councils (Wolfe [1948] 2001: 252; Schapiro 1977: 122, 125).

111. Schapiro (1977: 123).

112. Liebich (1997: 76).

113. Leggett (1986: 304, 305).

114. Daniels (1960: 93); Lewin (1989: 412); Graziosi (1996: 37); Suny (1998: 134).

115. Gill (1990: 59); Suny (1998: 140).

116. Schapiro (1977: 211–295); Suny (1998: 131–132).

117. Service (1979: 131, 150–154); Gill (1990: 195).

118. Daniels (1960: 304).

119. Easter (2000: 69–70).

120. Easter (2000: 70).

121. Carr (1950: 201); Schapiro (1971: 259); Rigby (1979).

122. Gill (1990). Also Fainsod (1958: 45, 49); Daniels (1960); Mawdsley (2005b: 189).

123. Rigby (1979: 185–186); Service (1995: 60–61); Mawdsley (2005b: 189).

124. Gerson (1976: 228); Werth (1999: 134); Boeva (2009: 46, 76–99); Gregory (2009: 86); Hagenloh (2009: 33).

125. Gregory (2009: 86).

126. Gerson (1976: 222); Werth (1999: 135); Getty and Naumov (2008: 34).

127. Pethybridge (1974: 115); Kotkin (2014: 440).

128. Daniels (1960: 210).

129. von Hagen (1990: 125, 308).

130. Leggett (1986); Boeva (2009: 50).

131. Jansen and Petrov (2002: 91); Gregory (2009: 188; 193).

132. Deutscher ([1959] 2003: 5).

133. Quoted in Gerson (1976: 222).

134. Kotkin (2014: 291).

135. Schapiro (1977: 212, 217).

136. Figes (2014: 775).

137. Graziosi (1996: 29–30).

138. Figes (2014: 756); also Werth (1999: 108–131). Most notably, in Ukraine, the anarchist Nestor Makhno organized a peasant army of 15,000 to battle the Bolsheviks (Figes 2014: 753).

139. Werth (1999: 108).

140. Figes (2014: 753).

141. Werth (1999: 111–112).

142. Figes (2014: 758).

143. Getzler (1983: 173–176).

144. Avrich (1970: 137); Werth (1999: 113).

145. Avrich (1970: 131).

146. Avrich (1970: 131).

147. Avrich (1970: 218).

148. Daniels (1960: 148).

149. Daniels (1960: 149).

150. Avrich (1970: 202–203); Werth (1999: 116); Figes (2014: 767).

151. Figes (2014: 769).

152. Figes (2014: 768).

153. von Hagen (1990: 291); Chuev (1993: 126); Kotkin (2014: 536). For several years after Lenin's exit, the country was in a "state of general unrest" (Daniels 1960: 220).

154. Many observers have drawn attention to Stalin's "complete mastery of the Party machine" after Lenin appointed him general secretary of the party in 1922

(Deutscher [1959] 2003: 231; Daniels 1960: 174; Kotkin 2014: 425). Although Stalin did not yet have the capacity to physically eliminate rivals, his control over the apparatus gave him enormous advantages in the struggle, including the ability to choose officials loyal to him, rig elections, and harass opposition.

155. Gill (1990: 7).

156. When Lenin became incapacitated in mid-1922, Trotsky was the "only leader who seemed plausible as a successor to Lenin" (Daniels 1960: 175).

157. Lenin wrote: "Stalin is too rude, and this fault . . . becomes insupportable in the office. I propose to the comrades to find a way to remove Stalin from that position" (quoted in Daniels 1960: 181).

158. Daniels (1960: 182).

159. Deutscher ([1959] 2003: 214).

160. Daniels (1960: 186); Schapiro (1971: 274).

161. Daniels (1960: 274); Schapiro (1971: 300); Kotkin (2014: 573).

162. Deutscher ([1959] 2003: 85, 78).

163. Daniels (1960: 240); Schapiro (1971: 288).

164. Daniels (1960: 278).

165. Daniels (1960: 277–280); Schapiro (1971: 305).

166. Daniels (1960: 123).

167. Daniels (1960: 286); Reiman (1987: 22); Getty and Naumov (2010: 26).

168. Schapiro (1971: 308). The demonstration was described as an "'antiparty rally' at a time when there was a direct threat of war" (Reiman 1987: 22).

169. Daniels (1960: 316–318).

170. Quoted in Daniels (1960: 318).

171. Daniels (1960: 363).

172. Daniels (1960: 169).

173. Reiman (1987: 100).

174. Daniels (1960: 398).

175. Daniels (1960: 307).

176. Daniels (1960); Gill (1990: 176–177).

177. Daniels (1960: 307).

178. Daniels (1960: 307–308, 402); Kotkin (2014: 654, 656).

179. Daniels (1960: 400, 231).

180. Fainsod (1958: 48); Deutscher ([1959] 2003: 230). For an analysis that views the internal opposition as somewhat stronger during this period, see Reiman (1987: 20–25).

181. Chuev (1993: 131, 135).

182. Kotkin (2014: 525); also Reiman (1987: 95). At the Twelfth Party Congress, Krupskaya voted with Stalin against Trotsky and kept her criticism of the leadership private. At the Fifteenth Party Congress in 1927, she failed to give any public backing to the United Opposition (Kotkin 2014: 615). Also Deutscher ([1959] 2003); Daniels (1960: 282).

183. Schapiro (1971: 288, 302); Gregory (2009: 146).

184. Gregory (2009: 150); Khlevniuk (2015: 84, 107).

185. Shearer and Khaustov (2015: 56–57).

186. Schapiro (1971: 307–308); Sontag (1975); Reiman (1987: 11); Hudson (2012a: 147–148).

187. Schapiro (1971: 307–308); Sontag (1975: 73); Hudson (2012a, 2012b); J. Harris (2013); Shearer (n.d.: 10–12).

188. Hudson (2012a: 148); Shearer (n.d.).

189. Quoted in Chuev (1993: 245); also Erlich (1960: 37, 51); Viola (1987: 25; 1996: 21); R. Tucker (1990: 74); Werth (1999: 147).

190. Viola (1987: 25).

191. Erlich (1960: 46); Reiman (1987: 7, 116).

192. Reiman (1987: 117).

193. Viola (1987: 21); Gill (1990: 113); Only 0.25 percent of rural inhabitants were party members in 1928; Kotkin (2014: 675).

194. Hudson (2012a; 2012b). Hudson's research has been criticized for relying on published police reports that may not accurately represent the situation at the time. However, our focus is not on the actual situation in the countryside but on the perceptions of Soviet leaders, which may have been shaped by such reports.

195. Hudson (2012a: 153).

196. Viola (1987: 25); Hughes (1991: 102–104); Kotkin (2014: 661–664).

197. Erlich (1960: 37, 51); R. Tucker (1990: 74); Chuev (1993: 245); Werth (1999: 147); J. Harris (2013: 42–43). For a detailed description of debates surrounding NEP, see Erlich (1960).

198. Daniels (1960: 358); Kotkin (2014: 661–664).

199. Daniels (1960: 324, 330); Reiman (1987: 38).

200. Viola (1987: 27); R. Tucker (1990: 71).

201. R. Tucker (1990: 108); Kotkin (2017: 91–92).

202. Lewin (1975: 11).

203. Allen (2003: 107).

204. Hunter (1973: 243); Suny (1998: 240).

205. Mawdsley (2005a: 47); Khlevniuk (2015: 183, 231).

206. Lewin (1975: 462).

207. Werth (1999: 146); Wemheuer (2014: 38); Shearer and Khaustov (2015: 89).

208. Viola (1996: viii, vii); also Lewin (1985: 142–143); Hudson (2012b: 114); Getty (2013: 220).

209. Viola (1996: 40).

210. Viola (1996: 133); Gregory (2009: 152).

211. Reiman (1987: 81); Viola (1996: viii); Werth (1999: 148).

212. Viola (1996: 125).

213. Werth (1999: 145).

214. Viola (1996: 4).

215. Reiman (1987: 55).

216. Davies (1980: 204, 243–248); Viola (2000: 2, 12, 29).

217. Lauchlan (2013: 17, 23); also Graziosi (1996: 49, 54); Wheatcroft (2007).

218. Graziosi (1996: 27–28, 33).

219. Shearer and Khaustov (2015: 117).

220. Shearer and Khaustov (2015: 8).

221. Lewin (1985: 155, 156); Conquest (1987); Werth (1999: 167).

222. Lewin (1975: 454).

223. Kotkin (2017: 198–204).

224. Getty and Naumov (2010: 196).

225. Getty and Naumov (2010: 242–243); Kotkin (2017: 305).

226. Kotkin (2017: 437) According to one estimate, shortly after the Terror, there were just under four million in labor camps and in exile (Getty and Naumov 2010: 241–243). Werth (1999: 238, 240) offers a lower figure of 1.67 million in camps in 1941.

227. In particular, the "mass operations," which targeted hundreds of thousands of former kulaks, certain ethnic populations, and anyone who had ever been associated with opposition activity, accounted for 90 percent of executions in 1937 and 1938 (Hagenloh 2013: 163; also 2009).

228. Khlevniuk (2015: 53).

229. Stalin argued that as the only socialist country in the world, Russia was surrounded by hostile enemy powers who were sending "armies of spies and subversives" on a mission to sabotage the socialist project (Werth 1999: 201).

230. Shearer and Khaustov (2015: 10).

231. Khlevniuk (1995: 172); Lenoe (2013: 196).

232. Khlevniuk (1995: 159).

233. Chuev (1993); Khlevniuk (1995: 169).

234. J. Harris (2003: 385).

235. Getty and Naumov (2010: 166).

236. Kotkin (2017: 397).

237. Getty and Naumov (2010: 166).

238. Getty and Naumov (2010: 169–170); Kotkin (2017: 52, 172, 415–420).

239. Kotkin (2017: 174, 426).

240. Werth (1999: 198); Kotkin (2017: 378).

241. A. Hill (2017: 690); Kotkin (2017: 378); also B. Taylor (2003: 154, 163–164).

242. Kotkin (2014: 376).

243. Kotkin (2017: 376, 619).

244. Getty and Naumov (2010: 177).

245. Khlevniuk (2009: 223); Fitzpatrick (2015: 135–139).

246. Khlevniuk (2009: 223).

247. Khlevniuk (2009: 218).

248. Werth (1999: 192, 194).

249. Shearer and Khaustov (2015: 9).

250. Fitzpatrick (2015: 137–139).

251. Getty and Naumov (2010: 176).

252. Getty and Naumov (2010: 178).

253. Werth (1999: 192, 194).

254. Getty and Naumov (2010: 199).

255. Scurr (2006: 318–358).

256. Khlevniuk (2015: 138); Kotkin (2017: 308, 372, 392).

257. Kotkin (2017: 437).

258. B. Taylor (2003: 160–161).

259. Getty and Naumov (2010: 8).

260. Getty and Naumov (2010: 140–141, 192, 194); Getty (2013: 218); Lauchlan (2013: 24); Viola (2017).

261. Getty and Naumov (2010: 114). The threat of a fifth column was the main public justification for the Terror (Getty and Naumov 2010: 171; Kotkin 2017: 427–428).

262. See Shulim (1977: 25); Kennedy (1988); Jones and Macdonald (2018: 662).

263. Getty and Naumov (2010: 137). In a somewhat similar vein, Fitzpatrick (2015: 115) argues that the Terror was made possible by the revolutionary character of the Bolshevik Party: "They belonged to a revolutionary party, and fighting enemies was what revolutionaries did."

264. Jansen and Petrov (2002: 91); Gregory (2009: 188, 193); Kotkin (2017: 394).

265. On rare examples of mid-level defections in the security services, see Jansen and Petrov (2002: 143–147); Khlevniuk (2009: 197, 199).

266. B. Taylor (2003: 160–161). Although Stalin's show trials were filled with lurid tales of assassination plots, there is no known instance of a serious assassination attempt against Stalin. See Khlevniuk (2009).

267. Nordlinger (1977).

268. B. Taylor (2003: 154).

269. Shirer (1960: 1316, 1319, 1339); Heinemann (2019).

270. Heinemann (2019).

271. Kotkin (2017: 426, 391).

272. Kotkin (2017: 413, 996n214).

273. Quoted in Mawdsley (2005a: 44).

274. Glantz and House (2015: 48) According to Overy, "Stalin remained utterly, almost obsessively, convinced that Germany would not invade" (1997: 70).

275. The USSR scrupulously abided by the pact, sending Germany petroleum products and other critical supplies until hours before the Nazi invasion (Glantz and House 2015: 49).

276. Overy (1997: 64); Glantz and House (2015: 45, 51).

277. As a result of purges, the Red Army was "chronically short of commanders at every level" (Glantz and House 2015: 10; also Mikoian 1999: 384). The Soviet war effort may have also been undermined by the purge of espionage organizations (Mikoian 1999: 384; Mawdsley 2005a: 32, 99), which weakened the state's "capability for analysis and warning" (Glantz and House 2015: 49).

278. Overy (1997: 77); Mawdsley (2005a: 81); Glantz and House (2015: 59).

279. Khrushchev (1990: 57); Overy (1997: 80).

280. Overy (1997: 117, 154); Mawdsley (2005a: 117).

281. Overy (1997: 85); Mawdsley (2005a: 100).

282. As Overy put it, "Few would have gambled on a Soviet victory" (1997: 156).

283. On lend-lease aid, see Glantz and House (2015: 197). On German errors, see Clark (1985: 108) and Glantz and House (2015: 66). On the role of territorial size and rough terrain, see Mawdsley (2005a: 45).

284. Lend-lease did not gain substantial traction until mid-1942, long after the invasion began (Mawdsley 2005a: 192–193; Glantz and House 2015: 358). Indeed, Russia "fought in isolation" during the first part of the war (Mawdsley 2005a: 186).

285. Indeed, support for German occupation was higher in the areas of Ukraine that suffered most from famine (Rozenas and Zhukov 2019: 575–576).

286. Revolution emerged in a context of wartime state collapse in Russia in 1917, Finland in 1918, Vietnam in 1945, Cambodia in 1975, and Afghanistan in the early 1990s. Revolutionary movements emerged as threats in the context of military aggression in Hungary in 1919, China after 1937, and Albania and Yugoslavia in the early 1940s.

287. Skocpol (1979).

288. Mawdsley (2005a: 44).

289. Khlevniuk (2015: 216).

290. Overy (1997: 117); Reese (2011: 175). It is possible that anti-Soviet activity was reduced by the brutality of the Nazi invaders. However, an explanation focusing on fear of the Nazis is not consistent with the fact that Soviet frontline soldiers defected in vast numbers to the Nazi side (Edele 2017: vii, 31). It is also not clear that information about Nazi atrocities reached Soviet populations in the first critical weeks of the invasion, which are the focus of the analysis here.

291. On civilian meddling and military coups, see Finer (1962) and Nordlinger (1977). Military defeat has been shown to increase the likelihood of a successful military coup (Bueno de Mesquita et al. 1992: 640, 643; Fearon 2004: 290; Chiozza and Goemans 2011; Weeks 2014).

292. Hellbeck (2015: 33, 37).

293. Mawdsley (2005a: 44); Khlevniuk (2015: 138); Kotkin (2017: 308, 372, 392).

294. Mawdsley (2005a: 49).

295. Mawdsley (2005a: 51).

296. Mawdsley (2005a: 47); Khlevniuk (2015: 185).

297. Overy (1997: 170, 171); Mawdsley (2005a: 42); Khlevniuk (2015: 183, 231).

298. Mawdsley (2005a: 46).

299. Zubkova (1998: 20); Mawdsley (2005a: 404).

300. Overy (1997: 250); Taubman (2003: 243); Gunitsky (2017: 157–158).

301. Werth (1999: 238). For a discussion of the expense of maintaining the Soviet Union's enormous penal system, see Werth (1999: 240–241); Gorlizki and Khlevniuk (2004: 123).

302. M. Djilas (1962); Taubman (2003: 211).

303. Gill (1990: 7); Gorlizki and Khlevniuk (2004: 113).

304. Richter (1994: 22).

305. Taubman (2003: 240).

306. Taubman (2003: 242).

307. Werth (1999: 252); Taubman (2003: 246).

308. Taubman (2003: 254).

309. Barsukov (2000: 52); Taubman (2003: 241, 259, 261). In 1957, following an attempted "antiparty" coup, Khrushchev mobilized the support of the party apparatus to sideline most of the remaining revolutionary generation, including Molotov, who had worked with Stalin since 1917.

310. Although the speech was intended only for Soviet delegates to the congress, the text of the speech quickly found its way into the public eye. On the secret speech and the decision-making behind it, see K. Smith (2017).

311. Richter (1994: 105); Taubman (2003: 382).

312. Taubman (2003: 382).

313. Richter (1994: 76); Zubkova (1998); Glantz and House (2015: 363).

314. Gorlizki and Khlevniuk (2004: 4). Although the regime remained brutal, there was nevertheless a steep decline in convictions for counterrevolutionary offenses (Gorlizki and Khlevniuk 2004: 5, 125). The regime's raison d'être evolved "from protecting a besieged party-state from internal and external enemies to protecting society as a whole from outside threats" (Richter 1994: 56).

315. Richter (1994: 77, 121).

316. The party had 441,851 primary party organizations in 1987 (Burant 1991: 312).

317. Yasin (1998: 168).

318. Svolik (2012).

319. Shelley (1996: 181–182).

320. Beissinger (2002: 70); Crump (2014: 101).

321. Barsukov (2000: 64).

322. Khrushchev also split up party structures into agricultural and industrial branches, a move that weakened the party machine and created deep opposition within the *nomenklatura.* See Richter (1994: 128) and Barsukov (2000: 62). We thank Mark Kramer for his analysis of the 1964 events and identification of sources.

323. Brezhnev had been "a trusted and chosen member of Khrushchev's entourage" since 1946 (Dornberg 1974: 87).

324. Sandle (2002: 171).

325. Mawdsley (2005b: 317); also Richter (1994: 53); Crump (2014: 67).

326. According to an unpublished survey of more than 2,000 cases of mass unrest between 1953 and 1983, special troops fired on protesters in half (6 of 12) of the instances in which they were mobilized between 1953 and 1964, but in just 1 of 21 cases between 1964 and 1983 (Alexeyeva and Chalidze 1985: 352).

327. Alexeyeva and Chalidze (1985: 352). We thank Mark R. Beissinger for providing us a copy of this study.

328. Amy Knight (1990); Murawiec and Gaddy (2002: 33).

329. See Dornberg (1974: 66); Werth (1999: 193); Khlevniuk (2009: 172); Fitzpatrick (2015: 141); Viola (2017).

330. Richter (1994: 44).

331. Bacon (2002: 11); Crump (2014: 59).

332. Richter (1994: 178, 179); Bacon (2002: 8).

333. Bacon (2002: 11, 15); Fowkes (2002: 69).

334. Blackwell (1979: 33–35).

335. Jowitt (1992: 142–143).

336. Bacon (2002: 2).

337. Jowitt (1992).

338. Svolik (2012).

339. Quoted in Chernyaev (2000: 160).

340. Ligachev (1996: 109–110).

341. Hough (1997: 268, 272).

342. A. Brown (1996: 274). Key policies, including the future of East Germany and the government's 1989 economic plan, were not even discussed at meetings (Hough 1997: 271). Instead, Gorbachev made decisions alone or in consultation with advisers outside the party leadership.

343. Ogushi (2008: 71–73).

344. Beissinger (2002).

345. Odom (1998: 312).

346. Odom (1998: 345).

347. Odom (1998: 320); also Lebed (1995: 404–405).

348. Lebed (1995: 404–405).

349. Daniels (1960: 304).

350. Hellbeck (2015: 33, 37).

351. Breslauer (1978); Bialer (1980); Hauslohner (1987); Cook and Dimitrov (2017).

352. Cook and Dimitrov (2017: 9).

353. Selznick (1952); Friedrich and Brzezinski (1965).

354. Holquist (2003: 643).

355. Lauchlan (2013).

Chapter 3

1. Dimitrov (2013: 8).

2. See Shambaugh (2008); Heilmann and Perry (2011); Vogel (2011); T. Bernstein (2013); Dimitrov (2013); Gallagher and Hanson (2013). Nathan (2003) and Walder (2004) contend that adaptiveness of the regime may be explained by the increasingly meritocratic character of the state bureaucracy and increased recruitment of highly educated individuals into the party.

3. Between 1978 and 2011, average GDP growth in China was nearly 9 percent a year (Dimitrov 2013: 21).

4. Although the Chinese military has played a central role in politics since 1949, it has never launched a serious coup attempt. Intervention into politics has always been done at the behest of party leaders (Shambaugh 2002: 18).

5. Fairbank (1987: 172).

6. Dreyer (2013: 74–117).

7. Fairbank (1987: 175, 181).

8. Marin (1996).

9. Dreyer (2013: 94–95).

10. Jordan (1976: 7, 14); Setzekorn (2018: 29).

11. J. Taylor (2011: 39, 44).

12. Dreyer (2013: 80–81).

13. Jordan (1976: 17, 29); Setzekorn (2018: 30–31, 35).

14. J. Harrison (1972: 83); Jordan (1976: 19, 263); J. Taylor (2011: 55).

15. J. Taylor (2011: 58–59); Dreyer (2013: 117–118, 139).

16. Jordan (1976: 6); J. Taylor (2011: 58); Dreyer (2013: 117).

17. Jordan (1976: 6); J. Taylor (2011: 55–62).

18. Wilbur (1983: 122); van de Ven (2003).

19. Jordan (1976: 34).

20. On the heterogeneity of the KMT coalition, see Jordan (1976: x–xi, 45). Also van de Ven (2003: 113).

21. Jordan (1976: 264); J. Taylor (2011: 55–62).

22. The first United Front generated considerable opposition within the CCP. See Chesneaux (1968: 243); J. Harrison (1972: 34); Pantsov (2000: 58–61); Pantsov and Levine (2012: 114).

23. Isaacs ([1938] 2010: 103–104).

24. Isaacs ([1938] 2010: 295); Meisner (1999: 23).

25. Chesneaux (1968: 256, 263); McDonald (1978: 207–214); Perry (1993: 80–84; 2007: 40).

26. Isaacs ([1938] 2010: 55–59); Chesneaux (1968: 264); McDonald (1978: 207–208); Zarrow (2005: 206). Strikes and protests took place in Chungking, Fuchow, Canton/Guangzhou, Amoy, Wuhan, Nanjing, Beijing, Tsingtao, and other cities (Chesneaux 1968: 273).

27. Chesneaux (1968: 266); Jordan (1976: 42, 56–57).

28. Jordan (1976: 35–52).

29. Jordan (1976: 61–62).

30. Isaacs ([1938] 2010: 96). As McDonald put it, "The armies of the Northern Expedition sowed organization in their wake as previous armies had sown devastation" (1978: 242). Also Fenby (2003: 124).

31. McDonald (1978: 250); also Isaacs ([1938] 2010: 95); Chesneaux (1968: 326–327).

32. J. Harrison (1972: 84–85); Jordan (1976: 111); Hofheinz (1977: 8, 10, 17, 57, 104); Meisner (1999: 25); Perry (2012: 7–8, 129). The party "filled the political vacuum" created by the Northern Expedition and the failure of the KMT to focus on this (X. Li 2007: 42). These associations were in many ways highly top-down affairs. Thus, they were most prevalent along major rail lines that were more accessible to outsiders (Hofheinz 1977: 130).

33. Hofheinz (1977: 31–35); Mao (2003).

34. Hofheinz (1977: 46).

35. Mao (2003: 15).

36. Jordan (1976: 284); Fenby (2003: 126); Pantsov and Levine (2012: 151, 160); Dreyer (2013: 137, 138).

37. McDonald (1978: 300).

38. Isaacs ([1938] 2010: 119); Chesneaux (1968: 357–361); Perry (1993: 84–87); Fenby (2003: 142).

39. Isaacs ([1938] 2010: 117–118).

40. Fenby (2003: 142); also Isaacs ([1938] 2010: 120–123); Zarrow (2005: 237).

41. Foreigners were convinced "that they were going to be murdered in their own beds by their own servants" (Isaacs [1938] 2010: 123). "The tales of fleeing missionaries, which grew taller by every mile as they traveled toward Shanghai, made churchgoing pillars of society shriek hysterically for blood" (Isaacs [1938] 2010: 124).

42. Isaacs ([1938] 2010: 123, 128).

43. Isaacs ([1938] 2010: 251–252); Perry (2007: 89–90); J. Taylor (2011: 66–68); Carradice (2018: 13–15).

44. J. Taylor (2011: 68); Perry (2012: 135); Dreyer (2013: 141–142).

45. P. Short (1999: 188).

46. Party membership fell from 58,000 in early 1927 to about 10,000 by year's end (Meisner 1999: 27; Pantsov and Levine 2012: 205).

47. Lary (2015: 5).

48. Pantsov and Levine (2012: 191–192). In the words of the Communist leader Zhang Guotao, "From this bloody lesson, the CCP learned that only armed force can deal with armed force" (quoted in P. Short 1999: 188).

49. Whitson (1973: 27); Hofheinz (1977: 55); Snow (1978: 359); Fenby (2003: 159–160); X. Li (2007: 37, 47); Hsu (2012: 52–53); Perry (2012: 136–137).

50. J. Becker (1998: 15).

51. Selden (1971: 34) notes that the KMT was able to control only those areas where transport and communications were better developed.

52. Averill (2006: 5); also Hofheinz (1967: 69); Selden (1971: 104); McDonald (1978: 5); Perry (1993, 2006, 2012).

53. Dreyer (2013: 7).

54. Dreyer (2013: 4–5).

55. J. Taylor (2011: 51).

56. J. Taylor (2011: 189, 296); Dreyer (2013: 5).

57. T. Wu (1976); J. Taylor (2011: 124–127, 256–257, 272).

58. Dorrill (1969).

59. Party discipline in the late 1920s was "lax" and undermined by "unruly independent rural soviets" (Whitson 1973: 44). See also P. Short (1999: 329).

60. This collection included groups led by He Long on the Hunan-Hubei border, Zhang Guotao north of the Yangtze, and Mao Zedong and Zhu De in the Jinggang Mountains. See Fenby (2003: 197); Averill (2006: 3); Wei (2012: 234).

61. Isaacs ([1938] 2010: 219–220); Byron and Pack (1992: 86).

62. Selden (1971: 47). For examples of Mao's insubordination during this period, see Whitson (1973); Hsu (2012: 111, 164); Pantsov and Levine (2012: 255, 256).

63. Hofheinz (1967: 69, 49, 53); Selden (1971: 57); Snow (1978: 159); Pantsov and Levine (2012: 211).

64. Hsu (2012: 76).

65. Hofheinz (1967).

66. Y. Wu (2014: 23); also Whitson (1973); X. Li (2007).

67. Hsu (2012: 98); also Chalmers Johnson (1962: 79–80).

68. Hsu (2012: 95–96). Indoctrination efforts were enhanced by increasing literacy among soldiers—which reached 60–70 percent in the 1930s (Snow 1978: 265).

69. Averill (2006: 163); Hsu (2012: 90–92).

70. X. Li (2007: 53). Much of the literature on party-military relations in China focuses on formal institutional structures such as the network of political commissars tasked with monitoring army loyalty (Joffe 1965: 57–58; Jencks 1981: 235–246; Shambaugh 1991: 550; X. Li 2007: 53). Although such institutions may be important, they do not appear to be the main source of tight party control. KMT commissars were widely viewed as "concubines" subservient to commanders (Whitson 1973: 440; Setzekorn 2018: 42). And although the CCP developed a pervasive system of political commissars in 1929 (Shambaugh 1991: 550; X. Li 2007: 53; Hsu 2012: 56), weak party control persisted for years afterward. See Shambaugh (1991: 531); Hsu (2012: 56). On the weakness of commissars, see Joffe (1965: 137; 1997: 42).

71. Whitson (1973: 49–64); Snow (1978); X. Li (2007: 53–57).

72. Salisbury (1985: 103).

73. Whitson (1973: 61); Salisbury (1985: 127); Hsu (2012: 219).

74. Barnouin and Yu (2006: 58); J. Taylor (2011: 111).

75. Snow (1978: 204–205); Salisbury (1985); B. Yang (1990); Shuyun (2006); Hsu (2012: 219); Pantsov and Levine (2012: 283).

76. Snow (1978: 204–205); Salisbury (1985); Hsu (2012: 219); Pantsov and Levine (2012: 288).

77. Salisbury (1985: 324–325); Fairbank (1987: 238); Hsu (2012: 215). Harrison Salisbury writes that the march created a "hard confidence" in the party leadership

and that, as a result of the Long March, faith in the revolution "hardened to steel" (1985: 324–325).

78. For a similar argument, see Shuyun (2006: 80).

79. Wei (2012: 232).

80. See Whitson (1973: 282–283); Salisbury (1985: 95–103); Shuyun (2006: 68).

81. Wei (2012: 242); also Salisbury (1985: 71, 109, 122–312); B. Yang (1990); Kampen (1989); Hsu (2012: 221). Zhou survived by quickly subordinating himself to Mao.

82. Whitson (1973: 51–54, 59–65, 132–140, 143–155); Salisbury (1985: 245); Wei (2012: 234).

83. Fenby (2003: 271); Pantsov and Levine (2012: 283–284).

84. Salisbury (1985: 271); also Whitson (1973: 140); Salisbury (1985: 311); B. Yang (1990: 207–208); X. Li (2007: 59); Hsu (2012: 231); Pantsov and Levine (2012: 287).

85. Salisbury (1985: 316).

86. Whitson (1973: 140); Salisbury (1985: 319–320); X. Li (2007: 63).

87. X. Li (2007: 57).

88. Salisbury (1985: 143).

89. Shambaugh (1991: 532); Yafeng (2008: 115).

90. Hinton (1966: 215); Shambaugh (1991: 530); Hsu (2012: 81).

91. Hofheinz (1977: 299). Also Joffe (1965: xii); Snow (1978: 296); Segal and Phipps (1990: 967); Ji (2001: 115); X. Li (2007: 46).

92. See J. Taylor (2011: 132, 136, 142).

93. Selden (1971: 122); J. Harrison (1972: 309, 315); Byron and Pack (1992: 159).

94. Byron and Pack (1992: 138); Meisner (1999: 33).

95. P. Short (1999: 265); Shuyun (2006: 57).

96. For analyses of Mao's centralization of power, see J. Harrison (1972: 289); Wylie (1980: 196); Teiwes (1987: 60); Teiwes and Sun (1995); Pantsov and Levine (2012: 290, 360).

97. Byron and Pack (1992: 159, 125).

98. P. Short (1999: 388); also Seybolt (1986: 51).

99. J. Harrison (1972: 337, 326); T. Wu (1992: 93).

100. Selden (1971: 194); also Wylie (1980: 184–187); Seybolt (1986: 48–50).

101. The military threat justified "rigid dogmas and orthodoxies in political and cultural life" (Meisner 1999: 50). Also Seybolt (1986: 58).

102. Seybolt (1986: 40–41); Lary (2015: 73).

103. Walder (2015: 31). The campaign was the "major initiative for unifying the Party and eventually the entire population behind [Mao's] leadership" and resulted in "disciplining and streamlining the CCP" (Harrison 1972: 309; also Seybolt 1986: 68; Huang 2000: 135). Although factionalism did not disappear, "all manner of control—orders, directives, complaints, reports and the like—flowed directly to and from Mao" (Huang 2000: 139).

104. Chalmers Johnson (1962: 1); Bianco (1971: 150); T. Wu (1992: 79); J. Taylor (2011: 171–173); Walder (2015: 20).

105. J. Taylor (2011: 142–143).

106. T. Wu (1976).

107. J. Taylor (2011: 142–143).

108. J. Taylor (2011: 149); Dreyer (2013: 303).

109. Classic accounts that emphasize the importance of the Japanese period include Chalmers Johnson (1962); Bianco (1971); and Selden (1971).

110. Bianco (1971: 150); T. Wu (1992: 79); Walder (2015: 20).

111. Chalmers Johnson (1962: 1).

112. Bianco (1971: 150); T. Wu (1992: 79).

113. Snow (1978: 236); Levine (1987: 193).

114. Chalmers Johnson (1962); Koss (2018: 183).

115. Pepper (1999); Westad (2003); Lary (2015); Walder (2015).

116. Dickson (1993: 56–59); J. Taylor (2011: 162–163); Dreyer (2013: 168, 173, 290).

117. J. Taylor (2011: 330).

118. Levine (1987: 229); Walder (2015: 33–34).

119. Whitson (1973: 302); Levine (1987: 88, 128); Fenby (2003: 476); Walder (2015: 16). On conscription, see Levine (1987: 152–156).

120. Fenby (2003: 484); Pantsov and Levine (2012: 350).

121. Westad (2003: 109).

122. Walder (2015: 39).

123. R. Bernstein (2014: 65).

124. Levine (1987: 204–205).

125. Levine (1987: 139–141).

126. Levine (1987: 90).

127. Hinton (1966); Westad (2003: 116).

128. Hinton (1966: 237); Fairbank (1987: 264); Levine (1987: 213); Pepper (1999: 277).

129. Pepper (1999: 288).

130. Westad (2003: 135); also Hinton (1966: 282).

131. Levine (1987: 212).

132. Westad (2003: 132).

133. Hinton (1966: 239, 243).

134. Hinton (1966: 282).

135. Hinton (1966: 282).

136. See Westad (2003: 116).

137. Levine (1987: 224).

138. Levine (1987: 224–228); Westad (2003: 127).

139. Hinton (1966: 189, 195); Levine (1987: 142); Pepper (1999: 298, 430).

140. Pepper (1999: 298).

141. Levine (1987: 218, 237). Also Hinton (1966: 170); Fairbank (1987: 265); Pepper (1999: 244, 329); Westad (2003: 116); Walder (2015: 45).

142. Zhang (1995: 37); Westad (2003: 305). In April 1949, the Chinese attacked and crippled British navy vessels that had been attempting to rescue British citizens trapped by the war (Westad 2003: 245; Lary 2015: 173).

143. Chen (1994: 33–38).

144. Meisner (1999: 83).

145. Lary (2015: 201).

146. Lary (2015: 189, 197, 240).

147. Lary (2015: 205).

148. Lary (2015: 205).

149. Chen (1994: 215).

150. Mao viewed Chinese policy in terms of international class struggle and agreed with the Soviet Union to play an active role in promoting revolution in the East—a stance that led to hostile relations with the United States (Chen 1994: 114, 121).

151. Fairbank (1987: 278); X. Li (2007: 80); Pantsov and Levine (2012: 386–387); Dikötter (2013: 142).

152. Teiwes (1987: 89).

153. Meisner (1999: 71); Perry (2007: 170).

154. Teiwes (1987: 89); Chen (1994: 221); Westad (2003: 297); Perry (2007: 170); Walder (2015: 52–53).

155. Teiwes (1987: 89); Chen (1994: 221).

156. Teiwes (1987: 89); Westad (2003: 297); Walder (2015: 53).

157. Walder (2015: 65).

158. J. Becker (1998: 51).

159. Walder (2015: 66); also Teiwes (1987: 87).

160. Chen (1994: 194); Westad (2003: 282); Walder (2015: 53, 66).

161. Meisner (1999: 72); Strauss (2006: 901); J. Yang (2008: 476).

162. Teiwes (1987: 89, 90); Chen (1994: 141).

163. J. Harrison (1972: 435); Meisner (1999: 98); Dikötter (2013: 75–76).

164. Meisner (1999: 98); Walder (2015: 50).

165. J. Harrison (1972: 435–436); P. Short (1999: 436); Dikötter (2013: 83).

166. Meisner (1999: 100). Not all repression or radical reform during this period can be directly tied to military conflict. In particular, the Anti-Rightist Campaign of 1957, which resulted in a purge of hundreds of thousands of intellectuals and technocrats, was not linked directly to military threat. See Fairbank (1987: 293); Teiwes (1987: 139).

167. Selden (1971: 278).

168. Hinton (1966: 323–357).

169. Pepper (1999: 244, 277, 289); Westad (2003: 131); Walder (2015: 47, 49).

170. Hinton (1966: 236–246).

171. J. Yang (2008: 13); Bramall (2011: 992).

172. Fairbank (1987: 299); Zhang (1995: 250); J. Yang (2008: 90).

173. Teiwes and Sun (1999: 70, 101); Chan (2001: 64); J. Yang (2008: 90).

174. J. Yang (2008: 101).

175. Chan (2001: 64); J. Yang (2008: xviii).

176. Teiwes and Sun (1999: 89).

177. Fairbank (1987: 304); J. Becker (1998: 85); Chan (2001: 14); Dikötter (2010: 29, 33).

178. Chan (2001: 68, 113, 121); Dikötter (2010: 27, 30).

179. Teiwes and Sun (1999: 114).

180. Teiwes and Sun (1999: 108); Chan (2001: 174).

181. Chan (2001: 256).

182. J. Becker (1998: 134); Chan (2001: 100, 176); J. Yang (2008: 28).

183. Chan (2001: 196); Dikötter (2010: 61).

184. J. Becker (1998: 70–76); Chan (2001: 123); J. Yang (2008: 207, 259); Dikötter (2010: 35).

185. Chan (2001: 123).

186. Chan (2001: 82); J. Yang (2008: 166); Dikötter (2010: 48).

187. Meisner (1999: 223).

188. Chan (2001: 82).

189. J. Becker (1998: 107).

190. J. Becker (1998: 106); J. Yang (2008: 174–177).

191. Chan (2001: 83).

192. Teiwes and Sun (1999: 109); Chan (2001: 145).

193. See J. Yang (2008: 119).

194. J. Becker (1998: 85); Dikötter (2010: 33).

195. Chan (2001: 146–148). As in Russia in the 1930s, peasants slaughtered animals rather than hand them over to the collective farms (J. Becker 1998: 134; Chan 2001: 89).

196. Chan (2001: 87, 138); also J. Becker (1998: 115–120). At the same time, China lacked the infrastructure to transport the grain collected, which was often left rotting in state granaries yards from starving peasants (J. Becker 1998: 143; J. Yang 2008: 46).

197. J. Becker (1998: 133).

198. Fairbank (1987: 303).

199. Lieberthal (1987: 294); J. Yang (2008: 504).

200. Teiwes and Sun (1999: 13, 96).

201. Teiwes and Sun (1999: 99, 188); Chan (2001: 60); J. Yang (2008: 89, 106).

202. Teiwes and Sun (1999: 112, 170); also J. Yang (2008: 93).

203. See especially J. Becker (1998); Teiwes and Sun (1999); Chan (2001); J. Yang (2008); Dikötter (2010).

204. Chan (2001: 136, 140).

205. During this period, the regime also demonstrated a striking capacity for rapid and massive population movements. In the fall of 1958, 47,000 teachers and students were sent to work on communal farms (Chan 2001: 137), and in May 1960 over 20 million urban residents were transferred to the countryside "without any significant turmoil" (J. Yang 2008: 445).

206. J. Yang (2008: 448, 451).

207. J. Yang (2008: 265, 478–482).

208. Chan (2001: 211, 220–221).

209. Chan (2001: 229–230); J. Yang (2008: 24, 36, 62, 71).

210. Joffe (1965: 85).

211. J. Yang (2008: 103); Dikötter (2010: 227).

212. J. Yang (2008: 482–484).

213. Nordlinger (1977: 88).

214. Joffe (1965: 85); also Lieberthal (1987: 307).

215. Joffe (1965: 88); also Lieberthal (1987: 307); Meisner (1999: 231).

216. Joffe (1965: 88).

217. J. Yang (2008: 380).

218. Dahm (1971: 224–225).

219. Meisner (1999: 231); Teiwes and Sun (1999: 202–212); J. Yang (2008: 358–360); Dikötter (2010: 92–93, 96).

220. Teiwes and Sun (1999: 203).

221. J. Yang (2008: 361–362); Dikötter (2010: 93).

222. J. Yang (2008: 382); also J. Becker (1998: 90–91). One exception was Peng's chief of staff, Huang Kechang, who backed Peng during the conference (Teiwes and Sun 1999: 205; Dikötter 2010: 94).

223. Joffe (1965: 149–150); Meisner (1999: 232).

224. Quoted in Gao (2007: 126–127).

225. Y. Wu (2014: xv).

226. Walder (2015: 196).

227. Huang (2000: 287).

228. Between 1962 and 1965, the party bureaucracy played an increasing role in shaping economic policy (Huang 2000: 256–259). Because of the degree of crisis on the one hand and Mao's commitment to the Great Leap Forward on the other, Liu Shaoqi and other party leaders reversed many Great Leap Forward policies without consulting Mao. This almost certainly heightened Mao's antipathy toward Liu and helped stimulate the Cultural Revolution (Huang 2000: 234–237).

229. Harding (1991: 133).

230. MacFarquhar and Schoenhals (2006: 117–131); Y. Wu (2014: 54); also Fairbank (1987: 328); Dikötter (2016).

231. MacFarquhar and Schoenhals (2006: 88–91).

232. Harding (1991: 152).

233. Harding (1991: 151); Teiwes and Sun (1996: 66).

234. MacFarquhar and Schoenhals (2006: 126).

235. Salisbury (1985: 327–341); Fairbank (1987: 320).

236. Walder (2015: 201).

237. Huang (2000: 284–285).

238. Huang (2000: 285–286); MacFarquhar and Schoenhals (2006: 156); Walder (2015: 202).

239. Walder (2015: 201).

240. Hofheinz (1977: 31–35); Mao (2003).

241. Huang (2000: 292–293).

242. Harding (1991: 133); Huang (2000: 302); Walder (2015: 203–204, 203); also MacFarquhar and Schoenhals (2006: 101, 156).

243. MacFarquhar and Schoenhals (2006: 154); Walder (2015: 235).

244. Y. Wu (2014: 101–102).

245. Esherick (2008: 117).

246. Harding (1991: 152).

247. Harding (1991: 162); Teiwes and Sun (1996: 72); MacFarquhar and Schoenhals (2006: 162–169, 214).

248. Walder (2015: 235).

249. Fairbank (1987: 328); Harding (1991: 160); Huang (2000: 295–296).

250. Teiwes and Sun (1996: 72); MacFarquhar and Schoenhals (2006: 176).

251. Teiwes and Sun (1996: 84); MacFarquhar and Schoenhals (2006: 231–232). The slogan "Drag out a small handful in the military!" was periodically used in early 1967 and appeared in a *Red Flag* editorial on August 1, 1967, the fortieth anniversary of the founding of the Red Army.

252. Schoenhals (2005: 280, 281, 278); also Fairbank (1987: 330); MacFarquhar and Schoenhals (2006: 214–216); Walder (2015: 250–252).

253. MacFarquhar and Schoenhals (2006: 215).

254. Schoenhals (2005: 284). For example, in Shanghai on August 4, armed factions attacked the Shanghai Diesel factory, resulting in a ten-hour battle that killed 983 people (Schoenhals 2005: 283).

255. Huang (2000: 305).

256. Harding (1991: 173).

257. Liu (1979: 817).

258. MacFarquhar and Schoenhals (2006: 245–246); Walder (2015: 253).

259. MacFarquhar and Schoenhals (2006: 388).

260. Walder (2015: 285).

261. Fairbank (1987: 330); MacFarquhar and Schoenhals (2006: 250–251); Walder (2015: 257–262).

262. MacFarquhar and Schoenhals (2006: 249–250). Rebellions and anarchy continued to beset significant parts of China in 1969 and 1970 (MacFarquhar and Schoenhals 2006: 301–302, 316–317).

263. MacFarquhar and Schoenhals (2006: 253–262); Walder (2015: 271–277).

264. Walder (2015: 285).

265. Teiwes and Sun (1996: 128); MacFarquhar and Schoenhals (2006: 293, 300).

266. Teiwes and Sun (1996: 91); Joffe (1997: 39). In August 1971, the PLA provided twenty-two of twenty-nine party first secretaries and a majority of cadres running provincial party bodies (MacFarquhar and Schoenhals 2006: 300).

267. MacFarquhar and Schoenhals (2006: 361).

268. MacFarquhar and Schoenhals (2006: 318).

269. Finer (1962: 20–21, 47, 79); Huntington (1968: 221); Nordlinger (1977).

270. Teiwes and Sun (1996: 52, 72); Schoenhals (2005: 292, 294).

271. MacFarquhar and Schoenhals (2006: 176, 191).

272. See Teiwes and Sun (1996: 80); Huang (2000: 309–311); MacFarquhar and Schoenhals (2006: 210–212); Walder (2015: 249–250).

273. Harding (1991: 132); Teiwes and Sun (1996: 61–62); MacFarquhar and Schoenhals (2006: 50).

274. Huang (2000: 311); MacFarquhar and Schoenhals (2006: 319).

275. For descriptions of the "Lin Biao incident," see especially Teiwes and Sun (1996: 152–160); MacFarquhar and Schoenhals (2006: 333–336).

276. Teiwes and Sun (1996: 83).

277. Teiwes and Sun (1996: 39); MacFarquhar and Schoenhals (2006: 333–336, 338). According to MacFarquhar and Schoenhals (2006: 335, 336), the four generals supposedly behind the plot had no knowledge of any plot against Mao. They also suggest that Lin Biao, who had taken sleeping pills and gone to bed on the night of the incident, might not have been fully aware of what was going on when his wife and son rushed him onto the plane.

278. Teiwes and Sun (1996: 130).

279. Teiwes and Sun (1996: 40). By all accounts, military leaders did not want responsibility for the economy and gave "considerable support" to the reassertion of civilian control after 1971 (Teiwes and Sun 1996: 133).

280. These were Jiang Qing, Zhang Chunqiao, Yao Wenyuan, and Wang Hongwen.

281. MacFarquhar and Schoenhals (2006: 450).

282. MacFarquhar and Schoenhals (2006: 443); Walder (2015: 312).

283. MacFarquhar and Schoenhals (2006: 443–444).

284. MacFarquhar and Schoenhals (2006: 443–449). By contrast, the Gang of Four—none of whom had participated in the Long March—had far weaker ties to the military (Liu 1979).

285. Vogel (2011: 654).

286. Dittmer (1978, 1990).

287. Nathan (2001: xvi); also Cheng (1990: 39); Dittmer (1990: 407, 409, 412).

288. Cheng (1990: 40).

289. Vogel (2011: 126).

290. For extensive discussions of Deng-era reforms, see Oi (1999); Huang (2000: 373–392); Shih (2008); Vogel (2011); Gewirtz (2017).

291. Among other things, the regime ceased to classify the population by class origins. See D. Zhao (2001: 42–43); Vogel (2011).

292. Cheng and White (1988); D. Zhao (2001: 49).

293. Huang (2000: 388, 399, 409); D. Zhao (2001: 98, 123, 127); Vogel (2011: 600–601); Pantsov and Levine (2015: 400).

294. See D. Zhao (2001); Pantsov and Levine (2015: 409).

295. Z. Zhao (2009); Pantsov and Levine (2015: 411).

296. D. Zhao (2001: 163); Vogel (2011: 635). Between May 13 and May 24, 8,205 hunger strikers were taken to the hospital (Vogel 2011: 652).

297. D. Zhao (2001: 170–173).

298. D. Zhao (2001: 172–173, 179); Z. Zhao (2009: 26).

299. D. Zhao (2001: 232–233).

300. D. Zhao (2001: 232–233). Ultimately, Yao Yilin and Li Peng supported the imposition of martial law while Zhao Ziyang and Hu Qili opposed it; Qiao Shi abstained. Deng was not an official member of the Politburo and thus did not vote. See Liang et al. (2001: 192–193); Z. Zhao (2009: 29–30).

301. Liang et al. (2001: 223, 253).

302. Liang et al. (2001: 253); Vogel (2011: 620).

303. See Liang et al. (2001: 265, 298, 321, 349).

304. Vogel (2011: 621). On the degree of military insubordination during the crisis, see Shambaugh (2002: 23–24).

305. Vogel (2011: 606); also Liang et al. (2001: 389).

306. Cheng (1990: 137-8); D. Zhao (2001: 213).

307. Liang et al. (2001: 305); Vogel (2011: 622).

308. Deng in remarks to U.S. government officials shortly after the crackdown. See Vogel (2011: 650).

309. Quoted in Cheng (1990: 137).

310. Liang et al. (2001: 370).

311. Cheng (1990: 137–138); D. Zhao (2001: 213).

312. D. Zhao (2001: 204); Vogel (2011: 631).

313. Liang et al. (2001: 385–398).

314. Cheng (1990: 138).

315. D. Zhao (2001: 8).

316. D. Zhao (2001: 146–147).

317. Vogel (2011: 632).

318. Agreements by student leaders to end the strike and leave the square were simply ignored by those who wanted to stay. Students even fought over access to the microphone in meetings with officials. See D. Zhao (2001: 180, 182, 189–190).

319. D. Zhao (2001: 196).

320. Vogel (2011: 668–669).

321. Vogel (2011: 664–692).

322. Barry Naughton, quoted in Ang (2020: 58).

323. Dickson (2008: 3). Also Shambaugh (2008: 112) and Minzner (2018: 6). Private entrepreneurs are now overrepresented in the national legislature (Hou 2019: 49–51).

324. Passages from government communications, quoted in Dickson (2008: 19).

325. Hou (2019: 2); Ang (2020: 59, 67).

326. Luqiu and Liu (2018: 389).

327. Manion (1993: 77).

328. Cheng and White (1998: 231–232); Vogel (2011: 645).

329. Vogel (2011: 644).

330. Cheng and White (1988).

331. Shambaugh (2008: 105).

332. Cheng and White (1998: 231).

333. Vogel (2011: 661); Lampton (2019: 30).

334. Xi Jinping once served as a secretary in the Central Military Commission but lacked anything like the intense combat experience that characterized the "elders." See Lampton (2019: 168).

335. Shambaugh (2002: 11).

336. Lampton (2019: 174–175); Wuthnow (2019: 19).

337. "Damaging Coup Rumours Ricochet across China," BBC News, March 22, 2012.

338. Pei (2016: 6, 8); also Walder (2018: 23).

339. Dickson (2008); Pei (2016: 6, 8).

340. Dickson (2014: 50).

341. See in particular Pei (2016: 264); Walder (2018).

342. Walder (2018: 30).

343. Ang (2020: 133–136).

344. Pei (2016: 1, 263, 266); Walder (2018: 25).

345. Walder (2018: 32); Lampton (2019: 189); Ang (2020: 202).

346. See World Bank Databank (n.d.).

347. Rowen (1996); Diamond (1999: 265); Hu (2000); Gilley (2004).

348. Freedom House (2008: 7).

349. Human Rights Watch (2008).

350. On the efficacy of Chinese controls over the internet, see M. Roberts (2018).

351. Ci (2019).

352. Shambaugh (2016: 122).

353. Shambaugh (2016: 122, 127).

354. Minzner (2018: 10, 14, 165).

355. Y. Li (2018: 2–3); Minzner (2018: 87).

356. Minzner (2018: 93).

357. Dickson (2008: 3–12).

358. Tsai (2011).

359. Wuthnow (2019).

360. Koss (2018).

361. Mattingly (2020: 16).

362. Mattingly (2020: 159).

363. Mattingly (2020: 121).

364. Economy (2018: 83).

365. Economy (2018: 80).

366. Y. Li (2018).

367. The measure of civil society strength is from the Varieties of Democracy's (version 9) Core Civil Society Index. This index captures the robustness of civil society on a scale of 0 (lowest) to 1 (highest) (Coppedge et al. 2019: 275).

Chapter 4

1. Quoted in J. Buchenau (2011: 92).

2. Schloming (1974: 170–171).

3. J. Meyer (1976: 64, 178); J. Buchenau (2011: 126); Joseph and Buchenau (2013: 102).

4. As Frank Tannenbaum observed, the Mexican Revolution was "anonymous. . . . No organized party presided at its birth. No great intellectuals prescribed its program, formulated its doctrine, outlined its objectives. . . . There is no Lenin in Mexico" ([1933] 1968: 115–119).

5. Magaloni (2006).

6. See Lozoya (1970: 22–27); Fuentes (1983: 28–59); Vázquez and Meyer (1985); de la Garza (1986: 45–47); Alan Knight (1986a, 1992b); Centeno (1994: 6); Soifer (2015: 96–107).

7. See Fuentes (1983: 47–48); Vázquez and Meyer (1985: 43–47, 65–70); Alan Knight (1992b: 102, 125–128).

8. Alan Knight (1992b: 101).

9. Soifer (2015: 170–220).

10. Ruíz (1980: 40–41); Alan Knight (1986a: 15–35).

11. Rugeley and Fallaw (2012: 6).

12. Alan Knight (1986a: 74–75).

13. Roughly 90 percent of peasant families were landless at the end of Díaz's rule (Wilkie 1967: 42; R. Hanson 1971: 27; F. Katz 1991: 94–99).

14. Alan Knight (1986a); F. Katz (1998: 90–101).

15. Lieuwen (1968: 9–11); Fuentes (1983: 77–78).

16. Alan Knight (1986a: 215).

17. Womack (1968: 91); Schloming (1974: 87–88); Ruíz (1980: 149–150).

18. Ruíz (1980: 144–145).

19. Wilkie (1967: 41–47); Ruíz (1980: 141–142).

20. Wilkie (1967: 43–47); Womack (1968: 86–90); Ruíz (1980: 140–152); Alan Knight (1986a: 232, 264–266, 278–281).

21. Womack (1968: 119–128); Schloming (1974: 96–97).

22. Alan Knight (1986a: 244).

23. Hart (1987: 253). Also Alan Knight (1986a: 262–264, 315).

24. Womack (1968: 86–88, 159–160); Alan Knight (1986a: 309–315); Gilly (2005: 74–75).

25. F. Katz (1998: 121–132).

26. F. Katz (1998: 126–127).

27. Alan Knight (1986a: 207–227, 284–352); Gilly (2005: 74–75).

28. Lieuwen (1968: 16–18); Alan Knight (1986a: 488–489); Easterling (2012: 63–66).

29. Alan Knight (1986b: 17–18, 103); F. Katz (1998: 219).

30. Womack (1968: 160); Schloming (1974: 112). According to Brading, Madero's killing "lit the fuse of the revolution" (1980: 8).

31. Alan Knight (1986b: 12–18, 58); F. Katz (1998: 198–212).

32. Alan Knight (1986b: 302); Joseph and Buchenau (2013: 74). The number of overall deaths is disputed, and some historians argue that the widely used figure of one million deaths is overstated (Rugeley and Fallaw 2012: 7–8). However, few scholars contest Alan Knight's (1986b: 302) claim that at least 200,000 people were killed in 1914–1915 alone.

33. Lieuwen (1968: 18–23).

34. Alan Knight (1986b: 215).

35. Alan Knight (1986b: 12–18, 58, 188); F. Katz (1998: 198–212). Whereas the Constitutionalists were liberal and nationalist, Villista and especially Zapatista forces were more radical, calling for land reform and other redistributive measures (Womack 1968; F. Katz 1998).

36. Alan Knight (1986b).

37. Brandenburg (1964: 53).

38. Alan Knight (1986b: 174–186); Womack (1991: 160–161).

39. Quoted in Alan Knight (1986b: 181).

40. Womack (1968: 331).

41. Alan Knight (1986b: 179, 215–216).

42. Womack (1968: 247).

43. Alan Knight (1986b: 178–186, 190–191).

44. Alan Knight (1986b: 123–124). Also Hart (1987: 372).

45. Womack (1968: 257).

46. Lieuwen (1968: 52).

47. Lieuwen (1968: 35); Alan Knight (1986b: 327–334, 431); F. Katz (1998: 494–497, 524).

48. Lieuwen (1968: 35); Womack (1968: 322–331).

49. See Schloming (1974: 147); Alan Knight (1986b: 209–215, 236–237); Camp (1992: 17).

50. See Brandenburg (1964: 54); Alan Knight (1986b: 215, 236–237, 442–444).

51. Lieuwen (1968).

52. Magaloni (2006).

53. See Schloming (1974: 84, 115–118); Brading (1980); Alan Knight (1980); Falcón (1984); Camp (1992); Fallaw (2012); Hernández Rodríguez (2014).

54. Lajous (1979: 65–66); Brading (1980: 8); Martínez Assad (1988: 7–8); Hernández Rodríguez (2014).

55. Prominent revolutionary generals included Abelardo Ródriguez in Baja California, Carlos Vidal in Chiapas, Rodrigo Queveda in Chihuahua, Manuel Pérez Treviño in Coahuila, Gabriel Barrios in Puebla, Saturnino Cedillo in San Luis Potosí, Adalberto Tejeda and Alejandro Mange in Veracruz, and Salvador Alvarado and Felipe Carrillo in Yucatán. See Schloming (1974: 115–118); Lajous (1979: 65–66); Falcón (1984, 1988); Fallaw (2012: 148–150); Martínez Assad (2013); Hernández Rodríguez (2014).

56. See Pansters (2005: 361); Fallaw (2012); and Hernández Rodríguez (2014).

57. Schloming (1974: 115–118); Lajous (1979: 66); and Martínez Assad (2013: 193–194).

58. Garrido (1982: 45, 56–60).

59. Garrido (1982: 38–40).

60. J. Buchenau (2011: 88).

61. Castro Martínez (1992: 37).

62. Garrido (1982: 41–45, 58–59).

63. Garrido (1982: 46–56); J. Buchenau (2011: 115–122).

64. Hernández Rodríguez (2014).

65. Rath (2012: 175).

66. Alan Knight (1986b: 448–449; 1992a: 131).

67. González Casanova (1981: 106).

68. See Garrido (1982: 51) and Alan Knight (1986b: 448–449).

69. Cline (1963: 137); Scott (1964: 128); Quirk (1973: 23); Alan Knight (1986a: 163); Joseph and Buchenau (2013: 7).

70. Quoted in Schloming (1974: 176).

71. Portes Gil (1964: 842).

72. See Ruíz (1980: 308–311); Alan Knight (1986b); Hodges and Gandy (2002: 6–7, 41–69); J. Meyer (2003: 32); J. Buchenau (2007, 2011).

73. See Ruíz (1980: 383–384, 400–403); Alan Knight (1986a: 163; 1986b: 497; 2014); Hodges and Gandy (2002); Joseph and Buchenau (2013: 7).

74. Ruíz (1980: 160).

75. Córdova (1973: 253). Also Ruíz (1980: 383–384).

76. According to Sarah Osten, anticlericalism was "the closest [the revolutionary elite] came to an ironclad ideological commitment" (2018: 241). Also Alan Knight (1986b: 395–396; 1994: 401); Bantjes Aróstegui (1994: 2–3; 1997); Fallaw (2012: 145–146).

77. Based on Camp (1997: 5).

78. Bantjes Aróstegui (1994: 12).

79. Tannenbaum (1971: 132); Fallaw (2013: 25).

80. See Mabry (1973: 18); Quirk (1973: 37–38); Alan Knight (1986b: 203, 499).

81. Tannenbaum (1971: 132). Also Portes Gil (1964: 565).

82. Quoted in Alan Knight (1994: 417).

83. D. Bailey (1974: 23); Alan Knight (1986b: 206, 499).

84. Bantjes Aróstegui (1997: 93, 99); also Quirk (1973: 23).

85. Schloming (1974: 114, 148–149); Alan Knight (1986a); Gilly (2005: 173–179); J. Buchenau (2011: 50–77).

86. Niemeyer (1974: 23–25); Schloming (1974: 114–118, 148–149); Trejo Delarbe and Yañez (1976: 134); Tutino (1986: 339).

87. Ruíz (1980: 308–311).

88. Quoted in R. Smith (1972: 21). Also Schloming (1974); Easterling (2012).

89. Alan Knight (1986a).

90. Ruíz (1980: 153, 159).

91. See Niemeyer (1974: 35–36, 58–59); Alan Knight (1986b: 471).

92. See Lieuwen (1968: 43); Neimeyer (1974: 217–222); Joseph and Buchenau (2013: 79–82).

93. Neimeyer (1974: 221).

94. See Niemeyer (1974: 216–224); Schloming (1974: 170–171); Hall (1981: 167–169, 179).

95. Lieuwen (1968: 42–43).

96. Schloming (1974: 170–171). Also Alan Knight (1986b: 470); Easterling (2012: 129).

97. Tannenbaum ([1933] 1968: 168–169; 1971: 105–112); Hall (1981: 179–181); Joseph and Buchenau (2013: 82).

98. Vernon (1965: 77–78); also L. Meyer (1972: 55–57).

99. Brandenburg (1964: 46); Niemeyer (1974: 103–114).

100. J. Meyer (1976: 14).

101. D. Bailey (1974: 23–25); Neimeyer (1974: 63–68, 88–97); J. Meyer (1976: 13–14).

102. D. Bailey (1974: 23–25).

103. D. Bailey (1974: 23–25).

104. Alan Knight (1986b: 455).

105. Osten (2018: 82–86).

106. Córdova (1973: 27).

107. Wilkie (1967: 56); Quirk (1973: 103); Hall (1981: 183).

108. Ruíz (1980: 158, 308–311). Also Schloming (1974: 173–174); Alan Knight (1986b: 174, 467).

109. Hall (1980: 137); Alan Knight (1986b: 466–467).

110. Ruíz (1980: 386–387).

111. R. Smith (1972: 79–83, 89); Vázquez and Meyer (1985: 124).

112. R. Smith (1972: 73–75).

113. Hall (1990: 191–192).

114. P. Henderson (1981); Alan Knight (1986b: 378–382).

115. Alan Knight (1986b: 378–382); P. Henderson (1981: 117–144).

116. Fowler Salamini (1991).

117. Alan Knight (1986b: 382–383).

118. On the Díaz rebellion, see P. Henderson (1981: 137, 144–145); on Peláez's army, see Fowler Salamini (1991: 198, 202–207) and J. Brown (1993: 293–299).

119. Tannenbaum (1971: 265–271).

120. R. Smith (1972: 133–137); Tardanico (1980: 71–73); Pozas Horcasitas (1982: 52).

121. L. Meyer (1972: 70–71); R. Smith (1972: 155–159, 169).

122. L. Meyer (1972: 70–71); R. Smith (1972: 150, 158).

123. F. Katz (1998: 197–198).

124. Hall (1981: 184–186, 217–240); Tamayo (2008: 21); Castro Martínez (2009: 65); J. Buchenau (2011: 97–98).

125. Hall (1981: 184–186); Castro Martínez (2009: 62–63); J. Buchenau (2011: 97–98).

126. See Lieuwen (1968: 54); Womack (1968: 357–363); Hall (1981: 242–245); Tamayo (2008: 24).

127. Garrido (1982: 44).

128. Lajous (1979: 14).

129. Tutino (1986: 6); J. Buchenau (2011: 106).

130. J. Buchenau (2011: 136).

131. Considered "the Great Compromiser," Obregón "reconciled revolutionary fervor with reactionary opposition, economic nationalism with the nation's position within the global capitalist system, and political centralization with the co-optation of regional leaders" (J. Buchenau 2011: 119).

132. L. Meyer (1972: 84–86); Vázquez and Meyer (1985: 129–130); Alan Knight (1986b: 518).

133. L. Meyer (1972: 100–102); R. Smith (1972: 222–223); Vázquez and Meyer (1985: 132).

134. Schloming (1974: 173–174); Hall (1980: 137); Alan Knight (1986b: 466–467).

135. J. Meyer (1991: 235); Hodges and Gandy (2002: 52).

136. Alan Knight (1991a: 97).

137. L. Meyer (1977: 93); Montes de Oca (1977: 50); Córdova (1995: 209–215).

138. F. Katz (1998: 731).

139. Tamayo (2008).

140. Hodges and Gandy (2002: 65–66); Tamayo (2008: 45–46).

141. Schloming (1974: 202); Hernández Chávez (2006: 238).

142. L. Meyer (1977: 93–94); Montes de Oca (1977: 50).

143. Beezley (2009: 9). Also Fowler Salamini (1980); Mendoza (1988); Joseph (2003); Osten (2018).

144. Tobler (1988: 508); J. Meyer (1991: 235).

145. L. Meyer (1978b: 212); Sherman (1997: 41, 56); Hodges and Gandy (2002: 53); Osten (2018).

146. Alan Knight (1986b: 186–188).

147. Hernández Chávez (2006: 258).

148. Lieuwen (1968: 73–77); J. Meyer (1991: 205–206); Castro Martínez (2009: 301–203).

149. About a third of the army's generals and about 40 percent of troops participated in the rebellion. See Lieuwen (1968: 75–76); Schloming (1974: 216–217); Castro Martínez (1992: 104–105); J. Buchenau (2011: 132).

150. Cosío Villegas (1981: 45).

151. Lieuwen (1968: 52–53); Tamayo (2008: 103); Castro Martínez (2009: 165–167); J. Buchenau (2011: 127–134).

152. Knight 1991b: 244.

153. Hamilton (1982: 71–72); Vázquez and Meyer (1985: 135); Joseph and Buchenau (2013: 98–99).

154. L. Meyer (1977: 16–24).

155. See R. Smith (1972: 236–237).

156. L. Meyer (1977: 24); Martínez Assad (1979: 22, 27).

157. L. Meyer (1972: 126; 1977: 20–23, 45); Lajous (1979: 17); Córdova (1995: 163–170).

158. Portes Gil (1964: 388, 397); Pozas Horcasitas (1982: 105–106).

159. L. Meyer (1972: 12); Pozas Horcasitas (1982: 105–106).

160. Portes Gil (1964: 397); L. Meyer (1972: 128); R. Smith (1972: 238).

161. L. Meyer (1972: 132–134).

162. R. Smith (1972: 259–263); Córdova (1995: 159–160).

163. Quirk (1973: 103, 119–120).

164. J. Buchenau (2011: 148).

165. J. Buchenau (2007: 125–126).

166. Reich (1995: 13).

167. J. Meyer (1976: 21–22); Camp (1997: 6–7).

168. D. Bailey (1974: 47); von Sauer (1974: 21–22); J. Meyer (1976: 22–24, 75–79); Ard (2003: 36).

169. D. Bailey (1974: 45); Tamayo (2008: 82); Joseph and Buchenau (2013: 100).

170. J. Meyer (1991: 205).

171. D. Bailey (1974: 52–53); Reich (1995: 12).

172. Quirk (1973: 153, 171); J. Meyer (1976: 41–43); Sherman (1997: 10).

173. Dulles (1961: 302, 308); Sherman (1997: 10).

174. J. Meyer (1976: 41–42). Also Dulles (1961: 529–531); Quirk (1973: 155). As a British diplomat put it at the time, the president had "decided . . . to go the whole hog and force a complete cessation of religious cult through the country" (quoted in J. Meyer 1976: 44).

175. J. Meyer (1976: 75–79).

176. Reich (1995: 13); Ard (2003: 37).

177. D. Bailey (1974: 64–66); Sherman (1997: 10).

178. J. Meyer (1976: 42).

179. Quirk (1973: 175–176); D. Bailey (1974: 302, 43–44).

180. Quirk (1973: 168–173); D. Bailey (1974: 43–44); Sherman (1997: 11).

181. J. Meyer (1976: 49–52).

182. J. Meyer (1976: 213).

183. L. Meyer (1978a: 11).

184. Quirk (1973: 203); D. Bailey (1974: 98–100); J. Meyer (1976: 70–75); Sherman (1997: 11).

185. Dulles (1961: 310); Mabry (1973: 20–21); Gonzales (2002: 212–214).

186. J. Meyer (1976: 52–57); Ard (2003: 39); Rugeley and Fallaw (2012: 8).

187. J. Meyer (1976: 64, 178); Joseph and Buchenau (2013: 102).

188. J. Meyer (1976: 106–107, 160–162); Sánchez Talanquer (2019: 316). In exchange for peasant militia support, the Calles government accelerated land redistribution. More land was distributed during the 1927–1929 Cristero War than in the previous seventeen years of revolution combined (J. Meyer 1976: 108–109).

189. J. Meyer (1991: 214).

190. Quirk (1973: 244–245); Reich (1995: 21–26); Sherman (1997: 71).

191. Tannenbaum (1971: 65).

192. Lieuwen (1968: 96–99); J. Buchenau (2007: 139–140, 2011: 153–155); Castro Martínez (2009: 369–377).

193. Sherman (1997: 18).

194. L. Meyer (1978a: 17). Also Córdova (1995: 23); J. Buchenau (2011: 162–163).

195. Córdova (1995: 23, 29–33); J. Buchenau (2007: 130–134, 145–147; 2011: 162–163).

196. Sánchez Talanquer (2017, 2019).

197. Lajous (1979: 23–26); Garrido (1982: 63–66); Córdova (1995: 29–33); Salmerón Sanginés (2000: 46); J. Buchenau (2007: 147–148); Sánchez Talanquer (2019).

198. Lajous (1979: 23–26); Garrido (1982: 69, 74); J. Buchenau (2007: 147–148).

199. Garrido (1982: 74–76).

200. See, for example, Garrido (1982).

201. The National Revolutionary Confederation was created for the 1922 midterm elections but collapsed the following year (Fuentes Díaz 1969: 215; Cosío Villegas 1981: 45; Garrido 1982: 47–48).

202. Garrido (1982: 56).

203. Fuentes Díaz (1969: 228); Garrido (1982: 64); Osten (2018: 198–202).

204. See Fuentes Díaz (1969: 215, 228–229); Garrido (1982: 47–48, 59–64, 71); Quintana (2010: 24); Osten (2018: 198–202).

205. Sánchez Talanquer (2017: 182; 2019: 316).

206. Sánchez Talanquer (2017: 319; 2019: 182). Also Alan Knight (1992a: 120).

207. Quoted in Sánchez Talanquer (2017: 319).

208. Quoted in Sánchez Talanquer (2017: 319).

209. Osten (2018); see also Falcón (1984); Salmerón Sangines (2000); Fallaw and Rugeley (2012).

210. Joseph (1980: 203–207); Tamayo (2008: 186–188); Osten (2018: 38–41).

211. Osten (2018: 39, 18–59).

212. Martínez Assad (1979: 164–165, 174–175); Osten (2018: 94, 135–146).

213. Osten (2018: 135–137, 144, 160).

214. Mendoza (1988: 92–93); Hernández Rodríguez (2014: 112).

215. See Buve (1980: 232); Fowler Salamini (1980: 185–188); Ramírez Rancaño (1988: 313); Tamayo (2008: 199); Rath (2013: 24); and Osten (2018: 75–79, 173). In other states, including Jalisco, San Luis Potosí, and Veracruz, revolutionary generals developed large peasant bases but did not build strong parties. See Ankerson (1980: 150–154); Fowler Salamini (1980: 174–189); Falcón (1984: 176–191); Tamayo (2008: 180–199).

216. Lajous (1979: 24–25, 165); Garrido (1982: 92–98).

217. Leal (1975: 53); Garrido (1982: 75, 83, 96–97); Salmerón Sanginés (2000: 63–64).

218. Garrido (1982: 72, 96); Salmerón Sanginés (2008: 3). Among the leading revolutionary caciques, only Adalberto Tejeda refused to join the party (Garrido 1982: 78, 83).

219. Lajous (1979: 25, 165); Garrido (1982: 97–98, 119–120); Hernández Chávez (2006: 246–247).

220. Garrido (1982: 92).

221. Sánchez Talanquer (2019: 307).

222. Lajous (1979: 66–68, 187); Garrido (1982: 92–103); Osten (2018: 244–245).

223. Lajous (1979: 66–68).

224. Lajous (1981: 66–67).

225. Osten (2018: 259).

226. Hernández Chávez (2006: 246).

227. Lajous (1979: 65–66); Fallaw (2012); Martínez Assad (2013); Hernández Rodríguez (2014). Sarah Osten (2018) argues, moreover, that regional party-building experiments in the 1920s served as models or organizational "blueprints" for the PRN. Thus, parties such as the PSS in Yucatán and the PRST in Tabasco not only demonstrated the "political value of institutionalized alliances with organized popular constituencies" (2018: 244) but also showed how the state could be used to both mobilize and control those popular constituencies (2018: 258–263). Indeed, Calles and his allies were "conspicuously influenced" by state-level socialist parties in their design of the PNR (Osten 2018: 2).

228. J. Buchenau (2007: 156).

229. Schloming (1974: 182–187).

230. Navarro (2010: 87).

231. Garrido (1982: 95); Salmerón Sanginés (2008: 19).

232. Lieuwen (1968: 103); Schloming (1974: 256); Garrido (1982: 91–95).

233. L. Meyer (1978a: 9); Lajous (1981: 71); Garrido (1982: 94–95).

234. Lajous (1979: 54).

235. Garrido (1982: 96).

236. L. Meyer (1978a: 60–63); Lajous (1979: 33–34); Salmerón Sanginés (2008: 17–18).

237. L. Meyer (1978a: 92); Salmerón Sanginés (2008: 18–21).

238. Lajous (1979: 72–76); Córdova (1995: 72–85).

239. Dulles (1961: 418–420); J. Buchenau (2007: 154).

240. Lajous (1979: 79).

241. Lajous (1979: 79); Peschard (1986: 209–210).

242. Sherman (1997: 23).

243. Garrido (1982: 147).

244. J. Buchenau (2007: 169).

245. Garrido (1982: 230, 171–175).

246. Córdova (1974: 116–117); Montes de Oca (1977: 51); Martínez Assad (1982: 158–159); Tobler (1988: 497).

247. Montes de Oca (1977: 51); Garrido (1982: 259–261).

248. Hellman (1983: 147–161).

249. Garrido (1982: 259–261); Middlebrook (1995).

250. Garrido (1982: 255); Hamilton (1982: 242–243).

251. Garrido (1982: 228–229).

252. González Casanova (1981: 113–114).

253. Serrano (1997).

254. Fuentes Díaz (1969: 287).

255. Alan Knight (1986b: 456); Aguilar Zinser (1990: 221–222); Loyo Camacho (2003: 66–67).

256. Ruíz (1980: 239–255).

257. Aguilar Zinser (1990: 221–223); Loyo Camacho (2003: 66–67); J. Buchenau (2011: 135).

258. Aguilar Zinser (1990: 222).

259. Wilkie (1967: 102–103).

260. Data from Correlates of War "National Material Capabilities" data set, version 5, https://correlatesofwar.org/data-sets/national-material-capabilities.

261. H. Jones (2014).

262. Brandenburg (1964: 54); Alan Knight (1986b: 208–209); Camp (1992: 17).

263. Camp (1992: 75–76).

264. Alan Knight (1986b: 184–192).

265. L. Meyer (1978b: 231–233); Córdova (1995: 262); Sherman (1997: 41).

266. Sherman (1997: 41).

267. Brandenburg (1964: 212); J. Meyer (1976: 20).

268. J. Meyer (1976: 75).

269. Quirk (1973: 244–245); Reich (1995: 21–26); Sherman (1997: 71).

270. Reich (1995: 28–29); Sherman (1997: 75).

271. J. Meyer (1976: 20); Sherman (1997: 34); Ard (2003: 40).

272. Campbell (1976: 38).

273. Sherman (1997: 35).

274. Campbell (1976: 71, 38); Bantjes Aróstegui (1997: 106).

275. Fallaw (2013: 17).

276. Fallaw (2013: 25).

277. Hellman (1983: 42–47); Mirón Lince (1986: 242–243).

278. Hellman (1983: 43). Also Mirón Lince (1986: 243); Tutino (1986: 8–9).

279. Trejo Delarbe and Yañez (1976: 135–141); Ruíz (1980: 294–299); Córdova (1995: 217–223).

280. Hamilton (1982: 147–161).

281. Trejo Delarbe and Yañez (1976: 145–146); Medina (1979: 151–175).

282. Alan Knight (1992a: 14).

283. Alan Knight (1993: 38); also Brandenburg (1964: 7–18).

284. Sánchez Talanquer (2019: 319–320).

285. Navarro (2010: 223). As one PRI leader put it, "The only political sin without pardon has been affiliation with the reactionary regime of Victoriano Huerta. We have forgiven everything else" (quoted in P. Smith 1979: 168).

286. Alan Knight (1992a: 134).

287. Alan Knight (1993: 39).

288. L. Meyer (1978a: 56).

289. Alan Knight (1993: 38).

290. Garrido (1982: 274–276).

291. Alan Knight (2003: 76).

292. Alan Knight (1993: 37).

293. Alan Knight (1992a: 134).

294. Navarro (2010: 250–254). Also Medina (1978: 113–114); Garrido (1982: 274–276). On Almazán, see Lieuwen (1968: 133–134) and Navarro (2010: 59–74). On Henríquez, see Servín (2001) and Navarro (2010: 219–220).

295. Navarro (2010: 199).

296. Langston (2002); Magaloni (2005: 124–129).

297. Magaloni (2006); K. Greene (2007).

298. Langston (2006).

299. Ackroyd (1991).

300. Lieuwen (1968); Camp (2005: 44–45).

301. Lieuwen (1968).

302. Camp (2005: 44–45).

303. Pozas Horcasitas (1982: 23–24); Falcón (1984, 1988); Fallaw (2012); Rugeley and Fallaw (2012); Martínez Assad (2013); Hernández Rodríguez (2014).

304. Camp (1992).

305. Lieuwen (1968: 102–108); Camp (1992: 22–23).

306. Camp (2005: 75).

307. Lieuwen (1968: 107–108); Rath (2013: 27). Thus, when President Cárdenas was criticized for creating a "military sector" of the ruling party in the late 1930s, he responded that he was "not bringing the military into politics. It [was] already there" (Piñeyro 1985: 56).

308. Brandenburg (1964: 101); Schloming (1974: 53); Camp (2005: 44–47, 76).

309. Lieuwen (1968); Camp (1984: 144–146; 1992: 190–191); Rath (2013: 169).

310. Camp (1992: 190; 2005: 45, 209, 225).

311. Camp (1984: 144–146; 1992: 190–191).

312. Camp (2005: 4, 7–8). Also Schloming (1974: 36–40, 317–318).

313. Serrano (1995: 428). Also Wager (1984: 88–89; 1995).

314. D. Bailey (1974: 302–303).

315. Ronfeldt (1984a); Ackroyd (1991); Serrano (1995: 432–434); Wager (1995).

316. Wager (1995: 103).

317. Ackroyd (1991: 81).

318. Ackroyd (1991). Revolutionary general Cedillo led a small rebellion in 1938, but he headed a private militia in the state of San Luis Potosí, rather than a sector of the army. See Lieuwen (1968: 126); Falcón (1988: 382–383); and Rath (2012: 187–188).

319. Ronfeldt (1984a); Ackroyd (1991); Serrano (1995: 432–434); Wager (1995).

320. Camp (2005: 95).

321. Camp (2005: 95).

322. Lieuwen (1968); Boils (1975, 1985).

323. Aguilar Zinser (1990: 221–222); Camp (1992: 219).

324. Lieuwen (1968: 146).

325. Boils (1975: 105). This is compared to 0.3 percent in Brazil and Venezuela, 0.4 percent in Peru, and 0.5 percent in Argentina and Chile (Boils 1975: 105).

326. Needler (1971: 67); Rath (2014: 98).

327. Wilkie (1967: 102–103).

328. Boils (1975: 105).

329. Rath (2014: 95).

330. Gillingham and Smith (2014: 8, 21).

331. Navarro (2010).

332. Aguayo Quezada (2001: 157).

333. Navarro (2010: 157–166).

334. Aguayo Quezada (2001: 68, 111–113); Navarro (2010: 185); Gillingham (2012: 93); H. Jones (2014: 220).

335. Aguayo Quezada (2001: 92–93); Gillingham (2012: 93).

336. Boils (1975: 115–120); Ronfeldt (1984a: 64–69; 1984b: 17); Aguayo Quezada (2001: 201); Rath (2013).

337. Camp (1992: 90).

338. See Ronfeldt (1984b: 12).

339. Sherman (1997: 75–76). Camp observed in the 1990s that the Church "[had] not used its potential for political mobilization . . . since the 1930s" (1997: 6).

340. Hamilton (1982: 101); Story (1986: 17–18).

341. Story (1986: 28–48).

342. Story (1987: 262).

343. J. Bailey (1988).

344. Vernon (1965: 165–170).

345. Luna et al. (1987: 15); Maxfield (1987: 2); Mizrahi (2003: 68–70).

346. Hellman (1983).

347. Tannenbaum (1971: 85).

348. González Casanova (1970: 134).

349. Aguayo Quezada (2001: 138).

350. Stevens (1987: 220).

351. Scott (1964: 321); Padgett (1966: 164–166).

352. Middlebrook (1995).

353. Medina (1979: 174–175).

354. Trejo Delarbe and Yañez (1976: 146); Medina (1979: 145).

355. Stevens (1987: 225–226); Middlebrook (1995).

356. Hamilton (1982).

357. Hamilton (1982).

358. F. Katz (1998: 738).

359. Story (1986: 91–92); Saragoza (1988).

360. Stevens (1987: 229).

361. Story (1986: 89); Saragoza (1988: 4, 161–165).

362. Escobar (1987: 73–74); Luna et al. (1987: 18–20).

363. Arriola and Galindo (1984: 137).

364. Magaloni (2006); K. Greene (2007).

365. Fuentes Díaz (1969: 328–335); Campbell (1976).

366. Basañez (1981: 171–182); Hellman (1983: 177–180).

367. Easterling (2012: 139).

368. González Casanova (1970: 134). For an excellent analysis of the causes and consequences of this power asymmetry, see K. Greene (2007).

369. Cline (1963: 167); González Casanova (1981: 122).

370. Aguayo Quezada (2001: 71).

371. Campbell (1976: 50–61); Sherman (1997).

372. Ankerson (1984: 168–169).

373. Sherman (1997).

374. Ard (2003: 64–65); Mizrahi (2003: 20–21).

375. Ard (2003: 85). Also Mabry (1973); Loaeza (1999).

376. Mabry (1973: 165–166); Camp (1997: 205–206).

377. Mabry (1973: 164); Ard (2003: 14, 78).

378. Mabry (1973: 191); Mizrahi (2003: 60–62).

379. Mizrahi (2003: 55).

380. Loaeza (1999: 242–243).

381. Mabry (1973: 184).

382. Cornelius (1987: 21). Also Hellman (1983); Collier and Collier (1991).

383. Padgett (1966: 109).

384. González Casanova (1981: 115, 130).

385. Klesner (1987: 104).

386. Castellanos (2007: 53).

387. González Casanova (1981: 128).

388. Scott (1964: 189–190); Fuentes Díaz (1969: 354). After 1952, the PP was co-opted by the PRI.

389. Magaloni (2006).

390. Magaloni (2006: 83).

391. Looney ([1978] 2018: 9).

392. Magaloni (2006).

393. L. Meyer (1978a: 110–131).

394. Haber (1992: 28–29).

395. Trejo Delarbe and Yañez (1976); J. Buchenau (2007: 170).

396. Trejo Delarbe and Yañez (1976: 136).

397. Lajous (1979: 143–146); Martínez Assad (2013: 197–201).

398. Lajous (1979: 106–122).

399. Lajous (1979: 142–143).

400. Córdova (1995: 323–345); J. Buchenau (2007: 163–166).

401. Alan Knight (1994a: 80–81).

402. Garrido (1982: 133–134, 197–201); Alan Knight (1991b: 253–254); J. Buchenau (2007: 81–82).

403. Alan Knight (1994a: 79–82).

404. Alan Knight (2003: 59).

405. Wilkie (1967: 72–79); Alan Knight (1994a: 79–82); Hernández Chávez (2006: 256–258).

406. See Córdova (1974: 100–104). As Raymond Vernon put it, "If any of Cárdenas' policies deserved to be called 'revolutionary,' they were his policies on land reform" (1965: 72).

407. Alan Knight (1991b: 258); J. Meyer (1991: 233–234).

408. Basañez (1981: 177).

409. Hamilton (1982: 177); Hernández Chávez (2006: 258).

410. Córdova (1974: 104).

411. González Casanova (1970: 48).

412. Eckstein (1982: 65–75).

413. L. Meyer (1978b: 212–213); Alan Knight (1986b: 96–104; 1991a: 103–104).

414. Bantjes Aróstegui (1997: 88).

415. Dulles (1961: 529–530); Mabry (1973: 24–25); Bantjes Aróstegui (1994: 3–5; 1997: 100–101, 107–110); Blancarte (2014: 71).

416. Bantjes Aróstegui (1997: 107).

417. Bantjes Aróstegui (1994: 4).

418. Sherman (1997: 40).

419. Bantjes Aróstegui (1997).

420. Bantjes Aróstegui (1997: 99–104).

421. See Dulles (1961: 619–620); Alan Knight (1994: 407); Bantjes Aróstegui (1997: 101, 106).

422. Bantjes Aróstegui (1997: 104).

423. Alan Knight (1994: 412); Bantjes Aróstegui (1997: 104).

424. Reich (1995: 45).

425. Mabry (1973: 24–25); Campbell (1976: 35–36); Blancarte (2014: 71).

426. Campbell (1976: 79); Bantjes Aróstegui (1997: 97).

427. Sánchez Talanquer (2017: 200–201).

428. Sherman (1997: 45–46); Fallaw (2013: 18).

429. Sherman (1997).

430. Alan Knight (1994a: 83–84).

431. Sherman (1997: 117, 101).

432. See L. Meyer (1972: 169–170, 200–216); H. Jones (2014: 5, 27).

433. Saragoza (1988: 191).

434. Fuentes Díaz (1969: 328–334); Campbell (1976); Sherman (1997).

435. Campbell (1976: 93–97, 116); J. Meyer (2003: 189–190, 210–225).

436. Michaels (1970: 75); von Sauer (1974: 39–40); Campbell (1976: 116); J. Meyer (2003: 275).

437. These were Argentina, Bolivia, Brazil, Chile, Cuba, the Dominican Republic, Ecuador, El Salvador, Guatemala, Nicaragua, Panama, Paraguay, and Peru.

438. Sherman (1997: 12).

439. Alan Knight (2014: 60).

440. Campbell (1976: 63–64, 72–78); Garrido (1982: 252).

441. Lieuwen (1968: 126); Boils (1975: 71); Falcón (1988: 382–383).

442. Lieuwen (1968: 126).

443. Rath (2012: 187–188).

444. Falcón (1988: 382–383).

445. Sherman (1997: 117).

446. Navarro (2010: 33).

447. Garrido (1982: 280–281); Sherman (1997: 123–124); Navarro (2010: 14–16).

448. Portes Gil (1964: 633); Lieuwen (1968: 133–134); Navarro (2010: 62–64).

449. Garrido (1982: 274, 279); Navarro (2010: 41, 76–78).

450. Portes Gil (1964: 633–634).

451. See Medina (1978: 133); Garrido (1982: 294); Navarro (2010: 52).

452. Navarro (2010: 51–57).

453. Campbell (1976: 132–135); Contreras (1981: 119).

454. Medina (1978: 126–130); Contreras (1981: 119); Garrido (1982: 294–295).

455. Tannenbaum (1971: 77); Medina (1978: 126–130).

456. Medina (1978: 121); Loaeza (1999: 178); Navarro (2010: 65–69).

457. See Gonzáles (1981: 131); Molinar Horcasitas (1991: 129).

458. Magaloni (2006).

459. Medina (1978); Sherman (1997: 129–133).

460. H. Jones (2014).

461. L. Meyer (1991); Mazza (2001).

462. Ackroyd (1991); Wager (1995).

463. E. Williams (1986: 150).

464. Langston (2002).

465. Medina (1979: 50).

466. Brandenburg (1964: 101).

467. Sánchez Gutiérrez (1988: 286–287); Navarro (2010: 201–203).

468. See Sánchez Gutiérrez (1988: 286–287); Servín (2001: 191–195, 261–267); Castellanos (2007: 45); Navarro (2010: 116, 219–220); Rath (2013: 96).

469. Bruhn (1997: 47).

470. Servín (2001: 336–345).

471. Servín (2001: 324, 349–353, 371–378, 385–391); Navarro (2010: 248–254).

472. Langston (2002).

473. Weldon (1997).

474. González Casanova (1970: 18–19).

475. González Casanova (1981: 135).

476. Collier and Collier (1991); Middlebrook (1995); Magaloni (2006); K. Greene (2007).

477. Magaloni (2006); K. Greene (2007).

478. Hellman (1983); Middlebrook (1995).

479. Wilkie (1967: 184–186); Stevens (1987: 220).

480. Boils (1975: 115–120); Ronfeldt (1984a); Rath (2013).

481. Aguayo Quezada (2001); Castellanos (2007).

482. Aguayo Quezada (2001: 119, 175).

483. Hellman (1983: 240–241); Aguayo Quezada (2001: 202).

484. Ronfeldt (1984a); Rath (2013).

485. Boils (1975: 115–120); Ronfeldt (1984a: 64–70); Rath (2013: 6–8, 99–103).

486. Stevens (1974: 122–124); Castellanos (2007: 168); Aguila and Bortz (2012: 207–208).

487. Stevens (1974: 125).

488. O'Donnell (1973); Linz and Stepan (1978).

489. These were Argentina, Bolivia, Brazil, Chile, the Dominican Republic, Ecuador, El Salvador, Guatemala, Honduras, Panama, Peru, and Uruguay.

490. See Collier and Collier (1991).

491. Joseph and Buchenau (2013: 163–164).

492. Guadarrama (1986: 106); Bruhn (1997: 49–51).

493. Scott (1964: 312); Joseph and Buchenau (2013: 164).

494. Bruhn (1997: 51–52).

495. Guadarrama (1986: 106); Bruhn (1997: 52).

496. Ramírez Rancaño (1981: 188–190); Hellman (1983: 163–164).

497. Ronfeldt (1984a: 64–65); Camp (2005: 108); Castellanos (2007: 23–63, 74–82).

498. Ronfeldt (1984b: 14); Aguayo Quezada (2001: 201).

499. Hellman (1983: 168–169). Also Aguayo Quezada (2001: 201); Castellano (2007: 171–183).

500. Stevens (1974: 204–215); Hellman (1983: 174–178).

501. P. Smith (1991: 359–360). Also Basañez (1981: 171–172); Joseph and Buchenau (2013: 164).

502. Stevens (1974: 228).

503. Joseph and Buchenau (2013: 164).

504. A Mexican press photographer, quoted in Poniatowska (1975: 323).

505. Stevens (1974: 236–237); Poniatowska (1975: 207); P. Smith (1991: 360–361).

506. Poniatowska (1975: 207); P. Smith (1991: 360–361).

507. Ronfeldt (1975: 2); E. Williams (1986: 145); Camp (2005: 29–33).

508. Camp (2005: 29–33).

509. J. Bailey (1988: 20).

510. Poniatowska (1975: 314).

511. Aguayo Quezada (2001: 139).

512. Joseph and Buchanau (2013: 169); Avina (2014).

513. Hellman (1983: 184–185).

514. Aguayo Quezada (2001); Castellanos (2007).

515. See González Casanova (1981: 141); P. Smith (1991: 361); Joseph and Buchenau (2013: 164–166).

516. P. Smith (1979); Camp (2002).

517. Benjamin (2013: 226).

518. Lieuwen (1968: 147).

519. See Camp (1985, 2002); Centeno (1994); Babb (2001).

520. K. Greene (2007).

521. Lieuwen (1968).

522. Magaloni (2006); K. Greene (2007).

523. Middlebrook (1995: 257–259).

524. Bruhn (1997: 118–120).

525. Collier (1992); Middlebrook (1995).

526. K. Greene (2007).

527. See J. Bailey (1988: 127); Saragoza (1988: 197); Lomelí Vanegas (2000: 447).

528. Loaeza (1999: 349–361); Mizrahi (2003: 71–72).

529. J. Bailey (1986: 124, 134); Maxfield (1987: 5–9); Loaeza (1999: 349–361).

530. Bravo Mena (1987: 102); Escobar (1987: 75).

531. Loaeza (1999: 330–331, 360–361); Mizrahi (2003: 72–75).

532. Loaeza (1999); Chand (2001); Ard (2003: 106–107).

533. Camp (1999: 136); Chand (2001: 203, 153, 195). A 1992 constitutional reform shored up the Church's legal standing and permitted greater Church involvement in public life.

534. Chand (2001: 194–195); Middlebrook (2001: 33); Olvera (2004: 415).

535. Trejo (2009, 2012).

536. Tamayo (1990: 128); Molinar (1991: 159–170, 201–202); Chand (2001) Olvera (2003a, 2003b, 2004).

537. Stevens (1987: 218).

538. Chand (2001: 35); T. Eisenstadt (2004: 54–55).

539. Bruhn (1997).

540. Castañeda (2000: 72–75).

541. Bruhn (1997: 118–120).

542. On the 1988 fraud, see Cornelius et al. (1989: 20–21); Gómez Tagle (1994); Bruhn (1997: 140–145); Castañeda (2000: 232–238).

543. Bruhn (1997: 148–149, 308).

544. Bruhn (1997: 149); Camp (2002: 169).

545. Serrano (1997: 143).

546. Bruhn (1997: 149); Camp (2005: 36).

547. Camp (1992: 83–84); Serrano (1995: 446).

548. Levitsky and Way (2010: 153–154).

549. Alcocer (1995); Gómez Tagle (2004); Magaloni (2005); Levitsky and Way (2010: 154–160).

550. Levitsky and Way (2010: 158).

551. Wager and Shultz (1995).

552. Dresser (1996); Chand (2001: 226).

553. Klesner (2004: 92); Magaloni (2005).

554. Becarra et al. (2000).

555. Collier (1992).

556. K. Greene (2007).

557. Magaloni (2006: 20, 47–49, 65–73).

Chapter 5

1. T. Smith (1978); Hyam (2006: 90).

2. By the 1980s, twenty-nine states in sub-Saharan Africa had adopted single-party constitutions (Bratton and van de Walle 1997: 8).

3. In a few cases, such as Burma and Indonesia, the anticolonial struggle was violent but postindependence governments did not pursue radical change.

4. Calculated from data in Casey et al. (2021).

5. Duncanson (1968: 138–139); Woodside (1976: 14–17); Lockhart (1989: 23–25); A. Short (1989: 2).

6. McAlister (1971: 241–242).

7. Buttinger (1967a: 15, 45); McAlister (1971: 45–47); Woodside (1976: 16–19, 137–140).

8. Frances Fitzgerald (1972: 53).

9. McAlister (1971: 45–47); Frances Fitzgerald (1972: 53–57).

10. More evidence that prerevolutionary Vietnam lacked favorable conditions for durable authoritarianism comes from South Vietnam, which was initially ruled by the nonrevolutionary autocracy of Ngo Dinh Diem. The Diem government inherited a weak state, with limited tax capacity, untrained security forces, and limited control over the national territory (Murti 1964: 126–131; Lockhart 1989: 269–271; Post 1989a: 221–234). Notwithstanding massive U.S. assistance (C. Thayer 1989), state and regime quickly unraveled in the face of communist insurgency. Diem fell prey to a coup in 1963, and a decade later the state collapsed.

11. Khánh (1982: 156–160); Duiker (1996: 42–43, 60–61).

12. J. Harrison (1982: 93); Pike (1986a: 22–23); Duiker (1996: 73–74).

13. Khánh (1982: 259–269); Lockhart (1989: 92–97).

14. Duncanson (1968: 155); McAlister (1971: 105); Khánh (1982: 291–292).

15. Buttinger (1967a: 278); McAlister (1971: 147–150, 164); Duiker (1995a: 45); Currey (1997: 86–88).

16. Pike (1978: 51); Duiker (1996: 88).

17. Tonnesson (1991: 288–290).

18. Khánh (1982: 299–230, 310); Duiker (1996: 86–88).

19. Chinh (1963: 31).

20. Tonnesson (1991: 381–388); Marr (1995: 388–400).

21. Pike (1978: 52).

22. Khánh (1982: 324). Also Fall (1968: 64); Lockhart (1989: 138).

23. Marr (2013: 442–446).

24. Duiker (1996: 108–11).

25. Porter (1993: 10–11); Duiker (1996: 108–111); Marr (2013: 140).

26. Pike (1966: 27–28); Marr (2013: 9).

27. Hodgkin (1981: 3).

28. Marr (1995: 4, 502–506).

29. Buttinger (1967a: 347–248); Post (1989a: 130); Duiker (2000: 325–326).

30. Chinh (1963: 21); Buttinger (1967a: 348); Kolko (1985: 40).

31. Murti (1964: 4–5); Duiker (1995a: 57; 1996: 120).

32. Buttinger (1967a: 316–330); Jamieson (1993: 197–199).

33. Marr (2013: 176–177).

34. Hammer (1954).

35. Fall (1967: 17); McAlister (1971: 297); J. Harrison (1982: 129).

36. Elliott (1980: 204).

37. Pike (1978: 77, 97; 1986a: 140); J. Harrison (1982: 115); Khánh (1982: 332); Vu (2014: 25).

38. Giap (1975: 84–87).

39. Turley (1982: 66); Lockhart (1989: 142); Marr (2013: 178).

40. Duiker (2000: 346–347).

41. Hammer (1954: 177); Turley (1982: 66); Lockhart (1989: 123–125, 146, 175).

42. Lockhart (1989: 175, 198–201, 225–229); Marr (2013: 156).

43. Pike (1966: 49); Duiker (1996: 142).

44. Marr (2013: 574).

45. Turley (1972a: 83–84); Currey (1997: 157–160).

46. Currey (1997: 157).

47. Lockhart (1989: 259); Post (1989a: 155–157, 181–184).

48. Lockhart (1989: 229).

49. Hammer (1954: 287); O'Ballance (1964: 195); Karnow (1983: 199); Pike (1986a: 39).

50. A. Short (1989: 328).

51. S. Tucker (1999: 75–76).

52. O'Ballance (1964: 243).

53. McAlister (1971: 216–217); Currey (1997: 108–109); Marr (2013: 405–408).

54. Pike (1966: 24; 1978: 27–28, 44); Buttinger (1967a: 320–322).

55. Fall (1955: 239–240); McAlister and Mus (1970: 84); J. Werner (1980: 107–108); Tonnesson (1991: 97).

56. Buttinger (1967a: 255–261); J. Werner (1980: 107–108).

57. Gheddo (1970: 172–173); Jamieson (1993: 213–215).

58. Pike (1966: 27, 48–49); Khánh (1982: 242–243); Jamieson (1993: 213–215).

59. Tonnesson (1991: 395); Marr (1995: 519–524; 2013: 404–427); Elliott (2003: 52).

60. Marr (2013: 390).

61. Fall (1954: 11–13); Buttinger (1967a: 408–412); Pike (1978: 81–82); J. Harrison (1982: 99–104); Marr (1995: 519).

62. Pike (1966: 44); Buttinger (1967a: 408–409); McAlister (1971: 192).

63. McAlister (1971: 191–192); Marr (2013: 409).

64. Woodside (1976: 189); J. Werner (1980: 125–126).

65. Currey (1997: 126); Marr (2013: 415).

66. Fall (1954: 13); R. Turner (1975: 43–44); J. Harrison (1982: 189); Currey (1997: 125–126).

67. Marr (2013: 497).

68. Buttinger (1967a: 412); Pike (1978: 82, 89); Currey (1997: 132, 146).

69. Lockhart (1989: 264); Post (1989a: 4–5, 214–220).

70. Hodgkin (1981: 336).

71. Buttinger (1967b: 771–772); Pike (1978: 77, 97); Post (1989a: 172); Vu (2014: 25). Also Fall (1954: 35); Porter (1975: 58); J. Harrison (1982: 115); Beresford (1988: 79).

72. Post (1989a: 168). Also Kattenburg (1975: 113); Pike (1978: 66–67); Marr (1995: 553).

73. Boudarel (1980: 138).

74. J. Harrison (1982: 223).

75. Also Turley (1972b: 26); Pike (1978: 72–77).

76. Porter (1993: 104); Currey (1997: 273).

77. Turley (1972a); Lockhart (1989); Duiker (1996: 170–175).

78. Turley (1972a: 143); Pike (1986a: 39); Currey (1997: 213).

79. Pike (1986a: 183–205). Also Turley (1975: 136; 1977: 223–235).

80. Pike (1978: 62).

81. Turley (1972a, 1977, 1982).

82. Turley (1977: 223–224); Pike (1986a: 343–360).

83. Turley (1977: 224).

84. Turley (1982: 62–63).

85. Pike (1986a: 181).

86. Pike (1986a: 243); Currey (1997: 213).

87. Fall (1954: 74). See especially Pike (1986a: 148–151).

88. Pike (1986a: 151–164); Turley (1988: 199).

89. Fall (1954: 41–42, 74); Turley (1975: 136–137).

90. Fall (1954: 41–42).

91. Pike (1978: 81–82). Also Buttinger (1967a: 412).

92. Khánh (1982: 327); Lockhart (1989: 4); Slater (2009: 235).

93. Kolko (1985: 18–20).

94. Kaye (1962: 107).

95. Slater (2009: 235).

96. Gheddo (1970: 13); Turley (1972a: 110–111); Moise (1983: 193).

97. Post (1989a: 285–286); Duiker (2000: 486).

98. Murti (1964: 73); Post (1989a: 150, 167); Hansen (2009: 179).

99. Fall (1968: 154); Gheddo (1970: 58–59); J. Harrison (1982: 213); Porter (1993: 39).

100. Gheddo (1970: 71); Porter (1993: 39); Hansen (2009: 180, 190).

101. Fall (1968: 154). Also Malarney (2003: 226).

102. Post (1989a: 291).

103. Vu (2017).

104. Pike (1978: 107).

105. Ninh (2002: 241).

106. Vien (1974: 134).

107. Moise (1983: 146, 210); Post (1989b: 28–30); Duiker (2000: 488).

108. Porter (1993: 58).

109. Post (1989b: 28, 25–30).

110. Beresford (1988: 59).

111. Fforde and Paine (1987: 36); Duiker (2000: 479–480).

112. Pike (1978: 108–109).

113. Pike (1978: 108–109); Moise (1983: 172–179).

114. Pike (1978: 109); Moise (1980: 95–99; 1983: 215).

115. Moise (1980: 93–95).

116. Moise (1983: 213–222); Kolko (1985: 566); Vu (2014: 24).

117. Moise (1983: 229–232).

118. Moise (1983: 230–241); Kolko (1985: 66).

119. Moise (1980: 93–95).

120. R. Turner (1975: 143); Moise (1976: 73, 78; 1983: 222); J. Harrison (1982: 149); Kolko (1985: 66); Szalontai (2005: 401); Vu (2014: 25).

121. Moise (1983); Duiker (2000: 476–480); Vu (2017).

122. Currey (1997: 221–222); L. Nguyen (2012: 34–35).

123. R. Turner (1975: 144–145); Moise (1980: 93–96).

124. Turley (1972a: 116–120); Pike (1978: 111–112); L. Nguyen (2012: 34–35).

125. Pike (1978: 111).

126. See Fall (1968: 157); R. Turner (1975: 166); Pike (1978: 111); J. Harrison (1982: 151); C. Thayer (1989: 93); Currey (1997: 222).

127. Lacouture (1968: 208); Pike (1978: 110); Post (1989a: 280); Duiker (2000: 222).

128. Post (1989b: 25); Porter (1993: 58); Margolin (1999b: 568, 587); Duiker (2000: 479–480).

129. Post (1989b: 168–188).

130. Post (1989b: 199, 224–225); Beresford (2003: 47). The percentage of peasant families living on cooperatives increased from less than 10 percent in 1957 to 88 percent in 1961 (R. Turner 1975: 189; Post 1989b: 21; 1989c: 27–28).

131. Post (1989c: 23–24); Porter (1993: 44–47).

132. Malarney (2003: 227–228).

133. Malarney (2003: 229–230).

134. Malarney (2003: 230).

135. Porter (1993: 177–178); Abuza (2001: 187–189); Malarney (2003: 248); C. Thayer (2009a: 52).

136. Fall (1968: 154); Gheddo (1970: 189); Malarney (2003: 26).

137. Turley (1972a: 63).

138. Duiker (1995a: 114).

139. Duiker (1995a: 115).

140. Vu (2017: 135).

141. Duiker (1996: 211–213; 2000: 513–514); L. Nguyen (2012: 51–53).

142. Vu (2017: 4).

143. Pike (1966: 111); Osborne (1970: 124–125); A. Short (1989: 260–261).

144. Duiker (1996: 224); Elliott (2003: 174–178).

145. L. Nguyen (2012: 63–66).

146. Vu (2017: 186).

147. Turley (1972a: 188–189); L. Nguyen (2006; 2012: 90–91); Vu (2017: 184–189).

148. L. Nguyen (2012: 89–91); Vu (2017: 178–208).

149. Kolko (1985: 257–296); Porter (1993: 24–28); S. Tucker (1999: 98, 116, 125); Turley (2009: 114–117); L. Nguyen (2012: 74–89).

150. Beresford (1988: 38); S. Tucker (1999: 120); L. Nguyen (2012: 76–77, 88).

151. L. Nguyen (2012: 109).

152. Kolko (1985: 308, 333–334); Currey (1997: 269); L. Nguyen (2012: 130–131).

153. Kolko (1985: 333–337, 371); Currey (1997: 269); Elliott (2003: 340–353); Turley (2009: 149); L. Nguyen (2012: 130).

154. Kolko (1985: 333–334); Post (1989d: 122).

155. L. Nguyen (2012: 155, 258–260).

156. Duiker (1995a: 244–250); Elliott (2003: 418–431); Turley (2009: 216–237).

157. Buttinger (1977: 149–150); Kolko (1985: 534–535); Turley (2009: 230).

158. Terzani (1976: 87).

159. Porter (1993: 29–30).

160. Most estimates of North Vietnamese deaths range from 800,000 to 1.3 million. See Buttinger (1977: 95); Pike (1978: 133); Luong (2003: 3); Turley (2009: 254).

161. J. Harrison (1982: 3); L. Nguyen (2006: 21).

162. Luong (2003: 2–3).

163. Turley (1972b: 36; 1993: 340–341); Porter (1993: 115–116); Duiker (1995b: 102–103); Brigham (2000: 90–91).

164. Turley (1972b: 26); Duiker (1983: 83–84, 94).

165. L. Nguyen (2006: 5–6; 2012: 76–81). Also Honey (1963: 19–39); Quinn-Judge (2004, 2005).

166. Kattenburg (1975: 114).

167. Pike (1978: 127); Beresford (1988: 86); Porter (1993: 105).

168. Pike (1978: 61–67).

169. Pike (1978: 61–67, 127–128, 141; 1986b: 48–49); Duiker (1983: 85); Post (1989b: 98–99).

170. Pike (1978: 66–67, 128); C. Thayer (1992a: 351); Porter (1993: 105).

171. Taylor and Botea (2008).

172. Post (1989a: 261; 1989b: 54).

173. Taylor and Botea (2008: 39–40).

174. Kerkvliet and Selden (1999: 103); B. McCormick (1999: 156–157); Taylor and Botea (2008: 39–40); Turley (2009: 129–130).

175. Fall (1968: 130–138).

176. Turley (1972a: 173–176).

177. Pike (1986a: 2, 64–65); Duiker (2000: 554).

178. Turley (1972b: 26–27).

179. Turley (1972a: 240; 1982: 73–74); Kattenburg (1975: 117); Pike (1986a: 1).

180. A. Bernstein (1990: 79).

181. Turley (2009: 129–130).

182. Pike (1978: 113–114); Turley (2009: 129–131).

183. Turley (1975: 157–158).

184. Turley (1972a: 237; 1975: 157–158); Pike (1986a: 194–195).

185. Turley (2009: 83).

186. Fforde and Paine (1987); L. Nguyen (2012: 196–197).

187. Turley (1972a: 3); Duiker (1995b: 117).

188. Kellen (1972: 106–107).

189. Jumper (1959); Buttinger (1967b: 865–875, 880–889); Duncanson (1968: 220–221).

190. Frances Fitzgerald (1972: 150–157); Beresford (1989: 95–96).

191. Pike (1966: 148); Duncanson (1968: 252); J. Harrison (1982: 226); S. Tucker (1999: 92).

192. Duiker (1995b: 110–111). Armed bands of former South Vietnamese soldiers and rump Cao Dai and Hoa Hao networks persisted but posed no threat to the regime (Duiker 1989: 11).

193. Pike (1978: 68–71, 97, 143).

194. Porter (1993: 58, 69); Vu (2014: 25–27).

195. Pike (1978: 133).

196. Pike (1978); Duiker (1983); Brigham (2000).

197. Brigham (2000: 104).

198. Duiker (1983: 95).

199. Pike (1978: 61–67; 1986b: 46–49); Beresford (1988: 88).

200. Pike (1986a: 1).

201. Pike (1986a: 92, 124); C. Thayer (2011: 65); Vu (2014: 28).

202. Pike (1986a: 1); S. Tucker (1999: 199).

203. L. Nguyen (2012: 81).

204. Turley (2009: 129–130); C. Thayer (2014).

205. Pike (1978: 114); Joiner (1990: 1064).

206. Long (1981: 15). Also C. Thayer (2014: 145–146).

207. Long (1981: 4–6, 11–19, 26–31).

208. Hayton (2010: 68–70).

209. C. Thayer (2014: 136, 145–146).

210. Turley (1975: 136; 1977: 223–235).

211. Pike (1986a: 353–360, 184).

212. Turley (1982: 63).

213. Frances Fitzgerald (1972: 150–157).

214. Duiker (1983: 112; 1996: 366); S. Tucker (1999: 197–198).

215. Evans and Rowley (1984: 228–229). Also Terzani (1976: 214–215); Long (1981: 21); Pike (1986a: 77–82).

216. Slater (2009: 228).

217. Slater (2009).

218. Gheddo (1970: 137–139); Terzani (1976: 259–262); Duiker (1989: 33).

219. Slater (2009: 238).

220. Duiker (1989: 33, 112); Porter (1993: 40).

221. Abuza (2001: 203–204); Malarney (2003: 251–252).

222. Abuza (2001: 13).

223. Slater (2009: 234).

224. Marr and White (1988: 1–2); Duiker (1989: 25; 1995a: 260); Marr (1991: 15–16).

225. Terzani (1976: 188–195, 220–221); Porter (1993: 174–175).

226. Duiker (1989: 13); Porter (1993: 165–166).

227. Tang (1986: 282); Jamieson (1993: 363–365); Porter (1993: 174–175).

228. Beresford (1989).

229. Beresford (1989: 103–110); Duiker (1989: 50–58; 1995b: 148); S. Tucker (1999: 197–198).

230. Duiker (1989: 51); S. Tucker (1999: 197–198).

231. Duiker (1989: 15; 1995b: 140–141); Desbarats (1990: 56–60).

232. Marr and White (1988: 7); Tri (1988); Duiker (1989: 58–63); Abuza (2001: 162).

233. Beresford (1988: 151–158; 2003: 59).

234. Beresford (1989: 112); Tri (1990: 37–38); Fforde and de Vylder (1996: 129).

235. H. Nguyen (2016: 33, 38). Also Cima (1989: 787); Duiker (1995a: 261–262).

236. Pike (1986a: 69–70); Duiker (1989: 158–175); Porter (1993: 202–205).

237. Duiker (1989: 229).

238. Duiker (1995a: 267); Kolko (1997: 23); S. Tucker (1999: 196–197).

239. Evans and Rowley (1984: 45–57, 148); Chandra (1986: 232–245).

240. Chandra (1986: 358).

241. Chandra (1986: 356–357); Duiker (1989: 188); S. Tucker (1999: 199–200).

242. Chandra (1986: 357, 361); Duiker (1989: 189–190; 1995b: 209).

243. Vu (2014: 34).

244. Evans and Rowley (1984: 248).

245. Chandra (1986: 397); Gough (1990: 391); Duiker (1995b: 140–141).

246. Duiker (1983: 95); Pike (1986b: 47); Porter (1993: 106).

247. Duiker (1983: 93).

248. Turley (1988: 201).

249. Pike (1986a: 138, 193); Cima (1990: 89).

250. C. Dixon (2004: 17).

251. Duiker (1989: 46–47).

252. Evans and Rowley (1984: 150, 244); C. Thayer (1987: 16; 1992a: 351); Vu (2014: 26).

253. Soviet aid declined from $4.3 billion between 1986 and 1990 to $110 million in 1991 (Chandra 1993: 23). Also Abuza (2001: 16); Hayton (2010: 6).

254. Fforde and de Vylder (1996).

255. Stern (1987: 477–479); Fforde (1993: 23); Fforde and de Vylder (1996: 243); Beresford (2003: 61–63).

256. Fforde and de Vylder (1996: 243); Beresford (2003: 62).

257. C. Thayer (1988: 30); Porter (1990: 81–84); Stern (1993); Abuza (2001: 96–97).

258. Malarney (2003: 235–245); Bouquet (2010).

259. C. Thayer (1992b: 111, 128); Jeong (1997); Abuza (2001: 236); Wischermann (2003); Wells-Dang (2014).

260. Wee (1991: 312–313); Stern (1993: 102–104); Kolko (1997: 126).

261. Kolko (1997: 127).

262. Wee (1991: 313); C. Thayer (1992a: 357–358); Heng (1998: 33); Marr (1998: 4–5).

263. Kolko (1997: 131–143).

264. Turley (1988: 201).

265. Abuza (2001); Slater (2009).

266. C. Thayer (1992a: 355–356; 1992b: 123–124); Abuza (2001: 169–171); Marr (2003: 281).

267. Jeong (1997: 155).

268. Porter (1993: 106–107); Elliott (1995: 418); Brigham (2000: 90–91).

269. Joiner (1990: 1064–1065); Abuza (2001: 215–218); C. Thayer (2014: 136–137).

270. Abuza (2001: 215–218); Hayton (2010: 68–70); C. Thayer (2014: 145–146).

271. Duiker (1989: 244).

272. Abuza (2001: 13–15); Slater (2009).

273. Abuza (2001: 13–15).

274. Elliott (1995: 416). Also Slater (2009).

275. Dollar (1999: 30).

276. Holmes (2007: 20).

277. Sidel (1997, 1998); Abuza (1998: 1114–1117); Truong (1998: 330).

278. Malesky (2014: 37).

279. Hiep (2016).

280. Hebbel (1993: 371).

281. Vu (2014: 36).

282. Gainsborough (2010: 135–155); Vu (2014: 37).

283. Vu (2014: 37); Vuving (2019).

284. Case (2016: 94); P. Nguyen (2017); Vuving (2017).

285. Vuving (2017: 429).

286. There were an estimated 140,000 community-based organizations in 2005 (C. Thayer 2009b: 5).

287. C. Thayer (2007: 387–388; 2014: 142); Hayton (2010: 127); Kerkvliet (2014).

288. C. Thayer (2009b: 15; 2014: 142); Hayton (2010: 127, 133).

289. C. Thayer (2009a: 55; 2009b: 16); Hayton (2010: 132).

290. C. Thayer (2009b: 18; 2010: 436). Also Hayton (2010: 132).

291. Kurfurst (2015); Morris-Jung (2015); Bui (2016).

292. Malesky (2014: 36); Kurfurst (2015: 137).

293. Kurfurst (2015: 143).

294. Kurfurst (2015: 137–138); H. Nguyen (2016: 40–43); Coxhead (2018); M. Nguyen (2018: 411).

295. H. Nguyen (2016: 40); C. Thayer (2018: 440); London (2019: 142).

296. H. Nguyen (2016: 39).

297. Slater (2009).

298. Taken from Varieties of Democracy (version 9) Core Civil Society Index. Averaged score 2000–2015. See Coppedge et al. (2019: 275).

299. Hayton (2010: 68–70); C. Thayer (2014: 136–137).

300. C. Thayer (2010: 438).

301. Kurfurst (2015: 153).

302. C. Dixon (2004: 23).

303. Entelis (1986: 7–18); Bennoune (1988: 17–19); H. Roberts (2003: 53, 113); Ruedy (2005: 32–43).

304. C. Moore (1970: 39–44, 79); Tlemcani and Hansen (1989: 115).

305. Leveau (1993: 248–249).

306. Volpi (2006: 443).

307. Adamson (1998: 98).

308. Quandt (1998: 120).

309. Horne ([1977] 2006); Stone (1997: 37).

310. Ottaway and Ottaway (1970: 31); Jackson (1977: 56); Stone (1997: 41); Evans (2012: 338).

311. Quandt (1969: 15); Ruedy (2005: 65).

312. Horne ([1977] 2006: 24–40); Jackson (1977: 15–21); Ruedy (2005: 145–150); Evans (2012: 87–91).

313. Jackson (1977: 16–23); Bennoune (1988: 81–84); Ruedy (2005: 153–157).

314. O'Ballance (1967: 63); Horne ([1977] 2006: 128); Ruedy (2005: 104, 164–165).

315. Jackson (1977: 27–30); Bennoune (1988: 85); Evans (2012: 179–181).

316. O'Ballance (1967: 44–49, 67, 108); Jackson (1977: 44–46); Galula (2006: 19); Evans (2012: 173).

317. Humbaraci (1966: 39–40); Quandt (1969: 92); Crenshaw Hutchinson (1978: 9–10).

318. Connelly (2002: 290–292); Ruedy (2005: 167–169); Evans (2012: 202–207).

319. Gallagher (1963: 133–138); Lewis (1973: 330–333); Adamson (1998: 78–79); Evans (2012: 129–130).

320. Quandt (1969: 126, 155); Lewis (1973: 330–333); Jackson (1977: 49, 54); Entelis (1986: 54–57).

321. Jackson (1977: 33, 50–52); Werenfels (2007: 34); Evans (2012: 129–130).

322. O'Ballance (1967: 68); Crenshaw Hutchinson (1978: 44); H. Roberts (1984: 7–8).

323. Jackson (1977: 34–39, 47); H. Roberts (1993: 125–128); Evans and Phillips (2007: 64, 207–209).

324. Entelis (1986: 52–53); Ageron (1991: 109–113); Galula (2006: 11–13, 61).

325. Ruedy (2005: 167–169); Galula (2006: 142–143); Evans (2012: 202–208).

326. Galula (2006: 142–143). Also O'Ballance (1967: 71); Jackson (1977: 52, 75); J. Hill (2009: 62).

327. Ruedy (2005: 267–269); Evans (2012: 207–209).

328. Humbaraci (1966: 51).

329. Jackson (1977: 75).

330. Quandt (1969: 135–138); Jackson (1977: 50–51); Ruedy (2005: 162).

331. Jackson (1977: 51).

332. Ruedy (2005: 169).

333. O'Ballance (1967: 120); Jackson (1977: 47–48); Tlemcani (1986: 64).

334. O'Ballance (1967: 216); Horne ([1977] 2006: 461–463); Galula (2006: 181).

335. J. Hill (2012: 8).

336. Connelly (2002).

337. Horne ([1977] 2006: 219, 234–235, 415–416); Connelly (2002); Galula (2006: 6).

338. J. Hill (2012: 9).

339. Connelly (2002).

340. Horne ([1977] 2006: 464–465).

341. Horne ([1977] 2006: 511); Ageron (1991: 125); Connelly (2002: 265).

342. Connelly (2002).

343. A. Harrison (1989).

344. Evans and Phillips (2007: 69). Also Horne ([1977] 2006: 486-497, 528–530); A. Harrison (1989: 81); Ageron (1991: 124–126).

345. Malley (1996: 134); Evans (2012: 314–319, 337).

346. Evans (2012: 318–320).

347. Clegg (1971: 39–40); Connelly (2002: 267–270); Ruedy (2005: 185, 195).

348. Clegg (1971: 39–40); Bennoune (1988: 97). Algeria's GDP contracted by 35 percent between 1960 and 1963 (Ruedy 2005: 195).

349. Gallagher (1963: 139); Humbaraci (1966: 4–5); C. Moore (1970: 122–123); Ruedy (2005: 105, 195).

350. Lewis (1963: 27); Clegg (1971: 39); Jackson (1977: 65).

351. C. Moore (1970: 122–123).

352. Horne ([1977] 2006: 536–538); Ruedy (2005: 191).

353. Jackson (1977: 56); Evans (2012: 333).

354. Horne ([1977] 2006: 537); Jackson (1977: 65).

355. Tlemcani (1986: 73); Ruedy (2005: 191).

356. Humbaraci (1966: 72); Ruedy (2005: 192).

357. Ruedy (2005: 192).

358. Quandt (1969:173); Jackson (1977: 73–74).

359. Merle (1967: 130–131); Tlemcani (1986: 78); Quandt (1969: 171–173); Jackson (1977: 72–73).

360. Gordon (1966: 73–74); Ottaway and Ottaway (1970: 22–23); Tlemcani (1986: 78–79).

361. C. Moore (1970).

362. Humbaraci (1966: 102); C. Moore (1970: 124–125); Jackson (1977: xvi, 52–54); Tlemcani (1986: 177).

363. Quandt (1969).

364. Gallagher (1963: 133–138); Gordon (1966: 74–75); Quandt (1969: 126, 154); Evans (2012: 129–130).

365. Entelis (1986: 54).

366. Quandt (1969: 167–168) identified "at least 10 relatively independent centers of authority" in the movement. Also Jackson (1977: 50–52); Ruedy (2005: 191).

367. Stone (1997: 37).

368. Evans and Phillips (2007: 69). Also Humbaraci (1966: 66); Jackson (1977: 51); Ruedy (2005: 181).

369. H. Roberts (1995: 266).

370. Ottaway and Ottaway (1970: 176–177); J. Hill (2016: 118).

371. Humbaraci (1966: 66).

372. Addi (1998: 50).

373. Volpi (2017: 116).

374. Addi (1998); Cook (2007).

375. As Hugh Roberts wrote, "The notion that the FLN ruled Algeria . . . was entirely erroneous" (2003: 354).

376. Quandt (1998: 63).

377. Stone (1997: 129). Also Derradji (2002: 399–400); Bouandel (2003: 3–6); Cook (2007: 30–33).

378. Bouandel (2003: 4–6).

379. Werenfels (2007: 67–68, 2).

380. J. Hill (2019: 1386).

381. Quandt (1969: 126); Horne ([1977] 2006: 137–138); Jackson (1977: 28–30).

382. Horne ([1977] 2006: 133–136); Crenshaw Hutchinson (1978: 6–8); H. Roberts (1984: 6–8).

383. Humbaraci (1966: 65); Horne ([1977] 2006: 133–136, 158, 221–222); Jackson (1977: 27).

384. H. Roberts (1984: 8).

385. Clegg (1971: 39–40).

386. Ottaway and Ottaway (1970: 40).

387. Stone (1997: 198–199); Quandt (1998: 29, 35–36).

388. Labat (1994); Willis (1996: 36); Stone (1997: 147–148).

389. H. Roberts (1988: 561–562); Willis (1996: 36–41).

390. Clegg (1971: 53–55); Crenshaw Hutchinson (1978: 12); H. Roberts (1993: 112–113).

391. C. Moore (1970: 36–37); Lawless (1984: 157).

392. Ottaway and Ottaway (1970: 81); Lewis (1973: 337); Byrne (2016: 73–78).

393. Byrne (2016: 128).

394. Quandt (1969: 165–166, 223–224); Byrne (2016: 133).

395. Byrne (2016: 2).

396. Clegg (1971).

397. Clegg (1971: 47–58); Bennoune (1988: 97, 104).

398. Clegg (1971: 39–56).

399. Ottaway and Ottaway (1970: 61); Vallin (1973: 53); Knauss (1980: 64); Byrne (2016: 155).

400. Byrne (2016: 155).

401. Ottaway and Ottaway (1970: 107).

402. Humbaraci (1966: 113); Clegg (1971: 55, 170, 183, 190); Bennoune (1988: 97, 104).

403. Clegg (1971).

404. Gordon (1966: 153–154); Ottaway and Ottaway (1970: 54); Clegg (1971: 59–60); Adamson (1998: 114).

405. Ottaway and Ottaway (1970: 60–67); Clegg (1971: 71–72); Tlemcani (1986: 95–105).

406. Ottaway and Ottaway (1970: 64–65).

407. Byrne (2016: 153).

408. Vallin (1973); Ruedy (2005: 198).

409. Knauss (1977: 66–67); Pfeifer (1985).

410. T. Smith (1975: 272–276); Knauss (1977: 70–76); Pfeifer (1985: 50–67); Ruedy (2005: 222–223).

411. T. Smith (1975: 271).

412. Bennoune (1988: 190); Stone (1997: 91–92); Ruedy (2005: 223).

413. Pfeifer (1985: 81); Ageron (1991: 140); Ruedy (2005: 223).

414. Ottaway and Ottaway (1970: 63–67); Clegg (1971: 71–74, 162–176); Tlemcani (1986: 95–105).

415. Mortimer (1970); Byrne (2016).

416. Byrne (2016).

417. Also Ottaway and Ottaway (1970: 147, 171); Mortimer (2015: 466–468).

418. Byrne (2016: 3).

419. Evans and Phillips (2007: 75); Torres-García (2013: 341).

420. Gallagher (1963: 242); Ottaway and Ottaway (1970: 154–156); Mortimer (2015: 469).

421. Gordon (1966: 222); Ruedy (2005: 211); Byrne (2016: 150).

422. Cavatorta (2009: 100); Byrne (2016: 238–241).

423. Byrne (2016: 150).

424. Byrne (2016: 148).

425. Byrne (2016: 148–149).

426. Ottaway and Ottaway (1970: 148–154).

427. Humbaraci (1966: 192–207); Heradslveil (1998: 91); Derradji (2002: 475).

428. Gordon (1966: 225); Humbaraci (1966: 197); Byrne (2016: 277).

429. Ottaway and Ottaway (1970: 151–152); Derradji (2002: 475).

430. Byrne (2016: 152).

431. Byrne (2016: 274–276).

432. Ruedy (2005: 206).

433. T. Smith (1975: 271–272); H. Roberts (1988: 573).

434. Ageron (1991: 140).

435. Ottaway and Ottaway (1970: 156–157); Byrne (2016: 240–242).

436. Quandt (1998: 84).

437. Gallagher (1963: 243).

438. Ottaway and Ottaway (1970: 148–154).

439. Gordon (1966: 232–234).

440. Bonora-Waisman (2003).

441. Humbaraci (1966: 192–200); Lawless (1984: 137).

442. Humbaraci (1966: 192).

443. Gordon (1966: 222); Entelis (1986: 196); Torres-García (2013: 341).

444. Torres-García (2013: 341); Byrne (2016: 216).

445. Humbaraci (1966: 145–146).

446. Humbaraci (1966: 143–146).

447. Torres-García (2013: 338); Byrne (2016: 219–222).

448. Entelis (1986: 54).

449. Also Quandt (1969: 167–174); H. Roberts (1984: 9–10); Werenfels (2007: 35).

450. Gordon (1966: 67).

451. Quandt (1969: 205); Jackson (1977: 82, 88); Stone (1997: 46–49).

452. Ottaway and Ottaway (1970: 80–81).

453. Quandt (1969: 212–213); Jackson (1977: 97–100).

454. Ottaway and Ottaway (1970: 80–81).

455. Ottaway and Ottaway (1970: 80–81, 87); Lewis (1973: 335–336); Jackson (1977: 178–179).

456. Gordon (1966: 150–151); Quandt (1969: 229–231); Ottaway and Ottaway (1970: 101–102); Jackson (1977: 188–189).

457. Jackson (1977: 198–200).

458. Ottaway and Ottaway (1970: 191–192); Cook (2007: 30).

459. Humbaraci (1966: 95).

460. Evans and Phillips (2007: 81).

461. Humbaraci (1966: 232); Quandt (1969: 241–247); Ottaway and Ottaway (1970: 191–192, 203); Ruedy (2005: 208).

462. Quandt (1969: 241, 244–247).

463. J. Hill (2009: 72).

464. Humbaraci (1966: 62–63); Lewis (1973: 338); Jackson (1977: 192); Tlemcani (1986: 93).

465. Stone (1997: 135); Werenfels (2007: 34).

466. J. Hill (2009: 182).

467. Jackson (1977: 191); Quandt (1998: 84).

468. Ottaway and Ottaway (1970: 161, 197–198); Stone (1997: 130–131).

469. Lewis (1973: 338); Zartman (1973: 214); Quandt (1998: 84).

470. Henry (2004: 71).

471. Horne ([1977] 2006: 133–136, 221–222); H. Roberts (1984: 6–7); Malley (1996: 129–130).

472. H. Roberts (1984: 6–8).

473. H. Roberts (1984: 8); Ottaway and Ottaway (1970: 81).

474. H. Roberts (1988: 573).

475. Jackson (1977: 174); Pfeifer (1985: 5); Ciment (1997: 40–41).

476. Ottaway and Ottaway (1970: 57–58, 131–142, 206–207); Jackson (1977: 112–113, 123–126, 195–197).

477. Jackson (1977: 177); Mezhoud (1993); J. Hill (2012: 12–16).

478. Willis (1996: 41); Derradji (2002: 297).

479. Stone (1997: 150–151).

480. Mortimer (1991: 577); Fuller (1995: 32).

481. Willis (1996: 46, 56–57); Layachi (2004: 49); J. Hill (2009: 131).

482. Mortimer (1991: 577–578).

483. Mortimer (1991: 578); Willis (1996: 61, 76); Stone (1997: 158–159).

484. Stone (1997: 159).

485. Evans and Phillips (2007: 85).

486. Humbaraci (1966: 231–233).

487. Humbaraci (1966: 232); Ottaway and Ottaway (1970: 191–192, 204); Jackson (1977: 202).

488. Quandt (1969: 240, 256–257); H. Roberts (1984: 11).

489. Quandt (1969: 256–237, 284–285); Entelis (1986: 168).

490. Quandt (1969: 260); Ottaway and Ottaway (1970: 352).

491. Entelis (1986: 60).

492. Vandewalle (1997: 34). Also Quandt (1998: 84); Cavatorta (2009: 89).

493. Evans and Phillips (2007: 87–88).

494. Willis (1996: 46–47, 66); Henry (2004: 77).

495. H. Roberts (1984: 31); Stone (1997: 58).

496. Quandt (1998: 29); Ruedy (2005: 232).

497. Cook (2007: 40).

498. Mezhoud (1993).

499. Mezhoud (1993).

500. Evans and Phillips (2007: 124).

501. Entelis (1986: 83); Fuller (1995: 32); Willis (1996: 76).

502. Tlemcani (1986: 196).

503. Ruedy (1994: 83).

504. Layachi (2004: 50).

505. Willis (1996: 70–72, 103); Stone (1997: 154–157).

506. Entelis (1986: 87–88); Willis (1996: 72); H. Roberts (2003: 158).

507. Evans and Phillips (2007: 125).

508. Stone (1997: 96–97); Ciment (1997: 50).

509. Entelis (1994: 228; 2011: 657); Ruedy (2005: 245–247).

510. Stone (1997: 63–64).

511. Willis (1996: 107–109); Stone (1997: 248); Evans and Phillips (2007: 102, 140–141).

512. Willis (1996: 110); Ruedy (2005: 249).

513. Ageron (1991: 143); Vandewalle (1992: 710); Ruedy (2005: 248).

514. Willis (1996: 112–121); Quandt (1998: 44–47); Volpi (2003: 43–44).

515. Salah Tahi (1992: 402); Willis (1996: 133, 155–157).

516. Mortimer (1991: 585); Zoubir (1995: 125).

517. Mortimer (1991: 586); Rouadjia (1995: 87–88); Willis (1996: 158).

518. "Algerian Election Tests Government," *New York Times*, December 26, 1991. Also Ruedy (2005: 254).

519. Mortimer (1991: 588–589); Cook (2007: 55–56).

520. Entelis (1994: 238); Ruedy (2005: 254).

521. Willis (1996: 179–180); Quandt (1998: 57).

522. Mortimer (1991: 591).

523. Willis (1996: 215–218); Stone (1997: 76–77).

524. Willis (1996: 230–232).

525. Martinez (2004: 18).

526. Willis (1996: 243–247); Cook (2007: 54–57).

527. Addi (1998: 47, 78); H. Roberts (2003: 248); Cook (2007: 39–40).

528. Willis (1996: 250–251); Stone (1997: 103).

529. Stone (1997: 103).

530. Willis (1996: 256); Stone (1997: 106–107).

531. Zartman (1994: 215); Willis (1996: 122); Ciment (1997: 93–95).

532. Malley (1996: 137); Willis (1996: 122–123); Stone (1997: 73); Volpi (2003: 48); Werenfels (2007: 12).

533. Martinez (2000: 161).

534. Martinez (2000: 161).

535. Shirley (1995: 29).

536. Willis (1996: 294); Werenfels (2007: 86).

537. Stone (1997: 106–107).

538. Willis (1996: 255–256); Stone (1997: 106–108); Derradji (2002: 319); Ruedy (2005: 259).

539. Willis (1996: 256–257, 267); Ciment (1997: 1); Stone (1997: 106–107).

540. Stone (1997: 108); Volpi (2003: 62).

541. Spencer (1994: 150); Ruedy (2005: 261).

542. Stone (1997: 184–185); Martinez (2000: 68–70); Evans and Phillips (2007: 82–84).

543. Willis (1996: 256–257); Stone (1997: 191–195); Heradslveil (1998: 55–65).

544. Willis (1996: 326–327).

545. Martinez (2000: 215); Ruedy (2005: 264); J. Hill (2012: 21).

546. H. Roberts (2007: 4); Werenfels (2007: 48); J. Hill (2009: 191).

547. Martinez (2004: 15); Ruedy (2005: 264); Cook (2007: 32); Werenfels (2007: 28); Cavatorta (2009: 3); Entelis (2011: 659); J. Hill (2012: 5).

548. Cavatorta (2009: 110–112).

549. Volpi (2003: 118–119); Cavatorta (2009: 150–169).

550. Volpi (2013); J. Hill (2016: 116).

551. Fuller (1995: 42); Martinez (2000: 59).

552. Martinez (2000: 147); Cook (2007: 27).

553. Volpi (2017: 85).

554. Willis (1996: 295).

555. Fuller (1995: 40); Willis (1996: 294); J. Hill (2016: 118).

556. Martinez (2000: 15); Werenfels (2007: 82); J. Hill (2019: 1387).

557. Quandt (1998: 61–62). Also Werenfels (2007: 55–56, 82); J. Hill (2019: 1387).

558. Quandt (1998: 61).

559. Fuller (1995: 93–96).

560. H. Roberts (1994).

561. H. Roberts (1995: 255); Willis (1996: 284); Stone (1997: 114–115).

562. Willis (1996: 346–355).

563. Ruedy (2005: 277); Volpi (2006: 448–449); J. Hill (2016: 124–125).

564. Werenfels (2007: 56); J. Hill (2016: 118).

565. Martinez (2000: 155–156).

566. J. Hill (2019: 1390).

567. J. Hill (2019: 1388).

568. Tlemcani (1986: 93); Martinez (2000: 148–156, 162; 2004: 24).

569. Achy (2013: 12); Volpi (2017: 146).

570. J. Hill (2012: 22).

571. Martinez (2004: 24); J. Hill (2012: 22).

572. Martinez (2000: 148–149; 2004: 18); Achy (2013: 12); J. Hill (2016: 99; 2019: 1391–1392).

573. Mortimer (2004; 2006: 163); Ruedy (2005: 278–279).

574. H. Roberts (2007: 2).

575. Martinez (2004: 21–22); Evans and Phillips (2007: 278–279).

576. Martinez (2004: 278–279).

577. Werenfels (2007: 138–141, 154).

578. Del Panta (2017).

579. J. Hill (2019: 1388).

580. Del Panta (2017: 1085).

581. Del Panta (2017: 1085).

582. Entelis (2011: 674); Del Panta (2017: 1085–1086).

583. Achy (2013).

584. Volpi (2013: 110–111; 2017: 85–86); Del Panta (2017: 1085, 1088); J. Hill (2019: 1386).

585. J. Hill (2019).

586. Government expenditure increased by 50 percent in 2011 (Achy 2013: 10–11). Also Volpi (2017).

587. Del Panta (2017).

588. Del Panta (2017: 109); International Crisis Group (2018: 3).

589. Werenfels (2007: 83).

590. Volpi (2020: 157).

591. Volpi (2020: 157–161).

592. Volpi (2020: 161–162).

593. Hadjor (1988: 43).

594. First (1970: 169); Rooney (1988: 27); Birmingham (1990: 15); Elischer (2013: 243).

595. Wallerstein (1964: 45); Hadjor (1988: 51); Rooney (1988: 43–44, 48); Birmingham (1990: 25).

596. Austin (1964); Bretton (1966: 75); First (1970: 170, 181); Howell and Rajasooria (1972: 9–11); Birmingham (1990: 15); Elischer (2013: 244).

597. Walton (2014: 225).

598. Arden-Clarke (1958: 31).

599. Arden-Clarke (1958: 31).

600. Colonial Governor Charles Arden-Clarke believed that the CPP's inclusion in the power structure provided the best defense against communism (Arden-Clarke 1958).

601. Addo-Fening (1972: 82).

602. Howell and Rajasooria (1972: 14).

603. Arden-Clarke (1958: 35); Howell and Rajasooria (1972: 14); Hadjor (1988: 58).

604. Rooney (1988: 122–123).

605. Wallerstein (1964: 57); Howell and Rajasooria (1972: 13); Rooney (1988: 34–35, 89); Hyam (2006: 150).

606. "Dr. Nkrumah's Policy of Independence," *The Times* (UK), October 26, 1953; Wallerstein (1964: 54); Howell and Rajasooria (1972: 19).

607. Howell and Rajasooria (1972: 19); Nwaubani (2001: 601).

608. Hyam (2006: 150).

609. Howell and Rajasooria (1972: 17).

610. Howell and Rajasooria (1972: 20–21).

611. Birmingham (1990: 63).

612. Quoted in S. Smith (1957: 363).

613. Barker (1968: 53–54); Hadjor (1988: 67); Birmingham (1990: 41, 46).

614. Bretton (1966: 75); Amonoo (1981: 6).

615. Hutchful (1973: 55–56); Baynham (1988: 65–66); Birmingham (1990: 89).

616. Bebler (1973: 31).

617. First (1970: 170).

618. Howell and Rajasooria (1972: 22); Rooney (1988: 139); Birmingham (1990).

619. Esseks (1971: 59); Howell and Rajasooria (1972: 21–22).

620. First (1970: 170–174); Esseks (1971: 60–61); Rooney (1988: 142, 188); Birmingham (1990: 9, 76–78).

621. David Brokensha, quoted in Wallerstein (1967: 45). Also Hutchful (1973: 59).

622. Rathbone (2000: 11).

623. Rooney (1988: 95–122); Rathbone (2000).

624. Barker (1968: 16); Howell and Rajasooria (1972: 50, 59); Rooney (1988: 169–180).

625. Nwaubani (2001: 605–606).

626. Rooney (1988: 169–176); Grilli (2017: 305).

627. Barker (1968: 98); First (1970: 182).

628. *Africa Report* (1964a: 25); First (1970: 174–176); Esseks (1971: 62–63).

629. Carol Johnson (1962); Howell and Rajasooria (1972: 50–52); Ahlman (2010: 70–77); Grilli (2017: 302).

630. Ahlman (2011: 29–30).

631. Nwaubani (2001: 601).

632. Howell and Rajasooria (1972: 57–58).

633. Ahlman (2011: 29–30).

634. Petchenkine (1993: 29); Nwaubani (2001: 612).

635. Nwaubani (2001: 614).

636. First (1970: 174, 176); Nwaubani (2001: 615).

637. First (1970: 193); Baynham (1988: 94).

638. Zolberg (1966); Rooney (1988: 57–58).

639. Wallerstein (1964: 60); Hadjor (1988: 61); Birmingham (1990: 47).

640. Zolberg (1966).

641. Zolberg (1966: 14, 95–98); First (1970: 182); Petchenkine (1993: 13–14, 21); McLaughlin and Owusu-Ansah (1995: 35).

642. Hutchful (1973: 48–56, 78); Baynham (1988: 66, 84); Birmingham (1990: 89).

643. Hutchful (1973: 70–71).

644. Bebler (1973: 31).

645. Barker (1968: 109, 113).

646. Barker (1968: 113).

647. First (1970: 183–184).

648. Howell and Rajasooria (1972: 48–49); Rooney (1988: 101, 103, 139).

649. First (1970: 183–184).

650. Barker (1968: 55).

651. Zolberg (1966: 98); First (1970: 186).

652. Zolberg (1966: 96–97); Barker (1968: 55); Hutchful (1973: 32); Amonoo (1981: 11–14); Petchenkine (1993: 13–14, 21).

653. W. Thompson (1966: 20); Austin (1972: 2); Dowse (1972: 17–18); Bebler (1973: 37).

654. Hutchful (1973: 72).

655. Gutteridge (1969: 98); Bebler (1973: 32–33); Baynham (1988: 60, 86, 155, 163).

656. Bebler (1973: 33).

657. Barker (1968: 8); First (1970: 183); Howell and Rajasooria (1972: 84); Hutchful (1973: 69); Baynham (1988: 90).

658. Gutteridge (1969: 105); Hutchful (1973: 89–90).

659. First (1970: 195); Hutchful (1973: 89); Baynham (1988: 140).

660. Kraus (1966: 19); Barker (1968: 194); First (1970: 195); Hutchful (1973: 89–90); Baynham (1988: 131–132, 140).

661. Barker (1968: 18); First (1970: 197); Baynham (1988: 138).

662. Bebler (1973: 34).

663. Hutchful (1973: 91–92).

664. Kraus (1966: 20); Baynham (1988: 143).

665. Gutteridge (1969: 105); Hutchful (1973: 91); Baynham (1988: 139, 73).

666. Hutchful (1973: 92).

667. Baynham (1988: 148); also Kraus (1966: 17); Barker (1968: 89); First (1970: 197).

668. Baynham (1988: 155).

669. Baynham (1988: 187, 193); Petchenkine (1993: 26).

670. Dowse (1972: 17–18).

671. CIA (1966); Bebler (1973: 37).

672. Barker (1968: 19).

673. Austin (1972: 2); Hutchful (1973: 34).

674. Barker (1968: 196–197, 207).

675. Rake (1965); First (1970: 175–177); Hutchful (1973: 35).

676. Barker (1968: 94); Bebler (1973: 34); Hutchful (1973: 85–87).

677. Baynham (1988: 133).

678. First (1970: 370).

679. Barker (1968: 83, 143, 149).

680. Barker (1968: 109, 113).

681. Bebler (1973: 32–33).

682. Dowse (1972: 17–18).

Chapter 6

1. On the vulnerability of sultanistic regimes to social revolution, see Skocpol and Goodwin (1989); Snyder (1992); and Chehabi and Linz (1998).

2. Pérez (1976a: 12–19, 32–54); Domínguez (1978: 13–19); Fermoselle (1987b: 105, 112–148).

3. Pérez (1976a); Domínguez (1978).

4. Domínguez (1998).

5. Pérez (1976a: 145–147); Fermoselle (1987b: 230); Domínguez (1998).

6. Thomas (1977: 215).

7. Padula (1993: 16–17); also Pérez (1976a: 145); Thomas (1977: 12, 158).

8. Bonachea and San Martín (1974: 88–89, 93, 106); Thomas (1977: 114–115).

9. Bonachea and San Martín (1974: 89, 93, 106); Thomas (1977: 126).

10. Pérez (1976a: 141–142).

11. Sweig (2002: 39).

12. Taber (1961: 244–245); Matthews (1975: 96); Thomas (1977: 192); Domínguez (1978: 121).

13. Goldenberg (1965: 157–159); Bonachea and San Martín (1974: 161–169); Llerena (1978: 134–139); Sweig (2002: 70–84, 90).

14. Farber (1976: 166–167); García-Pérez (2006: 70).

15. Bonsal (1971: 18); Domínguez (1998); Sweig (2002: 30–31, 171).

16. Bonsal (1971); Bonachea and San Martín (1974: 201).

17. Bonachea and San Martín (1974: 49–52, 142–144); Morán Arce (1980: 75–81, 135–154); Sweig (2002).

18. Bonachea and San Martín (1974: 113–130, 213–215); Fermoselle (1987b: 224–227); Sweig (2002: 19, 95–97).

19. Bonachea and San Martín (1974: 113–120); Sweig (2002: 19).

20. Morán Arce (1980: 224–225); Sweig (2002: 146–153).

21. Bonachea and San Martín (1974: 5, 146); Morán Arce (1980: 231–267); Sweig (2002: 148–152).

22. Bonachea and San Martín (1974: 230–233); Matthews (1975: 105); Domínguez (2020: 3).

23. Draper (1965: 24–25).

24. Barquín (1975: 616–617); Farber (2006: 118–119).

25. Domínguez (1978: 126); Morán Arce (1980: 277–279).

26. Pérez (2015: 243).

27. Domínguez (1998: 129–130).

28. Domínguez (1978: 128–130); Szulc (1986: 456).

29. Matthews (1975: 99); Thomas (1977: 221); Pérez (2015: 242, 252).

30. Pérez (1976a: 161); Barquín (1978: 12); Domínguez (1998).

31. Domínguez (1974: 217); Pérez (1976b: 257); Thomas (1977: 260); Guerra (2012: 16).

32. Thomas (1977: 256); Morán Arce (1980: 313–314); Domínguez (1998: 130–131).

33. Barquín (1975: 789–818, 833); Matthews (1975: 106); Pérez (1976a: 154–156).

34. Rabkin (1991: 21).

35. Bonachea and San Martín (1974: 291–294).

36. Sweig (2002: 177).

37. Bonachea and San Martín (1974: 312–313).

38. Barquín (1978: 26–41, 64–65, 84–85).

39. Pérez (1976b: 257); Thomas (1977: 247–248); Morán Arce (1980: 299–300).

40. Pérez (1976a: 165).

41. López-Fresquet (1966: 66).

42. Thomas (1977: 239, 246).

43. Bonachea and San Martín (1974: 322–325); Sweig (2002: 178).

44. Judson (1984: 228–229).

45. Paterson (1994: 231).

46. Barquín (1978: 92–99).

47. Thomas (1977: 283–284).

48. Huberman and Sweezy (1960: 84–85); Draper (1965: 118); Sweig (2002: 181); Klepak (2012: 181).

49. Matthews (1975: 235).

50. Thomas (1977: 413).

51. Fermoselle (1987b: 269); Klepak (2005: 42; 2015: 74).

52. San Martín and Bonachea (1989: 64); Greene Walker (2003: 349); Klepak (2012: 22).

53. Vellinga (1976: 246); Herrera Medina (2006: 33); Pérez (2015: 264).

54. Thomas (1977: 290–291); Fermoselle (1987b: 267); Rabkin (1991: 43).

55. Farber (1976: 215; 2006: 134); Judson (1984: 229).

56. Thomas (1977: 289).

57. Thomas (1977: 296–297); Domínguez (1978: 234); Evenson (1994).

58. Pérez (1976b: 259); Fermoselle (1987b: 267).

59. A. Suárez (1967: 227).

60. Karol (1970: 173–176); LeoGrande (1979: 458); Franqui (1984: 4).

61. Horowitz (1970: 6–11); Karol (1970: 171–172, 183); Gonzalez (1976).

62. Karol (1970: 171); LeoGrande (1979: 458); Franqui (1984: 4).

63. O'Connor (1970: 284); Fagen (1972: 27); Gonzalez (1974: 96).

64. Domínguez (1978: 376; also 1974, 1976a).

65. Matthews (1969: 323–324). Also Fagen (1972: 26); Gonzalez (1974: 96–98).

66. Sweig (2002: 176–177).

67. Bonachea and San Martín (1974: 325–326); Thomas (1977: 250–251, 287).

68. Quoted in Thomas (1977: 298); also Draper (1962: 53–55); García Montes and Avila (1970); Matthews (1975: 230–235); Thomas (1977: 224–225).

69. Gonzalez (1968: 44); García Montes and Avila (1970: 550); Thomas (1977: 298).

70. Ruíz (1968: 15); Bonsal (1971: 112); Welch (1985: 14); Rabkin (1991: 41).

71. Padula (1974: 421–424); Crahan (1985: 321; 1988: 207–209); Gómez Treto (1988); Kirk (1989).

72. Fernández (2003: 232).

73. Gómez Treto (1988: 13, 38–39).

74. Ruíz (1968: 142–145); Padula (1974).

75. Domínguez (1978: 147).

76. Padula (1974: 181–186, 208–211).

77. Thomas (1977: 275); Domínguez (1978: 67); Blasier (1985: 93).

78. Bonsal (1971: 43–45); Domínguez (1978: 67); Blasier (1985: 82–83).

79. Domínguez (1978: 145).

80. Fagen et al. (1968: 4).

81. Ruíz (1968: 15).

82. Fagen (1969: 3).

83. Castro espoused mainstream center-left ideas early in his career. Zeitlin and Schneer (1963: 57); Draper (1965: 5–6); Matthews (1969: 124; 1975: 146, 236–237); Horowitz (1975: 404–405).

84. Halperin (1972: 50); Szulc (1986: 331–332).

85. According to Domínguez, revolution required "not only extensive agrarian reforms but probably also major new state intervention in industry, at least in the sugar industry, in the public utilities, and in mining. Since there was heavy United States private investment in all of these areas the leaders concluded that a confrontation must surely follow" (1978: 145). Also Paterson (1994: 21–22).

86. Szulc (1986: 315).

87. Matthews (1969: 147).

88. Gonzalez (1974: 146–147); Domínguez (1989: 7).

89. Thomas (1977: 435–436); Domínguez (1978: 143).

90. O'Connor (1970: 91–93).

91. Huberman and Sweezy (1960: 119); Blasier (1971a: 60–61; 1985: 82–83); Matthews (1975: 163).

92. Farber (1976: 217; 2006: 135); Szulc (1986: 493).

93. Thomas (1977: 454–455); Pérez (2015: 255–256).

94. Padula (1974: 132–133).

95. Padula (1974: 146).

96. Franqui (1984: 79–80); Guerra (2012: 120–121).

97. Kirk (1985: 71–74, 99); Holbrook (2010: 265–267).

98. Kirk (1989: 80–81); Holbrook (2010: 266–269).

99. Bonsal (1971).

100. Farber (2006: 61).

101. Blight and Kornbluh (1998: 159); Latell (2007: 16); Rasenberger (2011: 40).

102. Rasenberger (2011: 55–56).

103. Blasier (1971a: 69).

104. Castro himself later said that Eisenhower's reaction to the May 1959 land reform convinced him that conflict with the United States was inevitable (Matthews 1975: 171–172).

105. Mesa-Lago (1971a: 278); Paterson (1994: 35).

106. Domínguez (1989: 6).

107. Thomas (1977: 495–503); Pérez (2015: 262).

108. Domínguez (1978: 146).

109. Pérez-Stable (2011a: 82); Pérez (2015: 257).

110. O'Connor (1970: 165); Thomas (1977: 519).

111. Thomas (1977: 519); Pérez (2015: 257–258).

112. Halperin (1972: 84–85); Domínguez (1978: 147); Evenson (1994: 179); Yaffe (2009: 15).

113. Goldenberg (1965: 193).

114. Halperin (1972: 2); Domínguez (1989: 6).

115. Meyer and Szulc (1962: 73).

116. Bonsal (1971: 16, 154–156); Robbins (1983: 139–145); W. Smith (1987: 53–54).

117. Also Robbins (1983: 139–145); W. Smith (1987: 53–54).

118. Halperin (1972: 130). Also A. Suárez (1967: 114–115); Robbins (1983: 139–145); W. Smith (1987: 53–54).

119. Domínguez (1989).

120. Domínguez (1989: 70, 113–118). Also Betancourt (1971).

121. Halperin (1972: 22, 318–345); del Aguila (1984: 104); Latell (2007: 7, 16, 186–190).

122. Draper (1962: 57).

123. LeoGrande (1982: 169); del Aguila (1984: 103–109); Domínguez (1989: 27, 70).

124. Del Aguila (1984: 102). Also Betancourt (1971: 106); Gleijeses (2009: 24).

125. Gleijeses (2009: 72).

126. Arboleya Cervera (1997: 46–47); Etcheverry and Gutierrez Oceguera (2008: 29–30).

127. Etcheverry and Gutierrez Oceguera (2008: 59–65).

128. Gilly (1964: 20–22); Szulc (1986: 575); Veláz Suárez (2008: 202).

129. Etcheverry and Gutierrez Oceguera (2008: 72–73). Also J. Suárez (1981: 33–59).

130. Herrera Medina (2006: 62); Etcheverry and Gutierrez Oceguera (2008: 72–73).

131. Meyer and Szulc (1962: 55–57, 85–93); Herrera Medina (2006: 9, 183–185); Etcheverry and Gutierrez Oceguera (2008: 23–24); Veláz Suárez (2008: 200).

132. Domínguez (1974: 214).

133. Domínguez (1978: 346); Escalante Font (2008: 187, 199); Etcheverry and Gutierrez Oceguera (2008: 21, 336).

134. Domínguez (1978: 346).

135. Szulc (1986: 576).

136. Kornbluh (1998: 172–173).

137. Blasier (1971a: 60–61).

138. Bonsal (1971: 151); Welch (1985: 52–53).

139. Blight and Kornbluh (1998); Kornbluh (1998); Bohning (2005); Rasenberger (2011).

140. Meyer and Szulc (1962: 114–115); Bonsal (1971: 135); Rasenberger (2011: 55–56).

141. See Thomas (1977: 581–593); Rasenberger (2011).

142. Thomas (1977: 590).

143. Thomas (1977: 584–593).

144. Thomas (1977: 589–593); Rasenberger (2011: 352).

145. Draper (1965: 135).

146. Quoted in Matthews (1975: 206).

147. Halperin (1972: 107–108).

148. Szulc (1986: 555).

149. Thomas (1977: 578).

150. Karol (1970: 233); Thomas (1977: 587); Kornbluh (1998: 21).

151. Meyer and Szulc (1962: 133); Franqui (1984: 127–128); Quirk (1993: 371).

152. Thomas (1977: 587).

153. Franqui (1984: 126).

154. Szulc (1986: 573–574); Blight and Kornbluh (1998: 116–123); Kornbluh (1998: 16); Bohning (2005: 72–106).

155. Paterson (1994: 259–261); Bohning (2005: 129, 138).

156. Domínguez (1989: 35).

157. López-Fresquet (1966: 178); Thomas (1977: 608–611); Bohning (2005: 112–113).

158. Thomas (1977: 608–611); Bohning (2005: 112–113).

159. Blight and Kornbluh (1998: 66).

160. Thomas (1977: 609–615); Domínguez (1989: 35); Gouré (1989b: 167–168).

161. Szulc (1986: 582).

162. Matthews (1969: 224).

163. Matthews (1975: 209–212); Thomas (1977: 619, 630).

164. Thomas (1977: 636).

165. Bohning (2005: 114).

166. Ayers (1976).

167. Bohning (2005: 9, 197, 234–238).

168. Escalante Font (2008); Etcheverry and Gutierrez Oceguera (2008).

169. Torres (1999).

170. Thomas (1977: 684).

171. Blasier (1985: 185).

172. Domínguez (1978: 148).

173. O'Connor (1970: 47–51, 91); del Aguila (1984: 49).

174. Guerra (2012: 77).

175. Franqui (1984: 114–115).

176. Fagen (1970a: 357); Gonzalez (1974: 96); Thomas (1977: 678–679).

177. Halperin (1972: 132–133); Gonzalez (1974: 125).

178. Fagen (1970b: 371–372); Halperin (1972: 132–133); LeoGrande (1979: 458).

179. Domínguez (1978: 210–211).

180. A. Suárez (1967: 139); Halperin (1972: 156); Thomas (1977: 595); LeoGrande (1979: 459).

181. Quoted in Fagen and Cornelius (1970: 360–363).

182. Fagen (1970: 357–358); Halperin (1972: 154–155); Gonzalez (1974: 103); Leo-Grande (1979: 461).

183. Matthews (1975: 228).

184. A. Suárez (1967: 33); Franqui (1984: 36); Fermoselle (1987b: 267).

185. Klepak (2012: 23, 27–28).

186. Klepak (2012: 25–28).

187. Domínguez (1978: 208).

188. San Martín and Bonachea (2003: 41).

189. Duncan (1993: 227–228).

190. Klepak (2012: xiii).

191. Rasenberger (2011: 108); Domínguez (2020: 5).

192. Klepak (2012: 38).

193. Domínguez (1982a: 47); Klepak (2012: 34).

194. Domínguez (1976b: 45).

195. Matthews (1969: 201).

196. Klepak (2008: 146).

197. Etcheverry and Gutierrez Oceguera (2008: 24–26, 176–177); Klepak (2008: 149–150).

198. Fermoselle (1987b: 274).

199. Domínguez and Mitchell (1977: 182).

200. Fagen (1969: 94–95); Domínguez (1989: 208–209).

201. Fagen (1969: 94, 73).

202. Fagen (1969: 77); Klepak (2012: 39).

203. Quoted in Blight and Kornbluh (1998: 118).

204. Horowitz (1975: 411).

205. Gómez Treto (1988: 13, 39).

206. Fernández (2003: 232).

207. Thomas (1977: 345); Farber (2006: 53).

208. Crahan (1988: 212). Also Goldenberg (1965: 207–208); Padula (1974: 457).

209. Padula (1974: 457–459); Kirk (1989: 80–81); Holbrook (2010: 268–269).

210. Jover Marimón (1971: 403); Kirk (1989: 82–83); Holbrook (2010: 265).

211. Kirk (1989: 83–84); Holbrook (2010: 270–271).

212. Gómez Treto (1988: 38).

213. Crahan (1985: 325–327); Arboleya Cervera (1997: 66–67); Holbrook (2010: 269).

214. Padula (1974: 483).

215. Padula (1974: 491); Crahan (1985: 327). The Church refused to condemn the invasion (Gómez Treto 1988: 91).

216. Gómez Treto (1988: 40).

217. Gómez Treto (1988: 40); Kirk (1989: 96).

218. Quoted in Holbrook (2010: 272–273).

219. Jover Marimón (1971: 404–405); Gómez Treto (1988: 41–42); Kirk (1989: 97); Holbrook (2010: 272–273).

220. Gómez Treto (1988: 45); Holbrook (2010: 273).

221. Kirk (1989: 99).

222. Gómez Treto (1988: 45).

223. Jover Marimón (1971: 402, 405); Nelson (1972: 162); Gómez Treto (1988: 46–47).

224. Jover Marimón (1971: 411–412); Domínguez (1978: 411).

225. Kirk (1985: 100; 1989: 109–126); Crahan (1988: 214).

226. Domínguez (1978: 411–413).

227. Montaner (2001: 96).

228. Jover Marimón (1971: 405).

229. Aranda (1968: 189–190); O'Connor (1970: 127–129).

230. Aranda (1968: 189–190); Thomas (1977: 661).

231. Eckstein (2003: 38).

232. Padula (1974: 572).

233. Domínguez (1978: 137).

234. Amaro and Mesa-Lago (1971: 366); Padula (1974: 321).

235. Padula (1974).

236. Fagen et al. (1968: 17); Domínguez (1978: 139–140).

237. Azicri (1988: 133); Pérez (2015: 277).

238. Gonzalez (1974: 171); Domínguez (1978: 140).

239. Arboleya Cervera (1997: 155–160, 210).

240. Draper (1965: 123).

241. Domínguez (1978: 137, 140).

242. Mesa-Lago (1971b: 503).

243. Quoted in Blight and Kornbluh (1998: 121).

244. Pérez-Stable (1992).

245. Horowitz (1970: 6–11); A. Suárez (1971: 12); Gonzalez (1976); Baloyra (1993).

246. Pérez-Stable (2011a: 156, 158).

247. Pérez-Stable (1993: 71). Also Halperin (1972: 158–159); Domínguez (1978: 330–334); LeoGrande (1978c, 1979, 1980).

248. LeoGrande (1978c).

249. Karol (1970: 456).
250. Matthews (1969: 321–322).
251. LeoGrande (1978c); Rabkin (1991: 68–71); Pérez-Stable (1993: 71–73).
252. Domínguez (1978: 197). Also Halperin (1981: 173); Rabkin (1991: 68–71). By the 1970s, the PCC had 16,000 cells (Domínguez 1978: 334). Party membership increased from 55,000 in 1969 to more than 500,000 in the mid-1980s (Pérez-Stable 1993: 73).
253. Domínguez (1978: 338); Pérez-Stable (2011a: 158).
254. Fagen (1972: 26); Gonzalez (1974: 96–98); Domínguez (1978: 342–345).
255. Matthews (1975: 235); Thomas (1977: 677); San Martín and Bonachea (2003: 43).
256. Gonzalez (1974: 104, 178); Thomas (1977: 678–679). The exception was President Dorticós.
257. Gonzalez (1974: 94).
258. Matthews (1969: 323–324).
259. Domínguez (1978: 241–242).
260. LeoGrande (1978c: 20–21).
261. Matthews (1975: 126).
262. Klepak (2012: 38).
263. Domínguez (1978: 208, 346; 1979: 59–60); Klepak (2008: 146; 2012: 25–38).
264. Domínguez (1978: 237; 1981: 128); Gonzalez and Ronfeldt (1986: 76).
265. Domínguez (1974: 215–216).
266. Fermoselle (1987b: 302); Gouré (1989b: 167–168).
267. San Martín and Bonachea (2003: 37).
268. Fermoselle (1987b: 325–328).
269. Gouré (1989a: 73–74; 1989c: 582–583, 591); Klepak (2012: 46–50).
270. Del Aguila (1989: 33); Schulz (1994b: 151).
271. Horowitz (1975: 411–412); Domínguez (1979: 39); Fernández (1989: 4, 8).
272. Domínguez (1979: 77, 57).
273. Domínguez (1989: 48).
274. Greene Walker (2003: 353–354). Also Latell (2007: 19); Domínguez (2020).
275. Klepak (2012: 41).
276. Thomas (1977: 475, 543).
277. Rodríguez (1993: 45, 35–68).
278. Horowitz (1971: 131).
279. Fagen (1969: 77); Thomas (1977: 544); Domínguez (1978: 208–209, 262).
280. Domínguez (1978: 205); Schulz (1994b: 151–152).
281. Klepak (2012: 41).
282. Domínguez (1976b: 57–61; 1978: 366); Espinosa (2003: 367–368); Greene Walker (2003: 345–347).
283. Domínguez (1974, 1976a); Matthews (1975: 16); LeoGrande (1978d).
284. Gonzalez (1974: 228); Vellinga (1976: 250); A. Suárez (1989: 154).
285. A. Suárez (1967: 76).
286. Domínguez (1974: 229).
287. Fermoselle (1987a); A. Suárez (1989: 139).
288. Fermoselle (1987a).

289. Pérez (1976b: 267–268); LeoGrande (1978d: 273–275).

290. Domínguez (1976b: 57); Pérez-Stable (2011a: 118–119).

291. Domínguez (1974: 232; 1978: 313, 375).

292. Klepak (2012: 36).

293. Domínguez (1974: 225–226; 1978: 365–366); LeoGrande (1978a: 206–208); Fermoselle (1987b: 285–286); Greene Walker (1993: 119–120); Klepak (2012: 36).

294. Greene Walker (1993: 114); Domínguez (2020).

295. Klepak (2005: 77).

296. LeoGrande (1978b: 279).

297. Domínguez (1974: 210; 1978: 342–345); LeoGrande (1978d).

298. Matos was not a long-standing veteran of the July 26 Movement (LeoGrande 1978d: 263).

299. LeoGrande (1978d: 265); Greene Walker (1994: 53; 2003: 360).

300. Domínguez (1978: 375); Mazarr (1989: 79).

301. Peters (2015: 146).

302. Crahan (1985: 337).

303. Jover Marimón (1971: 402–405); Crahan (1988: 224); Gómez Treto (1988: 13–14, 47); Kirk (1989: 103–104).

304. Domínguez (1978: 483); Gómez Treto (1988: 48).

305. Crahan (1988: 215).

306. Kirk (1989: 109–126).

307. Jover Marimón (1971: 409); Domínguez (1978: 411); Crahan (1988: 214–217); Gómez Treto (1988: 68, 91).

308. Domínguez (1978: 413).

309. Fermoselle (1987b: 298).

310. Mesa-Lago (1971b: 503); Domínguez (1978: 410).

311. Schulz (1994b: 152).

312. Pérez (2015: 263).

313. Gonzalez (1974: 144).

314. F. Thompson (2005: 314–316).

315. F. Thompson (2005: 314, 316).

316. Mesa-Lago (1993b: 149–150); Font (1997: 114).

317. Gouré (1989b: 167–168).

318. Halperin (1972: 39); Mesa-Lago (1993b). According to Mesa-Lago (1993b: 144), sugar subsidies totaled $13 billion and petroleum subsidies totaled at least $3 billion.

319. Gonzalez (1989: 642); Font (1997: 114); Sweig (2007: 47).

320. Domínguez (1989: 3).

321. Gonzalez and Ronfeldt (1992: 16); Abrahams and Lopez-Levy (2011: 219).

322. Matthews (1975: 40).

323. Reed (1992: 21).

324. LeoGrande (1978c: 20–21); Domínguez (1982b: 25; 1989: 254).

325. Domínguez (1985: 30; 1993b: 100).

326. Domínguez (1985: 30).

327. Baloyra and Morris (1993: 7–8); Pérez-Stable (2011a: 128–132).

328. Reed (1992: 161–176); Bardach (2009: 48, 202, 211); Pérez (2015: 253).

329. Gonzalez and Ronfeldt (1986: 75, 78); Greene Walker (2003: 360); Klepak (2012: 231).

330. Domínguez (1978: 375); Greene Walker (2003: 360); Klepak (2005: 237–239; 2012: 131–136).

331. Nelson (1972: 197).

332. Pérez-Stable (1993: 70).

333. Yaffe (2009: 264).

334. Frank Fitzgerald (1990: 49).

335. Mesa-Lago (1970: 82); Yaffe (2009: 264).

336. Thomas (1977: 670–671).

337. Thomas (1977: 669–671); Yaffe (2009: 63–67, 201–232).

338. Mesa-Lago (1972: 388, 391); Frank Fitzgerald (1990: 51); Yaffe (2009: 207–216).

339. Mesa-Lago (1970: 73–74).

340. Del Aguila (1984: 92).

341. Halperin (1981: 282).

342. Mesa-Lago (1970: 85–90).

343. Quirk (1993: 559).

344. Robbins (1983: 24–56, 152–154); del Aguila (1984: 102–109); Domínguez (1989: 70–71); Gleijeses (2009: 12).

345. Szulc (1986: 611).

346. Castro himself later described the jump into communism as his greatest error (Szulc 1989: 126).

347. Frank Fitzgerald (1990: 51); Pérez-Stable (2011a: 426).

348. Karol (1970: 426); Eckstein (2003: 38).

349. Mesa-Lago (1982: 115).

350. Halperin (1981: 294).

351. Robbins (1983: 156–165).

352. Szulc (1986: 606).

353. Halperin (1981: 310–316); del Aguila (1984: 110–111); Domínguez (1989: 73–77).

354. Halperin (1981: 294).

355. Del Aguila (1984: 94–95).

356. Gonzalez (1974: 208–209).

357. Pérez (2015: 270).

358. Del Aguila (1984: 94).

359. Pérez (2015: 270–271).

360. Domínguez (2020: 11).

361. Mesa-Lago (1971a: 305); Pérez (2015: 270–271).

362. Del Aguila (1984: 96).

363. Gonzalez (1974: 210–212); Halperin (1981: 325); del Aguila (1984: 96–99).

364. Quoted in del Aguila (1984: 99).

365. LeoGrande (1978c: 20–27).

366. Matthews (1969: 315–318); Gonzalez (1974: 139–141); Halperin (1981: 272–274).

367. Karol (1970: 468); del Aguila (1984: 93).

368. Baloyra and Lozano (1993: 273).

369. Domínguez (1974: 210; 1978: 342–345); LeoGrande (1978d: 263).

370. Nelson (1972: 206).

371. Del Aguila (1984: 98).

372. Robbins (1983: 269–270); W. Smith (1987: 82, 245–250).

373. Domínguez (1993b: 103); Klepak (2012: xv).

374. Frank Fitzgerald (1990: 134); Rodríguez (1993: 81).

375. Mesa-Lago (1988; 1993b: 134–137); Pérez-Stable (2011a: 125–127).

376. Domínguez (1993a: 119–120).

377. Frank Fitzgerald (1990: 137); Mesa-Lago (1993b: 134–137); Eckstein (2003: 60–65).

378. Mesa-Lago (1993b: 134–137).

379. Frank Fitzgerald (1990: 137); Azicri (2000: 69); Pérez-Stable (2011a: 125–127).

380. Azicri (2000: 67).

381. Oppenheimer (1992: 70–93); del Aguila (1993: 173); Latell (2007: 212–215); Klepak (2012: 53–54).

382. Oppenheimer (1992: 18); Espinosa (2003: 70); Domínguez (2020: 16).

383. Baloyra (1994: 26).

384. Greene Walker (1993: 128); Latell (2007: 207–208); Klepak (2012: 54).

385. Gonzalez and Ronfeldt (1992: 16).

386. Cardoso and Helwege (1992: 31); Baloyra and Lozano (1993: 265–266); Font (1997: 114). The USSR purchased 63 percent of Cuba's sugar exports and supplied nearly all its petroleum (Klepak 2012: 57).

387. Mazarr (1989: 65).

388. Reed (1992).

389. Schulz (1994b: 150); Font (1997: 118); Klepak (2012: 57); Pérez (2015: 303–305).

390. Eckstein (2003: 93); Klepak (2012: 58–59).

391. Quoted in Oppenheimer (1992: 414).

392. Domínguez (1993a: 124–125); Mesa-Lago (1993a: 3); Planas (1993).

393. Quoted in Mesa-Lago (1993b: 246).

394. Eckstein (2003: 93–98); Pérez (2015: 305–306).

395. Latell (2007: 233); Brenner et al. (2015: 25).

396. Baloyra and Morris (1993: 11–12).

397. Schulz (1994a: 175).

398. Pérez (2015: 327).

399. Eckstein (2003: 118–121).

400. Schulz (1994a: 179).

401. Klepak (2012: 80).

402. Latell (2007: 238); Pérez (2015: 327).

403. Aguirre (2002: 80–81); Bardach (2009: 217); Pérez-Stable (2011b: 27).

404. Latell (2007: 239).

405. Centeno and Font (1997: 217). Also Cardoso and Helwege (1992: 1); Kaufman Purcell (1992: 130).

406. Gonzalez and Ronfeldt (1992: 16); Schulz (1994b: 156–157); Pérez-Stable (1997: 29; 1999: 73).

407. Baloyra and Lozano (1993: 272–273).

408. Reed (1992: 161–176).

409. Sweig (2007: 55).

410. Greene Walker (1994: 53; 2003: 260); Klepak (2005: 237–239).

411. Jorge et al. (1991: 109–124); Schulz (1994b: 154); Millett (1996: 141, 147–150).

412. Millett (1996: 152).

413. Gonzalez and Ronfeldt (1992: 38, 41); Greene Walker (1994: 53); Latell (2003: 543); Bardach (2009: 186).

414. Gonzalez and Ronfeldt (1992: 37–38, 16); Klepak (2012: 131).

415. Del Aguila (2003: 426).

416. Eckstein (2003: 121).

417. Aguirre (2002: 80–81).

418. Baloyra (1994: 26).

419. Gonzalez and Ronfeldt (1992: 342); Planas (1994: 45).

420. Farber (1992: 342); Domínguez (1994: 16); Eckstein (2003: 118–119).

421. Schulz (1994b: 151–152).

422. Mesa-Lago (2003: 101).

423. Font (1997: 109, 123); Azicri (2000: 139–147); Pérez-López (2003: 185–188).

424. Fernández (2003: 227–232). Also Aguirre (2002); Crahan (2015: 89–92).

425. Del Aguila (1993: 170–171, 176); Aguirre (2002).

426. Fernández (2003: 239); Crahan and Armony (2007: 151); Abrahams and Lopez-Levy (2011: 98).

427. Mujal-León and Busby (2003: 504).

428. Abrahams and Lopez-Levy (2011: 96–97).

429. Abrahams and Lopez-Levy (2011: 97); Pérez-Stable (2011b: 94).

430. Abrahams and Lopez-Levy (2011: 97); Pérez-Stable (2011b: 95).

431. Abrahams and Lopez-Levy (2011: 98).

432. Latell (2007: 256).

433. Quoted in Whitehead (2016: 1666).

434. Sweig (2007: 40–41).

435. Latell (2007: 264).

436. LeoGrande (2015: 399–401); Pérez (2015: 353).

437. Brownlee (2007); Ghobadzadeh and Rahim (2016).

438. Kinzer (2003: 67).

439. Kinzer (2003); Takeyh (2014).

440. Katouzian (1998).

441. Abrahamian (1980: 23; 2008: 127–138); Katouzian (1998: 198–199); A. Milani (2011: 239–241).

442. Menashri (1990: 68–69); Katouzian (1998: 195–196); Abrahamian (2008: 125–126).

443. Abrahamian (2008: 126); Kaveh (2011: 74–76).

444. Arjomand (1988: 73); Katouzian (1998: 188); Abrahamian (2008: 132–133).

445. MERIP (1973); Abrahamian (1980: 24).

446. Moens (1991: 217).

447. Abrahamian (1980: 24).

448. Abrahamian (1980: 25); Bakhash (1990: 13).

449. Kaye et al. (2011: 11–12).

450. For example, the shah replaced the Muslim calendar with the royal one, introduced women's suffrage, and forbade women to wear the chador in universities (Abrahamian 1980: 25; Menashri 1990: 3).

451. Arjomand (1988: 85–86, 95); Moin (1999: 75, 83, 95–96, 119); Azimi (2014: 26, 29, 32–42).

452. Moin (1999: 92–93, 129–159).

453. Moin (1999: 120); Azimi (2014: 41). On Khomeini's rise, see Arjomand (1988: 91–102); Bakhash (1990: 19–51).

454. See Abrahamian (1982: 475–477); Moin (1999: 151–159); Brumberg (2001).

455. K. Harris (2017: 79).

456. Arjomand (1988: 177–183).

457. Arjomand (1988: 91–93).

458. Flood (1998: 103); Kurzman (2004: 37).

459. Arjomand (1988: 91–93); Menashri (1990: 24).

460. M. Milani (1994: 122).

461. A. Milani (2013).

462. See Arjomand (1988); Bakhash (1990); Kurzman (2004).

463. Bakhash (1990: 15).

464. Bakhash (1990: 16–18); Menashri (1990: 33–45); Rasler (1996).

465. Arjomand (1988: 123–125).

466. M. Milani (1994: 143).

467. Zabih (1988: 117).

468. Arjomand (1988: 126–127; Ostovar (2016: 41–42).

469. Moin (1999: 205); Ostovar (2016: 41–42).

470. Bakhash (1990: 164); Ostovar (2016: 42).

471. Bakhash (1990: 119).

472. Zabih (1988: 116).

473. Zabih (1988: 119).

474. M. Milani (1994: 179); Axworthy (2013: 185).

475. Arjomand (1988: 144, 163–164); Zabih (1988: 123); Bakhash (1990: 113).

476. Schahgaldian (1987: 17–28); Chuvin and Tripp (1988: 19); Cann and Danopoulos (1997: 275).

477. Kharsh (2002: 19).

478. Bakhash (1990: 289).

479. Menashri (1990: 28).

480. M. Milani (1994: 130).

481. M. Milani (1994: 130).

482. M. Milani (1994: 148); Axworthy (2013: 145); Ostovar (2016: 42).

483. M. Milani (1994: 201–202); Moin (1999: 224); Axworthy (2013: 152).

484. M. Milani (1994: 155).

485. M. Milani (1994: 201); Pourzand (2009–2010: 101–102).

486. Moin (1999: 212).

487. Moin (1999: 226).

488. M. Milani (1994: 166); Moin (1999: 229); Bowden (2006).

489. M. Milani (1994: 166).

490. Maloney (2015: 429–430).

491. Arjomand (1988: 139); Bakhash (1990: 149–150); M. Milani (1994: 161).

492. Bakhash (1990: 116).

493. M. Milani (1994: 172).

494. Bakhash (1990: 220); Alahmad and Keshavarzian (2010: 17); Ottolenghi (2011: 10); Axworthy (2013: 214).

495. Bakhash (1990: 219); M. Milani (1994: 187); Ottolenghi (2011: 10); Axworthy (2013: 214).

496. Bakhash (1990: 89).

497. M. Milani (1994: 190); Moin (1999: 252).

498. Bakhash (1990: 89); Katzman (1993: 81); Axworthy (2013: 146).

499. M. Milani (1994: 188); Moin (1999: 248).

500. Bakhash (1990: 161–164).

501. Arjomand (1988: 154, 173); M. Milani (1994: 188, 193). According to Ottolenghi, the Iranian repression was "as effective as the Bolsheviks' liquidation of their opponents in revolutionary Russia" (2011: 10).

502. Bakhash (1990: 221); Axworthy (2013: 215).

503. M. Milani (1994: 193); Ottolenghi (2011: 10).

504. Moin (1999: 231).

505. Schahgaldian (1987: 17–28); Chuvin and Tripp (1988: 19); Zabih (1988: 119); Cann and Danopoulos (1997: 275); Axworthy (2013: 148); Barany (2019: 54).

506. On the origins of the IRGC, see Schahgaldian (1987); Katzman (1993).

507. Schahgaldian (1987: 73); Katzman (1993: 7); Nader (2010: 59); Safshekan and Sabet (2010: 548).

508. Wehrey et al. (2009: 26); Pourzand (2009–2010: 99); Parsa (2020: 55–56).

509. Schahgaldian (1987: vii); Katzman (1993: 16); Nader (2010: 59).

510. Katzman (1993: 57, 1); Peterson (2010: 552).

511. Katzman (1993: 118).

512. Katzman (1993: 118, 119); Wehrey et al. (2009: 21).

513. Schahgaldian (1987: 81–82); Katzman (1993: 138); Hashemi and Postel (2010: xix); Saha (2014: 197–198); Ostovar (2016: 237).

514. Katzman (1993: 17, 35); Hashemi and Postel (2010: xix); Golkar (2012: 464); Ostovar (2016: 11); Barany (2019: 57).

515. Bakhash (1990: 109); Wehrey et al. (2009: 30); Safshekan and Sabet (2010: 548).

516. Schahgaldian (1987); Katzman (1993: 1, 52); Ostovar (2016: 47–48).

517. Katzman (1993: 30).

518. Bakhash (1990: 225).

519. Bakhash (1990: 129); Katzman (1993: 81).

520. Katzman (1993: 83).

521. Wehrey et al. (2009: 32–33); Golkar (2012: 460–461); Alfoneh (2013: 49).

522. Bakhash (1990: 237–239); M. Milani (1994: 192–193); Axworthy (2013: 240).

523. See CIA (1980); Kharsh (1990: 266); Robins (1990: 88); Moin (1999: 236).

524. Byman (2005: 91–92); Takeyh (2010: 373); Alahmad and Keshavarzian (2010: 21).

525. Byman (2005: 82, 83); Axworthy (2013: 222).

526. Byman (2005: 84–85); Axworthy (2013: 223); Ostovar (2016: 116).

527. Bakhash (1990: 280); Moin (1999: 285); Axworthy (2013: 298); Brumberg (2013).

528. Quoted in Chuvin and Tripp (1988: 48).

529. Wehrey et al. (2009: 23–25); Alahmad and Keshavarzian (2010: 17); Ostovar (2016: 235).

530. Byman (2005: 91–92).

531. Axworthy (2013: 189); also Kharsh (1990: 268); Menashri (1990: 71); Robins (1990: 85, 97); M. Milani (1994: 206).

532. M. Milani (1994: 207); Walt (1996); Takeyh (2010: 365); Axworthy (2013: 191).

533. M. Milani (1994: 206).

534. Axworthy (2013: 191).

535. Axworthy (2013: 191); Razoux and Elliott (2015: 23–26).

536. Axworthy (2013: 196, 208); Razoux and Elliott (2015: 113–117).

537. Takeyh (2010: 269).

538. The Basij provided up to 75 percent of Iran's frontline troops (Golkar 2012: 461).

539. Katzman (1993: 67); Alfoneh (2010: 62); Axworthy (2013: 218).

540. M. Milani (1994: 193).

541. Takeyh (2010: 371).

542. M. Milani (1994: 210).

543. CIA (1987: 15); Safshekan and Sabet (2010: 548).

544. Zabih (1988: 212); Bakhash (1990: 129); Alfoneh (2010: 63); Ottolenghi (2011: 12).

545. Cann and Danopoulos (1997: 276); Barany (2019: 55).

546. Sabet and Safshekan (2019: 96–97).

547. Bakhash (1990: 129); Wehrey et al. (2009: 22–23); Alahmad and Keshavarzian (2010: 20); Ottolenghi (2011: 9).

548. Ottolenghi (2011: 9).

549. Katzman (1993: 124–132). By 2020, the IRGC was said to control 25 percent of the economy (Parsa 2020: 55).

550. Alfoneh (2010: 62).

551. Saha (2014: 196); also Wehrey et al. (2009: 28).

552. Saha (2014: 197–198).

553. M. Milani (1994: 181); Takeyh (2010: 368).

554. Axworthy (2013: 283–288); Ehteshami (2017: 46).

555. Katzman (1993); Wehrey et al. (2009); Hashemi and Postel (2010: xix); Golkar (2012: 458); Ostovar (2016).

556. Katouzian (1998: 188).

557. Schahgaldian (1987: 17–28); Chuvin and Tripp (1988: 19); Cann and Danopoulos (1997: 275).

558. CIA (1984a); Zabih (1988: 143); M. Milani (1994: 150); Ward (2009: 230); Witoschek (2012: 28).

559. Zabih (1988: 144); Cann and Danopoulos (1997: 272).

560. Witoschek (2012: 29).

561. Moin (1999: 226).

562. Khalaji (2011: 139).

563. Khalaji (2011: 141); Moazami (2013: 150).

564. Khalaji (2011: 141).

565. Moazami (2013: 150).

566. "Who Rules Iran?," *New York Review of Books*, June 27, 2002; "Politics and Religion Blur in Struggle for Qom," *Financial Times*, February 6, 2009; Moazami (2013: 150); "Both Pluralism and Militants Gain Ground in Iran's Seminaries," *Religion Watch*, June 2017.

567. "Khamenei Pleads for Clerical Support in Qom," *Financial Times*, October 28, 2010; "More Senior Iranian Clerics Lambaste Government," *Radio Free Europe Documents and Publications*, December 30, 2010; "Battle of the Ayatollahs; Iran," *Economist*, May 4, 2019.

568. Gieling (1997: 783).

569. M. Milani (1994: 147, 155, 178); Moin (1999: 237); Axworthy (2013: 145).

570. Axworthy (2013: 272); Hovsepian-Bearce (2016: 52–53).

571. Moslem (2002); Brownlee (2007); Ansari (2010: 17); Ghobadzadeh and Rahim (2016).

572. Boroumand (2017: 40); Siavoshi (2017: 160–161); "The Irrelevance of Iran's Reformists," *Al Jazeera*, December 23, 2019; Parsa (2020: 58).

573. Bakhash (1990: 284–285); P. Jones (2011: 107); Moazami (2013: 150); Sabet and Safshekan (2019: 96–97).

574. CIA (1987: 14, 15); Saha (2014); Barany (2019: 54).

575. See Katzman (1993); Hashemi and Postel (2010: 421); Peterson (2010: 545–546); Ostovar (2016); Barany (2019).

576. K. Harris (2017: 44).

577. Katzman (1993: 35).

578. CIA (1984a).

579. Katzman (1993: 35).

580. Katzman (1993: 17); Hashemi and Postel (2010: xix); Golkar (2012: 464); Ostovar (2016: 11); Barany (2019: 57).

581. Sabet and Safshekan (2019: 97).

582. Quoted in Sabet and Safshekan (2019: 97).

583. Schahgaldian (1987); Naji (2008: 41).

584. Boroumand (2017: 40); "The Irrelevance of Iran's Reformists."

585. Moin (1999: 287).

586. CIA (1987: 20).

587. Moin (1999: 261); Brumberg (2001: 147–148). *Marja* (from *marj-e taqlid*—a source of emulation) is a Shiite religious title that bestows the right to make binding legal decisions—within the confines of Islamic law—for followers and lower-ranking clerics (Gieling 1997; Khalaji 2006: 1).

588. Axworthy (2013: 304, 320); Ehteshami (2017: 43).

589. P. Jones (2011: 105); Axworthy (2013: 304, 320); Ehteshami (2017: 43).

590. Moin (1999: 301); Axworthy (2013: 306).

591. Selbin (1993).

592. Siavoshi (2017: 138–139, 142, 150, 160).

593. Moin (1999: 265); Axworthy (2013: 305); Ehteshami (2017: 43); Golkar (2019).

594. Siavoshi (2017: 160–161). Eight years later, in 1997, Montazeri publicly questioned Khamenei's religious credentials and called for greater limits on the power of the supreme leader. Shortly before dying, he also supported protests against electoral fraud in 2009. See Alavi (1989: 7); Siavoshi (2017: 172–173, 181–185). These criticisms of the government are not considered defection because they fell short of calling for the elimination of clerical rule and because they occurred long after Montazeri had left the formal power structure.

595. Byman (2005: 100); Golkar (2011: 209).

596. See Golkar (2019).

597. Ghobadzadeh and Rahim (2016: 459–460); Boroumand (2017: 40).

598. Ghobadzadeh and Rahim (2016: 459–460).

599. P. Jones (2011: 108); Parsa (2020: 56).

600. See Golkar (2019).

601. Ostovar (2016: 151). Also Pourzand (2009–2010: 100); Golkar (2011: 208).

602. Golkar (2011: 211).

603. Nader (2010: 60); Ostovar (2016: 145–147); Forozan and Shahi (2017).

604. Wehrey et al. (2009: 28, 81–89).

605. Katzman (1993); Hashemi and Postel (2010: xix); Barany (2019: 57).

606. Amuzegar (2004: 76–77).

607. Amuzegar (2006: 57–59, 65).

608. Amuzegar (2006: 72); also Alfoneh (2008); Bakhash (2010: 18); Ostovar (2016: 156).

609. Alfoneh (2008); Bakhash (2010: 18); Ostovar (2016: 156).

610. Bakhash (2010: 18).

611. Axworthy (2013: 344–345).

612. Amuzegar (2004: 78–79); Alfoneh (2008); Pourzand (2009–2010: 101); Axworthy (2013: 348); Ostovar (2016: 157); Ehteshami (2017: 51).

613. Axworthy (2013: 353).

614. Bakhash (2010: 18); Barany (2019: 56).

615. Wehrey et al. (2009: 30); Safshekan and Sabet (2010: 548).

616. Amuzegar (2006: 57, 61).

617. Boroumand (2017: 40).

618. Amuzegar (2004); P. Jones (2011: 109).

619. Amuzegar (2004: 77–78, 86); "Khatami Warns against Constitutional Amendment," Kuwait News Agency, June 12, 2000.

620. "Khatami Vows to Put Down Student Protests in Iran," *AFP*, July 13, 1999; "Khatami Abandons Student Protesters: Iran's Pro-Democracy Activists Left Stunned, Confused as President Sides with Hard-Liners," *The Globe and Mail*, July 15, 1999.

621. Amuzegar (2004: 79).

622. "Iran Tightens Crackdown on Reformist Publications." *New York Times*, April 25, 2000; Amuzegar (2004: 82).

623. "Khatami Admits Reforms Have Failed," NBC News, December 6, 2004; Amuzegar (2004: 78–82).

624. Amuzegar (2004: 75); Parsa (2020: 57).

625. "Angry Iranian Students Lash Out at Khatami," *AFP*, July 15, 1999; "Khatami Abandons Student Protesters."

626. "Khatami Abandons Student Protesters"; Amuzegar (2004: 79).

627. "Khatami Should Resign, Says Nobel Peace Laureate," *The Guardian*, January 19, 2004; also "Reformers Critical of New Khatami Cabinet," Reuters, August 14, 2001.

628. Thus, turnout declined from 80 percent in 1997 to 67 percent in 2001 to 60 percent in 2005 (second round) (Iran Data Portal n.d.). Ahmadinejad appears to have been assisted by the Basij and the IRGC. See Naji (2008: 63); Sinkaya (2016: 165–170).

629. Afshari and Underwood (2009: 7); Ehteshami (2017: 64–66).

630. Axworthy (2013: 401–402); Ehteshami (2017: 64–68).

631. Ehteshami (2017: 72). For evidence of fraud, see Amnesty International (2009: 17); Mebane (2010: 14, 6); Ostovar (2016).

632. Afshari and Underwood (2009: 6–8).

633. Ansari (2010: ix); also Parsa (2020: 57).

634. A. Milani (2010: 41); Lachapelle et al. (2012: 19).

635. Saha (2014: 145); Ehteshami (2017: 77).

636. "Tehran Losing Iranians' Trust, Ex-Leader Says," *New York Times*, July 18, 2009.

637. Peterson (2010: 572); Ehteshami (2017: 77–78).

638. A. Milani (2010: 43).

639. Alfoneh (2010: 62).

640. Ostovar (2016: 185).

641. Alfoneh (2010: 62); Hashemi and Postel (2010: xix); Nader (2010: 61); Golkar (2012: 468); Ostovar (2016: 185–186); Barany (2019: 57).

642. A. Milani (2010: 43).

643. A. Milani (2010: 42); "With Brutal Crackdown, Iran Is Convulsed by Worst Unrest in 40 Years," *New York Times*, December 1, 2019.

644. See Amnesty International (2009: 11).

645. "Defiant Iranians Take to Streets," *Los Angeles Times*, July 31, 2009; A. Milani (2010: 43); Ehteshami (2017: 85).

646. Amnesty International (2009: 28–30).

647. Axworthy (2013: 409).

648. A. Milani (2010: 42).

649. "Iran Rounds Up Activists, Clamps Down in Streets," *Los Angeles Times*, December 29, 2009.

650. "Updates on Protests and Clashes in Iran," *New York Times*, December 27, 2009.

651. "Arrests by Iran in Bid to Quell Wide Protests," *New York Times*, February 10, 2010.

652. "Iran Executes Two Men on Charges of Sedition," *Los Angeles Times*, January 29, 2010; "Opposition Hardens Line inside Iran," *New York Times*, February 3, 2010.

653. A. Milani (2010: 41).

654. Saha (2014: 83).

655. Ostovar (2016: 186).

656. Peterson (2010: 541); Ostovar (2016: 186); Ehteshami (2017: 79).

657. Hashemi and Postel (2010: 421n25); Ostovar (2016: 186–187).

658. "Tehran Losing Iranians' Trust."

659. "Mousavi on the 'Green Path of Hope,'" *Frontline*, PBS, September 5, 2009.

660. Parsa (2020: 57).

661. "Mousavi Reportedly under House Arrest: Opposition Leader on Facebook: 'All My Communication . . . Has Been Cut Off,'" ABC News, June 27, 2009; "Mousavi on the 'Green Path of Hope.'"

662. Afshari and Underwood (2009: 9).

663. K. Harris (2012: 437); Barany (2019: 56); Parsa (2020: 57).

664. "Mousavi Reportedly under House Arrest."

665. Parsa (2020: 58).

666. K. Harris (2012: 443).

667. Parsa (2020: 59).

668. Boroumand (2017: 43).

669. Boroumand (2017: 41); Stevenson (2017).

670. Axworthy (2013: 381–385); Maloney (2015: 433); Ostovar (2016: 163); Nuclear Threat Initiative (2021).

671. Ostovar (2016: 198).

672. CRS (2020).

673. CRS (2020: 2).

674. Maloney (2015: 461–462); European Council on Foreign Relations (2019).

675. CRS (2020: 35, 64–65, 77).

676. CRS (2020: 24).

677. Maloney (2015: 470–471); CRS (2020: 64).

678. "What SWIFT Is and Why It Matters in the US-Iran Spat," *Al Jazeera*, November 5, 2018; CRS (2020: 54).

679. CRS (2020: 64); World Bank Databank (n.d.).

680. According to one survey, more than 90 percent of Iranians believed the government was not doing enough to fight corruption or keep food prices down, and nearly three-quarters believed the government was not doing enough to help the poor (Mohseni et al. 2018).

681. "Tens of Thousands of People Have Protested in Iran. Here's Why," *Washington Post*, January 3, 2018; Parsa (2020: 60).

682. Barany (2019: 54); Jones and Newlee (2019: 4).

683. "Iran's Top Leader Warns 'Thugs' as Protests Reach 100 Cities," ABC News, November 17, 2019; "The Guardian View on Iran's Protests: Unrest Is Crushed, Unhappiness Endures," *The Guardian*, November 26, 2019; "With Brutal Crackdown."

684. "Special Report: Iran's Leader Ordered Crackdown on Unrest—'Do Whatever It Takes to End It,'" Reuters, December 23, 2019.

685. "Iran Abruptly Raises Fuel Prices, and Protests Erupt," *New York Times*, November 15, 2019; "With Brutal Crackdown."

686. "With Brutal Crackdown."

687. "Iran's Leader Ordered Crackdown"; Parsa (2020: 60).

688. "With Brutal Crackdown."

689. "With Brutal Crackdown"; "Iran's Leader Ordered Crackdown."

690. See "One of the Worst Crackdowns in Decades Is Happening in Iran. Here's What We Know," CNN, December 3, 2019; "Iran's Leader Ordered Crackdown"; Parsa (2020: 54).

691. "With Brutal Crackdown."

692. "Irrelevance of Iran's Reformists"; see also "Iran's Green Movement Leader Demands Killers of Protesters Be Prosecuted," Radio Farda, November 30, 2019; "Karroubi to Khamenei: Take Responsibility for Failures of Past 30 Years," Middle East Institute, January 31, 2018.

693. See "Iran's Ex-President Khatami Walks a Tightrope during Protests," Radio Farda, November 28, 2019; also "The Irrelevance of Iran's Reformists."

694. Parsa (2020: 64–65).

695. Barany (2019: 57).

696. Cross (2010).

697. Ross (2001); Bellin (2004).

698. K. Harris (2017: 8–11).

699. M. Milani (1994: 205); Alamdari (2005); Saeidi (2009); K. Harris (2017: 28).

700. Forozan and Shahi (2017); Parsa (2020: 55).

701. K. Harris (2017: 173).

702. K. Harris (2017: 28).

703. Lachapelle et al. (2020).

704. Hashemi and Postel (2010: xviii–xix); also Daly (2012); Saha (2014); Barany (2019: 54).

705. Rabiei (2020: 157).

706. Parsa (2020: 65–66).

707. Kazemzadeh (2008: 198); K. Harris (2017: 182); Parsa (2020: 55, 65).

708. Moslem (2002); Brownlee (2007); Ghobadzadeh and Rahim (2016).

Chapter 7

1. On the Social Democrats' moderate and nonideological character, see Tőkés (1967: 171); Kenez (1971: 64).

2. Kaas and Lazarovics (1931: 172).

3. Kaas and Lazarovics (1931: 79); also Tőkés (1967: 85).

4. For example, Hungary was deprived of about 80 percent of its coal resources (Tőkés 1967: 85); also Kaas and Lazarovics (1931: 174).

5. Tőkés (1967: 87).

6. J. Dixon (1986: 34).

7. Kaas and Lazarovics (1931: 45–46); Eckelt (1965: 114); Tőkés (1967: 85).

8. Tőkés (1967: 87).

9. Kaas and Lazarovics (1931: 42, 37–38).

10. Tőkés (1967: 56–58).

11. Tőkés (1967: 56–61, 67).

12. Tőkés (1967: 67).

13. Zsuppán (1965: 316–317); Tőkés (1967: 79); Borsányi (1993: 86).

14. Zsuppán (1965: 319); Tőkés (1967: 85).

15. Zsuppán (1965: 321).

16. Tőkés (1967: 58); Borsányi (1993: 93).

17. Tőkés (1967: 58); Kenez (1971: 78); Doug Greene (2020).

18. Zsuppán (1965: 322).

19. Zsuppán (1965: 323); Tőkés (1967: 121); Borsányi (1993: 92, 100).

20. Kaas and Lazarovics (1931: 200).

21. Tőkés (1967: 129).

22. Kaas and Lazarovics (1931: 75); Eckelt (1965: 155); Jaszi (1969: 87).

23. Eckelt (1965: 156–157); Tőkés (1967: 126–127); Jaszi (1969: 87); Borsányi (1993: 114–115, 117).

24. Jaszi (1969: 96).

25. Doug Greene (2020).

26. Zsuppán (1965: 333).

27. Tőkés (1967: 134).

28. Kaas and Lazarovics (1931: 83–84); Tőkés (1967: 133); Borsányi (1993: 136).

29. Zsuppán (1965: 334); Tőkés (1967: 132); Borsányi (1993: 136).

30. See Zsuppán (1965); Tőkés (1967); Borsányi (1993); Doug Greene (2020).

31. Jaszi (1969: 88); Borsányi (1993: 139).

32. Jaszi (1969: 88).

33. Kenez (1971: 68). Thus, the major domestic and international policy initiatives during this period were driven by Kun. See, for example, Zsuppán (1965); Jaszi (1969: 127, 128); Molnar (1990: 19); Doug Greene (2020).

34. Tőkés (1967: 102, 137, 161, 171); Kenez (1971: 73); Doug Greene (2020).

35. At the unified party's first congress in June 1919, the Communists accounted for just a quarter of delegates (Tőkés 1967: 167).

36. Kenez (1971: 69).

37. Kenez (1971: 62, 65).

38. Zsuppán (1965: 315).

39. Doug Greene (2020).

40. Borsányi (1993: 154).

41. Borsányi (1993: 154); also Kaas and Lazarovics (1931: 208, 212); Hajdu (1979: 93).

42. Borsányi (1993: 152).

43. Tőkés (1967: 197–199); Hajdu (1979: 147); Borsányi (1993: 193–195); Doug Greene (2020).

44. Kenez (1971); Doug Greene (2020).

45. Urbas (1922: 63); Gerwarth (2008: 183).

46. Eckelt (1965: 278); Sakmyster (1975: 20); Bodo (2011: 138); Doug Greene (2020).

47. Molnar (1990: 28); Borsányi (1993: 156); Doug Greene (2020).

48. Tőkés (1967: 138, 139, 141); Jaszi (1969: 120, 128); Molnar (1990: 18).

49. Tőkés (1967: 139, 141); Jaszi (1969: 128); Kovrig (1979: 45–46); Molnar (1990: 18).

50. Dent (2018: 63–68).

51. Kaas and Lazarovics (1931: 98–129, 221).

52. Kaas and Lazarovics (1931: 102, 132–133, 154); Tőkés (1967: 159); Molnar (1990: 18).

53. Kaas and Lazarovics (1931: 140); Tőkés (1967: 193).

54. Kaas and Lazarovics (1931: 128).

55. Zsuppán (1965: 331).

56. Tőkés (1967: 187).

57. Kaas and Lazarovics (1931: 111); Tőkés (1967: 142); Jaszi (1969: 127); Molnar (1990: 19); Borsányi (1993: 93).

58. Tőkés (1967: 187).

59. Tőkés (1967: 187); Jaszi (1969: 127); Molnar (1990: 19).

60. Bodo (2011: 138).

61. Kaas and Lazarovics (1931: 127); Bodo (2011: 138).

62. Tőkés (1967: 143).

63. Tőkés (1967: 144); Borsányi (1993: 154).

64. Kaas and Lazarovics (1931: 262–263, 267); Tőkés (1967: 175, 184); Molnar (1990: 25).

65. Dominated by a "doomed oligarchy of utopian philosophers, orthodox fanatics, bewildered communist bureaucrats and ostracized socialists," the republic collapsed within a month (Tőkés 1967: 167, 191, 205; Molnar 1990: 28; Borsányi 1993: 174).

66. McAdams (2017: 123).

67. Tőkés (1967: 192–193).

68. Kaas and Lazarovics (1931: 190, 198); Borsányi (1993: 191).

69. Urbas (1922: 65); Kaas and Lazarovics (1931: 274); Sakmyster (1975: 20); Gerwath (2008: 186, 188).

70. Tőkés (1967: 193).

71. Tőkés (1967: 200); Borsányi (1993: 187, 188).

72. Molnar (1990: 28); Borsányi (1993: 156).

73. Borsányi (1993: 154).

74. Kaas and Lazarovics (1931: 297); Tőkés (1967: 204); Jaszi (1969: 153); Borsányi (1993: 201).

75. Tőkés (1967: 200, 205).

76. E. Becker (1998: 167). For a summary of estimates of the number who died under Pol Pot, see Margolin (1999a: 590).

77. E. Becker (1998: 71); Kiernan (2004: chap. 6); P. Short (2004: 139).

78. E. Becker (1998: 78–79).

79. Chandler (1992: 37–40); P. Short (2004: 63–66).

80. Chandler (1992: 62).

81. Chandler (1992: 67).

82. E. Becker (1998: 109).

83. Chandler (1992: 69).

84. E. Becker (1998: 107).

85. Margolin (1999a: 619).

86. P. Short (2004: 149).

87. Chandler (1992: 125); Margolin (1999a: 601); P. Short (2004: 100).

88. P. Short (2004: 326).

89. E. Becker (1998: 154, 242); P. Short (2004: 327).

90. Kiernan (2008: 26).

91. P. Short (2004: 205); Kiernan (2008: 55).

92. Chandler (1992: 73).

93. Chandler (1992: 81–83); Kiernan (2004: 266–268); P. Short (2004: 165).

94. Chandler (1992: 83–84); P. Short (2004: 166, 176).

95. E. Becker (1998: 111).

96. Chandler (1992: 85); P. Short (2004: 205).

97. P. Short (2004: 203–204).

98. Chandler (1992: 90, 91, 95); E. Becker (1998: 133).

99. P. Short (2004: 228).

100. Quoted in E. Becker (1998: 141–142).

101. E. Becker (1998: 141–142).

102. Chandler (1992: 97). One U.S. audit found that less than 10 percent of the aid designated for military salaries was actually distributed to soldiers (Deac 1997: 110).

103. P. Short (2004: 207).

104. Kiernan (2004: 378).

105. P. Short (2004: 251).

106. Shawcross (1979); Chandler (1992: 101); E. Becker (1998: 124); Kahin (2003: 312–313); P. Short (2004: 216, 264).

107. P. Short (2004: 215).

108. P. Short (2004: 209).

109. Chandler (1992: 101).

110. Chandler (1992: 99).

111. Chandler (1992: 101–105); E. Becker (1998: 148, 166); Kiernan (2004: 368–372); P. Short (2004: 235).

112. E. Becker (1998: 153).

113. E. Becker (1998: 154).

114. Kiernan (2008: 78).

115. Margolin (1999a: 632).

116. P. Short (2004: 271); Mertha (2014: 22).

117. Mertha (2014: 23).

118. P. Short (2004: 277); Kiernan (2008: 35–38).

119. E. Becker (1998: 193); Kiernan (2008: 39).

120. Chandler (1992: 97, 154); E. Becker (1998: 165); Margolin (1999a: 632); P. Short (2004: 205); Mertha (2014: 21–24).

121. Margolin (1999a: 632).

122. E. Becker (1998: 168); Kiernan (2008).

123. Pol Pot was only able to contact commanders in different regions via foot messengers (Chandler 1992: 84, 98); also Mertha (2014: 30).

124. E. Becker (1998: 139, 174, 203); P. Short (2004: 204, 304); Kiernan (2008: 75).

125. P. Short (2004: 275); Kiernan (2008: 34, 40, 53–54, 332); Mertha (2014: 29).

126. E. Becker (1998: 175); P. Short (2004: 304); Mertha (2014: 23).

127. Mertha (2014: 23).

128. E. Becker (1998: 173); Kiernan (2008: 63).

129. E. Becker (1998: 168); Margolin (1999a: 598).

130. P. Short (2004: 275); Kiernan (2008: 48–49).

131. Kiernan (2008: 49).

132. Margolin (1999a: 583).

133. P. Short (2004: 332–333); Mertha (2014: 24).

134. P. Short (2004: 313).

135. P. Short (2004: 288); also Margolin (1999a: 591).

136. Margolin (1999a: 577).

137. E. Becker (1998: 183).

138. E. Becker (1998: 254); Margolin (1999a: 591); Raszelenberg (1999: 67); Kiernan (2008: 55).

139. Kiernan (n.d.: 79).

140. P. Short (2004: 290).

141. E. Becker (1998: 166); Raszelenberg (1999: 66–67); P. Short (2004: 311).

142. Chandler (1992: 108).

143. P. Short (2004: 292).

144. Margolin (1999a: 584); P. Short (2004: 292, 347); Kiernan (2008: 186).

145. Margolin (1999a: 577).

146. E. Becker (1998: 166); Kiernan (2008: 187).

147. E. Becker (1998: 166–167); P. Short (2004: 291).

148. E. Becker (1998: 247).

149. Vickery (1983: 132); P. Short (2004: 325–326).

150. Chandler (1992: 128).

151. Margolin (1999a: 597, 599).

152. P. Short (2004: 316).

153. E. Becker (1998: 208); Margolin (1999a: 598); P. Short (2004: 346).

154. Ciorciari (2014: 221).

155. Chandler (1992: 125); E. Becker (1998: 144, 240, 241); P. Short (2004: 308); Mertha (2014: 103).

156. Mertha (2014: 73).

157. Margolin (1999a: 601).

158. Margolin (1999a: 620); Mertha (2014: 88–89).

159. Mertha (2014: 99).

160. E. Becker (1998: 240); Margolin (1999a: 601).

161. E. Becker (1998: 247); Margolin (1999a: 602); P. Short (2004: 353).

162. Margolin (1999a: 596).

163. Heuveline (1998); Etcheson (2005: 119).

164. Chandler (1992: 150).

165. P. Short (2004: 283).

166. P. Short (2004: 341).

167. E. Becker (1998: 165).

168. Raszelenberg (1999: 70).

169. So Phim, Vorn Vet, Chan Chakrey, and Cheng An were purged before the regime was defeated. Son Sen, Nuon Chea, Ta Mok, and Ieng Sary followed Pol Pot into exile in 1979 and remained loyal for more than a decade after the regime fell (see N. Thayer 1998).

170. E. Becker (1998: 276); Mertha (2014: 23, 41). According to Correlates of War data, Cambodia had among the highest number of soldiers per capita among all dictatorships in 1976, 1977, and 1978. We thank Jean Lachapelle for calculating this data.

171. Mertha (2014: 87).

172. E. Becker (1998: 176, 203, 298); Kiernan (2008: 54); Mertha (2014: 30–31).

173. Kiernan (2008: 322–324); Mertha (2014: 87).

174. Kiernan (2008: 322–324).

175. E. Becker (1998: 141, 142); P. Short (2004: 249); Etcheson (2005: 85); Mertha (2014: 29); Korstjens (2016: 141).

176. P. Short (2004: 281).

177. E. Becker (1998: 298).

178. Kiernan (2008: chap. 8) describes several purported coup plots that were mentioned by defectors and in confessions at the Toul Sleng death camp. However, he does not identify any clearly documented coup attempt. We also searched the Foreign Broadcast Information Service and cables and reports from the CIA but were unable to find any plausible instances of military efforts to overthrow Pol Pot.

179. P. Short (2004: 360).

180. P. Short (2004: 379). Hun Sen, who later led Cambodia, was a low-level Eastern Zone commander when he deserted to Vietnam in 1977 (E. Becker 1998: 305; P. Short 2004: 379). The more senior Heng Samrin, a zone deputy chief of staff, did not defect until the eve of the Vietnamese invasion (P. Short 2004: 386).

181. P. Short (2004: 354). These included a February 1977 uprising in Siem Reap by several hundred people armed with machetes, spears, and knives, which was quickly and brutally put down (Margolin 1999a: 633; Kiernan 2008: 342–344).

182. Margolin (1999a: 588).

183. Chandler (1992: 136).

184. P. Short (2004: 366).

185. Etcheson (2005).

186. P. Short (2004: 364, 368); see also Raszelenberg (1999: 67).

187. Margolin (1999a: 586); also Chandler (1992: 113); Kiernan (n.d.: 76). In one district, 40,000–70,000 inhabitants were executed for being "traitors collaborating with the CIA" (Margolin 1999a: 587).

188. Chandler (1992: 101); E. Becker (1998: 149); Kiernan (n.d.: 75).

189. E. Becker (1998: 242).

190. Raszelenberg (1999: 68); Kiernan (2008: 106–107; n.d.: 80–81).

191. E. Becker (1998: 293, 304).

192. Kiernan (2008: 63).

193. Chandler (1992: 3, 120, 141); E. Becker (1998: 304–305); P. Short (2004: 372, 375); Kiernan (2008: 357–366).

194. Chandler (1992: 3, 120, 141); P. Short (2004: 372, 375); Kiernan (2008: 357–366). Cambodian troops also carried out attacks against northeast Thailand and made territorial claims on Laos (E. Becker 1998: 291, 308; P. Short 2004: 372; Kiernan 2008: 366, 368).

195. P. Short (2004: 375).

196. Kiernan (2008: 389–390).

197. Chandler (1992: 151).

198. Kiernan (2008: 369–370).

199. P. Short (2004: 392).

200. P. Short (2004: 385).

201. P. Short (2004: 386).

202. P. Short (2004: 386).

203. E. Becker (1998: 314); Margolin (1999a: 587); P. Short (2004: 384–385); Kiernan (2008: 392–404).

204. Chandler (1992: 156); P. Short (2004: 385); Mertha (2014: 117).

205. E. Becker (1998: 264); P. Short (2004: 392) Kiernan (2008: 27); Mertha (2014: 55).

206. Ciorciari (2014); Mertha (2014).

207. E. Becker (1998: 318); P. Short (2004: 395–397).

208. E. Becker (1998: 325, 433); Gottesman (2003: 11, 7); P. Short (2004: 386); Kiernan (2008: 375, 442); Nhem (2013: 103).

209. Although the Khmer Rouge and the Vietnamese Communists were both revolutionary, the Vietnamese invasion could be seen as "counterrevolutionary" insofar as the CPK's ideology was rooted in anti-Vietnamese ethnic nationalism (Kiernan 2008: 26).

210. Mertha (2019).

211. Khalilzad (1997); Murshed (2006: 42).

212. Maley (2001: 8); Marsden (2002: 78–79); Rashid (2010: 85).

213. Nojumi (2008: 91); Ahmad (2017).

214. Coll (2004: 181); Nojumi (2008: 95).

215. Bearden (2001: 24). As many as 25,000 Arabs passed through Afghanistan during the war. Many of these were apparently Arab prisoners that Arab governments had released in the hope that they would never return (Coll 2004: 180, 201).

216. Bearden (2001: 24); Dorronsoro (2005: 276–277).

217. Khalilzad (1997); Dorronsoro (2005: 233); Murshed (2006: 42); Taylor and Botea (2008).

218. Nojumi (2008: 97).

219. Coll (2004: 263); Ahmad (2017: 60).

220. Coll (2004: 238).

221. Dorronsoro (2005: 299); Rashid (2010: 21–22); Ahmad (2017: 66).

222. Ahmad (2017: 74).

223. Coll (2004: 233).

224. Aisha Ahmad (2017: 76) estimates that there were 100 such checkpoints on the 500-kilometer road between Kandahar and Kabul. See also Rashid (2010: 22).

225. Rashid (2010: 97).

226. Coll (2004: 282–283; 2019: 66–67); Ahmad (2017: 67).

227. Coll (2019: 66, 69).

228. Maley (2001: 2); Coll (2004: 288).

229. Coll (2004: 288).

230. Rashid (2010: 17–18).

231. Rashid (2010: 31–32).

232. Barfield (2010: 257–258); Rashid (2010: 89, 111); Abbas (2014: 62, 67).

233. Dorronsoro (2005: 277).

234. Maley (1999: pt. 3); Marsden (2002: 63); Coll (2004: 284–285); Rashid (2010: 43).

235. Coll (2004: 284–285).

236. Davis (2001: 44); Ahmad (2017).

237. Ahmad (2017: 89).

238. Davis (2001: 46); Sullivan (2007: 102); Ahmad (2017: 89).

239. Coll (2004: 291).

240. Rashid (2010: 27–28).

241. Dorronsoro (2005: 267). For descriptions of the Taliban's rise, see Coll (2004: 291); Dorronsoro (2005: 246–256); Sullivan (2007: 102); Rashid (2010: 27–28); Ahmad (2017: 88–90).

242. Coll (2004: 285); Ahmad (2017: 88).

243. Coll (2004: 287; 2019: 95).

244. Coll (2004: 331; 2019: 47); Dorronsoro (2005: 245); Sullivan (2007: 105).

245. Marsden (2002: 124–136); Coll (2004: 228, 332); Sullivan (2007: 105).

246. Rashid (2010: 30).

247. Rashid (2010: 34).

248. Rashid (2010: 48).

249. Rashid (2010: 49–50).

250. Rashid (2010: 5).

251. Dorronsoro (2005: 273–274).

252. Dorronsoro (2005: 281–282).

253. Davis (2001: 51); Maley (2001: 11); Coll (2004: 500); Rashid (2010: 35).

254. Dorronsoro (2005: 287, 282).

255. Dorronsoro (2005: 278); Rashid (2010: 43). Most Taliban officials were "untrained for anything" (Rashid 2010: 32).

256. Rashid (2010: 101, 102). Government documents in the early days of the regime were written on cigarette boxes and old wrapping paper (Rashid 2010: 25).

257. Coll (2004: 500).

258. Marsden (2002: 51); Rashid (2010: 100).

259. Dorronsoro (2005: 327); Rashid (2010: 47).

260. Davis (2001: 54); Rashid (2010: 100).

261. Davis (2001: 54); Rashid (2010: 100).

262. Maley (2001: 15–16).

263. Barfield (2010: 261–262); Rashid (2010: 29).

264. Dupree (2001: 155); Marsden (2002: 88); Coll (2004: 334); Rashid (2010: 2).

265. Dupree (2001: 154).

266. Coll (2004: 334, 351).

267. Maley (2001: 15); Dorronsoro (2005: 285).

268. In the words of Ajmal Burhanzoi, a University of Toronto graduate student whose family lived in Afghanistan under the Taliban: "I was practicing [soccer] with my teammates early in the morning when we were approached by a group of Taliban. Their leader used his military knife to puncture our footballs and sliced one into two and put it on our coach's head as a hat—to humiliate and intimidate us. Our team never went back to practice again" (personal communication, April 14, 2020).

269. Dupree (2001); Coll (2004: 334, 351); Dorronsoro (2005: 290–291, 300–301); Barfield (2010: 261–262); Rashid (2010: 2, 4–5).

270. Marsden (2002: 53, 55); Dorronsoro (2005: 269); Barfield (2010: 263); Rashid (2010: 35, 73).

271. Maley (1999: pt. 5); Dorronsoro (2005: 292, 308).

272. Maley (1999: pt. 5); Coll (2004: 362); Rashid (2010: 65, 80).

273. Dorronsoro (2005: 274).

274. Dupree (2001: 147); Coll (2004: 363).

275. Sullivan (2007: 103); Rashid (2010: 112).

276. Coll (2004: 554–555); Rashid (2010: 76).

277. Bearden (2001: 24–25); Coll (2004: 227; 2019: 68); Dorronsoro (2005: 304–305).

278. Rashid (2010: 133).

279. Dorronsoro (2005: 305).

280. Coll (2004: 491); Rashid (2010: 134).

281. Coll (2004: 401). In the late 1990s, al-Qaeda contributed some $30 million to support the Taliban's war against the Northern Alliance (Coll 2004: 536; Nojumi 2008: 105, Rashid 2010: 139).

282. Nojumi (2008: 113).

283. Coll (2004: 380).

284. Coll (2004: 403, 537).

285. Marsden (2002: 147–148).

286. Coll 2004:414).

287. The Saudi Ministry of Religious Endowments continued to fund bin Laden's activities, however (Coll 2004: 414–415; Murshed 2006: 300–301).

288. Coll (2004: 482); Murshed (2006: 292–300); Barfield (2010: 265, 269).

289. Dorronsoro (2004: 236, 287, 299–300).

290. Coll (2004: 462).

291. Dupree (2001: 161).

292. Coll (2004: 524–525); Dorronsoro (2005: 321).

293. Dorronsoro (2005: 302–303, 309); Rashid (2010: 218).

294. Rashid (2010: 218).

295. Coll (2019: 67–68).

296. Coll (2019: 68).

297. Coll (2004: 473).

298. Coll (2019: 56); also Dorronsoro (2005: 312); Ahmed (2010).

299. Dorronsoro (2005: 323–325); Coll (2019: 93) At the same time, it is unclear whether the Taliban had the capacity to capture bin Laden if it had wanted to (Coll 2019: 62).

300. Giustozzi (2019: 18).

301. Giustozzi (2019: 34, 44, 53, 59, 110).

302. Giustozzi (2019: 46).

303. Watkins (2020: 13).

304. Giustozzi (2019: 37, 65, 68–70, 79, 91); Watkins (2020: 9).

305. Giustozzi (2019: 116, 153, 198, 247–249, 257).

306. Giustozzi (2019: 240–241); "How the Taliban Outlasted a Superpower: Tenacity and Carnage," *New York Times*, May 26, 2020.

307. "How the Taliban Outlasted a Superpower."

308. Watkins (2020: 5).

309. "Afghanistan: Taliban Announce New Rules for Women and Girls' Education," DW.com, September 12, 2021; "New Taliban Chancellor Bars Women from Kabul University," *New York Times*, September 27, 2021.

310. At the time of their revolutions, Hungary's population was 8 million (Statista .com), Cambodia's was 7.5 million, and Afghanistan's was 19 million (World Bank n.d.).

Chapter 8

1. Patch (1961), Huntington (1968), and Alan Knight (2003) make similar arguments.

2. Malloy (1970).

3. Corbett (1972).

4. Smith Ariñez (1960: 11); Zondag (1966: 69).

5. Malloy (1970: 189–190).

6. Tin exports generated between 75 and 95 percent of Bolivia's foreign exchange in the early twentieth century (Thorn 1971: 169; Knudson 1986: 22).

7. Thorn (1971: 169); Malloy (1971a: 6); Dunkerley (1984: 6–7).

8. Heath et al. (1969: 122).

9. Heath et al. (1969: 86–101); Kelley and Klein (1981: 76); García Arganarás (1992: 45).

10. Dunkerley (1984: 22).

11. Flores (1954: 119); Malloy (1970: 92); Eckstein (1983: 108); García Arganarás (1992: 45); Field (2014: 4–5).

12. H. Klein (1992: 188–226).

13. H. Klein (1968a: 109; 1992: 191); Corbett (1972: 24–27); Dunkerley (1984: 33–34).

14. Alexander (1958: 25–26); H. Klein (1971a: 204–217).

15. Burrier (2012: 8).

16. H. Klein (1971a: 204–226).

17. Patch (1961: 126).

18. H. Klein (1971a: 189, 204–217, 367–370; 1971b: 33–38); Mitchell (1977: 16); Antezana Ergueta (2017: 65).

19. H. Klein (1968b: 319–335); Malloy (1970: 87–95).

20. Malloy (1970: 120); Blasier (1985: 46–48).

21. Blasier (1971b: 46–61).

22. Patch (1961: 127); Dunkerley (1984: 33–34); Holtey (2012: 54).

23. Alexander (1958: 38–42); Malloy (1970: 127–134).

24. Malloy (1970: 134–150); H. Klein (1971b: 39).

25. H. Klein (1971a: 383–401); Crespo (1996: 125–126); Dorn (2011: 97–101).

26. Alexander (1958: 41, 96–97).

27. Quoted in Antezana Ergueta (2017: 71). Also Alexander (1958: 41–42); Crespo (1996: 128–129).

28. Malloy (1970: 156–157); Crespo (1996: 135–139); Antezana Ergueta (2017: 50, 100–103).

29. Antezana Ergueta (2017: 83–84).

30. Crespo (1996: 137–138); Antezana Ergueta (2017: 83–86).

31. Corbett (1972: 26–27); Malloy (1971b: 112).

32. Sanabria (1990: 51–52).

33. Prado Salmon (1984: 33).

34. Crespo (1996: 144).

35. Brill (1967: 14).

36. Dunkerley (1984: 48); Prado Salmon (1984: 38); Antezana Ergueta (2017: 87).

37. Prado Salmon (1984: 40); Antezana Ergueta (2017: 168).

38. Malloy (1970: 183).

39. Malloy (1971b: 117–118).

40. Selbin (1993: 35).

41. Mitchell (1977: 33); H. Klein (1992: 225).

42. Antezana Ergueta (2017: 89).

43. Malloy (1970: 158–163, 171–172); Mitchell (1977: 79–82).

44. Alexander (1982a: 127).

45. Malloy (1970: 180).

46. Brill (1967: 15–16).

47. Crespo (1996: 158).

48. Alexander (1958: 47); Dunkerley (1984: 48–49).

49. Malloy (1970: 184); Antezana Ergueta (2017: 182–183).

50. Burrier (2012: 9).

51. Eckstein (1976: 32).

52. Alexander (1982a: 16); H. Klein (1992: 237); Alan Knight (2003: 73).

53. Alan Knight (2003: 57).

54. Mitchell (1977: 44–47).

55. Alexander (1958: 122–125).

56. Malloy (1970: 145–157, 186–187); Alexander (2005: 74–90); Burrier (2012: 12).

57. Malloy (1970: 185; 1971b: 122–123).

58. David Greene (1965: 13); Malloy (1970: 145–157, 186–187); Alexander (2005: 89–90).

59. Zondag (1966: 51).

60. Malloy (1970: 201–202); Antezana Ergueta and Romero Bedregal (1973: 203–273).

61. Malloy (1971b: 127–128); Antezana Ergueta and Romero Bedregal (1973).

62. Malloy (1970: 283).

63. Malloy (1970: 283, 306). On MNR moderation, see Dunkerley (1984: 42); Selbin (1993: 34); Holtey (2012: 19–20, 80–84).

64. Heath et al. (1969: 40).

65. Dorn (2011: 30).

66. Malloy and Borzutsky (1982: 46).

67. Crespo (1996: 185).

68. Quoted in Burrier (2012: 10).

69. Lehman (2003: 108).

70. Dunkerley (1984: 42). One biographer described Paz as a "fiscal conservative" (Holtey 2012: 173).

71. Blasier (1971b).

72. Rabe (1988: 79); Lehman (1997: 199).

73. Zunes (2001: 35). Also Lehman (1997, 2003); Dorn (2011: 32).

74. Dorn (2011: 32).

75. Lehman (2003: 103). Also Burke and Malloy (1974: 69); Zondag (1982: 29–30); Zunes (2001: 40).

76. Blasier (1971b: 99); Burke and Malloy (1974: 52); Lehman (2003: 98).

77. Burke and Malloy (1974: 52).

78. H. Klein (1992: 233).

79. Dorn (2011: 170).

80. Dorn (2011: 171).

81. Malloy (1970); Antezana Ergueta (2017).

82. Dorn (2011: 163–166).

83. H. Klein (1992: 232).

84. Malloy (1970: 185–187).

85. Malloy (1970: 231–233; 1971a: 28–29); H. Klein (2011: 214).

86. Malloy (1971b: 112).

87. Alexander (1958: 123–125).

88. Thorn (1971: 169); Dunkerley (1984: 6–7).

89. Malloy (1971a: 6); Siekmeier (2004: 390).

90. Malloy (1970: 114).

91. Crespo (1996: 162–163).

92. Alexander (1958: 101); Malloy (1970: 174); Thorn (1971: 168–169).

93. Dorn (2011: 168).

94. García Arganarás (1992: 55); Lehman (1997: 199).

95. Malloy (1970: 195); Alexander (2005: 91–92).

96. Lehman (1997, 2003: 99–104); Siekmeier (2004).

97. Blasier (1985: 133). Also Siekmeier (2004).

98. Alexander (1958: 107, 116); Thorn (1971: 160).

99. Alexander (1958: 101, 107–108); Thorn (1971: 168–169); Holtey (2012: 80).

100. Dunkerley (1984: 65–66).

101. Justo (1967: 174); Malloy (1970: 203–204); Dunkerley (1984: 65–66).

102. Malloy (1971a: 28).

103. Dunkerley (1984: 67–72). Also Heath et al. (1969: 127–133); H. Klein (1992: 234–235).

104. Patch (1961: 129). Also Justo (1967: 174); Heath et al. (1969: 49).

105. Kelley and Klein (1981: 95).

106. Flores (1954: 120); Patch (1961: 124, 129); Heath et al. (1969: 383); Thorn (1971: 162).

107. Lanning (1969: 10); Eckstein (1983: 105); Malloy and Gamarra (1988: 2).

108. Eckstein (1983).

109. Heath et al. (1969: 274); Kelley and Klein (1981: 97).

110. Kelley and Klein (1981: 96–97).

111. Alexander (1958: 72); Thorn (1971: 160–161).

112. Alexander (1958: 73); Malloy (1970: 206).

113. Malloy (1970: 206).

114. Alexander (1958: 69–70); Thorn (1971: 62); Burrier (2012: 15).

115. Alexander (1958: 69–70); Heath et al. (1969: 51–59); Carter (1971: 244–245).

116. Dunkerley (1984: 73).

117. Patch (1961: 127).

118. Siekmeier (2004: 396); Dorn (2011: 179, 196).

119. Knudson (1986).

120. Dorn (2011: 190).

121. H. Klein (1971a: 404–405); Burrier (2012: 9).

122. Patch (1961: 131).

123. Malloy (1970: 231; 1971b: 126–129); Goodrich (1971: 16); Mitchell (1977: 91).

124. Brill (1967: 32, 36); Malloy (1970: 218); Dunkerley (1984: 97); Sanabria (1990: 100–101).

125. Alexander (1958: 239–240); Malloy (1970: 218, 267); Sanabria (1990: 101).

126. Patch (1961: 131); Mitchell (1977: 71); Knudson (1986: 329).

127. Blasier (1971b, 1985).

128. On the U.S. response to the revolution, see Blasier (1971b, 1985); Lehman (1997); Siekmeier (2004).

129. Blasier (1971b: 100); Lehman (2003: 97); Dorn (2011: 203).

130. Dorn (2011: 203).

131. Blasier (1971b: 100); Dorn (2011).

132. Blasier (1971b); Siekmeier (2004); Dorn (2011); Field (2014: 6).

133. Lehman (1997: 191).

134. See Lehman (1997: 192).

135. Dorn (2011: 167).

136. Lehman (1997: 192, 198); Dorn (2011: 170–174).

137. Blasier (1985: 131).

138. Lehman (2003: 99–100, 108); Dorn (2011: 178–183).

139. Lehman (1997: 192); Dorn (2011: 183, 186–189).

140. Lehman (2003: 102).

141. Blasier (1971b: 72).

142. Lehman (1997: 203–205).

143. Zunes (2001).

144. Blasier (1985: 137); Lehman (1997: 185).

145. David Greene (1965: 3); Eckstein (1976: 37).

146. Blasier (1971b: 54–55).

147. Zunes (2001).

148. Alan Knight (2003: 69).

149. Corbett (1972: 31, 65); Dunkerley (1984: 48–49).

150. Alexander (1958: 149–150); Malloy (1970: 231); Prado Salmon (1984: 44–48).

151. Brill (1967: 16–17); Justo (1967: 162); Corbett (1972: 31, 59–61).

152. Brill (1967: 15–16); Corbett (1972: 29); Queiser Morales (1992: 80, 122).

153. Alexander (1958: 150); Brill (1967: 17, 30); Corbett (1972: 59–61).

154. Alexander (1958: 146–150); Knudson (1986: 329).

155. Brill (1967: 17).

156. Lanning (1969: 10).

157. Alexander (1958: 47, 106); Blasier (1971b: 93); Dunkerley (1984: 50); Field (2014: 25).

158. Blasier (1971b: 93); Corbett (1972: 30–31); Dunkerley (1984: 50).

159. Corbett (1972: 65, 30).

160. Malloy (1970: 181).

161. Alexander (1958: 146–147); Prado Salmon (1984: 41–44).

162. Corbett (1972: 31); Prado Salmon (1984: 55–56).

163. Corbett (1972: 31); Prado Salmon (1984: 54–56); Field (2014: 12).

164. Queiser Morales (1992: 80–81); Whitehead (2003: 39); Holtey (2012: 84).

165. Blasier (1971b: 96).

166. Brill (1967: 30); Alexander (1982a: 126).

167. Brill (1967: 56, 30).

168. Malloy (1970: 180).

169. Brill (1967: 56, 30).

170. Malloy (1970: 180); Corbett (1972: 31); Prado Salmon (1984: 44).

171. Malloy (1970: 181); Corbett (1972: 65); Prado Salmon (1984).

172. Zondag (1966: 52); Heath et al. (1969: 385); Burrier (2012: 9).

173. Heath et al. (1969: 385).

174. Malloy (1970: 262).

175. Malloy (1970: 234–235); Zondag (1982: 32).

176. Alan Knight (2003: 72–73).

177. Hennessy (1964: 199); Crespo (1996: 66).

178. Brill (1967: 32, 36); Malloy (1970: 235).

179. Crespo (1996: 172–173).

180. Malloy (1970: 235). Also Guerra (2004: 235–236).

181. Guerra (2004: 236).

182. Hennessy (1964: 199); Malloy (1970: 235).

183. Malloy (1970: 234–235).

184. Robert J. Alexander reported 771 political prisoners in the wake of a Falange rebellion in 1953 (1958: 230–233).

185. Malloy (1970: 234).

186. Malloy (1970: 251–252, 262); Whitehead (2003: 36–37); Holtey (2012: 130).

187. Knudson (1986: 329).

188. Alexander (1982a: 127).

189. Malloy (1971b: 126–129).

190. Grindle (2003: 5).

191. Prado Salmon (1984: 49); Field (2014: 25).

192. Corbett (1972: 65, 30–31).

193. Corbett (1972); Prado Salmon (1984).

194. Brill (1967: 30).

195. Alexander (1982a: 126).

196. Alan Knight (2003: 67).

197. Kelley and Klein (1981: 128).

198. David Greene (1965: 25); Zondag (1966: 51).

199. Eckstein (1976: 31); Dunkerley (1984: 100–101); B. Werner (2020).

200. Eckstein (1976: 31). Also Malloy (1970: 250–251; 1971a: 38); Dunkerley (1984: 100–101).

201. Malloy (1970: 333).

202. Zondag (1966: 201).

203. Zondag (1966: 55–57); Crespo (1996: 202–203).

204. Alexander (1958: 267–269).

205. Malloy (1970: 237–238); Alexander (2005: 100).

206. Alexander (1958: 206–221); Thorn (1971: 183–184); Zondag (1982: 34).

207. Dunkerley (1984: 87).

208. Blasier (1971b); Zunes (2001).

209. Malloy (1970: 237–238); H. Klein (1992: 242–243).

210. Malloy (1970: 238).

211. Malloy (1971b: 132–133).

212. Malloy (1971b: 132–138).

213. Crespo (1996: 204).

214. Alexander (1958: 54, 218–219); Mitchell (1977: 65–70).

215. Alexander (1958: 219).

216. Malloy (1970: 240); Corbett (1972: 33–34); Knudson (1986: 326–329).

217. Blasier (1971b: 93).

218. Corbett (1972: 35–36); Field (2014: 25).

219. Mitchell (1977: 92).

220. Crespo (1996: 237).

221. Field (2014: 142–143).

222. Zondag (1966: 65).

223. Blasier (1971b: 86–87); Alexander (2005: 110); Field (2014).

224. Burrier (2012: 21–22); Field (2014: 3).

225. Malloy (1970: 298–300); Blasier (1971b); Field (2014).

226. Malloy (1971b: 139).

227. Malloy (1970: 298–300); Dunkerley (1984: 104–105); Holtey (2012: 130).

228. Malloy (1971b: 142).

229. Malloy (1971a: 45); Corbett (1972: 35–36); Alexander (2005: 114); Field (2014: 76).

230. Dunkerley (1984: 114).

231. Dunkerley (1984: 114); Queiser Morales (1992: 123); Burrier (2012: 23).

232. Corbett (1972: 35); Eckstein (1976: 37–38); Burrier (2012: 23).

233. Field (2014: 49).

234. H. Klein (1971a: 406).

235. Crespo (1996: 244–245); Field (2014: 32–33).

236. Dunkerley (1984: 111); Alexander (2005: 111–112).

237. García Arganarás (1992: 66); Field (2014: 39–97).

238. Holtey (2012: 146–147); Field (2014: 39–97). Although Vice President Lechín initially backed the government, he was eventually pulled into opposition by his union base (Malloy 1970: 300–301; Mitchell 1977: 89–90).

239. Alexander (2012: xii).

240. Dunkerley (1984: 118); Crespo (1996: 248).

241. Mitchell (1977: 92).

242. Blasier (1971b: 96–97).

243. Blasier (1971b: 96–97); Alexander (1982a: 128); Zondag (1982: 36–37).

244. Mitchell (1977: 93–94).

245. Brill (1967: 22–23).

246. Mitchell (1977: 93).

247. Crespo (1996: 248).

248. Malloy (1970: 312).

249. Mitchell (1977: 95); Field (2014: 145, 151).

250. Justo (1967: 198).

251. Brill (1967: 40).

252. Brill (1967: 39); Malloy (1971b: 143–144).

253. Field (2014: 143–169).

254. Holtey (2012: 150).

255. Field (2014: 166–169).

256. Brill (1967: 41–43); Malloy (1971b: 144); Field (2014: 167, 173–181).

257. Brill (1967: 41–43); Field (2014: 180–181).

258. Malloy (1970: 309).

259. H. Klein (1971a: 406); Alexander (1982b: 62); Field (2014: 145).

260. Brill (1967: 16, 23, 30–32); Blasier (1971b: 95); Corbett (1972: 30–31).

261. Field (2014: 190).

262. Mitchell (1977: 99).

263. Malloy (1971b: 145). Also Mitchell (1977: 100–101); Malloy and Gamarra (1988: 10–13).

264. Antezana Ergueta (2017: 188).

265. Álvarez Montalván (1994: 15).

266. Booth (1985: 18–19); Álvarez Montalván (1994: 19–21).

267. Booth (1985: 15–34).

268. Barbosa Miranda (2010: 174).

269. Booth (1985: 40–45).

270. Millett (1977: 61–78, 136); Barbosa Miranda (2010: 174–180).

271. Millett (1977: 169–185).

272. Booth (1998).

273. Booth (1998).

274. Black (1981: 34).

275. "Somoza's Legacy: Plundered Economy," *Washington Post*, November 30, 1979; Walker (1991b: 6).

276. Weber (1981: 30).

277. Black (1981: 51–55); Álvarez Montalván (1994: 43–44).

278. Black (1981: 50–51).

279. Black (1981: 47, 51–52).

280. Kirk (1992: 34–36); Spalding (1994: 43–48).

281. Booth (1985: 59–60); Walker (2003: 27–28).

282. Zimmermann (2000: 78–80).

283. Booth (1985: 140, 147); Zimmermann (2000: 80–82); Barbosa Miranda (2010: 292–295).

284. Pineda (1980: 125–126); Weber (1981: 21); Zimmermann (2000: 97, 187).

285. Christian (1985: 27).

286. Booth (1985: 141–142).

287. Black (1981: 59–60); Booth (1985: 81).

288. Booth (1985: 81–83); Everingham (1996).

289. Booth (1985: 108, 134); P. Williams (1985: 352); Foroohar (1989: 80–82); Kirk (1992: 82–97).

290. Dodson and Montgomery (1982: 166–174); Dodson and O'Shaughnessy (1990: 120–124); Mulligan (1991: 117–137).

291. Booth (1985: 141–143).

292. Black (1981: 88–97).

293. Kagan (1996: 31).
294. Booth (1985: 143–144).
295. Jarquín (2019: 96).
296. Pastor (1987: 44–45); Kagan (1996: 38).
297. Cardenal (2013: 65).
298. Weber (1981: 41–47).
299. Booth (1985: 160–165); Christian (1985: 51).
300. Booth (1985: 103–106); Everingham (1996: 140).
301. Booth (1985: 145, 165).
302. Dodson and Montgomery (1982: 173–174); Foroohar (1989: 117–142).
303. Booth (1985: 165–166).
304. Pastor (1987: 68–79).
305. Christian (1985: 70–82); Pastor (1987: 82–83).
306. Booth (1985: 168–169).
307. Jarquín (2019: 72–73).
308. Diederick (1981: 208–236).
309. Christian (1985: 84).
310. Somoza (1980: 240).
311. Booth (1985: 170).
312. Booth (1985: 135–137); Everingham (1996: 160–169).
313. Chavarria (1982: 34); Booth (1985: 173).
314. Booth (1985: 177).
315. Booth (1985: 175–177).
316. See Pastor (1987); Kagan (1996).
317. Pastor (1987: 121–126).
318. Pastor (1987: 120–141); Kagan (1996: 92–98).
319. Pastor (1987: 134–135, 145).
320. Booth (1985: 177).
321. Somoza (1980: 387).
322. Pastor (1987: 147–152); Jarquín (2019: 91–96).
323. Pastor (1987: 151); Ramírez (2007: 113).
324. Quoted in Pastor (1987: 151).
325. Pastor (1987: 151).
326. Gilbert (1988: 12).
327. Kinzer (1991: 72).
328. Diederick (1981: 321).
329. Christian (1985: 115).
330. Pastor (1987: 152).
331. Christian (1985: 116); Kinzer (1991: 72).
332. Quoted in Kinzer (1991: 73).
333. O'Kane (1990: 172).
334. Christian (1985: 117); Gilbert (1988: 12); Jarquín (2019: 96).
335. Chavarria (1982: 37); Kinzer (1991: 78–79).
336. O'Kane (1990: 173–175, 187–189).
337. Christian (1985: 133); O'Kane (1990); Reding (1991: 18).
338. Barbosa Miranda (2010).

339. See Gorman (1982: 131); Cajina (1997: 87-88); Barbosa Miranda (2010: 343-349).

340. Guzman (1996: 159); Cajina (1997: 99); Barbosa Miranda (2010: 343-349).

341. Black (1981: 225); Cajina (1997: 93).

342. Jarquín (2019: 4).

343. Gorman (1981: 140).

344. Booth (1985: 187-188).

345. Christian (1985: 122-123).

346. Quoted in Christian (1985: 121).

347. Christian (1985: 169-172).

348. Jarquín (2019: 114).

349. Gorman (1981: 144).

350. Walker (1991a: 82). Also Barbosa Miranda (2010: 350-355).

351. Booth (1985: 176); Prevost (1991: 111); Vanden and Prevost (1993: 114).

352. Booth (1985: 165). Also Kinzer (1991: 73, 173-177, 188-189).

353. Petras (1979: 14).

354. P. Williams (1985: 347-359); Dodson and O'Shaughnessy (1990: 3-7); Kirk (1992: 34-36, 82-97).

355. Kirk (1992: 101).

356. Lewellen (1989: 18); Dodson and O'Shaughnessy (1990: 148-149); Kirk (1992: 102-109, 139).

357. Gooren (2010: 52).

358. Christian (1985: 225-226).

359. Nichols (1982: 194); Close (1988: 70).

360. R. Harris (1987: 12); Walker (1991b: 10).

361. Kagan (1996: 411).

362. Christian (1985: 124-125); Kinzer (1991: 76); Spalding (1994: 66).

363. Black (1981: 207); Gilbert (1988: 106-107); Farhi (1990: 117); Spalding (1994: 66-67, 196).

364. See Spalding (1994, 1998); Everingham (1996: 170).

365. Spalding (1998: 156-159).

366. Mahoney (2001).

367. Colburn (1986); Luciak (1995: 104-105); Everingham (1996: 170).

368. Nichols (1982: 193-196).

369. Nichols (1982: 193-196); Kagan (1996: 411).

370. Christian (1985: 25); Weaver and Barnes (1991: 120-121); Everingham (1996).

371. Booth (1985: 90, 104-106, 194-204); Weaver and Barnes (1991: 111-121).

372. See Weber (1981: 54-60); Gilbert (1988); Everingham (1996); Jarquín (2019).

373. Gilbert (1988: 178).

374. Booth (1985: 158); Gilbert (1988); Zimmermann (2000: 61-67, 73-74).

375. Weber (1981: 76).

376. Zimmermann (2000).

377. See Miranda (1993: 97-113); Ramírez (2007: 122); Jarquín (2019: 132).

378. Quoted in Jarquín (2019: 132).

379. Zimmermann (2000: 9); Jarquín (2019: 123-124).

380. Jarquín (2019: 105). Also Gilbert (1988: 38, 109-110); Ramírez (2007).

381. Farhi (1990); K. Roberts (1990).

382. Ramírez (2007: 161).

383. Pastor (1987: 157). Also Berryman (1984: 238); Jarquín (2019: 132).

384. Quoted in Kagan (1996: 122).

385. Ramírez (2007); Jarquín (2019).

386. Irvin (1983: 127–128); Christian (1985: 124–125); Farhi (1990: 121).

387. Everingham (1996: 169).

388. Spalding (1994: 66).

389. Irvin (1983: 127).

390. Spalding (1987).

391. Spalding (1987; 1994: 66–67).

392. Weber (1981: 86).

393. Two progressive priests joined the revolutionary cabinet: Foreign Minister Miguel D'Escoto and Culture Minister Ernesto Cardenal.

394. Christian (1985: 213–214).

395. Quoted in Christian (1985: 214).

396. Berryman (1984); Dodson (1986: 44).

397. Gilbert (1988: 135–152).

398. Deere and Marchetti (1985: 91–93); Baumeister (1991: 237–239).

399. Christian (1985: 249).

400. See Deere and Marchetti (1985: 79); Baumeister (1991: 236–237); Spalding (1994: 81–83).

401. Baumeister (1991: 235); Spalding (1994: 84, 205).

402. Baumeister (1991: 236–237).

403. Baumeister (1991: 237).

404. Gilbert (1988: 101).

405. See Dickey (1985: 42); Colburn (1986: 56–59); Langlois (1997).

406. Deere and Marchetti (1985).

407. Deere and Marchetti (1985: 76–81, 90–93, 99); Baumeister (1991: 238); Ramírez (2007: 229); Jarquín (2019: 163–165).

408. Langlois (1997: 706–707). Also Deere and Marchetti (1985: 94); Miranda (1993: 233–234); Ramírez (2007: 229).

409. Bendaña (1982).

410. Miranda (1993: 70–74).

411. Quoted in Kinzer (1991: 186).

412. Jaime Wheelock, quoted in Kinzer (1991: 119).

413. Sergio Ramírez, quoted in Kagan (1996: 196).

414. Miranda (1993: 32–33, 70); Kagan (1996: 160–161); Jarquín (2019: 138–140).

415. Quoted in Kagan (1996: 303).

416. Dickey (1985: 72–75); Pastor (1987: 180–181).

417. Dickey (1985: 75). Also Pastor (1987: 180–181); Kagan (1996: 160–161).

418. Quoted in Jarquín (2019: 140).

419. Pastor (1987: 184–186).

420. Miranda (1993: 72, 155); Cajina (1997: 83–85); Ramírez (2007: 141–142).

421. Quoted in Jarquín (2019: 125).

422. Cajina (1997: 84).

423. Kinzer (1991: 96); Ramírez (2007: 150); Jarquín (2019: 137).

424. Pastor (1987: 194); Miranda (1993: 156–157); Kagan (1996: 192).

425. Kagan (1996: 192).

426. Pastor (1987: 194).

427. Quoted in Kinzer (1991: 96).

428. Kagan (1996: 127–128). Also Pastor (1987: 158, 161).

429. Pastor (1987: 190).

430. Robinson (1992: 12–13).

431. Kornbluh (1991: 327).

432. Kornbluh (1991: 326–329).

433. Kinzer (1991: 142, 249–250); Walker (1991b: 85).

434. Quoted in Kornbluh (1991: 326).

435. See Dickey (1985); Radu (1986); Morales Carazo (1989); Langlois (1997); T. Brown (2001).

436. Morales Carazo (1989: 33); Kinzer (1991: 137).

437. Morales Carazo (1989: 30–38); T. Brown (2001).

438. T. Brown (2001: 86–91).

439. Morales Carazo (1989: 5); Jarquín (2019: 166).

440. Kinzer (1991: 141).

441. Morales Carazo (1989: 47); Kinzer (1991: 138–144); T. Brown (2001: 81–83).

442. Pastor (1987: 213).

443. See Langlois (1997); T. Brown (2001).

444. Colburn (1986: 56–59).

445. Dickey (1985: 142).

446. Baumeister (1991: 238); Langlois (1997: 706–707); Jarquín (2019: 163–165).

447. Langlois (1997: 699–703, 709).

448. Conroy (1987: 55); Oquist (1992: 8); Cajina (1997: 21).

449. See Miranda (1993); Cajina (1997: 83–85); Ramírez (2007: 141–142).

450. Christian (1985: 193).

451. Gilbert (1988: 163).

452. Gilbert (1988: 122); Miranda (1993: 36–37, 109, 158, 259); Ramírez (2007: 142).

453. Miranda (1993: 13–14, 224).

454. Christian (1985: 187–189); Miranda (1993: 29–31).

455. Ramírez (2007: 113); also Miranda (1993: 19–21).

456. Kinzer (1991: 79).

457. Cajina (1997).

458. Dickey (1985: 269). Also Ramírez (2007: 141–142).

459. Cajina (1997: 85).

460. Spalding (1994: 99).

461. Booth (1985: 262). On plans for a smaller army, see Gorman (1982: 125) and Cajina (1997: 262).

462. Benítez et al. (1988: 314–315); Walker (1991a: 86; 1991b: 81–86); Cajina (1997: 103–108).

463. Booth (1985: 263); Close (1988: 176); Walker (1991b: 86).

464. Close (1988: 176); Walker (1991b: 81–86); Miranda (1993: 119).

465. Lacayo Oyanguren (2005: 140); also Miranda (1993: 100–101).

466. Dickey (1985: 269).

467. Vanden (1991: 312); Walker (1991a: 87); Kagan (1996: 254–255).

468. Langlois (1997: 698–699).

469. Cruz (1989); Kornbluh (1991: 343); Robinson (1992). The CIA reportedly paid off opposition parties to boycott the 1984 elections (Kornbluh 1991: 343).

470. Christian (1985: 220–221, 231–232); Lewellen (1989: 15); Dodson and O'Shaughnessy (1990: 218–219); Kinzer (1991: 203).

471. Booth (1985: 214); Foroohar (1989: 209–211).

472. Kinzer (1991: 199); Kagan (1996: 409).

473. Dickey (1985: 132–143).

474. Booth (1985: 207, 210); Christian (1985: 178–190); Kinzer (1991); Spalding (1994: 70–71).

475. Close (1985: 154); Cruz (1989: 66–76); Martí i Puig (1997: 90).

476. Miranda (1993: 187); Spalding (1994: 70–71, 214–215); Luciak (1995: 38–39).

477. Spalding (1994: 214–215).

478. Farhi (1990: 111, 121–122).

479. T. Brown (2001: 163–165).

480. Quoted in Christian (1985: 184).

481. Deere and Marchetti (1985: 98–100); Baumeister (1991: 235).

482. Spalding (1994: 78).

483. Kinzer (1991: 202–203); Kirk (1992: 168–169).

484. In 1983, Pope John Paul II was invited to visit Nicaragua, where, during a public mass for hundreds of thousands of people, he embraced the Church hierarchy and sharply criticized the regime. See Kirk (1992: 148–149); Cardenal (2013: 383–384).

485. Gilbert (1988: 146).

486. Vanden (1991: 312); Miranda (1993: 118–123, 133); Ramírez (2007: 161).

487. See Gilbert (1988: 170); Miranda (1993: 120, 127–133, 161).

488. Quoted in Miranda (1993: 161).

489. Kagan (1996: 415).

490. Kagan (1996: 410).

491. Dodson (1991: 178); Kirk (1992: 189–190).

492. Linfield (1991: 279–280).

493. Linfield (1991: 280–282); Kirk (1992: 189–190).

494. Vargas (1991: 44–45).

495. Spalding (1994: 98–101).

496. Ricciardi (1991: 259–260); Ramírez (2007: 163); Jarquín (2019: 214–215).

497. See Vanden (1991: 311–313); Kagan (1996: 527–529); Jarquín (2019: 202–250).

498. Kirk (1992: 177–209).

499. Kinzer (1991: 353); Kagan (1996: 550–553).

500. Edmisten (1990: 99–102); Linfield (1991: 280–282).

501. Spalding (1994: 97, 98–122).

502. Spalding (1994: 105–121, 254).

503. Miranda (1993: 244–248); Kagan (1996: 355–357).

504. Cajina (1997: 23–24).

505. Close (1985: 154; 1988: 133); Martí i Puig (1997: 90).

506. LASA (1984); Close (1999: 22–27).

507. Reding (1991).

508. Jarquín (2019: 193).

509. Gilbert (1988: 49–52); Miranda (1993: 13–14, 19–26); Martí i Puig (2009: 35–37).

510. Kinzer (1991: 79).

511. Quoted in Selbin (1993: 84).

512. Prevost (1991: 108–109); Miranda (1993: 24–31); Cajina (1997: 183).

513. Christian (1985: 187–189); Miranda (1993: 22–31).

514. Pastor (2002: 119–122). Also Kinzer (1991: 302–303, 351).

515. Kinzer (1991: 302–303).

516. Cruz (1989: 183, 246); Miranda (1993: 24–26).

517. Christian (1985: 273); Cruz (1989: 72–75, 110–111).

518. Kinzer (1991: 295).

519. Close (1988: 176); Walker (1991b: 81–86); Miranda (1993: 119).

520. Walker (1991b: 86–87); Miranda (1993: 118–119); Cajina (1997: 103–108); Premo (1997: 68).

521. Walker (1991a: 86–87); Herrera Zúñiga (1994: 122); Cajina (1997: 107–108); Premo (1997: 65).

522. Kinzer (1991: 179–180, 185); Miranda (1993: 189–191).

523. Gilbert (1988: 70). Also Benítez et al. (1988: 316); Serra (1991: 51–54).

524. Christian (1985: 70).

525. Gorman (1982: 131); Cajina (1997: 125).

526. Cajina (1997: 116–121).

527. Cajina (1997: 183, 99); Barbosa Miranda (2010: 346–349).

528. Guzman (1996: 159–160).

529. Gilbert (1988: 63, 83); Guzman (1996: 159–160); Cajina (1997: 99, 107, 121, 320); Barbosa Miranda (2010: 346–349).

530. Black (1981: 225).

531. Cajina (1997: 126).

532. Miranda (1993: 207).

533. Cajina (1997: 119–120); Barbosa Miranda (2010: 347–348).

534. Cajina (1997: 119–121); Barbosa Miranda (2010: 347–348).

535. Walker (1991a: 8).

536. Cajina (1997: 125).

537. Walker (2003: 150).

538. Miranda (1993); Cajina (1997).

539. Christian (1985: 273–279, 265).

540. Gilbert (1988: 149).

541. Gilbert (1988: 143–144).

542. Kinzer (1991: 199).

543. Spalding (1998: 181).

544. Spalding (1994: 214–215; 1998: 148–169).

545. Booth (1985: 215, 230–231); Kinzer (1991: 237); Linfield (1991: 279–280).

546. Christian (1985: 288); Kinzer (1991: 353); Valdivia (1991: 360).

547. Stahler-Sholk (1997: 82).

548. Cajina (1997: 23).

549. Kagan (1996: 570); Jarquín (2019: 214–215).

550. Vanden (1991: 313).

551. K. Roberts (1990); Kagan (1996: 527–529).

552. Pastor (2002: 217–229).

553. K. Roberts (1990: 96–97); Jarquín (2019: 202–250).

554. Jarquín (2019).

555. Kinzer (1991: 382–386).

556. Levitsky and Way (2010: 141–145).

557. Kinzer (1991: 387–388).

558. Miranda (1993: 273); Cajina (1997: 19–20); Orozco (2002: 89).

559. Weaver and Barnes (1991); LeoGrande (1992); Orozco (2002: 83).

560. Council of Freely Elected Heads of Government (1990); Leiken (1990).

561. Cajina (1997: 23–26).

562. Spalding (1997: 252; 1998: 163).

563. Vargas (1991: 80–81).

564. Oquist (1992: 34).

565. Kinzer (1991: 391).

566. UNO received $3.5 million in overt U.S. government assistance, as well as a reported $5 million from the CIA (Oquist 1992; Robinson 1992; Selbin 1993: 110).

567. Pastor (2002).

568. MacQueen (1997); Chabal (2003: 19); Mendy (2003: 38–41).

569. Hance (1967: 24).

570. Clarence-Smith (1975: 151–152).

571. Hance (1967: 24).

572. Aaby (1978); Chabal (1983); Fistein (2011).

573. Chabal (2003: 40, 46).

574. Chilcote (1977: 32); Chabal (2003: 44–45, 66–67, 155–172).

575. Chabal (2003: 56–57).

576. Zartman (1964: 9); MacQueen (1997: 18, 27); Dhada (1998: 572).

577. Dhada (1998: 572, 574); Reno (2011: 44).

578. Reno (2011: 44–45).

579. MacQueen (1997: 37); Chabal (2003: 83–89).

580. Chabal (2003: 19–20); Fistein (2011: 446).

581. Hodges (1979: 4).

582. Forrest (1992: 26–27); Chabal (2003: 9–20); International Crisis Group (2008: 2). About 2,000 European civilians lived in the colony (MacQueen 1997: 37).

583. Lopes (1987: 68).

584. Lyon (1980: 159); Forrest (1987: 101); Chabal (2003: 40, 46); Embaló (2012: 258).

585. Davidson (1981: 73); Chabal (2003: 73–74, 78).

586. Chabal (2003: 79, 82).

587. Goldstone (1998: 213); Chabal (2003: 79).

588. Dhada (1998: 576, 578). The FARP expanded to 5,000 by the mid-1960s.

589. Lopes (1987: 31); Dhada (1993: 25); International Crisis Group (2008: 5).

590. *Africa Report* (1964b: 27); Dhada (1998: 572–574); Chabal (2003: 76–77).

591. *Africa Confidential* (1968: 5); Dhada (1998: 574–576, 580).

592. Apparently, a limiting factor was the expense of supplying troops with beer (Dhada 1998: 584–585).

593. Davidson (1981: 79); MacQueen (1997: 77); Dhada (1998: 582); Chabal (2003: 107–120).

594. Zartman (1967: 69); Chabal (2003: 92, 93); Reno (2011: 45).

595. Zartman (1967: 68–69); Davidson (1981: 90–93, 129).

596. Reno (2011: 44).

597. Schoenmakers (1987: 131); Dhada (1993: 73, 75).

598. Lopes (1987: 97); International Crisis Group (2008: 7).

599. U.S. Department of State (1973); Davidson (1974).

600. Aaby (1978: 8).

601. *Africa Report* (1972: 11).

602. Chilcote (1977: 35); Davidson (1981: 101); Dhada (1993: 72–73, 91); Chabal (2003: 111, 113).

603. Lopes (1987: 72, 85–86); Dhada (1998: 586); Chabal (2003: 77); Reno (2011: 46).

604. Dhada (1998: 583–584).

605. Marcum (1967: 17); *Africa Confidential* (1972: 2); Davidson (1981); Chabal (1983: 192); MacQueen (1997: 98); Dhada (1998: 583, 585).

606. Chabal (2003: 96, 124).

607. Chabal (2003: 96, 125–130).

608. MacQueen (1997: 42); Chabal (2003: 103); Reno (2011: 46).

609. Chabal (2003: 132, 133); Reno (2011: 46).

610. Chabal (2003: 130–131).

611. *Africa Confidential* (1974: 5); Bergerol (1975: 18); MacQueen (1997: 99, 104, 109).

612. Forrest (2005: 250, 255).

613. Embaló (2012: 260); Havik (2012: 55); "The Status of Human Rights Organizations in Sub-Saharan Africa: Guinea-Bissau," University of Minnesota Human Rights Library, n.d., http://hrlibrary.umn.edu/africa/gbissau.htm.

614. Washington (1980: 20); Okafor (1988: 134).

615. Aaby (1978: 19); Davidson (1981: 170–172); Lopes (1987: 98–101).

616. Chilcote (1977: 36); Washington (1980: 20).

617. Washington (1980: 21); also Aaby (1978: 8).

618. Washington (1980: 21).

619. *Africa Confidential* (1977: 6); *Africa Report* (1987: 38); Topouzis (1989: 50).

620. *Africa Confidential* (1977: 7).

621. Lopes (1987: 107); also Andelman (1970); Aaby (1978: 14); Gomes (1986: 18); Dhada (1993: 55).

622. Davidson (1981: 65); Lopes (1987: 118).

623. *Africa Confidential* (1977: 6).

624. *Africa Confidential* (1977: 7); Topouzis (1989: 50).

625. *Africa Confidential* (1978: 6); Hodges (1979: 7).

626. Keefe (1977: 267).

627. *Africa Confidential* (1978: 7); Hodges (1979: 8–9).

628. *Africa Confidential* (1978: 7); MacQueen (1997: 222).

629. Washington (1980: 20); Davidson (1981: 170–172); Okafor (1988: 134).

630. Legum (1975: 8); Hodges (1979: 5).

631. Also Somerville (1986: 47–51); Hanlon (1990: 128, 129); MacQueen (1997: 216); Tvedten (1997: 38); Heywood (2000: 205–207); Hodges (2004: 9); Malache et al. (2005: 174–175); Reno (2011: 56–61).

632. Hodges (1979: 5).

633. Chaliand (1969: 48, 84); Chabal (1983: 191; 2003: 105); Lopes (1987: 69); Forrest (1992: 36); Dhada (1998: 577, 578); Embaló (2012: 258, 259).

634. Guinea-Bissau "achieved its independence with no infrastructure, industry, or trained personnel; less than 600 km of paved roads; [and] half a dozen bridges in a country crossed by dozens of rivers" (Gomes 1986: 17). Also Hodges (1979: 4); Davidson (1981: 90); Okafor (1988: 125).

635. Fistein (2011: 445); Mesfin (2019: 5).

636. Zartman (1967); Rudebeck (1974: 132); Dhada (1993: 18–27, 119–120); Chabal (2003: 79, 80, 100).

637. See data from Correlates of War "National Material Capabilities" data set, version 5, https://correlatesofwar.org/data-sets/national-material-capabilities.

638. Chabal (2003: 132, 133); Reno (2011: 46).

639. P. Munslow (1981: 112).

640. Embaló (2012: 258); Havik (2012: 57).

641. Lopes (1987: 117).

642. Forrest (1992: 57).

643. Lopes (1987: 133–134).

644. Hodges (1979: 6); P. Munslow (1981: 112–113); Forrest (1992: 47, 55, 99).

645. Keefe (1977: 267); *Africa Report* (1981: 24).

646. Chaliand (1969: 48); Chabal (2003: 139–140).

647. Topouzis (1989); Dhada (1998: 586).

648. Forrest (1987: 100); Dhada (1993: 128).

649. P. Munslow (1981: 112); *Africa Report* (1981: 24); Frempong (2005: 6); "The Status of Human Rights Organizations in Sub-Saharan Africa."

650. *Africa Confidential* (1980: 4–5); Chabal (1983: 199); Forrest (1987: 102).

651. Forrest (1987: 104).

652. *Africa Confidential* (1980: 4–5); Forrest (1987: 105).

653. *Africa Report* (1986: 34); Forrest (1987: 109); Embaló (2012: 261).

654. *Africa Report* (1986: 34).

655. Embaló (2012: 261–262).

656. Levitsky and Way (2010).

657. Forrest (2005: 251).

658. Forrest (2005: 251).

659. Forrest (2005: 253).

660. Embaló (2012: 264–265).

661. Forrest (2005: 256); Embaló (2012: 264–269).

662. Forrest (2005: 257).

663. Legum (1975: 8).

664. Saul (1985: 24); MacQueen (1997: 44, 45); Newitt (2002: 190); Nuvunga (2017: 65).

665. Way et al. (2019).

666. Somerville (1986: 56–58); Tvedten (1997: 44); Hodges (2004: 50).

667. Field (2014: 6).

668. Blasier (1985: 141–142); Field (2014: 14).

Chapter 9

1. In Iran, the clerical government maintained the prerevolutionary army but built the powerful Islamic Revolutionary Guard, which it tightly controlled—and relied heavily upon for the regime's security.

2. Regimes in Afghanistan, Cambodia, and Hungary did not survive their respective reactive sequence and thus cannot provide a test of this part of the argument.

3. Shelley (1996: 181–182).

4. Beissinger (2002: 70); Crump (2014: 101).

5. The Algerian regime, which also failed to develop strong authoritarian pillars, survived for longer but was unstable.

6. Although the revolutionary government attempted to nationalize some factories and expropriate some large landholdings, it was legalistic, committed to private property, and sensitive to the reactions of foreign businesses. See Upton (1980: 358–390); Tikka (2014: 97–98); Engelstein (2018: 283).

7. Huntington (1968: 270–273).

8. Seton Watson (1956).

9. Pirjevec (2018: 64).

10. R. McCormick (2015).

11. Perica (2002: 96); Pirjevec (2018: 64–84).

12. Ulam (1952: 102); Denitch (1976: 466).

13. Pirjevec (2018: 70, 81); also Ulam (1952: 74); Denitch (1976: 467); Benson (2001: 75); Biondich (2011: 146–147).

14. Ulam (1952: 74); Denitch (1976: 467); Benson (2001: 75); Biondich (2011: 146–147).

15. Denitch (1976: 469–471); H. Williams (2020: 394).

16. Ulam (1952: 74); Denitch (1976: 467); Benson (2001: 75); Biondich (2011: 146–147); H. Williams (2020: 394–398).

17. These included Croats, Montenegrins, Muslims, Serbs, and Slovenes.

18. A. Djilas (1995: 116–117); Biondich (2011: 147); Hoare (2011: 202).

19. Ulam (1952: 34, 82); Seton Watson (1956: 220); Perica (2002: 96); Obradović (2013: 381); Trifković (2016: 254, 269–279); Pirjevec (2018: 75, 81, 142).

20. Trifković (2016: 254, 269); Piffer (2018: 439).

21. Ulam (1952: 124); Pirjevec (2018: 59); H. Williams (2020: 396).

22. Ulam (1952: 34, 82); Seton Watson (1956: 220); A. Djilas (1995: 122); Perica (2002: 96); Obradović (2013: 381); Trifković (2016: 254, 269–279); Pirjevec (2018: 75, 81, 142).

23. Pirjevec (2018: 152).

24. Seton Watson (1956: 220).

25. Ulam (1952: 81–82).

26. Ulam (1952: 34, 82); Seton Watson (1956: 220); Banac (1988: 158); Dimitrijevic (2019: 11); Nielson (2020: 19). In the mid-1960s, UDBA had dossiers on more than a third of the working population (Dimitrijevic 2019: 25).

27. Pirjevec (2018: 202, 220).

28. Denitch (1976: 470, 473).

29. Jonjić (2007: 111); Pirjevec (2018: 151); Janjetovic (2020: 403).

30. Denitch (1976: 470, 473); Mirescu (2015: 102); Pirjevec (2018: 153, 144).

31. Pirjevec (2018: 160); Piffer (2019: 431–432); Janjetovic (2020: 406).

32. Barnett (2006: 82); Pirjevec (2018: 153–154); Janjetovic (2020: 403).

33. Obradović (2013: 380); Janjetovic (2020: 404).

34. Pirjevec (2018: 165); Janjetovic (2020: 403).

35. Murray (1953); Palmer (2000: 200); Mirescu (2015: 83).

36. Matijevic (2006: 131–132); K. Buchenau (2014: 62, 64).

37. Murray (1953: 23); Palmer (2000: 203); Jonjić (2007: 136); Mirescu (2015: 99).

38. Palmer (2000: 218–219); Matijevic (2006: 137–138); Jonjić (2007: 112); Mirescu (2015: 100). Attacks on clergy grew so widespread that Tito had to publicly call for a halt to physical assaults (Volf 1989: 25).

39. Matijevic (2006: 138).

40. Murray (1953); Pirjevec (2018: 161, 164).

41. Basta (2010: 96).

42. Jonjić (2007: 112).

43. Niebuhr (2017: 285); Pirjevec (2018: 168); Unkovski-Korica (2020: 463).

44. Niebuhr (2017: 286); Pirjevec (2018: 169).

45. Niebuhr (2017: 292).

46. Mehilli (2011: 52).

47. Niebuhr (1987: 287–291); Pirjevec (2018: 156).

48. Pirjevec (2018: 163).

49. Barnett (2006: 84); Niebuhr (2017: 286); Pirjevec (2018: 163–166).

50. Quoted in Pirjevec (2018: 167).

51. Niebuhr (2017: 292); Pirjevec (2018: 169, 170).

52. Ulam (1952: 80–83, 115); Banac (1988: 126); Perović (2007); Janjetovic (2020: 407).

53. Banac (1988: 133); Pirjevec (2018: 214, 220).

54. Thorpe (1998: 641–642).

55. Ulam (1952: 80–83, 115); Banac (1988: 160); Barnett (2006: 85–86); Pirjevec (2018: 194); Dimitrijevic (2019: 11).

56. Stalin's comment was reported by Khrushchev. See Banac (1988: 117); Pirjevec (2018: 191); also Ulam (1952: 115).

57. Banac (1988).

58. Banac (1988: x, 147–149); Pirjevec (2018: 184). In addition, Banac (1988: x, 151, 153, 157) estimates that about a fifth of the KPJ rank and file supported the Cominform decision to expel Yugoslavia, in part because they expected Stalin to come out on top. The KPJ at the time also feared that there was significant "clandestine" support for the Cominform in the military (Banac 1988: 159).

59. Barnett (2006: 87).

60. Ulam (1952: 98); also Banac (1988: 137).

61. Ulam (1952: 124, 132); Banac (1988: x); Benson (2001: 95); Previšić (2020: 71).

62. Ulam (1952: 124); Banac (1988: 128); Benson (2001: 95); Previšić (2020: 71).

63. Banac (1988: 124); Pirjevec (2018: 191).

64. Ulam (1952: 83, 109, 124); Banac (1988: 119, 158); Irvine (1991: 337); Barnett (2006: 87); Pirjevec (2018: 187, 196); Previšić (2020: 71).

65. Vladisavljević (2008: 54).

66. Banac (1988: 137–142); Pirjevec (2018: 216); Dimitrijevic (2019: 18). Most notable among the decentralizing reforms was the introduction of workers' "self-management," which was intended to replace central planning and give elected groups of employees a voice in running enterprises. See Basta (2010: 97–98); Unkovski-Korica (2020: 464–465).

67. Estrin (1991: 190).

68. Matijevic (2006: 122); Janjetovic (2020: 405).

69. Ramet (1982: 256); Perica (2002: 536).

70. Ramet (1982: 260); Matijevic (2006: 129–130).

71. Burg (1986: 172); Perica (2002: 542–556).

72. G. Klein (1975: 351); Benson (2001: 111–112); Basta (2010: 99–100); Mirescu (2015: 103).

73. Singleton (1972: 176); G. Klein (1975: 357); Pickering and Baskin (2008: 526).

74. Hasan (1981: 64); Irvine (2008: 161); Pickering and Baskin (2008: 526).

75. Benson (2001: 122); Irvine (2008: 155–157).

76. Irvine (2008: 155).

77. G. Klein (1975: 359–360).

78. Irvine (2008: 149).

79. Other leading members of the revolutionary generation who died or retired in the late 1970s or early 1980s included Edvard Kardelj from Slovenia, Vladimir Bakarić from Croatia, and Miloš Minić and Petar Stambolić from Serbia (Vladisavljević 2008: 45).

80. OECD (1988: 9); Vladisavljević (2008: 1, 47–54).

81. OECD (1988: 9); Vladisavljević (2008: 46–47); Ritter (2017: 143–144).

82. LeBor (2004).

83. Sell (2002); LeBor (2004); Vladisavljević (2008).

84. Mirescu (2015: 107); Ragazzi (2017).

85. The APL (called the Communist Party until 1948) was created by Yugoslav agents in Albania in 1941 but gained effective autonomy during the conflict. See Prifti (1978: 200); Vickers (2011: 160); Fevziu (2016: 128). By the time it gained power in 1944, the APL had been shaped much more by wartime mobilization than by Yugoslav assistance (Mitrojorgji 2020: 372).

86. Hibbert (1991: 58).

87. Hibbert (1991: 115); Fevziu (2016: 68). Italy occupied Albania in 1939 and was replaced by German forces following the fall of Mussolini in 1943.

88. Mehilli (2011: 35); Fevziu (2016: 90).

89. Prifti (1978: 16, 218); Hibbert (1991: 16, 23, 118); Mehilli (2011: 11, 35). Military size from Correlates of War "National Material Capabilities" data set, version 5, https://correlatesofwar.org/data-sets/national-material-capabilities.

90. Prifti (1978: 16); Hibbert (1991: 16, 23); Mehilli (2011: 11); Fevziu (2016: 95).

91. Prifti (1978: 195); Hibbert (1991: 115, 235); Fevziu (2016: 78, 83).

92. Biberaj (1990: 15); Mehilli (2011: 56).

93. Biberaj (1990: 19); Hibbert (1991: 233); Fevziu (2016: 108).

94. Prifti (1978: 14); Hibbert (1991: 234); Mehilli (2011: 52); Fevziu (2016: 124–125).

95. See Fevziu (2016: 139); Niebuhr (2017).

96. Fevziu (2016: 148–149).

97. Mehilli (2020: 448–449).

98. Fevziu (2016: 172–173).

99. Biberaj (1990: 44). Data from Correlates of War "National Material Capabilities" data set. Albania ranked among the top ten most militarized autocracies (in terms of military personnel per capita) until 1972 and was in the top twenty until the regime collapsed in 1992.

100. Fevziu (2016: 160).

101. Mehilli (2011: 11).

102. Mehilli (2011: 9).

103. Mehilli (2020: 448).

104. Mehilli (2011); Fevziu (2016: 148–149); Marku (2020).

105. See detailed descriptions of these events in Mehilli (2011: 16–22; 2020: 449–450).

106. Mehilli (2011: 50).

107. Mehilli (2020: 451).

108. Biberaj (1990: 25); Fevziu (2016: 151).

109. Skendi (1962); Marku (2020).

110. Prifti (1978: 218).

111. Soares de Oliveira (2015: 95).

112. L. Henderson (1979: 249); Soares de Oliveira (2015: 117).

113. Somerville (1986: 29–40, 45).

114. Somerville (1986: 50–53).

115. Somerville (1986: 47–48); Heywood (2000: 205–207); Hodges (2004: 9).

116. T. Young (1988: 171).

117. Somerville (1986: 51); Tvedten (1997: 38).

118. Hodges (2004: 9).

119. Tvedten (1997: 41). Although the end of the Cold War brought a peace accord in 1994, Savimbi withdrew from the agreements after losing elections and the war continued until Savimbi's death in 2002. See Tvedten (1997: 41).

120. Tvedten (1997: 42).

121. Somerville (1986: 56–58); Tvedten (1997: 44); Hodges (2004: 50).

122. Somerville (1986: 48).

123. Tvedten (1997: 42).

124. Sogge (2009: 12); also Hodges (2004: 72–73).

125. Smaldone (1991: 212).

126. Somerville (1986: 54).

127. Soares de Oliveira (2015: 91).

128. Hodges (2004: 88–94); Soares de Oliveira (2015: 104–105, 121).

129. Soares de Oliveira (2015: 99–101).

130. Hodges (2004).

131. Shore (1974: 5–6); Emerson (2014: 21).

132. MacQueen (1997: 44); Derluguian (2012: 82, 91).

133. Simpson (1993: 316); Hall and Young (1997: 17).

134. See Shore (1974: 7); Henriksen (1978); B. Munslow (1983: 82); Sumich and Honwana (2007: 18).

135. Newitt (2002: 192).

136. "2d Night of Mozambique Strife Is Intense," *New York Times*, December 19, 1975; CIA (1985); Malache et al. (2005: 174).

137. Sumich and Honwana (2007: 9).

138. Hanlon (1990: 46–49).

139. Hanlon (1990: 122, 128–131); Simpson (1993: 325).

140. Newitt (2002: 190); Reno (2011: 56–57).

141. Hanlon (1990: 76); Reno (2011: 56–57).

142. Saul (1985: 12); Simpson (1993: 325); Malache et al. (2005: 163, 166, 174, 175); Reno (2011: 59–61, 63).

143. Emerson (2014: 24).

144. Kempton (1991: 21); Newitt (2002: 190); Nuvunga (2017: 65).

145. Hall and Young (1997: 19); Malache et al. (2005: 162).

146. Saul (1985: 91); Emerson (2014: 91).

147. Malache et al. (2005: 179–183).

148. At the same time, Mozambican civil society was otherwise weak (Civicus Moniter n.d.: 11). For example, the country's main trade union federation was founded by Frelimo and maintained close ties to the government. Thus, we code destruction of independent power centers as partial.

149. See "2d Night of Mozambique Strife."

150. Bartolli and Mutisi (2014: 168). Also "Former Mozambican Army Chief Denies Coup Charge," Reuters, August 17, 1992.

151. Manning (2005: 234–235); Levitsky and Way (2010: 250–251). Frelimo won the 2019 presidential election with 73 percent of the vote and captured nearly three-quarters of parliament.

152. Reyntjens (2004: 209); Jowell (2014: 278).

153. Reyntjens (2004: 209, 204; 2013: 253).

154. Human Rights Watch (1999); Lakin and Beloff (2014: 52); Reyntjens (2016); Roessler and Verhoeven (2016: 109).

155. Moss (2014: 436–441).

156. Moss (2014: 441); Kelley (2017: 113–114).

157. Mgbako (2005: 205); Samset (2011: 273); Moss (2014: 236–241); S. Turner (2014).

158. Prunier (2009: 26, 56, 68); Roessler and Verhoeven (2016: 137).

159. Roessler and Verhoeven (2016: 127, 136).

160. Prunier (2009: 26, 56, 68); Roessler and Verhoeven (2016: 306).

161. Pottier (2002: 183); Reyntjens (2004: 195–196); Kelley (2017: 127–128).

162. Reyntjens (2004: 195).

163. A year later, when Kabila broke with the RPF and began supporting the Interahamwe, the RPF invaded *again*. The conflict ended in 2002 after the Congo

government agreed to halt support for the insurgents. See Prunier (2009: chaps. 6–8); Roessler and Verhoeven (2016).

164. Reyntjens (2004: 183); Purdeková (2011: 485); Jowell (2014: 278).

165. Correlates of War "National Material Capabilities" data set.

166. Jowell (2014: 282).

167. Jowell (2014: 284).

168. Reyntjens (2004: 183); Purdeková (2011: 487–489).

169. Ingelaere (2014); Bentrovato (2015).

170. Purdeková (2011: 482).

171. Reyntjens (2004: 193); Purdeková (2011: 492–493).

172. Van Hoyweghen (1996: 379, 395–400).

173. Jowell (2014: 279).

174. In 1995, Prime Minister Faustin Twagiramungu and Interior Minister Seth Sendashonga resigned and went into exile. In 2000, National Assembly Speaker Joseph Sebarenzi was forced to resign after denouncing government abuse. A month later, Prime Minister Pierre-Célestin Rwigema was expelled and sought asylum in the United States. In 2004, the RPF general secretary, Theogene Rudasingwa, fled to the United States after falling out with Kagame. Patrick Karegeya, the former head of external intelligence, was jailed for eighteen months after breaking with Kagame and then escaped to South Africa. See Human Rights Watch (2000); Reyntjens (2004: 180–182; 2015: 24); "Rwandan Army Spokesperson Arrested over Indiscipline," *BBC Monitoring Africa*, May 5, 2005; "Rwanda; Former ESO Chief Flees," *Africa News*, November 28, 2007; Prunier (2009: 45).

175. Reyntjens (2015: 25).

176. Pool (2001: 63); Tareke (2009: 63).

177. Gebre-Medhin (1984: 54); Stewart (2021: 98, 100–103, 108–109, 122).

178. Connell (2001: 356–357); Pool (2001: 59); Stewart (2021: 110, 120–133).

179. Stewart (2021: 112–115).

180. Joireman (1996: 273); Makki (1996: 493); Tronvoll (1998: 471); Rock (2000: 224); Pool (2001: 188); Kibreab (2009b: 40–41).

181. Tronvoll (1998: 481).

182. Pool (2001: 109).

183. Reid (2011: 193); Calchi Novati (2021: 16).

184. Reid (2011: 232–233).

185. Reid (2011: 232); see also Lefebvre (1995); Tareke (2009: 344).

186. Abbink (2003: 223).

187. Reid (2011: 233).

188. Abbink (2003); Reid (2011: 221).

189. Abbink (2003: 220); Tareke (2009: 346).

190. Connell (1997: 67); Reid (2011: 232).

191. Makki (1996: 478).

192. Pool (2001: 60). The state even imposed a tax on Eritrean diaspora. Economist Intelligence Unit (2016).

193. Steves (2003: 125); Kibreab (2009a).

194. Kibreab (2009a: 44); Reid (2011: 229); Landinfo (2015: 7–9).

195. Kibreab (2009a: 49).

196. Correlates of War "National Material Capabilities" data set.

197. Calculated from Correlates of War, "National Material Capabilities" data set.

198. Tareke (2009: 69).

199. Pool (2001: 152).

200. Woldemariam (2018: 179–181).

201. For example, the regime's security forces fired on disabled veterans who were protesting their terrible living conditions, killing five (Mengisteab and Yohannes 2005: 14).

202. On the 1993 action, see Mengisteab and Yohannes (2005: 19); on the 2013 action, see International Crisis Group (2013).

203. Tronvoll and Mekonnen (2014: 11).

204. Tareke (2009: 65); see also Iyob (1995: 124).

205. Shinn (2003).

206. Human Rights Watch (2009, 2019).

207. AllAfrica (2001); Home Office (2004: 6.75); Human Rights Watch (2019).

208. AllAfrica (2001); See Home Office (2004: 4.25); Human Rights Watch (2019). According to Amnesty International, most have died in prison. See "Amnesty Urges Immediate Release to Detained Eritrean Politicians, Ministers," *Sudan Tribune*, September 17, 2011.

209. Eritrea Focus (2019).

210. These cases are Albania, Angola, Eritrea, Mozambique, Rwanda, and Yugoslavia.

211. This includes Mozambique, which failed to build a strong state or destroy all independent institutions, but nevertheless has a combined score of two out of three pillars.

212. Selznick (1952); Friedrich and Brzezinski (1965: 3, 15).

213. Selznick (1952); Friedrich and Brzezinski (1965).

214. Garrido (1982).

215. A similar argument is made by Slater (2010) and Slater and Fenner (2011).

216. Fagen (1969); Selbin (1993).

217. Selbin (1993: 13).

218. Cook and Dimitrov (2017).

219. Magaloni (2006); Waldner (2017).

220. Skocpol (1979: 288); Beissinger (2022).

221. S. Hanson (2010: 53); Roessler and Verhoeven (2016: 33); McAdams (2017); Vu (2017).

222. Golan (1988); M. Katz (1990); Roessler and Verhoeven (2016: 34).

223. Beissinger (2022).

224. Beissinger (2022) also argues that other structural changes at the end of the twentieth century, including urbanization, the decline of interstate war, and the weakening of landed elites, made social revolutions less likely.

225. Roessler and Verhoeven (2016: 43). For example, Museveni's National Resistance Movement, which won power in Uganda in 1986, chose "reformist over revolutionary goals," maintaining friendly relations with neighboring states and becoming an "exemplar of the Washington Consensus" (C. Young 2001: 209; Kasfir 2005: 275; Mwenda 2007: 29–30). Similarly, the TPLF in Ethiopia, which was originally a

Marxist movement, embraced market liberalization and maintained friendly relations with the United States and most of its neighbors (J. Young 1997: 167, 209; Prendergast and Duffield 1999: 49; Hagmann and Abbink 2011: 582; Clapham 2017: 69).

226. The Khmer Rouge received critical assistance from Vietnam during its rise. The Chinese Communist Party and revolutionary movements in Angola, Guinea-Bissau, and Mozambique benefited from significant Soviet bloc support. In Vietnam and Yugoslavia, powerful revolutionary movements emerged without significant communist support but obtained communist assistance near the end of their armed struggles for power.

227. For example, see Bueno de Mesquita et al. (2005).

228. Skocpol (1979: 170).

229. Slater (2009, 2010); Levitsky and Way (2010, 2012); LeBas (2011).

230. LeBas (2011).

231. Slater (2010).

232. Levitsky and Way (2010, 2012); Slater (2010); LeBas (2011).

233. Also Levitsky and Way (2010, 2012); Slater (2010); LeBas (2011).

234. Reuter and Gandhi (2011).

235. See Slater (2010); LeBas (2011).

236. Slater (2010: 5).

237. Jamestown Foundation (2011).

238. Decalo (1976: 107–108).

239. Heilbrunn (1997); Seely (2005: 368).

240. Svolik (2012: 5).

241. Way et al. (2019).

242. For a more detailed account, see Way et al. (2019).

243. Quoted in Barany (2012: 238). Also Gutteridge (1969: 24–29).

244. Lupogo (2001: 79).

245. Bienen (1968: 59); CIA (1983b); Barany (2012: 240–241; 2014: 610).

246. CIA (1984b). In addition, it created a new Chinese-trained security service, the Tanzanian Intelligence and Security Service, as well as a party-controlled people's militia (CIA 1975, 1983b). See also Barany (2014: 610).

247. CIA (1983a, 1983b).

248. See Slater (2010); Slater and Fenner (2011).

249. See Greitens (2016).

250. Beissinger (2022: 4).

251. Rotberg (2003); Sarkees et al. (2003: 52–53); Münkler (2004); Roessler and Verhoeven (2016: 86).

252. Bearden (2001: 24); Dorronsoro (2005: 276–277); Nojumi (2008: 91); Ahmad (2017).

253. Khalilzad (1997); Dorronsoro (2005: 233); Murshed (2006: 42); Taylor and Botea (2008).

254. Warrick (2015: 117–120).

255. Stern and Berger (2015: 16–17); Warrick (2015: 119).

256. Warrick (2015: 167).

257. Warrick (2015: 243).

258. Stern and Berger (2015: 45–46).

259. Stern and Berger (2015: 47–49).

260. Stern and Berger (2015: 186). At its height, ISIS nominally controlled the lives of up to 12 million people. "ISIS Caliphate Crumbles as Last Village in Syria Falls," *New York Times*, March 23, 2019. Because ISIS never controlled a state capital or was recognized internationally, it is, according to our coding rules, a regional rebellion and thus not included in the list of revolutionary regimes.

261. "ISIS Caliphate Crumbles."

262. "ISIS Caliphate Crumbles."

263. Giustozzi (2019: 240–241); "How the Taliban Outlasted a Superpower: Tenacity and Carnage," *New York Times*, May 26, 2020.

Aaby, Peter. 1978. *The State of Guinea-Bissau: African Socialism or Socialism in Africa?* Scandinavian Institute of African Studies Research Report no. 45.

Abbas, Hassan. 2014. *The Taliban Revival: Violence and Extremism on the Pakistan Afghanistan Frontier.* New Haven, CT: Yale University Press.

Abbink, Jon. 2003. "Badme and the Ethio-Eritrean Border: The Challenge of Demarcation in the Post-War Period." *Africa: Rivista trimestrale di studi e documentazione dell'Istituto italiano per l'Africa e l'Oriente* 58, no. 2: 219–231.

Abrahamian, Ervand. 1980. "Structural Causes of the Iranian Revolution." *MERIP Reports* 87 (May): 21–26.

Abrahamian, Ervand. 1982. *Iran between Two Revolutions.* Princeton, NJ: Princeton University Press.

Abrahamian, Ervand. 2008. *A History of Modern Iran.* New York: Cambridge University Press.

Abrahams, Harlan, and Arturo Lopez-Levy. 2011. *Raúl Castro and the New Cuba: A Close-Up View of Change.* Jefferson, NC: McFarland.

Abuza, Zachary. 1998. "Leadership Transition in Vietnam since the Eighth Party Congress: The Unfinished Congress." *Asian Survey* 38, no. 12: 1105–1121.

Abuza, Zachary. 2001. *Renovating Politics in Contemporary Vietnam.* Boulder, CO: Lynne Rienner.

Acharya, Avidit, Matthew Blackwell, and Maya Sen. 2016. "Explaining Causal Findings without Bias: Detecting and Assessing Direct Effects." *American Political Science Review* 110, no. 3: 512–529.

Achy, Lahcen. 2013. *The Price of Stability in Algeria.* Beirut: Carnegie Middle East Center.

Ackroyd, William S. 1991. "Military Professionalism, Education, and Political Behavior in Mexico." *Armed Forces and Society* 18, no. 1: 81–96.

Adamson, Kay. 1998. *Algeria: A Study in Competing Ideologies.* London: Cassell.

Addi, Lauhouari. 1998. "Algeria's Army, Algeria's Agony." *Foreign Affairs* 77, no. 4: 44–53.

Addo-Fening, Robert. 1972. "Gandhi and Nkrumah: A Study of Non-Violence and Non-Co-operation Campaigns in India and Ghana as an Anti-colonial Strategy." *Transactions of the Historical Society of Ghana* 13, no. 1: 65–85.

Adelman, Jonathan R. 1982. "Toward a Typology of Communist Civil-Military Relations." In Jonathan R. Adelman, ed., *Communist Armies in Politics.* Boulder, CO: Westview Press.

Adelman, Jonathan R. 1985. *Revolution, Armies and War: A Political History.* Boulder, CO: Lynne Rienner.

Africa Confidential. 1968. "Portuguese Guinea: More War than Most." 8, no. 3: 5.

Africa Confidential. 1972. "Portuguese Africa: Facing the Music." 13, no. 1: 2.

Africa Confidential. 1974. "Guinea-Bissau: The New State." 15, no. 22: 5.

Africa Confidential. 1977. "Guinea-Bissau: Political Divergence." 18, no. 8: 6.

Africa Confidential. 1978. "Guinea-Bissau: Western Influence Grows." 19, no. 20: 6.

Africa Confidential. 1980. "Guinea-Bissau: The Cape Verdian Downfall." 21, no. 24: 4–5.

Africa Report. 1964a. "Ghana Revisited." February 1: 25.

Africa Report. 1964b. "Portuguese Guinea." October: 27.

Africa Report. 1972. "Africa Day by Day: May 19." June: 11.

Africa Report. 1981. "Guinea-Bissau Coup Leaders to Try Cabral." January–February: 24.

Africa Report. 1986. "Guinea-Bissau: Vieira Foils Another Coup." January–February: 34.

Africa Report. 1987. "Guinea-Bissau: Trading Places." November–December: 38.

Afshari, Ali, and Graham Underwood. 2009. "Iran in Ferment: The Green Wave." *Journal of Democracy* 20, no. 4: 6–10.

Ageron, Charles-Robert. 1991. *Modern Algeria: A History from 1830 to the Present*. London: Hurst.

Aguayo Quezada, Sergio. 2001. *La charola: Una historia de los servicios de inteligencia en México*. Mexico City: Raya en el Agua/Grijalbo.

Aguila, Marcos, and Jeffrey Bortz. 2012. "The Rise of Gangsterism and *Charrismo*: Labor Violence and the Postrevolutionary Mexican State." In Will G. Pansters, ed., *Violence, Coercion, and State-Making in Twentieth-Century Mexico: The Other Half of the Centaur*. Stanford, CA: Stanford University Press.

Aguilar Zinser, Adolfo. 1990. "Civil-Military Relations in Mexico." In Louis W. Goodman, Johanna Mendelson Forman, and Juan Rial, eds., *The Military and Democracy: The Future of Civil-Military Relations in Latin America*. Lexington, MA: Lexington Books.

Aguirre, Benigno E. 2002. "Social Control in Cuba." *Latin American Politics and Society* 44, no. 2: 67–98.

Ahlman, Jeffrey. 2010. "The Algerian Question in Nkrumah's Ghana, 1958–1960: Debating 'Violence' and 'Nonviolence' in African Decolonization." *Africa Today* 57, no. 2: 66–84.

Ahlman, Jeffrey. 2011. "Road to Ghana: Nkrumah, Southern Africa and the Eclipse of a Decolonizing Africa." *Kronos* 37, no. 1: 23–40.

Ahmad, Aisha. 2017. *Jihad & Co.: Black Markets and Islamist Power*. New York: Oxford University Press.

Ahmed, Naseem. 2010. "General Musharaf's Taliban Policy 1999–2008." *The Dialogue* 5, no. 2: 1–29.

Alahmad, Nida, and Arang Keshavarzian. 2010. "A War on Multiple Fronts." *Middle East Report* 40, no. 4: 16–28.

Alamdari, Kazem. 2005. "The Power Structure of the Islamic Republic of Iran: Transition from Populism to Clientelism, and Militarization of the Government." *Third World Quarterly* 26, no. 8: 1285–1301.

Alavi, Bahram. 1989. "Rival Government Factions Emerge Clearly as Iran's Post-Khomeini Power Struggle Begins." *The Washington Report on Middle East Affairs*, May.

Albats, Evgeniia. 1994. *The State within a State: The KGB and Its Hold on Russia*. New York: Farrar, Straus, Giroux.

Albertus, Michael. 2015. *Autocracy and Redistribution: The Politics of Land Reform*. New York: Cambridge University Press.

Alcocer, Jorge V. 1995. "Recent Electoral Reforms in Mexico: Prospects for a Real Multiparty Democracy." In Riordan Roett, ed., *The Challenge of Institutional Reform in Mexico*. Boulder, CO: Lynne Rienner.

Alexander, Robert J. 1958. *The Bolivian National Revolution*. New Brunswick, NJ: Rutgers University Press.

Alexander, Robert J. 1982a. *Bolivia: Past, Present, and Future of Its Politics*. New York: Praeger.

Alexander, Robert J. 1982b. "The Labor Movement during and since the 1952 Revolution." In Jerry R. Landman, ed., *Modern-Day Bolivia: Legacy of the Revolution and Prospects for the Future*. Tempe: Center for Latin American Studies, Arizona State University.

Alexander, Robert J. 2005. *A History of Organized Labor in Bolivia*. Westport, CT: Praeger.

Alexander, Robert J. 2012. "Introduction." In Joseph C. Holtey, ed., *Victor Paz Estenssoro: A Political Biography*. Scotts Valley, CA: CreateSpace Independent Publishing Platform.

Alexeyeva, Liudmilla, and Valery Chalidze. 1985. *Mass Unrest in the USSR*. Office of Net Assessment of the Department of Defense, report no. 19 (August).

Alfoneh, Ali. 2008. "The Revolutionary Guards' Role in Iranian Politics." *Middle East Quarterly*, Fall: 3–14.

Alfoneh, Ali. 2010. "The Basij Resistance Force." In Robin Wright, ed., *The Iran Primer: Power, Politics, and U.S. Policy*. Washington, DC: United States Institute of Peace Press.

Alfoneh, Ali. 2013. *Iran Unveiled: How the Revolutionary Guards Is Turning Iran from Theocracy into Military Dictatorship*. Washington, DC: AEI Press.

AllAfrica. 2001. "Eritrea: Party Puts Its Case against Dissidents." September 26. https://allafrica.com/stories/200109260023.html.

Allen, Robert C. 2003. *Farm to Factory: A Reinterpretation of the Soviet Industrial Revolution*. Princeton, NJ: Princeton University Press.

Álvarez Montalván, Emilio. 1994. *Las fuerzas armadas en Nicaragua: Sinopsis histórica 1821–1994*. Managua: Jorge Eduardo Arellano.

Amaro, Nelson, and Carmelo Mesa-Lago. 1971. "Inequality and Classes." In Carmelo Mesa-Lago, ed., *Revolutionary Change in Cuba*. Pittsburgh: University of Pittsburgh Press.

Amnesty International. 2009. *Iran: Election Contested, Repression Compounded*. London: Amnesty International Publications.

Amonoo, Benjamin. 1981. *Ghana 1957–1966: Politics of Institutional Dualism*. Boston: Allen and Unwin.

Amuzegar, Jahangir. 2004. "Khatami: A Folk Hero in Search of Relevance." *Middle East Policy* 11, no. 2: 75–93.

Amuzegar, Jahangir. 2006. "Khatami's Legacy: Dashed Hopes." *Middle East Journal* 60, no. 1: 57–74.

Andelman, David. 1970. "Amilcar Cabral: Pragmatic Revolutionary Shows How an African Guerilla War Can Be Successful." *Africa Report*, May: 18–19.

Ang, Yuen Yuen. 2020. *China's Gilded Age: The Paradox of Economic Boom and Vast Corruption*. Cambridge: Cambridge University Press.

Ankerson, Dudley. 1980. "Saturnino Cedillo: A Traditional Caudillo in San Luis Potosi 1890–1938." In D. A. Brading, ed., *Caudillo and Peasant in the Mexican Revolution*. Cambridge: Cambridge University Press.

Ankerson, Dudley. 1984. *Agrarian Warlord: Saturnino Cedillo and the Mexican Revolution in San Luis Potosí*. DeKalb: Northern Illinois University Press.

Ansari, Ali. 2010. *Crisis of Authority: Iran's 2009 Presidential Election*. London: Chatham House.

Antezana Ergueta, Luis. 2017. *La revolución del 9 de Abril de 1952*. La Paz: Plural Editores.

Antezana Ergueta, Luis, and Hugo Romero Bedregal. 1973. *Historia de los sindicatos campesinos: Un proceso de integración nacional en Bolivia*. La Paz: Servicio Nacional de Reforma Agraria.

Aranda, Sergio. 1968. *La revolución agraria en Cuba*. Mexico City: Siglo Veintiuno.

Arboleya Cervera, Jesús. 1997. *La contrarevolución cubana*. Havana: Editorial de Ciencias Sociales.

Ard, Michael J. 2003. *An Eternal Struggle: How the National Action Party Transformed Mexican Politics*. Westport, CT: Praeger.

Arden-Clarke, Charles. 1958. "Eight Years of Transition in Ghana." *African Affairs* 57, no. 226: 29–37.

Arjomand, Said. 1988. *The Turban for the Crown: The Islamic Revolution in Iran*. New York: Oxford University Press.

Arriola, Carlos, and Juan Gustavo Galindo. 1984. "Los empresarios y el Estado en México (1976–1982)." *Foro Internacional* 25, no. 2: 118–137.

Ash, Timothy Garton. 1993. *The Magic Lantern: The Revolution of '89 Witnessed in Warsaw, Budapest, Berlin, and Prague*. New York: Random House.

Austin, Dennis. 1964. *Politics in Ghana, 1946–60*. London: Oxford University Press.

Austin, Dennis. 1972. "Introduction." In Dennis Austin and Robin Luckham, eds., *Politicians and Soldiers in Ghana 1966–1972*. London: Frank Cass.

Averill, Stephen C. 2006. *Revolution in the Highlands: China's Jinggangshan Base Area*. Lanham, MD: Rowman and Littlefield.

Avina, Alexander. 2014. *Specters of Revolution: Peasant Guerrillas in the Cold War Mexican Countryside*. Oxford: Oxford University Press.

Avrich, Paul. 1970. *Kronstadt, 1921*. Princeton, NJ: Princeton University Press.

Axworthy, Michael. 2013. *Revolutionary Iran: A History of the Islamic Republic*. New York: Oxford University Press.

Ayers, Bradley Earl. 1976. *The War That Never Was: An Insider's Account of CIA Operations against Cuba*. Indianapolis, IN: Bobbs-Merrill.

Azicri, Max. 1988. *Cuba: Politics, Economics and Society*. London: Pinter Publishers.

Azicri, Max. 2000. *Cuba Today and Tomorrow: Reinventing Socialism*. Gainesville: University Press of Florida.

Azimi, Fakhreddin. 2014. "Khomeini and the 'White Revolution.'" In A. Adib-Moghaddam, ed., *A Critical Introduction to Khomeini*. Cambridge: Cambridge University Press.

Ba, Wilbur W. 2012. *Survival through Adaptation: The Chinese Red Army and the Encirclement Campaigns, 1927–1936*. Fort Leavenworth, KS: Combat Studies Institute Press, U.S. Army Combined Arms Center.

Babb, Sarah. 2001. *Managing Mexico: Economists from Nationalism to Neoliberalism*. Princeton, NJ: Princeton University Press.

Bacon, Edwin. 2002. "Reconsidering Brezhnev." In Edwin Bacon, ed., *Brezhnev Reconsidered*. New York: Palgrave Macmillan.

Bailey, David C. 1974. *Viva Crísto Rey! The Cristero Rebellion and the Church-State Conflict in Mexico*. Austin: University of Texas Press.

Bailey, John J. 1986. "The Impact of Major Groups on Policy-Making Trends in Government-Business Relations in Mexico." In Roderic A. Camp, ed., *Mexico's Political Stability: The Next Five Years*. Boulder, CO: Westview Press.

Bailey, John J. 1988. *Governing Mexico: The Statecraft of Crisis Management*. New York: St. Martin's Press.

Bakhash, Shaul. 1990. *The Reign of the Ayatollahs: Iran and the Islamic Revolution*. Rev. ed. New York: Basic Books.

Bakhash, Shaul. 2010. "The Six Presidents." In Robin Wright, ed., *The Iran Primer: Power, Politics, and U.S. Policy*. Washington, DC: United States Institute of Peace Press.

Baloyra, Enrique A. 1993. "Socialist Transitions and Prospects for Change in Cuba." In Enrique A. Baloyra and James A. Morris, eds., *Conflict and Change in Cuba*. Albuquerque: University of New Mexico Press.

Baloyra, Enrique A. 1994. "Where Does Cuba Stand?" In Donald E. Schulz, ed., *Cuba and the Future*. Westport, CT: Greenwood Press.

Baloyra, Enrique A., and Roberto Lozano. 1993. "Soviet-Cuban Relations: The New Environment and Its Impact." In Enrique A. Baloyra and James A. Morris, eds., *Conflict and Change in Cuba*. Albuquerque: University of New Mexico Press.

Baloyra, Enrique A., and James A. Morris. 1993. "Introduction." In Enrique A. Baloyra and James A. Morris, eds., *Conflict and Change in Cuba*. Albuquerque: University of New Mexico Press.

Banac, Ivo. 1988. *With Stalin against Tito: Cominformist Splits in Yugoslav Communism*. Ithaca, NY: Cornell University Press.

Bantjes Aróstegui, Adrian. 1994. "Religión y revolución en México, 1929–1940." *Boletín* 15: 1–22.

Bantjes Aróstegui, Adrian. 1997. "Idolatry and Iconoclasm in Revolutionary Mexico: The De-Christianization Campaigns, 1929–1940." *Mexican Studies / Estudios Mexicanos* 13, no. 1: 87–120.

Barany, Zoltan. 2012. *The Soldier and the Changing State: Building Democratic Armies in Africa, Asia, Europe, and the Americas*. Princeton. NJ: Princeton University Press.

Barany, Zoltan. 2014. "How Post-Colonial Armies Came About: Comparative Perspectives from Asia and Africa." *Journal of Asian and African Studies* 49, no. 5: 597–616.

Barany, Zoltan. 2019. "Who Will Shield the Imams? Regime Protection in Iran and the Middle East." *Middle East Policy* 26, no. 1: 49–59.

Barbosa Miranda, Francisco. 2010. *Historia militar de Nicaragua: Antes del siglo XV al XXI*. Managua: HISPAMER.

Bardach, Ann Louise. 2009. *Without Fidel: A Death Foretold in Miami, Havana, and Washington*. New York: Scribner.

Barfield, Thomas. 2010. *Afghanistan: A Cultural and Political History*. Princeton, NJ: Princeton University Press.

Barker, Peter. 1968. *Operation Cold Chop: The Coup That Toppled Nkrumah*. Accra: Ghana Publishing Corporation.

Barnett, Neil. 2006. *Tito*. London: Haus Publishing.

Barnouin, Barbara, and Chenggen Yu. 2006. *Zhou Enlai: A Political Life*. Hong Kong: Chinese University Press.

Barquín, Ramón M. 1975. *Las luchas guerrilleras en Cuba.* Vol. 2. Madrid: Playor.

Barquín, Ramón M. 1978. *El dia que Fidel Castro se apoderó de Cuba.* San Juan, Puerto Rico: Editorial Rambar.

Barsukov, Nikolai. 2000. "The Rise to Power." In William Taubman, Sergei Khrushchev, and Abbott Gleason, eds., *Nikita Khrushchev.* New Haven, CT: Yale University Press.

Bartolli, Andrea, and Martha Mutisi. 2014. "Merging Militaries: Mozambique." In Roy Licklider, ed., *New Armies from Old: Merging Competing Militaries after Civil Wars.* Washington, DC: Georgetown University Press.

Basañez, Miguel. 1981. *La lucha por la hegemonía en México, 1968–1980.* Mexico City: Siglo Veitniuno.

Basta, Karlo. 2010. "Non-ethnic Origins of Ethnofederal Institutions: The Case of Yugoslavia." *Nationalism and Ethnic Politics* 16, no. 1: 92–110.

Baumeister, Eduardo. 1991. "Agrarian Reform." In Thomas W. Walker, ed., *Revolution and Counterrevolution in Nicaragua.* Boulder, CO: Westview Press.

Baynham, Simon. 1988. *The Military and Politics in Nkrumah's Ghana.* Boulder, CO: Westview Press.

Bearden, Milton. 2001. "Afghanistan, Graveyard of Empires." *Foreign Affairs* 80, no. 6: 17–30.

Bebler, Anton, ed. 1973. *Military Rule in Africa: Dahomey, Ghana, Sierra Leone, and Mali.* New York: Praeger.

Becarra, Ricardo, Pedro Salazar, and José Woldenberg. 2000. *La mecánica del cambio político en México: Elecciones, partidos y reformas.* Mexico City: Cal y Arena.

Becker, Elizabeth. 1998. *When the War Was Over: Cambodia and the Khmer Rouge Revolution.* New York: PublicAffairs.

Becker, Jaime, and Jack Goldstone. 2005. "How Fast Can You Build a State? State Building in Revolutions." In Matthew Lange and Dietrich Rueschemeyer, eds., *States and Development: Historical Antecedents of Stagnation and Advance.* New York: Palgrave Macmillan.

Becker, Jasper. 1998. *Hungry Ghosts: Mao's Secret Famine.* New York: Henry Holt.

Beezley, William H. 2009. "The Role of State Governors in the Mexican Revolution." In Jürgen Buchenau and William H. Beezley, eds., *State Governors in the Mexican Revolution, 1910–1952: Portraits in Conflict, Courage, and Corruption.* Lanham, MD: Rowman and Littlefield.

Beissinger, Mark R. 2002. *Nationalist Mobilization and the Collapse of the Soviet State: A Tidal Approach to the Study of Nationalism.* New York: Cambridge University Press.

Beissinger, Mark R. 2022. *The Revolutionary City: Urbanization and the Global Transformation of Rebellion.* Princeton, NJ: Princeton University Press.

Bellin, Eva. 2004. "The Robustness of Authoritarianism in the Middle East: Exceptionalism in Comparative Perspective." *Comparative Politics* 36, no. 2: 139–157.

Bellin, Eva. 2012. "Reconsidering the Robustness of Authoritarianism in the Middle East: Lessons from the Arab Spring." *Comparative Politics* 44, no. 2: 127–149.

Bendaña, Alejandro. 1982. "The Foreign Policy of the Nicaraguan Revolution." In Thomas W. Walker, ed., *Nicaragua in Revolution.* New York: Praeger.

Benítez, Raúl, Lucrecia Lozano, Ricardo Córdova, and Antonio Cavalla. 1988. "Fuerzas armadas, sociedad y pueblo: Cuba y Nicaragua." In Augusto Varas, ed., *La autonomía militar en América Latina.* Caracas: Editorial Nueva Sociedad.

Benjamin, Thomas. 2013. "The Mexican Revolution: One Century of Reflections." In Douglas W. Richmond and Sam W. Haynes, eds., *The Mexican Revolution: Conflict and Consolidation, 1910–1940*. College Station: Texas A&M University Press.

Bennoune, Mahfoud. 1988. *The Making of Contemporary Algeria, 1830–1987*. Cambridge: Cambridge University Press.

Benson, L. 2001. *Yugoslavia: A Concise History*. New York: Palgrave Macmillan.

Bentrovato, Denise. 2015. "Rwanda, Twenty Years On: Assessing the RPF's Legacy through the Views of the Great Lakes Region's New Generation." *Cahiers d'études africaines* 55, no. 218: 231–254.

Benvenuti, Francesco. 1988. *The Bolsheviks and the Red Army, 1918–1922*. Translated by Christopher Woodall. New York: Cambridge University Press.

Beresford, Melanie. 1988. *Vietnam: Politics, Economics and Society*. London: Pinter Publishers.

Beresford, Melanie. 1989. *National Unification and Economic Development in Vietnam*. London: Macmillan.

Beresford, Melanie. 2003. "Economic Transition, Uneven Development, and the Impact of Reform on Regional Inequality." In Hy V. Luong, ed., *Postwar Vietnam: Dynamics of a Transforming Society*. Lanham, MD: Rowman and Littlefield.

Bergerol, Jane. 1975. "Guinea Bissau: Facing Independent Realities." *Africa Report* 28, no. 4: 18–20.

Bernstein, Alvin. 1990. "Military Cooperation and Technology Transfer between the Soviet Union and Vietnam." In Thai Quang Trung, ed., *Vietnam Today: Assessing the New Trends*. New York: Taylor and Francis.

Bernstein, Richard. 2014. *China 1945: Mao's Revolution and America's Fateful Choice*. New York: Vintage.

Bernstein, Thomas. 2013. "Resilience and Collapse in China and the Soviet Union." In Martin K. Dimitrov, ed., *Why Communism Did Not Collapse: Understanding Authoritarian Resilience in Asia and Europe*. New York: Cambridge University Press.

Berryman, Phillip. 1984. *The Religious Roots of Rebellion: Christians in the Central American Revolutions*. London: SCM Press.

Betancourt, Ernesto F. 1971. "Exporting the Revolution to Latin America." In Carmelo Mesa-Lago, ed., *Revolutionary Change in Cuba*. Pittsburgh: University of Pittsburgh Press.

Bialer, Seweryn. 1980. *Stalin's Successors: Leadership, Stability, and Change in the Soviet Union*. New York: Cambridge University Press.

Bianco, Lucien. 1971. *Origins of the Chinese Revolution, 1915–1949*. Stanford, CA: Stanford University Press.

Biberaj, Elez. 1990. *Albania: A Socialist Maverick*. Boulder, CO: Westview Press.

Bienen, Henry. 1968. "Public Order and the Military in Africa: Mutinies in Kenya, Uganda, and Tanganyika." In Henry Bienen, ed., *The Military Intervenes: Case Studies in Political Development*. New York: Russell Sage Foundation.

Biondich, Mark. 2011. *The Balkans: Revolution, War, and Political Violence since 1878*. Oxford: Oxford University Press.

Birmingham, David. 1990. *Kwame Nkrumah*. London: Cardinal.

Black, George. 1981. *Triumph of the People: The Sandinista Revolution in Nicaragua*. London: Zed Press.

Blackwell, Robert. 1979. "Cadres Policy in the Brezhnev Era." *Problems of Communism* 28, no. 2: 29–42.

Blancarte, Roberto. 2014. "Intransigence, Anti-Communism, and Reconciliation: Church/State Relations in Transition." In Paul Gillingham and Benjamin T. Smith, eds., *Dictablanda: Politics, Work, and Culture in Mexico, 1938–1968*. Durham, NC: Duke University Press.

Blasier, Cole. 1971a. "The Elimination of United States Influence." In Carmelo Mesa-Lago, ed., *Revolutionary Change in Cuba*. Pittsburgh: University of Pittsburgh Press.

Blasier, Cole. 1971b. "The United States and the Revolution." In James M. Malloy and Richard S. Thorn, eds., *Beyond the Revolution: Bolivia since 1952*. Pittsburgh: University of Pittsburgh Press.

Blasier, Cole. 1985. *The Hovering Giant: U.S. Responses to Revolutionary Change in Latin America, 1910–1985*. Pittsburgh: University of Pittsburgh Press.

Blaydes, Lisa. 2010. *Elections and Distributive Politics in Mubarak's Egypt*. Cambridge: Cambridge University Press.

Blight, James G., and Peter Kornbluh, eds. 1998. *Politics of Illusion: The Bay of Pigs Invasion Reexamined*. Boulder, CO: Lynne Rienner.

Bodo, Bela. 2011. "The White Terror in Hungary, 1919–1921: The Social Worlds of Paramilitary Groups." *Austrian History Yearbook* 42 (April): 133–163.

Boeva, Liubov'. 2009. *"Osobennaya kasta": VChK-OGPU i ukreplenie kommunisticheskogo rezhima v gody nepa*. Moscow: AIRO-XX.

Bohning, Don. 2005. *The Castro Obsession: U.S. Covert Operations against Cuba, 1959–1965*. Washington, DC: Potomac Books.

Boils, Guillermo. 1975. *Los militares y la política en México (1915–1974)*. Mexico City: Ediciones El Caballito.

Boils, Guillermo. 1985. "Los militares in México (1965–1985)." *Revista mexicana de sociología* 47, no. 1: 169–185.

Bonachea, Rámon L., and Marta San Martín. 1974. *The Cuban Insurrection, 1952–1959*. New Brunswick, NJ: Transaction Publishers.

Bonora-Waisman, Camille. 2003. *France and the Algerian Conflict: Issues in Democracy and Political Stability, 1988–1995*. Aldershot, UK: Ashgate.

Bonsal, Philip W. 1971. *Cuba, Castro, and the United States*. Pittsburgh: University of Pittsburgh Press.

Booth, John A. 1985. *The End and the Beginning: The Nicaraguan Revolution*. 2nd ed. Boulder, CO: Westview Press.

Booth, John A. 1998. "The Somoza Regime in Nicaragua." In Houchang E. Chehabi and Juan J. Linz, eds., *Sultanistic Regimes*. Baltimore: Johns Hopkins University Press.

Boroumand, Ladan. 2017. "Iran's 2017 Election: Waning Democratic Hopes." *Journal of Democracy* 28, no. 4: 38–45.

Borsányi, Gyorgy. 1993. *The Life of a Communist Revolutionary, Béla Kun*. New York: Columbia University Press.

Bosworth, Richard J. B. 2002. *Mussolini*. London: A & C Black.

Bouandel, Toucef. 2003. "Political Parties and the Transition from Authoritarianism: The Case of Algeria." *Journal of Modern African Studies* 41, no. 1: 1–22.

Boudarel, Georges. 1980. "Influences and Idiosyncrasies in the Line and Practice of the Viet Communist Party." In William S. Turley, ed., *Vietnamese Communism in Comparative Perspective*. Boulder, CO: Westview Press.

Bouquet, Mathieu. 2010. "Vietnamese Party-State and Religious Pluralism since 1986: Building the Fatherland?" *Sojourn: Journal of Social Issues in Southeast Asia* 25, no. 1: 90–108.

Bowden, Mark. 2006. *Guests of the Ayatollah: The Iran Hostage Crisis: The First Battle in America's War with Militant Islam*. New York: Grove Press.

Box-Steffensmeier, Janet M., Suzanna De Boef, and Kyle A. Joyce. 2006. "Event Dependence and Heterogeneity in Duration Models: The Conditional Frailty Model." *Political Analysis* 15, no. 3: 237–256.

Brading, D. A. 1980. "Introduction: National Politics and the Populist Tradition." In D. A. Brading, ed., *Caudillo and Peasant in the Mexican Revolution*. Cambridge: Cambridge University Press.

Bramall, Chris. 2011. "Agency and Famine in China's Sichuan Province, 1958–1962." *The China Quarterly* 208: 990–1008.

Brandenburg, Frank R. 1964. *The Making of Modern Mexico*. Englewood Cliffs, NJ: Prentice-Hall.

Bratton, Michael, and Nicolas van de Walle. 1997. *Democratic Experiments in Africa: Regime Transitions in Comparative Perspective*. New York: Cambridge University Press.

Bravo Mena, Luis Felipe. 1987. "COPARMEX and Mexican Politics." In Sylvia Maxfield and Ricardo Anzaldúa Montoya, eds., *Government and Private Sector in Contemporary Mexico*. La Jolla: Center for U.S.-Mexican Studies, University of California, San Diego.

Brenner, Philip, Marguerite Rose Jiménez, John M. Kirk, and William M. LeoGrande. 2015. "Introduction: History as Prologue: Cuba before 2006." In Philip Brenner, Marguerite Rose Jiménez, John M. Kirk, and William M. LeoGrande, eds., *A Contemporary Cuba Reader: The Revolution under Raúl Castro*. Lanham, MD: Rowman and Littlefield.

Breslauer, George W. 1978. "On the Adaptability of Soviet Welfare-State Authoritarianism." In Karl W. Ryavec, ed., *Soviet Society and the Communist Party*. Amherst: University of Massachusetts Press.

Bretton, Henry L. 1966. *The Rise and Fall of Kwame Nkrumah: A Study of Personal Rule in Africa*. London: Pall Mall Press.

Brigham, Robert K. 2000. "Revolutionary Heroism and Politics in Postwar Vietnam." In Charles E. Neu, ed., *After Vietnam: Legacies of a Lost War*. Baltimore: Johns Hopkins University Press.

Brill, William H. 1967. *Military Intervention in Bolivia: The Overthrow of Paz Estenssoro and the MNR*. Washington, DC: Institute for the Comparative Study of Political Systems.

Brinks, Daniel, Steven Levitsky, and María Victoria Murillo. 2019. *Understanding Institutional Weakness: Power and Design in Latin American Institutions*. New York: Cambridge University Press.

Brinton, Crane. (1938) 1965. *The Anatomy of Revolution*. 3rd ed. New York: Vintage Books.

Brown, Archie. 1996. *The Gorbachev Factor*. Oxford: Oxford University Press.

Brown, Jonathan. 1993. *Oil and Revolution in Mexico*. Berkeley: University of California Press.

Brown, Timothy C. 2001. *The Real Contra War*. Norman: University of Oklahoma Press.

Brownlee, Jason. 2007. *Authoritarianism in an Age of Democratization*. New York: Cambridge University Press.

Bruhn, Kathleen. 1997. *Taking on Goliath: The Emergence of a New Left Party and the Struggle for Democracy in Mexico*. University Park: Pennsylvania State University Press.

Brumberg, Daniel. 2001. *Reinventing Khomeini: The Struggle for Reform in Iran*. Chicago: University of Chicago Press.

Brumberg, Daniel. 2013. "Iran's Successes and Failures—34 Years Later." United States Institute of Peace, *The Iran Primer*, February 9. https://iranprimer.usip.org/blog/2013/feb/09/iran's-successes-and-failures-34-years-later.

Buchenau, Jürgen. 2007. *Plutarco Elías Calles and the Mexican Revolution*. Lanham, MD: Rowman and Littlefield.

Buchenau, Jürgen. 2011. *The Last Caudillo: Alvaro Obregón and the Mexican Revolution*. Malden, MA: Wiley-Blackwell.

Buchenau, Klaus. 2014. "The Serbian Orthodox Church." In Lucian N. Leustean, ed., *Eastern Christianity and Politics in the Twenty-First Century*. London: Routledge.

Bueno de Mesquita, Bruce, Randolph M. Siverson, and Gary Woller. 1992. "War and the Fate of Regimes: A Comparative Analysis." *American Political Science Review* 86, no. 3: 638–646.

Bueno de Mesquita, Bruce, Alastair Smith, Randolph M. Siverson, and James D. Morrow. 2005. *The Logic of Political Survival*. Cambridge, MA: MIT Press.

Bui, Thiem Hai. 2016. "The Influence of Social Media in Vietnam's Elite Politics." *Journal of Current Southeast Asian Affairs* 35, no. 2: 89–112.

Burant, Stephen. 1991. "The Communist Party." In Raymond E. Zickel, ed., *Soviet Union: A Country Study*. 2nd ed. Washington, DC: Federal Research Division, Library of Congress.

Burg, Steven L. 1986. "Elite Conflict in Post-Tito Yugoslavia." *Soviet Studies* 38, no. 2: 170–193.

Burke, Melvin, and James M. Malloy. 1974. "From National Populism to National Corporatism: The Case of Bolivia (1952–1970)." *Studies in Comparative International Development* 9, no. 1: 49–73.

Burrier, Grant. 2012. "Aborted Corporatism: The Case of Bolivia under the Movimiento Nacionalista Revolucionario (MNR, 1952–64)." *Bolivian Research Review* 9, no. 1: 1–39.

Buttinger, Joseph. 1967a. *Vietnam: A Dragon Embattled*. Vol. 1, *From Colonialism to the Vietminh*. New York: Praeger.

Buttinger, Joseph. 1967b. *Vietnam: A Dragon Embattled*. Vol. 2, *Vietnam at War*. New York: Praeger.

Buttinger, Joseph. 1977. *Vietnam: The Unforgettable Tragedy*. New York: Horizon Press.

Buve, Raymond. 1980. "State Governors and Peasant Mobilization in Tlaxcala." In D. A. Brading, ed., *Caudillo and Peasant in the Mexican Revolution*. Cambridge: Cambridge University Press.

Byman, Daniel. 2005. *Deadly Connections: States That Sponsor Terrorism*. New York: Cambridge University Press.

Byrne, Jeffrey James. 2016. *Mecca of Revolution: Algeria, Decolonization, and the Third World Order*. New York: Oxford University Press.

Byron, John, and Robert Pack. 1992. *The Claws of the Dragon: Kang Sheng—the Evil Genius behind Mao and His Legacy of Terror in People's China*. New York: Simon and Schuster.

Cajina, Roberto J. 1997. *Transición política y reconversión militar en Nicaragua, 1990–1995*. Managua: CRIES.

Calchi Novati, Gian Paolo. 2021. "The Lines of Tension in the Horn and the Ethiopia-Eritrea Case." In Andrea de Guttry, Harry H. G. Post, and Gabriella Venturini, eds., *The 1998–2000 Eritrea-Ethiopia War and Its Aftermath in International Legal Perspective*. The Hague: T.M.C. Asser Press.

Callahan, Mary P. 2005. *Making Enemies: War and State Building in Burma*. Ithaca, NY: Cornell University Press.

Camp, Roderic A. 1984. "Generals and Politicians in Mexico: A Preliminary Comparison." In David F. Ronfeldt, ed., *The Modern Mexican Military: A Reassessment*. La Jolla: Center for U.S.-Mexican Studies, University of California, San Diego.

Camp, Roderic A. 1985. *Intellectuals and the State in Twentieth-Century Mexico*. Austin: University of Texas Press.

Camp, Roderic A. 1992. *Generals in the Palacio: The Military in Modern Mexico*. New York: Oxford University Press.

Camp, Roderic A. 1997. *Crossing Swords: Politics and Religion in Mexico*. New York: Oxford University Press.

Camp, Roderic A. 1999. *Politics in Mexico: The Decline of Authoritarianism*. New York: Oxford University Press.

Camp, Roderic A. 2002. *Mexico's Mandarins: Crafting a Power Elite for the Twenty-First Century*. Berkeley: University of California Press.

Camp, Roderic A. 2005. *Mexico's Military on the Democratic Stage*. Westport, CT: Praeger Security International.

Campbell, Hugh G. 1976. *La derecha radical en México, 1929–1949*. Mexico City: SepSetentas.

Cann, Rebecca, and Constantine Danopoulos. 1997. "The Military and Politics in a Theocratic State: Iran as a Case Study." *Armed Forces & Society* 24, no. 2: 269–288.

Capoccia, Giovanni. 2016. "Critical Junctures." In Orfeo Fioretos, Tulia Falleti, and Adam Sheingate, eds., *The Oxford Handbook of Historical Institutionalism*. New York: Oxford University Press.

Capoccia, Giovanni, and R. Daniel Keleman. 2007. "The Study of Critical Junctures: Theory, Narrative, and Counterfactuals in Historical Institutionalism." *World Politics* 59, no. 3: 341–369.

Cardenal, Ernesto. 2013. *La revolución perdida*. 3rd ed. Managua: Anama.

Cardoso, Eliana, and Ann Helwege. 1992. *Cuba after Communism*. Cambridge, MA: MIT Press.

Carr, Edward. 1950. *The Bolshevik Revolution, 1917–1923*. Vol. 1. New York: Macmillan.

Carradice, Phil. 2018. *The Shanghai Massacre: China's White Terror, 1927*. South Yorkshire, UK: Pen and Sword Books.

Carter, Jeff, Michael Bernhard, and Glenn Palmer. 2012. "Social Revolution, the State and War: How Revolutions Affect War-Making Capacity and Interstate War Outcomes." *Journal of Conflict Resolution* 56, no. 3: 439–466.

Carter, William B. 1971. "Revolution and the Agrarian Sector." In James M. Malloy and Richard S. Thorn, eds., *Beyond the Revolution: Bolivia since 1952*. Pittsburgh: University of Pittsburgh Press.

Case, William. 2016. "Vietnam in 2015: Factional Battles, Economic Tailwinds, and Neighborhood Jitters." *Asian Survey* 56, no. 1: 93–100.

Casey, Adam E. 2020. *The Durability of Client Regimes: Foreign Sponsorship and Autocracies, 1946–2010*. Doctoral dissertation, University of Toronto.

Casey, Adam E., Jean Lachapelle, and Lucan Way. 2021. "National Liberation and Decolonization." Paper prepared for the International Studies Association Annual Meeting (virtual), April 9.

Castañeda, Jorge G. 2000. *Perpetuating Power: How Mexican Presidents Were Chosen*. New York: New Press.

Castellanos, Laura. 2007. *México armado, 1943–1981*. Mexico City: Ediciones Era.

Castro Martínez, Pedro. 1992. *Adolfo de la Huerta y la revolución mexicana*. Mexico City: Instituto Nacional de Estudios Históricos de la revolución mexicana.

Castro Martínez, Pedro. 2009. *Álvaro Obregón: Fuego y cenizas de la revolución mexicana*. Mexico City: Ediciones Era.

Cavatorta, Francesco. 2009. *The International Dimension of the Failed Algerian Transition: Democracy Betrayed?* Manchester, UK: Manchester University Press.

Centeno, Miguel Ángel. 1994. *Democracy within Reason: Technocratic Revolution in Mexico*. University Park: Pennsylvania State University Press.

Centeno, Miguel Ángel, and Mauricio Font. 1997. "Reflections: May 1, 1996." In Miguel Ángel Centeno and Mauricio Font, eds., *Toward a New Cuba? Legacies of a Revolution*. Boulder, CO: Lynne Rienner.

Chabal, Patrick. 1983. "Party, State, and Socialism in Guinea-Bissau." *Canadian Journal of African Studies / Revue Canadienne des Études Africaines* 17, no. 2: 189–210.

Chabal, Patrick. 2003. *Amilcar Cabral: Revolutionary Leadership and People's War*. Trenton, NJ: Africa World Press.

Chaguaceda, Armando. 2015. "The Promise Besieged: Participation and Autonomy in Cuba." In Philip Brenner, Marguerite Rose Jiménez, John M. Kirk, and William M. LeoGrande, eds., *A Contemporary Cuba Reader: The Revolution under Raúl Castro*. Lanham, MD: Rowman and Littlefield.

Chaliand, Gerard. 1969. *Armed Struggle in Africa: With the Guerrillas in "Portuguese" Africa*. Translated by David Rattray and Robert Leonhardt. New York: Monthly Review Press.

Chamberlin, William. 1935. *The Russian Revolution, 1917–1921*. New York: Palgrave Macmillan.

Chan, Alfred L. 2001. *Mao's Crusade: Politics and Policy Implementation in China's Great Leap Forward*. New York: Oxford University Press.

Chand, Vikram. 2001. *Mexico's Political Awakening*. Notre Dame, IN: University of Notre Dame Press.

Chandler, David. 1992. *Brother Number One: A Political Biography of Pol Pot*. Boulder, CO: Westview Press.

Chandra, Nayan. 1986. *Brother Enemy: The War after the War*. San Diego, CA: Harcourt Brace Jovanovich.

Chandra, Nayan. 1993. "Indochina beyond the Cold War: The Chill from Eastern Europe." In Borje Ljunggren, ed., *The Challenge of Reform in Indochina*. Cambridge, MA: Harvard Institute for International Development.

Chavarria, Ricardo E. 1982. "The Nicaraguan Insurrection." In Thomas W. Walker, ed., *Nicaragua in Revolution*. New York: Praeger.

Chehabi, Houchang E., and Juan J. Linz, eds. 1998. *Sultanistic Regimes*. Baltimore: Johns Hopkins University Press.

Cheibub, José Antonio, Jennifer Gandhi, and James Raymond Vreeland. 2010. "Democracy and Dictatorship Revisited." *Public Choice* 143, no. 1/2: 67–101.

Chen, Jian. 1994. *China's Road to the Korean War: The Making of the Sino-American Confrontation*. New York: Columbia University Press.

Cheng, Chu-yuan. 1990. *Behind the Tiananmen Massacre*. Boulder, CO: Westview Press.

Cheng, Li, and Lynn White. 1988. "The Thirteenth Central Committee of the Chinese Communist Party: From Mobilizers to Managers." *Asian Survey* 28, no. 4: 371–399.

Cheng, Li, and Lynn White. 1998. "The Fifteenth Central Committee of the Chinese Communist Party: Full-Fledged Technocratic Leadership with Partial Control by Jiang Zemin." *Asian Survey* 38, no. 3: 231–264.

Chernyaev, Anatoly. 2000. *My Six Years with Gorbachev*. University Park: Pennsylvania State University Press.

Chesneaux, Jean. 1968. *The Chinese Labor Movement, 1919–1927*. Stanford, CA: Stanford University Press.

Chilcote, Ronald H. 1977. "Guinea-Bissau's Struggle: Past and Present." *Africa Today* 24, no. 1: 31–39.

Chinh, Truong. 1963. *Primer for Revolt: The Communist Takeover in Viet-Nam*. New York: Praeger.

Chiozza, Giacomo, and H. E. Goemans. 2011. *Leaders and International Conflict*. New York: Cambridge University Press.

Chorley, Katharine. (1943) 1973. *Armies and the Art of Revolution*. Boston: Beacon Press.

Christian, Shirley. 1985. *Nicaragua: Revolution in the Family*. New York: Random House.

Chuev, Felix. 1993. *Molotov Remembers: Inside Kremlin Politics: Conversations with Felix Chuev*. Chicago: Ivan R. Dee.

Chuvin, Shahram, and Charles Tripp. 1988. *Iran and Iraq at War*. London: I. B. Taurus.

Ci, Jiwei. 2019. "Without Democracy, China Will Rise No Farther." *Foreign Affairs*, October 4.

CIA. 1966. "Army Overthrows Nkrumah Regime in Ghana." *Weekly Review of Current Intelligence*, February 25.

CIA. 1975. "East Africa: Outside Influence and Potential Conflict." DCI/NOI 1076-75. Central Intelligence Agency, 05/07/1975, Secret. Declassified March 9, 2006. CREST no. CIA-RDP79R01142A000500070002-5.

CIA. 1980. "Iran: Exporting the Revolution. An Intelligence Estimate." March 30. https://www.cia.gov/library/readingroom/docs/CIA-RDP81B00401R000500100001-8.pdf.

CIA. 1983a. "Kenya-Uganda-Tanzania: Uneasy Neighbors." Intelligence Assessment, Office of African and Latin American Analysis, Central Intelligence

Agency, 06/06/1983, Secret. Declassified July 8, 2011. CREST no. CIA-RDP 84S00552R000300070002-9.

CIA. 1983b. "The Tanzanian Military: Nyerere's Uncertain Shield." Intelligence Assessment, Office of African and Latin American Analysis, Central Intelligence Agency, ALA 83-10089, June 7, 1983, Secret. Declassified June 22, 2011. CREST no. CIA-RDP84S00552R000200150003-0.

CIA. 1984a. "The Iranian Armed Forces: Clerical Control and Military Effectiveness." Intelligence Assessment, NESA 84-10261C, September, Top Secret. Declassified April 21, 2009. CREST no. CIA-RDP85T00314R000300010003-6.

CIA. 1984b. "Tanzania: Nyerere under Fire." Intelligence Assessment, Office of African and Latin American Analysis, Central Intelligence Agency, ALA 84-10109, November 1, 1984, Secret. Declassified March 4, 2010. CREST no. CIA-RDP85S00317R000300070003-8.

CIA. 1985. "Mozambique: Machel's Embattled Regime." Intelligence Assessment, Directorate of Intelligence, Central Intelligence Agency, April 1, 1982, Secret. Declassified January 5, 2007. CREST no. CIA-RDP83B00225R000100160001-3.

CIA. 1987. "Iran's Revolutionary Guard: Armed Pillar of the Islamic Republic." NESA 87-10004, January, Secret. Declassified May 8, 2012. CREST no. CIA-RDP06T00412R000606580001-5.

Cima, Ronald J. 1989. "Vietnam's Economic Reform: Approaching the 1990s." *Asian Survey* 29, no. 8: 786–799.

Cima, Ronald J. 1990. "Vietnam in 1989: Initiating the Post-Cambodia Period." *Asian Survey* 30, no. 1: 88–95.

Ciment, James. 1997. *Algeria: The Fundamentalist Challenge.* New York: Facts on File.

Civicus Moniter. n.d. *Mozambican Civil Society Within: Evaluation, Challenges, Opportunities and Action.* Maputo, Mozambique: Fundação para o Desenvolvimento da Comunidade. https://www.civicus.org/media/CSI_Mozambique_Country _Report.pdf.

Ciorciari, John D. 2014. "China and the Pol Pot Regime." *Cold War History* 14, no. 2: 215–235.

Clapham, Christopher. 2017. *The Horn of Africa: State Formation and Decay.* London: Hurst.

Clarence-Smith, W. G. 1975. *The Third Portuguese Empire, 1825–1975: A Study in Economic Imperialism.* Manchester, UK: University of Manchester Press.

Clark, Alan. 1985. *Barbarossa: The Russian-German Conflict, 1941–45.* New York: HarperCollins.

Clegg, Ian. 1971. *Workers' Self-Management in Algeria.* New York: Monthly Review Press.

Cline, Howard F. 1963. *Mexico: Revolution to Evolution, 1940–1960.* New York: Oxford University Press.

Close, David. 1985. "The Nicaraguan Elections of 1984." *Electoral Studies* 4, no. 2: 152–158.

Close, David. 1988. *Nicaragua: Politics, Economics and Society.* London: Pinter Publishers.

Close, David. 1999. *Nicaragua: The Chamorro Years.* Boulder, CO: Lynne Rienner.

Cohen, Stephen F. 1980. *Bukharin and the Bolshevik Revolution: A Political Biography, 1888–1938.* New York: Oxford University Press.

Colburn, Forrest D. 1986. *Post-Revolutionary Nicaragua: State, Class, and the Dilemmas of Agrarian Policy.* Berkeley: University of California Press.

Colgan, Jeff. 2012. "Measuring Revolution." *Conflict Management and Peace Science* 29, no. 4: 444–467.

Coll, Steve. 2004. *Ghost Wars: The Secret History of the CIA, Afghanistan, and bin Laden.* New York: Penguin.

Coll, Steve. 2019. *Directorate S: The C.I.A. and America's Secret Wars in Afghanistan and Pakistan.* New York: Penguin.

Collier, Ruth Berins. 1992. *The Contradictory Alliance: State-Labor Relations and Regime Change in Mexico.* Berkeley: International and Area Studies, University of California, Berkeley.

Collier, Ruth Berins, and David Collier. 1991. *Shaping the Political Arena: Critical Junctures, the Labor Movement, and Regime Dynamics in Latin America.* Princeton, NJ: Princeton University Press.

Colton, Timothy J. 1979. *Commissars, Commanders, and Civilian Authority: The Structure of Soviet Military Politics.* Cambridge, MA: Harvard University Press.

Connell, Dan. 1997. "After the Shooting Stops: Revolution in Postwar Eritrea." *Race & Class* 38, no. 4: 57–78.

Connell, Dan. 2001. "Inside the EPLF: The Origins of the 'People's Party' and Its Role in the Liberation of Eritrea." *Review of African Political Economy* 28, no. 89: 345–364.

Connelly, Matthew. 2002. *A Diplomatic Revolution: Algeria's Fight for Independence and the Origins of the Post–Cold War Era.* Oxford: Oxford University Press.

Conquest, Robert. 1987. *The Harvest of Sorrow: Soviet Collectivization and the Terror-Famine.* New York: Oxford University Press.

Conroy, Michael E. 1987. "Patterns of Changing External Trade in Revolutionary Nicaragua: Voluntary and Involuntary Trade Diversification." In Rose J. Spalding, ed., *The Political Economy of Revolutionary Nicaragua.* Boston: Allen and Unwin.

Contreras, Ariel José. 1981. "Estado y sociedad civil en el proceso electoral de 1940." In Carlos Martínez Assad, ed., *La sucesión presidencial en México, 1928–1988.* Mexico City: Nueva Imagen.

Cook, Linda J., and Martin K. Dimitrov. 2017. "The Social Contract Revisited: Evidence from Communist and State Capitalist Economies." *Europe-Asia Studies* 69, no. 1: 8–26.

Cook, Steven A. 2007. *Ruling but Not Governing: The Military and Political Development in Egypt, Algeria, and Turkey.* Baltimore: Johns Hopkins University Press.

Coppedge, Michael, et al. 2019. "V-Dem Codebook v9." In *Varieties of Democracy (V-Dem) Project.* Gothenburg, Sweden: University of Gothenburg, V-Dem Institute.

Corbett, Charles D. 1972. *The Latin American Military as a Socio-political Force: Case Studies of Bolivia and Argentina.* Coral Gables, FL: Center for Advanced International Studies, University of Miami.

Córdova, Arnaldo. 1973. *La ideología de la revolución mexicana.* Mexico City: Ediciones Era.

Córdova, Arnaldo. 1974. *La política de masas del cardenismo.* Mexico City: Serie Popular Era.

Córdova, Arnaldo. 1995. *La revolución en crisis: La aventura del maximato.* Mexico City: Cal y Arena.

Cornelius, Wayne A., Jr. 1987. "Political Liberalization in an Authoritarian Regime: Mexico, 1976–1985." In Judith Gentleman, ed., *Mexican Politics in Transition.* Boulder, CO: Westview Press.

Cornelius, Wayne A., Jr. Judith Gentleman, and Peter H. Smith. 1989. "Overview: The Dynamics of Political Change in Mexico." In Wayne A. Cornelius, Judith Gentleman, and Peter H. Smith, eds., *Mexico's Alternative Political Futures.* La Jolla: Center for U.S.-Mexican Studies, University of California, San Diego.

Cosío Villegas, Daniel. 1981. *El sistema político mexicano: Las posibilidades de cambio.* Mexico City: Cuadernos de Joaqu Mortiz.

Council of Freely Elected Heads of Government. 1990. *Observing Nicaragua's Elections, 1989–1990.* Atlanta: Carter Center of Emory University.

Coxhead, Ian. 2018. "Vietnam in 2017: Flying Fast in Turbulence." *Asian Survey* 58, no. 1: 149–157.

Crahan, Margaret E. 1985. "Cuba: Religion and Revolutionary Institutionalization." *Journal of Latin American Studies* 17, no. 2: 319–340.

Crahan, Margaret E. 1988. "Cuba: Religion and Revolutionary Institutionalization." In Sergio G. Roca, ed., *Socialist Cuba: Past Interpretations and Future Challenges.* Boulder, CO: Westview Press.

Crahan, Margaret E. 2015. "Religion and Civil Society in Cuba, 1959–2013." In Philip Brenner, Marguerite Rose Jiménez, John M. Kirk, and William M. LeoGrande, eds., *A Contemporary Cuba Reader: The Revolution under Raúl Castro.* Lanham, MD: Rowman and Littlefield.

Crahan, Margaret E., and Ariel C. Armony. 2007. "Rethinking Civil Society and Religion in Cuba." In Bert Hoffmann and Laurence Whitehead, eds., *Debating Cuban Exceptionalism.* New York: Palgrave Macmillan.

Crenshaw Hutchinson, Martha. 1978. *Revolutionary Terrorism: The FLN in Algeria, 1954–1962.* Stanford, CA: Hoover Institution Press.

Crespo, Alfonso. 1996. *Hernán Siles Zuazo: El hombre de abril.* La Paz: Ediciones Plural.

Cross, Kevin. 2010. "Why Iran's Green Movement Faltered: The Limits of Information Technology in a Rentier State." *SAIS Review* 30, no. 2: 162–187.

CRS (Congressional Research Service). 2020. *Iran Sanctions.* RS 20817. https://fas .org/sgp/crs/mideast/RS20871.pdf.

Crump, Thomas. 2014. *Brezhnev and the Decline of the Soviet Union.* New York: Routledge.

Cruz, Arturo, Jr. 1989. *Memoirs of a Counterrevolutionary: Life with the Contras, the Sandinistas, and the CIA.* New York: Doubleday.

Currey, Cecil B. 1997. *Victory at Any Cost: The Genius of Viet Nam's General Vo Nguyen Giap.* Washington, DC: Potomac Books.

Dahm, Bernhard. 1971. *History of Indonesia in the Twentieth Century.* London: Pall Mall Press.

Daly, Brendan. 2012. "Regime Change in Iran?" *Middle East Quarterly*, Spring: 81–86.

Daniels, Robert V. 1960. *The Conscience of the Revolution: Communist Opposition in Soviet Russia.* Cambridge, MA: Harvard University Press.

Darch, Colin. 2018. *Historical Dictionary of Mozambique.* Lanham, MD: Rowman and Littlefield.

Davidson, Basil. 1974. "Guinea: Bissau and the Cape Verde Islands: The Transition from War to Independence." *Africa Today* 21, no. 4: 5–20.

Davidson, Basil. 1981. *The People's Cause: A History of Guerrillas in Africa*. London: Longman.

Davies, R. W. 1980. *The Socialist Offensive: The Collectivization of Soviet Agriculture, 1929–1930*. Cambridge, MA: Harvard University Press.

Davis, Anthony. 2001. "How the Taliban Became a Military Force." In William Maley, ed., *Fundamentalism Reborn? Afghanistan and the Taliban*. New York: New York University Press.

de la Garza, Luis Alberto. 1986. "El Mexico postindependiente." In Luis Alberto de la Garza et al., eds., *Evolución del estado mexicano*, tomo 1, *Formación 1810–1910*. Mexico City: Ediciones El Caballito.

Deac, Wilfred. 1997. *Road to the Killing Fields: The Cambodian War of 1970–1975*. College Station: Texas A&M University Press.

Decalo, Samuel. 1976. *Coups and Army Rule in Africa: Studies in Military Style*. New Haven, CT: Yale University Press.

Deere, Carmen Diana, and Peter Marchetti. 1985. "The Peasantry and the Development of Sandinista Agrarian Policy, 1979–1984." *Latin American Research Review* 20, no. 3: 75–109.

del Aguila, Juan M. 1984. *Cuba: Dilemmas of a Revolution*. Boulder, CO: Westview Press.

del Aguila, Juan M. 1989. "The Changing Character of Cuba's Armed Forces." In Jaime Suchlicki, ed., *The Cuban Military under Castro*. Coral Gables, FL: Institute of Interamerican Studies, Graduate School of International Studies, University of Miami, North-South Center.

del Aguila, Juan M. 1993. "The Politics of Dissidence: A Challenge to the Monolith." In Enrique A. Baloyra and James A. Morris, eds., *Conflict and Change in Cuba*. Albuquerque: University of New Mexico Press.

del Aguila, Juan M. 2003. "The Cuban Armed Forces: Changing Roles, Continued Loyalties." In Irving Louis Horowitz and Jaime Suchlicki, eds., *Cuban Communism, 1959–2003*. New Brunswick, NJ: Transaction Publishers.

Del Panta, Gianni. 2017. "Weathering the Storm: Why Was There No Arab Uprising in Algeria?" *Democratization* 24, no. 6: 1085–1102.

Denitch, Bogdan. 1976. "Violence and Social Change in the Yugoslav Revolution: Lessons for the Third World?" *Comparative Politics* 8, no. 3: 465–478.

Dent, Bob. 2018. *Painting the Town Red: Politics and the Arts during the 1919 Hungarian Soviet Republic*. London: Pluto Press.

Derluguian, Georgi. 2012. "The Social Origins of Good and Bad Governance: Reinterpreting the 1968 Schism in Frelimo." In Eric Morier-Genoud, ed., *Sure Road? Nationalisms in Angola, Guinea-Bissau and Mozambique*. Leiden: Brill.

Derradji, Abder Rahmane. 2002. *A Concise History of Political Violence in Algeria, 1954–2000: Brothers in Faith, Enemies in Arms*. Bk. 2. Lewiston, NY: Edwin Mellen Press.

Desbarats, Jacqueline. 1990. "Human Rights: Two Steps Forward One Step Back." In Thai Quang Trung, ed., *Vietnam Today: Assessing the New Trends*. New York: Taylor and Francis.

Deutscher, Isaac. (1954) 2003. *The Prophet Armed: Trotsky, 1879–1921*. New York: Verso.

Deutscher, Isaac. (1959) 2003. *The Prophet Outcast: Trotsky 1929–1940*. New York: Verso.

Dhada, Mustafa. 1993. *Warriors at Work: How Guinea Was Really Set Free*. Niwot: University Press of Colorado.

Dhada, Mustafa. 1998. "The Liberation War in Guinea-Bissau Reconsidered." *Journal of Military History* 62, no. 3: 571–593.

Diamond, Larry J. 1999. *Developing Democracy: Toward Consolidation*. Baltimore: Johns Hopkins University Press.

Dickey, Christopher. 1985. *With the Contras: A Reporter in the Wilds of Nicaragua*. New York: Simon and Schuster.

Dickson, Bruce. 1993. "The Lessons of Defeat: The Reorganization of the Kuomintang on Taiwan, 1950–52." *China Quarterly* 133: 56–84.

Dickson, Bruce. 2008. *Wealth into Power: The Communist Party's Embrace of China's Private Sector*. Cambridge: Cambridge University Press.

Dickson, Bruce. 2014. "Who Wants to Be a Communist? Career Incentives and Mobilized Loyalty in China." *China Quarterly* 217: 42–68.

Diederick, Bernard. 1981. *Somoza and the Legacy of U.S. Involvement in Central America*. New York: E. P. Dutton.

Dikötter, Frank. 2010. *Mao's Great Famine: The History of China's Most Devastating Catastrophe, 1958–1962*. New York: Walker.

Dikötter, Frank. 2013. *The Tragedy of Liberation: A History of the Chinese Revolution 1945–1957*. London: Bloomsbury.

Dikötter, Frank. 2016. *The Cultural Revolution: A People's History, 1962–1976*. New York: Bloomsbury.

Dimitrijevic, Bojan. 2019. "Intelligence and Security Services in Tito's Yugoslavia. 1944–1966." *Istorija 20 veka* 37, no. 2: 9–28.

Dimitrov, Martin K. 2013. "Understanding Communist Collapse and Resilience." In Martin K. Dimitrov, ed., *Why Communism Did Not Collapse: Understanding Authoritarian Resilience in Asia and Europe*. New York: Cambridge University Press.

Dittmer, Lowell. 1978. "Bases of Power in Chinese Politics: A Theory and an Analysis of the Fall of the 'Gang of Four.'" *World Politics* 31, no. 1: 26–60.

Dittmer, Lowell. 1990. "Patterns of Elite Strife and Succession in Chinese Politics." *China Quarterly* 123: 405–430.

Dix, Robert. 1983. "Varieties of Revolution." *Comparative Politics* 15, no. 3: 281–293.

Dixon, Chris. 2004. "State, Party and Political Change in Vietnam." In Duncan McCargo, ed., *Rethinking Vietnam*. London: RoutledgeCurzon.

Dixon, Joe C. 1986. *Defeat and Disarmament: Allied Diplomacy and the Politics of Military Disarmament*. Newark: University of Delaware Press.

Djilas, Aleksa. 1995. "Tito's Last Secret." *Foreign Affairs* 74, no. 4: 116–122.

Djilas, Milovan. 1962. *Conversations with Stalin*. Translated by Michael B. Petrovich. New York: Harcourt, Brace and World.

Dodson, Michael. 1986. "The Politics of Religion in Revolutionary Nicaragua." *Annals of the American Academy of Political and Social Science* 483 (January): 36–49.

Dodson, Michael. 1991. "Religion and Revolution." In Thomas W. Walker, ed., *Revolution and Counterrevolution in Nicaragua*. Boulder, CO: Westview Press.

Dodson, Michael, and T. S. Montgomery. 1982. "The Churches in the Nicaraguan Revolution." In Thomas W. Walker, ed., *Nicaragua in Revolution*. New York: Praeger.

Dodson, Michael, and Laura Nuzzi O'Shaughnessy. 1990. *Nicaragua's Other Revolution: Religious Faith and Political Struggle*. Chapel Hill: University of North Carolina Press.

Dollar, David. 1999. "The Transformation of Vietnam's Economy: Sustaining Growth in the 21st Century." In Jennie I. Litvack and Dennis A. Rondinelli, eds., *Market Reform in Vietnam: Building Institutions for Development*. Westport, CT: Quorum Books.

Domínguez, Jorge I. 1974. "The Civic Soldier in Cuba." In Catherine M. Kelleher, ed., *Political-Military Systems: Comparative Perspectives*. Beverly Hills, CA: Sage Publications.

Domínguez, Jorge I. 1976a. "The Civic Soldier in Cuba." In Abraham F. Lowenthal, ed., *Armies and Politics in Latin America*. New York: Holmes and Meier.

Domínguez, Jorge I. 1976b. "Institutionalization and Civil-Military Relations in Cuba." *Cuban Studies* 6, no. 1: 39–65.

Domínguez, Jorge I. 1978. *Cuba: Order and Revolution*. Cambridge, MA: Harvard University Press.

Domínguez, Jorge I. 1979. "The Armed Forces and Foreign Relations." In Cole Blasier and Carmelo Mesa-Lago, eds., *Cuba in the World*. Pittsburgh: University of Pittsburgh Press.

Domínguez, Jorge I. 1981. "Political and Military Limitations and Consequences of Cuban Policies in Africa." In Carmelo Mesa-Lago and June S. Belkin, eds., *Cuba in Africa*. Pittsburgh: Center for Latin American Studies, University of Pittsburgh.

Domínguez, Jorge I. 1982a. "The Cuban Army." In Jonathan R. Adelman, ed., *Communist Armies in Politics*. Boulder, CO: Westview Press.

Domínguez, Jorge I. 1982b. "Revolutionary Politics: The New Demands for Orderliness." In Jorge I. Domínguez, ed., *Cuba: Internal and International Affairs*. Beverly Hills, CA: Sage Publications.

Domínguez, Jorge I. 1985. "Succession in Cuba: Institutional Strengths and Weaknesses." In Jaime Suchlicki, ed., *Problems of Succession in Cuba*. Coral Gables, FL: Institute of Interamerican Studies, Graduate School of International Studies, University of Miami, North-South Center.

Domínguez, Jorge I. 1989. *To Make a World Safe for Revolution: Cuba's Foreign Policy*. Cambridge, MA: Harvard University Press.

Domínguez, Jorge I. 1993a. "The Political Impact on Cuba of the Reform and Collapse of Communist Regimes." In Carmelo Mesa-Lago, ed., *Cuba after the Cold War*. Pittsburgh: University of Pittsburgh Press.

Domínguez, Jorge I. 1993b. "The Secrets of Castro's Staying Power." *Foreign Affairs* 72, no. 2: 97–107.

Domínguez, Jorge I. 1994. "Leadership Strategies and Mass Support: Cuban Politics before and after the 1991 Communist Party Congress." In Jorge Pérez-López, ed., *Cuba at a Crossroads: Politics and Economics after the Fourth Party Congress*. Gainesville: University Press of Florida.

Domínguez, Jorge I. 1998. "The Batista Regime in Cuba." In Houchang E. Chehabi and Juan J. Linz, eds., *Sultanistic Regimes*. Baltimore: Johns Hopkins University Press.

Domínguez, Jorge I. 2020. "Cuban Military and Politics." In *Oxford Research Encyclopedia of Politics*. New York: Oxford University Press.

Domínguez, Jorge I., and Christopher Mitchell. 1977. "The Roads Not Taken: Institutionalization and Political Parties in Cuba and Bolivia." *Comparative Politics* 9, no. 2: 173–195.

Dorn, Glenn J. 2011. *The Truman Administration and Bolivia*. University Park: Pennsylvania State University Press.

Dornberg, John. 1974. *Brezhnev: The Masks of Power*. New York: Basic Books.

Dorrill, William F. 1969. "The Fukien Rebellion and the CCP: A Case of Maoist Revisionism." *China Quarterly* 37: 31–53.

Dorronsoro, Gilles. 2005. *Revolution Unending: Afghanistan, 1979 to the Present*. London: Hurst.

Dowse, Robert. 1972. "Military and Police Rule." In Dennis Austin and Robin Luckham, eds., *Politicians and Soldiers in Ghana 1966–1972*. London: Frank Cass.

Draper, Theodore. 1962. *Castro's Revolution: Myths and Realities*. New York: Praeger.

Draper, Theodore. 1965. *Castroism: Theory and Practice*. New York: Praeger.

Dresser, Denise. 1996. "Treading Lightly and without a Stick: International Actors and the Promotion of Democracy in Mexico." In Tom Farer, ed., *Beyond Sovereignty: Collectively Defending Democracy in the Americas*. Baltimore: Johns Hopkins University Press.

Dreyer, Edward L. 2013. *China at War, 1901–1949*. New York: Routledge.

Duiker, William J. 1983. *Vietnam: Nation in Revolution*. Boulder, CO: Westview Press.

Duiker, William J. 1989. *Vietnam since the Fall of Saigon*. Updated ed. Athens: Ohio University Center for International Studies.

Duiker, William J. 1995a. *Sacred War: Nationalism and Revolution in Vietnam*. New York: McGraw-Hill.

Duiker, William J. 1995b. *Vietnam: Revolution in Transition*. Boulder, CO: Westview Press.

Duiker, William J. 1996. *The Communist Road to Power in Vietnam*. 2nd ed. Boulder, CO: Westview Press.

Duiker, William J. 2000. *Ho Chi Minh*. New York: Hyperion.

Dulles, John W. F. 1961. *Yesterday in Mexico: A Chronicle of the Revolution, 1919–1936*. Austin: University of Texas Press.

Duncan, W. Raymond. 1993. "Cuban-U.S. Relations and Political Contradictions in Cuba." In Enrique A. Baloyra and James A. Morris, eds., *Conflict and Change in Cuba*. Albuquerque: University of New Mexico Press.

Duncanson, Dennis J. 1968. *Government and Revolution in Vietnam*. London: Oxford University Press.

Dunkerley, James. 1984. *Rebellion in the Veins: Political Struggle in Bolivia, 1952–82*. London: Verso.

Dunn, John. 1972. *Modern Revolutions: An Introduction to the Analysis of a Political Phenomenon*. Cambridge: Cambridge University Press.

Dunning, Thad. 2008. *Crude Democracy: Natural Resource Wealth and Political Regimes*. New York: Cambridge University Press.

Dupree, Nancy Hatch. 2001. "Afghan Women under the Taliban." In William Maley, ed., *Fundamentalism Reborn? Afghanistan and the Taliban*. New York: New York University Press.

Easter, Gerald M. 2000. *Reconstructing the State: Personal Networks and Elite Identity in Soviet Russia*. New York: Cambridge University Press.

Easterling, Stuart. 2012. *The Mexican Revolution: A Short History, 1910–1920*. Chicago: Haymarket Books.

Eckelt, Frank. 1965. *The Rise and Fall of the Béla Kun Regime in 1919*. Doctoral dissertation, New York University. ProQuest.

Eckstein, Susan. 1976. *The Impact of a Revolution: A Comparative Analysis of Mexico and Bolivia*. London: Sage Publications.

Eckstein, Susan. 1982. "The Impact of Revolution on Social Welfare in Latin America." *Theory and Society* 11, no. 1: 43–94.

Eckstein, Susan. 1983. "Transformation of a 'Revolution from Below'—Bolivia and International Capital." *Comparative Studies in Society and History* 25, no. 1: 105–135.

Eckstein, Susan. 2003. *Back from the Future: Cuba under Castro*. New York: Routledge.

Economist Intelligence Unit. 2016. "'Diaspora Tax' Draws More Criticism." August 31. http://country.eiu.com/article.aspx?articleid=34564387&Country=Eritrea&topic=Economy&subtopic=Forecast&subsubtopic=External+sector.

Economy, Elizabeth. 2018. *The Third Revolution: Xi Jinping and the New Chinese State*. Oxford: Oxford University Press.

Edele, Mark. 2017. *Stalin's Defectors: How Red Army Soldiers Became Hitler's Collaborators*. New York: Oxford University Press.

Edmisten, Patricia Taylor. 1990. *Nicaragua Divided: La Prensa and the Chamorro Legacy*. Pensacola: University of West Florida Press.

Edwards, Lyford P. 1927. *The Natural History of Revolution*. Chicago: University of Chicago Press.

Ehteshami, Anoushiravan. 2017. *Iran: Stuck in Transition*. New York: Routledge.

Eisenstadt, S. N. 1992. "The Breakdown of Communist Regimes and the Vicissitudes of Modernity." *Daedalus* 121, no. 2: 21–41.

Eisenstadt, S. N. 1978. *Revolution and the Transformation of Societies: A Comparative Study of Civilizations*. New York: Free Press.

Eisenstadt, Todd A. 2004. *Courting Democracy in Mexico: Party Strategies and Electoral Institutions*. New York: Cambridge University Press.

Elischer, Sebastian. 2013. *Political Parties in Africa: Ethnicity and Party Formation*. New York: Cambridge University Press.

Elliott, David W. P. 1980. "Institutionalizing the Revolution: Vietnam's Search for a Model of Development." In William S. Turley, ed., *Vietnamese Communism in Comparative Perspective*. Boulder, CO: Westview Press.

Elliott, David W. P. 1995. "Vietnam Faces the Future." *Current History* 94, no. 596: 412–419.

Elliott, David W. P. 2003. *The Vietnamese War: Revolution and Social Change in the Mekong Delta, 1930–1975*. Armonk, NY: M. E. Sharpe.

Embaló, Birgit. 2012. "Civil-Military Relations and Political Order in Guinea-Bissau." *Journal of Modern African Studies* 50, no. 2: 253–281.

Emerson, Stephen A. 2014. *The Battle for Mozambique: The Frelimo-Renamo Struggle, 1977–1992*. West Midlands, UK: Helion.

Engelstein, Laura. 2018. *Russia in Flames: War, Revolution, Civil War, 1914–1921*. New York: Oxford University Press.

Entelis, John P. 1986. *Algeria: The Revolution Institutionalized*. Boulder, CO: Westview Press.

Entelis, John P. 1994. "Islam, Democracy, and the State: The Reemergence of Authoritarian Politics in Algeria." In John Ruedy, ed., *Islamism and Secularism in North Africa*. New York: St. Martin's Press.

Entelis, John P. 2011. "Algeria: Democracy Denied, and Revived?" *Journal of North African Studies* 16, no. 4: 653–678.

Eritrea Focus. 2019. "Eritrea: A Message to the 'G-4'—on the 18th Anniversary of the 'G-11' Disappearance." September 19. https://www.asmarino.com/ai-commentary/5205 -eritrea-a-message-to-the-g-4-on-the-18th-anniversary-of-the-g-11-disappearance.

Erlich, Alexander. 1960. *The Soviet Industrialization Debate, 1924–1928*. Cambridge, MA: Harvard University Press.

Escalante Font, Fabián. 2008. "La contrarrevolución en los primeros años de la revolución cubana." In Enrique Oltuski Ozacki, Héctor Rodríguez Llompart, and Eduardo Torres-Cuevas, eds., *Memorias de la revolución II*. Havana: Imagen Contemporánea.

Escobar, Saúl David. 1987. "Rifts in the Mexican Power Elite, 1976–1986." In Sylvia Maxfield and Ricardo Anzaldúa Montoya, eds., *Government and Private Sector in Contemporary Mexico*. La Jolla: Center for U.S.-Mexican Studies, University of California, San Diego.

Esherick, Joseph. 2008. "Forum: Mao and the Cultural Revolution in China: Commentaries on *Mao's Last Revolution* and a Reply by the Authors: Commentary by Joseph W. Esherick, University of California, San Diego." *Journal of Cold War Studies* 10, no. 2: 116–119.

Espinosa, Juan Carlos. 2003. "Vanguard of the State: The Cuban Armed Forces in Transition." In Irving Louis Horowitz and Jaime Suchlicki, eds., *Cuban Communism, 1959–2003*. New Brunswick, NJ: Transaction Publishers.

Esseks, John D. 1971. "Political Independence and Economic Decolonization: The Case of Ghana under Nkrumah." *Western Political Quarterly* 24, no. 1: 59–64.

Estrin, Saul. 1991. "Yugoslavia: The Case of Self-Managing Market Socialism." *Journal of Economic Perspectives* 5, no. 4: 187–194.

Etcheson, Craig. 2005. *After the Killing Fields*. Westport, CT: Praeger.

Etcheverry, Pedro Vázquez, and Santiago Gutiérrez Oceguera. 2008. *Bandidismo: Derrota de la CIA en Cuba*. Havana: Editorial Capitan San Luis.

European Council on Foreign Relations. 2019. "Meeting the Challenge of Secondary Sanctions." Policy Brief, June 25. https://ecfr.eu/publication/meeting_the _challenge_of_secondary_sanctions/.

Evans, Grant, and Kelvin Rowley. 1984. *Red Brotherhood at War: Vietnam, Cambodia, and Laos since 1975*. London: Verso.

Evans, Martin. 2012. *Algeria: France's Undeclared War*. Oxford: Oxford University Press.

Evans, Martin, and John Phillips. 2007. *Algeria: Anger of the Dispossessed*. New Haven, CT: Yale University Press.

Evenson, Debra. 1994. *Revolution in the Balance: Law and Society in Contemporary Cuba*. Boulder, CO: Westview Press.

Everingham, Mark. 1996. *Revolution and the Multiclass Coalition in Nicaragua*. Pittsburgh: University of Pittsburgh Press.

Fagen, Richard R. 1969. *The Transformation of Political Culture in Cuba*. Stanford, CA: Stanford University Press.

Fagen, Richard R. 1970a. "The Integrated Revolutionary Organizations." In Richard R. Fagen and Wayne A. Cornelius Jr., eds., *Political Power in Latin America: Seven Confrontations*. Englewood Cliffs, NJ: Prentice-Hall.

Fagen, Richard R. 1970b. "The New Communist Party and the Return of Escalante." In Richard R. Fagen and Wayne A. Cornelius Jr., eds., *Political Power in Latin America: Seven Confrontations*. Englewood Cliffs, NJ: Prentice-Hall.

Fagen, Richard R. 1972. "Continuities in Cuban Revolutionary Politics." *Monthly Review* 23, no. 11: 24–28.

Fagen, Richard R., Richard A. Brody, and Thomas O'Leary. 1968. *Cubans in Exile: Disaffection and the Revolution*. Stanford, CA: Stanford University Press.

Fagen, Richard R., and Wayne A. Cornelius Jr., eds. 1970. *Political Power in Latin America: Seven Confrontations*. Englewood Cliffs, NJ: Prentice-Hall.

Fainsod, Merle. 1958. *Smolensk under Soviet Rule*. Cambridge, MA: Harvard University Press.

Fairbank, John K. 1987. *The Great Chinese Revolution, 1800–1985*. New York: Harper and Row.

Falcón, Ramona. 1984. *Revolución y caciquismo: San Luis Potosí, 1910–1938*. Mexico City: El Colegio de México.

Falcón, Ramona. 1988. "Saturnino Cedillo: El último gran cacique militar." In Carlos Martínez Assad, ed., *Estadistas, caciques y caudillos*. Mexico City: Instituto de Investigaciones Sociales.

Fall, Bernard B. 1954. "The Viet-Minh Regime: Government and Administration in the Democratic Republic of Vietnam." Data paper no. 14, Department of Far Eastern Studies, Cornell University.

Fall, Bernard B. 1955. "The Political-Religious Sects of Viet-Nam." *Pacific Affairs* 28, no. 3: 235–253.

Fall, Bernard B. 1967. *Street without Joy*. 4th ed. New York: Schocken Books.

Fall, Bernard B. 1968. *The Two Vietnams: A Political and Military Analysis*. 6th ed. New York: Praeger.

Fallaw, Ben. 2012. "Eulogio Ortiz: The Army and the Antipolitics of Postrevolutionary State Formation, 1920–1935." In Ben Fallaw and Terry Rugeley, eds., *Forced Marches: Soldiers and Military Caciques in Modern Mexico*. Tucson: University of Arizona Press.

Fallaw, Ben. 2013. *Religion and State Formation in Revolutionary Mexico*. Durham, NC: Duke University Press.

Fallaw, Ben, and Terry Rugeley, eds. 2012. *Forced Marches: Soldiers and Military Caciques in Modern Mexico*. Tucson: University of Arizona Press.

Farber, Samuel. 1976. *Revolution and Reaction in Cuba*. Middletown, CT: Wesleyan University Press.

Farber, Samuel. 1992. "Castro under Siege." *World Policy Journal* 9, no. 2: 329–348.

Farber, Samuel. 2006. *The Origins of the Cuban Revolution Reconsidered*. Chapel Hill: University of North Carolina Press.

Farhi, Farideh. 1990. *States and Urban-Based Revolutions: Iran and Nicaragua.* Urbana: University of Illinois Press.

Fearon, James D. 2004. "Why Do Some Civil Wars Last So Much Longer than Others?" *Journal of Peace Research* 41, no. 3: 275–301.

Fenby, Jonathan. 2003. *Chiang Kai-shek: China's Generalissimo and the Nation He Lost.* New York: Carrol and Graf.

Fermoselle, Rafael. 1987a. *Cuban Leadership after Castro: Biographies of Cuba's Top Generals.* Miami: Ediciones Universal.

Fermoselle, Rafael. 1987b. *The Evolution of the Cuban Military, 1492–1986.* Miami: Ediciones Universal.

Fernández, Damián. 1989. "Historical Background: Achievements, Failures, and Prospects." In Jaime Suchlicki, ed., *The Cuban Military under Castro.* Coral Gables, FL: Institute of Interamerican Studies, Graduate School of International Studies, University of Miami, North-South Center.

Fernández, Damián. 2003. "Searching for Civil Society in Cuba." In Irving Louis Horowitz and Jaime Suchlicki, eds., *Cuban Communism, 1959–2003.* New Brunswick, NJ: Transaction Publishers.

Fevziu, B. 2016. *Enver Hoxha: The Iron Fist of Albania.* London: I. B. Tauris.

Fforde, Adam. 1993. "The Vietnamese Economy in 1992: Development and Prospects." In Carlyle A. Thayer and David G. Marr, eds., *Vietnam and the Rule of Law.* Canberra: Department of Political and Social Change, Australian National University.

Fforde, Adam, and Stefan de Vylder. 1996. *From Plan to Market: The Economic Transition in Vietnam.* Boulder, CO: Westview Press.

Fforde, Adam, and Suzanne H. Paine. 1987. *The Limits of National Liberation: Problems of Economic Management in the Democratic Republic of Vietnam.* London: Croom Helm.

Field, Thomas C. 2014. *From Development to Dictatorship: Bolivia and the Alliance for Progress in the Kennedy Era.* Ithaca, NY: Cornell University Press.

Figes, Orlando. 2014. *A People's Tragedy: The Russian Revolution 1891–1924.* London: The Bodley Head.

Finer, Samuel. 1962. *The Man on Horseback: The Role of the Military in Politics.* London: Pall Mall Press.

First, Ruth. 1970. *The Barrel of a Gun: Political Power in Africa and the Coup d'Etat.* London: Penguin.

Fischer, Bernd. 1999. *Albania at War: 1939–1945.* West Lafayette, IN: Purdue University Press.

Fistein, David. 2011. "Guinea-Bissau: How a Successful Social Revolution Can Become an Obstacle to Subsequent State-Building." *International Journal of African Historical Studies* 44, no. 3: 443–455.

Fitzgerald, Frances. 1972. *Fire in the Lake: The Vietnamese and the Americans in Vietnam.* Boston: Little, Brown.

Fitzgerald, Frank T. 1990. *Managing Socialism: From Old Cadres to New Professionals in Revolutionary Cuba.* New York: Praeger.

Fitzpatrick, Sheila. 1984. "Origins of Stalinism: How Important Was the Civil War?" *Acta Slavica Iaponica* 2: 105–125.

Fitzpatrick, Sheila. 1989. "New Perspectives on the Civil War." In Diane P. Koenker, William G. Rosenberg, and Ronald Grigor Suny, eds., *Party, State, and Society in the Russian Civil War: Explorations in Social History.* Bloomington: Indiana University Press.

Fitzpatrick, Sheila. 1999. *Everyday Stalinism: Ordinary Life in Extraordinary Times: Soviet Russia in the 1930s.* New York: Oxford University Press.

Fitzpatrick, Sheila. 2008. *The Russian Revolution.* New York: Oxford University Press.

Fitzpatrick, Sheila. 2015. *On Stalin's Team: The Years of Living Dangerously in Soviet Politics.* Princeton, NJ: Princeton University Press.

Flood, Patrick. 1998. *The Effectiveness of UN Human Rights Institutions.* Westport, CT: Praeger.

Flores, Edmundo. 1954. "Land Reform in Bolivia." *Land Economics* 30, no. 2: 112–124.

Font, Mauricio. 1997. "Crisis and Reform in Cuba." In Miguel Ángel Centeno and Mauricio Font, eds., *Toward a New Cuba? Legacies of a Revolution.* Boulder, CO: Lynne Rienner.

Foran, John, ed. 1997. *Theorizing Revolutions.* London: Routledge.

Foran, John. 2005. *Taking Power: On the Origins of Third World Revolutions.* New York: Cambridge University Press.

Foran, John, and Jeff Goodwin. 1993. "Revolutionary Outcomes in Iran and Nicaragua: Coalition Fragmentation, War, and the Limits of Social Transformation." *Theory and Society* 22, no. 2: 209–247.

Foroohar, Manzar. 1989. *The Catholic Church and Social Change in Nicaragua.* Albany: State University of New York Press.

Forozan, Hesam, and Afshin Shahi. 2017. "The Military and the State in Iran: The Economic Rise of the Revolutionary Guards." *Middle East Journal* 71, no. 1: 67–86.

Forrest, Joshua. 1987. "Guinea-Bissau since Independence: A Decade of Domestic Power Struggles." *Journal of Modern African Studies* 25, no. 1: 95–116.

Forrest, Joshua. 1992. *Guinea-Bissau: Power, Conflict, and Renewal in a West African Nation.* Boulder, CO: Westview Press.

Forrest, Joshua. 2005. "Democratization in a Divided Urban Political Culture." In Leonardo A. Villalón and Peter VonDoepp, eds., *The Fate of Africa's Democratic Experiments: Elites and Institutions.* Bloomington: Indiana University Press.

Fowkes, Ben. 2002. "The National Question in the Soviet Union under Brezhnev: Policy and Response." In Edwin Bacon, ed., *Brezhnev Reconsidered.* New York: Palgrave Macmillan.

Fowler Salamini, Heather. 1980. "Revolutionary Caudillos in the 1920s: Francisco Múgica and Adalberto Tejeda." In D. A. Brading, ed., *Caudillo and Peasant in the Mexican Revolution.* Cambridge: Cambridge University Press.

Fowler Salamini, Heather. 1991. "Caciquismo and the Mexican Revolution: The Case of Manuel Peláez." In Roderick A. Camp, Charles A. Hale, and Josefina Zoraida Vázquez, eds., *Los intelectuales y el poder en México.* Mexico City: Colegio de México.

Franqui, Carlos. 1984. *Family Portrait with Fidel: A Memoir.* New York: Random House.

Freedom House. 2008. *Freedom in the World 2008.* New York: Freedom House. https://freedomhouse.org/sites/default/files/2020-02/Freedom_in_the_World_2008_complete_book.pdf.

Frempong, A. K. 2005. "The Internal and Regional Dynamics of the Cycle of War and Peace in Guinea-Bissau." Paper prepared for the Lusophonie in Africa CODESRIA International Colloquium, Luanda, Angola.

Friedrich, Carl J., and Zbigniew K. Brzezinski. 1965. *Totalitarian Dictatorship and Autocracy.* Cambridge, MA: Harvard University Press.

Fuentes, Gloria. 1983. *El ejercito mexicano.* Mexico City: Grijalbo.

Fuentes Díaz, Vicente. 1969. *Los partidos políticos en México.* Mexico City: Editorial Altiplano.

Fuller, Graham E. 1995. *Algeria: The Next Fundamentalist State?* Santa Monica, CA: Rand Corporation.

Gainsborough, Martin. 2010. *Vietnam: Rethinking the State.* London: Zed Books.

Gallagher, Charles F. 1963. *The United States and North Africa: Morocco, Algeria, and Tunisia.* Cambridge, MA: Harvard University Press.

Gallagher, Mary, and Jonathan K. Hanson. 2013. "Authoritarian Survival, Resilience, and the Selectorate Theory." In Martin K. Dimitrov, ed., *Why Communism Did Not Collapse: Understanding Authoritarian Resilience in Asia and Europe.* New York: Cambridge University Press.

Galula, David. 2006. *Pacification in Algeria, 1956–1958.* Santa Monica, CA: Rand Corporation.

Gandhi, Jennifer. 2008. *Political Institutions under Dictatorship.* Cambridge: Cambridge University Press.

Gandhi, Jennifer, and Adam Przeworski. 2007. "Authoritarian Institutions and the Survival of Autocrats." *Comparative Political Studies* 40, no. 11: 1279–1301.

Gao, Wenqian. 2007. *Zhou Enlai: The Last Perfect Revolutionary.* New York: PublicAffairs.

García Arganarás, Fernando. 1992. "Bolivia's Transformist Revolution." *Latin American Perspectives* 73, no. 2: 44–71.

García Montes, Jorge, and Antonio Alonso Avila. 1970. *Historia del Partido Comunista de Cuba.* Miami: Ediciones Universal.

García-Pérez, Gladys Marel. 2006. *Insurrección y revolución (1952–1959).* Havana: Ediciones Unión.

Garrido, Luis Javier. 1982. *El partido de la revolución institucionalizada: La formación del nuevo estado en México (1928–1945).* Mexico City: Siglo Veintiuno.

Gebre-Medhin, Jordan. 1984. "Nationalism, Peasant Politics, and the Emergence of a Vanguard Front in Eritrea." *Review of African Political Economy*, no. 30: 48–57.

Geddes, Barbara. 1999. "What Do We Know about Democratization after Twenty Years?" *Annual Review of Political Science* 2, no. 1: 115–144.

Geddes, Barbara, Joseph Wright, and Erica Frantz. 2014. "Autocratic Breakdown and Regime Transitions: A New Data Set." *Perspectives on Politics* 12, no. 2: 313–331.

Geddes, Barbara, Joseph Wright, and Erica Frantz. 2018. *How Dictatorships Work: Power, Personalization, and Collapse.* Cambridge: Cambridge University Press.

Gerson, Lennard D. 1976. *The Secret Police in Lenin's Russia.* Philadelphia: Temple University Press.

Gerwarth, Robert. 2008. "The Central European Counter-Revolution: Paramilitary Violence in Germany, Austria and Hungary after the Great War." *Past & Present* 200, no. 1: 175–209.

Getty, J. Arch. 2013. "Pre-election Fever: The Origins of the 1937 Mass Operations." In James Harris, ed., *The Anatomy of Terror: Political Violence under Stalin.* New York: Oxford University Press.

Getty, J. Arch, and Oleg V. Naumov. 2008. *Yezhov: The Rise of Stalin's "Iron Fist."* New Haven, CT: Yale University Press.

Getty, J. Arch, and Oleg V. Naumov. 2010. *The Road to Terror: Stalin and the Self-Destruction of the Bolsheviks, 1932–1939.* New Haven, CT: Yale University Press.

Getzler, Israel. 1983. *Kronstadt 1917–1921: The Fate of a Soviet Democracy.* New York: Cambridge University Press.

Gewirtz, Julian. 2017. *Unlikely Partners: Chinese Reformers, Western Economists, and the Making of Global China.* Cambridge, MA: Harvard University Press.

Gheddo, Piero. 1970. *The Cross and the Bo-Tree: Catholics and Buddhists in Vietnam.* New York: Sheed and Ward.

Ghobadzadeh, Naser, and Lily Zubaidah Rahim. 2016. "Electoral Theocracy and Hybrid Sovereignty in Iran." *Contemporary Politics* 22, no. 4: 450–468.

Giap, Vo Nguyen. 1975. *Unforgettable Days.* Hanoi: Foreign Languages Publishing House.

Gieling, Saskia. 1997. "The 'Marja'iya' in Iran and the Nomination of Khamanei in December 1994." *Middle Eastern Studies* 33, no. 4: 777–787.

Gilbert, Dennis. 1988. *Sandinistas.* New York: Basil Blackwell.

Gill, Graeme. 1990. *The Origins of the Stalinist Political System.* New York: Cambridge University Press.

Gilley, Bruce. 2004. *China's Democratic Future: How It Will Happen and Where It Will Lead.* New York: Columbia University Press.

Gillingham, Paul. 2012. "Who Killed Crispín Aguilar? Violence and Order in the Post-revolutionary Countryside." In Will G. Pansters, ed., *Violence, Coercion, and State-Making in Twentieth-Century Mexico: The Other Half of the Centaur.* Stanford, CA: Stanford University Press.

Gillingham, Paul, and Benjamin T. Smith. 2014. "The Paradoxes of Revolution." In Paul Gillingham and Benjamin T. Smith, eds., *Dictablanda: Politics, Work, and Culture in Mexico, 1938–1968.* Durham, NC: Duke University Press.

Gilly, Adolfo. 1964. *Inside the Cuban Revolution.* New York: Monthly Review Press.

Gilly, Adolfo. 2005. *The Mexican Revolution.* New York: New Press.

Giustozzi, Antonio. 2019. *The Taliban at War: 2001–2018.* New York: Oxford University Press.

Glantz, David M., and Jonathan M. House. 2015. *When Titans Clashed: How the Red Army Stopped Hitler.* Lawrence: University Press of Kansas.

Gleijeses, Piero. 2009. *The Cuban Drumbeat: Castro's Worldview: Cuban Foreign Policy in a Hostile World.* London: Seagull Books.

Goemans, H. E., Kristian Skrede Gleditsch, and Giacomo Chiozza. 2009. "Introducing Archigos: A Dataset of Political Leaders." *Journal of Peace Research* 46, no. 2: 269–283.

Golan, Galia. 1988. *The Soviet Union and National Liberation Movements in the Third World.* London: Unwin Hyman.

Goldenberg, Boris. 1965. *The Cuban Revolution and Latin America.* New York: Praeger.

Goldfrank, Walter. 1975. "World System, State Structure, and the Onset of the Mexican Revolution." *Politics and Society* 5, no. 4: 417–439.

Goldfrank, Walter. 1979. "Theories of Revolution and Revolution without Theory: The Case of Mexico." *Theory and Society* 7, no. 1/2: 135–165.

Goldstone, Jack. 1980. "Theories of Revolution: The Third Generation." *World Politics* 32, no. 3: 425–453.

Goldstone, Jack. 1991. *Revolution and Rebellion in the Early Modern World*. Berkeley: University of California Press.

Goldstone, Jack. 1998. *The Encyclopedia of Political Revolutions*. London: Routledge.

Goldstone, Jack. 2001. "Toward a Fourth Generation of Revolutionary Theory." *Annual Review of Political Science* 4: 139–187.

Goldstone, Jack. 2014. *Revolutions: A Very Short Introduction*. Oxford: Oxford University Press.

Goldstone, Jack, Ted Robert Gurr, and Farrokh Moshiri, eds. 1991. *Revolutions of the Late Twentieth Century*. Boulder, CO: Westview Press.

Golkar, Saeid. 2011. "Politics of Piety: The Basij and Moral Control of Iranian Society." *Journal of the Middle East and Africa* 2, no. 2: 207–219.

Golkar, Saeid. 2012. "Organization of the Oppressed or Organization for Oppressing: Analysing the Role of the Basij Militia of Iran." *Politics, Religion & Ideology* 13, no. 4: 455–471.

Golkar, Saeid. 2019. "Iran after Khamenei: Prospects for Political Change." *Middle East Policy Council* 26, no. 1: 75–88.

Gomes, Adelino. 1986. "Cabral's Dream." *Africa Report*, January–February: 15–20.

Gómez Tagle, Silvia. 1994. *De la alquimia al fraude en las elecciones mexicanas*. Mexico City: García y Valadés.

Gómez Tagle, Silvia. 2004. "Public Institutions and Electoral Transparency in Mexico." In Kevin J. Middlebrook, ed., *Dilemmas of Political Change in Mexico*. London: Institute of Latin American Studies, University of London.

Gómez Treto, Raúl. 1988. *The Church and Socialism in Cuba*. Maryknoll, NY: Orbis Books.

Gonzales, Michael J. 2002. *The Mexican Revolution, 1910–1940*. Albuquerque: University of New Mexico Press.

Gonzalez, Edward. 1968. "Castro's Revolution, Cuban Communist Appeals, and the Soviet Response." *World Politics* 21, no. 1: 39–68.

Gonzalez, Edward. 1974. *Cuba under Castro: The Limits of Charisma*. Boston: Houghton Mifflin.

Gonzalez, Edward. 1976. "Political Succession in Cuba." *Studies in Comparative Communism* 9, nos. 1–2: 80–107.

Gonzalez, Edward. 1989. "The Cuban and Soviet Challenge in the Caribbean Basin." In Irving Louis Horowitz, ed., *The Cuban Revolution*. New Brunswick, NJ: Transaction Publishers.

Gonzalez, Edward, and David F. Ronfeldt. 1986. *Castro, Cuba, and the World*. Santa Monica, CA: Rand Corporation.

Gonzalez, Edward, and David F. Ronfeldt. 1992. *Cuba Adrift in a Postcommunist World*. Santa Monica, CA: Rand Corporation.

González Casanova, Pablo. 1970. *Democracy in Mexico*. Oxford: Oxford University Press.

González Casanova, Pablo. 1981. *El estado y los partidos políticos en México*. Mexico City: Ediciones Era.

Goodrich, Carter. 1971. "Bolivia in Time of Revolution." In James M. Malloy and Richard S. Thorn, eds., *Beyond the Revolution: Bolivia since 1952*. Pittsburgh: University of Pittsburgh Press.

Goodwin, Jeff. 2001. *No Other Way Out: States and Revolutionary Movements, 1945–1991*. Cambridge: Cambridge University Press.

Gooren, Henri. 2010. "Ortega for President: The Religious Rebirth of Sandinismo in Nicaragua." *European Review of Latin American and Caribbean Studies* 89: 47–63.

Gordon, David. 1966. *The Passing of French Algeria*. London: Oxford University Press.

Gorlizki, Yoram, and Oleg V. Khlevniuk. 2004. *Cold Peace: Stalin and the Soviet Ruling Circle, 1945–1953*. New York: Oxford University Press.

Gorman, Stephen M. 1981. "Power and Consolidation in the Nicaraguan Revolution." *Journal of Latin American Studies* 13, no. 1: 133–149.

Gorman, Stephen M. 1982. "The Role of the Revolutionary Armed Forces." In Thomas W. Walker, ed., *Nicaragua in Revolution*. New York: Praeger.

Gottesman, Evan. 2003. *Cambodia after the Khmer Rouge: Inside the Politics of Nation Building*. New Haven, CT: Yale University Press.

Gough, Kathleen. 1990. *Political Economy in Vietnam*. Berkeley, CA: Folklore Institute.

Gouré, Leon. 1989a. "Cuban Military Doctrine and Organization." In Jaime Suchlicki, ed., *The Cuban Military under Castro*. Miami: North-South Center, University of Miami.

Gouré, Leon. 1989b. "Soviet-Cuban Military Relations." In Jaime Suchlicki, ed., *The Cuban Military under Castro*. Miami: North-South Center, University of Miami.

Gouré, Leon. 1989c. "'War of all the People': Cuba's Military Doctrines." In Irving Louis Horowitz, ed., *The Cuban Revolution*. 7th ed. New Brunswick, NJ: Transaction Publishers.

Graziosi, Andrea. 1996. *The Great Soviet Peasant War: Bolsheviks and Peasants, 1917–1933*. Cambridge, MA: Ukrainian Research Institute, Harvard University.

Greene, David G. 1965. "Revolution and the Rationalization of Reform in Bolivia." *Inter-American Economic Affairs* 19, no. 5: 3–25.

Greene, Doug Enna. 2020. "Lenin's Boys: A Short History of Soviet Hungary." *Cosmonaut*, August 21. https://cosmonaut.blog/2020/08/21/lenins-boys-a-short-history-of-soviet-hungary.

Greene, Kenneth. 2007. *Why Dominant Parties Lose: Mexico's Democratization in Comparative Perspective*. New York: Cambridge University Press.

Greene Walker, Phyllis. 1993. "Political-Military Relations since 1959." In Enrique A. Baloyra and James A. Morris, eds., *Conflict and Change in Cuba*. Albuquerque: University of New Mexico Press.

Greene Walker, Phyllis. 1994. "The Cuban Armed Forces and Transition." In Donald E. Schulz, ed., *Cuba and the Future*. Westport, CT: Greenwood Press.

Greene Walker, Phyllis. 2003. "Political-Military Relations from 1959 to the Present." In Irving Louis Horowitz and Jaime Suchlicki, eds., *Cuban Communism, 1959–2003*. New Brunswick, NJ: Transaction Publishers.

Gregory, Paul. 2009. *Terror by Quota: State Security from Lenin to Stalin*. New Haven, CT: Yale University Press.

Greitens, Sheena Chestnut. 2016. *Dictators and Their Secret Police: Coercive Institutions and State Violence*. New York: Cambridge University Press.

Grilli, Matteo. 2017. "Nkrumah, Nationalism, and Pan-Africanism: The Bureau of African Affairs Collection." *History in Africa* 44: 295–307.

Grindle, Merilee S. 2003. "1952 and All That: The Bolivian Revolution in Comparative Perspective." In Merilee S. Grindle and Pilar Domingo, eds., *Proclaiming Revolution: Bolivia in Comparative Perspective*. London: Institute of Latin American Studies, University of London.

Guadarrama, Rocio. 1986. "Los inicios de la estabilización." In Cristina Puga et al., eds., *Evolución del estado mexicano, tomo 3, Consolidación 1940–1983*. Mexico City: Ediciones El Caballito.

Guerra, Lillian. 2012. *Visions of Power in Cuba: Revolution, Redemption, and Resistance, 1959–1971*. Chapel Hill: University of North Carolina Press.

Guerra Mercado, Juan. 2004. "Autonomía universitaria: Apuntes para una revisión histórica." *Temas sociales* 25: 233–244.

Gunitsky, Seva. 2017. *Aftershocks: Great Powers and Domestic Reforms in the Twentieth Century*. Princeton, NJ: Princeton University Press.

Gurr, Ted Robert. 1970. *Why Men Rebel*. Princeton, NJ: Princeton University Press.

Gurr, Ted Robert. 1988. "War, Revolution, and the Growth of the Coercive State." *Comparative Political Studies* 21, no. 1: 45–65.

Gutteridge, William. 1969. *The Military in African Politics*. London: Methuen.

Guzman, Luis Humberto. 1996. "Nicaragua's Armed Forces: An Assessment of Their Political Power." In Richard L. Millett and Michael Gold-Biss, eds., *Beyond Praetorianism: The Latin American Military in Transition*. Coral Gables, FL: North-South Center Press, University of Miami.

Haber, Stephen H. 1992. "Assessing the Obstacles to Industrialisation: The Mexican Economy, 1830–1940." *Journal of Latin American Studies* 24, no. 1: 1–32.

Haber, Stephen H., and Victor Menaldo. 2011. "Do Natural Resources Fuel Authoritarianism? A Reappraisal of the Resource Curse." *American Political Science Review* 105, no. 1: 1–26.

Hadjor, Kofi Buenor. 1988. *Nkrumah and Ghana: The Dilemma of Post-Colonial Power*. London: Kegan Paul International.

Hagenloh, Paul. 2009. *Stalin's Police: Public Order and Mass Repression in the USSR, 1926–1941*. Baltimore: Johns Hopkins University Press.

Hagenloh, Paul. 2013. "'Mass Operations' under Lenin and Stalin." In James Harris, ed., *The Anatomy of Terror: Political Violence under Stalin*. New York: Oxford University Press.

Haggard, Stephan, and Robert R. Kaufman. 1995. *The Political Economy of Democratic Transitions*. Princeton, NJ: Princeton University Press.

Hagmann, Tobias, and Jon Abbink. 2011. "Twenty Years of Revolutionary Democratic Ethiopia, 1991 to 2011." *Journal of Eastern African Studies* 5, no. 4: 579–595.

Hajdu, Tibor. 1979. *The Hungarian Soviet Republic*. Budapest: Akadémiai Kiadó.

Hall, Linda B. 1980. "Alvaro Obregon and the Agrarian Movement, 1912–1920." In D. A. Brading, ed., *Caudillo and Peasant in the Mexican Revolution*. Cambridge: Cambridge University Press.

Hall, Linda B. 1981. *Alvaro Obregon: Power and Rebellion in Mexico, 1911–1920*. College Station: Texas A&M University Press.

Hall, Linda B. 1990. "Banks, Oil, and the Reinstitutionalization of the Mexican State, 1920–1924." In Jaime E. Rodríguez O., ed., *The Revolutionary Process in Mexico: Essays on Political and Social Change, 1880–1940*. Los Angeles: UCLA Latin American Center Publications, University of California, Los Angeles.

Hall, Margaret, and Tom Young. 1997. *Confronting Leviathan: Mozambique since Independence*. Athens: Ohio University Press.

Halliday, Fred. 1999. *Revolution and World Politics*. London: Palgrave.

Halperin, Maurice. 1972. *The Rise and Decline of Fidel Castro*. Berkeley: University of California Press.

Halperin, Maurice. 1981. *The Taming of Fidel Castro*. Berkeley: University of California Press.

Hamilton, Nora. 1982. *The Limits of State Autonomy: Post-Revolutionary Mexico*. Princeton, NJ: Princeton University Press.

Hammer, Ellen J. 1954. *The Struggle for Indochina*. Stanford, CA: Stanford University Press.

Hance, William. 1967. "Three Economies." *Africa Report*, November: 23–30.

Hanlon, Joseph. 1990. *Mozambique: The Revolution under Fire*. London: Zed Books.

Hansen, Peter. 2009. "Bac Di Cu: Catholic Refugees from the North of Vietnam and Their Role in the Southern Republic, 1954–1959." *Journal of Vietnamese Studies* 4, no. 3: 173–211.

Hanson, Roger D. 1971. *The Politics of Mexican Development*. Baltimore: Johns Hopkins University Press.

Hanson, Stephen E. 2010. *Post-Imperial Democracies: Ideology and Party Formation in Third Republic France, Weimar Germany, and Post-Soviet Russia*. New York: Cambridge University Press.

Harding, Harry. 1991. "The Chinese State in Crisis." In Roderick MacFarquhar and John K. Fairbank, eds., *The Cambridge History of China*, vol. 15, *The People's Republic*, pt. 2, *Revolutions within the Chinese Revolution, 1966–1982*. New York: Cambridge University Press.

Harris, James. 2003. "Was Stalin a Weak Dictator?" *Journal of Modern History* 75, no. 2: 375–386.

Harris, James. 2013. "Intelligence and Threat Perception: Defending the Revolution, 1917–1937." In James Harris, ed., *The Anatomy of Terror: Political Violence under Stalin*. New York: Oxford University Press.

Harris, Kevan. 2012. "Brokered Exuberance of the Middle Class: An Ethnographic Analysis of Iran's 2009 Green Movement." *Mobilization* 17, no. 4: 435–455.

Harris, Kevan. 2017. *A Social Revolution: Politics and the Welfare State in Iran*. Berkeley: University of California Press.

Harris, Richard. 1987. "The Revolutionary Transformation of Nicaragua." *Latin American Perspectives* 14, no. 1: 3–18.

Harrison, Alexander. 1989. *Challenging De Gaulle: The O.A.S. and the Counterrevolution in Algeria, 1954–1962*. New York: Praeger.

Harrison, James Pinkney. 1972. *The Long March to Power: A History of the Chinese Communist Party, 1921–72*. New York: Macmillan.

Harrison, James Pinckney. 1982. *The Endless War: Fifty Years of Struggle in Vietnam*. New York: Free Press.

Hart, John Mason. 1987. *Revolutionary Mexico: The Coming and Process of the Mexican Revolution*. Berkeley: University of California Press.

Hasan, Sabiha. 1981. "Yugoslavia's Foreign Policy under Tito." *Pakistan Horizon* 34, no. 4: 62–103.

Hashemi, Nader, and Danny Postel. 2010. "Introduction." In Nader Hashemi and Danny Postel, eds., *The People Reloaded: The Green Movement and the Struggle for Iran's Future*. Brooklyn, NY: Melville House.

Hauslohner, Peter. 1987. "Gorbachev's Social Contract." *Soviet Economy* 3: 54–89.

Havik, Philip J. 2012. "Virtual Nations and Failed States: Making Sense of the Labyrinth." In Eric Morier-Genoud, ed., *Sure Road? Nationalisms in Angola, Guinea-Bissau and Mozambique*. Leiden: Brill.

Hayton, Bill. 2010. *Vietnam: Rising Dragon*. New Haven, CT: Yale University Press.

Heath, Dwight B., Charles J. Erasmus, and Hans C. Bueschler. 1969. *Land Reform and Social Revolution in Bolivia*. New York: Praeger.

Hebbel, Hollis C. 1993. "The Vietnamese Military's Changing Role." *Southeast Asian Affairs* 1993: 364–372.

Heilbrunn, John. 1997. "Commerce, Politics and Business Associations in Benin and Togo." *Comparative Politics* 29, no. 4: 473–492.

Heilmann, Sebastian, and Elizabeth J. Perry. 2011. "Embracing Uncertainty: Guerrilla Policy Style and Adaptive Governance in China." In Sebastian Heilmann and Elizabeth J. Perry, eds., *Mao's Invisible Hand: The Political Foundations of Adaptive Governance in China*. Cambridge, MA: Harvard University Press.

Heinemann, Winfred. 2019. *Unternehmen "Walküre": Eine Militärgeschichte des 20. Juli 1944*. Göttingen: Druck und Bindung.

Hellbeck, Jochen. 2015. *Stalingrad: The City That Defeated the Third Reich*. New York: PublicAffairs.

Hellman, Judith Adler. 1983. *Mexico in Crisis*. New York: Holmes and Meier.

Henderson, Lawrence W. 1979. *Angola: Five Centuries of Conflict*. Ithaca, NY: Cornell University Press.

Henderson, Peter V. N. 1981. *Félix Díaz, the Porfirians, and the Mexican Revolution*. Lincoln: University of Nebraska Press.

Heng, Russell Hiang-Khng. 1998. "Media in Vietnam and the Structure of Its Management." In David G. Marr, ed., *Mass Media in Vietnam*. Canberra: Department of Political and Social Change, Australian National University.

Hennessy, C. A. M. 1964. "Shifting Forces in the Bolivian Revolution." *The World Today* 20, no. 5: 197–207.

Henriksen, Thomas H. 1978. "Marxism and Mozambique." *African Affairs* 77, no. 309: 441–462.

Henry, Clement. 2004. "Algeria's Agonies: Oil Rent Effects in a Bunker State." *Journal of North African Studies* 9, no. 2: 68–81.

Heradslveil, Daniel. 1998. *Political Islam in Algeria*. Oslo: Norwegian Institute of International Affairs.

Hernández Chávez, Alicia. 2006. *Mexico: A Brief History*. Berkeley: University of California Press.

Hernández Rodríguez, Rogelio. 2014. "Strongmen and State Weakness." In Paul Gillingham and Benjamin T. Smith, eds., *Dictablanda: Politics, Work, and Culture in Mexico, 1938–1968*. Durham, NC: Duke University Press.

Herrera Medina, José R. 2006. *Operación Jaula: Contragolpe en el Escambray*. Havana: Editorial Verde Olivo.

Herrera Zúñiga, René. 1994. *Nicaragua, el derrumbe negociado*. Mexico City: El Colegio de México.

Herspring, Dale R. 1996. *Russian Civil-Military Relations*. Bloomington: Indiana University Press.

Heuveline, Patrick. 1998. "'Between One and Three Million': Towards the Demographic Reconstruction of a Decade of Cambodian History (1970–79)." *Population Studies* 51, no. 1: 49–65.

Heywood, Linda. 2000. *Contested Power in Angola, 1840s to the Present*. Rochester, NY: University of Rochester Press.

Hibbert, Reginald. 1991. *Albania's National Liberation Struggle: The Bitter Victory*. London: Pinter Publishers.

Hiep, Le Hong. 2016. "Vietnam in 2015: Challenges Persist amidst Hope for Change." *Southeast Asian Affairs* 2016: 363–378.

Hill, Alexander. 2017. *The Red Army and the Second World War*. New York: Cambridge University Press.

Hill, Jonathan. 2009. *Identity in Algerian Politics: The Legacy of Colonial Rule*. Boulder, CO: Lynne Rienner.

Hill, Jonathan. 2012. "Remembering the War of Liberation: Legitimacy and Conflict in Contemporary Algeria." *Small Wars and Insurgencies* 23, no. 1: 4–31.

Hill, Jonathan. 2016. *Democratization in the Maghreb*. Edinburgh: Edinburgh University Press.

Hill, Jonathan. 2019. "The Evolution of Authoritarian Rule in Algeria: Linkage versus Organizational Power." *Democratization* 26, no. 8: 1382–1398.

Hinton, William. 1966. *Fanshen: A Documentary of Revolution in a Chinese Village*. Middlesex, UK: Penguin Books.

Ho, Daniel E., Kosuke Imai, Gary King, and Elizabeth A. Stuart. 2007. "Matching as Nonparametric Preprocessing for Reducing Model Dependence in Parametric Causal Inference." *Political Analysis* 15, no. 3: 199–236.

Hoare, Marko. 2011. "The Partisans and the Serbs." In Sabrina Ramet and Ola Listhaug, eds., *Serbia and the Serbs in World War Two*. New York: Palgrave Macmillan.

Hodges, Donald C., and Ross Gandy. 2002. *Mexico, the End of the Revolution*. Westport, CT: Praeger.

Hodges, Tony. 1979. "Guinea-Bissau: Five Years of Independence." *Africa Report*, January–February: 4–9.

Hodges, Tony. 2004. *Angola: Anatomy of an Oil State*. Oxford: James Curry.

Hodgkin, Thomas. 1981. *Vietnam: The Revolutionary Path*. London: Macmillan.

Hofheinz, Roy. 1967. "The Autumn Harvest Insurrection." *China Quarterly* 32: 37–87.

Hofheinz, Roy. 1977. *The Broken Wave: The Chinese Communist Peasant Movement, 1922–1928*. Cambridge, MA: Harvard University Press.

Holbrook, Joseph. 2010. "The Catholic Church in Cuba, 1959–1962: The Clash of Ideologies." *International Journal of Cuban Studies* 2, no. 3/4: 264–275.

Holmes, Leslie. 2007. "Vietnam in Comparative Communist and Postcommunist Perspective." In Stephanie Balme and Mark Sidel, eds., *Vietnam's New Order: International Perspectives on the State and Reform in Vietnam*. New York: Palgrave Macmillan.

Holquist, Peter. 2002. *Making War, Forging Revolution: Russia's Continuum of Crisis, 1914–1921*. Cambridge, MA: Harvard University Press.

Holquist, Peter. 2003. "Violent Russia, Deadly Marxism? Russia in the Epoch of Violence, 1905–21." *Kritika* 4, no. 3: 627–652.

Holtey, Joseph C., ed. 2012. *Victor Paz Estenssoro: A Political Biography*. Scotts Valley, CA: CreateSpace Independent Publishing Platform.

Home Office. 2004. *Eritrea Report*. Country Information and Policy Unit Immigration and Nationality Directorate, United Kingdom.

Honey, P. J. 1963. *Communism in Vietnam*. Cambridge, MA: MIT Press.

Horne, Alistair. (1977) 2006. *A Savage War of Peace: Algeria 1954–1962*. New York: New York Review Books.

Horowitz, Irving Louis. 1970. "Cuban Communism." In Irving Louis Horowitz, ed., *Cuban Communism*. New Brunswick, NJ: Transaction Publishers.

Horowitz, Irving Louis. 1971. "The Political Sociology of Cuban Communism." In Carmelo Mesa-Lago, ed., *Revolutionary Change in Cuba*. Pittsburgh: University of Pittsburgh Press.

Horowitz, Irving Louis. 1975. "Military Origins of the Cuban Revolution." *Armed Forces and Society* 1, no. 4: 402–418.

Hou, Yue. 2019. *The Private Sector in Public Office: Selective Property Rights in China*. New York: Cambridge University Press.

Hough, Jerry. 1997. *Democratization and Revolution in the USSR, 1985–1991*. Washington, DC: Brookings Institution.

Hovsepian-Bearce, Yvette. 2016. *The Political Ideology of Ayatollah Khamenei: Out of the Mouth of the Supreme Leader of Iran*. New York: Routledge.

Howell, Thomas, and Jeffrey P. Rajasooria. 1972. *Ghana and Nkrumah*. New York: Facts on File.

Hsu, Wilbur W. 2012. "Survival through Adaptation: The Chinese Red Army and the Encirclement Campaigns, 1927–1936." Thesis presented to the Faculty of the U.S. Army Command and General Staff College, Fort Leavenworth, KS.

Hu, Shaohua. 2000. *Explaining Chinese Democratization*. Westport, CT: Praeger.

Huang, Jing. 2000. *Factionalism in Chinese Communist Politics*. New York: Cambridge University Press.

Huberman, Leo, and Paul M. Sweezy. 1960. *Cuba: Anatomy of a Revolution*. New York: Monthly Review Press.

Hudson, Hugh, Jr. 2012a. "The 1927 Soviet War Scare: The Foreign Affairs–Domestic Policy Nexus Revisited." *Soviet and Post-Soviet Review* 39, no. 2: 145–165.

Hudson, Hugh, Jr. 2012b. *Peasant, Political Police, and the Early Soviet State*. New York: Palgrave Macmillan.

Hughes, James. 1991. *Stalin, Siberia and the Crisis of the NEP*. Cambridge: Cambridge University Press.

Human Rights Watch. 1998. *Sudan: Global Trade, Local Impact: Arms Transfers to All Sides in the Civil War in Sudan*. Human Rights Watch Reports 10, no. 4 (August). https://www.hrw.org/legacy/reports98/sudan/Sudarm988.htm#TopOfPage.

Human Rights Watch. 1999. *Leave None to Tell the Story: Genocide in Rwanda*. Human Rights Watch Reports, March. https://www.hrw.org/reports/1999/rwanda/index.htm#TopOfPage.

Human Rights Watch. 2000. *Rwanda: The Search for Security and Human Rights Abuses*. Human Rights Watch Reports, 12, no. 1 (April). https://www.hrw.org/reports/2000/rwanda/Rwan004.htm#TopOfPage.

Human Rights Watch. 2008. "China: Crackdown Violates Olympic Promises." Human Rights Watch News, February 6. https://www.hrw.org/news/2008/02/06/china-crackdown-violates-olympic-promises.

Human Rights Watch. 2009. "Service for Life: State Repression and Indefinite Conscription in Eritrea." Human Rights Watch Reports, April 16. https://www.hrw.org/report/2009/04/16/service-life/state-repression-and-indefinite-conscription-eritrea.

Human Rights Watch. 2019. "Never to Be Seen Again in Eritrea? Eritrea's Endless Incommunicado Detention of Critics." Human Rights Watch Dispatches, September 18. https://www.hrw.org/news/2018/09/18/never-be-seen-again-eritrea.

Humbaraci, Arslan. 1966. *Algeria: The Revolution That Failed.* New York: Praeger.

Hunter, Holland. 1973. "The Overambitious First Soviet Five-Year Plan." *Slavic Review* 32, no. 2: 237–257.

Huntington, Samuel. 1968. *Political Order in Changing Societies.* New Haven, CT: Yale University Press.

Huntington, Samuel. 1970. "Social and Institutional Dynamics of One-Party Systems." In Samuel Huntington and Clement H. Moore, eds., *Authoritarian Politics in Modern Society: The Dynamics of Established One-Party Systems.* New York: Basic Books.

Hutchful, Eboe. 1973. *Military Rule and the Politics of Demilitarization in Ghana 1966–1969.* Doctoral dissertation, University of Toronto.

Hyam, Ronald. 2006. *Britain's Declining Empire: The Road to Decolonisation, 1918–1968.* Cambridge: Cambridge University Press.

Iacus, Stefano M., Gary King, and Gisueppe Porro. 2012. "Casual Inference without Balance Checking: Coarsened Exact Matching." *Political Analysis* 20, no. 1: 1–24.

Ihonvbere, Julius O. 1996. *Economic Crisis, Civil Society, and Democratization: The Case of Zambia.* Trenton, NJ: Africa World Press.

Imai, Kosuke, and Marc Ratkovic. 2014. "Covariate Balancing Propensity Score." *Journal of the Royal Statistical Society, Series B (Statistical Methodology)* 76, no. 1: 243–263.

Ingelaere, Bert. 2014. "What's on a Peasant's Mind? Experiencing RPF State Reach and Overreach in Post-Genocide Rwanda (2000–10)." *Journal of Eastern African Studies* 8, no. 2: 214–230.

International Crisis Group. 2008. "Guinea-Bissau: In Need of a State." July 2. https://www.crisisgroup.org/africa/west-africa/guinea-bissau/guinea-bissau-need-state.

International Crisis Group. 2013. "Eritrea: When Is a Mutiny Not a Mutiny?" January 24. https://www.crisisgroup.org/africa/horn-africa/eritrea/eritrea-when-mutiny-not-mutiny.

International Crisis Group. 2018. "Breaking Algeria's Economic Paralysis." November 19. https://www.crisisgroup.org/middle-east-north-africa/north-africa/algeria/192-breaking-algerias-economic-paralysis.

Irvin, George. 1983. "Nicaragua: Establishing the State as the Centre of Accumulation." *Cambridge Journal of Economics* 7: 125–139.

Irvine, Jill. 1991. "Tito, Hebrang, and the Croat Question, 1943–1944." *East European Politics & Societies* 5, no. 2: 306–340.

Irvine, Jill. 2008. "The Croatian Spring and the Dissolution of Yugoslavia." In Lenard Cohen and Jasna Dragović-Soso, eds., *State Collapse in South-Eastern Europe.* West Lafayette, IN: Purdue University Press.

Isaacs, Harold R. (1938) 2010. *The Tragedy of the Chinese Revolution*. Chicago: Haymarket Books.

Iyob, Ruth. 1995. *The Eritrean Struggle for Independence: Domination, Resistance, and Nationalism, 1941–1993*. Cambridge: Cambridge University Press.

Jackson, Henry F. 1977. *The FLN in Algeria: Party Development in a Revolutionary Society*. Westport, CT: Greenwood Press.

Jamestown Foundation. 2011. "Alawi Control of the Syrian Military Key to Regime's Survival." *Terrorism Monitor* 9, no. 23. https://www.refworld.org/docid/4e3fb2452.html.

Jamieson, Neil L. 1993. *Understanding Vietnam*. Berkeley: University of California Press.

Janjetovic, Zoran. 2020. "An Oppressive Liberation: Yugoslavia 1944–1948." In John R. Lampe and Ulf Brunnbauer, eds., *The Routledge Handbook of Balkan and Southeast European History*. London: Routledge.

Janos, Andrew C. 1970. "The One-Party State and Social Mobilization: East Europe between the Wars." In Samuel Huntington and Clement H. Moore, eds., *Authoritarian Politics in Modern Society: The Dynamics of Established One-Party Systems*. New York: Basic Books.

Jansen, Marc, and Nikolai Petrov. 2002. *Stalin's Loyal Executioner: People's Commissar Nikolai Ezhov, 1895–1940*. Stanford, CA: Hoover Institute Press.

Jarquín, Mateo Cayetano. 2019. *A Latin American Revolution: The Sandinistas, the Cold War, and Political Change in the Region, 1977–1990*. Doctoral dissertation, Harvard University.

Jaszi, Oscar. 1969. *Revolution and Counter-Revolution in Hungary*. New York: Howard Fertig.

Jencks, Harlan. 1981. "China's Civil-Military Relations, 1949–1980." In Morris Janowitz, ed., *Civil-Military Relations: Regional Perspectives*. Thousand Oaks, CA: Sage.

Jeong, Yeonsik. 1997. "The Rise of State Corporatism in Vietnam." *Contemporary Southeast Asia* 19, no. 2: 152–171.

Ji, You. 2001. "China: From Revolutionary Tool to Professional Military." In Muthiah Alagappa, ed., *Military Professionalism in Asia: Conceptual and Empirical Perspectives*. Honolulu, HI: East-West Center.

Joffe, Ellis. 1965. *Party and Army: Professionalism and Political Control in the Chinese Officer Corps, 1949–1964*. Cambridge, MA: Harvard University Press.

Joffe, Ellis. 1997. "Party-Army Relations in China: Retrospect and Prospect." In David Shambaugh and Richard Yang, eds., *China's Military in Transition*. New York: Oxford University Press.

Johnson, Carol A. 1962. "Conferences of Independent African States." *International Organization* 16, no. 2: 426–429.

Johnson, Chalmers. 1962. *Peasant Nationalism and Communist Power: The Emergence of Revolutionary China 1937–1945*. Stanford, CA: Stanford University Press.

Johnson, Chalmers. 1966. *Revolutionary Change*. Boston: Little, Brown.

Johnson, Chalmers. 1982. *Revolutionary Change*. 2nd ed. Stanford, CA: Stanford University Press.

Joiner, Charles A. 1990. "The Vietnam Communist Party Strives to Remain the 'Only Force.'" *Asian Survey* 30, no. 11: 1053–1065.

Joireman, Sandra Fullerton. 1996. "The Minefield of Land Reform: Comments of the Eritrean Land Proclamation." *African Affairs* 95, no. 379: 269–285.

Jones, Colin, and Simon Macdonald. 2018. "Robespierre, York, and Pisistratus during the French Revolutionary Terror." *The Historical Journal* 61, no. 3: 643–672.

Jones, Halbert. 2014. *The War Has Brought Peace to Mexico: World War Two and the Consolidation of the Post-Revolutionary State*. Albuquerque: University of New Mexico Press.

Jones, Peter. 2011. "Succession and the Supreme Leader in Iran." *Survival* 53, no. 6: 105–126.

Jones, Seth, and Danika Newlee. 2019. "Iran's Protests and the Threat to Domestic Stability." *CSIS Briefs*, November.

Jonjić, Tomislav. 2007. "Organized Resistance to the Yugoslav Communist Regime in Croatia in 1945–1953." *Review of Croatian History* 1: 109–145.

Jordan, Donald A. 1976. *Northern Expedition: China's National Revolution of 1926–28*. Honolulu: University of Hawaii Press.

Jorge, Antonio, Jaime Suchlicki, and Adolfo Leyva de Varona, eds. 1991. *Cuba in a Changing World*. Coral Gables, FL: Institute of Interamerican Studies, Graduate School of International Studies, University of Miami, North-South Center.

Joseph, Gilbert M. 1980. "Caciquismo and the Revolution: Carrillo Puerto in Yucatán." In D. A. Brading, ed., *Caudillo and Peasant in the Mexican Revolution*. Cambridge: Cambridge University Press.

Joseph, Gilbert M. 2003. *Revolution from Without: Yucatán, Mexico, and the United States, 1880–1924*. Durham, NC: Duke University Press.

Joseph, Gilbert M., and Jürgen Buchenau. 2013. *Mexico's Once and Future Revolution: Social Upheaval and the Challenge of Rule since the Late Nineteenth Century*. Durham, NC: Duke University Press.

Jover Marimón, Mateo. 1971. "The Church." In Carmelo Mesa-Lago, ed., *Revolutionary Change in Cuba*. Pittsburgh: University of Pittsburgh Press.

Jowell, Marco. 2014. "Cohesion through Socialization: Liberation, Tradition and Modernity in the Forging of the Rwanda Defense Force (RDF)." *Journal of Eastern African Studies* 8, no. 2: 278–293.

Jowitt, Ken. 1992. *New World Disorder: The Leninist Extinction*. Berkeley: University of California Press.

Judson, C. Fred. 1984. *Cuba and the Revolutionary Myth: The Political Education of the Cuban Rebel Army, 1953–1963*. Boulder, CO: Westview Press.

Jumper, Roy. 1959. "Sects and Communism in South Vietnam." *Orbis* 3: 85–96.

Justo, Liborio. 1967. *Bolivia: La revolución derrotada*. Cochabamba: Rojas Araujo.

Kaas, Albert, and Fedor de Lazarovics. 1931. *Bolshevism in Hungary: The Béla Kun Period*. London: Grant Richards.

Kagan, Robert. 1996. *A Twilight Struggle: American Power and Nicaragua, 1997–1990*. New York: Free Press.

Kahin, George McTurnan. 2003. *Southeast Asia: A Testament*. London: RoutledgeCurzon.

Kalugin, Oleg. 1994. *The First Directorate: My 32 Years in Intelligence and Espionage Against the West*. New York: St. Martin's Press.

Kampen, Thomas. 1989. "The Zunyi Conference and Further Steps in Mao's Rise to Power." *China Quarterly* 117: 118–134.

Karnow, Stanley. 1983. *Vietnam: A History*. New York: Penguin.

Karol, K. S. 1970. *Guerrillas in Power: The Course of the Cuban Revolution*. New York: Hill and Wang.

Kasfir, Nelson. 2005. "Guerrillas and Civilian Participation: The National Resistance Army in Uganda, 1981–86." *Journal of Modern African Studies* 43, no. 2: 271–296.

Katouzian, Homa. 1998. "The Pahlavi Regime in Iran." In Houchang E. Chehabi and Juan J. Linz, eds., *Sultanistic Regimes*. Baltimore: Johns Hopkins University Press.

Kattenburg, Paul M. 1975. "DRV External Relations in the New Revolutionary Phase." In Joseph J. Zasloff and MacAlister Brown, eds., *Communism in Indochina: New Perspectives*. Lexington, MA: Lexington Books.

Katz, Friedrich. 1991. "The Liberal Revolution and the Porfiriato." In Leslie Bethell, ed., *Mexico since Independence*. Cambridge: Cambridge University Press.

Katz, Friedrich. 1998. *The Life and Times of Pancho Villa*. Stanford, CA: Stanford University Press.

Katz, Mark N., ed. 1990. *The USSR and Marxist Revolutions in the Third World*. Cambridge: Cambridge University Press.

Katzman, Kenneth. 1993. *The Warriors of Islam: Iran's Revolutionary Guard*. Boulder, CO: Westview Press.

Kaufman Purcell, Susan. 1992. "Collapsing Cuba." *Foreign Affairs* 17, no. 1: 130–145.

Kaveh, Moravej. 2011. *The SAVAK and the Cold War: Counter-Intelligence and Foreign Intelligence (1957–1968)*. Doctoral thesis, University of Manchester.

Kaye, Dalia Dassa, Alireza Nader, and Parisa Roshan. 2011. *Israel and Iran: A Dangerous Rivalry*. Santa Monica, CA: Rand Corporation.

Kaye, William. 1962. "A Bowl of Rice Divided: The Economy of North Vietnam." In P. J. Honey, ed., *North Vietnam Today: Profile of a Communist Satellite*. New York: Praeger.

Kazemzadeh, Masoud. 2008. "Intra-elite Factionalism and the 2004 Majles Elections in Iran." *Middle Eastern Studies* 44, no. 2: 189–214.

Keefe, Eugene. 1977. *Area Handbook for Portugal*. Washington, DC: Foreign Area Studies of American University.

Keep, John. 1976. *The Russian Revolution: A Study in Mass Mobilization*. New York: W. W. Norton.

Kellen, Konrad. 1972. "1971 and Beyond: The View from Hanoi." In Joseph J. Zasloff and Allen E. Goodman, eds., *Indochina in Conflict: A Political Assessment*. Lexington, MA: Lexington Books.

Kelley, Jonathan, and Herbert S. Klein. 1981. *Revolution and the Rebirth of Inequality: A Theory Applied to the National Revolution in Bolivia*. Berkeley: University of California Press.

Kelley, Thomas. 2017. "Maintaining Power by Manipulating Memory in Rwanda." *Fordham International Law Journal* 41, no. 1: 79–134.

Kempton, Daniel R. 1991. "Africa in the Age of Perestroika." *Africa Today* 38, no. 3: 7–29.

Kenez, Peter. 1971. "Coalition Politics in the Hungarian Soviet Republic." In Andrew C. Janos and William D. Slottman, eds., *Revolution in Perspective: Essays on the Hungarian Soviet Republic of 1919*. Berkeley: University of California Press.

Kennedy, Michael. 1988. *The Jacobin Clubs in the French Revolution: The Middle Years*. Princeton, NJ: Princeton University Press.

Kerkvliet, Benedict J. 2014. "Government Repression and Toleration of Dissidents in Contemporary Vietnam." In Jonathan D. London, ed., *Politics in Contemporary Vietnam: Party, State, and Authority Relations*. London: Palgrave Macmillan.

Kerkvliet, Benedict, and Mark Selden. 1999. "Agrarian Transformation in China and Vietnam." In Anita Chan, Benedict Kerkvliet, and Jonathan Unger, eds., *Transforming Asian Socialism: China and Vietnam Compared*. Lanham, MD: Rowman and Littlefield.

Khalaji, Mehdi. 2006. *The Last Marja: Sistani and the End of Traditional Religious Authority in Shiism*. Washington Institute for Near East Policy, Policy Focus no. 59, September.

Khalaji, Mehdi. 2011. "Iran's Regime of Religion." *Journal of International Affairs* 11, no. 1: 131–147.

Khalilzad, Zalmay. 1997. "Anarchy in Afghanistan." *Journal of International Affairs* 51, no. 1: 37–56.

Khánh, Huynh Kim. 1982. *Vietnamese Communism, 1925–1945*. Ithaca, NY: Cornell University Press.

Kharsh, Efraim. 1990. "Geopolitical Determinism: The Origins of the Iran-Iraq War." *Middle East Journal* 44, no. 2: 256–268.

Kharsh, Efraim. 2002. *Essential Histories: Iran-Iraq War 1980–1988*. Oxford: Osprey Publishing.

Khlevniuk, Oleg V. 1995. "The Objectives of the Great Terror." In Julian Cooper, Maureen Perrie, and E. A. Rees, eds., *Soviet History, 1917–53: Essays in Honour of R. W. Davies*. New York: St. Martin's Press.

Khlevniuk, Oleg V. 2009. *Master of the House: Stalin and His Inner Circle*. Translated by Nora Seligman Favorov. New Haven, CT: Yale University Press.

Khlevniuk, Oleg V. 2015. *Stalin: New Biography of a Dictator*. Translated by Nora Seligman Favorov. New Haven, CT: Yale University Press.

Khrushchev, Nikita. 1990. *Khrushchev Remembers: The Glasnost Tapes*. Boston: Little, Brown.

Kibreab, Gaim. 2009a. "Forced Labor in Eritrea." *Journal of Modern African Studies* 47, no. 1: 41–72.

Kibreab, Gaim. 2009b. "Land Policy in Post-Independence Eritrea: A Critical Reflection." *Journal of Contemporary African Studies* 27, no. 1: 37–56.

Kiernan, Ben. 2004. *How Pol Pot Came to Power: Colonialism, Nationalism, and Communism in Cambodia, 1930–1975*. 2nd ed. New Haven, CT: Yale University Press.

Kiernan, Ben. 2008. *The Pol Pot Regime: Race, Power, and Genocide in Cambodia under the Khmer Rouge, 1975–79*. New Haven, CT: Yale University Press.

Kiernan, Ben. n.d. "The Cambodian Genocide, 1975–1979." https://www.niod.nl/sites/niod.nl/files/Cambodian%20genocide.pdf.

King, Gary, James Honaker, Anne Joseph, and Kenneth Scheve. 2001. "Analyzing Incomplete Political Science Data: An Alternative Algorithm for Multiple Imputation." *American Political Science Review* 95, no. 1: 49–69.

King, Gary, Christopher Lucas, and Richard A. Nielsen. 2017. "The Balance–Sample Size Frontier in Matching Methods for Causal Inference." *American Journal of Political Science* 61, no. 2: 473–489.

Kinzer, Stephen. 1991. *Blood of Brothers: Life and War in Nicaragua*. New York: G. P. Putnam's Sons.

Kinzer, Stephen. 2003. *All the Shah's Men: An American Coup and the Roots of Middle East Terror*. Hoboken, NJ: John Wiley and Sons.

Kirk, John M. 1985. "From Counterrevolution to *Modus Vivendi*: The Church in Cuba, 1959–84." In Sandor Halebsky and John M. Kirk, eds., *Cuba: Twenty-Five Years of Revolution, 1959–1984*. New York: Praeger.

Kirk, John M. 1989. *Between God and the Party: Religion and Politics in Revolutionary Cuba*. Tampa: University of South Florida Press.

Kirk, John M. 1992. *Politics and the Catholic Church in Nicaragua*. Gainesville: University Press of Florida.

Klein, George. 1975. "The Role of Ethnic Politics in the Czechoslovak Crisis of 1968 and the Yugoslav Crisis of 1971." *Studies in Comparative Communism* 8, no. 4: 339–369.

Klein, Herbert S. 1968a. "The Crisis of Legitimacy and the Origins of Social Revolution: The Bolivian Experience." *Journal of Inter-American Studies* 10, no. 1: 102–116.

Klein, Herbert S. 1968b. *Origines de la revolución nacional boliviana: La crisis de la generación del Chaco*. La Paz: Editorial "Juventud."

Klein, Herbert S. 1971a. *Parties and Political Change in Bolivia, 1880–1952*. Cambridge: Cambridge University Press.

Klein, Herbert S. 1971b. "Prelude to the Revolution." In James M. Malloy and Richard S. Thorn, eds., *Beyond the Revolution: Bolivia since 1952*. Pittsburgh: University of Pittsburgh Press.

Klein, Herbert S. 1992. *Bolivia: The Evolution of a Multi-ethnic Society*. New York: Oxford University Press.

Klein, Herbert S. 2011. *A Concise History of Bolivia*. 2nd ed. Cambridge: Cambridge University Press.

Klepak, Hal. 2005. *Cuba's Military 1990–2005: Revolutionary Soldiers during Counter-Revolutionary Times*. New York: Palgrave Macmillan.

Klepak, Hal. 2008. "Cuba." In Stuart Farson, Peter Gill, Mark Phythian, and Schlomo Shapiro, eds., *PSI Handbook of Global Security and Intelligence: National Approaches*, vol. 1, *The Americas and Asia*. Westport, CT: Praeger.

Klepak, Hal. 2012. *Raúl Castro and Cuba: A Military Story*. New York: Palgrave Macmillan.

Klepak, Hal. 2015. "The Revolutionary Armed Forces: Loyalty and Efficiency in the Face of Old and New Challenges." In Philip Brenner, Marguerite Rose Jiménez, John M. Kirk, and William M. LeoGrande, eds., *A Contemporary Cuba Reader: The Revolution under Raúl Castro*. Lanham, MD: Rowman and Littlefield.

Klesner, Joseph L. 1987. "Changing Patterns of Electoral Participation and Official Party Support in Mexico." In Judith Gentleman, ed., *Mexican Politics in Transition*. Boulder, CO: Westview Press.

Klesner, Joseph L. 2004. "The Structure of the Mexican Electorate: Social, Attitudinal, and Partisan Bases of Vicente Fox's Victory." In Jorge I. Domínguez and Chappell Lawson, eds., *Mexico's Pivotal Democratic Election: Candidates, Voters, and the Presidential Campaign of 2000*. Stanford, CA: Stanford University Press.

Knauss, Peter R. 1977. "Algeria's 'Agrarian Revolution': Peasant Control or Control of Peasants?" *African Studies Review* 20, no. 3: 65–78.

Knauss, Peter R. 1980. "Algeria under Boumedienne: The Mythical Revolution." In Isaac James Mowoe, ed., *The Performance of Soldiers as Governors: African Politics and the African Military*. Washington, DC: University Press of America.

Knight, Alan. 1980. "Peasant and Caudillo in Revolutionary Mexico, 1910–1917." In D. A. Brading, ed., *Caudillo and Peasant in the Mexican Revolution.* Cambridge: Cambridge University Press.

Knight, Alan. 1986a. *The Mexican Revolution.* Vol. 1, *Porfirians, Liberals and Peasants.* Lincoln: University of Nebraska Press.

Knight, Alan. 1986b. *The Mexican Revolution.* Vol. 2, *Counter-Revolution and Reconstruction.* Lincoln: University of Nebraska Press.

Knight, Alan. 1990. "Revolutionary Project, Recalcitrant People: Mexico, 1910–1940." In Jaime E. Rodríguez O., ed., *The Revolutionary Process in Mexico: Essays on Political and Social Change, 1880–1940.* Los Angeles: UCLA Latin American Center Publications, University of California, Los Angeles.

Knight, Alan. 1991a. "Land and Society in Revolutionary Mexico: The Destruction of the Great Haciendas." *Mexican Studies* 7, no. 1: 73–104.

Knight, Alan. 1991b. "The Rise and Fall of Cardenismo, c. 1930–c. 1946." In Leslie Bethell, ed., *Mexico since Independence.* Cambridge: Cambridge University Press.

Knight, Alan. 1992a. "Mexico's Elite Settlement: Conjuncture and Consequences." In John Higley and Richard Gunther, eds., *Elites and Democratic Consolidation in Latin America and Southern Europe.* Cambridge: Cambridge University Press.

Knight, Alan. 1992b. "The Peculiarities of Mexican History: Mexico Compared to Latin America, 1821–1992." *Journal of Latin American Studies* 24: 99–144.

Knight, Alan. 1993. "State Power and Political Stability in Mexico." In Neil Harvey, ed., *Mexico: Dilemmas of Transition.* London: Institute of Latin American Studies, University of London.

Knight, Alan. 1994a. "Cardenismo: Juggernaut or Jalopy?" *Journal of Latin American Studies* 26, no. 1 (February): 73–107.

Knight, Alan. 1994b. "Popular Culture and the Revolutionary State in Mexico, 1910–1940?" *Hispanic American Historical Review* 74, no. 3: 393–444.

Knight, Alan. 2003. "The Domestic Dynamics of the Mexican and Bolivian Revolutions." In Merilee S. Grindle and Pilar Domingo, eds., *Proclaiming Revolution: Bolivia in Comparative Perspective.* London: Institute of Latin American Studies, University of London.

Knight, Alan. 2014. "The End of the Mexican Revolution? From Cárdenas to Avila Camacho, 1937–1941." In Paul Gillingham and Benjamin T. Smith, eds., *Dictablanda: Politics, Work, and Culture in Mexico, 1938–1968.* Durham, NC: Duke University Press.

Knight, Amy. 1990. *The KGB: Police and Politics in the Soviet Union.* Boston: Unwin Hyman.

Knight, Amy. 1991. "Internal Security." In Raymond E. Zickel, ed., *Soviet Union: A Country Study.* 2nd ed. Washington, DC: Federal Research Division, Library of Congress.

Knight, Amy. 1996. *Spies without Cloaks: The KGB's Successors.* Princeton, NJ: Princeton University Press.

Knudson, Jerry W. 1986. *Bolivia: Press and Revolution, 1932–1964.* Lanham, MD: University Press of America.

Kolko, Gabriel. 1985. *Anatomy of a War: Vietnam, the United States, and the Modern Historical Experience.* New York: Free Press.

Kolko, Gabriel. 1997. *Vietnam: Anatomy of a Peace*. London: Routledge.

Kornbluh, Peter. 1991. "The U.S. Role in the Counterrevolution." In Thomas W. Walker, ed., *Revolution and Counterrevolution in Nicaragua*. Boulder, CO: Westview Press.

Kornbluh, Peter. 1998. *Bay of Pigs Declassified: The Secret CIA Report on the Invasion of Cuba*. New York: New Press.

Korstjens, Sandra. 2016. "Smashing the Enemies: The Organization of Violence in Democratic Kampuchea." In Uğur Ümit Üngör, ed., *Genocide: New Perspectives on Its Causes, Courses and Consequences*. Amsterdam: Amsterdam University Press.

Koss, Daniel. 2018. *Where the Party Rules: The Rank and File of China's Communist State*. Cambridge: Cambridge University Press.

Kotkin, Stephen. 2014. *Stalin*. Vol. 1, *Paradoxes of Power, 1878–1928*. New York: Penguin.

Kotkin, Stephen. 2017. *Stalin*. Vol. 2, *Waiting for Hitler, 1929–1941*. New York: Penguin.

Kovrig, Bennet. 1979. *Communism in Hungary: From Kun to Kádár*. Stanford, CA: Hoover Institution Press.

Kraus, Jon. 1966. "The Men in Charge." *Africa Report*, April: 16–20.

Kurfurst, Sandra. 2015. "Networking Alone? Digital Communications and Collective Action in Vietnam." *Journal of Current Southeast Asian Affairs* 34, no. 3: 123–150.

Kurzman, Charles. 2004. *The Unthinkable Revolution in Iran*. Cambridge, MA: Harvard University Press.

Labat, Severine. 1994. "Islam and Islamists: The Emergence of New Types of Politico-Religious Militants." In John Ruedy, ed., *Islamism and Secularism in North Africa*. New York: St. Martin's Press.

Lacayo Oyanguren, Antonio. 2005. *La difícil transición nicaragüense: En el gobierno con Doña Violeta*. Managua: Fundación UNO.

Lachapelle, Jean, Steven Levitsky, Lucan Way, and Adam E. Casey. 2020. "Social Revolution and Authoritarian Durability." *World Politics* 72, no. 4: 557–600.

Lachapelle, Jean, Lucan Way, and Steven Levitsky. 2012. "Crisis, Coercion, and Authoritarian Durability: Explaining Diverging Responses to Anti-regime Protest in Egypt and Iran." Working Paper vol. 127, Center on Democracy, Development, and the Rule of Law, Stanford University.

Lacouture, Jean. 1968. *Ho Chi Minh: A Political Biography*. New York: Vintage Books.

Lajous, Alejandra. 1979. *Los orígenes del partido único en México*. Mexico City: Universidad Nacional Autónoma de México.

Lajous, Alejandra. 1981. "La primera campaña del PNR y la oposición vasconcelista." In Carlos Martínez Assad, ed., *La sucesión presidencial en México, 1928–1988*. Mexico City: Nueva Imagen.

Lakin, Samantha, and Jonathan Beloff. 2014. "Leadership Mindsets: The Social and Political Development of the Rwandan Patriotic Front (RPF) of the Past Twenty Years." *Journal of African Union Studies* 3, no. 3: 47–67.

Lall, Ranjit. 2016. "How Multiple Imputation Makes a Difference." *Political Analysis* 24, no. 4: 414–433.

Lampton, David. 2019. *Following the Leader: Ruling China, from Deng Xiaoping to Xi Jinping*. Berkeley: University of California Press.

Landinfo. 2015. "Report: Eritrea: National Service." March 23. https://www.refworld.org/pdfid/56cd5e574.pdf.

Langlois, Robert. 1997. "Becoming a Contra": The Dilemma of Peasants during the Revolution in Nicaragua." *International Journal* 52, no. 4: 695–713.

Langston, Joy. 2002. "Breaking Out Is Hard to Do: Exit, Voice, and Loyalty in Mexico's One-Party Hegemonic Regime." *Latin American Politics and Society* 44, no. 3: 61–88.

Langston, Joy. 2006. "The Birth and Transformation of the Dedazo in Mexico." In Gretchen Helmke and Steven Levitsky, eds., *Informal Institutions and Democracy: Lessons from Latin America*. Baltimore: Johns Hopkins University Press.

Lanning, Eldon. 1969. "Governmental Capabilities in a Revolutionary Situation: The MNR in Bolivia." *Inter-American Economic Affairs* 23, no. 2: 3–22.

Lary, Diana. 2015. *China's Civil War: A Social History, 1945–1949*. New York: Cambridge University Press.

LASA (Latin American Studies Association). 1984. *The Electoral Process in Nicaragua: Domestic and International Influences: The Report of the LASA Delegation to Observe the Nicaraguan General Election of November 4, 1984*. Pittsburgh: LASA.

Latell, Brian, 2003. "The United States and Cuba: Future Security Issues." In Irving Louis Horowitz and Jaime Suchlicki, eds., *Cuban Communism, 1959–2003*. New Brunswick, NJ: Transaction Publishers.

Latell, Brian. 2007. *After Fidel: Raul Castro and the Future of Cuba's Revolution*. New York: Palgrave Macmillan.

Lauchlan, Iain. 2013. "The Chekist Origins of the Great Terror." In James Harris, ed., *The Anatomy of Terror: Political Violence under Stalin*. New York: Oxford University Press.

Lawless, Richard. 1984. "Algeria: The Contradictions of Rapid Industrialization." In Richard Lawless and Allan Findlay, eds., *North Africa: Contemporary Politics and Economic Development*. London: Croom Helm.

Lawson, George. 2019. *Anatomies of Revolution*. New York: Cambridge University Press.

Layachi, Azzedine. 2004. "Political Liberalization and the Islamist Movement in Algeria." *Journal of North African Studies* 9, no. 2: 46–67.

Leal, Juan Felipe. 1975. "The Mexican State 1915–1973: A Historical Interpretation." *Latin American Perspectives* 2, no. 2: 48–63.

LeBas, Adrienne. 2011. *From Protest to Parties: Party-Building and Democratization in Africa*. Oxford: Oxford University Press.

Lebed, Aleksandr. 1995. *Za derzhavu obidno!* Moscow: Moskovskaia Pravda.

LeBor, Adam. 2004. *Milosevic: A Biography*. New Haven, CT: Yale University Press.

Lee, Terence. 2015. *Defect or Defend: Military Responses to Popular Protests in Authoritarian Asia*. Baltimore: Johns Hopkins University Press.

Lefebvre, Jeffrey A. 1995. "Post–Cold War Clouds on the Horn of Africa: The Eritrea-Sudan Crisis." *Middle East Policy* 4, no. 1–2: 34–49.

Leggett, George. 1986. *The Cheka: Lenin's Political Police*. Oxford: Oxford University Press.

Legum, Colin. 1975. "National Liberation in Southern Africa." *Problems of Communism* 24: 1–20.

Lehman, Kenneth. 1997. "Revolutions and Attributions: Making Sense of Eisenhower Administration Policies in Bolivia and Guatemala." *Diplomatic History* 21, no. 2: 185–213.

Lehman, Kenneth. 2003. "Braked but Not Broken: The United States and Revolutionaries in Mexico and Bolivia." In Merilee S. Grindle and Pilar Domingo, eds., *Proclaiming Revolution: Bolivia in Comparative Perspective*. London: Institute of Latin American Studies, University of London.

Leiken, Robert S. 1990. "Old and New Politics in Managua." *Journal of Democracy* 1, no. 3: 26–38.

Lenoe, Matthew. 2013. "Fear, Loathing, Conspiracy: The Kirov Murder as Impetus for Terror." In James Harris, ed., *The Anatomy of Terror: Political Violence under Stalin*. New York: Oxford University Press.

LeoGrande, William M. 1978a. "A Bureaucratic Approach to Civil-Military Relations in Communist Political Systems." In Dale R. Herspring and Ivan Volgyes, eds., *Civil-Military Relations in Communist Systems*. Boulder, CO: Westview Press.

LeoGrande, William M. 1978b. "Civil-Military Relations in Cuba: Party Control and Political Socialization." *Studies in Comparative Communism* 11, no. 3: 278–291.

LeoGrande, William M. 1978c. "Continuity and Change in the Cuban Political Elite." *Cuban Studies* 8, no. 2: 1–31.

LeoGrande, William M. 1978d. "The Politics of Revolutionary Development: Civil-Military Relations in Cuba, 1959–1976." *Journal of Strategic Studies* 1: 260–294.

LeoGrande, William M. 1979. "Party Development in Revolutionary Cuba." *Journal of Interamerican Studies and World Affairs* 21, no. 4: 457–480.

LeoGrande, William M. 1980. "The Communist Party of Cuba since the First Congress." *Journal of Latin American Studies* 12, no. 2: 397–419.

LeoGrande, William M. 1982. Foreign Policy: The Limits of Success." In Jorge I. Domínguez, ed., *Cuba: Internal and International Affairs*. Beverly Hills, CA: Sage Publications.

LeoGrande, William M. 1992. "Political Parties and Postrevolutionary Politics in Nicaragua." In Louis W. Goodman, William M. LeoGrande, and Johanna Mendelson Forman, eds., *Political Parties and Democracy in Central America*. Boulder, CO: Westview Press.

LeoGrande, William M. 2015. "Cuba's Perilous Political Transition in the Post-Castro Era." *Journal of Latin American Studies* 47, no. 2: 377–405.

LeRiche, M., and M. Arnold. 2012. *South Sudan: From Revolution to Independence*. London: Hurst.

Leveau, Remy. 1993. "Reflections on the State in the Maghreb." In George Joffé, ed., *North Africa: Nation, State, and Region*. London: Routledge.

Levine, Steven I. 1987. *Anvil of Victory: The Communist Revolution in Manchuria: 1945–1948*. New York: Columbia University Press.

Levitsky, Steven, and María Victoria Murillo. 2009. "Variation in Institutional Strength." *Annual Review of Political Science* 12: 115–133.

Levitsky, Steven, and Lucan Way. 2006. "Leverage versus Linkage: Rethinking the International Dimension of Regime Change." *Comparative Politics* 38, no. 4: 379–400.

Levitsky, Steven, and Lucan Way. 2010. *Competitive Authoritarianism: Hybrid Regimes after the Cold War*. New York: Cambridge University Press.

Levitsky, Steven, and Lucan Way. 2012. "Beyond Patronage: Violent Struggle, Ruling Party Cohesion, and Authoritarian Durability." *Perspectives on Politics* 10, no. 4: 869–889.

Lewellen, Ted C. 1989. "Holy and Unholy Alliances: The Politics of Catholicism in Revolutionary Nicaragua." *Journal of Church and State* 31, no. 1: 15–33.

Lewin, Moshe. 1975. *Russian Peasants and Soviet Power: A Study of Collectivization*. New York: W. W. Norton.

Lewin, Moshe. 1985. *The Making of the Soviet System: Essays in the Social History of Interwar Russia*. London: Methuen.

Lewin, Moshe. 1989. "The Civil War: Dynamics and Legacy." In Diane P. Koenker, William G. Rosenberg, and Ronald Grigor Suny, eds., *Party, State, and Society in the Russian Civil War: Explorations in Social History*. Bloomington: Indiana University Press.

Lewis, William H. 1963. "Algeria: The Plight of the Victor." *Current History* 44, no. 257: 22–28.

Lewis, William H. 1973. "The Decline of Algeria's FLN." In I. William Zartman, ed., *Man, State, and Society in the Contemporary Maghrib*. New York: Praeger.

Li, Xiaobing. 2007. *A History of the Modern Chinese Army*. Lexington: University Press of Kentucky.

Li, Yao. 2018. *Playing by the Informal Rules: Why the Chinese Regime Remains Stable despite Rising Protests*. Cambridge: Cambridge University Press.

Liang, Zhang, comp. 2001. *The Tiananmen Papers: The Chinese Leadership's Decision to Use Force against Their Own People—in Their Own Words*. Edited by Andrew Nathan and Perry Link. New York: PublicAffairs.

Lieberthal, Kenneth. 1987. "The Great Leap Forward and the Split in the Yan'an Leadership." In Roderick MacFarquhar and John K. Fairbank, eds., *The Cambridge History of China*, vol. 14, *The People's Republic*, pt. 1, *The Emergence of Revolutionary China, 1949–1965*. New York: Cambridge University Press.

Liebich, Andre. 1997. *From the Other Shore: Russian Social Democracy after 1921*. Cambridge, MA: Harvard University Press.

Lieuwen, Edwin. 1968. *Mexican Militarism: The Political Rise and Fall of the Revolutionary Army*. Albuquerque: University of New Mexico Press.

Ligachev, Yegor. 1996. *Inside Gorbachev's Kremlin*. Boulder, CO: Westview Press.

Lincoln, W. Bruce. 1999. *Red Victory: A History of the Russian Civil War*. New York: Da Capo Press.

Linfield, Michael. 1991. "Human Rights." In Thomas W. Walker, ed., *Revolution and Counterrevolution in Nicaragua*. Boulder, CO: Westview Press.

Linz, Juan J., and Alfred Stepan, eds. 1978. *The Breakdown of Democratic Regimes*. Baltimore: Johns Hopkins University Press.

Lipset, Seymour Martin. 1959. "Some Social Requisites of Democracy: Economic Development and Political Legitimacy." *American Political Science Review* 53, no. 1: 69–105.

Liu, Alan P. 1979. "The 'Gang of Four' and the Chinese People's Liberation Army." *Asian Survey* 19, no. 9: 817–837.

Llerena, Mario. 1978. *The Unsuspected Revolution: The Birth and Rise of Castroism*. Ithaca, NY: Cornell University Press.

Loaeza, Soledad. 1999. *El Partido Acción Nacional: La larga marcha, 1939–1993: Oposición leal y partido de protesta*. Mexico City: Fondo de Cultura Económica.

Lockhart, Greg. 1989. *Nation in Arms: The Origins of the People's Army of Vietnam*. Sydney: Allen and Unwin.

Lomelí Vanegas, Leonardo. 2000. "El PRI durante el gobierno de Luis Echeverría." In Miguel Gonzáles Compeán and Leonardo Lomelí Vanegas, eds., *El partido de la revolución: Institución y conflicto (1928–1999)*. Mexico City: Fondo de Cultura Económica.

London, Jonathan D. 2019. "Vietnam in 2018: Consolidating Market Leninism." *Asian Survey* 59, no. 1: 140–146.

Londregan, John B., and Keith T. Poole. 1990. "Poverty, the Coup Trap, and the Seizure of Executive Power." *World Politics* 42, no. 2: 151–183.

Long, Nguyen, with Harry H. Kendall. 1981. "After Saigon Fell: Daily Life under the Vietnamese Communists." Research paper. Berkeley: Institute of East Asian Studies, University of California, Berkeley.

Looney, Robert. (1978) 2018. *Mexico's Economy: A Policy Analysis with Forecasts to 1990*. London: Routledge.

Lopes, Carlos. 1987. *Guinea Bissau: From Liberation Struggle to Independent Statehood*. Translated by Michael Wolfers. Boulder, CO: Westview Press.

López-Fresquet, Rufo. 1966. *My 14 Months with Castro*. Cleveland: World Publishing Company.

Lorgen, Christy Cannon. 2000. "Villagisation in Ethiopia, Mozambique, and Tanzania." *Social Dynamics* 26, no. 2: 171–198.

Loyo Camacho, Martha Beatriz. 2003. *Joaquín Amaro y el proceso de institucionalización del ejército mexicano, 1917–1931*. Mexico City: UNAM.

Lozoya, Jorge Alberto. 1970. *El ejército mexicano (1911–1965)*. Mexico City: El Colegio de México.

Luciak, Ilja A. 1995. *The Sandinista Legacy: Lessons from a Political Economy in Transition*. Gainesville: University Press of Florida.

Lueders, Hans, and Ellen Lust-Okar. 2018. "Multiple Measurements, Elusive Agreement, and Unstable Outcomes in the Study of Regime Change." *Journal of Politics* 80, no. 2: 736–741.

Luna, Matilde, Ricardo Tirado, and Francisco Valdés. 1987. "Businessmen and Politics in Mexico, 1982–1986." In Sylvia Maxfield and Ricardo Anzaldúa Montoya, eds., *Government and Private Sector in Contemporary Mexico*. La Jolla: Center for U.S.-Mexican Studies, University of California, San Diego.

Luong, Hy V. 2003. "Postwar Vietnamese Society: An Overview of Transformational Dynamics." In Hy V. Luong, ed., *Postwar Vietnam: Dynamics of a Transforming Society*. Lanham, MD: Rowman and Littlefield.

Lupogo, Herman. 2001. "Tanzania: Civil-Military Relations and Political Stability." *African Security Review* 10, no. 1: 75–86.

Luqiu, Rose Luwei, and Chuyu Liu. 2018. "'New Social Class' or Old Friends? A Study of Private Entrepreneurs in the National People's Congress of China." *Journal of East Asian Studies* 18: 389–400.

Lust-Okar, Ellen. 2007. *Structuring Conflict in the Arab World: Incumbents, Opponents, and Institutions*. New York: Cambridge University Press.

Luttwak, Edward. 2016. *Coup d'État: A Practical Handbook*. Cambridge, MA: Harvard University Press.

Lyon, Judson. 1980. "Marxism and Ethnonationalism in Guinea-Bissau." *Ethnic and Racial Studies* 3, no. 2: 156–167.

Lyons, Terrence. 2016a. "From Victorious Rebels to Strong Authoritarian Parties: Prospects for Post-War Democratization." *Democratization* 23, no. 6: 126–141.

Lyons, Terrence. 2016b. "The Importance of Winning: Victorious Insurgent Groups and Authoritarian Politics." *Comparative Politics* 42, no. 2: 167–184.

Mabry, Donald J. 1973. *Mexico's Acción Nacional: A Catholic Alternative to Revolution.* Syracuse, NY: Syracuse University Press.

MacFarquhar, Roderick, and Michael Schoenhals. 2006. *Mao's Last Revolution.* Cambridge, MA: Harvard University Press.

MacQueen, Norrie. 1997. *The Decolonization of Portuguese Africa.* London: Longman.

Magaloni, Beatriz. 2005. "The Demise of Mexico's One-Party Dominant Regime: Elite Choices and the Masses in the Establishment of Democracy." In Frances Hagopian and Scott Mainwaring, eds., *The Third Wave of Democratization in Latin America: Advances and Setbacks.* New York: Cambridge University Press.

Magaloni, Beatriz. 2006. *Voting for Autocracy: Hegemonic Party Survival and Its Demise in Mexico.* New York: Cambridge University Press.

Magaloni, Beatriz. 2008. "Credible Power-Sharing and the Longevity of Authoritarian Rule." *Comparative Political Studies* 41, no. 4/5: 715–741.

Magaloni, Beatriz, Jonathan Chu, and Eric Min. 2013. *Autocracies of the World 1950–2012.* Version 1.0. Data set. Center on Democracy, Development and the Rule of Law, Stanford University. https://cddrl.fsi.stanford.edu/research/autocracies_of_the_world_dataset/.

Mahoney, James. 2001. "Path Dependent Explanations of Regime Change: Central America in Comparative Perspective." *Studies in Comparative International Development* 36, no. 1: 111–141.

Mainwaring, Scott, and Aníbal Pérez-Liñán. 2013. *Democracies and Dictatorships in Latin America: Emergence, Survival, and Fall.* New York: Cambridge University Press.

Makki, Fouad. 1996. "Nationalism, State Formation and the Public Sphere: Eritrea 1991–96." *Review of African Political Economy* 23, no. 70: 475–497.

Malache, Adriano, Paulino Macaringue, and Joao-Paulo Borges Coelho. 2005. "Profound Transformations and Regional Conflagrations: The History of Mozambique's Armed Forces from 1975–2005." In Martin Rupiya, ed., *Evolutions and Revolutions: A Contemporary History of Militaries in Southern Africa.* Pretoria: Institute for Security Studies.

Malarney, Shaun Kingsley. 2003. "Return to the Past? The Dynamics of Contemporary Religious and Ritual Transformation." In Hy V. Luong, ed., *Postwar Vietnam: Dynamics of a Transforming Society.* Lanham, MD: Rowman and Littlefield.

Malesky, Edmund. 2014. "Vietnam in 2013: Single-Party Politics in the Internet Age." *Asian Survey* 54, no. 1: 30–38.

Maley, William. 1999. "The Foreign Policy of the Taliban." Council on Foreign Relations, July 6. https://www.cfr.org/report/foreign-policy-taliban.

Maley, William. 2001. "Introduction: Interpreting the Taliban." In William Maley, ed., *Fundamentalism Reborn? Afghanistan and the Taliban.* New York: New York University Press.

Malley, Robert. 1996. *The Call from Algeria: Third Worldism, Revolution, and the Turn to Islam.* Berkeley: University of California Press.

Malloy, James M. 1970. *Bolivia: The Uncompleted Revolution.* Pittsburgh: University of Pittsburgh Press.

Malloy, James M. 1971a. *Bolivia's MNR: A Study of a National Popular Movement in Latin America.* Buffalo: Council on International Studies, State University of New York at Buffalo.

Malloy, James M. 1971b. "Revolutionary Politics." In James M. Malloy and Richard S. Thorn, eds., *Beyond the Revolution: Bolivia since 1952.* Pittsburgh: University of Pittsburgh Press.

Malloy, James M., and Sylvia Borzutsky. 1982. "The Praetorianization of the Revolution: 1964–1967." In Jerry R. Landman, ed., *Modern-Day Bolivia: Legacy of the Revolution and Prospects for the Future.* Tempe: Center for Latin American Studies, Arizona State University.

Malloy, James M., and Eduardo Gamarra. 1988. *Revolution and Reaction: Bolivia, 1964–1985.* New Brunswick, NJ: Transaction Books.

Maloney, Suzanne. 2015. *Iran's Political Economy since the Revolution.* New York: Cambridge University Press.

Mampilly, Zachariah C. 2011. *Rebel Rulers: Insurgent Governance and Civilian Life during War.* Ithaca, NY: Cornell University Press.

Manion, Melanie. 1993. *Retirement of Revolutionaries in China: Public Policies, Social Norms, Private Interests.* Princeton, NJ: Princeton University Press.

Manning, Carrie L. 2001. "Competition and Accommodation in Post-Conflict Democracy: The Case of Mozambique." *Democratization* 8, no. 2: 140–168.

Manning, Carrie L. 2002. *The Politics of Peace in Mozambique: Post-Conflict Democratization, 1992–2000.* Westport, CT: Praeger.

Manning, Carrie L. 2005. "Assessing Adaptation to Democratic Politics in Mozambique: The Case of Frelimo." In Leonardo A. Villalón and Peter VonDoepp, eds., *The Fate of Africa's Democratic Experiments: Elites and Institutions.* Bloomington: Indiana University Press.

Mao Zedong. 2003. "Mao Zedong's Report on the Peasant Movement in Hunan, March 1927." In Jussi Hanhimäki and Odd Arne Westad, eds., *The Cold War: A History in Documents and Eyewitness Accounts.* New York: Oxford University Press.

Marcum, John. 1967. "Three Revolutions." *Africa Report,* November: 8–22.

Margolin, Jean-Louis. 1999a. "Cambodia: The Country of Disconcerting Crimes." In Stéphane Courtois et al., eds., *The Black Book of Communism: Crimes, Terror, Repression.* Cambridge, MA: Harvard University Press.

Margolin, Jean-Louis. 1999b. "Vietnam and Laos: The Impasse of War Communism." In Stéphane Courtois et al., eds., *The Black Book of Communism: Crimes, Terror, Repression.* Cambridge, MA: Harvard University Press.

Marin, Brian. 1996. *The Shanghai Green Gang: Politics and Organized Crime, 1919–1937.* Berkeley: University of California Press.

Marku, Ylber. 2020. "Communist Relations in Crisis: The End of Soviet-Albanian Relations, and the Sino-Soviet Split, 1960–1961." *International History Review* 42, no. 4: 813–832.

Marr, David G. 1991. "Where Is Vietnam Coming From?" In Dean Forbes, Terence H. Hull, David G. Marr, and Brian Brogran, eds., *Doi Moi: Vietnam's Renovation: Policy and Performance.* Canberra: Research School of Pacific Studies, Australian National University.

Marr, David G. 1995. *Vietnam 1945: The Quest for Power*. Berkeley: University of California Press.

Marr, David G. 1998. "Introduction." In David G. Marr, ed., *Mass Media in Vietnam*. Canberra: Department of Political and Social Change, Australian National University.

Marr, David G. 2003. "A Passion for Modernity: Intellectuals and the Media." In Hy V. Luong, ed., *Postwar Vietnam: Dynamics of a Transforming Society*. Lanham, MD: Rowman and Littlefield.

Marr, David G. 2013. *Vietnam: State, War and Revolution (1945–1946)*. Berkeley: University of California Press.

Marr, David G., and Christine Pelzer White. 1988. "Introduction." In David G. Marr and Christine Pelzer White, eds., *Postwar Vietnam: Dilemmas in Socialist Development*. Ithaca, NY: Southeast Asia Program, Cornell University.

Marsden, Peter. 2002. *The Taliban: War and Religion in Afghanistan*. London: Zed Books.

Marshall, Monty G., Ted Robert Gurr, and Keith Jaggers. 2018. "Polity IV Project: Political Regime Characteristics and Transitions, 1800–2017." Version p4v2017. Codebook, http://www.systemicpeace.org/inscr/p4manualv2017.pdf. Database, http://www.systemicpeace.org/inscr/p4v2017.xls.

Martí i Puig, Salvador. 1997. *La revolución enredada: Nicaragua, 1977–1996*. Madrid: Los Libros de la Catarata.

Martí i Puig, Salvador. 2009. "El Frente Sandinista de Liberación Nacional: Análisis de una mutación." In Salvador Martí i Puig and David Close, eds., *Nicaragua y el FSLN [1979–2009]: ¿Qué queda de la revolución?* Barcelona: Ediciones Bellaterra.

Martinez, Luis. 2000. *The Algerian Civil War, 1990–1998*. New York: Columbia University Press.

Martinez, Luis. 2004. "Why the Violence in Algeria?" *Journal of North African Studies* 9, no. 2: 14–27.

Martínez Assad, Carlos. 1979. *El laboratorio de la revolución: El Tabasco garridista*. Mexico City: Siglo Veintiuno.

Martínez Assad, Carlos. 1982. "Los caudillos regionales y el poder central." In Carlos Martínez Assad, Mario Ramírez Rancaño, and Ricardo Pozas Horcasitas, eds., *Revolucionarios fueron todos*. Mexico City: Fondo de Cultura Económica.

Martínez Assad, Carlos. 1988. "Introducción." In Carlos Martínez Assad, ed. *Estadistas, Caciques y Caudillos*. Mexico City: Instituto de Investigaciones Sociales.

Martínez Assad, Carlos. 2013. "Back to Centralism, 1920–1940." In Douglas W. Richmond and Sam W. Haynes, eds., *The Mexican Revolution: Conflict and Consolidation, 1910–1940*. College Station: Texas A&M University Press.

Matijevic, Margareta. 2006. "Religious Communities in Croatia." *Review of Croatian History* 2, no. 1: 117–140.

Matthews, Herbert L. 1969. *Fidel Castro*. New York: Simon and Schuster.

Matthews, Herbert L. 1975. *Revolution in Cuba: An Essay in Understanding*. New York: Charles Scribner's Sons.

Mattingly, Daniel. 2020. *The Art of Political Control in China*. Cambridge: Cambridge University Press.

Mawdsley, Evan. 2005a. *The Russian Civil War*. New York: Pegasus Books.

Mawdsley, Evan. 2005b. *The Thunder in the East: The Nazi-Soviet War 1941–1945.* London: Hodder Arnold.

Maxfield, Sylvia. 1987. "Introduction." In Sylvia Maxfield and Ricardo Anzaldúa Montoya, eds., *Government and Private Sector in Contemporary Mexico.* La Jolla: Center for U.S.-Mexican Studies, University of California, San Diego.

Mazarr, Michael J. 1989. "Prospects for Revolution in Post-Castro Cuba." *Journal of Interamerican Studies and World Affairs* 31, no. 4: 61–90.

Mazza, Jacqueline. 2001. *Don't Disturb the Neighbors: The United States and Democracy in Mexico, 1980–1995.* New York: Routledge.

McAdams, A. James. 2017. *Vanguard of the Revolution: The Global Idea of the Communist Party.* Princeton, NJ: Princeton University Press.

McAlister, John, Jr. 1971. *Vietnam: The Origins of Revolution.* Garden City, NY: Doubleday.

McAlister, John, Jr., and Paul Mus. 1970. *The Vietnamese and Their Revolution.* New York: Harper and Row.

McCormick, Barrett L. 1999. "Political Change in China and Vietnam: Coping with the Consequences of Economic Reform." In Anita Chan, Benedict Kerkvliet, and Jonathan Unger, eds., *Transforming Asian Socialism: China and Vietnam Compared.* Lanham, MD: Rowman and Littlefield.

McCormick, Robert B. 2015. *Croatia under Ante Pavelić: America, the Ustaše and Croatian Genocide.* London: I. B. Tauris.

McDonald, Angus W. 1978. *The Urban Origins of Rural Revolution: Elites and the Masses in Hunan Province, China, 1911–1927.* Berkeley: University of California Press.

McLaughlin, James L., and David Owusu-Ansah. 1995. "Historical Setting." In LaVerle Berry, ed., *Ghana: A Country Study.* Washington, DC: Federal Research Division, Library of Congress.

Mebane, Walter R. 2010. "Fraud in the 2009 Presidential Election in Iran?" *Chance* 23, no. 1: 6–15.

Medina, Luis. 1978. *Historia de la revolución mexicana, periodo 1940–1952.* Vol. 18, *Del cardenismo al avilacamachismo.* Mexico City: El Colegio de México.

Medina, Luis. 1979. *Historia de la revolución mexicana, periodo 1940–1952.* Vol. 20, *Civilismo y modernización del autoritarismo.* Mexico City: El Colegio de México.

Mehilli, Elidor. 2011. "Defying Destalinization: Albania's 1956." *Journal of Cold War Studies* 13, no. 4: 4–56.

Mehilli, Elidor. 2020. "Enver Hoxha's Albania: Yugoslav, Soviet, and Chinese Relations and Ruptures." In John R. Lampe and Ulf Brunnbauer, eds., *The Routledge Handbook of Balkan and Southeast European History.* London: Routledge.

Meisner, Maurice. 1999. *Mao's China and After: A History of the People's Republic.* New York: Free Press.

Menashri, David. 1990. *Iran: A Decade of War and Revolution.* New York: Holmes & Meier.

Mendoza, Arturo Alvarado. 1988. "Perfil político de Emilio Portes Gil." In Carlos Martínez Assad, ed., *Estadistas, caciques y caudillos.* Mexico City: Instituto de Investigaciones Sociales.

Mendy, Peter. 2003. "Portugal's Civilizing Mission in Colonial Guinea-Bissau: Rhetoric and Reality." *International Journal of African Historical Studies* 36, no. 1: 35–58.

Meng, Xiao-Li, and Donald B. Rubin. 1992. "Performing Likelihood Ratio Tests with Multiply-Imputed Data Sets." *Biometrika* 79, no. 1: 103–111.

Mengisteab, Kidane, and Okbazghi Yohannes. 2005. *Anatomy of an African Tragedy: Political, Economic and Foreign Policy Crisis in Post-Independence Eritrea.* Trenton, NJ: Red Sea Press.

MERIP (Middle East Research and Information Project). 1973. "Iran: The Shah Buys Some Stability." *MERIP Reports,* no. 16: 21–22.

Merle, Robert. 1967. *Ben Bella.* London: Michael Joseph.

Mertha, Andrew. 2014. *Brothers in Arms: Chinese Aid to the Khmer Rouge, 1975–1979.* Ithaca, NY: Cornell University Press.

Mertha, Andrew. 2019. "Rectification." In Christian Sorace, Ivan Franceschini, and Nicholas Loubere, eds., *Afterlives of Chinese Communism: Political Concepts from Mao to Xi.* Canberra: Australian National University Press.

Mesa-Lago, Carmelo. 1970. "The Revolutionary Offensive." In Irving Louis Horowitz, ed., *Cuban Communism.* New Brunswick, NJ: Transaction Publishers.

Mesa-Lago, Carmelo. 1971a. "Economic Policies and Growth." In Carmelo Mesa-Lago, ed., *Revolutionary Change in Cuba.* Pittsburgh: University of Pittsburgh Press.

Mesa-Lago, Carmelo. 1971b. "Present and Future of the Revolution." In Carmelo Mesa-Lago, ed., *Revolutionary Change in Cuba.* Pittsburgh: University of Pittsburgh Press.

Mesa-Lago, Carmelo. 1972. "Economic Significance of Unpaid Labor in Socialist Cuba." In Rolando E. Bonachea and Nelson P. Valdes, eds., *Revolution in Cuba.* New York: Anchor Books.

Mesa-Lago, Carmelo. 1982. "The Economy: Caution, Frugality, and Resilient Ideology." In Jorge I. Domínguez, ed., *Cuba: Internal and International Affairs.* Beverly Hills, CA: Sage Publications.

Mesa-Lago, Carmelo. 1988. "The Cuban Economy in the 1980s: The Return of Ideology." In Sergio G. Roca, ed., *Socialist Cuba: Past Interpretations and Future Challenges.* Boulder, CO: Westview Press.

Mesa-Lago, Carmelo. 1993a. "The Economic Effects on Cuba of the Downfall of Socialism in the USSR and Eastern Europe." In Carmelo Mesa-Lago, ed., *Cuba after the Cold War.* Pittsburgh: University of Pittsburgh Press.

Mesa-Lago, Carmelo. 1993b. "Introduction: Cuba, the Last Communist Warrior." In Carmelo Mesa-Lago, ed., *Cuba after the Cold War.* Pittsburgh: University of Pittsburgh Press.

Mesa-Lago, Carmelo. 2003. "The Cuban Economy in 1999–2001: Evaluation of Performance." In Irving Louis Horowitz and Jaime Suchlicki, eds., *Cuban Communism, 1959–2003.* New Brunswick, NJ: Transaction Publishers.

Mesfin, Elshaddai. 2019. "Guinea Bissau: Conflict Insight." Peace and Security Report. Institute for Peace and Security Studies, Addis Ababa University. https://media .africaportal.org/documents/guinea_bissau_conflict_insights_vol_1-_conflict _insight.pdf.

Meyer, Jean A. 1976. *The Cristero Rebellion: The Mexican People between Church and State 1926–1929.* Cambridge: Cambridge University Press.

Meyer, Jean A. 1991. "Revolution and Reconstruction in the 1920s." In Leslie Bethell, ed., *Mexico since Independence.* Cambridge: Cambridge University Press.

Meyer, Jean A. 2003. *El sinarquismo, el cardenismo, y la iglesia*. Mexico City: Tusquets Editoriales.

Meyer, Karl E., and Tad Szulc. 1962. *The Cuban Invasion: Chronicle of a Disaster*. New York: Praeger.

Meyer, Lorenzo. 1972. *Mexico and the United States in the Oil Controversy, 1917–1942*. Austin: University of Texas Press.

Meyer, Lorenzo. 1977. "Historical Roots of the Authoritarian State in Mexico." In José Luis Reyna and Richard S. Weinert, eds., *Authoritarianism in Mexico*. Philadelphia: Institute for the Study of Human Issues.

Meyer, Lorenzo. 1978a. *Historia de la revolución mexicana, periodo 1928–1934*. Vol. 7, *Los inicios de la institucionalización, la política del Maximato*. Mexico City: El Colegio de México.

Meyer, Lorenzo. 1978b. *Historia de la revolución mexicana, periodo 1928–1934*. Vol. 8, *El conflicto social y los gobiernos del Maximato*. Mexico City: El Colegio de México.

Meyer, Lorenzo. 1991. "Mexico: The Exception and the Rule." In Abraham F. Lowenthal, ed., *Exporting Democracy: The United States and Latin America*. Baltimore: Johns Hopkins University Press.

Mezhoud, Salem. 1993. "*Glasnost* the Algerian Way: The Role of Berber Nationalists in Political Reform." In George Joffé, ed., *North Africa: Nation, State, and Region*. London: Routledge.

Mgbako, Chi Adanna. 2005. "Ingando Solidarity Camps: Reconciliation and Political Indoctrination in Post-Genocide Rwanda." *Harvard Human Rights Journal* 18: 201–224.

Michaels, Albert L. 1970. "The Crisis of Cardenismo." *Journal of Latin American Studies* 2, no. 1: 55–79.

Middlebrook, Kevin J. 1995. *The Paradox of Revolution: Labor, the State, and Authoritarianism in Mexico*. Baltimore: Johns Hopkins University Press.

Middlebrook, Kevin J. 2001. "Party Politics and Democratization in Mexico: The Partido Acción Nacional in Comparative Perspective." In Kevin J. Middlebrook, ed., *Party Politics and the Struggle for Democracy in Mexico: National and State-Level Analyses of the Partido Acción Nacional*. La Jolla: Center for U.S.-Mexican Studies, University of California, San Diego.

Mikoian, Anastas. 1999. *Tak bylo: Razmyshleniia o minuvshen*. Moscow: Vagrius.

Milani, Abbas. 2010. "The Green Movement." In Robin Wright, ed., *The Iran Primer: Power, Politics, and U.S. Policy*. Washington, DC: United States Institute of Peace Press.

Milani, Abbas. 2011. *The Shah*. New York: Palgrave Macmillan.

Milani, Abbas. 2013. "Iran: The Genealogy of a Failed Transition." In Michael McFaul and Kathryn Stoner-Weiss, eds., *Transitions to Democracy: A Comparative Perspective*. Baltimore: Johns Hopkins University Press.

Milani, Mohsen. 1994. *The Making of Iran's Islamic Revolution: From Monarchy to Islamic Republic*. Boulder, CO: Westview Press.

Millett, Richard L. 1977. *Guardians of the Dynasty*. Maryknoll, NY: Orbis Books.

Millett, Richard L. 1996. "From Triumph to Survival: Cuba's Armed Forces in an Era of Transition." In Richard L. Millett and Michael Gold-Biss, eds., *Beyond Praetorianism: The Latin American Military in Transition*. Coral Gables, FL: North-South Center Press, University of Miami.

Minzner, Carl. 2018. *End of an Era: How China's Authoritarian Revival Is Undermining Its Rise*. New York: Oxford University Press.

Miranda, Roger, with William Ratliff. 1993. *The Civil War in Nicaragua: Inside the Sandinistas*. New Brunswick, NJ: Transaction Publishers.

Mirescu, Alexander. 2015. "A Curious Case of Cooperation and Coexistence: Church-State Engagement and Oppositional Free Spaces in Communist Yugoslavia and East Germany." *Hungarian Historical Review* 4, no. 1: 82–113.

Mirón Lince, Rosa María. 1986. "Cárdenas en el poder (II)." In Javier Garciadiego Dantan et al., eds., *Evolución del estado mexicano*, tomo 2, *Reestructuración 1910–1940*. Mexico City: Ediciones El Caballito.

Mitchell, Christopher. 1977. *The Legacy of Populism in Bolivia: From the MNR to Military Rule*. New York: Praeger.

Mitrojorgji, Lejnar. 2020. "The Albanian Communist Party from Prewar Origins to Wartime Resistance and Power." In John R. Lampe and Ulf Brunnbauer, eds., *The Routledge Handbook of Balkan and Southeast European History*. London: Routledge.

Mizrahi, Yemile. 2003. *From Martyrdom to Power: The Partido Acción Nacional in Mexico*. Notre Dame, IN: University of Notre Dame Press.

Moazami, Behrooz. 2013. *State, Religion, and Revolution in Iran, 1796 to the Present*. New York: Palgrave Macmillan

Moens, Alexander. 1991. "President Carter's Advisers and the Fall of the Shah." *Political Science Quarterly* 106, no. 2: 211–237.

Mohseni, Ebrahim, Nancy Gallagher, and Clay Ramsay. 2018. *Iranian Public Opinion after the Protests*. Center for International Studies and Security, University of Maryland. https://cissm.umd.edu/research-impact/publications/iranian-public-opinion-after-protests-questionnaire.

Moin, Baqer. 1999. *Khomeini: Life of the Ayatollah*. New York: St. Martin's Press.

Moise, Edwin E. 1976. "Land Reform and Land Reform Errors in North Vietnam." *Pacific Affairs* 49, no. 1: 70–92.

Moise, Edwin E. 1980. "'Class-ism' in North Vietnam, 1953–1956." In William S. Turley, ed., *Vietnamese Communism in Comparative Perspective*. Boulder, CO: Westview Press.

Moise, Edwin E. 1983. *Land Reform in China and North Vietnam: Consolidating the Revolution at the Village Level*. Chapel Hill: University of North Carolina Press.

Molinar Horcasitas, Juan. 1991. *El tiempo de la legitimidad: Elecciones, autoritarismo y democracia en México*. Mexico City: Cal y Arena.

Molnar, Miklos. 1990. *From Béla Kun to János Kádár: Seventy Years of Hungarian Communism*. New York: Berg.

Montaner, Carlos Alberto. 2001. *Journey to the Heart of Cuba: Life as Fidel Castro*. New York: Algora.

Montes de Oca, Rosa Elena. 1977. "The State and the Peasants." In José Luis Reyna and Richard S. Weinert, eds., *Authoritarianism in Mexico*. Philadelphia: Institute for the Study of Human Issues.

Moore, Barrington. 1966. *Social Origins of Dictatorship and Democracy: Lord and Peasant in the Making of the Modern World*. Boston: Beacon Press.

Moore, Clement H. 1970. *Politics in North Africa: Algeria, Morocco, and Tunisia*. Boston: Little, Brown.

Morales Carazo, Jaime. 1989. *La Contra*. Mexico City: Editorial Planeta.

Morán Arce, Lucas. 1980. *La revolución cubana: Una versión rebelde*. San Juan: Universidad Católica.

Morgan, Stephen L., and Christopher Winship. 2015. *Counterfactuals and Causal Inference: Methods and Principles for Social Research*. 2nd ed. New York: Cambridge University Press.

Morris-Jung, Jason. 2015. "Vietnam's Online Petition Movement." *Southeast Asian Affairs* 2015: 402–415.

Morrison, Kevin M. 2009. "Oil, Nontax Revenue, and the Redistributional Foundations of Regime Stability." *International Organization* 63, no. 1: 107–138.

Mortimer, Robert A. 1970. "The Algerian Revolution in Search of the African Revolution." *Journal of Modern African Studies* 8, no. 3: 363–387.

Mortimer, Robert A. 1991. "Islamic and Multiparty Politics in Algeria." *Middle East Journal* 45, no. 4: 575–593.

Mortimer, Robert A. 2004. "Bouteflika and the Challenge of Political Stability." In Ahmed Aghrout and Redha M. Bougherira, eds., *Algeria in Transition: Reforms and Development Prospects*. London: RoutledgeCurzon.

Mortimer, Robert A. 2006. "State and Army in Algeria: The 'Bouteflika Effect.'" *Journal of North African Studies* 11, no. 2: 155–171.

Mortimer, Robert A. 2015. "Algerian Foreign Policy: From Revolution to National Interest." *Journal of North African Studies* 20, no. 3: 466–482.

Moslem, Mehdi. 2002. *Factional Politics in Post-Khomeini Iran*. Syracuse, NY: Syracuse University Press.

Moss, Sigrun M. 2014. "Beyond Conflict and Spoilt Identities: How Rwandan Leaders Justify a Single Recategorization Model for Post-Conflict Reconciliation." *Journal of Social and Political Psychology* 2, no. 1: 435–449.

Mujal-León, Eusebio, and Joshua W. Busby. 2003. "Much Ado about Something? Regime Change in Cuba." In Irving Louis Horowitz and Jaime Suchlicki, eds., *Cuban Communism, 1959–2003*. New Brunswick, NJ: Transaction Publishers.

Mulligan, Joseph E. 1991. *The Nicaraguan Church and the Revolution*. Kansas City, MO: Sheed and Ward.

Münkler, Herfried. 2004. *The New Wars*. Cambridge: Cambridge University Press.

Munslow, Barry. 1983. *Mozambique: The Revolution and Its Origins*. New York: Longman.

Munslow, Peter. 1981. "The 1980 Coup in Guinea Bissau." *Review of African Political Economy*, no. 21: 109–113.

Murawiec, Laurent, and Clifford Gaddy. 2002. "The Higher Police: Vladimir Putin and His Predecessors." *The National Interest*, no. 67: 29–36.

Murray, John. 1953. "Tito and the Catholic Church." *Irish Quarterly Review* 42, no. 165: 23–38.

Murshed, S. Iftikhar. 2006. *Afghanistan: The Taliban Years*. London: Bennett and Bloom.

Murti, B. S. N. 1964. *Vietnam Divided: The Unfinished Struggle*. New York: Asia Publishing House.

Mwenda, Andrew M. 2007. "Personalizing Power in Uganda." *Journal of Democracy* 18, no. 3: 23–37.

Nader, Alireza. 2010. "The Revolutionary Guards." In Robin Wright, ed., *The Iran Primer: Power, Politics, and U.S. Policy*. Washington, DC: United States Institute of Peace Press.

Nafziger, Steven, and Peter Lindert. 2013. "Russian Inequality on the Eve of the Revolution." https://web.williams.edu/Economics/wp/Nafziger_Lindert_Inequality_Sept2013.pdf.

Naji, Kasra. 2008. *Ahmadinejad: The Secret History of Iran's Radical Leader*. Berkeley: University of California Press.

Nathan, Andrew J. 2001. "Introduction: The Documents and Their Significance." In Zhang Liang, comp., *The Tiananmen Papers*, ed. Andrew Nathan and Perry Link. New York: PublicAffairs.

Nathan, Andrew J. 2003. "Authoritarian Resilience." *Journal of Democracy* 14, no. 1: 6–17.

Navarro, Aaron. W. 2010. *Political Intelligence and the Creation of Modern Mexico (1938–1954)*. University Park: Pennsylvania State University Press.

Needler, Martin C. 1971. *Politics and Society in Mexico*. Albuquerque: University of New Mexico Press.

Nelson, Lowry. 1972. *Cuba: The Measure of a Revolution*. Minneapolis: University of Minnesota Press.

Newitt, Malyn. 2002. "Mozambique." In Patrick Chabal, David Birmingham, Joshua Forrest, Malyn Newitt, Gerhard Seibert, and Elisa Silva Andrade, eds., *A History of Postcolonial Africa*. London: Hurst.

Nguyen, Hai Hong. 2016. "Resilience of the Communist Party of Vietnam's Authoritarian Regime since Doi Moi." *Journal of Current Southeast Asian Affairs* 35, no. 2: 31–55.

Nguyen, Lien-Hang T. 2006. "The War Politburo: North Vietnam's Diplomatic and Political Road to the Tet Offensive." *Journal of Vietnamese Studies* 1, no. 1–2: 4–58.

Nguyen, Lien-Hang T. 2012. *Hanoi's War: An International History of the War for Peace in Vietnam*. Chapel Hill: University of North Carolina Press.

Nguyen, Manh Hung. 2018. "Vietnam in 2017: Power Consolidation, Domestic Reforms, and Coping with New Geopolitical Challenges." *Southeast Asian Affairs* 2018: 406–428.

Nguyen, Phuong. 2017. "Vietnam in 2016: Searching for a New Ethos." *Southeast Asian Affairs* 2017: 408–419.

Nhem, Boraden. 2013. *The Khmer Rouge: Ideology, Militarism, and the Revolution That Consumed a Generation*. Santa Barbara, CA: Praeger.

Nichols, John Spicer. 1982. "The News Media in the Nicaraguan Revolution." In Thomas W. Walker, ed., *Nicaragua in Revolution*. New York: Praeger.

Niebuhr, Robert. 2017. "Enlarging Yugoslavia: Tito's Quest for Expansion, 1945–1948." *European History Quarterly* 47, no. 2: 284–310.

Nielson, Christian. 2020. *Yugoslavia and Political Assassinations*. London: Bloomsbury Academic.

Niemeyer, Eberhardt, Jr. 1974. *Revolution at Querétaro: The Mexican Constitutional Convention of 1916–1917*. Austin: University of Texas Press.

Ninh, Kim N. B. 2002. *A World Transformed: The Politics of Culture in Revolutionary Vietnam, 1945–1965*. Ann Arbor: University of Michigan Press.

Nojumi, Neamatollah. 2008. "The Rise and Fall of the Taliban." In Robert Crews and Amin Tarzi, eds., *The Taliban and the Crisis of Afghanistan*. Cambridge, MA: Harvard University Press.

Nome, Frida, and Kari Vogt. 2008. "Islamic Education in Qom: Contemporary Developments." *Acta Orientalia* 69: 35–75.

Nordlinger, Eric A. 1977. *Soldiers in Politics: Military Coups and Governments*. Englewood Cliffs, NJ: Prentice-Hall.

Nuclear Threat Initiative. 2021. "Iran." https://www.nti.org/learn/countries/iran/.

Nuvunga, Adriano. 2017. "From Former Liberation Movement to Four Decades in Government: The Maintenance of the Frelimo State." In Redie Bereketeab, ed., *National Liberation Movements as Governments in Africa*. London: Routledge.

Nwaubani, Ebere. 2001. "Eisenhower, Nkrumah and the Congo Crisis." *Journal of Contemporary History* 36, no. 4: 599–622.

O'Ballance, Edgar. 1964. *The Indo-China War 1945-1954: A Study in Guerrilla Warfare*. London: Faber and Faber.

O'Ballance, Edgar. 1967. *The Algerian Insurrection, 1954-62*. London: Faber and Faber.

Obradović, Marija. 2013. "From Revolutionary to Clientelistic Party: The Communist Party of Yugoslavia, 1945–1952." *East European Politics and Societies and Cultures* 27, no. 3: 376–399.

O'Connor, James. 1970. *The Origins of Socialism in Cuba*. Ithaca, NY: Cornell University Press.

Odom, William. 1998. *The Collapse of the Soviet Military*. New Haven, CT: Yale University Press.

O'Donnell, Guillermo. 1973. *Modernization and Bureaucratic-Authoritarianism: Studies in South American Politics*. Berkeley: Institute of International Studies, University of California, Berkeley.

O'Donnell, Guillermo, and Philippe C. Schmitter. 1986. *Transitions from Authoritarian Rule: Tentative Conclusions about Uncertain Democracies*. Baltimore: Johns Hopkins University Press.

OECD (Organization for Economic Cooperation and Development). 1988. *OECD Economic Surveys: Yugoslavia*. Paris: OECD.

Ogushi, Atsushi. 2008. *The Demise of the Soviet Communist Party*. London: Routledge.

Oi, Jean C. 1999. *Rural China Takes Off: Institutional Foundations of Economic Reform*. Berkeley: University of California Press.

Okafor, F. O. E. 1988. "The PAIGC and the Economic Development of Guinea Bissau: Ideology and Reality." *The Developing Economies* 26, no. 2: 125–140.

O'Kane, Trish. 1990. "The New World Order." *NACLA Report on the Americas* 24, no. 1: 28–31.

Olvera, Alberto J. 2003a. "Las tendencies generales de desarrollo de la sociedad civil en México." In Alberto J. Olvera, ed., *Sociedad civil, esfera pública y democratización en América Latina*. Xalapa, Mexico: Universidad Veracruzana.

Olvera, Alberto J. 2003b. "Movimientos sociales prodemocráticos y esfera pública en México: El caso de Alianza Cívica." In Alberto J. Olvera, ed., *Sociedad civil, esfera pública y democratización en América Latina*. Xalapa, Mexico: Universidad Veracruzana.

Olvera, Alberto J. 2004. "Civil Society in Mexico at Century's End." In Kevin J. Middlebrook, ed., *Dilemmas of Political Change in Mexico*. London: Institute of Latin American Studies, University of London.

Oppenheimer, Andres. 1992. *Castro's Final Hour: The Secret Story behind the Coming Downfall of Communist Cuba*. New York: Simon and Schuster.

Oquist, Paul. 1992. "Sociopolitical Dynamics of the 1990 Nicaraguan Elections." In Vanessa Castro and Gary Prevost, eds., *The 1990 Elections in Nicaragua and Their Aftermath*. Lanham, MD: Rowman and Littlefield.

Orozco, Manuel. 2002. *International Norms and Mobilization of Democracy: Nicaragua in the World*. Aldershot, UK: Ashgate.

Osborne, Milton. 1970. *Region of Revolt: Focus on Southeast Asia*. Adelaide: Pergamon Press.

Osinsky, Pavel, and Jari Eloranta. 2014. "Why Did the Communists Win or Lose? A Comparative Analysis of the Revolutionary Civil Wars in Russia, Finland, Spain, and China." *Sociological Forum* 29, no. 2: 318–341.

Osten, Sarah. 2018. *The Mexican Revolution's Wake: The Making of a Political System, 1920–1929*. New York: Cambridge University Press.

Ostovar, Afshon. 2016. *Vanguard of the Imam: Religion, Politics and Iran's Revolutionary Guard*. New York: Oxford University Press.

Ottaway, David, and Marina Ottaway. 1970. *Algeria: The Politics of a Socialist Revolution*. Berkeley: University of California Press.

Ottolenghi, Emanuelle. 2011. *The Pasdaran: Inside Iran's Islamic Revolutionary Guard Corps*. Washington, DC: Foundation for Defense of Democracies.

Overy, Richard. 1997. *Russia's War*. New York: Penguin Books.

Padgett, L. Vincent. 1966. *The Mexican Political System*. Boston: Houghton Mifflin.

Padula, Alfred. 1974. *The Fall of the Bourgeoisie: Cuba, 1959–1961*. Doctoral dissertation, University of New Mexico.

Padula, Alfred. 1993. "Cuban Socialism: Thirty Years of Controversy." In Enrique A. Baloyra and James A. Morris, eds., *Conflict and Change in Cuba*. Albuquerque: University of New Mexico Press.

Paige, Jeffrey. 1975. *Agrarian Revolution: Social Movements and Export Agriculture in the Underdeveloped World*. New York: Free Press.

Palmer, Peter. 2000. *The Communists and the Roman Catholic Church in Yugoslavia, 1941–1946*. Doctoral dissertation, University of Oxford.

Pantsov, Alexander V. 2000. *The Bolsheviks and the Chinese Revolution: 1919–1927*. Honolulu: University of Hawaii Press.

Pantsov, Alexander V., and Steven I. Levine. 2012. *Mao: The Real Story*. New York: Simon and Schuster.

Pantsov, Alexander V., and Steven I. Levine. 2015. *Deng Xiaoping: A Revolutionary Life*. New York: Oxford University Press.

Parsa, Misagh. 2020. "Authoritarian Survival: Iran's Republic of Repression." *Journal of Democracy* 31, no. 3: 54–68.

Pastor, Robert A. 1987. *Condemned to Repetition: The United States and Nicaragua*. Princeton, NJ: Princeton University Press.

Pastor, Robert A. 2002. *Not Condemned to Repetition: The United States and Nicaragua*. Boulder, CO: Westview Press.

Patch, Richard. 1961. "Bolivia: The Restrained Revolution." *Annals of the Academy of Political and Social Science* 334: 123–132.

Paterson, Thomas G. 1994. *Contesting Castro: The United States and the Triumph of the Cuban Revolution.* New York: Oxford University Press.

Pei, Minxen. 2016. *China's Crony Capitalism: The Dynamics of Regime Decay.* Cambridge, MA: Harvard University Press.

Pepinsky, Thomas. 2009. *Economic Crises and the Breakdown of Authoritarian Regimes: Indonesia and Malaysia in Comparative Perspective.* New York: Cambridge University Press.

Pepinsky, Thomas. 2014. "The Institutional Turn in Comparative Authoritarianism." *British Journal of Political Science* 44, no. 4: 631–653.

Pepper, Suzanne. 1999. *Civil War in China: The Political Struggle, 1945–1949.* Lanham, MD: Rowman and Littlefield.

Pérez, Louis, Jr. 1976a. *Army Politics in Cuba, 1898–1958.* Pittsburgh: University of Pittsburgh Press.

Pérez, Louis, Jr. 1976b. "Army Politics in Socialist Cuba." *Journal of Latin American Studies* 8, no. 2: 251–271.

Pérez, Louis, Jr. 2015. *Cuba: Between Reform and Revolution.* New York: Oxford University Press.

Pérez-López, Jorge F. 2003. "Waiting for Godot: Cuba's Stalled Reforms and Continuing Economic Crisis." In Irving Louis Horowitz and Jaime Suchlicki, eds., *Cuban Communism, 1959–2003.* New Brunswick, NJ: Transaction Publishers.

Pérez-Stable, Marifeli. 1992. "Charismatic Authority, Vanguard Party Politics, and Popular Mobilizations: Revolution and Socialism in Cuba." *Cuban Studies* 22: 2–26.

Pérez-Stable, Marifeli. 1993. "'We Are the Only Ones and There Is No Alternative': Vanguard Party Politics in Cuba, 1975–1991." In Enrique A. Baloyra and James A. Morris, eds., *Conflict and Change in Cuba.* Albuquerque: University of New Mexico Press.

Pérez-Stable, Marifeli. 1997. "The Invisible Crisis: The Exhaustion of Politics in 1990s Cuba." In Miguel Ángel Centeno and Mauricio Font, eds., *Toward a New Cuba? Legacies of a Revolution.* Boulder, CO: Lynne Rienner.

Pérez-Stable, Marifeli. 2011a. *The Cuban Revolution: Origins, Course, and Legacy.* New York: Oxford University Press.

Pérez-Stable, Marifeli. 2011b. *The United States and Cuba: Intimate Enemies.* New York: Routledge.

Perica, Vjekoslav. 2002. *Balkan Idols: Religion and Nationalism in Yugoslav States.* New York: Oxford University Press

Perlmutter, Amos. 1977. *The Military and Politics in Modern Times: On Professionals, Praetorians, and Revolutionary Soldiers.* New Haven, CT: Yale University Press.

Perlmutter, Amos, and William M. LeoGrande. 1982. "The Party in Uniform: Toward a Theory of Civil-Military Relations in Communist Political Systems." *American Political Science Review* 76, no. 4: 778–789.

Perry, Elizabeth J. 1993. *Shanghai on Strike: The Politics of Chinese Labor.* Stanford, CA: Stanford University Press.

Perry, Elizabeth J. 2007. *Patrolling the Revolution: Worker Militias, Citizenship, and the Modern Chinese State.* Lanham, MD: Rowman and Littlefield.

Perry, Elizabeth J. 2012. *Anyuan: Mining China's Revolutionary Tradition*. Berkeley: University of California Press.

Peschard, Jacqueline. 1986. "El Maximato." In Javier Garciadiego Dantan et al., eds., *Evolución del estado mexicano*, tomo 2, *Reestructuración 1910–1940*. Mexico City: Ediciones El Caballito.

Petchenkine, Youry. 1993. *Ghana: In Search of Stability, 1957–1992*. Westport, CT: Praeger.

Peters, Philip. 2015. "Cuba's Entrepreneurs: Foundation of a New Private Sector." In Philip Brenner, Marguerite Rose Jiménez, John M. Kirk, and William M. Leo-Grande, eds., *A Contemporary Cuba Reader: The Revolution under Raúl Castro*. Lanham, MD: Rowman and Littlefield.

Peterson, Scott. 2010. *Let the Swords Encircle Me: Iran—a Journey behind the Headlines*. New York: Simon and Schuster.

Pethybridge, Roger. 1974. *The Social Prelude to Stalinism*. London: Macmillan.

Petras, James. 1979. "Whither the Nicaraguan Revolution?" *Monthly Review* 31, no. 5: 1–22.

Pettee, George. 1938. *The Process of Revolution*. New York: Harper and Brothers.

Pfeifer, Karen. 1985. *Agrarian Reform under State Capitalism in Algeria*. Boulder, CO: Westview Press.

Pickering, Paula M., and Mark Baskin. 2008. "What Is to Be Done? Succession from the League of Communists of Croatia." *Communist and Post-Communist Studies* 41, no. 4: 521–540.

Piffer, Tommaso. 2018. "Stalin, the Western Allies and Soviet Policy towards the Yugoslav Partisan Movement, 1941–4." *Journal of Contemporary History* 54, no. 2: 420–441.

Pike, Douglas. 1966. *Vietcong: The Organization and Techniques of the National Liberation Front of South Vietnam*. Cambridge: Center for International Studies, Massachusetts Institute of Technology.

Pike, Douglas. 1978. *History of Vietnamese Communism, 1925–1976*. Stanford, CA: Hoover Institution Press.

Pike, Douglas. 1986a. *PAVN: People's Army of Vietnam*. Novato, CA: Presidio Press.

Pike, Douglas. 1986b. "Political Institutionalization in Vietnam." In Robert A. Scalapino, Seizaburo Sato, and Jusuf Wanandi, eds., *Asian Political Institutionalization*. Berkeley: Institute of East Asian Studies, University of California, Berkeley.

Pineda, Empar. 1980. *La revolución nicaragüense: Presentación y selección de textos*. Madrid: Editorial Revolución.

Piñeyro, Jose Luis. 1985. *Ejercito y sociedad en México: Pasado y presente*. Puebla: Universidad Autónoma de Puebla.

Pirjevec, Jože. 2018. *Tito and His Comrades*. Madison: University of Wisconsin Press.

Planas, J. Richard. 1993. "The Impact of Soviet Reforms on Cuban Socialism." In Enrique A. Baloyra and James A. Morris, eds., *Conflict and Change in Cuba*. Albuquerque: University of New Mexico Press.

Planas, J. Richard. 1994. "Why Does Castro Survive?" In Donald E. Schulz, ed., *Cuba and the Future*. Westport, CT: Greenwood Press.

Poniatowska, Elena. 1975. *Massacre in Mexico*. New York: Viking.

Pool, David. 2001. *From Guerrillas to Government: The Eritrean People's Liberation Front*. Athens: Ohio University Press.

Porter, Gareth. 1975. "The Paris Agreement and Revolutionary Strategy in South Viet-nam." In Joseph J. Zasloff and MacAlister Brown, eds., *Communism in Indochina: New Perspectives*. Lexington, MA: Lexington Books.

Porter, Gareth. 1990. "The Politics of 'Renovation' in Vietnam." *Problems of Communism* 39, no. 3: 72–88.

Porter, Gareth. 1993. *Vietnam: The Politics of Bureaucratic Socialism*. Ithaca, NY: Cornell University Press.

Portes Gil, Emilio. 1964. *Autobiografía de la revolución mexicana*. Mexico City: Instituto Mexicano de Cultura.

Post, Ken. 1989a. *Revolution, Socialism and Nationalism in Viet Nam*. Vol. 1, *An Interrupted Revolution*. Aldershot, UK: Dartmouth.

Post, Ken. 1989b. *Revolution, Socialism and Nationalism in Viet Nam*. Vol. 2, *Viet Nam Divided*. Aldershot, UK: Dartmouth.

Post, Ken. 1989c. *Revolution, Socialism and Nationalism in Viet Nam*. Vol. 3, *Socialism in Half a Country*. Aldershot, UK: Dartmouth.

Post, Ken. 1989d. *Revolution, Socialism and Nationalism in Viet Nam*. Vol. 5, *Winning the War and Losing the Peace*. Aldershot, UK: Dartmouth.

Pottier, Johan. 2002. *Re-imagining Rwanda: Conflict, Survival, and Disinformation in the Late Twentieth Century*. New York: Cambridge University Press.

Pourzand, Azadeh. 2009–2010. "Change They Don't Believe In: The Political Presence of the Basij in the Islamic Republic of Iran." *Harvard Kennedy School Review* 10: 99–103.

Pozas Horcasitas, Ricardo. 1982. "De la ruptura del diejo régimen a la creación del nuevo orden." In Carlos Martínez Assad, Mario Ramírez Rancaño, and Ricardo Pozas Horcasitas, eds., *Revolucionarios fueron todos*. Mexico City: Fondo de Cultura Económica.

Prado Salmon, Gary. 1984. *Poder y fuerzas armada, 1949–1982*. La Paz: Editorial Los Amigos del Libro.

Premo, Daniel. 1997. "The Redirection of the Armed Forces." In Thomas W. Walker, ed., *Nicaragua without Illusions: Regime Transition and Structural Adjustment in the 1990s*. Wilmington, DE: Scholarly Resources.

Prendergast, John, and Mark Duffield. 1999. "Liberation Politics in Ethiopia and Eritrea." In Taisier M. Ali and Robert O. Matthews, eds., *Civil Wars in Africa: Roots and Resolution*. Montreal: McGill–Queen's University Press.

Previšić, Martin. 2020. "The 1948 Split and a New Round of Factional Struggles within the Communist Party of Yugoslavia: Parallel Biographies and Histories." In Tvrtko Jakovina and Martin Previšić, eds., *The Tito-Stalin Split 70 Years After*. Zagreb: University of Zagreb; Ljubljana: University of Ljubljana.

Prevost, Gary. 1991. "The FSLN as Ruling Party." In Thomas W. Walker, ed., *Revolution and Counterrevolution in Nicaragua*. Boulder, CO: Westview Press.

Prifti, Peter R. 1978. *Socialist Albania since 1944: Domestic and Foreign Developments*. Cambridge, MA: MIT Press.

Pringle, Robert W. 2000. "Andropov's Counterintelligence State." *International Journal of Intelligence and Counterintelligence* 13, no. 2: 193–203.

Prunier, Gerard. 2009. *Africa's World War: Congo, the Rwandan Genocide, and the Making of a Continental Catastrophe*. New York: Oxford University Press.

Przeworski, Adam, Michael E. Alvarez, José Antonio Cheibub, and Fernando Limongi. 2000. *Democracy and Development: Political Institutions and Well-Being in the World, 1950–1990*. New York: Cambridge University Press.

Purdeková, Andrea. 2011. "'Even If I Am Not Here, There Are So Many Eyes': Surveillance and State Reach in Rwanda." *Journal of Modern African Studies* 49, no. 3: 475–497.

Quandt, William B. 1969. *Revolution and Political Leadership: Algeria, 1954–1968*. Cambridge, MA: MIT Press.

Quandt, William B. 1998. *Between Bullets and Ballots: Algeria's Transition from Authoritarianism*. Washington, DC: Brookings Institution Press.

Queiser Morales, Waltraud 1992. *Bolivia: Land of Struggle*. Boulder, CO: Westview Press.

Quinn-Judge, Sophie. 2004. "Rethinking the History of the Vietnamese Communist Party." In Duncan McCargo, ed., *Rethinking Vietnam*. London: RoutledgeCurzon.

Quinn-Judge, Sophie. 2005. "The Ideological Debate in the DRV and the Significance of the Anti-party Affair, 1967–68." *Cold War History* 5, no. 4: 479–500.

Quintana, Alejandro. 2010. *Maximino Ávila Camacho and the One-Party State: The Taming of Caudillismo and Caciquismo in Post-Revolutionary Mexico*. Lanham, MD: Lexington Books.

Quirk, Robert E. 1973. *The Mexican Revolution and the Catholic Church*. Bloomington: Indiana University Press.

Quirk, Robert E. 1993. *Fidel Castro*. New York: W. W. Norton.

Rabe, Stephen. 1988. *Eisenhower and Latin America: The Foreign Policy of Anti-Communism*. Chapel Hill: University of North Carolina Press.

Rabiei, Kamran. 2020. "Protest and Regime Change: Different Experiences of the Arab Uprisings and the 2009 Iranian Presidential Election Protests." *International Studies* 57, no. 2: 144–170.

Rabinowitch, Alexander. 1976. *The Bolsheviks Come to Power: The Revolution of 1917 in Petrograd*. New York: W. W. Norton.

Rabkin, Rhoda. 1991. *Cuban Politics: The Revolutionary Experiment*. New York: Praeger.

Radu, Michael. 1986. "The Origins and Evolution of the Nicaraguan Insurgencies, 1979–1985." *Orbis* 29: 821–840.

Ragazzi, Francesco. 2017. *Governing Diasporas in International Relations: The Transnational Politics of Croatia and Former Yugoslavia*. London: Routledge.

Rake, Alan. 1965. "Ghana's Economic Crisis." *Africa Report* 10, no. 3: 47–48.

Ramet, Pedro. 1982. "Catholicism and Politics in Socialist Yugoslavia." *Religion in Communist Lands* 10, no. 3: 256–274.

Ramírez, Sergio. 2007. *Adiós Muchachos*. Barcelona: Penguin Random House.

Ramírez Rancaño, Mario. 1981. "La candidatura de Gustavo Díaz Ordaz." In Carlos Martínez Assad, ed., *La sucesión presidencial en México, 1928–1988*. Mexico City: Nueva Imagen.

Ramírez Rancaño, Mario. 1988. "Violencia en Tlaxcala bajo el gobierno de Adolfo Bonilla." In Carlos Martínez Assad, ed., *Estadistas, caciques y caudillos*. Mexico City: Instituto de Investigaciones Sociales.

Rasenberger, Jim. 2011. *Brilliant Disaster: JFK, Castro, and America's Doomed Invasion of Cuba's Bay of Pigs*. New York: Scribner.

Rashid, Ahmed. 2010. *Taliban: Militant Islam, Oil and Fundamentalism in Central Asia*. New Haven, CT: Yale University Press.

Rasler, Karen. 1996. "Concessions, Repression, and Political Protest in the Iranian Revolution." *American Sociological Review* 61, no. 1: 132–152.

Raszelenberg, Patrick. 1999. "The Khmers Rouges and the Final Solution." *History and Memory* 11, no. 2: 62–93.

Rath, Thomas. 2012. "Revolutionary Citizenship against Institutional Inertia: *Cardenismo* and the Mexican Army, 1934–1940." In Ben Fallaw and Terry Rugeley, eds., *Forced Marches: Soldiers and Military Caciques in Modern Mexico*. Tucson: University of Arizona Press.

Rath, Thomas. 2013. *Myths of Demilitarization in Postrevolutionary Mexico, 1920–1960*. Chapel Hill: University of North Carolina Press.

Rath, Thomas. 2014. "Camouflaging the State: The Army and the Limits of Hegemony in PRIísta Mexico, 1940–1960." In Paul Gillingham and Benjamin T. Smith, eds., *Dictablanda: Politics, Work, and Culture in Mexico, 1938–1968*. Durham, NC: Duke University Press.

Rathbone, Richard. 2000. *Nkrumah and the Chiefs: The Politics of Chieftaincy in Ghana 1951–60*. Oxford: James Currey.

Razoux, Pierre, and Nicholas Elliott. 2015. *The Iran-Iraq War*. Cambridge, MA: Belknap Press of Harvard University Press.

Reding, Andrew. 1991. "The Evolution of Governmental Institutions." In Thomas W. Walker, ed., *Revolution and Counterrevolution in Nicaragua*. Boulder, CO: Westview Press.

Reed, Gail. 1992. *Island in the Storm: The Cuban Communist Party's Fourth Congress*. Melbourne: Ocean Press.

Rees, E. A. 2000. "The Great Terror: Suicide or Murder?" *Russian Review* 59, no. 3: 446–450.

Reese, Robert R. 2011. *Why Stalin's Soldiers Fought: The Red Army's Effectiveness in World War II*. Lawrence: University Press of Kansas.

Reich, Peter Lester. 1995. *Mexico's Hidden Revolution: The Catholic Church in Law and Politics since 1929*. Notre Dame, IN: University of Notre Dame Press.

Reid, Anthony. 1974. *The Indonesian National Revolution 1945–1950*. London: Longman.

Reid, Richard. 2011. *Frontiers of Violence in North-East Africa: Genealogies of Conflict since c. 1800*. New York: Oxford University Press.

Reiman, Michal. 1987. *The Birth of Stalinism: The USSR on the Eve of the "Second Revolution."* Bloomington: Indiana University Press.

Reno, William. 2011. *Warfare in Independent Africa*. Cambridge: Cambridge University Press.

Reuter, Ora John. 2017. *The Origins of Dominant Parties: Building Authoritarian Institutions in Post-Soviet Russia*. New York: Cambridge University Press.

Reuter, Ora John, and Jennifer Gandhi. 2011. "Economic Performance and Elite Defection from Hegemonic Parties." *British Journal of Political Science* 41, no. 1: 83–110.

Reyntjens, Filip. 2004. "Rwanda, Ten Years On: From Genocide to Dictatorship." *African Affairs* 103, no. 411: 177–210.

Reyntjens, Filip. 2013. *Political Governance in Post-Genocide Rwanda*. New York: Cambridge University Press.

Reyntjens, Filip. 2015. "Rwanda: Progress or Powder Keg?" *Journal of Democracy* 26, no. 3: 19–33.

Reyntjens, Filip. 2016. "(Re-)imagining a Reluctant Post-Genocide Society: The Rwandan Patriotic Front's Ideology and Practice." *Journal of Genocide Research* 18, no. 1: 61–81.

Ricciardi, Joseph. 1991. "Economic Policy." In Thomas W. Walker, ed., *Revolution and Counterrevolution in Nicaragua*. Boulder, CO: Westview Press.

Richter, James. 1994. *Khrushchev's Double Bind: International Pressures and Domestic Coalition Politics*. Baltimore: Johns Hopkins University Press.

Rigby, T. H. 1979. *Lenin's Government: Sovnarkom 1917–1922*. New York: Cambridge University Press.

Ritter, David. 2017. "Yugoslavia." In Donatella della Porta, Teije Hidde Donker, Bogumila Hall, Emin Poljarevic, and Daniel P. Ritter, eds., *Social Movements and Civil War When Protests for Democratization Fail*. London: Routledge.

Rivero, Rigoberto. 1966. "Professionalism in the Cuban Armed Forces." *Military Review* 46, no. 3: 13–19.

Robbins, Carla Anne. 1983. *The Cuban Threat*. New York: McGraw-Hill.

Roberts, Hugh. 1984. "The Politics of Algerian Socialism." In Richard Lawless and Allan Findlay, eds., *North Africa: Contemporary Politics and Economic Development*. London: Croom Helm.

Roberts, Hugh. 1988. "Radical Islam and the Dilemma of Algerian Nationalism: The Embattled Arians of Algiers." *Third World Quarterly* 10, no. 2: 556–589.

Roberts, Hugh. 1993. "The FLN: French Conceptions, Algerian Realities." In George Joffé, ed., *North Africa: Nation, State, and Region*. London: Routledge.

Roberts, Hugh. 1994. "Algeria between Eradicators and Conciliators." *Middle East Report*, no. 189: 24–27.

Roberts, Hugh. 1995. "Algeria's Ruinous Impasse and the Honorable Way Out." *International Affairs* 71, no. 2: 247–267.

Roberts, Hugh. 2003. *The Battlefield: Algeria 1988–2002: Studies in a Broken Polity*. London: Verso.

Roberts, Hugh. 2007. "Demilitarizing Algeria." Carnegie Papers, no. 86. Washington, DC: Carnegie Endowment for International Peace.

Roberts, Kenneth. 1990. "Bullying and Bargaining: The United States, Nicaragua, and Conflict Resolution in Central America." *International Security* 15, no. 2: 67–102.

Roberts, Margaret E. 2018. *Censored: Distraction and Diversion inside China's Great Firewall*. Princeton, NJ: Princeton University Press.

Robins, Philip. 1990. "Iraq: Revolutionary Threats and Regime Responses." In John L. Esposito, ed., *The Iranian Revolution: Its Global Impact*. Miami: Florida International University Press.

Robinson, William I. 1992. *A Faustian Bargain: U.S. Intervention in the Nicaraguan Elections and American Foreign Policy in the Post–Cold War Era*. Boulder, CO: Westview Press.

Rock, June. 2000. "The Land Issue in Eritrea's Reconstruction and Development." *Review of African Political Economy* 27, no. 84: 221–234.

Rodríguez Menier, Juan Antonio. 1993. *Cuba por dentro: El Minint*. Miami: Ediciones Universal.

Roessler, P., and H. Verhoeven. 2016. *Why Comrades Go to War: Liberation Politics and the Outbreak of Africa's Deadliest Conflict*. New York: Oxford University Press.

Rolandsen, O. H., and M. W. Daly. 2016. *A History of South Sudan: From Slavery to Independence*. New York: Cambridge University Press.

Ronfeldt, David F. 1975. "The Mexican Army and Political Order since 1940." Rand Corporation Paper, August. Santa Monica, CA: Rand Corporation.

Ronfeldt, David F. 1984a. "The Mexican Army and Political Order since 1940." In David F. Ronfeldt, ed., *The Modern Mexican Military: A Reassessment*. La Jolla: Center for U.S.-Mexican Studies, University of California, San Diego.

Ronfeldt, David F. 1984b. "The Modern Mexican Military: An Overview." In David F. Ronfeldt, ed., *The Modern Mexican Military: A Reassessment*. La Jolla: Center for U.S.-Mexican Studies, University of California, San Diego.

Rooney, David. 1988. *Kwame Nkrumah: The Political Kingdom in the Third World*. London: I. B. Tauris.

Ross, Michael. 2001. "Does Oil Hinder Democracy?" *World Politics* 53, no. 3: 325–361.

Ross, Michael. 2012. *The Oil Curse: How Petroleum Wealth Shapes the Development of Nations*. Princeton, NJ: Princeton University Press.

Ross, Michael L., and Paasha Mahdavi. 2015. "Oil and Gas Data, 1932–2014." Harvard Dataverse, V2. doi: 10.7910/DVN/ZTPW0Y.

Rotberg, Robert. 2003. "Failed States, Collapsed States, Weak States: Causes and Indicators." In Robert Rotberg, ed., *State Failure and State Weakness in a Time of Terror*. Washington, DC: Brookings Institution Press.

Rouadjia, Ahmed. 1995. "Discourse and Strategy of the Algerian Islamist Movement." In Laura Guazzone, ed., *The Islamist Dilemma: The Political Role of Islamist Movements in the Contemporary Arab World*. Reading, UK: Ithaca Press.

Rowen, Henry S. 1996. "The Short March: China's Road to Democracy." *The National Interest*, no. 45: 61–70.

Rozenas, Arturas, and Yuri M. Zhukov. 2019. "Mass Repression and Political Loyalty: Evidence from Stalin's 'Terror by Hunger.'" *American Political Science Review* 113, no. 2: 569–583.

Rudebeck, Lars. 1974. *Guinea Bissau: A Study of Political Mobilization*. Uppsala: Scandinavian Institute of African Studies.

Ruedy, John. 1994. "Continuities and Discontinuities in the Algerian Confrontation with Europe." In John Ruedy, ed., *Islamism and Secularism in North Africa*. New York: St. Martin's Press.

Ruedy, John. 2005. *Modern Algeria: The Origins and Development of a Nation*. Bloomington: Indiana University Press.

Rugeley, Terry, and Ben Fallaw. 2012. "Redrafting History: The Challenges of Scholarship on the Mexican Military Experience." In Ben Fallaw and Terry Rugeley, eds., *Forced Marches: Soldiers and Military Caciques in Modern Mexico*. Tucson: University of Arizona Press.

Ruíz, Ramón Eduardo. 1968. *Cuba: The Making of a Revolution*. Amherst: University of Massachusetts Press.

Ruíz, Ramón Eduardo. 1980. *The Great Rebellion: Mexico, 1905–1924*. New York: W. W. Norton.

Sabet, Farzan, and Roozbeh Safshekan. 2019. "The Revolutionary Guard in Iranian Domestic and Foreign Power Politics." In Shahram Akbarzadeh, ed., *Routledge Handbook of International Relations in the Middle East*. London: Routledge.

Saeidi, Ali. 2009. "Iranian Para-governmental Organizations (Bonyads)." Middle East Institute. https://www.mei.edu/publications/iranian-para-governmental-organizations-bonyads.

Safshekan, Roozbeh, and Farzan Sabet. 2010. "The Ayatollah's Praetorians: The Islamic Revolutionary Guard Corps and the 2009 Election Crisis." *Middle East Journal* 64, no. 4: 543–558.

Saha, Sparsha. 2014. *Iran's Situations: Military Violence, Protests, and Group Dynamics*. Doctoral dissertation, Harvard University.

Sakmyster, Thomas L. 1975. "Army Officers and Foreign Policy in Interwar Hungary, 1918–41." *Journal of Contemporary History* 10, no. 1: 19–40.

Salah Tahi, Mohand. 1992. "The Arduous Democratization Process in Algeria." *Journal of Modern African Studies* 30, no. 3: 397–419.

Salisbury, Harrison. 1985. *The Long March: The Untold Story*. New York: HarperCollins.

Salmerón Sanginés, Pedro. 2000. "La fundación (1928–1933)." In Miguel Gonzáles Compeán and Leonardo Lomelí Vanegas, eds., *El partido de la revolución: Institución y conflicto (1928–1999)*. Mexico City: Fondo de Cultura Económica.

Salmerón Sanginés, Pedro. 2008. "El primer candidato del partido de Estado: La 'Invención' de Pascual Ortiz Rubio y la lealtad institucional de Aarón Sáenz." *Boletín* 57 (January–April): 2–21.

Samset, Ingrid. 2011. "Building a Repressive Peace: The Case of Post-Genocide Rwanda." *Journal of Intervention and Statebuilding* 5, no. 3: 265–283.

San Martín, Marta, and Ramón L. Bonachea. 1989. "Military Dimensions of the Cuban Revolution." In Irving Louis Horowitz, ed., *The Cuban Revolution*. New Brunswick, NJ: Transaction Publishers.

San Martín, Marta, and Ramón L. Bonachea. 2003. "Guerrillas at War." In Irving Louis Horowitz and Jaime Suchlicki, eds., *Cuban Communism, 1959–2003*. New Brunswick, NJ: Transaction Publishers.

Sanabria, Floren G. 1990. *La revolución del 9 de Abril*. La Paz: Editora Proinsa.

Sánchez Gutiérrez, Arturo. 1988. "Los militares en la década de los cincuenta." *Revista mexicana de sociología* 50, no. 3: 269–293.

Sánchez Talanquer, Mariano. 2017. *States Divided: History, Conflict, and State Foundation in Mexico and Colombia*. Doctoral dissertation, Cornell University.

Sánchez Talanquer, Mariano. 2019. "Las huellas del pasado: Legados representativos de la era del PRI." In Mariano Sánchez Talanquer and Ricardo Becerra Laguna, eds., *Las caras de Jano: Noventa años del Partido Revolucionario Institucional*. Mexico City: CIDE.

Sandle, Mark. 2002. "Brezhnev and Developed Socialism: The Ideology of *Zastoi*?" In Edwin Bacon, ed., *Brezhnev Reconsidered*. New York: Palgrave Macmillan.

Saragoza, Alex M. 1988. *The Monterrey Elite and the Mexican State 1880–1940*. Austin: University of Texas Press.

Sarkees, Meredith Reid, and Frank Whelon Wayman. 2010. *Resort to War: 1816–2007*. Washington, DC: CQ Press.

Sarkees, Meredith Reid, Frank Whelon Wayman, and J. David Singer. 2003 "Interstate, Intra-state, and Extra-state Wars: A Comprehensive Look at Their Distribution over Time, 1816–1997." *International Studies Quarterly* 47, no. 1: 49–70.

Saul, John S. 1985. *A Difficult Road: The Transition to Socialism in Mozambique*. New York: Monthly Review Press.

Schahgaldian, Nikola B. 1987. *The Iranian Military under the Islamic Republic*. Santa Monica, CA: Rand Corporation.

Schapiro, Leonard. 1971. *The Communist Party of the Soviet Union*. New York: Vintage Books.

Schapiro, Leonard. 1977. *The Origin of the Communist Autocracy: Political Opposition in the Soviet State First Phase, 1917–1922*. Cambridge, MA: Harvard University Press.

Schloming, Gordon Clark. 1974. *Civil-Military Relations in Mexico, 1910–1940*. Doctoral dissertation, Columbia University.

Schoenbaum, David. 1966. *Hitler's Social Revolution: Class and Status in Nazi Germany, 1933–1939*. New York: W. W. Norton.

Schoenhals, Michael. 2005. "'Why Don't We Arm the Left?' Mao's Culpability for the Cultural Revolution's 'Great Chaos' of 1967." *China Quarterly* 182: 277–300.

Schoenmakers, Hans. 1987. "Old Men and New State Structures in Guinea Bissau." *Journal of Legal Pluralism and Unofficial Law* 19, no. 25–26: 99–138.

Schulz, Donald E. 1994a. "Postscript: The Cuban Crisis in the Summer of 1993—an Opportunity for the United States?" In Donald E. Schulz, ed., *Cuba and the Future*. Westport, CT: Greenwood Press.

Schulz, Donald E. 1994b. "The United States and Cuba: From a Strategy of Conflict to Constructive Engagement." In Donald E. Schulz, ed., *Cuba and the Future*. Westport, CT: Greenwood Press.

Scott, Robert E. 1964. *Mexican Government in Transition*. Urbana: University of Illinois Press.

Scurr, Ruth. 2006. *Fatal Purity: Robespierre and the French Revolution*. New York: Holt.

Seely, Jennifer. 2005. "The Legacies of Transition Governments: Post-Transition Dynamics in Benin and Togo." *Democratization* 12, no. 3: 357–377.

Segal, Gerald, and John Phipps. 1990. "Why Communist Armies Defend Their Parties." *Asian Survey* 30, no. 10: 959–976.

Selbin, Eric. 1993. *Modern Latin American Revolutions*. Boulder, CO: Westview Press.

Selbin, Eric. 2010. *Revolution, Rebellion, Resistance: The Power of Story*. London: Zed Books.

Selden, Mark. 1971. *The Yenan Way in Revolutionary China*. Cambridge, MA: Harvard University Press.

Sell, Louis. 2002. *Slobodan Milosevic and the Destruction of Yugoslavia*. Durham, NC: Duke University Press.

Selznick, Philip. 1952. *The Organizational Weapon: A Study of Bolshevik Strategy and Tactics*. New York: McGraw-Hill.

Serra, Luis Hector. 1991. "The Grass-Roots Organizations." In Thomas W. Walker, ed., *Revolution and Counterrevolution in Nicaragua*. Boulder, CO: Westview Press.

Serrano, Mónica. 1995. "The Armed Branch of the State: Civil-Military Relations in Mexico." *Journal of Latin American Studies* 27, no. 2: 423–448.

Serrano, Mónica. 1997. "Estado y fuerzas armadas en México." In Marcelo Cavarozzi, ed., *México en el desfiladero: Los años de Salinas*. Mexico City: Juan Pablos Editor.

Service, Robert. 1979. *The Bolshevik Party in Revolution: A Study in Organisational Change, 1917–1923*. New York: Barnes and Noble Books.

Service, Robert. 1985. *Lenin: A Political Life*. Vol. 1, *The Strengths of Contradiction*. Bloomington: Indiana University Press.

Service, Robert. 1991. *Lenin: A Political Life*. Vol. 2, *Worlds in Collision*. Bloomington: Indiana University Press.

Service, Robert. 1995. *Lenin: A Political Life*. Vol. 3, *The Iron Ring*. Bloomington: Indiana University Press.

Servín, Elisa. 2001. *Ruptura y oposición: El movimiento henriquista, 1945–1954*. Mexico City: Cal y Arena.

Seton Watson, Hugh. 1956. *The East European Revolution*. New York: Praeger.

Setzekorn, Eric. 2018. *The Rise and Fall of an Officer Corps: The Republic of China Military, 1942–1955*. Norman: University of Oklahoma Press.

Sewell, William H. 1985. "Ideologies and Social Revolutions: Reflections on the French Case." *Journal of Modern History* 57, no. 1: 57–85.

Seybolt, Peter J. 1986. "Terror and Conformity: Counterespionage Campaigns, Rectification, and Mass Movements, 1942–1943." *Modern China* 12, no. 1: 39–73.

Shah, Aqil. 2014. *The Army and Democracy: Military Politics in Pakistan*. Cambridge, MA: Harvard University Press.

Shambaugh, David. 1991. "The Soldier and the State in China: The Political Work System in the People's Liberation Army." *China Quarterly* 127: 527–568.

Shambaugh, David. 2002. *Modernizing China's Military: Progress, Problems, and Prospects*. Berkeley: University of California Press.

Shambaugh, David. 2008. *China's Communist Party: Atrophy and Adaptation*. Berkeley: University of California Press.

Shambaugh, David. 2016. "Contemplating China's Future." *Washington Quarterly* 39, no. 3: 121–130.

Shawcross, William. 1979. *Sideshow: Kissinger, Nixon and the Destruction of Cambodia*. London: Andre Deutsch.

Shearer, David. n.d. "Stalin at War: Patterns of Violence and Foreign Threat." Manuscript, University of Delaware.

Shearer, David, and Vladimir Khaustov. 2015. *Stalin and the Lubianka: A Documentary History of the Political Police and Security Organs in the Soviet Union, 1922–1953*. New Haven, CT: Yale University Press.

Shelley, Louise. 1996. *Policing Soviet Society: The Evolution of State Control*. London: Routledge.

Sherman, John. 1997. *The Mexican Right: The End of Revolutionary Reform, 1929–1940*. Westport, CT: Praeger.

Shih, Victor C. 2008. *Factions and Finance in China: Elite Conflict and Inflation*. Cambridge: Cambridge University Press.

Shinn, David. 2003. "Terrorism in East Africa and the Horn: An Overview." *Journal of Conflict Studies* 23, no. 2: 79–91.

Shirer, William. 1960. *The Rise and Fall of the Third Reich*. Greenwich CT: Fawcett Crest Books.

Shirley, Edward G. 1995. "Is Iran's Present Algeria's Future?" *Foreign Affairs* 74, no. 3: 28–44.

Shore, Herbert. 1974. "Mondlane, Machel and Mozambique: From Rebellion to Revolution." *Africa Today*, Winter: 3–12.

Short, Anthony. 1989. *Origins of the Vietnam War*. London: Longman.

Short, Philip. 1999. *Mao: A Life*. London: Hodder and Stoughton.

Short, Philip. 2004. *Pol Pot: Anatomy of a Nightmare*. New York: Macmillan.

Shulim, Joseph. 1977. "Robespierre and the French Revolution." *American Historical Review* 82, no. 1: 20–38.

Shuyun, Sun. 2006. *The Long March*. New York: Penguin Press.

Siavoshi, Sussan. 2017. *Montazeri: The Life and Thought of Iran's Revolutionary Ayatollah*. New York: Cambridge University Press.

Sidel, Mark. 1997. "Generational and Institutional Transition in the Vietnamese Communist Party: The 1996 Congress and Beyond." *Asian Survey* 37, no. 5: 481–495.

Sidel, Mark. 1998. "Vietnam in 1997: A Year of Challenges." *Asian Survey* 38, no. 1: 80–90.

Siekmeier, James F. 2004. "Trailblazer Diplomat: Bolivian Ambassador Víctor Andrade Uzquiano's Efforts to Influence U.S. Policy, 1944–1962." *Diplomatic History* 28, no. 3: 385–406.

Simpson, Mark. 1993. "Foreign and Domestic Factors in the Transformation of Frelimo." *Journal of Modern African Studies* 31, no. 2: 309–337.

Singer, J. David. 1988. "Reconstructing the Correlates of War Dataset on Material Capabilities of States, 1816–1985." *International Interactions* 14, no. 2: 115–132.

Singh, Naunihal. 2014. *Seizing Power: The Strategic Logic of Military Coups*. Baltimore: Johns Hopkins University Press.

Singleton, F. 1972. "The Roots of Discord in Yugoslavia." *The World Today* 28, no. 4: 170–180.

Sinkaya, Bayram. 2016. *The Revolutionary Guards in Iranian Politics*. London: Routledge.

Skendi, Stavro. 1962. "Albania and the Sino-Soviet Conflict." *Foreign Affairs* 40, no. 3: 471–478.

Skocpol, Theda. 1979. *States and Social Revolutions*. New York: Cambridge University Press.

Skocpol, Theda. 1982. "Rentier State and Shi'a Islam in the Iranian Revolution." *Theory and Society* 11, no. 3: 265–283.

Skocpol, Theda. 1988. "Social Revolutions and Mass Military Mobilization." *World Politics* 40, no. 4: 147–168.

Skocpol, Theda, ed. 1994. *Social Revolutions in the Modern World*. New York: Cambridge University Press.

Skocpol, Theda, and Jeff Goodwin. 1989. "Explaining Revolutions in the Contemporary Third World." *Politics and Society* 17, no. 4: 485–509.

Slater, Dan. 2009. "Revolutions, Crackdowns, and Quiescence: Communal Elites and Democratic Mobilization in Southeast Asia." *American Journal of Sociology* 115, no. 1: 203–254.

Slater, Dan. 2010. *Ordering Power: Contentious Politics, State-Building, and Authoritarian Durability in Southeast Asia*. New York: Cambridge University Press.

Slater, Dan, and Sofia Fenner. 2011. "State Power and Staying Power: Infrastructural Mechanisms and Authoritarian Durability." *Journal of International Affairs* 65, no. 1: 15–29.

Slater, Dan, and Erika Simmons. 2010. "Informative Regress: Critical Antecedents in Comparative Politics." *Comparative Political Studies* 43, no. 7: 886–917.

Slater, Dan, and Nicholas Rush Smith. 2016. "The Power of Counterrevolution: Elitist Origins of Political Order in Postcolonial Asia and Africa." *American Journal of Sociology* 121, no. 5: 1472–1516.

Smaldone, Joseph P. 1991. "National Security." In Thomas Coehlo, ed., *Angola: A Country Study*. Washington, DC: Federal Research Division, Library of Congress.

Smele, Jonathan. 2016. *The "Russian" Civil Wars, 1916–1926: Ten Years That Shook the World*. New York: Oxford University Press.

Smith, Benjamin. 2005. "Life of the Party: The Origins of Regime Breakdown and Persistence under Single-Party Rule." *World Politics* 57, no. 3: 421–451.

Smith, Benjamin. 2007. *Hard Times in the Lands of Plenty: Oil Politics in Iran and Indonesia*. Ithaca, NY: Cornell University Press.

Smith, Kathleen. 2017. *Moscow 1956: The Silenced Spring*. Cambridge, MA: Harvard University Press.

Smith, Peter H. 1979. *Labyrinths of Power: Political Recruitment in Twentieth-Century Mexico*. Princeton, NJ: Princeton University Press.

Smith, Peter H. 1991. "Mexico since 1947: Dynamics of an Authoritarian Regime." In Leslie Bethell, ed., *Mexico since Independence*. Cambridge: Cambridge University Press.

Smith, Robert Freeman. 1972. *The United States and Revolutionary Nationalism in Mexico, 1916–1932*. Chicago: University of Chicago Press.

Smith, S. A. 1957. "The Independence of Ghana." *Modern Law Review* 20, no. 4: 347–363.

Smith, Tony. 1975. "The Political and Economic Ambitions of Algerian Land Reform, 1962–1974." *Middle East Journal* 29, no. 3: 259–278.

Smith, Tony. 1978. "A Comparative Study of French and British Decolonization." *Comparative Studies in Society and History* 20, no. 1: 70–102.

Smith, Wayne S. 1987. *The Closest of Enemies: A Personal and Diplomatic Account of U.S-Cuban Relations since 1957*. New York: W. W. Norton.

Smith Ariñez, Eduardo. 1960. *Veinte años de revolución en Bolivia*. Lima: Ediciones Raiz.

Snow, Edgar. 1978. *Red Star over China*. New York: Grove Press.

Snyder, Richard. 1992. "Explaining Transitions from Neopatrimonial Dictatorships." *Comparative Politics* 24, no. 4: 379–399.

Snyder, Richard. 1998. "Path Out of Sultanistic Regimes: Combining Structural and Voluntarist Perspectives." In Houchang E. Chehabi and Juan J. Linz, eds., *Sultanistic Regimes*. Baltimore: Johns Hopkins University Press.

Soares de Oliveira, Ricardo 2015. *Magnificent and Beggar Land: Angola since the Civil War*. New York: Oxford University Press.

Sogge, David. 2009. "Angola: 'Failed' yet 'Successful.'" Working paper, no. 81 Madrid: FRIDE.

Soifer, Hillel David. 2012. "The Causal Logic of Critical Junctures." *Comparative Political Studies* 45, no. 12: 1572–1597.

Soifer, Hillel David. 2015. *State Building in Latin America*. New York: Cambridge University Press.

Somerville, Keith. 1986. *Angola: Politics, Economics and Society*. Boulder, CO: Lynne Rienner.

Somoza, Anastasio. 1980. *Nicaragua Betrayed*. Boston: Western Islands Publishers.

Sontag, John P. 1975. "The Soviet War Scare of 1926–27." *The Russian Review* 34, no. 1: 66–77.

Spalding, Rose J., ed. 1987. *The Political Economy of Revolutionary Nicaragua*. Boston: Allen and Unwin.

Spalding, Rose J. 1994. *Capitalists and Revolution in Nicaragua: Opposition and Accommodation, 1979–1993*. Chapel Hill: University of North Carolina Press.

Spalding, Rose J. 1997. "The Economic Elite." In Thomas W. Walker, ed., *Nicaragua without Illusions: Regime Transition and Structural Adjustment in the 1990s*. Wilmington, DE: Scholarly Resources.

Spalding, Rose J. 1998. "Revolution and the Hyperpoliticized Business Peak Association: Nicaragua and el Consejo Superior de la Empresa Privada." In Francisco Durand and Eduardo Silva, eds., *Organized Business, Economic Change, and Democracy in Latin America*. Coral Gables, FL: North-South Center Press, University of Miami.

Spencer, Claire. 1994. "Algeria in Crisis." *Survival* 36, no. 2: 149–163.

Stahler-Sholk, Richard. 1997. "Structural Adjustment and Resistance: The Political Economy of Nicaragua under Chamorro." In Gary Prevost and Harry E. Vanden, eds., *The Undermining of the Sandinista Revolution*. New York: St. Martin's Press.

Stern, Jessica, and J. M. Berger. 2015. *ISIS: The State of Terror*. New York: HarperCollins.

Stern, Lewis M. 1987. "The Scramble toward Revitalization: The Vietnamese Communist Party and the Economic Reform Program." *Asian Survey* 27, no. 4: 477–493.

Stern, Lewis M. 1993. *Renovating the Vietnamese Communist Party: Nguyen Van Linh and the Programme for Organizational Reform, 1987–1991*. New York: St. Martin's Press.

Stevens, Evelyn P. 1974. *Protest and Response in Mexico*. Cambridge, MA: MIT Press.

Stevens, Evelyn P. 1987. "'The Opposition' in Mexico: Always a Bridesmaid, Never Yet the Bride." In Judith Gentleman, ed., *Mexican Politics in Transition*. Boulder, CO: Westview Press.

Stevenson, Jonathan. 2017. "Iran under Rouhani: Increasing Constraint." *Strategic Comments* 23, no. 7: vi–vii.

Steves, Franklin. 2003. "Regime Change and War: Domestic Politics and the Escalation of the Ethiopia-Eritrea Conflict." *Cambridge Review of International Affairs* 16, no. 1: 119–133.

Stewart, Megan. 2021. *Governing for Revolution: Social Transformation in Civil War*. New York: Cambridge University Press.

Stone, Martin. 1997. *The Agony of Algeria*. New York: Columbia University Press.

Story, Dale. 1986. *Industry, the State, and Public Policy in Mexico*. Austin: University of Texas Press.

Story, Dale. 1987. "The PAN, the Private Sector, and the Future of the Mexican Opposition." In Judith Gentleman, ed., *Mexican Politics in Transition*. Boulder, CO: Westview Press.

Strauss, Julia. 2006. "Morality, Coercion and State Building by Campaign in the Early PRC: Regime Consolidation and After, 1949–1956." *China Quarterly* 188: 891–912.

Suárez, Andrés. 1967. *Cuba: Castroism and Communism, 1959–1966*. Cambridge, MA: MIT Press.

Suárez, Andrés. 1971. "Leadership, Ideology, and Political Party." In Carmelo Mesa-Lago, ed., *Revolutionary Change in Cuba*. Pittsburgh: University of Pittsburgh Press.

Suárez, Andrés. 1989. "Civil-Military Relations in Cuba." In Jaime Suchlicki, ed., *The Cuban Military under Castro*. Coral Gables, FL: Institute of Interamerican Studies, Graduate School of International Studies, University of Miami, North-South Center.

Suárez, José Amador. 1981. *La lucha contra bandidos en Cuba*. Havana: Editorial Letras Cubanas.

Sullivan, Daniel P. 2007. "Tinder, Spark, Oxygen, Fuel: The Mysterious Rise of the Taliban." *Peace Research* 44, no. 1: 93–108.

Sumich, Jason, and João Honwana. 2007. "Strong Party, Weak State? Frelimo and State Survival through the Mozambican Civil War: An Analytical Narrative on State-Making." Crisis States Research Centre Working Paper no. 23. London School of Economics.

Suny, Ronald Grigor. 1972. *The Baku Commune, 1917–1918: Class and Nationality in the Russian Revolution*. Princeton, NJ: Princeton University Press.

Suny, Ronald Grigor. 1998. *The Soviet Experiment: Russia, the USSR, and the Successor States*. New York: Oxford University Press.

Suny, Ronald Grigor. 2020. *Stalin: Passage to Revolution*. Princeton, NJ: Princeton University Press.

Svolik, Milan W. 2012. *The Politics of Authoritarian Rule*. Cambridge: Cambridge University Press.

Swain, Geoffrey. 2014. *Trotsky and the Russian Revolution*. New York: Routledge.

Sweig, Julia A. 2002. *Inside the Cuban Revolution: Fidel Castro and the Urban Underground*. Cambridge, MA: Harvard University Press.

Sweig, Julia A. 2007. "Fidel's Final Victory." *Foreign Affairs* 86, no. 1: 39–56.

Szalontai, Balazs. 2005. "Political and Economic Crisis in North Vietnam, 1955–56." *Cold War History* 5, no. 4: 395–426.

Szulc, Tad. 1986. *Fidel: A Critical Portrait*. New York: William Morrow.

Szulc, Tad. 1989. "Fidelismo." In Irving Louis Horowitz, ed., *The Cuban Revolution*. New Brunswick, NJ: Transaction Publishers.

Taber, Robert. 1961. *M-26: Biography of a Revolution*. New York: Lyle Stuart.

Takeyh, Ray. 2010. "The Iran-Iraq War: A Reassessment." *Middle East Journal* 64, no. 3: 365–383.

Takeyh, Ray. 2014. "What Really Happened in Iran: The CIA, the Ouster of Mosaddeq, and the Restoration of the Shah." *Foreign Affairs* 93, no. 4: 2–12.

Tamayo, Jaime. 1990. "Neoliberalism Encounters *Neocardenismo*." In Joe Foweraker and Ann. L Craig, eds., *Popular Movements and Political Change in Mexico*. Boulder, CO: Lynne Rienner.

Tamayo, Jaime. 2008. *El Obregonismo y los movimientos sociales: La conformación del estado moderno en México (1920–1924)*. Guanajuato: Universidad de Guadalajara.

Tang, Truong Nhu. 1986. *A Vietcong Memoir*. New York: Vintage Books.

Tannenbaum, Frank. (1933) 1968. *Peace by Revolution: An Interpretation of Mexico*. New York: Columbia University Press.

Tannenbaum, Frank. 1971. *Mexico: The Struggle for Peace and Bread*. New York: Knopf.

Tardanico, Richard. 1980. "Revolutionary Nationalism and State Building in Mexico, 1917–1924." *Politics and Society* 10, no. 1: 59–86.

Tareke, Gebru. 2009. *The Ethiopian Revolution: War in the Horn of Africa*. New Haven, CT: Yale University Press.

Taubman, William. 2003. *Khrushchev: The Man and His Era*. New York: W. W. Norton.

Taylor, Brian D. 2003. *Politics and the Russian Army: Civil-Military Relations, 1689–2000*. New York: Cambridge University Press.

Taylor, Brian D., and Roxana Botea. 2008. "Tilly Tally: War-Making and State-Making in the Contemporary Third World." *International Studies Review* 10, no. 1: 27–56.

Taylor, Jay. 2011. *The Generalissimo: Chiang Kai-shek and the Struggle for Modern China*. Cambridge, MA: Belknap Press of Harvard University Press.

Teiwes, Frederick C. 1987. "Establishment and Consolidation of the New Regime." In Roderick MacFarquhar and John K. Fairbank, eds., *The Cambridge History of China*, vol. 14, *The People's Republic*, pt. 1, *The Emergence of Revolutionary China, 1949–1965*. New York: Cambridge University Press.

Teiwes, Frederick C., and Warren Sun. 1995. "From a Leninist to a Charismatic Party: The CCP's Changing Leadership, 1937–1945." In Tony Saich and Hans van de Ven, eds., *New Perspectives on the Chinese Communist Revolution*. Armonk, NY: M. E. Sharpe.

Teiwes, Frederick C., and Warren Sun. 1996. *The Tragedy of Lin Biao: Riding the Tiger during the Cultural Revolution 1966–1971*. London: Hurst.

Teiwes, Frederick C., and Warren Sun. 1999. *China's Road to Disaster: Mao, Central Politicians, and Provincial Leaders in the Unfolding of the Great Leap Forward, 1955–1959*. Armonk, NY: M. E. Sharpe.

Terzani, Tiziano. 1976. *Giai Phong! The Fall and Liberation of Saigon*. New York: St. Martin's Press.

Thayer, Carlyle A. 1987. "Vietnam's Sixth Party Congress: An Overview." *Contemporary Southeast Asia* 9, no. 1: 12–22.

Thayer, Carlyle A. 1988. "The Regularization of Politics: Continuity and Change in the Party's Central Committee, 1951–1986." In David G. Marr and Christine Pelzer White, eds., *Postwar Vietnam: Dilemmas in Socialist Development*. Ithaca, NY: Southeast Asia Program, Cornell University.

Thayer, Carlyle A. 1989. *War by Other Means: National Liberation and Revolution in Viet-Nam 1954-60*. Sydney: Allen and Unwin.

Thayer, Carlyle A. 1992a. "The Challenges Facing Vietnamese Communism." *Southeast Asian Affairs* 1992: 349–364.

Thayer, Carlyle A. 1992b. "Political Reform in Vietnam: Doi Moi and the Emergence of Civil Society." In Robert F. Miller, ed., *The Development of Civil Society in Communist Systems*. Sydney: Allen and Unwin.

Thayer, Carlyle A. 2007. "Vietnam: The Tenth Party Congress and After." *Southeast Asian Affairs* 2007: 381–397.

Thayer, Carlyle A. 2009a. "Political Legitimacy of Vietnam's One Party-State: Challenges and Responses." *Journal of Current Southeast Asian Affairs* 28, no. 4: 47–70.

Thayer, Carlyle A. 2009b. "Vietnam and the Challenge of Political Civil Society." *Contemporary Southeast Asia* 31, no. 1: 1–27.

Thayer, Carlyle A. 2010. "Political Legitimacy in Vietnam: Challenge and Response." *Politics and Policy* 38, no. 3: 423–444.

Thayer, Carlyle A. 2011. "Military Politics in Contemporary Vietnam: Political Engagement, Corporate Interests, and Professionalism." In Marcus Mietzner, ed., *The*

Political Resurgence of the Military in Southeast Asia: Conflict and Leadership. London: Routledge.

Thayer, Carlyle A. 2014. "The Apparatus of Authoritarian Rule in Vietnam." In Jonathan D. London, ed., *Politics in Contemporary Vietnam: Party, State, and Authority Relations*. London: Palgrave Macmillan.

Thayer, Carlyle A. 2018. "Force Modernization: Vietnam." *Southeast Asian Affairs* 2018: 419–444.

Thayer, Nate. 1998. "End of Story?" *Far Eastern Economic Review* 161, no. 51: 23–24.

Thomas, Hugh. 1977. *The Cuban Revolution*. New York: Harper and Row.

Thompson, Frank W. 2005. "Cuban Economic Performance in Retrospect." *Review of Radical Political Economics* 37, no. 3: 311–319.

Thompson, W. Scott. 1966. "New Directions in Ghana." *Africa Report*, November: 18–22.

Thorn, Richard S. 1971. "The Economic Transformation." In James M. Malloy and Richard S. Thorn, eds., *Beyond the Revolution: Bolivia since 1952*. Pittsburgh: University of Pittsburgh Press.

Thorpe, Andrew. 1998. "Comintern 'Control' of the Communist Party of Great Britain, 1920–43." *English Historical Review* 113, no. 452: 637–662.

Tikka, Marko. 2014. "Warfare and Terror in 1918." In T. Tepora and A. Roselius, eds., *The Finnish Civil War 1918: History, Memory, Legacy*. Boston: Brill.

Tilly, Charles. 1978. *From Mobilization to Revolution*. Reading, MA: Addison-Wesley.

Tlemcani, Rachid. 1986. *State and Revolution in Algeria*. Boulder, CO: Westview Press.

Tlemcani, Rachid, and William W. Hansen. 1989. "Development and the State in Post-Colonial Algeria." *Journal of Asian and African Studies* 24, no. 1–2: 114–133.

Tobler, Hans Werner. 1988. "Peasants and the Shaping of the Revolutionary State." In Friedrich Katz, ed., *Riot, Rebellion, and Revolution: Rural Social Conflict in Mexico*. Princeton, NJ: Princeton University Press.

Toft, Monica Duffy. 2016. "Ending Civil Wars: A Case for Rebel Victory?" *International Security* 34, no. 4: 7–36.

Tőkés, Rudolf. 1967. *Béla Kun and the Hungarian Soviet Republic*. New York: Praeger.

Tonnesson, Stein. 1991. *The Vietnamese Revolution of 1945: Roosevelt, Ho Chi Minh and de Gaulle in a World at War*. Oslo: International Peace Research Institute.

Topouzis. Daphne. 1989. "Guinea Bissau: Shifting Course." *Africa Report*, September–October: 49–51.

Torigian, Joseph. 2016. *Prestige, Manipulation, and Coercion: Elite Power Struggles and the Fate of Three Revolutions*. Doctoral dissertation, Massachusetts Institute of Technology.

Torres, María de los Angeles. 1999. *In the Land of the Mirrors: Cuban Exile Politics in the United States*. Ann Arbor: University of Michigan Press.

Torres-García, Ana. 2013. "U.S. Diplomacy and the North African 'War of the Sands.'" *Journal of North African Studies* 18, no. 2: 324–348.

Trejo, Guillermo. 2009. "Religious Competition and Ethnic Mobilization in Latin America: Why the Catholic Church Promotes Indigenous Movements in Mexico." *American Political Science Review* 103, no. 3: 323–342.

Trejo, Guillermo. 2012. *Popular Movements in Autocracies: Religion, Repression, and Indigenous Collective Action in Mexico*. New York: Cambridge University Press.

Trejo Delarbe, Raul, and Aníbal Yañez. 1976. "The Mexican Labor Movement: 1917–1975." *Latin American Perspectives* 3, no. 1: 133–153.

Tri, Vo Nhan. 1988. "Party Policies and Economic Performance: The Second and Third Five-Year Plans Examined." In David G. Marr and Christine Pelzer White, eds., *Postwar Vietnam: Dilemmas in Socialist Development*. Ithaca, NY: Southeast Asia Program, Cornell University.

Tri, Vo Nhan. 1990. "The Renovation Agenda: Groping in the Dark." In Thai Quang Trung, ed., *Vietnam Today: Assessing the New Trends*. New York: Taylor and Francis.

Trifković, Gaj, 2016. "'Damned Good Amateurs': Yugoslav Partisans in the Belgrade Operation 1944." *Journal of Slavic Military Studies* 29, no. 2: 253–278.

Trimberger, Ellen Kay. 1978. *Revolution from Above: Military Bureaucrats and Development in Japan, Turkey, Egypt, and Peru*. New Brunswick, NJ: Transaction Books.

Tronvoll, Kjetil. 1998. "The Process of Nation-Building in Post-War Eritrea: Created from Below or Directed from Above?" *Journal of Modern African Studies* 36, no. 3: 461–482.

Tronvoll, Kjetil, and Daniel R. Mekonnen. 2014. *The African Garrison State: Human Rights and Political Development in Eritrea*. London: James Currey.

Truong, David H. D. 1998. "Striving towards 'Doi Moi' II." *Southeast Asian Affairs* 1998: 328–333.

Tsai, Kellee S. 2011. *Capitalism without Democracy*. Ithaca, NY: Cornell University Press.

Tucker, Robert C. 1990. *Stalin in Power*. New York: W. W. Norton.

Tucker, Spencer C. 1999. *Vietnam*. London: UCL Press.

Turley, William S. 1972a. *Army, Party and Society in the Democratic Republic of Vietnam: Civil-Military Relations in a Mass-Mobilization System*. Doctoral dissertation, University of Washington.

Turley, William S. 1972b. "The DRV since the Death of Ho Chi Minh: The Politics of a Revolution in Transition." In Joseph J. Zasloff and Allen E. Goodman, eds., *Indochina in Conflict: A Political Assessment*. Lexington, MA: Lexington Books.

Turley, William S. 1975. "The Political Role and Development of the People's Army of Vietnam." In Joseph J. Zasloff and MacAlister Brown, eds., *Communism in Indochina: New Perspectives*. Lexington, MA: Lexington Books.

Turley, William S. 1977. "Origins and Development of Communist Military Leadership in Vietnam." *Armed Forces and Society* 3, no. 2: 219–244.

Turley, William S. 1982. "The Vietnamese Army." In Jonathan R. Adelman, ed., *Communist Armies in Politics*. Boulder, CO: Westview Press.

Turley, William S. 1988. "The Military Construction of Socialism: Postwar Roles of the People's Army of Vietnam." In David G. Marr and Christine Pelzer White, eds., *Postwar Vietnam: Dilemmas in Socialist Development*. Ithaca, NY: Southeast Asia Program, Cornell University.

Turley, William S. 1993. "Political Renovation in Vietnam: Renewal and Adaptation." In Borje Ljunggren, ed., *The Challenge of Reform in Indochina*. Cambridge, MA: Harvard Institute for International Development.

Turley, William S. 2009. *The Second Indochina War: A Concise Political and Military History*. Lanham, MD: Rowman and Littlefield.

Turner, Robert F. 1975. *Vietnamese Communism: Its Origins and Development*. Stanford, CA: Hoover Institution Press.

Turner, Simon. 2014. "Making Good Citizens from Bad Life in Post-Genocide Rwanda." *Development and Change* 45, no. 3: 415–433.

Tutino, John. 1986. *From Insurrection to Revolution in Mexico: Social Bases of Agrarian Violence, 1750–1940.* Princeton, NJ: Princeton University Press.

Tvedten, Inge. 1997. *Angola: Struggle for Peace and Reconstruction.* Boulder, CO: Westview Press.

Ulam, Adam. 1952. *Titoism and the Cominform.* Cambridge, MA: Harvard University Press.

Unkovski-Korica, Vladimir. 2020. "Yugoslavia's Third Way: The Rise and Fall of Self-Management." In John R. Lampe and Ulf Brunnbauer, eds., *The Routledge Handbook of Balkan and Southeast European History.* London: Routledge.

Upton, A. F. 1980. *The Finnish Revolution, 1917–1918.* Minneapolis: University of Minnesota Press.

Urbas, Emmanuel. 1922. "The White Terror in Hungary." *Current History* 17, no. 1: 59–69.

U.S. Department of State, Bureau of Intelligence and Research. 1973. "Portuguese Guinea: Rebels Establish Government." October 5. Washington, DC: U.S. Department of State. https://2001-2009.state.gov/documents/organization/66985.pdf.

Vachudova, Milada. 2005. *Europe Undivided: Democracy, Leverage and Integration after Communism.* Oxford: Oxford University Press.

Valdivia, Angharad N. 1991. "The U.S. Intervention in Nicaraguan and Other Latin American Media." In Thomas W. Walker, ed., *Revolution and Counterrevolution in Nicaragua.* Boulder, CO: Westview Press.

Vallin, Raymond. 1973. "Muslim Socialism in Algeria." In I. William Zartman, ed., *Man, State, and Society in the Contemporary Maghrib.* New York: Praeger.

van de Ven, Hans. 2003. *War and Nationalism in China, 1925–1945.* London: Routledge.

Van Hoyweghen, Saskia. 1996. "The Disintegration of the Catholic Church of Rwanda: A Study of the Fragmentation of Political and Religious Authority." *African Affairs* 95, no. 380: 379–401.

Vanden, Harry E. 1991. "Foreign Policy." In Thomas W. Walker, ed., *Revolution and Counterrevolution in Nicaragua.* Boulder, CO: Westview Press.

Vanden, Harry E., and Gary Prevost. 1993. *Democracy and Socialism in Sandinista Nicaragua.* Boulder, CO: Lynne Rienner.

Vandewalle, Dirk. 1992. "At the Brink: Chaos in Algeria." *World Policy Journal* 9, no. 4: 705–717.

Vandewalle, Dirk. 1997. "Islam in Algeria: Religion, Culture, and Opposition in a Rentier State." In John L. Esposito, ed., *Political Islam: Revolution, Radicalism, or Reform?* Boulder, CO: Lynne Rienner.

Vargas, Oscar René. 1991. *Nicaragua: Los partidos políticos y la búsqueda de un nuevo modelo.* Managua: Centro de Investigación y Desarrollo ECOTEXTURA.

Vázquez, Josefina Zoraida, and Lorenzo Meyer. 1985. *The United States and Mexico.* Chicago: University of Chicago Press.

Veláz Suárez, Aníbal. 2008. "La lucha contra bandidos." In Enrique Oltuski Ozacki, Héctor Rodríguez Llompart, and Eduardo Torres-Cuevas, eds., *Memorias de la revolución II.* Havana: Imagen Contemporánea.

Vellinga, M. L. 1976. "The Military and the Dynamics of the Cuban Revolutionary Process." *Comparative Politics* 8, no. 2: 245–271.

Vernon, Raymond. 1965. *The Dilemma of Mexico's Development: The Roles of the Private and Public Sectors.* Cambridge, MA: Harvard University Press.

Vickers, M. 2011. *The Albanians: A Modern History.* London: I. B. Tauris.

Vickery, Michael. 1983. "Democratic Kampuchea: Themes and Variations." In David Chandler and Ben Kiernan, eds., *Revolution and Its Aftermath in Kampuchea*. New Haven, CT: Yale University Southeast Asia Studies.

Vien, Nguyen Khac. 1974. *Tradition and Revolution in Vietnam*. Berkeley, CA: Indochina Resource Center.

Viola, Lynne. 1987. *Best Sons of the Fatherland: Workers in the Vanguard of Soviet Collectivization*. New York: Oxford University Press.

Viola, Lynne. 1996. *Peasant Rebels under Stalin: Collectivization and the Culture of Peasant Resistance*. New York: Oxford University Press.

Viola, Lynne. 2000. "The Role of the OGPU in Dekulakization, Mass Deportations, and Special Resettlement in 1930." Carl Beck Papers in Russian & East European Studies, no. 1406.

Viola, Lynne. 2017. *Stalinist Perpetrators on Trial: Scenes from the Great Terror in Soviet Ukraine*. Oxford: Oxford University Press.

Vladisavljević, Nebojša. 2008. *Serbia's Antibureaucratic Revolution: Milošević, the Fall of Communism and Nationalist Mobilization*. London: Palgrave Macmillan.

Vogel, Ezra. 2011. *Deng Xiaoping and the Transformation of China*. Cambridge, MA: Harvard University Press.

Volf, Miroslav. 1989. "Church, State, and Society: Reflections on the Life of the Church in Contemporary Yugoslavia." *Transformation* 6, no. 1: 24–31.

Volpi, Frédéric. 2003. *Islam and Democracy: The Failure of Dialogue in Algeria*. London: Pluto Press.

Volpi, Frédéric. 2006. "Algeria's Pseudo-Democratic Politics: Lessons for Democratization in the Middle East." *Democratization* 13, no. 3: 442–455.

Volpi, Frédéric. 2013. "Algeria versus the Arab Spring." *Journal of Democracy* 24, no. 3: 104–115.

Volpi, Frédéric. 2017. *Revolution and Authoritarianism in North Africa*. New York: Oxford University Press.

Volpi. Frédéric. 2020. "Algeria: When Elections Hurt Democracy." *Journal of Democracy* 31, no. 2: 152–165.

von Hagen, Mark. 1990. *Soldiers in the Proletarian Dictatorship: The Red Army and the Soviet Socialist State, 1917–1930*. Ithaca, NY: Cornell University Press.

von Sauer, Franz A. 1974. *The Alienated "Loyal" Opposition: Mexico's Partido Acción Nacional*. Albuquerque: University of New Mexico Press.

Vu, Tuong. 2014. "Persistence amid Decay: The Communist Party of Vietnam at 83." In Jonathan D. London, ed., *Politics in Contemporary Vietnam: Party, State, and Authority Relations*. London: Palgrave Macmillan.

Vu, Tuong. 2017. *Vietnam's Communist Revolution: The Power and Limits of Ideology*. New York: Cambridge University Press.

Vuving, Alexander L. 2017. "The 2016 Leadership Change in Vietnam and Its Long-Term Implications." *Southeast Asian Affairs* 2017: 421–435.

Vuving, Alexander L. 2019. "Vietnam in 2018: A Rent-Seeking State on Correction Course." *Southeast Asian Affairs* 2019: 375–393.

Wager, Stephen. J. 1984. "Basic Characteristics of the Modern Mexican Military." In David F. Ronfeldt, ed., *The Modern Mexican Military: A Reassessment*. La Jolla: Center for U.S.-Mexican Studies, University of California, San Diego.

Wager, Stephen J. 1995. "The Mexican Military Approaches the 21st Century: Coping with a New World Order." In Donald E. Schulz and Edward J. Williams, eds., *Mexico Faces the 21st Century*. Westport, CT: Greenwood Press.

Wager, Stephen J., and Donald E. Schulz. 1995. "The Zapatista Revolt and Its Implications for Civil-Military Relations and the Future of Mexico." In Donald E. Schulz and Edward J. Williams, eds., *Mexico Faces the 21st Century*. Westport, CT: Greenwood Press.

Walder, Andrew G. 2004. "The Party Elite and China's Trajectory of Change." *China: An International Journal* 2, no. 2: 189–209.

Walder, Andrew G. 2015. *China under Mao: A Revolution Derailed*. Cambridge, MA: Harvard University Press.

Walder, Andrew G. 2018. "Back to the Future? Xi Jinping as an Anti-bureaucratic Crusader." *China: An International Journal* 16, no. 3: 18–34.

Waldner, David. 2017. "A Coalitional Theory of Autocratic Regime Survival." Paper prepared for the Annual Meeting of the American Political Science Association, San Francisco, CA, August 31–September 1.

Walker, Thomas W. 1991a. "The Armed Forces." In Thomas W. Walker, ed., *Revolution and Counterrevolution in Nicaragua*. Boulder, CO: Westview Press.

Walker, Thomas W. 1991b. "Introduction." In Thomas W. Walker, ed., *Revolution and Counterrevolution in Nicaragua*. Boulder, CO: Westview Press.

Walker, Thomas W. 2003. *Nicaragua: Living in the Shadow of the Eagle*. Boulder, CO: Westview Press.

Waller, J. Michael. 2004. "Russia: Death and Resurrection of the KGB." *Demokratizatsiya* 12, no. 3: 333–355.

Wallerstein, Immanuel. 1964. *The Road to Independence: Ghana and the Ivory Coast*. Paris: Mouton.

Wallerstein, Immanuel. 1967. "Ghana as a Model." *Africa Report*, May: 43–46.

Walt, Stephen. 1996. *Revolution and War*. Ithaca, NY: Cornell University Press.

Walton, Calder. 2014. *Empire of Secrets: British Intelligence, the Cold War, and the Twilight of Empire*. New York: Overlook Press.

Ward, Steven R. 2009. *Immortal: A Military History of Iran and Its Armed Forces*. Washington, DC: Georgetown University Press.

Warrick, Joby. 2015. *Black Flags: The Rise of ISIS*. New York: Doubleday.

Washington, Shirley. 1980. "New Institutions for Development in Guinea Bissau." *The Black Scholar* 11, no. 5: 14–23.

Washington, Shirley. 1984. "South Africa Obstructs Angola's Search for Peace." *The Black Scholar* 15, no. 6: 23–32.

Watkins, Andrew. 2020. *Taliban Fragmentation: Fact, Fiction, and Future*. Peaceworks, no. 160. Washington, DC: United States Institute of Peace. https://www.usip.org/publications/2020/03/taliban-fragmentation-fact-fiction-and-future.

Way, Lucan, Steven Levitsky, and Adam E. Casey. 2019. "Military Origins and Coups." Paper presented at the Annual Meeting of the American Political Science Association, Washington, DC, August 29–September 1.

Weaver, Eric, and William Barnes. 1991. "Opposition Parties and Coalitions." In Thomas W. Walker, ed., *Revolution and Counterrevolution in Nicaragua*. Boulder, CO: Westview Press.

Weber, Henri. 1981. *Nicaragua: The Sandinista Revolution*. London: Verso.

Wee, Tan Kee. 1991. "Vietnam at the Crossroads in 1990." *Southeast Asian Affairs* 1991: 311–320.

Weeks, Jessica. 2014. *Dictators at War and Peace*. Ithaca, NY: Cornell University Press.

Wehrey, Frederic, Jerrold D. Green, Brian Nichiporuk, Alireza Nader, Lydia Hansell, Rasool Nafisi, and S. R. Bohandy. 2009. *The Rise of the Pasdaran: Assessing the Domestic Roles of Iran's Islamic Revolutionary Guards Corps*. Santa Monica, CA: Rand Corporation.

Wei, William. 2012. "'Political Power Grows out of the Barrel of a Gun': Mao and the Red Army." In David A. Graff and Robin Higham, eds., *A Military History of China*. Lexington: University Press of Kentucky.

Welch, Richard E., Jr. 1985. *Response to Revolution: The United States and the Cuban Revolution, 1959–1961*. Chapel Hill: University of North Carolina Press.

Weldon, Jeffrey. 1997. "Political Sources of Presidencialismo in Mexico." In Scott Mainwaring and Matthew Soberg Shugart, eds., *Presidentialism and Democracy in Latin America*. New York: Cambridge University Press.

Wells-Dang, Andrew. 2014. "The Political Influence of Civil Society in Vietnam." In Jonathan D. London, ed., *Politics in Contemporary Vietnam: Party, State, and Authority Relations*. London: Palgrave Macmillan.

Wemheuer, Felix. 2014. *Famine Politics in Maoist China and the Soviet Union*. New Haven, CT: Yale University Press.

Werenfels, Isabelle. 2007. *Managing Instability in Algeria: Elites and Political Change since 1995*. London: Routledge.

Werner, Bridgette K. 2020. "Between Autonomy and Acquiescence: Negotiating Rule in Revolutionary Bolivia, 1953–1958." *Hispanic American Historical Review* 100, no. 1: 93–121.

Werner, Jayne. 1980. "Vietnamese Communism and Religious Sectarianism." In William S. Turley, ed., *Vietnamese Communism in Comparative Perspective*. Boulder, CO: Westview Press.

Werth, Nicolas. 1999. "A State against Its People: Violence, Repression, and Terror in the Soviet Union." In Stéphane Courtois et al., eds., *The Black Book of Communism: Crimes, Terror, Repression*. Cambridge, MA: Harvard University Press.

Westad, Odd Arne. 2003. *Decisive Encounters: The Chinese Civil War, 1946–1950*. Stanford, CA: Stanford University Press.

Weyland, Kurt. 2019. *Revolution and Reaction: The Diffusion of Authoritarianism in Latin America*. New York: Cambridge University Press.

Wheatcroft, Stephen. 2007. "Agency and Terror: Evdokimov and Mass Killing in Stalin's Great Terror." *Australian Journal of Politics and History* 53, no. 1: 20–43.

Whitehead, Laurence. 2003. "The Bolivian National Revolution: A Comparison." In Merilee S. Grindle and Pilar Domingo, eds., *Proclaiming Revolution: Bolivia in Comparative Perspective*. London: Institute of Latin American Studies, University of London.

Whitehead, Laurence. 2016. "The 'Puzzle' of Autocratic Resilience/Regime Collapse: The Case of Cuba." *Third World Quarterly* 37, no. 9: 1666–1682.

Whitson, William W. 1973. *The Chinese High Command: A History of Communist Military Politics, 1927–1971*. London: Macmillan.

Wickham-Crowley, Timothy. 1992. *Guerrillas and Revolution in Latin America*. Princeton, NJ: Princeton University Press.

Wilbur, C. Martin. 1983. *The Nationalist Revolution in China, 1923–1928*. Cambridge: Cambridge University Press.

Wilcox, Wayne. 1965. "The Pakistan Coup of 1958." *Pacific Affairs* 38, no. 2: 142–163.

Wilkie, James W. 1967. *The Mexican Revolution: Federal Expenditure and Social Change since 1910*. Berkeley: University of California Press.

Williams, Edward J. 1986. "The Evolution of the Mexican Military and Its Implications for Civil-Military Relations." In Roderic A. Camp, ed., *Mexico's Political Stability: The Next Five Years*. Boulder, CO: Westview Press.

Williams, Heather. 2020. "Partisans and Chetniks in Occupied Yugoslavia." In John R. Lampe and Ulf Brunnbauer, eds., *The Routledge Handbook of Balkan and Southeast European History*. London: Routledge.

Williams, Philip J. 1985. "The Catholic Hierarchy in the Nicaraguan Revolution." *Journal of Latin American Studies* 17, no. 2: 341–369.

Willis, Michael. 1996. *The Islamist Challenge in Algeria: A Political History*. New York: New York University Press.

Wischermann, Jorg. 2003. "Vietnam in the Era of Moi Moi: Issue-Oriented Organizations and Their Relationship to the Government." *Asian Survey* 43, no. 5: 867–889.

Witoschek, G. 2012. "Sleeping Beauty or Cinderella? Iran's Conventional Military—the Artesh—and the Evolution of Its Legitimacy over Three Decades of the Mullahs Regimes." Master of Defence Studies, Canadian Forces College. https://www.cfc .forces.gc.ca/259/290/298/286/witoschek.pdf.

Woldemariam, Michael. 2018. *Insurgent Fragmentation in the Horn of Africa: Rebellion and Its Discontents*. New York: Cambridge University Press.

Wolf, Eric. 1969. *Peasant Wars of the Twentieth Century*. New York: Harper and Row.

Wolfe, Bertram D. (1948) 2001. *Three Who Made Revolution: A Biographical History of Lenin, Trotsky, and Stalin*. New York: Cooper Square Press.

Womack, John, Jr. 1968. *Zapata and the Mexican Revolution*. New York: Vintage Books.

Womack, John, Jr. 1991. "The Mexican Revolution, 1910–1920." In Leslie Bethell, ed., *Mexico since Independence*. Cambridge: Cambridge University Press.

Woodside, Alexander B. 1976. *Community and Revolution in Modern Vietnam*. Boston: Houghton Mifflin.

World Bank. n.d. Databank. Available at https://databank.worldbank.org/home.aspx.

Wu, Tien-wei. 1976. *The Sian Incident: A Pivotal Point in Modern Chinese History*. Ann Arbor: University of Michigan Press.

Wu, Tien-wei. 1992. "The Chinese Communist Movement." In James C. Hsiung and Steven I. Levine, eds., *China's Bitter Victory: The War with Japan 1937–1945*. Armonk, NY: M. E. Sharpe.

Wu, Yiching. 2014. *The Cultural Revolution at the Margins: Chinese Socialism in Crisis*. Cambridge, MA: Harvard University Press.

Wuthnow, Joel. 2019. *China's Other Army: The People's Armed Police in an Era of Reform*. Washington, DC: National Defense University Press.

Wylie, Raymond F. 1980. *The Emergence of Maoism: Mao Tse-tung, Ch'en Po-ta, and the Search for Chinese Theory, 1935–1945*. Stanford, CA: Stanford University Press.

Yafeng, Xia. 2008. "Forum: Mao and the Cultural Revolution in China: Commentaries on *Mao's Last Revolution* and a Reply by the Authors: Commentary by Yafeng Xia." *Journal of Cold War Studies* 10, no. 2: 108–116.

Yaffe, Helen. 2009. *Che Guevara: The Economics of Revolution*. London: Palgrave Macmillan.

Yang, Benjamin. 1990. *From Revolution to Politics: Chinese Communists on the Long March*. Boulder, CO: Westview Press.

Yang, Jisheng. 2008. *Tombstone: The Great Chinese Famine, 1958–1962*. New York: Farrar, Straus and Giroux.

Yasin, Yevgenii. 1998. "How the Chinese Path of Reform Failed in the USSR." In Michael Ellman and Vladimir Kontorovich, eds., *The Destruction of the Soviet Economic System: An Insiders' History*. Armonk, NY: M. E. Sharpe.

Yasmann, Victor and Vladislov Zubok. 1998. "The KGB Documents and Soviet Collapse: Part II." Washington DC: National Council for Eurasian and East European Research. https://www.ucis.pitt.edu/nceeer/1998-813-15-2-Yasman.pdf.

Young, Crawford. 2001. "Review: Uganda under Museveni." *African Studies Review* 44, no. 2: 207–210.

Young, John. 1997. *Peasant Revolution in Ethiopia: The Tigray People's Revolutionary Front, 1971–1991*. New York: Cambridge University Press.

Young, Tom. 1988. "The Politics of Development in Angola and Mozambique." *African Affairs* 87, no. 347: 165–184.

Zabih, Sepehr. 1988. *The Iranian Military in Revolution and War*. New York: Routledge.

Zarrow, Peter. 2005. *China in War and Revolution, 1895–1949*. London: Routledge.

Zartman, I. William. 1964. "Africa's Quiet War: Guinea Bissau." *Africa Report*, 9 no. 2: 8–12.

Zartman, I. William. 1967. "Guinea: The Quiet War Goes On." *Africa Report* 12, no. 8: 67–72.

Zartman, I. William. 1973. "The Algerian Army in Politics." In I. William Zartman, ed., *Man, State, and Society in the Contemporary Maghrib*. New York: Praeger.

Zartman, I. William. 1994. "The Challenge of Democratic Alternatives in the Maghrib." In John Ruedy, ed., *Islamism and Secularism in North Africa*. New York: St. Martin's Press.

Zeitlin, Maurice, and Robert Schneer. 1963. *Cuba: A Tragedy in Our Hemisphere*. New York: Grove Press.

Zhang, Shu Guang. 1995. *Mao's Military Romanticism: China and the Korean War, 1950–1953*. Lawrence: University Press of Kansas.

Zhao, Dingxin. 2001. *The Power of Tiananmen: State-Society Relations and the 1989 Beijing Student Movement*. Chicago: University of Chicago Press.

Zhao, Ziyang. 2009. *Prisoner of the State: The Secret Journal of Premier Zhao Ziyang*. New York: Simon and Schuster.

Zimmermann, Matilde. 2000. *Sandinista: Carlos Fonseca and the Nicaraguan Revolution*. Durham, NC: Duke University Press.

Zolberg, Aristide. 1966. *Creating Political Order: The Party-States of West Africa*. Chicago: Rand McNally.

Zolberg, Aristide. 1968. "Military Intervention in the New States of Tropical Africa." In Henry Bienen, ed., *The Military Intervenes: Case Studies in Political Development*. New York: Russell Sage Foundation.

Zondag, Cornelius H. 1966. *The Bolivian Economy, 1952–65: The Revolution and Its Aftermath.* New York: Frederick A. Praeger.

Zondag, Cornelius H. 1982. "Bolivia's 1952 Revolution: Initial Impact and U.S. Involvement." In Jerry R. Landman, ed., *Modern-Day Bolivia: Legacy of the Revolution and Prospects for the Future.* Tempe: Center for Latin American Studies, Arizona State University.

Zoubir, Yahia H. 1995. "Stalled Democratization of an Authoritarian Regime: The Case of Algeria." *Democratization* 2, no. 2: 109–139.

Zsuppán, Ferenc Tibor. 1965. "The Early Activities of the Hungarian Communist Party, 1918–19." *Slavonic and East European Review* 43, no. 101: 314–344.

Zubkova, Elena. 1998. *Russia after the War: Hopes, Illusion, and Disappointments, 1945–1957.* Armonk, NY: M. E. Sharpe.

Zunes, Stephen. 2001. "The United States and Bolivia: The Taming of a Revolution, 1952–1957." *Latin American Perspectives* 28, no. 5: 33–49.

Note: Page numbers in *italics* indicate figures and tables.

party-army fusion (*continued*)
  high-intensity coercion and, 41; Mexico
  and, 137–38, 146; Nicaragua and, 289,
  305; revolutionary durability theory and,
  1, 18–20, 31, 38, 41, 321–22, 340–41, 353;
  Vietnam and, 170
party cards, 36, 59
Party for African Independence in Guinea-
  Bissau and Cape Verde (PAIGC), 27,
  42, 274, 308–16, 320, 322
Party of the Democratic Revolution (PRD),
  153
Party of the Poor, 150
party-state complex: Ghana and, 198–99;
  Guinea-Bissau and, 313–14, 316; Mexico and, 136–43, 152; revolutionary
  durability theory and, 346; USSR and,
  56–58; Vietnam and, 169–70
Pastor, Robert A., 300
Pastora, Eden, 304
Patiño, 275
Paz, Octavio, 150
Paz Estenssoro, Victor: Bolivia and, 275–89,
  316, 322, 325; Bolivian Workers Central
  (COB) and, 278–80, 282–84, 286–87,
  289; mining and, 275–81, 276, 285,
  287–88; overthrow of, 275; second
  term of, 287; state-building and,
  283–84
peasants: Bolivia and, 275–81, 285–86, 322;
  China and, 89–92, 96–103, 154;
  communism and, 60, 64, 89–90, 96,
  99, 165, 252, 256, 327; Eritrea and,
  340; Hungary and, 251–55; Institutional Revolutionary Party (PRI) and,
  133, 135, 140–42, 143, 148–51, 154, 275,
  286; Khmer Rouge and, 256–57, 260;
  labor camps and, 65; land reform and,
  35, 97–100, 119–20, 123, 126–27, 135,
  144, 154, 165, 279–80, 340; Mexico
  and, 119, 121, 123, 126–35, 141, 144,
  146, *344*; mobilization of, 21, 28, 47,
  55, 102, 119, 121, 123, 126–35, 141,
  144, 146, 161, 275–76, 278, 281, 323,
  327; National Peasant Confederation
  (CNC) and, 133, 135; Nicaragua and,
  289, 297, 299–300; radicalism and,
  14, 28–29, 97, 99, 117, 119, 123–28, 131,
  144, 150, 165, 182–83, 251–52, 209, 275,
  279–81, 297, 300, 328, 336, 340; Red
  Army and, 35, 55, 64, 96, 119, 126–27,

129, 135, 149, 161, 275, 278; Socialist
  Revolutionaries (SRs) and, 14, 22, 48–52,
  55, 65; USSR and, 46–49, 55–60, 63–67,
  73, 323, 334, 336; Vietnam and, 161,
  165–66, 171; villagization of, 334
Peláez, Manuel, 125
Peng Dehuai, 103
People's Army of Vietnam (PAVN), 19, 161
People's Daily (newspaper), 109
People's Fadai, 232
People's Liberation Army (PLA), 90, 96,
  103, 105–7
People's Liberation Movement, 14
People's Revolutionary Armed Forces
  (FARP), 309–10, 313
Pereira, Aristides, 311
Pérez Serantes, Enrique, 215
Perlmutter, Amos, 19
Persian Gulf, 2, 190, 235–36, 247, 320
Peru, 139, 146, 210, 280, 324
Pham Hong, 163, 172
Pham Van Dong, 163
Philippines, 7
Piłsudski, Józef, 63
Pioneers, 64
Poland, 23, 63–64, 71, 74, 210, 226, 333
polarization: China and, 89–90, 110, 113;
  Cuba and, 324; elite cohesion and,
  16–17, 30, 42, 147–51, 247, 337, 346,
  351–52; existential threat and, 17,
  337, 351–52; Ghana and, 200; Iran
  and, 244, 247, 249, 321; Mexico and,
  143–51, 154; polarization and, 244,
  247, 249, 321; revolutionary durability
  theory and, 4, 16–17, 29–30, 42
police: Algeria and, 180, 193; Bolivia and,
  276–78, 283; China and, 89, 114; Cuba
  and, 206–7, 212, 218; Guinea-Bissau
  and, 309; Hungary and, 252; Iran and,
  246; loyal coercive apparatus and, 18,
  24; Mexico and, 119–20, 135, 139, 142;
  Nicaragua and, 293–94, 301, 304–5;
  radicalism and, 13, 82, 84, 119; religious,
  268; revolutionary durability theory and,
  5, 13, 18–19, 24, 317, 329, 332, 335–36,
  340; secret, 52, 57, 180, 218, 301, 304,
  329, 332, 335; Taliban and, 268; USSR
  and, 47–48, 52, 54, 57, 60, 64, 71, 75,
  81–84; Vietnam and, 162, 169
Politburo: communism and, 80, 217;
  military and, 1, 79, 104, 164, 172, 219;

A NOTE ON THE TYPE

———◆———

THIS BOOK has been composed in Miller, a Scotch Roman typeface designed by Matthew Carter and first released by Font Bureau in 1997. It resembles Monticello, the typeface developed for The Papers of Thomas Jefferson in the 1940s by C. H. Griffith and P. J. Conkwright and reinterpreted in digital form by Carter in 2003.

Pleasant Jefferson ("P. J.") Conkwright (1905–1986) was Typographer at Princeton University Press from 1939 to 1970. He was an acclaimed book designer and AIGA Medalist.